◎◎ tripadvisor

The Best
by travellers like you

Visit TripAdvisor for millions of candid reviews by real travellers.
Find the best places to eat, stay, and play... wherever you go.

Top-Rated Hotels

1 Casa Claver Loft Boutique Hotel ◎◎◎◎◎
Cartagena
"Felt like we were staying with rich friends"

2 Hotel Casa D'mer ◎◎◎◎◎
Taganga
"Spotless, stylish and cheaper than the rest"

3 La Casa de Farol Hotel Boutique ◎◎◎◎◎
Santa Marta
"Classy and incredible... wonderful place!"

Popular Restaurants

1 hostería shardana ◎◎◎◎◎
Bogota
"Amazing hospitality... loved the open fire"

2 Andrés Carne de Res ◎◎◎◎◎
Chia
"Great fun and the food was fantastic"

3 Cevichería Trattoria Donde Wippy ◎◎◎◎◎
Cartagena
"On the pricier side, but great food"

Amazing Things to Do

1 Aquantis Bed Breakfast & Diving ◎◎◎◎◎
Taganga
"New equipment, faultless safety procedures"

2 Gold Museum (Museo del Oro) ◎◎◎◎◎
Bogotá
"Magnificently designed and organized spot"

3 Walled City ◎◎◎◎◎
Cartagena
"Safe and tranquil... gorgeous at night"

tripadvisor.co.uk | tripadvisor.it | tripadvisor.es | tripadvisor.de | tripadvisor.fr | tripadvisor.se | nl.tripadvisor.com
tripadvisor.dk | tripadvisor.ie | tripadvisor.no | pl.tripadvisor.com | tripadvisor.ru
Ratings were accurate as of April 2011 and may change over time. Visit tripadvisor.co.uk online for current ratings.

Footprint story

It was 1921

Ireland had just been partitioned, the British miners were striking for more pay and the federation of British industry had an idea. Exports were booming in South America – how about a handbook for businessmen trading in that far away continent? The Anglo-South American Handbook was born that year, written by W Koebel, the most prolific writer on Latin America of his day.

1924

Two editions later the book was 'privatized' and in 1924, in the hands of Royal Mail, the steamship company for South America, it became The South American Handbook, subtitled 'South America in a nutshell'. This annual publication became the 'bible' for generations of travellers to South America and remains so to this day. In the early days travel was by sea and the Handbook gave all the details needed for the long voyage from Europe. What to wear for dinner; how to arrange a cricket match with the Cable & Wireless staff on the Cape Verde Islands and a full account of the journey from Liverpool up the Amazon to Manaus: 5898 miles without changing cabin!

1939

As the continent opened up, the South American Handbook reported the new Pan Am flying boat services, and the fortnightly airship service from Rio to Europe on the Graf Zeppelin. For reasons still unclear but with extraordinary determination, the annual editions continued through the Second World War.

1970s

Many more people discovered South America and the backpacking trail started to develop. All the while the Handbook was gathering fans, including literary vagabonds such as Paul Theroux and Graham Greene (who once sent some updates addressed to "The publishers of the best travel guide in the world, Bath, England").

1990s

During the 1990s the company set about developing a new travel guide series using this legendary title as the flagship. By 1997 there were over a dozen guides in the series and the Footprint imprint was launched.

2000s

The series grew quickly and there were soon Footprint travel guides covering more than 150 countries. In 2004, Footprint launched its first thematic guide: *Surfing Europe*, packed with colour photographs, maps and charts. This was followed by further thematic guides such as *Diving the World, Snowboarding the World, Body and Soul escapes, Travel with Kids* and *European City Breaks*.

2011

Today we continue the traditions of the last 90 years that have served legions of travellers so well. We believe that these help to make Footprint guides different. Our policy is to use authors who are genuine experts who write for independent travellers; people possessing a spirit of adventure, looking to get off the beaten track.

Colombia Handbook

Anna Maria Espsäter

After years of negative headlines, Colombia is at long last coming into its own. Blessed with such a variety of natural landscapes, from arid deserts and vast savannahs to snow-capped volcanoes and white-sand beaches, Colombia offers a staggering array of experiences. As the only country in South America to have both a Caribbean and a Pacific coastline, a relaxing beach holiday can be enjoyed on either coast; raging rivers and deep caves have turned the area surrounding San Gil into a mecca for adventure sports enthusiasts; the Amazon jungle in the far south is a paradise for nature lovers; and the Zona Cafetera, where the majority of Colombia's 'black gold' is produced, offers authentic stays at coffee *fincas*, amidst abundant greenery and stunning mountain scenery.

Although nature is a great draw, the cities aren't to be missed either: vibrant and lively, Colombia has some of the best urban culture and nightlife in Latin America. Bogotá's Gold Museum, Cali's salsa clubs and Medellín's Plaza Botero are all well worth visiting.

It is rumoured that no other country on the continent has a greater variety of music genres and most of these can be enjoyed at the numerous fiestas held in even the tiniest of villages throughout the year. These festivals are a legacy of the mixed heritage of indigenous, European and African cultures, all of which have helped shape and create modern-day Colombia. Cultural icons such as sculptor Fernando Botero and writer Gabriel García Márquez – even perhaps drug baron Pablo Escobar – capture the imagination. Prepare to be dazzled by the sheer diversity of this country.

This page Colombia is the only South American country to have both Caribbean and Pacific beaches.

Previous page The beautiful one-storey colonial houses in Cartagena were originally home to the artisan classes.

Punta Gallinas ⑥
Península de
la Guajara

Santa Marta○ ⑤
Barranquilla○ Ciudad
Perdida
Cartagena○ ④

Maicao○

Mompós○

PANAMA

Sincelejo○

Montería○

○Turbo

Río Cauca

Santa Fe de
Antioquia○

Bahía Solano○

Quibdó○

Istmina○

Medellín○ ⑦

Manizales○

Pereira○ ⑨
⑧ Parque
Nacional
Los Nevados

Villa de Leiva○ ○Tunja

Bucaramanga○
○San Gil
③

Río Magdalena

Aracua○

Río Meta

② Zipaquirá

□ ①
BOGOTA

Pacific
Ocean

Buenaventura○

Cali○ ⑩
⑫
Tierradentro

⑪
Popayán○

San Agustín○

Pasto○ ○Mocoa

○Ipiales Puerto Asis

○ Garzón

○ Florencia

Río Guaviare

Mitú
○

Río Vaupés

Río Apaporis

Leguizamo
○

ECUADOR

Río Putumayo

Río Caquetá

N

100 km
100 miles

PERU

Tarapacá○

Leticia○
Río Amazonas

Tumaco○

4

Highlights See colour maps at back of book

aribbean Sea

VENEZUELA

Puerto
Carreño

Río Orinoco

Puerto
nírida

BRAZIL

1 La Candelaria
Stroll through the
capital city's vibrant
historic centre.
➤ See page 54

2 Zipaquirá
Wonder at this
imposing cathedral,
carved inside an
ancient salt mine.
➤ See page 86

3 San Gil Discover
the extreme within,
abseiling, rafting,
caving or paragliding
in Colombia's adven-
ture sports capital.
➤ See page 111

4 Cartagena Explore
the fortified old centre,
teeming with historical
buildings, then laze
on the beautiful
beaches nearby.
➤ See page 138

5 Ciudad Perdida
Climb the 1300 stone
steps and trek through
the jungle to this
hidden archaeological
site. ➤ See page 183

6 Punta Gallinas
Experience the other-
worldly landscape and
solitary sand dunes
of South America's
northernmost point.
➤ See page 195

7 Medellín Enjoy
Colombia's city of
eternal spring, taking
a turn in its tango bars
or partying all night
in Parque Lleras.
➤ See page 214

8 La Zona Cafetera
Stay on an authentic
coffee *finca*, learning
about all things coffee.
➤ See page 252

**9 Los Nevados
National Park** Wander
the *páramo*, and get up
close and personal with
some of Colombia's
highest peaks.
➤ See page 259

10 Cali Practise your
sleek moves and dance
the night away in
Cali's salsatecas.
➤ See page 286

11 Popayán Admire
the whitewashed
colonial houses or
take a dip in the
nearby hot springs.
➤ See page 304

**12 Tierradentro and
San Agustín** Feel
Colombia's ancient
cultures come to life,
exploring hidden
tombs and mysterious
statues. ➤ See pages
307 and 317

5

Valle de los Cojines, an enormous valley filled with 'pillow plants' and surrounded by the snow tops of the Sierra Nevada El Cocuy.

In Colombia there are more festivals, parties and carnivals than there are days in the year.

Contents

↘ **1 Introduction**
4 Highlights map

↘ **11 Essentials**
12 Planning your trip
17 Getting there
19 Getting around
23 Sleeping
25 Eating and drinking
29 Festivals and events
31 Responsible travel
33 Essentials A-Z

↘ **45 Bogotá & around**
54 Sights
68 Listings
83 Around Bogotá

↘ **89 North of Bogotá**
92 Boyacá Department
111 Santander Department
126 Norte de Santander
   Department

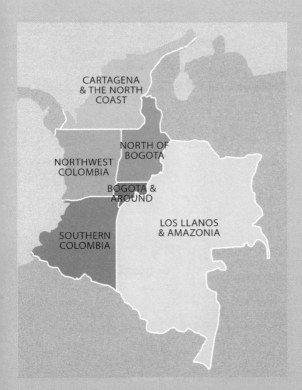

CARTAGENA
& THE NORTH
COAST

NORTH OF
BOGOTÁ

NORTHWEST
COLOMBIA

BOGOTA &
AROUND

LOS LLANOS
& AMAZONIA

SOUTHERN
COLOMBIA

↘ 135 **Cartagena & the North Coast**
138 Cartagena
157 Around Cartagena
170 Barranquilla
175 Santa Marta and around
191 East to Venezuela
200 San Andrés and
   Providencia

↘ 211 **Northwest Colombia**
214 Medellín
237 Around Medellín
248 Department of Chocó
252 La Zona Cafetera

↘ 283 **Southern Colombia**
286 Cauca Valley
304 Popayán and Tierradentro
317 San Agustín and around
323 Far south

↘ 333 **Los Llanos & Amazonia**
336 Los Llanos
340 Amazonia

↘ 349 **Background**
350 History
355 Modern Colombia
359 Culture
370 People
371 Land and environment

↘ 383 **Footnotes**
384 Basic Spanish
   for travellers
389 Index
395 Advertisers' index
396 Acknowledgements
397 About the author
400 Credits

Contents

12 Planning your trip
  12 Where to go
  15 Itineraries
  15 When to go
  16 What to do

17 Getting there
  17 Air
  18 River
  18 Road
  18 Sea

19 Getting around
  19 Air
  20 Rail
  20 Road
  22 Maps

23 Sleeping

25 Eating and drinking
  25 Regional specialities
  27 Restaurants
  27 Drinks

29 Festivals and events

31 Responsible travel

33 Essentials A-Z

Footprint features

21 Driving in Colombia
24 Sleeping price codes
26 Eating price codes
30 Bizarre festivals
32 How big is your footprint?
36 Colombian Spanish

Essentials

Planning your trip

Where to go

A country as large and varied as Colombia has a great many sights worth visiting. A comprehensive look at the country will require a good deal of time and planning. If you have limited time and want to see as much as possible, you could consider air travel. If you have more time, there are good Pullman and minibuses.

You will almost certainly arrive in the country via Bogotá or Cartagena, so a look at these two cities is a good place to start.

Bogotá

Like most capital cities, at least in Latin America, Bogotá is crowded, noisy, polluted and disorganized. Yet it is a proud, cosmopolitan city with impressive modern buildings and services. The historical centre, La Candelaria, has a wealth of fine colonial churches and buildings. For a great view of the city, take the cable car to the top of Monserrate. A visit to the Gold Museum, with its dazzling collection of pre-Columbian art, is a mind-boggling experience. There is excellent accommodation in all categories. Bogotá is the best place for information on the whole country and has comprehensive transport links. Places to visit nearby include Guatavita, Zipaquirá, the many towns down to the west towards the Río Magdalena, and the parks of Chicaque, Chingaza and Sumapaz (check for security). You may decide to spend the night in one of these places and there is plenty of good accommodation on offer. Midweek stays can be particularly good value.

Cartagena

Cartagena is more relaxed than Bogotá, though it is not without the problems of a big modern city. It is colonial Spain's finest legacy in the Americas, impressive in every respect. Spend several days here as there is so much to see. It is also the best base for visits to the Caribbean coast and the islands: check out the beaches and the watersports available. Beaches along the coast and on the offshore islands can be visited, as can the strange mud volcanoes nearby. To the northeast, Barranquilla has its own attractions, including a spectacular carnival, perhaps the finest in Latin America after Rio de Janeiro. Mompós is a superb colonial town that can be visited from either Barranquilla or Cartagena, but you will have to stay overnight. Cartagena is also the gateway to San Andrés, a popular island resort, and to the charming neighbouring island of Providencia.

Medellín

Medellín, with its recent history of over-industrialization and violent drug cartels behind it, is now a modern, vibrant city with many new buildings that complement the old, restored architecture. There is plenty of modern art to see, fascinating places to visit in the surrounding Department of Antioquia and friendly, outgoing people to meet. The *paisas* (as the locals are known) leave the city at the weekends and head for the countryside; tourists should follow their lead. Santa Fe de Antioquia, a remarkable, preserved colonial town, is an easy day trip but you will almost certainly want to stay the night. The journey to Rionegro takes you through some beautiful countryside, and to the west of Medellín, El Peñol, the towering black rock overlooking Guatapé and its huge lake, should not be missed. There are many delightful places with lakes and waterfalls in this region. To the

New on iPad

oo tripadvisor®

Find places travellers trust
- Hotels
- Restaurants
- Things to do
- Flights
- Forums

Write a Review

The #1 Essential Travel Download*
Get TripAdvisor Mobile - **FREE**

- Browse millions of traveller reviews, photos & maps
- Find hotels, restaurants & things to do
- See what's nearby
- Apps available for iPhone, Android, Nokia, Palm Pre, & Windows Mobile

* From "iPhone Travel Apps: 10 Essential Downloads" on Frommers.com

southwest of Medellín is Jericó and particularly recommended for a visit is Jardín, truly a garden village. Medellín is also the jumping-off point for Quibdó, the Chocó and the northern part of Colombia's Pacific coast.

Cali

The 'capital' of the south, Cali is about the same size as Medellín and has a similar unhappy past. However, it is now reinvigorated and has an attractive, lively atmosphere, which springs from its interesting mix of inhabitants. The locals have combined to make this the finest popular music centre of the continent and this is well illustrated by their passion for salsa. The Farallones National Park is a few kilometers to the west. To the north is Darién; with its Calima museum and lake it is a recommended trip. Buenaventura is accessible from Cali, as is the central section of the Pacific coast and the island of Gorgona.

The rest of Colombia

A quarter of the population live in the four cities listed above, but to find the heart of Colombia you must look elsewhere. The country is strongly regionalized and this stems from the rugged terrain and its early history, when many different indigenous groups lived separately. All roads do not lead to Bogotá; hence the importance today of the *departamentos* and their capitals. In the 19th century some were independent countries for a short time (eg Antioquia) and these were often Spanish settlements. The fierce pride of the later inhabitants ensured the preservation of their heritage and virtually all are worth a visit, but of particular interest are Popayán, Tunja, Pereira, Neiva and Bucaramanga.

Smaller places that express even better the feel of colonial Colombia are spread around the western part of the country. They include Villa de Leiva, Santa Fe de Antioquia, Mompós, Monguí and Barichara. If you are looking for fine scenery, it is all here: from deserts (La Guajira and Tatacoa) to the wettest area of the Americas (Chocó); from one of the hottest places in South America (Norte de Santander) to the snows of the Nevados.

For beach lovers, Colombia has two long coastlines that give access to plenty of palm-fringed tropical paradises. Thanks to increased security, the Darién's Caribbean coastline has opened up to visitors and isolated villages such as Capurganá and Sapzurro are rewarding destinations for the intrepid traveller, as are the villages of Bahía Solano and Nuquí on the Pacific coast. Offshore are many coral islands. Further afield, the island of Providencia is full of culture and laid-back charm, and its Seaflower Bioreserve barrier reef offers some of the best and most extensive diving in the Caribbean. There are deep river gorges (Chicamocha), high mountain chains (Cocuy and Sierra de Santa Marta) and many areas of fine *páramo* for walking and trekking. Colombia also has its own stretch of Amazon, and Leticia is recommended as a good, well-organized place to experience the jungle. In addition to all this, there are 56 national parks spread throughout the country.

Some particularly outstanding attractions that it would be a pity to miss are: the archaeological sites of Ciudad Perdida, San Agustín and Tierradentro; the wax palms above Salento; the flamingos near Riohacha; the mud volcanoes near Arboletes; the wonderful rich green countryside of the Zona Cafetera; the Gold Museum in Bogotá; the walled city in Cartagena; El Peñol rock; Parque Botero in Medellín; Las Lajas sanctuary; and the Zipaquirá salt cathedral.

Two weeks

The fast northern loop To see as much as possible in such a short space of time will require air travel and some pre-planning. Most visitors to Colombia make a beeline for its sparkling Caribbean coast. Start by flying from Bogotá to Santa Marta and the beaches of Tayrona National Park. After a few days unwinding it's a short hop along the coast to Cartagena. Spend a couple of days exploring the labyrinthine walled city before relaxing on Playa Blanca or the coral island of the Islas del Rosario (depending on your budget). The colonial town of Mompós is a worthwhile (though travel-heavy) stopover on the way to Medellín. After taking in the Antioquian capital's culture and nightlife, spend a few days sampling the department's beautiful traditional villages, such as Santa Fe de Antioquia or Guatapé, before catching a plane back to Bogotá.

Three weeks

The more leisurely northern loop An extra week allows for more bus travel and a chance to see Colombia's interior up close. Start by exploring Bogotá and its colonial sector, La Candelaria. A visit to the Gold Museum is a must. It's then a short bus ride to Villa de Leiva, with the magnificent Zipaquirá salt cathedral a convenient stopover. Soak up Villa de Leiva's colonial atmosphere over a couple of days and explore its many surrounding attractions before heading up to San Gil for some rafting, kayaking and hiking. The neighbouring village of Barichara will provide more colonial architecture. From San Gil, make your way up to Santa Marta and follow the same loop as above as far as Medellín and on to Bogotá, stopping off at the Río Claro Nature Reserve en route.

Four weeks or more

The figure of eight A month or more will give you the opportunity to see a good chunk of the country – though you will have to travel fast. Start by following the northern loop described above and then from Bogotá, take a bus due south stopping off at the Tatacoa desert for a night under the stars. From nearby Neiva it's a hard day's slog (but a worthwhile one) to Tierradentro. Spend a couple of days exploring the extraordinary tombs in the surrounding hills before heading down to San Agustín for a well-earned rest in one of the town's many comfortable country *hostales* and for some horse riding in its stunning countryside. From San Agustín it's a spectacular drive to the dazzling white city of Popayán, which has several attractions in its environs such as the market at Silvia. From here, head to the salsa-mad city of Cali, but try and be there for the weekend. Next, venture into the 'coffee zone' for a stay on a coffee *finca*. The village of Salento and the Valle de Cocora are a must if you find yourself in this region, as are the snowy peaks of Los Nevados. From here it's an nine-hour bus journey or a short flight back to Bogotá.

When to go

The climate varies little in Colombia and other than the Chocó (northwest Colombia) where it rains almost daily, you will see plenty of sun year-round. There are no seasons to speak of and temperatures are dictated mainly by altitude. However, travellers should take note that between March and September is the rainy season in the eastern departments, which can make travel difficult because of landslides and flooding. See page 375 for more detailed information on climate.

The best time for a visit is December to February, on average the driest months. It's worth remembering, though, that this is holiday season for many Colombians and prices rise significantly in the most popular places, and transport, including domestic flights, can be busy. During this period, a number of major annual fiestas are held, for example in January in the south (Popayán and Pasto) and in February, at the opposite end of the country, Barranquilla Carnival. These events bring the locals out in force and it is a fun time to visit. Equally, Easter is a local holiday time and almost every town has superb celebrations. In July and August, accommodation prices tend to rise because of school holidays.

What to do

Hiking

Colombia's varied topography offers a wealth of options for the hiking enthusiast. Everything from jungle treks and scampers over glacier fields to leisurely strolls through Arcadian landscapes can be enjoyed here. In Los Nevados and El Cocuy, Colombia has a couple of mountain ranges to rival any along the Andean chain. Other national parks such as Puracé offer countless waterfalls, lakes and trails to explore. To get up close and personal with tropical wildlife the Colombian Amazon is the place to go. Reserva Natural Palmarí (actually in Brazil but best accessed from Leticia), offers guided jungle walks ranging from one to 72 hrs. **Sal Si Puedes**, T1-2833765, and **Corporación Clorofila Urbana**, T1-6168711, www.cloro filaurbana.org, are 2 of several walking clubs that organize walks in the countryside just outside Bogotá and further afield.

Diving

With 2 extensive coastlines it's not surprising that Colombia offers myriad diving opportunities. Top of the list for aquatic aficionados must be the San Andrés and Providencia archipelago, which boasts the third-largest barrier reef in the world. The several dive shops dotted around the 2 islands offer huge choice for exploring this underwater wonderland. The Caribbean coast is known for its large brain coral and the fishing village of Taganga has established itself as a dive centre. There are coral islands off Cartagena and Tolú while Capurganá on the Darién coast has some excellent dive sites. On the Pacific coast, Bahía

Solano offers the chance to explore a scuttled navy vessel. Further south the ex-prison island of Gorgona has countless exotic fish and turtles, while the remote island of Malpelo is heaven for hammerhead shark fans.

Parapenting

Squeezed between the Andean mountain ranges of the Central and Eastern cordilleras that create a very effective wind tunnel, the Mesa de Ruitoque near Bucaramanga is the perfect place for parapenting. With 2 very professional schools, 1 of which even has its own hostel, this is the perfect place to learn how to glide the sky. Nearby San Gil has 2 excellent locations for paragliding, 1 of which involves a flight over the spectacular Chicamocha Canyon.

Rafting and kayaking

The town of San Gil has become the unofficial capital of the Colombian adventure sports scene. 3 whitewater rivers flow through or near it, offering a range of levels to satisfy everyone from the timid beginner to the seasoned adrenalin junkie. There are many companies offering professional and safety-conscious guidance and equipment, as well as new thrills such as hydrospeed, best described as whitewater boogie boarding. In southern Colombia, the village of San Agustín catches the Magdalena river at its wildest, while Cubarral on the Ariari River near Villavicencio is another popular rafting destination.

Operators are listed in the relevant places throughout the book.
See page 124 for San Gil operators.

Getting there

Air

International flights arrive principally at Bogotá and Cartagena, but there are also direct flights to Medellín, Cali, Pereira, Barranquilla and San Andrés. Fares are significantly lower in the low season, outside the peaks times of Easter, July, August and December to mid-January.

From Europe
There are direct flights to Bogotá from Paris with **Air France** (www.airfrance.com), from Frankfurt with Lufthansa (www.lufthansa.com), from Madrid with **Avianca** (www.avianca.com), and **Iberia** (www.iberia.com). Flights from London go via Europe or the USA.

From North America
Continental (www.continental.com) has direct flights from New York, Cleveland and Houston. **American Airlines** (www.aa.com) flies direct from Miami to Bogotá. **Delta** (www.delta.com) flies via Atlanta. **Spirit Air** (www.spiritair.com) has flights from the US to Cartagena, Medellín and Bogotá. **Air Canada** (www.aircanada.com) flies direct to Bogotá from Toronto.

From Australia and New Zealand
LAN (www.lan.com) has connections with Sydney and Auckland via Santiago in Chile.

From Latin America
Avianca (www.avianca.com) has direct connections with Bogotá from Buenos Aires, Caracas, Lima, Mexico City, Panama City, Quito, Santiago and San José. **TACA** (www.taca.com) flies direct to Bogotá from Lima, Montevideo and San José and from Lima to Medellín. **Copa** (www.copaair.com) has direct flights from Panama City. **Aerolíneas Argentinas** (www.aerolineas.com.ar) has two flights a week, Wednesday and Friday, between Buenos Aires and Bogotá. **LAN** has direct connections from Santiago.

Discount travel agents

In the UK
Dial A Flight, T0844-811 4444, www.dialaflight.com. Discount flight specialists.
GAP Adventures, T0844-272 0000, www.gapadventures.com. GAP year and adventure specialist.
Journey Latin America, T020-8747 8315, www.journeylatinamerica.co,uk. Latin America specialist, tailor-made and group tours.

STA Travel, T0871-230 0040, www.statravel.co.uk. Specialists in low-cost student/youth flights and tours, student IDs and insurance.
Trailfinders,T0845-054 6060, www.trailfinders.com.
Tucan Travel, T020-8896 1600, www.tucantravel.com. Tailor-made tours and adventure travel.

In North America
Air Brokers International, T01-800-883 3273, www.airbrokers.com. Consolidator

and specialists in Round the World and Circle Pacific tickets.

Discount Airfares Worldwide On-Line, www.etn.nl/discount.htm. A hub of consolidator and discount agent links.

STA Travel, T1-800-781 4040, www.statravel.com. Branches in Los Angeles, New York, San Diego, Boston, Chicago, Seattle ,Washington DC and a number of other US locations.

In Australia and New Zealand
Contours Travel, T1300-135 391, www.contourstravel.com.au.
Flight Centre, in Australia, T133133, www.flightcentre.com.au; in New Zealand, T0800-243 544, www.flightcentre.co.nz.
STATravel, in Australia, T134 782, www.statravel.com.au; in New Zealand, T0800-474 400, www.statravel.co.nz.
Trailfinders, T1300-780212, www.trailfinders.com.au.
Travel.com.au, T1300-130483, www.travel.com.au.

River

Colombia shares borders with Brazil and Peru at Leticia on the Amazon. It is possible to cross from these countries by ferry, but the journey can be time consuming. **Amazon Cruise Lines** ⓘ *www.amazoncruiselines.com*, operates between Iquitos and Leticia.

Road

The main Colombia–Venezuela crossings are at Cúcuta–San Antonio (page 129) and Maicao–Paraguachón for Maracaibo (page 196). The border with Ecuador is crossed at Ipiales–Rumichaca (page 329). ▶▶ *See Visas and immigration, page 42.*

Foot
If travelling independently on foot, there are many more places for entering or leaving Colombia. These include from Ecuador via Puerto Asís, from Panama via the Darién Gap and from Venezuela across the Río Orinoco, none of which are advised at the moment under current security circumstances.

Sea

Colombia can be reached from Ecuador entering via Tumaco. There are various ways to reach Colombia from Panama by sea but only the Capurganá route is currently considered safe.

Getting around

Air

Colombia has a well-established national airline network with several competing airlines. Internal flights are increasingly competitively priced and if you have little time, flying is a worthwhile option. **Avianca, Aires, Satena** and **Easyfly** are the main carriers, the latter a low-cost airline, with an expanding network of routes. There are also several regional airlines such as **Aerolíneas de Antioquia**, which serve smaller destinations.

A useful search engine for sourcing cheap flights is **www.despegar.com**. It may be worth using a travel agent to look for flights as they often have discount arrangements with certain airlines, or book online for good last-minute deals, as well as advance purchase fares. **Doble Vía** ① *T211 2754*, and **Vivir Volando** ① *T601 4676, www.vivirvolando.com*, in Bogotá, and **Destino Colombia** ① *www.destinocolombia.com*, in Medellín and Cartagena, are recommended.

Domestic airlines

Copa Airlines, Cra 10, No 27-51, Loc 165, Bogotá, T342 7221, www.copaair.com. Colombia's second largest airline after it was bought out by Panamanian carrier **Copa**. Flies to most of the main destinations.
Aires, T294 0300 (Bogotá), T01-900 331 9440 (rest of the country), www.aires.aero. Smaller airline with services to some of the remoter destinations as well as the main ones.
Avianca, El Dorado airport, Bogotá, T413-9862, www.avianca.com. Offices in every major city in Colombia. The country's national airline, Avianca flies to most destinations. The drawback is that all connections must go via Bogotá.
Easyfly, T414 8111 (in Bogotá) www.easyfly.com.co. New budget airline with cheap flights to obscure destinations near popular tourist cities.
Satena, Av Eldorado 103-08, Entrada 1, interior 11, Bogotá, T605 2222 (T01-8000 331 7100, rest of the country), www.satena.com. Government-owned airline with flights to most destinations.

Rail

Colombia used to have an extensive railway system but due to lack of funding most of the lines have fallen into disrepair or are used purely for cargo. There are two exceptions. On weekends, a tourist train runs north from La Sabana station in downtown Bogotá, stopping at Usaquén and continuing to the salt cathedral at Zipaquirá and Cajicá. See www.turistren.com.co for more information.

The Tren Turístico Café y Azúcar, another tourist train, operates only at weekends and public holidays between Cali, Buga and La Tebaida. Another line leaves Cali for La Cumbre, on the way to Buenaventura. See www.trenturisticocafeyazucar.com.co for more information.

Sadly, an attempt to resuscitate a third railway line between Santa Marta and Gabriel García Márquez's hometown of Aracataca appears to have stuttered to a halt. Dubbed 'The Yellow Train of Macondo', the line was opened in 2007 to a great fanfare with 'Gabo' himself aboard for its maiden voyage but a regular service has so far failed to materialize.

Road

While there are few motorways, the main roads in Colombia are mostly in good condition and journeys are generally comfortable, although landslides frequently close roads after rains. From Bogotá two roads run north towards the coast. To the northeast, a road heads high over the mountains of Boyacá and up to Bucaramanga before straightening up as it makes towards the Sierra Nevada de Santa Marta. Another road climbs northeast from here toward Cúcuta and the Venezuelan border.

A second road leaves Bogotá to the northwest and joins the Magdalena River Valley at Honda. It follows the river until it reaches a fork at Puerto Triunfo. The eastern artery cuts back towards Bucaramanga. The western branch leads to Medellín.

Medellín is on the course of the Pan-American Highway, the single, continuous road that links most of the countries in the Americas, beginning in Canada and ending in Chile (interrupted only by the Darién Gap jungle between Panama and Colombia). In Colombia, after Darién, it begins again at Turbo and runs due south, passing through Medellín, the Zona Cafetera, Cali, Popayán, Pasto and reaches Ecuador via Ipiales.

There are two further main roads exiting Bogotá. One runs southeast over (and under) high mountain passes towards Villavicencio and the Llanos. The other heads south towards Neiva. It eventually joins up with the Pan-American Highway at Pasto but not before tackling some treacherous terrain around Mocoa.

Bus

On the main routes, the bus network is comprehensive and buses are generally comfortable and efficient. Arriving at one of the large bus stations, the choice of carriers can be daunting, but it also has its advantages as there are frequent services and competition between different companies can sometimes allow for a bit of haggling.

There is usually a choice of operators along main routes, with varying degrees of quality and speed. The cheapest, *corrientes*, are essentially local buses, stopping frequently, uncomfortable and slow but offering plenty of local colour. *Pullman* or *servicio de lujo* (luxury) are long-distance buses, usually with air conditioning, toilets and DVDs (almost always violent pirate films dubbed into Spanish). *Colectivos*, also known as *vans* or *busetas*, are usually 12-20 seat vehicles but also seven-seater cars, pick-up trucks or taxis,

Driving in Colombia

If there is one rule that is always adhered to on Colombian roads it is that 'might is right'. Colombians may have impeccable manners in personal exchanges but when they step into a car, like Jekyll and Hyde, their character transforms. Overtaking around blind corners, ignoring traffic lights – anything goes. The worst culprits are truck drivers who seem to treat their job as a permanent rally. They are closely followed by bus drivers, with the rest not far behind. In cities, especially Bogotá, pedestrians have few rights. So mind how you go, look both ways twice when crossing the road, sit tight on the bus or in a taxi, and cross your fingers.

rather cramped but fast, saving several hours on long journeys. The latter are also known as *por puestos* (pay-by-the-seat) and will not leave until all the places have been filled. It is also possible to order a *'puerta-a-puerta'* (door-to-door) service with some companies. The cost of tickets is relatively high by Latin American standards. Fares shown in the text are middle of the range but should be treated as no more than a guide. These are some of the best known operators: **Berlinas del Fonce**, www.berlinasdelfonce.com, **Bolivariano**, www.bolivariano.com.co, **Copetran**, www.copetran.com.co, **Expreso Brasilia**, www.expreso brasilia.com, **Expreso Palmira**, www.expresopalmira.com.co.

Car

With a good road network, self-driving is becoming an increasingly popular way of seeing Colombia. It's an especially good way of exploring rural areas such as the Zona Cafetera where public transport will only take you between the main cities. The kind of motoring you do will depend on the car you set out with. While a normal car will reach most places of interest, high ground clearance is useful for badly surfaced or unsurfaced roads and for fording rivers. Four-wheel drive vehicles are recommended for flexibility in mountain and jungle territory. Wherever you travel you should expect from time to time to find roads that are badly maintained, damaged or closed during the wet season; expect delays because of floods and landslides. There is also the possibility of delays due to major roadworks. Do not plan your schedule too tightly. There are *peajes* (toll stations) every 60-100 km or so on major roads: tolls depend on distance and type of vehicle, but start around US$3. Motorcycles and bicycles don't have to pay. For excellent information in Spanish and English, including all the toll costs, see www.viajaporcolombia.com.

Safety Before taking a long journey, ask locally about the state of the road and check if there are any safety issues. Roads are not always signposted. Avoid night journeys; the roads may not be in good condition, lorry and bus drivers tend to be reckless, and animals often stray onto the roads. Police and military checks can be frequent in troubled areas, keep your documents handy. In town, try to leave your car in an attended *parqueadero* (car park), especially at night. Only park in the street if there is someone on guard, tip US$0.50.

Spare no ingenuity in making your car impenetrable. Your model should be like an armoured van: anything less secure can be broken into by the determined and skilled thief. Avoid leaving your car unattended except in a locked garage or guarded parking space. Adult minders or street children will generally protect your car fiercely in exchange for a tip. Be sure to note down key numbers and carry spares of the most important ones (but don't keep all spares inside the vehicle).

Documents National driving licences may be used by foreigners in Colombia. International drivers licences are also accepted. Carry driving documents with you at all times.

When you cross the border into Colombia, make sure you keep any papers you are given; you will be asked to produce them when you leave. Bringing a car in by sea or air is much more complicated: you will usually be required to hire an agent to clear it through customs, which can be a slow and expensive process. To bring a car into Colombia, you must have documents proving ownership of the vehicle, and a tourist card/transit visa. These are normally valid for 90 days and must be applied for at the Colombian consulate in the country that you will be leaving for Colombia. A *carnet de passages* is recommended when entering with a European registered vehicle.

Insurance for the vehicle against accident, damage or theft is best arranged in the country of origin, but it is getting increasingly difficult to find agencies who offer this service. In Latin American countries it is very expensive to insure against accident and theft.

Fuel prices are around US$4.70 per gallon for standard petrol, US$4.10 per gallon for super and US$5.40 per gallon for diesel. Prices are likely to fluctuate in the current economic climate.

Car hire Car hire, though relatively expensive, especially if you are going to the more remote areas and need 4WD or specialist vehicles, is convenient for touring, and the better hotels all have safe parking. The main international car rental companies are represented at principal airports but may be closed on Saturday afternoons and Sundays. There are also local firms in most of the departmental capitals. In addition to passport and driver's licence, a credit card may be asked for as additional proof of identity (Visa, MasterCard, American Express), and to secure a returnable deposit to cover any liability not covered by the insurance. Check the insurance carefully; it may not cover you beyond a certain figure, nor for 'natural' damage such as flooding. Ask if extra cover is available. You should be given a diagram showing any scratches and other damage on the car before you hired it.

Maps

A decent map can be difficult to find but sound out the nearest tourist office and they should be able to provide at least a map of the town.

There are few road maps but the *Guía Rutas de Colombia*, available at all toll booths, provides a relatively decent map, www.rutascolombia.com (in Spanish). Try also major bookstores such as **Pan-Americana**.

The **Instituto Geográfico Agustín Codazzi** ① *www.igac.gov.co*, produces general and specialist maps of the country. Unfortunately, this institution is receiving increasingly less funding from the government and many maps may be out of date.

Sleeping

In Colombia there are a number of quite exceptional hotels that are well worth seeking out. They are usually in colonial towns and not necessarily very expensive. There is a small network of youth hostels, of varying quality and used extensively by Colombian groups, but international members are welcome. Increasingly more budget accommodation and backpackers' hostels are opening up, as well as many chic boutique hotels, often in restored colonial buildings.

There are many names in Colombia for hotels including *posada, pensión, residencia, hostal, hostería, hospedaje, hospedería, mesón* and *hotelito*. Ignore them all and simply look at the price range for what to expect. *Motels* are almost always pay-by-the-hour 'love hotels' (see page 245) for use by illicit lovers, couples still living with their parents, or prostitutes and their clients. Most of the time, especially with the more expensive drive-in ones on the outskirts of town, the names will provide an obvious enough clue (eg 'Passion Motel'), but this is not always the case. Some *residencias* also double up as *acostaderos*, or love hotels. It's best to avoid these.

The more expensive hotels add on 16% IVA (VAT) to bills. Strictly speaking foreigners should be exempt from this but there seems to be some confusion about the application of this law. Raise the matter with your hotel and you may well get a discount. Some hotels add a small insurance charge.

From 15 December to mid- or late January, and 15 June to 31 August, some hotels in main holiday centres may increase prices by as much as 50%. In some hotels outside the main cities you can only stay (very cheaply) at *en pensión* rates, but no allowance is made for missing a meal.

The Colombian hotel federation, **COTELCO** ① *www.cotelco.org*, has lists of authorized prices for all member hotels, which can be consulted at tourist offices. In theory, new laws require all hotels to be registered, but to date this is incomplete particularly with regard to cheaper hotels. Most hotels in Colombia charge US$3 to US$10 for extra beds for children, up to a maximum (usually) of four beds per room. Prices are normally displayed at reception, but in quiet periods it is always worth negotiating and ask to see the room before committing.

When booking a hotel from an airport or bus station, try to speak to the hotel yourself; most will understand at least simple English and possibly French, German or Italian. If you use an official tourist agent, you will probably pay a little more as a booking fee. If you accept help from anyone else, you could be putting yourself at risk.

In cheaper hotels, beware of electric shower heaters, which can be dangerous through faulty wiring. Hotels are sometimes checked by the police for drugs. Make sure they do not remove any of your belongings. You do not need to show them any money. Cooperate but be firm about your rights.

Toilets may suffer from inadequate water supplies. In all cases, however, do not flush paper down the toilet bowl but use the receptacle provided. Carry toilet paper with you as cheaper establishments as well as restaurants, bars, etc may not provide it, or make an additional charge for it.

Sleeping price codes

LL over US$200	L US$151-200	AL US$101-150
A US$66-100	B US$46-65	C US$31-45
D US$21-30	E US$12-20	F US$7-11
G US$6 and under		

Price codes refer to the cost of a double room in high season, including taxes.

Camping

Local tourist authorities have lists of official campsites, but they are seldom signposted on main roads, so can be hard to find. Permission to camp with tent, campervan or car may be granted by landowners in less populated areas. Many *haciendas* have armed guards protecting their property, which can add to your safety. Do not camp on private land without permission. Those in campervans can camp by the roadside, but it is not particularly safe and it can be difficult to find a secluded spot. If you have a vehicle, it is possible to camp at truck drivers' restaurants or sometimes at police or army posts. Check very carefully before deciding to camp: you may be exposing yourself to significant danger. Some hostels, particularly in rural areas, also offer camping and often provide tents and other equipment at an additional cost, but are still cheaper than dorm beds.

Youth hostels

La Federación Colombiana de Albergues Juveniles ⓘ *www.fcaj.org.co*, is affiliated to the International Youth Hostel Federation (IYHF) and has 12 hostels around the country, with a **main office** ⓘ *Cra 15 No 124-17, Torre B, Oficina 201, Bogotá, T612 6422*. Apart from two hostels in Bogotá, there are others in Armenia, Cartagena, Medellín, Montenegro, Paipa, Santa Marta and Manizales. Hostels are often full at holiday periods, December to January and June to mid-July; it's best to telephone in advance during these times. Otherwise, it's usually possible to arrive without a reservation. Membership can be taken out in Colombia: Hostelling International Cards are recognized and qualify for discounts. See also the **Colombian Hostel Association** ⓘ *www.colombianhostels.com*, which has hostels in Bogotá, Bucaramanga, Cartagena, Cali, Manizales, Medellín, Mompós, San Gil, Salento, San Agustín, Taganga, Valledupar and Villa de Leiva. **Hostel Trail Latin America** ⓘ *Cra 11, No 4-16, Popayán, T831 7871, www.hosteltrail.com*, is an online network of hostels and tour companies in South America providing information on locally run businesses for backpackers and independent travellers.

Homestays

In many places, it is possible to stay with a local family; check with the local tourist office to see what is available. This is a good option for those interested in learning Spanish informally in a family environment. However, if you take formal classes, you should have a student visa (see Visas and immigration, page 42). See also box, page 255.

Eating and drinking

Colombia has yet to reach international renown for its cuisine, but food is becoming more of a draw with gastronomy festivals such as Otro Sabor in Medellín changing the culinary landscape of the country. Even though you can now find most regional specialities available in all the major cities, there are many local variations to sample in different parts of Colombia.

Some of the standard items on the menu are: *sancocho*, a meat stock (may be fish on the coast) with potato, corn (on the cob), yucca, sweet potato and plantain. *Arroz con pollo* (chicken and rice), one of the standard Latin American dishes, is excellent in Colombia. *Carne asada* (grilled beefsteak), usually an inexpensive cut, is served with *papas fritas* (chips) or rice and you can ask for a vegetable of the day. *Sobrebarriga* (belly of beef) is served with varieties of potato in a tomato and onion sauce. *Huevos pericos,* eggs scrambled with onions and tomatoes, are a popular, cheap and nourishing snack available almost anywhere, especially favoured for breakfast. *Tamales* are meat pies made by folding a maize dough round chopped pork mixed with potato, rice, peas, onions and eggs wrapped in banana leaves (which you don't eat) and steamed. Other ingredients may be added such as olives, garlic, cloves and paprika. Colombians eat *tamales* for breakfast with hot chocolate. *Empanadas* are another popular snack; these are made with chicken or various other meats, or vegetarian filling, inside a maize dough and deep fried in oil. *Patacones* are cakes of mashed and baked *platano* (large green banana). *Arepas* are standard throughout Colombia; these are flat maize griddle cakes often served instead of bread or as an alternative. *Pan de bono* is cheese flavoured bread. *Almojábanas*, a kind of sour milk/cheese bread roll, great for breakfast when freshly made. *Buñuelos* are 4-6 cm balls of wheat flour and eggs mixed and deep-fried, also best when still warm. *Arequipe* is a sugar-based brown syrup used with desserts and in confectionary, universally savoured by Colombians. *Brevas* (figs) with *arequipe* are one of the most popular desserts.

Regional specialities

Bogotá and Cundinamarca *Ajiaco de pollo* (or *ajiaco santafereño*) is a delicious chicken stew with maize, manioc (yucca), three types of potato, herbs (including *guascas*) and sometimes other vegetables, served with cream and capers, and pieces of avocado. It is a Bogotá speciality. *Chunchullo* (tripe), and *morcilla* (blood sausage) are popular dishes. *Cuajada con melado (melao)* is a dessert of fresh cheese served with cane syrup, or *natas* (based on the skin of boiled milk).

Boyacá *Mazamorra* is a meat and vegetable soup with broad and black beans, peas, varieties of potato and cornflour. *Care* (or *mazamorro* in Antioquia and elsewhere) is a milk and maize drink, which, to confuse matters further is known as *peto* in Cundinamarca. *Puchero* is a stew based on chicken with potatoes, yucca, cabbage, turnips, corn (on the cob) and herbs. *Cuchuco*, another soup with pork and sweet potato. *Masato* is a slightly fermented rice beverage. *Longaniza* (long pork sausage) is also very popular.

Eating price codes

Santander and Norte de Santander *Mute* is a traditional soup of various cereals including corn. Goat, often served with *pepitoria* (its innards) and pigeon appear in several local dishes. *Hormigas culonas* (large-bottomed black ants) is the most famous culinary delight of this area, served toasted, and particularly popular in Bucaramanga at Easter time. Locals claim they have aphrodisiacal powers. *Bocadillo veleño* is similar to quince jelly but made from guava. It takes its name from Vélez, but can be found elsewhere in Colombia. *Rampuchada* is a north Santander stew based on the fish of the Zulia river which flows into Venezuela. *Hallacas* are cornmeal turnovers with different meats and whatever else is to hand inside, typical of neighbouring Venezuela, like an oversized *tamal*. Dishes featuring chickpeas and goat's milk are popular in this part of Colombia. *Carne oreada* is salted dried meat marinated in a *panela* (unrefined sugarcane) and pineapple sauce and has the consistency of beef jerky.

Cartagena and the north coast Fish is naturally a speciality in the coastal regions. In *Arroz con coco*, rice here is prepared with coconut. *Cazuela de mariscos*, a soup/stew of shellfish and white fish, maybe including octopus and squid, is especially good. *Sancocho de pescado* is a fish stew with vegetables, usually simpler and cheaper than *cazuela*. *Chipichipi*, a small clam found along the coast in Barranquilla and Santa Marta, is a standard local dish served with rice. *Empanada* (or *arepa*) *de huevo*, is deep fried with eggs in the middle and is a good light meal. *Canasta de coco* is a good local sweet: pastry containing coconut custard flavoured with wine and surmounted by meringue.

Tolima *Lechona*, suckling pig with herbs is a speciality of Ibagué. *Viudo de pescado* is a dish based on small shellfish from the Opía (a local) river. *Achira* is a kind of hot biscuit.

Antioquia *Bandeja paisa* consists of various types of gut-busting pork cuts or other grilled meats, *chorizo* (sausage), *chicharrón* (pork crackling), sometimes an egg, served with rice, beans, potato, manioc and a green salad; this has now been adopted in other parts of the country. *Natilla*, a sponge cake made from cornflour and *salpicón*, a tropical fruit salad.

Cali and south Colombia In contrast to most of Colombia, menus tend not to include potato (in its many forms). Instead, emphasis is on corn, plantain, rice and avocado with the usual pork and chicken dishes. *Manjar blanco*, made from milk and sugar or molasses, served with biscuit is a favourite dessert. *Cuy*, *curí* or *conejillo de Indias* (guinea pig), is typical of the southern department of Nariño. *Mazorcas* (baked corn-on-the-cob) are typical of roadside stalls in southern Colombia.

Restaurants

In the main cities (Bogotá, Cartagena, Medellín and Cali) you will find a limitless choice of menu and price. The other departmental capitals have a good range of specialist restaurants and all the usual fast-food outlets, Colombian and international. Only in the smaller towns and villages, not catering for tourists, will you find a modest selection of places to eat. Watch out for times of opening in the evenings, some city areas may tend to close around 1800 (eg La Candelaria in Bogotá, although this is changing fast, with more places open late), and times may be different at weekends. On Sundays it can be particularly difficult to eat in a restaurant and even hotel restaurants may be closed.

The basic Colombian meal of the day is at lunchtime, the *almuerzo* or *menú ejecutivo/del día*, with soup, main course and fruit juice or *gaseosa* (soft drink). If you are economizing, ask for the *plato del día*, *bandeja* or *plato corriente* (just the main dish). This can be found everywhere, many restaurants will display the menu and cost in the window.

The cheapest food can be found in markets (when they are open), from street stalls in most downtown areas and at transport terminals, but bear in mind it might not be safe or agree with you. The general rules apply: keep away from uncooked food and salads, and eat fruit you have peeled yourself. Watch what the locals are eating as a guide to the best choice. Wash it down with something out of a sealed bottle. Having said that, take it easy with dishes that are unfamiliar especially if you have arrived from a different climate or altitude. On the other hand, you may find that fresh fruit drinks, wherever prepared, are irresistible in which case you will have to take your chances! ▸▸ *See Health, page 34.*

Restaurants are more difficult to evaluate than hotels because, as everywhere, they come, change and go. We try to give you a tested choice at all available price levels. Food is generally good, occasionally very good. Note that more expensive restaurants may add a discretionary 16% IVA tax to the bill.

Most of the bigger cities have specific vegetarian restaurants and you will find them listed in the text. The **Govinda** chain is widely represented. Be warned that they are normally open only for lunch. In towns and villages you will have to ask for special food to be prepared.

Drinks

Colombian coffee is always mild. *Tinto*, the national small cup of black coffee, is taken at all hours. The name is misleading; don't expect to get a glass of red. If you want it strong, ask for *café cargado*; a *tinto doble* is a large cup of black coffee. Coffee with milk is called *café perico*; *café con leche* is a mug of milk with coffee added. If you want a coffee with less milk, order *tinto y leche aparte* and they will bring the milk separately.

Tea is popular but herbal rather than Indian or Chinese: ask for (*bebida*) *aromática*, flavours include *limonaria*, *orquídea* and *manzanilla*. If you want Indian tea, *té Lipton en agua* should do the trick. *Té de menta* (mint tea) is another of many varieties available but you may have to go to an upmarket café or *casa de té*, which can be found in all of the bigger cities. Chocolate is also drunk: *chocolate Santafereño* is often taken during the afternoon in Bogotá with snacks and cheese. *Agua de panela* (hot water with unrefined sugar) is a common beverage, also made with limes, milk, or cheese.

Bottled soft drinks are universal and standard, commonly called *gaseosas*. If you want non-carbonated, ask for *sin gas*. Again you will find that many of the special fruits are used for bottled drinks. Water comes in bottles, cartons and small plastic packets, or even plastic bags: all safer than out of the tap, although tap water is generally of a reasonable quality.

Many acceptable brands of beer are produced, until recently almost all produced by the Bavaria group. Each region has a preference for different brands. The most popular are Aguila, Club Colombia, Costeño and Poker. Club Colombia won the prestigious Monde Selection 'Grand Gold Medal with Palm Leaves' in 2008, marking it out as one of the best beers in the world. The Bogota Beer Company has its own small brewery in Chapinero and has several bars around the city serving delicious draught beer modelled on British and German ales.

A traditional drink in Colombia is *chicha*. It is corn-based but sugar and/or *panela* are added and it is boiled. It is served as a non-alcoholic beverage, but if allowed to ferment over several days, and especially if kept in the fridge for a while, it becomes very potent.

The local rum is good and cheap; ask for *ron*, not *aguardiente*. One of the best rums is Ron Viejo de Caldas, another (dark) is Ron Medellín. Try *canelazo* cold or hot rum with water, sugar, lime and cinnamon. As common as rum is *aguardiente* (literally 'fire water'), a white spirit distilled from sugar cane. There are two types, with *anís* (aniseed) or without. Local table wines include Isabella; none is very good. Wine is very expensive, as much as US$15 in restaurants for an acceptable bottle of Chilean or Argentine wine, more for European and other wines.

Warning Care should be exercised when buying imported spirits in some bars and small shops. It has been reported that bottles bearing well-known labels have been 'recycled' and contain a cheap and poor imitation of the original contents and can be dangerous. You are probably safe purchasing in supermarkets. Also note that ice may not be made from drinking water.

Fruit and juices

Colombia has an exceptional range and quality of fruit – another aspect of the diversity of altitude and climate. Fruits familiar in northern and Mediterranean climates are here, though with some differences, including: *manzanas* (apples); *bananos* (bananas); *uvas* (grapes); *limones* (limes; lemons, the larger yellow variety, are rarely seen); *mangos* (mangoes); *melones* (melons); *naranjas* (oranges; usually green or yellow in Colombia); *duraznos* (peaches); and *peras* (pears).

Then there are the local fruits: *chirimoyas* (a green fruit, white inside with pips); *curuba* (banana passion fruit); *feijoa* (a green fruit with white flesh, high in vitamin C); *guayaba* (guava); *guanábana* (soursop); *lulo* (a small orange fruit); *maracuyá* (passion fruit); *mora* (literally 'black berry' but dark red more like a loganberry); *papaya*; the delicious *pitahaya* (taken either as an appetizer or dessert); *sandía* (watermelon); *tomate de árbol* (tree tomato, several varieties normally used as a fruit); and many more.

All of these fruits can be served as juices, either with milk (hopefully fresh) or water (hopefully bottled or sterilized). Most hotels and restaurants are careful about this and you can watch the drinks being prepared on street stalls. You will be surprised how delicious these drinks are and the adventurous can experiment to find their favourite. Fruit yoghurts are nourishing and cheap; Alpina brand is good; *crema* style is best. Also, Kumis is a type of liquid yoghurt. Another drink you must try is *champús*, a corn base, with fruit, *panela*, cloves and cinnamon added.

Festivals and events

There are more festivals, parties and carnivals in Colombia than days in the year. Every city, town and village has at least three or four annual events in which local products and traditions are celebrated with music, dancing and raucous revelry (these are listed throughout the book). Below are some of the most significant. ▸▸ *See also Background, page 368.*

January

2-3 Jan Feria de Manizales, www.feriademanizales.gov.co. Festivities include horse parades, beauty pageants, bullfighting and general celebration of all things coffee.

5-6 Jan Carnaval de los Blancos y Negros, www.carnavaldepasto.org. The city of Pasto celebrates one of Latin America's oldest carnivals in which everyone daubs each other with black grease and white flour to commemorate the emancipation of black slaves. Celebrations begin late Dec with communal water fights and floats. There is dancing, parades and lots of costumes.

5-10 Jan Carnaval del Diablo. The town of Ríosucio in Caldas has celebrated this homage to the devil every 2 years since 1915. The whole town effectively becomes a masked ball as locals dress up as devils and other characters in a festival in which Hispanic, black and indigenous traditions collide.

20 Jan Corraleja de Sincelejo. Jan is bullfighting season in Colombia and many towns hold events. Most famous of these is the Corraleja at Sincelejo, a sometimes brutal show in which the town's youth display their bravura against 40 bulls released into a ring. Injuries – even deaths – are frequent.

End Jan Hay Festival Cartagena, www.hayfestival.com/cartagena. A branch of the UK's Hay Festival turns Cartagena into a focus for all things literary during 4 days.

February

2 Feb Fiesta de Nuestra Señora de la Candelaria. Celebrated in towns, including Cartagena and Medellín, this religious cult festival was inherited from the Canary Islands, where 2 goat herders witnessed the apparition of the Virgin Mary holding a green candle.

February-March

Barranquilla Carnival (movable), www.carnavaldebarranquilla.org. Beginning 4 days before Ash Wed, this is one of the best carnivals in South America. 4 days of partying are compulsory by law and involve parades and plenty of dancing.

March

Concurso Mundial de la Mujer Vaquera, www.mundialmujervaquera.com. The women of the Llanos prove their cowboy skills during 3 days.

March-April

Semana Santa (Holy Week) (movable). Celebrated all over Colombia, but the processions in Popayán, Mompós and Pamplona are particularly revered.

April

26-30 Apr Festival de la Leyenda Vallenata, www.festivalvallenato.com. One of the most important music festivals in Colombia, 4 days of hard partying in Valledupar culminate in the selection of the best *vallenato* musician.

June-July

22 Jun-2 Jul Festival Folclórico y Reinado Nacional del Bambuco. The city of Neiva hosts *Bambuco* dancing competitions and various parades in which bikini-clad beauty queens float downriver on boats while up to 5000 (often) drunken women ride horses through Neiva's streets. It culminates in the crowning of a *Bambuco* queen.

28 Jun-2 Jul Torneo Internacional del Joropo, www.torneointernacionaldeljoropo.com. The city of Villavicencio gives itself over to a celebration of *llanero* culture

Bizarre festivals

García Márquez once said, "five Colombians in a room invariably turns into a party". It could also be said that a couple of hundred Colombians in a village invariably turns into a fiesta. Colombians will use almost anything as a pretext for a celebration. Below are some of the most bizarre.

Festival del Burro, San Antero, Córdoba
The people of the Caribbean coastal town of San Antero love their donkeys. So much so that they have a festival dedicated to them. Each year around Easter time the town's donkeys are paraded through the streets – in drag. Some wear lipstick and mascara, feather boas and pearl necklaces, while others sport jeans or bikinis, and the best get-up wins a prize. They have even built a Burrodome, a special stadium where man and beast can hang out drinking beer and listen to *vallenato*.

Yipao, Armenia, Quindío, October
Willys jeeps first arrived in Colombia in 1946 from the United States and they have become the most popular vehicles in the Zona Cafetera's hilly countryside thanks to their robust handling and capacity to carry weights far beyond their size. Colombians demonstrate their admiration for these Second World War army jeeps by holding *yipaos* – competitions in which Willys' owners must try to load as much produce as is physically possible onto their vehicles and parade down the street, often performing wheelies as they go. The most popular of the *yipaos* is held in Armenia each October as part of the city's annual fiesta but the largest is in Calaracá in July, which in 2006 set a Guinness World Record for the largest jeep parade with over 370 Willys jeeps taking part.

Tomatina, Sutamarchán, Boyacá
The premise of this festival is very simple: dump a bunch of tomatoes in a field and get several thousand people to throw them at each other. In 2008, the local authorities estimated that 10 tons of tomatoes were thrown, squashed and pulped during this messy fight, which takes place each June. This festival probably took its cue from the Tomatína in Buñol, near Valencia in Spain, which claims to be the world's largest vegetable fight.

with more than 3000 couples dressed in traditional outfits dance *joropo* in the streets, a large horse parade, a beauty contest and *coleo* (a type of rodeo) making up the events.

August
First 2 weeks of Aug Feria de las Flores. Concerts, street parties, antique car parades, a *Paso Fino* horse parade and the *Desfile de Silleteros*, in which flower-growers file through the streets carrying their elaborate displays mounted on wooden 'chairs', have made this festival in Medellín a world-renowned event.
Aug Festival del Viento y de las Cometas (most windy weekend in Aug). Villa de Leiva's enormous cobbled plaza fills with hundreds of kite-fliers displaying models of all shapes and sizes. Competition is fierce.

September
Sep Jazz al Parque Bogotá's parks resonate to the sound of pianos, saxophones and trumpets during this festival that has grown exponentially since it first began in 1996. Musicians from all over the world converge on Colombia's capital for a weekend.
20 Sep-9 Oct Fiestas de San Pacho, www.sanpacho.org. For 20 days in late Sep/early Oct, the streets of Quibdó in Chocó convert themselves into a big party venue to

commemorate the death of Saint Francis of Assisi. Religious processions, parades and *sancocho* cookouts all combine in this fusion of Catholicism and African customs.

October
Encuentro Mundial del Coleo,
www.mundialcoleo.com.co. More than 40,000 people descend on Villvicencio each year to watch mounted cowboys display their skills at *coleo*, a sport not dissimilar to rodeo that involves upending bulls by grabbing them by the tail and twisting until they fall over.

November
Late Nov-early Dec El Pirarucú de Oro This music festival in Leticia reflects the Colombian Amazon capital's position on the edge of 2 frontiers. With influences from Brazil and Peru, the festival hosts a competition that celebrates music from the region.
First 2 weeks of Nov Independence of Cartagena and Concurso Nacional de la Belleza. Cartagena celebrates being the first department to win Independence from the Spanish each 11 Nov with parades and traditional dancing in the streets. This has been somewhat supplanted by the National Beauty Pageant in which the winner will go on to represent Colombia at Miss Universe.

December
7-8 Dec Festival de Luces The skies above Villa de Leiva are lit by one of the best pyrotechnic shows in Colombia while the streets are illuminated by hundreds of candles in this most picturesque of festivals.
25-30 Dec Feria de Cali, www.feriadecali.com. What started as a bullfighting festival involving the best Spanish and South American matadors is now a city-wide party where Cali's self-imposed title of 'capital of salsa' is reaffirmed every year. The festival is opened by an impressive *Paso Fino* horse parade.

Public holidays

1 Jan New Year's Day
6 Jan Epiphany*
19 Mar St Joseph*
Easter Maundy Thursday; Good Friday
1 May Labour Day
May Ascension Day* (6 weeks and a day after Easter Sunday)
May/Jun Corpus Christi* (9 weeks and a day after Easter Sunday)
29 Jun Saint Peter and Saint Paul*
30 Jun Sacred Heart*
20 Jul Independence Day
7 Aug Battle of Boyacá
15 Aug Assumption*
12 Oct Columbus' arrival in America*
1 Nov All Saints' day*
11 Nov Independence of Cartagena*
8 Dec Immaculate Conception
25 Dec Christmas Day
* When these do not fall on a Mon, the public holiday will be on the following Mon. Public holidays are known as *puentes* (bridges).

Responsible travel

The benefits of international travel are self evident for both hosts and travellers: employment, understanding of different cultures and business and leisure opportunities. At the same time there is clearly a downside to the industry. Where visitor pressure is high and/or poorly regulated, there can be adverse impacts on society and the natural environment. Paradoxically, this is as true in undeveloped and pristine areas (where culture and the natural environment are less 'prepared' for even small numbers of visitors) as in major resorts.

How big is your footprint?

The point of a holiday is, of course, to have a good time, but if it's relatively guilt-free as well, that's even better. Perfect ecotourism would ensure a good living for local inhabitants, while not detracting from their traditional lifestyles, encroaching on their customs or spoiling their environment. Perfect ecotourism probably doesn't exist, but everyone can play their part. Here are a few points worth bearing in mind:

• Think about where your money goes and be fair and realistic about how cheaply you travel. Try to put money into local people's hands; drink local beer or fruit juice rather than imported brands and stay in locally owned accommodation wherever possible.

• Haggle with humour and appropriately. Remember that you want a fair price, not the lowest one.

• Think about what happens to your rubbish. Take biodegradable products and a water bottle filter. Be sensitive to limited resources like water, fuel and electricity.

• Help preserve local wildlife and habitats by respecting rules and regulations, such as sticking to footpaths, not standing on coral and not buying products made from endangered plants or animals.

• Don't treat people as part of the landscape; they may not want their picture taken. Ask first and respect their wishes.

• Learn the local language and be mindful of customs and norms. It can enhance your travel experience and you'll earn respect and be more readily welcomed by local people.

• And finally, use your guidebook as a starting point, not the only source of information. Talk to local people, then discover your own adventure.

Vulnerable places in Colombia

Leticia The Amazon's vast array of species are under threat from hunting and tourism. Seek out tour guides with sound environmental practice and do not buy any animal products as souvenirs.

San Agustín Unsurprisingly, this town has become increasingly popular thanks to its mysterious sculptures and majestic countryside. Unfortunately, with mass tourism comes litter and damage. Be sure to take your rubbish home and do not climb on the stones.

Islas del Rosario The coral reefs of the Caribbean coast are already showing signs of damage from global warming. Snorkellers and divers can avoid contributing further by not stepping on the coral and ensuring that boats drop anchor on sand rather than coral.

The travel industry is growing rapidly and increasingly its impact is becoming apparent. These impacts can seem remote and unrelated to an individual trip or holiday, but individual choice and awareness can make a difference in many instances and, collectively, travellers are having a significant effect in shaping a more responsible and sustainable industry.

Of course travel can have beneficial impacts and this is something to which every traveller can contribute. Many national parks are part funded by receipts from visitors. Similarly, travellers can promote patronage and protection of important archaeological sites and heritage through their interest and contributions via entrance and performance fees. They can also support small-scale enterprises by staying in locally run hotels and hostels, eating in local restaurants and by purchasing local goods, supplies and arts and crafts.

Essentials A-Z

Accident and emergency

Contact the relevant emergency service and your embassy in Bogotá. Make sure you obtain police/medical reports in order to file insurance claims.

Emergency services

Police: T112 or 123 (from mobiles); **Ambulance**: T132; **Fire**: T119; **Red Cross ambulance and traffic accidents**: T127; **CAI Police**: T156.

If you have problems with theft or other forms of crime, contact a **Centro de Atención Inmediata (CAI)** office for assistance. Only at a CAI police office is it possible to report a theft and get the relevant paperwork, not at other police stations. In Bogotá the CAI office is: downtown, Cra 24 No 82-77, T742 3536, La Candelaria, Cra 7 y C6.

Children

Travel with children can bring you into closer contact with Colombian families and, generally, presents no special problems – in fact the path may even be smoother for family groups. Officials are sometimes more amenable where children are concerned and they are pleased if your child knows a little Spanish. Many museums and attractions offer discounts for children. For more detailed advice on travelling with children, see Footprint's *Travel with Kids*.

Bus travel

Remember that a lot of time can be spent waiting for and riding buses, which are sometimes crowded and uncomfortable. You should take reading material as it is difficult to find and expensive. Local comic strips are a good way for older children to learn a bit of Spanish. But reading on the bus itself, especially on winding mountain roads, may make children (and adults) nauseous.

Fares

On long-distance buses you pay for each seat, and there are no half-price fares. For shorter trips it is cheaper, if less comfortable, to seat small children on your knee. Sometimes there are spare seats that children can occupy after tickets have been collected.

Food

It is easiest to take food with you on longer trips than to rely on meal regular stops where the food may not be to taste. It's best stick to simple things like bread and fruit while you are on the road. Biscuits, packaged junk food and bottled drinks abound. In restaurants, you may be able to buy a *media porción* (half portion), or divide a full-size helping between 2 children.

Customs

Customs checks take place at airports and frontiers for both arriving and leaving travellers (see Visas and immigration, page 42). There are sometimes additional checks at the flight gate before departure. Do not carry drugs or firearms of any kind and take care that no-one tampers with your baggage.

Disabled travellers

Provision for the disabled is limited, but increasing, in Colombia. Wheelchairs and assistance are available at major airports. Modern and public buildings are being provided with ramps and relevant lifts, and some streets have sidewalk breaks that are usually adequate for wheelchairs. More hotels and restaurants now have disabled access, rooms and toilets.

But, of course, only a minority of disabled people are wheelchair-bound and it is now widely acknowledged that disabilities do not stop you from enjoying a great holiday. Some travel companies specialize in exciting holidays, tailor-made for individuals depending on their level of ability.

For general information, consult the **Global Access – Disabled Travel Network**, www.globalaccessnews.com.

Drugs

As is all too well known, Colombia is part of a major drug producing and smuggling route and still produces roughly 80% of the world's cocaine. Police and customs activities have greatly intensified and smugglers increasingly try to use innocent carriers. Do not carry packages for other people without checking the contents (indeed taking suspicious packages or gift-wrapped presents of your own through customs could give problems). Be very polite if approached by policemen, or if your hotel room is raided by police looking for drugs. Colombians who offer you drugs may well be setting you up for the police, who are very active on the north coast and San Andrés island, and other tourist resorts. There are established penalties, which include prison, fines and deportation of any foreigner caught using any drug.

Electricity

110 Volts AC, alternating at 60 cycles per second. A voltage converter may be required if your device does not run on 110 Volts. Most sockets accept both continental European (round) and North American (flat) 2-pin plugs.

Embassies and consulates

Visit www.cancilleria.gov.co for a full list of addresses.

Health

See your GP or travel clinic at least 6 weeks before departure for general advice on travel risks and vaccinations. Try phoning a specialist travel clinic if your own doctor is unfamiliar with health conditions in Colombia. Make sure you have sufficient medical travel insurance, get a dental check, know your own blood group and if you suffer a long-term condition such as diabetes or epilepsy, obtain a Medic Alert bracelet/necklace (www.medicalert.co.uk). If you wear glasses, take a copy of your prescription.

Vaccinations

It is advisable to vaccinate against polio, tetanus, diphtheria, typhoid, hepatitis A, and also rabies if going to more remote areas. If visiting the Amazon you will most likely be asked to produce a yellow fever certificate at the airport in Leticia and may well be turned away if you can't, or you will be made to have the vaccination on the spot (not recommended). Malaria and dengue fever are a danger in the Amazon and other tropical areas such as the Darién and Chocó. Specialist advice should be taken on the best anti-malarials to use.

Health risks

The most common cause of travellers' **diarrhoea** is from eating contaminated food. In Colombia, drinking water is rarely the culprit, although it's best to be cautious (see below). Swimming in sea or river water that has been contaminated by sewage can also be a cause; ask locally if it is safe. Diarrhoea may be also caused by viruses, bacteria (such as E-coli), protozoal (such as giardia), salmonella and cholera. It may be accompanied by vomiting or by severe abdominal pain. Any kind of diarrhoea responds well to the replacement of water and salts. Sachets of rehydration salts can be bought in most chemists and can be dissolved in boiled water. If the symptoms persist, consult a doctor. Tap water in the major cities is in theory safe to drink but it may be advisable to err on the side of caution and drink only bottled or boiled water. Avoid having ice in drinks unless you trust that it is from a reliable source.

Travelling in high altitudes can bring on **altitude sickness**. On reaching heights above 3000 m, the heart may start pounding and the traveller may experience shortness of breath. Smokers and those with underlying heart or lung disease are often hardest hit. Take it easy for the first few days, rest and drink plenty of water, you will feel better soon. It is essential to get acclimatized before undertaking long treks or arduous activities.

Mosquitoes are more of a nuisance than a serious hazard but some, of course, are carriers of serious diseases such as **malaria**, so it is sensible to avoid being bitten as much as possible. Sleep off the ground and use a mosquito net and some kind of insecticide. Mosquito coils release insecticide as they burn and are available in many shops, as are tablets of insecticide, which are placed on a heated mat plugged into a wall socket.

If you get sick

Contact your embassy or consulate for a list of doctors and dentists who speak your language, or at least some English. Doctors and health facilities in major cities are also listed in the Directory sections of this book. Good-quality healthcare is available in the larger centres of Colombia but it can be expensive, especially hospitalization. Make sure you have adequate insurance (see below).

Useful websites
www.btha.org British Travel Health Association.
www.cdc.gov US government site that gives excellent advice on travel health and details of disease outbreaks.
www.fco.gov.uk British Foreign and Commonwealth Office travel site has useful information on each country, people, climate and a list of UK embassies/consulates.

www.fitfortravel.scot.nhs.uk A-Z of vaccine/health advice for each country.
www.travelhealth.co.uk Independent travel health site with advice on vaccination, travel insurance and health risks.

Insurance

Travel insurance is a must for all visitors to Colombia. Always take out insurance that covers both medical expenses and baggage loss, and read the small print carefully before you set off. Check that all the activities you may end up doing are covered. Mountaineering, for example, is excluded from many policies; also make sure that coverage is not excluded at high altitude. Check if medical coverage includes air ambulance and emergency flights back home. Be aware of the payment protocol: in Colombia you will have to pay out of your own pocket and later request reimbursement from the insurance company. Before paying for any medical services, insist on getting a fully itemized invoice. In case of baggage loss, have the receipts for expensive personal effects like cameras and laptops on file, take photos of these items, note the serial numbers and be sure to leave unnecessary valuables at home. Keep the insurance company's telephone number with you and get a police report for any lost or stolen items.

Internet

Public internet access is available in many but not all areas of Colombia; small towns and villages may not have connectivity. As elsewhere, however, the internet has completely replaced postal and telephone services for most travellers. Cyber cafés are frequented not only by tourists, but also by many locals, and sometimes get crowded and noisy. Keep an eye on your belongings.

Both the cost and speed of access vary, with the best service generally

Colombian Spanish

Colombians display a sometimes excessive inclination for politeness.

Nowhere is this more evident than in their language. Colombian Spanish is characterized by a punctilious, sometimes archaic, courteousness. Step inside any shop or taxi in the interior (the coast has its own rules, separate from the rest of the country) and you are likely to be bombarded by forms of address such as *'a la orden'* (at your service), *'que esté bien'* (may you be well), *'con mucho gusto'* (with pleasure); in departments such as Boyacá, you may even be addressed as *'su merced'* (your mercy).

And politeness isn't only for strangers. They even use the third person, formal *usted* (you) with their children or spouses.

Although things are changing, most Colombians speak little English, or any other foreign language, so it's up to the traveller to make the effort to learn some Spanish. Without any language skills, you will feel like someone peering through the keyhole at the country. But Colombians are so gregarious that with just a modest knowledge of the language they will talk at you for hours and the Colombian accent is one of the easiest to understand.

When first arriving in Colombia, it's a good idea to start your trip with some lessons at a language school. With that in mind, see the relevant sections throughout the book for listings of language schools.

---

available in the largest cities. Hourly rates are usually US$1-4. Many hotels now have free Wi-Fi available, as do cafés, bars, restaurants and some public spaces such as parks. Keep your wits about you if using Wi-Fi spots outdoors, not all are safe. Most main airports have free Wi-Fi throughout, but connectivity can be erratic.

Language → *For a list of useful Spanish words and phrases, see page 384.*

The official language of Colombia is Spanish and it is spoken by the majority of the population. However, there are also some 60 aboriginal languages spoken by the indigenous communities. A form of creole English is spoken on the islands of San Andrés and Providencia. English, or any other foreign language, is increasingly spoken even off the beaten track, but even a basic knowledge of Spanish will infinitely enhance your journey and make communication that much easier. So it's well worth learning the basics before you arrive – or take a course at the start of

your trip (see below). Note that if you are intending to do any formal studies, you must obtain a student visa (see Visas and immigration, page 42), which can be obtained once in the country.

Amerispan, 1334 Walnut St, 6th floor, Philadelphia, PA 19107, USA, T215-7511100/T1-800-879 6640, www.amerispan.com, offers Spanish immersion and volunteer programmes throughout Latin America, including in Bogotá, Cartagena and Medellín.

Cactus Language Travel Holidays, T0845-130 4775 (UK), www.cactuslanguage.com offers Spanish language courses often combined with activities such as salsa or gastronomy in different parts of Colombia, including Bogotá, Cartagena and Leticia.

LGBT travellers

Colombia has some of the most progressive laws in favour of homosexuality in Latin America. While same-sex marriages and civil unions are yet to be legalized, common-law marriage (registered partnership), property and inheritance rights for same-sex couples were approved by the Constitutional Court in 2007. Most of the big cities have gay neighbourhoods. Bogotá in particular has a large and thriving gay scene, centred around Chapinero. But outside of the big cities homosexuality has little acceptance. It is therefore prudent to respect local sensibilities.

Media

Magazines

Best is probably *Semana*, www.semana.com and *Cambio*, www.cambio.com.co (set to relaunch), owned by *El Tiempo* newspaper (see below). Bogotá has an excellent English-language magazine, *The City Paper*, www.thecitypaperbogota.com, distributed in hotels, hostels and bars.

Newspapers

Most of the major cities have a paper, usually with a regional bias.
Bogotá: *El Tiempo*, www.eltiempo.com, *El Espectador*, www.elespectador.com, *La República*, www.larepublica.com.co.
Cartagena: *El Heraldo*, www.elheraldo.co.
Cali: *El País*, www.elpais.com.co, *Nuevo Diario Occidente*, www.diariooccidente.com.co, *El Pueblo*.
Medellín: *El Mundo*, www.elmundo.com, *El Colombiano*, www.elcolombiano.com.

Radio

Colombia has a wealth of radio stations. Try **W Radio**, www.wradio.com.co, for up-to-the-minute news. You may be able to pick up the **BBC World Service** or **Voice of America** with a long-wave radio.

Television

Colombia has some 25 TV stations including regional ones, but the 2 principal stations are **RCN** (state owned) and **Caracol** (private). Colombian TV is well known for its 'soaps' (*telenovelas*), which are exported to other Spanish-speaking countries. Satellite TV with access to **CNN** and **CNN en Español** is available in even the cheapest hotels.

Money → *US$1 = 1785 pesos; UK£1 =2886 pesos; €1=2542 pesos (Jun 2011) . See www.xe.com.*

Colombia's currency is the *peso*. The following denominations of banknotes circulate: 50,000, 20,000, 10,000, 5000, 2000 and 1000, as well as coins worth 500, 200, 100 and 50. Large bills may be hard to use in small towns so carry plenty of notes in small dominations (10,000 and below). Watch out for forged notes. The 50,000-peso note should smudge colour if it is real, if not, refuse to accept it.

There is a variety of ways for visitors to bring their funds to Colombia. You are strongly advised to combine 2 or more of these, so as not to be stuck if there are problems Always carry some US$ cash; they will work when and where all else fails.

ATMs and credit cards

As it is unwise to carry large quantities of cash in Colombia, credit cards are widely used, especially MasterCard and Visa; Diners Club is also accepted. American Express (Amex) is only accepted in expensive places in Bogotá. Many banks accept Visa (Visaplus and ATH logos) and Cirrus/MasterCard (Maestro and Multicolor logos) to advance pesos against the card, or through ATMs. There are ATMs for Visa and MasterCard everywhere but you may have to try several machines before you find one that works. Most **Carulla** and **Exito** supermarkets have ATMs.

The ATM system is different to banks in Europe; the machine does not retain your card during the withdrawal. Insert your card for scanning and withdraw immediately, then proceed as normal. If your card is not immediately given back, do not proceed with the transaction and do not type in your pin number. Money has been stolen from accounts when cards have been retained.

ATMs dispense a frustratingly small amount of cash at a time. The maximum withdrawal is often 300,000 pesos (about US$150), which can accrue heavy bank charges over a period of time. For larger amounts try: **Davivienda** (500,000 per visit) and **Bancolombia** (400,000 per visit).

If planning to use credit and debit cards be sure to warn your bank back at home in advance as they may think it has been stolen and block your card. Find out how much your bank charges for foreign withdrawals. It may be worthwhile opening an account with a bank that does not have a high fee e.g. **Nationwide** in the UK.

Credit card loss or theft: Visa call collect to T0800-891 725; MasterCard T0800-964767.

Note Only use ATMs in supermarkets, malls or where a security guard is present. Don't ask a taxi driver to wait while you use an ATM. Be particularly vigilant around Christmas time when thieves may be on the prowl.

Exchange

Cash (preferably US$ or euro) and TCs can, in theory, be exchanged in any bank, except the **Banco de la República**. In smaller places it's best to go early; take your passport. It can be difficult to buy and sell large amounts of sterling, even in Bogotá.

In most sizeable towns there are *casas de cambio* (exchange bureaux), which are quicker to use than banks but sometimes charge higher commission. US$ and euro are readily accepted but other international currencies can be harder to change.

Hotels may give very poor rates of exchange, especially if you are paying in dollars. It is dangerous to change money on the streets and you may well be given counterfeit pesos. Also in circulation are counterfeit US$ bills. You must present your passport when changing money (a photocopy is not normally accepted).

When leaving Colombia, try to sell your pesos before or at the border, as it may be difficult to change them in other countries.

Traveller's cheques

When changing TCs, you will need to show your passport and you may be asked for a photocopy (take a supply of photocopies with you). The procedure is always slow, sometimes involving finger printing and photographs. The best currency to take is US$; preferably in small denominations. Sterling TCs are practically impossible to change. To change Amex TCs, use major banks; you may have to provide proof of purchase. Obtaining reimbursement for lost Amex TCs can be straightforward if you have the numbers recorded. You may be asked for proof of purchase, as well as a *diligencia de queja* (police certificate) explaining the circumstances of loss; apply to the offices of their representatives Expreso Viajes & Turismo in Bogotá at C 85, No 20-32, T593 4949, Mon-Fri 0800-1800, Sat 0900-1200. Banks may be unwilling to change TCs in remote areas, so always have some local currency (and US$ for emergencies). TCs are not normally accepted in hotels, restaurants or shops.

Cost of living

Prices are generally lower than Europe and North America for services and locally produced items, but more expensive for imported and luxury goods. Modest, basic accommodation costs about US$10-12 per person per night in Bogotá, Cartagena, Santa Marta and colonial cities like Villa de Leiva, Popayán or Santa Fe de Antioquia, but a few dollars less elsewhere. A *menú del día* (set lunch) costs about US$2-3 and breakfast US$1.75-2. A la carte meals are usually good value and fierce competition keeps prices relatively low. Internet cafés charge US$1-4 per hr.

Opening hours

Business hours are generally Mon-Fri 0800-1200, 1400-1700, Sat 0900-1200. A longer siesta may be taken in small towns and tropical areas. **Banks** in larger cities do not close for lunch. Most businesses such as banks and airline offices close for official holidays while **supermarkets** and street markets may stay open. This depends a lot on where you are, so enquire locally.

Police and the law

You are required to carry your passport at all times, although this is seldom asked for outside border areas. In the event of a vehicle accident in which anyone is injured, all drivers involved are usually detained until blame has been established, which may take several weeks. Never offer to bribe a police officer. If an official suggests that a bribe must be paid before you can proceed on your way, be patient and they may relent.

In general, however, there are few hassles and most police are helpful to travellers.

Post and courier

There are 2 parallel services; **Deprisa**, operated by the national airline **Avianca**, and **4-72**, previously known as Correos de Colombia or Adpostal. Both have offices in major cities but only **4-72** can be found in small towns and rural areas. Both will take parcels for overseas. Prices are usually similar but not always identical for overseas mail. Anything important should be registered.**Servientrega**, **DHL** and **Fedex** also handle overseas parcels.

Safety

Travellers confirm that the vast majority of Colombians are polite, honest and will go out of their way to help visitors and make them feel welcome. In general, anti-gringo sentiments are rare.

Drugs and scams
Visitors should keep in mind that Colombia is part of a major cocaine-smuggling route and avoid any involvement. See Drugs, page 34, for further details.

There have been reports of travellers being victims of *burundanga*, a drug obtained from a white flower, native to Colombia. At present, the use of this drug appears to be confined to major cities. It is very nasty, almost impossible to see or smell. It leaves the victim helpless and at the will of the culprit. Usually, the victim is taken to ATMs to draw out money. Be wary of accepting cigarettes, food and drink from strangers at sports events or on buses. In bars watch your drinks very carefully.

Other Colombian scams may involve fake police and taxicabs and there are variations in most major cities.

Theft
Pickpockets, bag snatchers and bag slashers are always a hazard for tourists, especially in crowded areas such as markets or the downtown cores of major cities. There have been reports of assaults in the Candelaria area of Bogotá, especially at night. Keep alert and avoid swarms of people. You should likewise avoid deserted areas, such as parks or plazas after hours. Be especially careful arriving at or leaving from bus stations. As a rule these are often the most dangerous areas of most towns and are obvious places to catch people carrying a lot of important belongings.

Leave unnecessary documents and valuables at home. Those you bring should be carried in a money-belt or pouch, including your passport, airline tickets, credit and debit cards. Hide your main cash supply in several different places. If one stash is lost or stolen, you will still have the others to fall back on. Never carry valuables in an ordinary pocket, purse or day-pack. Keep cameras in bags or day-packs and generally out of sight. Do not wear expensive wrist watches or jewellery. If you are wearing a shoulder-bag or day-pack in a crowd, carry it in front of you.

Hotel security
The cheapest hotels are usually found near markets and bus stations but these are also the least safe areas of most Colombian towns.

Look for something a little better if you can afford it, and if you must stay in a suspect area, try to return to your hotel before dark. If you trust your hotel, then you can leave any valuables you don't need in their safe-deposit box, but always keep an inventory of what you have deposited. If you don't trust the hotel, change to one you feel safe in. An alternative to leaving valuables with the hotel administration is to lock everything in your pack and secure that in your room; a light bicycle chain or cable and a small padlock will provide at least a psychological deterrent for would-be thieves. Even in an apparently safe hotel, never leave valuable objects strewn about your room.

Guerrillas

The government has had considerable success in its fight against left-wing guerrillas such as the **FARC**, but the internal armed conflict in Colombia is almost impossible to predict and the security situation changes from day to day. For this reason, it is essential to consult regularly with locals for up-to-date information. Taxi and bus drivers, local journalists, soldiers at checkpoints, hotel owners and Colombians who actually travel around their country are usually good sources of reliable information. Since 2002, incidents of kidnapping and homicide rates in major cities have been declining. Travelling overland between towns, especially during the holiday season and bank holiday weekends, has in general become much safer due to increased military and police presence along main roads. However, the government has launched a major offensive against the guerrillas (especially in the south) and in some areas fighting between the armed forces and guerrilla groups has intensified.

Women travellers

Unaccompanied foreign women may be objects of some curiosity. Don't be unduly scared – or flattered. Avoid arriving anywhere after dark. Remember that for a single woman a taxi at night can be as dangerous as wandering around alone. If you accept a

social invitation, make sure that someone knows the address and the time you left. Ask if you can bring a friend (even if you do not). As elsewhere, watch your alcohol intake at parties with locals, especially if you are on your own. A good general rule is to always look confident and pretend you know where you are going, even if you do not. Don't tell strangers where you are staying.

Student travellers

If you are in full-time education you are entitled to an **International Student Identity Card (ISIC)**, which is sold by student travel offices and agencies in 70 countries. The ISIC may give you special prices on transport and access to a variety of other concessions and services, although these are relatively uncommon in Colombia. Teachers are entitled to an **International Teacher Identity Card (ITIC)**. Both are available from www.isic.org. If undertaking any form of study in Colombia, you will need a student visa (see Visas and immigration, page 42).

Tax

Departure tax is US$33, and is not included in any airline tickets. Visitors who stay longer than 2 months pay a reduced fee of US$23. International Airport Tax and the Revenue stamp can be paid in Colombian pesos, at the equivalent current exchange rate for IATA dollars for the day.

VAT/IVA is 16%. Ask for an official receipt if you want it documented. Some hotels and restaurants add IVA onto bills, but foreigners do not officially have to pay (see page 23).

Telephone → Country code +57.

National and international calls can be made from the many public phone offices found throughout all major cities and even in rural towns. You are assigned a cabin, place your calls, and pay on the way out. There is usually a screen that tells you how much you are spending. Prices vary considerably. You can also make calls from street vendors who hire out their mobile phones (usually signposted '*minutos*').

It is relatively inexpensive to buy a pay-as-you go SIM card for your mobile phone. Calls are on the whole cheap but there is a complicated system for making calls from mobiles. For calling landlines, dial the 1-digit area code, followed by the 7-digit number, if outside the area you are calling.

Time

GMT -5 all year round.

Tipping

A voluntary charge is added to most bills but you can ask to have this taken off if you are not happy with the service.

Tourist information

Contact details for tourist offices and other information resources are given in the relevant sections throughout the text. The Colombian government is making a big push to promote tourism and most *alcaldías* (municipalities) have some sort of tourist office, whose staff are invariably very helpful but the qualifications of staff, resources available and standards of service vary enormously in smaller towns. Keep your expectations modest and you may be pleasantly surprised. Useful website: www.colombia.travel has plenty of up-to-date and useful information.

Websites

www.clubhaciendasdelcafe.com Extensive list of coffee *fincas* in the Zona Cafetera.

www.colombianhostels.com.co Network of Colombian backpackers' hostels.
www.conexcol.com Colombian search engine covering many topics. (Spanish only)
www.despegar.com Cheap flights website for travel within Latin America.
www.gobiernoenlinea.gov.co Government website with information on new laws and citizen rights, in Spanish and English.
www.hosteltrail.com/colombia Reviews of hostels, tour agencies and destinations.
www.ideam.gov.co Weather and climate information.
www.igac.gov.co Instituto Geográfico Agustín Codazzi Official maps of Colombia.
www.invias.gov.co Instituto Nacional de Vías (National Road Institute). Current details on the state of the roads with maps, etc.
www.lab.org.uk Latin American Bureau site, based in the UK. Publishes books and holds talks on Latin American issues.
www.poorbuthappy.com/colombia Closed down in Apr 2010, but the archives are still available online. Increasingly out of date.
www.posadasturisticasdecolombia.com.co Information on places to stay in Colombia, including the Chocó.
www.presidencia.gov.co The government website.
www.quehubo.com Listings site.

Tour operators

In the UK
4 & 5*South America Travel, T0800-011-2959 www.southamerica.travel.
Colombia57 Tours, Travel and Logistics, T0800 789157 (UK free phone), www.colombia57.com.
Dragoman, T01728-861 133, www.dragoman.co.uk.
Exodus Travels, T0845-869 9152, www.exodus.co.uk.
Exploratory Overland Expeditions, T01865-573987, www.eoe.org.uk.

Explore, T0845-013 1537, www.explore.co.uk.

Intrepid Travel, T0203-147 7777, www.intrepidtravel.com.

Journey Latin America, T020-8747 8315, www.journeylatinamerica.co.uk.

LATA (Latin American Travel Association), info@lata.org, www.lata.org. Useful country information and listing of UK operators specializing in Latin America.

In North America

4&5*South America Travel, T1800-747 4540, www.southamerica.travel.

GAP Adventures, T1888-800 4100, www.gapadventures.com.

See Colombia Travel, 11491 SW 20th St, Miami Fl, 33025-6639, T1-800-553-8701 (toll free), T0207-101-9467 (UK) www.seecolombia.travel.

In South America

Surtrek, Av Amazonas 897 y Wilson, Quito, Ecuador, T593-2250 0530, www.surtrek.com.

Visas and immigration

When entering the country, you will be given a copy of your DIAN (customs) luggage declaration. Keep it safe; you may be asked for it when you leave. If you receive an entry card when flying in and lose it while in Colombia, apply to any **DAS** office (see Visa extensions, below) who should issue one and re-stamp your passport for free. Normally, passports are scanned by a computer and no landing card is issued, but passports still must be stamped on entry. Note that to leave Colombia you must get an exit stamp from the DAS. They often do not have offices at the small border towns, so try to get your stamp in a main city.

It is highly recommended that you photocopy your passport details, including entry stamps which, for added insurance, you can have witnessed by a notary. Always carry a photocopy of your passport with you, as you may be asked for identification. This is a valid substitute for most purposes though not, for example, for cashing TCs or drawing cash across a bank counter. Generally acceptable for identification (eg to enter government buildings) is a driving licence, provided it is plastic, of credit card size and has a photograph. For more information, check with your consulate.

Tourist visas

Tourists are normally given 30 days permission to stay on entry. If you intend to stay more than 30 days, make sure you ask for longer and you can be granted up to 90 days, but 60 days is more common.

Nationals of Bulgaria, Russia and the Middle East (except Israel), Asian countries (except Japan, South Korea, Philippines, Indonesia and Singapore), Haiti, Nicaragua, and all African countries need a visa to visit Colombia. If in doubt, check regulations before leaving your home country. Visas are issued only by Colombian consulates. When a visa is required you must present a valid passport, 3 photographs on white background, the application form (in duplicate), US$13-40 or equivalent (price varies according to nationality), onward tickets, and a photocopy of all the documents (allow 2 weeks maximum).

Visa extensions

If not granted at the border, an extension (*salvoconducto*) can be applied for at the DAS (security police) office in any major city. The *salvoconducto* is only issued once for a period of 30 days, costs around US$36 and is usually processed within 24 hrs. It is best to apply 2-3 days before your visa expires. Bring 2 recent photos and copies of your passport. If you overstay on any type of visa, you will be charged a fine, minimum US$55 up to US$800. The **DAS** office in Bogotá is Cra 28 No 17A-00, T408 8000, www.das.gov.co (see page 81). Arrive early in the morning, expect long queues and a painfully slow bureaucratic process. DAS does not accept cash payments; these are made at the appropriate bank with special payments slips.

Alternatively, if you have good reason to stay longer (eg for medical treatment), apply at the embassy in your home country before leaving. If you wish to stay between 7-10 days longer on a tourist visa, go to a DAS

office with your onward ticket and they will usually grant you a free extension on the spot. An onward ticket may be asked for at land borders or Bogotá international airport. You may be asked to prove that you have sufficient funds for your stay.

Student and business visas

If you are going to take a Spanish course, you must have a student visa. You may not study on a tourist visa. A student visa can be obtained while in Colombia on a tourist visa. Proof of sufficient funds is necessary (US$400-600 for a 6-month stay is usually deemed sufficient). You must be first enrolled in a course from a bona fide university to apply for a student visa.

Various business and other temporary visas are needed for foreigners who have to reside in Colombia for a length of time. The **Ministerio de Relaciones Exteriores** (not DAS), C 10 No 5-51, Palacio de San Carlos, T01800-093 8000 or 382 6999, www.cancilleria.gov.co, Mon-Fri 0800-1745, processes student and some work visas. In general, Colombian work visas can only be obtained outside Colombia at the appropriate consulate and or embassy.

You must register work and student visas at a DAS office within 15 days of obtaining them, otherwise you will be liable to pay a hefty fine. Visas must be used within

3 months. Supporting documentary requirements for visas change frequently. Check with the appropriate consulate in good time before your trip.

Weights and measures

Colombia uses the metric system, but US gallons for petrol.

Wildlife and national parks

National parks
See also Background, page 381.
National parks are administered by Unidad Administrativa Especial del Sistema de Parques Nacionales Naturales (UAESPNN). The main office is at the Ministerio del Medio Ambiente, Vivienda y Desarrollo Territorial, Oficina de Ecoturismo, Carrera 10, No 20-30, piso 1, Bogotá, T01 353 2400 ext 138-139, www.parquesnacionales.gov.co, Mon-Fri 0800-1745. Staff can provide information about facilities and accommodation, and have maps. If you intend to visit the parks, this is a good place to start and ask for up-to-date details and to obtain a permit (see below). The *National Parks Guide* is attractive and informative, US$15, providing lavishly illustrated scientific information. There is a library and research unit (*Centro de Documentación*) for more information. Permits are obtainable here and at the many offices near the parks themselves.

Permits are required to visit the parks (usually free) and admission is charged at park entrances. Some prices vary according to high and low seasons. High season includes: weekends, Jun-Jul, Dec-Jan, public holidays and Semana Santa.

Other useful addresses include:
Asociación Red Colombiana de Reservas Naturales de la Sociedad Civil, C 2 A, No 26-103, San Fernando, Cali, T558 5046, a network of privately owned nature reserves that work with local people to build a sustainable model of environmentally friendly tourism. Instituto Colombiano de Antropología e Historia, Calle 12, No 2-41, T286 0021, www.icanh.gov.co, Mon-Fri 0800-1700, also has useful information.

Volunteering
Volunteers can apply to work as park rangers at some national parks; details are available from the UAESPNN office in Bogotá (see above). There are 20 or so parks participating in the scheme (minimum 30 days); Corales del Rosario National Park has been particularly recommended. If you have a specific or professional scientific interest and would like to study in one of the parks, bring a letter from an educational or research institution from your home country indicating your subject of interest.

Websites
www.coama.org.co Details of conservation projects in the Amazon and Orinoco regions.
www.conservation.org Conservation International site. Click on "In the field" and "South America" for details about projects in Colombia.
www.humboldt.org.co Site of Institute Von Humboldt, probably the most important environment research organization in Colombia. An excellent site with descriptions of the different ecosystems in the country and projects with ethnic communities (in Spanish).
www.iucn.org International Union for the Conservation of Nature. One of the best sites for information on biodiversity protection worldwide with links to South America/Colombia including projects in protected areas and national parks.
www.minambiente,gov.co Colombia Ministry of the Environment. Environmental legislation and general information.
www.natura.org.co Fundación Natura for scientific information on several national parks where they have projects.
www.survivalinternational.org Information on indigenous communities in Colombia.

Contents

48 Ins and outs
53 Background

54 Sights
54 La Candelaria
63 Monserrate
64 Downtown Bogotá
67 North of the centre

68 Listings

83 Around Bogotá
83 Southwest to Parque
Natural Chicaque
83 Bogotá to Honda
85 Guatavita
86 Zipaquirá
87 Listings

Footprint features

46 Don't miss ...
61 Antanas Mockus
62 Emeralds
65 Cementerio Central
84 The legend of El Dorado
85 Policarpa Salavarrieta

At a glance

◉ **Getting around** TransMilenio colectivo or taxi in Bogotá. Bus to outlying areas.

◉ **Time required** 3-4 days to explore city highlights, 1-2 weeks for excursions.

☼ **Weather** Cool and rainy most of the year in Bogotá, warmer in the surrounding low-lying regions.

✕ **When not to go** Good all year.

Don't miss ...

1 Strolling around the historic centre of La Candelaria, page 54.

2 Haggling for emeralds, page 62.

3 Exploring the treasures of the Gold Museum, page 62.

4 The hilltop sanctuary of Monserrate, page 63.

5 The Botanical Garden, page 66.

6 Watching the flower sellers at Paloquemao market, page 66.

7 The majestic salt cathedral at Zipaquirá, page 96.

Colombia's capital is a vast, sprawling, traffic-choked metropolis set high in a valley surrounded by the mountains of the Cordillera Oriental. Thanks to some enterprising local governance, Bogotá has undergone something of a renaissance in the past 15 years and has become one of the most exciting capitals in Latin America, its nightlife, dining, fashion and culture equal to anything that Buenos Aires or Rio de Janeiro can offer. However, it's a city that still suffers from extremes of wealth and poverty, a city where air-conditioned, tinted-windowed cars stand bumper to bumper with rubbish-collecting horse and carts and where the conspicuous consumption on show in the enormous, flashy shopping centres and the gated communities of the north of the city stand in stark contrast to the depressing shanty towns to the south and east.

To the north is effectively a new city, characterized by the opulent restaurants, bars and nightclubs of the Zona G, Zona T and Parque 93.

The old centre is La Candelaria, a rabbit warren of colonial buildings, narrow, cobbled streets, theatres, universities and countless cafés buzzing with intellectual debate. La Candelaria is home to one of Latin America's most impressive cultural attractions, the Gold Museum, a dazzling display of pre-Columbian treasures. Outside the noisy, polluted centre there are numerous attractions and pretty towns to visit, perfect for day or weekend excursions, most impressive of which is the extraordinary salt cathedral at Zipaquirá.

Ins and outs → *Colour map 2, C5.*

Getting there → *Phone code: 1. Population: 9,600,000. Altitude 2625 m. Average temperature 14°C.*
Air The International airport has two terminals, **El Dorado**, currently being expanded and the **Puente Aéreo**, the latter 1 km before the main terminal. Both are on Avenida El Dorado. Most international flights arrive at El Dorado; however some **Avianca** flights from the USA come into the Puente Aéreo. The arrival procedure is much the same at both terminals. If you are changing planes in Bogotá, there is complimentary transport between terminals.

El Dorado ① *T425 1000, www.elnuevodorado.com*, has comfortable departure areas where the usual duty-free shops are of a high standard. There are many snack bars and restaurants on the first floor and free Wi-Fi throughout, although connectivity can be erratic. International calls can be made from **Telecom** on the first floor, which is open until 2100, and accepts credit cards. There is a post office in the main arrivals lounge and two tourist offices run by the city tourist authority, one on the right near the international arrivals exit and the other in a similar position near the domestic arrivals exit. They are open daily during normal hours. Hotel and general information is available. Exchange rates are marginally less favourable than in the city, but pesos cannot be changed back into dollars at the airport without receipts. The **Banco Popular** by the barrier changes traveller's cheques (they may request copy of purchase receipt) and there is a *casa de cambio* alongside, which changes cash only. They may not be open at holiday times. When closed, ask airport police where to change money. Car hire counters are opposite the *casa de cambio*. Allow at least two hours for checking in and going through the comprehensive security. There is no baggage deposit. You no longer need to reconfirm most flights, especially if booked online, but double check with travel agent at the time of booking. Use only uniformed porters.

Puente Aéreo has ATMs which accept international credit cards. There is a **Presto** fast-food restaurant, **Telecom** with international call facilities but no exchange service and an internet café. Otherwise, services are similar to those at El Dorado.

The taxi fare from airport to city is a fixed charge, US$10.50, more at night and early morning. Make sure you get a registered taxi, normally yellow, found to your right as you leave the main terminal. You can also go left to the far end of the main terminal to domestic arrivals where you can get a ticket from the booth just inside the building, which will fix the price of your journey – recommended. There is a separate taxi rank outside. You will be expected to tip if you are helped with any luggage. Unofficial taxis are not advisable. Use only uniformed porters. There are *colectivos* (US$0.80-1.25 plus luggage per person) to the centre. In the city centre take buses and black and red *colectivos* marked 'Aeropuerto' to the airport. Watch belongings inside and outside airport, especially at night. ›› *See Getting around, below, and Transport, page 78, for further details.*

Bus The long-distance bus terminal is **Terminal de Transportes** ① *near Av Boyacá at C 33B, No 69-59, T423 3600, www.terminaldetransportes.gov.co, there is also access from Cra 68.* To get into town take buses marked 'Centro' or 'Germania'. The 'Germania' bus goes up through the centre and La Candelaria. Taxi fares from the terminal to the city are about US$5-6, depending on the destination, with a surcharge at night and on public holidays. Go to the appropriate exit and obtain a slip from a vending booth, which shows the exact fare to your destination. Do not take unofficial taxis, which are normally touting for particular hotels.

Getting around

Visitors should not be too active for the first 24 hours. Some people get dizzy at Bogotá's altitude. Be careful with food and alcohol for a day or two. Walking in the downtown area and in Candelaria is recommended, as distances are short and the traffic is heavy. North Bogotá is more spacious and buses and taxis are more convenient. Between the two and elsewhere, transport is necessary.

TransMilenio This is Bogotá's highly successful traffic-busting transport system, inaugurated in 2001 and currently being expanded, consisting of articulated buses on dedicated lanes. It can be a little baffling to work out at first but it's a quick, cheap way to get around once you get the hang of it. It runs north to south along Autopista Norte and Avenida Caracas with branches to various destinations in the west of the city. There is a branch along Calle 80 and a link to La Candelaria (Parque de Los Periodistas on Avenida Jiménez de Quesada with a stop at the Gold Museum). *Corriente* services stop at all principal road intersections while *expresos* have limited stops. The journey from the centre to the north takes less than 30 minutes. Journey cost US$0.85. Using the TransMilenio is a good, quick way of getting around the city but it tends to be crowded. See www.transmilenio.gov.co for more details.

Local bus Bus fares are from US$0.65 up, depending on length of route and time of day. Most buses have day/night tariff advertised in the window. *Busetas* charge a little more. There are some red and white *ejecutivo* routes with plush seats, at US$0.70. Fares are a bit higher at night and on holidays. Urban buses are not good for sightseeing because you will most likely be standing.

Car rental Whilst not cheap, if you are in the city for several days this could be a good option. ▸▸ *See details under Transport, page 80.*

Taxi Taxis are the best way to get between sectors of the city, and at night are recommended for all journeys. All taxis have meters: insist that they are used. The starting charge is US$2.20 and an average fare from North Bogotá to the centre US$6. ▸▸ *See details under Transport, page 80.*

Orientation

The Calles (abbreviated 'C', or 'Cll') run at right angles across the Carreras ('Cra' or 'K'). It is easy enough to find a place once the address system, which is used throughout Colombia, is understood. The address C 13, No 12-45 would be the building on Calle 13 between Carrera 12 and 13 at 45 paces from Carrera 12; however *transversales* (Tra) and *diagonales* (Diag) can complicate the system. The Avenidas (Av), broad and important streets, may be either Calles (like 26) or Carreras (like 14) or both (like 19 which is Calle in the Centre and Carrera in the North). Avenida Jiménez de Quesada, one of Bogotá's most well known streets, owes its curves and bends to having been built over a river-bed (which, incidentally was opened up again in 2000). The Calles in the south of the city are marked 'Sur' or 'S'; this is an integral part of the address and must be quoted.

To the east lie the mountains of the eastern cordillera, a useful landmark for getting your bearings. Most of the interesting parts of the city follow the foot of the cordillera in a north–south line. **La Candelaria**, full of character, occupies the area bounded by Avenida Jiménez de Quesada, Calle 6, Carrera 3 and Carrera 10. There is some modern infill but many of the houses are well preserved in colonial style, one or two storeys high with tiled roofs, projecting eaves, wrought ironwork and carved balconies. The main colonial churches, palaces and museums are concentrated around and above the Plaza Bolívar.

1 Bogotá orientation

Sleeping	Hotel Lord 5	Al Wadi 7
Casa Medina 1	Las Terrazas 6	Artesano 21
Casona del Patio 2		Criterión 8
Diamante Central Park 3	Eating	Estrella de los Ríos 12
El Cafecito 4	Archie's Pizza 1	H Sasson 2

Some hotels are found in this part, more along the margins, eg Avenida Jiménez de Quesada. **Note** The street names in La Candelaria are reportedly set to change in 2011. Check new street names with local tourist boards or on the Proexport website,

La Casa de las Sopas **14**	Bars & clubs	TransMilenio route
La Cigale **15**	LOV **22**	
La Hamburguesería **16**	In Vitro **23**	
Mini-mal **18**	Son Salomé **25**	
Tábula **20**	Theatrón **26**	

➡ **Bogotá maps**
1 **Bogotá orientation, page 50**
2 **La Candelaria, page 56**
3 **Downtown Bogotá, page 64**
4 **North Bogotá, page 67**

www.colombia.travel. **Downtown Bogotá** runs in a band northeast along Carrera 7 from Avenida Jiménez de Quesada to Calle 26. It is a thorough mix of styles including modern towers and run-down colonial and later buildings, together with a few notable exceptions. The streets are full of life, but can be paralysed by traffic at busy times. The pavements can be congested too, particularly Carrera 7 and Avenida 19. From Calle 50 to Calle 68 is **El Chapinero**, once the outskirts of the city and now a commercial district with a sprinkling of old, large mansions. It also doubles up as the epicentre of Bogotá's thriving gay scene, known as 'Chapigay', with many bars and clubs. Next to the National Park, along La Séptima (Carrera 7) is **La Merced**, a cluster of English country-style houses. A few blocks further south, along Carrera 4 between Calle 25 and Calle 27, is the Bohemian area of **La Macarena**, formerly inhabited by struggling artists but now becoming increasingly fashionable with many good restaurants and bars. Beyond Calle 60, the main city continues north to a comparatively new district, **North Bogotá**, which is split into various points of interest. Most of the best hotels, restaurants and embassies are in this area, which is regarded as the safest in Bogotá. Between Carrera 4 and Carrera 5 and Calle 68 and Calle 71 is what is known as the **Zona G** (for 'gourmet'), home to some of Bogotá best (and most expensive) restaurants. The T-shaped pedestrianized area made up by Calle 83 and Carrera 13 is **Bogotá's Zona Rosa** (also known as the Zona T) with many fashionable bars, clubs and restaurants. Further north the streets around **Parque 93** have some of the most expensive bars and restaurants in the city, while at the very limits of the city, off Carrera 7 between Calle 117 and Calle119, is **Usaquen**, formerly a satellite town of Bogotá with a pleasant plaza, and a popular evening and weekend excursion for *rolos* (as *bogotanos* are sometimes called), looking to get a break from the metropolis.

Safety

As in any city of this size, take care not to tempt thieves by careless displays of money or valuables. Also, anyone approaching you with questions, offering to sell something or making demands, may well be a thief or a con-artist. Beware, they may be well-dressed and plausible, may pose as plain-clothes officials, and often work in pairs. Read the Safety section in Essentials carefully and the comments in the various paragraphs below. Especially recommended is to take taxis, preferably radio taxis, if travelling in the city at night. Also, do not forget to watch where you are going, especially in the wet. Potholes in both roads and pavements can be very deep. La Candelaria district is relatively safe by day, but there have been several reports of muggings and robberies by night. You may be hassled by beggars. If returning to your hotel at night, take a taxi and keep the doors locked. Watch out for con-men in and near the Plaza de Bolívar. Best to ignore anyone who approaches – a wave of the hand is sufficient.

If you have problems with theft or other forms of crime, contact a **Centro de Atención Inmediata** (CAI) ⓘ *downtown C 60 y Cra 9, T217 7472, La Candelaria, Cra 7 y C6, there are many offices throughout the city, or T156, for assistance.* Only at a CAI police office is it possible to report a theft and get the relevant paperwork, not at other police stations.

Tourist information

There are 16 tourist information kiosks dotted around the city, as well as one mobile unit. **La Candelaria** ⓘ *Plaza Bolívar, Cra 8, No 10-83, T283 7115, Mon-Sat 0800-1800, Sun 1000-1600.* Also has internet connection with first 15 minutes free for tourists. Good local guide books and maps, friendly and helpful. **El Dorado airport** ⓘ *International terminal T413 8238, daily 0900-2100. National terminal T414 7935, daily 0900-2100.*

Bus station ⓘ *Módulo 5, local 127, T295 4460, Mon-Sat 0700-1900, Sun 1000-1600.* **Centro Internacional** ⓘ *Cra 13, No 26-62, T286 2248, 0700-1700.* **Unicentro shopping centre** ⓘ *Av 15 No 123-30, Entrada 8, 1st floor, T612 1967, daily 0900-2100.* There is also the **Colombia Tourist Board – Proexport** ⓘ *C 28, No 13A-15, piso 35, T427 9000, www.colombia.travel. Their website has mobile downloads at http://m.colombia.travel.*

The **National Parks Office** ⓘ *Cra 10, No 20-30, p1, T353 2400 ext. 138-139, www.parquesnacionales.gov.co, Mon-Fri 0800-1745,* though for accommodation in many of them you must contact Aviatur who hold concessions in the most popular locations, www.concesionesparquesnaturales.com. Full details are given on page 44.

Note Most museums and tourist attractions are open Tuesday to Sunday around 0900-1700, but may be closed for a period in the middle of the day. Times are frequently changed. Entry is often free but may be a modest US$2 or so. Very little is open on Mondays. The best time to visit the churches is before or after Mass (not during). Mass times are 0700, 1200 and 1800.

Best time to visit
Bogotá is an all-year-round-city. Holiday times such as Easter and Christmas are quiet, but attractions are closed, as many are on Monday if they have been open over the weekend.

Climate Bogotá has a temperate climate; hot in the middle of the day but normally much cooler at night, when a light sweater or even a coat may be required. Theoretically there is a wet season from April to November but there is not much rain in the middle of the year and there can be showers at any time.

Background

The city of Santa Fe de Bogotá (also written Santafé and with or without accent) was founded by Gonzalo Jiménez de Quesada on 6 August 1538 in territory inhabited by the indigenous Muisca. The name of the king, Bacatá, was adopted for the new city. In 1575, Philip II of Spain confirmed the city's title as the 'very noble and very loyal city of Santafé de Bogotá', adopting the name of Jiménez de Quesada's birthplace of Santa Fe in Andalucía. It was the capital of the Viceroyalty of Nueva Granada in 1740. After Independence in 1819, Bogotá became the capital of Gran Colombia, a confederation of what is today Venezuela, Ecuador, Panama and Colombia and remained capital of Colombia as the other republics separated.

For much of the 19th century, Bogotá suffered from isolation in economic terms mainly due to distance and lack of good transport. Population in 1850 was no more than 50,000. By 1900, however, a tram system unified the city and railways connected it to the Río Magdalena. Migrants from the Colombian countryside flocked to the city and by 1950, the population was 500,000, and the move to develop the north of the city accelerated. Since then it has re-emphasized its position as the dominant city in Colombia.

The official name of the city is now simply Bogotá, the urban area of the metropolis is known as the Distrito Capital (DC), and it is also the capital of the surrounding Department of Cundinamarca.

Sights

La Candelaria → *For listings, see pages 68-82.*

The Plaza de Bolívar, marked out by the city's founders (as Plaza Mayor), is at the heart of the historic centre. Around the plaza are the narrow streets and mansions of the **Barrio La Candelaria**, the historical and cultural heart of the city occupying the area of some 70 city blocks to the south of Avenida Jiménez de Quesada, north of Calle 6 and east of Carrera 10 (see map). Because the main commercial and residential focus of the city moved down the hill and to the north early on, much of the original colonial town remains. It is one of the best-preserved major historical centres in Latin America, and as such has attracted artists, writers and academics to fill the sector with theatres, libraries and universities, for which Colombia has a very high reputation in the Spanish-speaking world. There are some delightful sights, especially the colonial houses with their barred windows, carved doorways, red-tiled roofs and sheltering eaves. The local authorities are helping to preserve and renovate properties and the cobbled streets, a feature of La Candelaria. Many of the best of Bogotá's churches and colonial buildings are in this district. Some hotels are found in this part, more along the margins, for example on Avenida Jiménez de Quesada. The streets are relatively uncrowded and safe, although care should be exercised after dark. West of Carrera 10 and south of Calle 6 it's seedier and not recommended for pedestrians.

Plaza Bolívar and around

Plaza de Bolívar is the central square of Bogotá, with a statue of the Liberator at its centre. The **cathedral** ① *open Mon-Sat 0900-1000, Sun 0900-1400*, stands on the northeast corner of the square. The first was completed in 1553 to replace a small chapel where Fray Domingo de las Casas said the first Mass in Bogotá. The present building was constructed between 1807 and 1823. It has a fine, spacious interior, redecorated (1998) in cream and gold with high ceilings across three naves. There are lateral chapels in classical style, a notable choir loft of carved walnut, wrought silver on the altar of the Chapel of El Topo and elaborate candelabras. Treasures and relics include paintings attributed to Ribera and the banner brought by Jiménez de Quesada to Bogotá in the sacristy, which also houses portraits of past archbishops. There are monuments to Jiménez and to Antonio Nariño inside the cathedral. **Gregorio Vázquez de Arce y Ceballos** (1638-1711), the most notable painter in colonial Colombia, is buried in one of the chapels near the altar. A number of his paintings can be seen in the cathedral. Next to it is the **Capilla del Sagrario** ① *Cra 7, No 10-40, T341 1954 (closed Sat), Mass is celebrated at 0800 and 1700 during the week*, built at the end of the 17th century. There are two aisles with wooden balconies above and a fine red/gilt ceiling and screen. The inside of the dome was painted by Ricardo Acevedo Bernal. There are several paintings by Gregorio Vázquez de Arce y Ceballos. Next door is the **Palacio Arzobispal** ① *Cra 7, No 10-20*, with splendid bronze doors, and opposite, at the bottom of Calle 10, is **Colegio de San Bartolomé** ① *Cra 7, No 9-96*, originally Bogotá's oldest university, founded in 1573, where many notable Colombians of the past were educated, including Antonio Nariño, Antonio Ricaurte and General Santander. The imposing early-20th-century classical building, now an important secondary school, fits appropriately into the corner of Plaza Bolívar.

On the south side of the Plaza Bolívar is the **Capitolio Nacional**, originally the site of the Viceroy's Palace. In 1846, Thomas Reed, born in Tenerife and educated in England, was commissioned to build the Capitolio, but it was fraught with difficulties from the start. Construction was suspended in 1851, to be recommenced in 1880 by Pietro Cantini, who finished the façade to the original design in 1911. The rest was finally 'finished' in 1927 by Alberto Manrique Martín. Many other architects and engineers were involved at various times. In fact it is still being restored, now by the Instituto Nacional de Vías (National Road Institute), which has a department that specializes in maintaining national monuments. The Capitolio houses several ministries, the Supreme Court (Palacio de Justicia, see below), Consejo de Estado and Congress. On the corner of Carrera 8/Calle 10 is the **Casa de Los Comuneros** ① *Cra 8 No 9-83, T327 4900, restricted access, make appointment.* The building dates from the 17th century when it housed commercial premises with living quarters above and typical wrought-iron balconies. There are also preserved examples of later modifications to the building from the 19th and 20th centuries. It now belongs to the Instituto Distrital de Cultura y Turismo and includes the main tourist office of the city.

The **Alcaldía** ① *Cra 8, No 10-65, www.bogota.gov.co,* Bogotá's city hall, is on the west side of the plaza. It is known as the Liévano Building, and is in the French style of the early 20th century. Until 1960, the ground floor galleries were business premises. On the north side of the plaza you will see the **Palacio de Justicia.** The former building was badly damaged when the Army recaptured it from the M19 guerrillas who attacked and took it over in 1985. Eventually it was pulled down and a new one was completed in April 1999.

On the northeast corner of Calle 11/Carrera 7 is the **Museo 20 de Julio**, also known as the **Casa del Florero** ① *C 11, No 6-94, T2826647, Tue-Fri, 0900-1700, Sat and Sun 1000-1515, US$1.50, reduction for ISIC cards,* in a colonial house, which houses the famous flower vase that featured in the 1810 revolution. The owner of the vase, the Spaniard José González Llorente refused to lend the vase for the decoration of the main table at an event in honour of Antonio Villavicencio, a prominent Creole (person born in Latin America of Spanish descent). This snub was used as a pretext by the Creoles for the rebellion against the Spaniards which led to the independence nine years later of Nueva Granada. A copy of the Declaration of Independence is on display. The museum has collections of the Independence War period, including documents and engravings and some fine portraits of Simón Bolívar. Two doors above the museum (Calle 11 No 6-42) is an attractive inner courtyard, now a restaurant, which is worth a look.

Just off the plaza is **Iglesia de San Ignacio** ① *C 10 No 6-35,* built by the Jesuits between 1605 and 1635 with plans from Rome. Over the choir and the galleries is a rich ceiling in Moorish style and emeralds from Muzo in Boyacá were used in the monstrance. Paintings by Gregorio Vázquez de Arce y Ceballos are in the nave. Opposite is the **Plazuela de Rufino Cuervo**, one of the few colonial squares in La Candelaria, a garden of trees and flowers with balconied buildings around and the dome of the Capilla del Sagrario, visible above. The Palacio Arzobispal (Cardinal's Palace) is to the left. To the right of the square is The **Museo de Trajes Regionales** ① *C 10, No 6-20, T2826531, www.museodetrajes regionales.com, Mon-Fri 1000-1630, Sat 1000-1600, US$1,50,* with a display of present and past regional dress, and a collection of handwoven textiles showing pre-Columbian techniques. This is the house where Manuela Sáenz, Bolívar's mistress, lived. At the back of the square is **La Imprenta**, where Antonio Nariño's translation of Thomas Paine's 'Rights of Man' was published in 1794. This had a profound influence on the growing demand for Independence from Spain (see above). You can read an extract from the text in Spanish on the wall of the building.

2 La Candelaria

Quinta de Bolívar

To Monserrate

Av Circunvalar

Media Torta

Universidad de los Andes

Parque La Concord

Parque Germania

Cra 1

Av Jiménez de Quesada

Las Aguas

Cra 3A

Parque de los Periodistas

Plazoleta del Rosario

Parque Santander

Museo del Oro

A

B

C

D

1   3

2

3

N

100 metres
100 yards

Sights ○

Alcaldía **34** *D5*
Biblioteca Luis Angel
   Arango **8** *C4*
Camarín del Carmen **48** *C5*
Capilla del Sagrado **22** *C5*
Capitolio Nacional **33** *D5*
Casa de Los Comuneros **32** *D5*
Casa de Moneda **9** *C4*
Casa de Poesía Silva **1** *B3*
Cathedral **23** *C4*
Colegio de San Bartolomé
   19 *C5*
Colegio Mayor de Nuestra
   Señora del Rosario **38** *C3*
Colegio Salesiano
   León XIII **47** *C5*
Corporación La Candelaria
   4 *B4*
Donación Botero **46** *C4*
Fundación Rafael Pombo
   11 *C5*
Iglesia de La Candelaria **7** *B4*
Iglesia de la Veracruz **43** *C3*
Iglesia de Nuestra Señora
   María del Carmen **25** *C5*
Iglesia de San Agustín **26** *C6*
Iglesia de San Francisco **41** *C3*

Iglesia de San Ignacio **15** *C5*
La Bordalita **39** *C3*
La Imprenta **18** *C5*
La Tercera Orden **44** *C2*
Museo 20 de Julio (Casa del
   Florero) **36** *C4*
Museo Arqueológico **24** *C6*
Museo de Arte Colonial **14** *C5*
Museo de Artes y Tradiciones
   Populares **28** *D6*
Museo del Oro **45** *C3*
Museo del Siglo XIX **29** *D6*
Museo de Trajes
   Regionales **17** *C5*
Museo Militar **10** *C5*
Observatorio Astronómico
   30 *D5*
Palacio Arzobispal **21** *C5*
Palacio de Justicia **35** *D4*
Palacio de Nariño **27** *C6*
Palacio de San Carlos **13** *C5*
Palacio de San Francisco
   42 *D3*
Palacio de
   Telecomunicaciones **37** *D4*
Plaza de Bolívar **20** *D5*
Plaza del Chorro de
   Quevedo **2** *B4*
Plazuela de Rufino Cuervo
   16 *C5*
Santa Clara **31** *D5*
Teatro Colón **12** *C5*
Teatro Libre de Bogotá **3** *B4*

Sleeping ●

17 Route House **12** *A3*
Abadía Colonial **1** *B4*
Alegría's Hostel **13** *B5*
Ambala **2** *C3*
Casa Platypus **3** *B2*
The Cranky Croc **11** *B3*

Hostal Fátima **4** *B3*
Hostal Sue **5** *B3*
Hostal Sue Candelaria **6** *B3*
Hotel de la Opera **7** *C5*
Platypus **9** *B3*
San Sebastián **10** *B3*

Eating

Asociación Construimos
  Futuro **1** *B3*
La Cicuta **5** *A5*
La Paella **2** *C4*
La Totuma **3** *B3*
Moros y Cristianos **4** *B5*

Rosita **6** *B3*
Sopas de Mamá y Postres
  de la Abuela **7** *D5*
Yumi Yumi **8** *B2*

Bars & clubs

Escobar y Rosas **9** *B3*
Quiebra Canto **10** *C2*

🚈 TransMilenio

Opposite, on the corner of Calle 10/Carrera 6 is the **Museo de Arte Colonial** ① *Cra 6, No 9-77, T314 6017/286 6768, Tue-Fri 0900-1700, Sat-Sun 1000-1600, free in 2011, US$1.50 from 2012*, one of the finest colonial buildings in Colombia. It belonged originally to the Society of Jesus, and was once the seat of the oldest University in Colombia and of the National Library. It has a splendid collection of colonial art and paintings, including a whole room of works by Gregorio Vázquez de Arce y Ceballos, all kinds of silver, furniture, glassware and utensils of the time. Particularly impressive is the collection of portable writing cabinets with inlay marquetry in one of the upstairs rooms. There is a private chapel and two charming patios.

East of Carrera 6

Further up Calle 10, at No 5-51, is the **Palacio de San Carlos**, where Bolívar lived for a time. He is said to have planted the now huge walnut tree in the courtyard. On 25 September 1828, there was an attempt on his life and his mistress, Manuela Sáenz, thrust him out of the window (a plaque facing Calle 10 marks the event) and he was able to hide for two hours under the stone arches of the bridge across the Río San Agustín, now Calle 7. Santander, suspected of complicity, was arrested and banished. Later, it was the home of the presidents of Colombia at various times until 1980. At present it houses the Ministry of Foreign Affairs. Opposite is the **Teatro Colón** ① *C 10, No 5-32*, which opened in 1892 on the 400th anniversary of Columbus' discovery of America. It presents operas, ballets, plays and concerts and is the home of the Colombian Symphony Orchestra which performs there regularly. The auditorium is late 19th century, lavishly decorated and seats 1200. Guided tours can be arranged Mondays-Fridays 0900-1700 or ask if you can have a look around when the theatre is not in use. Next door is the **Fundación Rafael Pombo** ① *C 10/Cra 5-22*, named after the writer of children's books, who lived here. The foundation is dedicated to services to children, including a library, workshops and a film studio.

Across Carrera 5 is the **Museo Militar** ① *C 10 No 4-92, Tue-Sun 0900-1630, free*. The building was originally constructed to house part of the National University but is now a museum devoted to the Colombian armed forces and has a interesting collection of weapons. There is also a detailed presentation of the Independence campaign of 1819.

One block north is the **Casa de Moneda (The Mint)** ① *C 11, No 4-93, www.lablaa.org, Mon-Sat 1000-1900, Sun and holidays 1000-1700, closed Tue, free*. The mint was established on this site in 1620 and the present building dates from 1753, constructed with traditional materials including stone and adobe. Note the courtyard and thick walled arcades. The exhibition traces the history of currency from the earliest trading in gold, salt and tumbago to the present day. There is good commentary (much also in English) with interactive exhibits. The hoard of 1630 coins, known as the *Tesoro del Mesuno*, which was found in 1936 on a small island in the Río Magdalena, is displayed. There is a coin and banknote exhibition upstairs and occasional extra art shows. Next door, a permanent display of Fernando Botero's work was opened in 2000 as **Museo Botero** ① *C 11 4-41, www.lablaa.org, Mon-Sat 0900-1900, Sun 1000-1700, closed Tue, free*, with three salons of his sculptures and paintings as well as an impressive collection of works by Picasso, Matisse, Lucian Freud, Henry Moore, Dalí and Giacometti, among others. Well worth a visit.

Opposite and running the full block between Carrera 4 and Carrera 5 is the **Biblioteca Luis Angel Arango** ① *C 11, No 4-14, Mon-Sat 0800-2000, Sun 0800-1600, free; also has free internet service available for 30 mins but it's in great demand*. A facility of the Banco de la República, this library has one of the best collections in Latin America. There are research rooms, art galleries and three reading rooms. The cafeteria on the sixth floor has a good view and reasonable food. They also have premises on the other side of Calle 11. There is a splendid concert hall, where public concerts are usually cheap or free. The library is very popular with students, who will be found queuing an hour before it opens at 0800 to secure a study place in the reading room. On the corner of Calle 11/Carrera 4 is **Iglesia de La Candelaria**, part of an Augustinian friary originally established in 1560. This is an 18th-century three-nave colonial church with some fine carving and a gilded reredos. The structure is in poor shape and desperate steps have been taken to buttress the southwest corner.

A few blocks north of here is **Casa de Poesía Silva** ① *C 14, No 3-41, T2865710, www.casadepoesiasilva.com, Mon-Fri 0900-1300, 1400-1800, free*. The poet José Asunción Silva lived here until his death in 1895. This is a good introduction to the restored colonial house, with a peaceful garden patio. There is a museum, bookshop and a fine audio and book library with taped readings of almost every Spanish-speaking author. CDs can be bought in the bookshop. There are also lectures and poetry readings.

From the Casa de Poesía to Calle 14/Carrera 2, turn right up a delightful narrow alleyway (Callejón del Embudo) to the **Plaza del Chorro de Quevedo**, which is believed to be the centre of the Muisca village of Teusaquillo (or Tibsaquillo) and was certainly where Jiménez de Quesada took possession of the territory in the name of King Charles of Spain to form the kingdom of New Granada on 6 August 1538. The centre of the city later moved down to flatter ground (around what is now the Parque Santander), but a commemorative chapel (now a cultural centre) was built on the corner of this plaza and many other houses were built around and below. The name dates from about 1800 when Father Francisco Quevedo provided a *chorro* (well) for the local people. From time to time during the day you will see many students here taking a break from their studies at the several universities nearby, adding to the activity (and the safety) of the area until around 2000 in the evening.

Down Calle 13 is the first home of the **Teatro Libre de Bogotá** ① *C 13, No 2-44, T2814834, www.teatrolibre.com*. It still houses a professional acting school with occasional public performances. The main home of this company is now in Chapinero (see page 66). Also on this street is the **Corporación La Candelaria** ① *C 13, No 2-58, T336-0888*, part of the government of the Barrio and an information point. Look in at the attractive colonial patio, with its trees and lawns. At present, under the guidance of the Corporacíon, efforts are being made to reinstate the 'cobbled' streets with modern techniques but with very successful results. They have another office across the street which also has information and sells T-shirts, etc.

South of Plaza Bolívar

One block south of the plaza is the museum of **Santa Clara** ① *Cra 8, No 8-91, T337 6762, Tue-Fri 0900-1700, Sat and Sun 1000-1600, free in 2011, US$1 from 2012*, formerly the church of the convent of Clarissa nuns, built between 1619 and 1630 and preserved very much as it was in the 17th century. There is a comprehensive collection of religious art, including paintings by Gregorio Vázquez de Arce y Ceballos, and some fine interior decoration with coffered ceilings and lattice screens and windows behind which the nuns attended Mass concealed from the public. Note the extensive remains of the original wall paintings. Though discreet signs on the walls tell you what to look for, a guide is a great help, ask at the entrance. Concerts are occasionally staged here.

Opposite is the **Observatorio Astronómico**, built in 1802, one of the first in Latin America, while further south, at Carrera 8/Calle 8 is the **Museo del Siglo XIX** ① *Cra 8, No 7-93, T281 7362, Mon-Fri 0830-1300 and 1400-1700, Sat 0900-1300, US$1.75*, formerly a private house, renovated in the Republican style around 1880. It was acquired by Bancafé in 1977 and now has a collection of 19th-century paintings, clothes and furniture. The *Botica de los pobres* is a fascinating recreation of a 'poor man's chemist' shop of the period. Note the decoration of the rooms on the second floor and the staircase woodwork. A 19th-century-style coffee shop was opened in 2000, which has good coffee to order, mini sandwiches and snacks – not cheap, but very pleasant. There are newspapers and books to read.

The entrance to the **Palacio** (or **Casa**) **de Nariño**, the presidential palace, is on Calle 7. It has a spectacular interior with a fine collection of contemporary Colombian paintings. Enquire if there are guided tours. The ceremonial guard is normally changed Monday, Wednesday, Friday and Sunday at 1730.

Opposite is the **Iglesia de San Agustín** ① *Cra 7 6-25, T246 4195, Mon-Fri 0700-1800, Sun 0800-1900, closed Sat, free*, built between 1637 and 1668, the tower being a later addition. It is strongly ornamented with an interesting coffered ceiling in the crypt. Note the ceilings in the nave and also the chandeliers. It was restored in 1988 and inside has a bright, cheerful appearance. There are several paintings by Gregorio Vázquez de Arce y Ceballos. The Image of Jesus was proclaimed Generalissimo of the army in 1812.

East of here is the **Museo Arqueológico** ① *Cra 6, No 7-43, Tue-Fri 0830-1700, Sat 0900-1600, free*, which is sponsored by the Banco Popular. This is the restored mansion of the Marqués de San Jorge, which is itself a beautiful example of 17th-century Spanish colonial architecture. The museum is arranged in themes rather than periods and is not well labelled. However it is an impressive and comprehensive collection of decorated ceramics from all the early cultures of Colombia. The restored murals of the original house are also interesting.

A block further east is the **Iglesia de Nuestra Señora María del Carmen** ① *Cra 5, No 8-36, T342 0972*, the most striking church in Bogotá. The architecture is bright and interesting with a graceful western tower and fine cupola over the transept, all in red and white, brick/stone construction. It has been repainted to brighten up this corner of La Candelaria. Inside the red/white motif continues with elegant arches and an impressive altar. The stained-glass windows, unusually illustrating fruit and flowers, are slanted to give maximum light to the congregation and the windows in the apse are particularly fine. The overall impression of freshness and light is emphasized by the detail in the rose windows of the clerestory and the intricate ornamentation inside and outside the building. Time your visit to see inside; Masses are normally at 0700, 1200 and 1800. Next to the church along Carrera 5 is the **Colegio Salesiano Leon XIII**, a boys college. Inside, a cobbled 'street' leads upwards with three courtyards and the buildings of the former Carmelite community on the left, all in the same style as the church, now serving the school. On the corner of Carrera 5/Calle 9 is the former Carmelite chapel with its bell tower above and a rounded balcony on Calle 9 housing the altar of the chapel. This building, known as the **Camarín del Carmen** ① *entrance at Calle 9, No 4-93*, was faithfully restored as a colonial building in 1957 and is now used as a theatre.

North of Plaza Bolívar

From Plaza Bolívar, Carrera 7 (La Séptima), which was the first important street of Bogotá, runs four blocks to Avenida Jiménez de Quesada, connecting the administrative centre of the city with Parque Santander, the first residential area and now the commercial hub of the capital. This street is locally known as the Calle Real del Comercio. On the corner of Carrera 7/Calle 12A is the **Palacio de Telecomunicaciones**, the headquarters of the

Antanas Mockus

In the early 1990s, Bogotá had a reputation as a world capital of anarchic disorder. It was choked with traffic and pollution, kidnappings, murders and car bombings were rife, while much of the population suffered abject poverty.

Enter 'anti-politician' Antanas Mockus, the son of Lithuanian immigrants and a former mathematics professor at the Universidad Nacional de Colombia who served as Mayor of Bogotá for two terms (1995-1997 and 2001-2003) and oversaw the city's transformation into a place where citizens felt safe to walk the streets.

Mockus first came to public attention when he dropped his pants and mooned a class of students in order to get their attention. His time in office would be full of equally imaginative stunts.

Many felt that it would take a superhero to restore a sense of moral fibre to a society apparently falling apart at the seams and Mockus took them at their word, often dressing up in spandex and a cape, taking on the character of 'Supercitizen'.

To combat *bogotanos'* disregard for the highway code he employed 420 mime artists to mock and shame motorists into heeding stoplights and pedestrian crossings, believing that Colombians were more afraid of ridicule than being fined. When there was a water shortage in the city he starred in an ad on TV in which he was shown turning off the water while he soaped in the shower.

To tackle gun crime he offered an amnesty on guns in exchange for food and had the melted metal from the weapons recast as spoons for babies. He also encouraged a 'Ladies' Night' in which men were asked to stay at home while their wives went out on the town.

While many mocked Mockus, labelling him little more than a clown, many of his initiatives were effective. Homicide rates fell from 80 per 100,000 to 23 per 100,000 during his tenure, while traffic accidents decreased by 50% and water usage by 40%. His government managed to provide a sewage system that reached 100% of the population, up from 78%. He even managed to leave a US$700 million surplus to his successor, partly aided by his success in persuading 63,000 people to pay a voluntary extra 10% tax. Diagnosed with Parkinson's disease in 2010, he still ran for president the same year, finishing second in the polling and only losing to current president Juan Manuel Santos in the runoff election.

country's postal services on the site of the colonial church of Santo Domingo. In the building there is the **Museo Postal** ⓘ *Mon-Fri 0830-1630*. Up Calle 13 and left at Carrera 6 there are two universities: **La Gran Colombia**, and **Colegio Mayor de Nuestra Señora del Rosario** near the corner at Calle 14, No 6-25. The latter school is the second oldest in Bogotá, was founded by Father Cristóbal de Torres of the order of Santo Domingo in the 16th century and is a typical cloistered school of the period. **José Celestino Mutis**, the botanist, taught natural sciences and medicine here. You can buy a good cheap lunch at the cafeteria and great crêpes. Alongside is the chapel of the Order – **La Bordalita**. Inside is an embroidered Virgin made by Queen Isabel de Borbón for Father Cristóbal on his appointment as Archbishop of Santa Fe de Bogotá. The elegant façade has some fine stone carvings above the entrance.

Museo de Bogotá ⓘ *Cra 4 10-18, T352 1865, www.museodebogota.gov.co, Tue-Fri 0900-1800, Sat-Sun 1000-1700, free*, is Bogotá's own museum depicting the history of the city. It's housed inside Casa Sámano.

Emeralds

Thinking about buying a diamond? Think again. A fine emerald is a much rarer gemstone, and the finest emeralds in the world hail from Colombia. Like diamonds, emeralds are evaluated according to the four 'C's – Colour, Clarity, Cut and Carat weight – although colour, not clarity, is considered the most important attribute. A dark green emerald is considered the most precious variety, although they range in colour. Unlike other gemstones all emeralds have flaws or 'inclusions'.

However, rather than detracting from their value, inclusions are said to give an emerald its personality.

If you are in the market for a stone, go to Avenida Jiménez in Bogotá, which is the heart of Colombia's unofficial emerald exchange. The emeralds sold here come from Colombia's three most prolific mines – Muzo, Coscuez and Chivor – all located in the cloudforests of Boyacá, just a few hours to the north. These mines have a long history that dates back to AD 1000, long before the Spanish invasion. To catch a glimpse of some exquisite examples of emerald jewellery from pre-Hispanic times, check out the **Museo del Oro** in Bogotá, see below.

Although not strictly in the Barrio de La Candelaria, the cluster of interesting buildings around the **Parque Santander** are appropriately part of Old Bogotá, with three of the finest churches in Colombia. After crossing Jiménez de Quesada, the **Iglesia de San Francisco** ① *Mon-Fri 0700-1800, Sat-Sun 0700-1300, 1630-1930*, is immediately to your left. It is an interesting mid-16th-century church with paintings of famous Franciscans, choir stalls, a famous ornate gold high altar (AD1622), and a fine Lady Chapel with blue and gold ornamentation. The remarkable ceiling is in Spanish-*Mudéjar* (Moorish) style. Try to see this church when fully illuminated. Behind it along Avenida Jiménez de Quesada is the **Palacio de San Francisco** ① *Av Jiménez No 7-50*, built between 1918 and 1933 for the Gobernación de Cundinamarca, on the site of the Franciscan friary. Designed in the Republican style, it has a fine façade and competed to some degree with the Capitolio Nacional. It is now part of the Rosario University. Next to the San Francisco church and overlooking Parque Santander is the **Iglesia de la Veracruz**, first built eight years after the founding of Bogotá, rebuilt in 1731, and again in 1904. In 1910 it became the Panteón Nacional e Iglesia de la República. José de Caldas, the famous scientist, was buried under the church along with many other patriots, victims of the Spanish 'Reign of Terror' around 1815. It has a bright white and red interior and a fine decorated ceiling. Fashionable weddings are held here. Across Calle 16 is the third major church **La Tercera Orden**, a colonial church famous for its carved woodwork along the nave and a high balcony, massive wooden altar reredos, and confessionals. It was built by the Third Franciscan Order in the 17th century, hence the name.

Museo del Oro On the northeast corner of the Parque de Santander is the **Museo del Oro** (the Gold Museum) ① *C16 No 5-41, T343 2233, www.banrep.gov.co/museo-del-oro, Tue-Sat 0900-1800 (leave by 1900), Sun and holidays 1000-1600 (leave by 1700), US$1.50, free on Sun*, in the splendid premises of the Banco de la República. This collection is a 'must', and is perhaps the finest museum in all of South America. There are more than 35,000 pieces of pre-Columbian gold work in the total collection, most of which is held here. The rest is divided between other regional Museos de Oro (all of which are worth a visit), sponsored by the Banco de la República throughout Colombia. Many thousands of pieces are displayed.

On two upper floors, a full display is made of the dozen or so pre-Spanish indigenous groups that have been identified in Colombian territory, and how they found and worked gold and other metals. It is a fascinating story, illustrated by many examples of their work. They used techniques, some might say, unsurpassed by goldsmiths of today.

The first display floor sets the scene, each culture set in its geographical and historical environment, explaining the characteristics of their art. There are illustrative models including one of Ciudad Perdida as it would have looked when inhabited. In each section there are helpful portable boards with explanatory notes in English. The second floor has many more examples of the extraordinary goldwork of these pre-Columbian peoples. The centrepiece of the exhibition is the Salón Dorado, a glittering display of 8000 pieces inside an inner vault – an unforgettable experience.

On the ground floor there is a souvenir/bookshop, and exhibition rooms. Audio guides can be hired at the ticket office. On the first floor, 20-minute films are shown throughout the day, times and languages are displayed.

Monserrate → *For listings, see pages 68-82.*

ⓘ *T284 5700 (answer service also in English), www.cerromonserrate.com; the fare up to Monserrate Mon-Sat before 1700 is US$7 adult and child return, after 1700 US$8.50, Sun US$4. The funicular works Mon-Sat 0745-1145, every 30 mins; the cable car operates Mon-Sat 1200-2400 every 20 mins; funicular Sun and holidays 0600-1830, cable car 0900-1700. Times change frequently.*

There is a very good view of the city from the top of Monserrate (3152 m), the lower of the two peaks rising sharply to the east. It is reached by a funicular railway and a cable car. The convent at the top is a popular shrine and pilgrimage site. At the summit, near the church, a platform gives a bird's-eye view of the city's tiled roofs and of the plains beyond stretching to the rim of the Sabana. Sunrise and sunset can be spectacular. The **Calle del Candelero**, a reconstruction of a Bogotá street of 1887, has plenty of street stalls and snack bars. Behind the church are popular picnic grounds. There are two upmarket touristy restaurants at the top, both overpriced and closed Sunday. If you wish to walk up, possibly the safest time is at the weekend about 0500, before the crowds arrive but when there are people about. At this time you will catch the sunrise. The path is dressed stone and comfortably graded all the way up with refreshment stalls at weekends every few metres. It takes about one and a quarter hours up (if you don't stop), but at the time of writing the path was closed due to lack of maintenance funds; it's due to reopen later in the year.

Safety It is best not to walk to the top of Monserrate alone; and do not display cameras openly. On no account walk down in the dark. On weekdays it is not recommended to walk up and especially not down. You should also take a bus or taxi to the foot of the hill Monday to Friday and, at all times, from the bottom station into town. There are usually taxis waiting by the footbridge across the road. There have been reports of tourists being mugged at the summit and the bottom, even during the day. The walk up to Guadalupe, the higher peak opposite Monserrate, is not recommended.

Quinta de Bolívar

ⓘ *C 20, No 2-91 Este, T336 6419, www.quintadebolivar.gov.co, Tue-Sat 0900-1700, Sun 1000-1600, US$1.50, reductions for students and children, guided tours.*

At the foot of Monserrate is the Quinta de Bolívar, a fine colonial mansion with splendid gardens and lawns. There are several cannons captured at the battle of Boyacá. The elegant house, once Bolívar's home, is now a museum showing some of his personal possessions and paintings of events in his career. Opposite the Quinta is the attractive campus of the prestigious private university, Los Andes.

Downtown Bogotá → *For listings, see pages 68-82.*

Downtown Bogotá, the old commercial centre with shops, offices and banks, runs in a band northwards from Avenida Jiménez de Quesada. It is very patchy, with a thorough mix of architectural styles, including modern towers and colonial buildings in various states of repair. This commercial hub narrows to a thin band of secondary shops extending between Carrera 7 and Avenida Caracas to around Calle 60. The streets are full of life; they are also often paralysed by traffic and choked with fumes. The pavements can be very congested too, particularly Carrera 7 and Avenida (Calle)19, but the former is closed to traffic every Sunday 0700-1400, creating a totally different atmosphere. Many of the budget hotels and some of the better ones are found in this area, which is not that safe, although standards are improving.

The commercial centre of Bogotá has been weakened in recent years by the migration north of company headquarters and offices, yet the area seems busier than ever. For the visitor there are plenty of attractions. For the immediate area of Parque de Santander, see La Candelaria, page 54.

3 Downtown Bogotá

Bogotá maps
1 Bogotá orientation, page 50
2 La Candelaria, page 56
3 Downtown Bogotá, page 64
4 North Bogotá, page 67

200 metres
200 yards

Sleeping
Bacatá
Clásico Hotel del Parque 2
Quinta de Bolívar 5
San Francisco 3

Tequendama 4

Eating
Café La Bohème 4
Enobra 1

Food Rice 2
La Juguetería 3

Bars & clubs
The End Bar 5

Cementerio Central

The tomb of Leo S Kopp in Bogotá's Cementerio Central has something of a cult following. Kopp, of German origin, founded Bavaria Beer, Colombia's largest brewery. Famously generous, he was known to find employment for anyone who came and asked him.

It appears that his capacity for giving continues after his death. On any given day it's not uncommon to see the poor and the unemployed laying flowers at his grave or kissing the magnificent bronze statue that guards it. Rumour has it that the statue retains its radiance thanks to a civil servant who, having prayed at the feet of Kopp's statute, was rewarded with a job and now shows his gratitude by secretly cleaning and shining the effigy.

Iglesia de San Diego ① *Cra 7, No 26-37*, built around 1606 by the Franciscans, with a chapel to the Virgin added in 1629. There is a fine statue of Our Lady in the chapel dedicated to the countryside (which surrounded it when it was built). The monastery was built about 1560, and the fine Moorish ceiling can still be seen. Local craft items are sold in part of the old San Diego monastery adjacent to the church.

Iglesia de Nuestra Señora de las Aguas ① *Cra 3, No 18-66*. This charming 17th-century church has a wide façade with seven bells overlooking a small park and Avenida Jiménez de Quesada. The name refers to the San Francisco river, which now flows under the avenida. It has a single nave and a baroque altar, with a wood carving of tropical fruits at its base. The convent next door has been inhabited by Dominicans for over a century. It has served as a hospital and a school since then, now it is occupied by **Artesanías de Colombia** ① *Cra 2 No 18A-58, www.artesaniasdecolombia.com.co*, one of the best places to buy local crafts.

Teatro Jorge Eliécer Gaitán ① *Cra 7, No 22-47, T334 6800, www.teatrojorgeeliecer.gov.co*, built in art-deco style around 1945 as a movie house, it is now one of the biggest theatres in the country, holding an audience of over 1500 for shows, concerts and theatre productions.

Museo Nacional ① *Cra 7, No 28-66, T381 6470, www.museonacional.gov.co, Tue-Sat 1000-1800, Sun 1000-1700, free in 2011, US$1.75 from 2012 (pensioners free), various tours available*; founded by Santander in 1823 and later moved to this building, a former prison built around 1900, designed by Thomas Reed (see Capitolio Nacional). It houses a well-displayed archaeological collection, one of the best in the country. Even if you are short of time, try to see this display. There is a collection of gold items in the vault. The top floor has a fine art section, comprising 20th-century national paintings and sculptures. Expensive but good café and tasty cakes. There are also salads and desserts named after exhibits.

Museo de Arte Moderno ① *C 24, No 6-00, T286 0466, www.mambogota.com, Tue-Sat 1000-1800, Sun 1100-1700, US$1.50, half price for students*, has an appropriately modern building, inaugurated in 1953. It has an interesting, well-displayed collection of modern Colombian artists, with sculptures, graphic arts and more represented. Good café and bookshop. If you want to photograph in the museum you must obtain permission from the office.

Parque de la Independencia

Parque de la Independencia is popular at weekends though not recommended for visits during the week. In the park is the **Planetarium** ① *Diagonal 27 6-81, T3344546, www.planetariodebogota.gov.co, Tue-Sun 1030-1600, open bank holiday Mon, free entrance, events US$1.50*, offering lectures, courses, seminars, and a public astronomical show. There are occasional son et lumière shows, and there's also a good **internet café** ① *US$1 per hr.* Beside the park is the **Plaza de Toros (Bull Ring)** ① *9 Parque de los Mártires (Park of the Martyrs), Cra 14 (Av Caracas)/C10-11*, with a monument, on the site of the Plaza in which the Spanish shot many patriots during the struggle for Independence.

Chapinero and around

The centre of Bogotá comes to a natural end where Carreras 7 to 13 come together beyond the Centro Internacional, a large complex that includes the Tequendama Hotel. In the link between Central and North Bogotá, there are a number of places of interest.

Casa Museo Jorge Eliécer Gaitán ① *C 42, No 15-52, Tue-Fri 0900-1700, Sat-Sun 1000-1400, free*, is the former residence of the populist leader whose assassination in April 1948 triggered the infamous 'Bogotazo', at the outset of La Violencia. The museum is dedicated to this period of Colombia's history.

Instituto Nacional de Investigaciones Geológico-Mineras (INGEOMINAS) ① *Diagonal 53, No 34-53, T220 0200, www.ingeominas.gov.co*, has a library and pleasant museum. It is in the corner of the Universidad National campus, close to other Earth Science institutions including the Instituto Geográfico Agustín Codazzi.

Museo de los Niños ① *Cra 60 No 63-27, T225 7587, www.museodelosninos.org.co, US$1, Tue-Fri 1½-hr tours at 0830, 1030, 1330 and 1530, Sat, Sun and holidays 0930-1530, guided tours*, natural sciences explained for children.

Museo de Arte y Cultura Colsubsidio ① *C 36 No 5A-19, T340 0770, www.colsubsidio. com*, has exhibitions of contemporary artists, and other special events.

Teatro Nacional ① *C 71, No 10-25, T217 4577, www.teatronacional.com.co*, has traditional presentations by national and international artists and important facilities for training young people. They have other premises in North Bogotá (C 95 No 47-15).

Teatro Libre de Bogotá ① *Cra 11 No 61-80, T217 1988, www.teatrolibre.com*, has frequent presentations, formerly in La Candelaria where they still have a base.

Jardín Botánico José Celestino Mutis ① *C 63 No 68-95, T437 7060, www.jbb.gov.co, Tue-Fri 0800-1700, Sat, Sun and hols 0900-1700, US$2.50 adult, US$1.50 child*, are interesting and well-organized botanical gardens that have a collection of over 5000 native orchids, plus roses, gladioli and trees from all over the country. If you can't get to the national parks, you can at least see many of the local species here. It has a fine documentation centre with resident experts.

Maloka Centro Interactivo de Ciencia y Tecnología ① *Cra 68D, No 24A-51, T427 2707, www.maloka.org, daily 1000-1900, US$10.25, including cinema*, is a complex of science exhibits and instructive entertainment for all ages. There are over 200 exhibits in nine halls, a 135° large-screen cinema, internet rooms, restaurants and other facilities. A full visit takes about three hours.

Along Calle 26 with Carrera 16 is the **Cementerio Central**, an oval-shaped construction full of large mausoleums and pine trees. This is Bogotá's principal cemetery, built between 1830 and 1929 and many of Colombian history's most influential figures are buried here, including Luis Carlos Galán, a liberal politician and journalist who was assassinated during the drug wars of the late 1980s, and leader of the M19 guerrilla group Carlos Pizarro, also murdered. Round the corner from the inner ellipse is the grave of Leo S Kopp, founder of Bavaria, Colombia's largest beer company. Presided over by an impressive bronze statue, the site has something of a cult following (see box, page 65).

Nearby is the **Plaza del Mercado de Paloquemao** ① *Av 19 with Cra 25*, an enormous covered market with over 1800 stalls selling fruit and vegetables, meats, herbs and flowers as well as some handicrafts. To catch the flower market in full flow, visit between 0500 and 1000 – Friday and Sunday are the best days.

North of the centre → *For listings, see pages 68-82.*

Beyond Calle 60, the main city continues north to a comparatively new area, North Bogotá, where there has been great commercial expansion with the development of wealthy suburbs. Most of the best hotels and restaurants are in this area, which is regarded as the safest in Bogotá. The T-shaped area made up by Calle 83 and Carrera 13 is the **Zona Rosa**, also known as the Zona T. Many bars, clubs and restaurants can be found here. Small towns, such as Chapinero, **Chicó** and Usaquén have been absorbed, and the city now extends north to around Calle 200. Many commercial and financial companies have moved here but most government offices and many businesses remain downtown.

North Bogotá is noted for its huge, lavish shopping malls, which have sprung up in the last few years. They are worth a visit even if the prices don't grab you. The **Hacienda Santa Bárbara** ⓘ *Cra 7 115-60, www.haciendasantabarbara.com.co,* has been constructed within a large country mansion, and parts of the colonial architecture, arches, and stone floors have been incorporated. Even some of the old gardens have been retained.

4 North Bogotá

Bogotá maps
1 Bogotá orientation, page 50
2 La Candelaria, page 56
3 Downtown Bogotá, page 64
4 North Bogotá, page 67

❶ TransMilenio

500 metres
500 yards

Sleeping 🛏
Andino Royal 1
Morrison Hotel 2
Viaggio Suites 3
Windsor House 4

Eating 🍴
80 Sillas 5
Camino del Café 8
El Corral Gourmet 6
K-Listo 9
La Hamburguesería 11

Salto del Angel 12
Wok 13

Bars & clubs 🍸
Alma 14

Museo de 'El Chicó' Mercedes Sierra de Pérez ① *Cra 7, No 93-01, www.museodelchico.com, Mon-Fri 1000-1700, Sat 0800-1200, guided tours US$1.75,* formerly the **Hacienda de El Chicó**, is a fine example of colonial architecture. It contains a worldwide collection of mostly 18th-century porcelain, furniture and paintings.

Usaquén

Usaquén was once one of the more important towns, but has now been absorbed by the growing metropolis of Bogotá. The small plaza in the centre has become an attractive shopping and restaurant area, popular in the evenings. The railway station can be used for the tourist train to Zipaquirá at weekends (see Transport, page 80, for more details). **World Trade Center** ① *C 100, No 8A-49, T657 8757, www,wtcbogota.com.co,* is a large convention and exhibition centre with all the usual services. The **Bogotá Royal Hotel** is alongside.

◉ Bogotá listings → *Phone code: 1.*

Hotel and guesthouse prices

LL over US$200	**L** US$151-200	**AL** US$101-150
A US$66-100	**B** US$46-65	**C** US$31-45
D US$21-30	**E** US$12-20	**F** US$7-11
G US$6 and under		

Restaurant prices

�託⫯⫯ over US$12	⫯⫯ US$6-12	⫯ under US$6

⊜ Sleeping

Accommodation is plentiful in Bogotá. All 3 sections of the city have top-class and middle-range hotels but budget travellers will find more choice in the **Downtown** and **La Candelaria** areas. If possible, book hotels in advance, even if only from the airport or bus terminal. For hostel organizations, see page 24.

Taxi drivers at the airport or bus station occasionally say that the hotel you have chosen is 'closed', 'not known', etc, especially the cheaper ones listed in La Candelaria. Insist they take you to the right address.

Note During 2011 there has been a spate of attacks targeting backpacker hostels in La Candelaria. Muggings by armed gangs and one incidence of sexual assault at hostels have been reported. The Candelaria Hostel Association has been urging the police to take measures, but at the time of writing security had not improved and visitors are advised to check the situation with local hostel owners.

La Candelaria *p54, map p56*
L Hotel de la Opera, C 10, No 5-72, T336 2066, www.hotelopera.com.co. This privately owned hotel was previously the residency of Simón Bolívar's personal guard. Spread out over 2 buildings; 1 colonial, 1 Republican, now joined together, this is Colombian opulence at its best, with period pieces adorning its exquisite rooms. It has 2 rooftop restaurants with superb views as well as a sauna, Turkish bath, jacuzzi, gym, bar and pool. The junior suites have original bathtubs.
A Abadía Colonial, C 11, No 2-32, T341 1884, www.abadiacolonial.com. Fine colonial building in the heart of La Candelaria. Comfortable rooms if a little small. Best to ask for a street-facing room as otherwise they have no windows. Has Wi-Fi, cable TV, safe and a restaurant serving Italian food.
A Casa Platypus, Cra 3, No 16-28, T281 1801, www.casaplatypus.com. From the owner of the **Platypus Hostel**, this hotel is aimed at 'the parents of backpackers' or 'flash packers'. In a beautiful colonial building overlooking the Parque de los Periodistas, it has excellent rooms, a kitchen and a fine roof terrace with views of Monserrate. Wi-Fi and good breakfasts. Highly recommended.
B Ambalá, Cra 5, No 13-46, T342 6384, www.hotelambala.net. In a pretty colonial building, Ambalá's rooms are clean but a little small and with dated decor.

San Sebastián, Av Jiménez, No 3-97, T243 8937. The lobby of this hotel has some amusing Picasso imitation murals and it was plainly a fashionable location in its time but those days are long gone. The rooms are a little dated but it's functional and has hot water, internet, Wi-Fi and good writing desks as well as good views of Monserrate. Breakfast included.

C-E 17 Route House, Cra 1 15A-16, T284 5068, www.17routehouse.com. Small hostel with room for 10 people, specializing in adventure tourism and biking. Does a different typical breakfast every day and the price includes a bike tour of Bogotá. Friendly.

D Alegrías Hostel, Cra 2 9-46, T286 8047, www.alegriashostel.com. New hostel in the heart of La Candelaria, set around a pleasant patio. 10- and 7-bed dorms (**F**) available.

D The Cranky Croc, C 15, No 3-46, T342 2438, www.crankycroc.com. This Aussie-run hostel is located in a beautiful 300-year-old building, carefully restored to retain many of the original features. Excellent facilities include Wi-Fi and internet (for a charge), free luggage storage and a lounge with a fireplace. Has several private rooms with bathrooms and dorms with bunks (**F**). Restaurant with different breakfast menus and good cocktails.

D Hostal Fátima, C 14, No 2-24, T281 6389, www.hostalfatima.com. **Fátima** is a maze of brightly coloured rooms and sunny patios with lots of stained-glass windows and potted plants. It has lots of added bonuses such as a sauna and jacuzzi, a TV room and even a dance studio teaching contemporary and jazz dance, yoga and pilates. Has several private rooms with bathrooms as well as dorms with bunks (**F**). Nice bar, also open to the public. Offers IH and student discounts. Long-term stays available soon, ask at reception.

D Hostal Sue, C 16, No 2-55 and **Hostal Sue Candelaria**, Cra 3, No 14-18, T334 8894 and T341 2647, www.hostalsue.com. Both have excellent facilities, including Wi-Fi, internet, kitchen, free lockers, hot water, laundry service and places to relax in hammocks.

The Candelaria one has a ping-pong table too. The difference between them is that they attract different crowds: the 1st is for a younger crowd, keener on partying, the 2nd for those seeking a quieter atmosphere. Dorms with bunks (**F**) available.

D Platypus, C 16, No 2-43, T352 0127, www.platypusbogota.com. As the first backpackers' hostel to open in Colombia, the **Platypus** has built a reputation for having all the facilities you would expect, such as internet access and Wi-Fi, a book exchange and a kitchen. A string of other hostels have since opened up in the Candelaria offering similar services but what still makes the **Platypus** stand out is owner Germán Escobar's excellent knowledge of Colombia. Private rooms with bathrooms and several dorms with bunks (**F**).

Downtown Bogotá *p64, map p64*
The downtown area of Bogotá suffers from petty crime and muggings by night.

LL-L Tequendama, Cra 10, No 26-21, T382 0300, www.cptequendama.com.co. Colombia's largest hotel, recently refurbished, the Tequendama has been witness to some of Colombia's most important political events since its inauguration in 1953. With 2 restaurants, a spa, new pool, Wi-Fi throughout and large rooms and suites, it is well equipped for the conferences it invariably hosts.

A Bacatá, C 19, No 5-20, T283 8300, www.hotelbacata.com.co. Another traditional Bogotá hotel, **Bacatá** has large rooms with minibar, cable TV and Wi-Fi, as well as a sauna, gym and pizzeria.

A Clásico Hotel del Parque, C 24 No 4A-79 (esq Cra 5), T284 2200, www.hoteldel parqueclasico.com. In the heart of the Centro Internacional, this 1980s hotel has had little work done on it since it was built but it does have a pool, sauna, Wi-Fi and breakfast included.

A San Francisco, Cra 10, No 23-63, T286 1677, www.sfcol.com. This modern hotel has good-sized rooms, a restaurant,

Wi-Fi, free breakfasts and free transfer to and from the airport. Welcome drink upon arrival.

B Quinta de Bolívar, Cra 4, No 17-59, T337 6500, www.hotelquintadebolivar.com. Located on the edge of La Candelaria, this Republican-era building has cosy rooms and breakfast is included. Wi-Fi, sauna and jacuzzi.

Chapinero and around *p66, map p50*
LL Casa Medina, Cra 7, No 69A-22, T312 0299, www.hotelescharleston.com. Built in 1945 by Santiago Medina, with its stone columns and carved wooden doors this hotel is Bogotá at its most refined. It has a gym, Wi-Fi, iPod docks, a gym and a fine restaurant in a wooden panelled room. A new tower has been added with 34 additional rooms.

A Casona del Patio, Cra 8, No 69-24, T212 8805, www.lacasonadelpatio.net. With 24 immaculate rooms set around a sunny patio and well situated near the Zona G, this is one of the best mid-range options in Bogotá. Has cable TV and Wi-Fi. Recommended.

B Las Terrazas, C 54A, No 3-12, T255 5777. Well placed in a quiet area of Chapinero Alto, this hotel is popular with foreigners. The building is an interesting shape, a kind of half pyramid, meaning that each room has a large balcony with excellent views of the city. Has Wi-Fi and cable TV. First 2 floors are student residences.

C Diamante Central Park, C 53, No 10-78, T210 2463. In the heart of El Chapinero, this hotel is a bit of an ugly block but is nonetheless pretty good value. Has Wi-Fi, cable TV and safes in each room.

C Hotel Lord, C 63, No 14-62, T255 0530, www.hotel-lord.com. Popular with Colombian businessmen, some of the rooms are a little small and have only windows onto corridors but the street-facing ones are good value with cable TV and good light. Has an internet room and a restaurant.

D-F El Cafecito, Cra 6, No 34-70, T285 8308, www.cafecito.net. From the owners of the popular hostals in Ecuador, **El Cafecito** offers an excellent alternative to staying in La Candelaria. Well located in the English architecture neighbourhood of La Merced and near the restaurants of La Macarena and the clubs of Carrera 7, the building has an interesting history, having once been an asphalt factory belonging to mayoral candidate Moreno de Caro. It has an excellent Wi-Fi-enabled café serving crêpes and cocktails and several individually decorated rooms with and without private bathrooms, as well as bunks in dorms. Good choice of brunch served until 1600 and pleasant garden. Recommended.

North of the centre *p67, map p67*
LL Andino Royal, C 85, No 12-28, T651 3100, www.hotelesroyal.com. Well placed between Parque 93 and the Zona Rosa, this modern hotel has all the conveniences you would expect including a gym, Wi-Fi and cable TV. The rooms are light and airy with large windows.

LL Morrison Hotel, C 84 Bis, No 13-54, T266 3111, www.morrisonhotel.com. Conveniently located near the Zona T, this recently refurbished hotel, with a contemporary British design, has large rooms with Wi-Fi, LCD TVs and thermo-acoustic windows. It looks out onto the beautiful Parque León de Greiff. Bar and restaurant have also recently been added to the premises.

L Windsor House, C 95, No 9-97, T634 3630, www.hotelesestelar.com. English-style luxury hotel with large rooms. Some have jacuzzis, all have a safe, minibar and use of a gym and Turkish bath. Wi-Fi and restaurant.

AL-A Viaggio Suites, Cra 18, No 86A-36, Edificio Virrey, T236 1712, www.viaggio. com.co. Excellent value short-term and medium-let apartments. Spacious, modern and clean with fitted kitchens, daily house keeper and breakfast included. All apartments have Wi-Fi and laundry service. Prices drop for longer stays. There is no sign outside, ring the door bell. Has a second building at Cra 18 93A-60. Recommended.

🍴 Eating

Restaurants are spread throughout the city. The more exotic and fashionable places to eat are in **North Bogotá** but La Candelaria has its bistros and good value, typical Colombian food, as well as recent additions of more upmarket restaurants. Take local advice if you want to eat really cheaply in markets or from street stalls. Increasingly restaurants in La Candelaria are also open in the evenings.

La Candelaria p54, map p56
La Cicuta, C 9 No 1-95, T283 0229. The French chef cooks up a storm in this lovely restaurant, overlooking a beautiful garden. Good vegetarian options and also perfect steaks.

La Paella, C 11, No 5-13. Opposite the Centro Cultural García Márquez, this restaurant serves Spanish food and specializes in paellas.

Rosita, C 13A, No 1A-36. On the lovely Plazoleta Chorro de Quevedo, this is a great little breakfast and lunchtime spot. Sells cookbooks and has a café with desserts next door.

Asociación Construimos Futuro, C 15A, No 2-21. Good breakfasts served up by a neighbourhood co-operative. Has Wi-Fi.

La Totuma, Cra 2, No 13A-58. On the hip Callejón del Embudo, this restaurant serves economic sushi and other Japanese dishes. Colourful surroundings.

Moros y Cristianos, C 9, N0 3-11. Cuban food served in a sunny, glass-covered patio. Live music Fri-Sun nights.

Sopas de Mamá y Postres de la Abuela, Cra 9, No 10-59. A real *rolo* institution, this restaurant serves traditional Colombian broths such as *ajiaco* and *sancocho* in a beautiful 2nd-floor gallery with stained-glass windows and large panelled wooden doors. Its other speciality is puddings.

Yumi Yumi, Cra 3, No 16-40. Tiny hole-in-the-wall restaurant serving sandwiches, crêpes, Thai curries on Tue nights, fruit juices and always has a 2x1 offer for their cocktails. Open late most nights and offers free tickets to clubs in the Zona Rosa.

Downtown Bogotá p64, map p64
Enobra, Cra 4A, No 26A-37. Fashionable, chic restaurant with sparse decor serving tapas and various cuts of steak.

La Juguetería, C 27, No 4A-03, T341 1188. A bit of an **Andrés Carne de Res** but in town, **La Juguetería** cooks up excellent steaks in a frankly slightly disturbing atmosphere: the restaurant's decoration theme is toys and dolls and they hang everywhere. Some of the tables are even made out of dolls' heads.

Café La Bohème, C 27 5-28, T286 8463. Bohemian, French-inspired café, open Mon-Sat, serving breakfasts, coffees and drinks. Has Wi-Fi.

Food Rice, Cra 4A, No 26A-13. This restaurant has a simple but effective formula: it only does rice, but rice dishes from around the world, everything from Chinese to Malaysian to Indian. There are some good vegetarian options. Does home delivery.

Chapinero and around p66, map p50
Bogotá has several gastronomic zones. The Zona 'G' ('G' stands for gourmet) is much talked about, but **La Macarena**, comprising several blocks along Carrera 4, has several very good restaurants at more reasonable prices. Formerly an area frequented by artists, it is now becoming increasingly hip. All of Cra 4 and side streets leading up to it are packed with a number of new, tasty-looking restaurants.

Criterión, C 69A, No 5-75, T310 2810. This restaurant has minimalist decor and a French-influenced menu of dishes such as *foie gras*, goat's cheese salad, shellfish and various types of steak as well as a large wine list.

Estrella de los Ríos, C 26B, No 4-50, T337 4037, www.estrelladelosrios.com. Costeña Estrella calls her small place an 'anti-restaurant'. Her idea is that your dining experience should feel much like she is cooking for you at home. Hence, you must book 24 hrs in advance and she reserves the right to turn you away if she doesn't like you! Estrella, the author of several cookbooks, conjures up *costeño* and Cuban food in her intimate kitchen for US$55 for 5 courses, excluding alcohol. Highly recommended.

¶¶ H Sasson, C 6517-04, www.harryssasson. com. Harry Sasson is one of Colombia's best known chefs and owns a number of Bogotá's most popular restaurants. H Sasson does contemporary Asian food such as crispy duck and curries in stylish surroundings.

¶¶ Archie's, C 82 13-07, www.archies pizzas.com. A pizza chain that does some of the best gourmet pizzas in all of South America. Pricey, but worth it. Excellent range, outdoor seating, even has a breakfast pizza.

¶¶ Artesano, Cra 4A, No 27-12. Artesano, specializing in 'woodfire cuisine', does a wide range of pizzas, fish and chicken dishes, all cooked 'a la leña'.

¶¶ La Cigale, C 69A, No 4-93, T400 9906, www.lacigale.com.co. This French restaurant does all the Gallic specialities you would expect, including terrines and magret de canard.

¶¶ Mini-mal, Cra 4A, No 57-52, T347 5464, www.mini-mal.org. As the name suggests, the focus of this restaurant/bar/design shop is on minimalism. The menu is contemporary Colombian cuisine with alternative takes on Pacific, Caribbean, Andean and Amazonian recipes.

¶¶ Tábula, C 29 bis, No 5-90. Gourmet international menu in stylish surroundings a couple of blocks from La Macarena.

¶ Al Wadi, C 27, No 4-14. Healthy Lebanese food, including kebabs, falafel and various types of rice.

¶ El Cafecito, Cra 6, No 34-70, www.cafecito. net. Café belonging to the hostel of the same name, El Cafecito has an excellent varied menu that includes rosti, pancakes, salads, sandwiches, world coffees and good teas as well as a variety of cocktails. All of this is served in the fine surroundings of an English-style mansion in La Merced.

¶ La Casa de las Sopas, C 34, No 13-20. Excellent lunchtime venue serving traditional Colombian soups and broths, including ajiaco, mondongo and sancocho.

¶ La Hamburguesería, Cra 4A, No 27-27, www.lahamburgueseria.com This fast-food chain is becoming increasingly popular in Bogotá for the quality of its hamburgers and hotdogs. There are several more outlets spread around town. Does home delivery.

North of the centre p67, map p67
North of C 76 there are 3 popular areas for eating and drinking. The **Zona T**, also known as the **Zona Rosa** is a T-shaped pedestrianized area, comprising C 83 and Cra 13, and has some of Bogotá's best restaurants and bars. Further north is **Parque 93** (www.parque93. com), for many years the most exclusive address in Bogotá, although some of Colombia's chain restaurants are now beginning to encroach upon its territory. Beyond, on C 117 with Cra. 6A (used to be part of Cra 7) and Cra 7 is Usaquén, formerly a town in its own right but now a part of the big metropolis, and a popular venue for evening and weekend dining. Cra 6A in particular is home to a number of new restaurants springing up.

¶¶ El Corral Gourmet, C 93A, No 12-57. This popular Colombian burger chain is a cut and some more above McDonald's. It serves mainly large hamburgers as well as onion rings and other side orders.

¶¶ Salto del Angel, Cra 13, No 93A-45, T3450304, www.saltodelangel.com.co. This enormous restaurant on Parque 93 has a large varied menu of steaks, ceviches and picking food as well as some international options which include fish and chips. At weekends, after dinner, the tables are cleared and it becomes a popular upmarket disco.

¶¶ Wok, Cra 13, No 82-74. Fashionable Asian cuisine restaurant.

¶ K-Listo, C 83, No 12A-36. Fast-food chain serving stuffed arepas and empanadas.

Usaquén p68, map p67
¶¶ 80 Sillas, C 118, No 6A-05, T619 2471. All kinds of ceviches and other seafood served in wooden elevated patios with encroaching ferns.

Camino del Café, Cra 6, No 117-26. easant café with outdoor terrace and i-Fi. Good coffees, sandwiches, snacks, e creams and cocktails.

La Hamburguesería, C 118, No 6A-40, 214 1943. This hamburger diner, part of popular Bogotá franchise, has very good urgers as well as salads, club sandwiches nd soups. It often has live music at e weekends.

) Bars and clubs

3ogotá *p48, maps p50, p56, p64 and p67* Most bars and clubs are concentrated in he Cra 11-13, C 80-86 region, known as the Zona Rosa – a lively, upmarket area where many restaurants open late. Some of these have live entertainment. Further south along Cra 7, from C 32 up to C 59 draws an edgier crowd of filmmakers, artists and students.

The area of **La Candelaria** has little to offer in the way of nightlife, Wed-Fri are the best nights.

Alma Bar, C 85, No 12-51, T622 8289. Open Wed-Sat 2130-0245, entry US$10, 1st drink US$3. A relatively new bar/club playing jazz, house and funk, while Wed night is salsa night.

The End, Centro Internacional Tequendama, piso 30, Cra 7 and C 29. The best place for late drinking.

Escobar y Rosas, Cra 4, No 15-01, La Candelaria. In a converted old chemist is packed on Fri-Sat nights with a student crowd.

In Vitro, C 59, No 6-38. What started as a weekly meeting of friends to show their short films and documentaries has developed into one of Bogotá's hippest clubs. Shows short films during the week while the weekends are reserved for an eclectic mix of salsa, rock'n'roll and indie music. Tue and Wed night are especially popular as entrance is free. Frequented by filmmakers, artists and students.

LOV (Lost on Vibes) nightclub, Cra 7 No 32-16, www.lovnightclub.com.

Formerly Cha Cha, housed in the old Hilton hotel.

QuiebraCanto, Cra 5, No 17-76, La Candelaria. In a colonial house, plays world music, funk and salsa to a friendly crowd and is best on Wed and Thu nights.

Son Salomé, Cra 7, No 40-31, Piso 2. No cover and cheap drinks Popular salsa venue.

Theatron, C 58, No 10-32, www.theatronde pelicula.com. In an old cinema theatre, this spectacular gay venue, spread out over 4 floors and with a capacity of 4000 has to be seen to be believed. It includes a rooftop garden and several different rooms playing everything from *vallenato* to electronic music. It accepts straight couples but beyond a certain point within the building it's men only.

🎭 Entertainment

Bogotá *p48, maps p50, p56, p64 and p67* *Guía del Ocio* (known as *GO*, www.goguiade locio.com.co) has listings on restaurants and clubs, as does *Plan B*, formerly a newspaper, now only online (www.planb.com.co) and *Vive.in* (www.vive.in).

Cinema

Consult *El Espectador*, *El Tiempo* or *PlanB* magazine for listings; there are frequent programme changes.

Cine Bar Lumière, Cra 14, No 85-59, T6360485. US$4 weekends and holidays, cheaper mid-week, comfortable airplane-style seats, food and drink.

Cine Bar Paraíso, Cra 6, No 120A-56, T2155316, www.cinemaparaiso.com.co (Usaquén).

Cinemanía, Cra14, No 93A-85, T621 0122, mainstream and foreign art films.

In Vitro, C 59, No 6-38, www.invitrovisual.com, is a popular nightclub that also shows Colombian and international arthouse films during the week.

Museo de Arte Moderno (see page 65) shows Colombian and foreign films every day, all day.

There are cinema complexes in the principal shopping centres (see below). The best are **Centro Comercial Andino, Unicentro**, and **Atlantis**. Most have discounted rates on Tue. For programme times call **CineColombia**, T404 2463, www.cinecolombia.com.

Foreign films are shown on weekend mornings in some commercial cinemas and there are many small screening rooms running features. Admission US$4.50-8. There is an international film festival in Oct (**Festival de Cine de Bogotá**, www.bogo cine.com) and a **European film festival** (Eurocine, www.eurocine.com).

⊛ Festivals and events

Bogotá *p48, maps p50, p56, p64 and p67*
There are many local religious festivals and parades at Easter and Christmas.
Jan Fiesta de los Reyes Magos
(Three Kings), in the suburb of Egipto (up the hill to the east of Candelaria), has traditional processions.
Mar Iberoamerican Theatre Festival, www.festivaldeteatro.com.co, a biennial event (next 2012) hosted by Bogotá.
May Feria Internacional del Libro (book fair) is held in Corferias, Cra 37 No, 24-67, www.feriadellibro.com.
Apr, May, Jun Temporada de Opera y Zarzuela is held in the Teatro Colón in with international artists.
In **Jun-Jul** there is **Rock al Parque**, the biggest annual rock festival in Latin America (www.rockalparque.gov.co).
Aug-Sep Opera season.
Sep Candelaria Festival, with street theatre, music and dance events. Also the **Festival Internacional de Jazz** takes place.
Dec Expoartesanía fair, at Corferias (www.expoartesanias.com). An excellent selection of arts and crafts and regional food from across Colombia. Highly recommended.

⊙ Shopping

Bogotá *p48, maps p50, p56, p64 and p67*
There is a 16% value-added tax on all purchases. Heavy duty plastic for covering rucksacks etc, is available at several shops around C 16 and Av Caracas; some have heat-sealing machines to make bags to size. In **Barrio Gaitán**, Cr 30 y C 65, are rows of leather shops. This is an excellent area to buy made-to-measure leather jackets, good value; not safe at night, go during the day. Designer labels are cheaper in Colombia than in Europe.

Bookshops
Books in Colombia are generally expensive.
Ateneo, C 82, No 13-19, in the north of the city. Good selection of Colombian titles, knowledgeable staff.
Authors, C 70, No 5-23, T2177788, www.authors.com.co. Run by American owner, sells English-language books, good selection, friendly staff. Café attached.
Exopotamia, C 70, No 4-47. Good selection of books and Latin music, also branch in Biblioteca Luis Angel Arango in Candelaria.
Forum, No 93A, No 13A-49, just off Parque 93, www.forum.com.co. Foreign magazines, CDs, pleasant atmosphere.
Librería Central, C 94, No 13-92. Some English- and German-language books.
Librería Nacional, www.librerianacional. com, bookstores across town eg Unicentro and Santa Bárbara shopping centres. Good Colombian history and current affairs section and some foreign press.
Panamericana, Cra 7, No 14-09, www.panamericana.com.co. Disorganized, but has some guidebooks and maps. Other branches in the city.
Taschen, Cra 40 No 20A-89. Art books, small selection of English books and foreign magazines. Also at **Museum of Modern Art**.
Villegas Editores, Av 82, No 11-50, int 3, www.villegaseditores.com. Great coffee-table books on Colombia.

Newspapers

US and European newspapers can be bought at **Librería Oma**, at **Tacos de la 19**, near the corner of Cra 7/C (Av) 19, or at **Papeles La Candelaria**, C 11, No 3-89, open daily, also has internet, fax and sells Latin-American cultural magazines, US, European and other papers 2 days after publication.

There are several excellent English-language newspapers, eg The *City Paper*, www.thecitypaperbogota.com, for good travel stories on Colombia. It's available at many hotels, hostels, embassies and popular bars such as the **Bogota Beer Company**. There is also the *Bogotá Daily*, www.bogotadaily.com.

Camping equipment

Monodedo, Cra 16, No 82-22, T616 3467, www.monodedo.com. Good selection of camping and climbing equipment. Enquire here for information about climbing in Colombia.

Computer repair

Tempo's System, C 79, No 16-22, Local 4, piso 2, T691 9707, temposystem@gmail.com. Ask for Ever Rodríguez, an excellent, trustworthy technician. Also try nearby **Unilago** shopping centre.

Handicrafts

Artesanías de Colombia, Claustro de Las Aguas, next to the Iglesia de las Aguas, Cra 2, No 18A-58; Cra 11 No 84-12 by CC Andino; and in **Plaza de los Artesanos**, Tr 48, No 63A-52, www.artesaniasdecolombia.com.co. Beautiful but expensive designer crafts.
Tienda Fibrarte, Cra 3, No 11-24. *Artesanías* from around Colombia and Latin America. Good fique products, coca tea. Credit cards accepted.
Galería Cano, Ed Bavaria, Cra 13, No 27-98 (Torre B, Int 1-19), also at Unicentro, Loc 218 and at the Airport, www.galeriacano.com.co. Sell textiles, pottery, and gold and gold-plated replicas of some of the jewellery on display in the **Gold Museum**.

Markets

Mercado de Pulgas (flea market), Cra 7/C 24, in car park beside **Museo de Arte Moderno**, on Sun and holidays 0800-1700. A better flea market can be found at the **Usaquén market** around the plaza on Sun, also a good arts and crafts market at the top of the hill in Usaquén.
Pasaje Rivas, C10 y Cra10. Persian-style bazaar. Hammocks, ceramics, cheap. A small arts and crafts market is open on most days opposite **Hotel Tequendama** in the centre.
Paloquemao food market, Cra 27, entre C19 y 22. Bogotá's huge central market, good to visit just to see the sheer abundance of Colombia's tropical fruits and flowers. Cheap stalls serving *menú del día*. Safe. Flower section best between 0500 and 1000.
San Andresito, Cra 38 y C12. Popular contraband market, cheap alcohol, designer sports labels, electrical goods, football shirts. Relatively safe.

Jewellery

The pavements and cafés along Av Jiménez, below Cra 7, and on Plazoleta del Rosario are used on weekdays (especially Fri) by emerald dealers. Rows of jewellers and emerald shops also along C 12 with Cra 6. Great expertise is needed in buying: there are bargains, but synthetics and forgeries abound.
Emerald Trade Centre, Av Jiménez, No 5-43, p 1. German/English spoken.
GMC Galería Minas de Colombia, C20, No 0-86, T281 6523, www.galeriaminasde colombia.com, at foot of Monserrate diagonal from Quinta de Bolívar. Good selection of jewellery at reasonable prices.
La Casa de la Esmeralda, C 30, No 16-18. Wide range of stones.

Photography

Poder Fotográfico, Cra 5, No 20-58 Ap 101, T3429678, for good developing in 2-3 hrs, used by professionals, also camera repairs. Other photo shops nearby. **Foto Japón**, www.fotojapon.com, branches all over the city, gives free film, branch at Cra 7, No 14-32.

Shopping malls

Avenida Chile CC, Av Chile (C 72), No 10-34, www.avenidachilecentrocomercial.com, is another good shopping centre;
Bulevar Niza, Cra 52, No 125A-59;
Centro Comercial Andino, Cra 11, No 82-71, www.centroandino.com.co;
Centro Comercial Unilago, Cra 15, No 78-33, www.unilago.com. For computers, gadgets and repairs.
Hacienda Santa Bárbara, Cra 7 No 115-60, www.haciendasantabarbara.com.co;
Unicentro, a large shopping centre on Cra 15, No 123-30, www.unicentrobógota.com (take 'Unicentro' bus from centre, going north on Cra 10 takes about 1 hr).

Exito, **Pomona** and **Carulla** chains are probably Bogotá's best supermarket groups.

▲ Activities and tours

Bogotá *p48, maps p50, p56, p64 and p67*
Biking
Bogotá Bike Tours, Cra 3 No 12-72, T281 9924, www.BogotaBikeTours.com, offers bilingual bike tours around Bogotá, as well as mountain bike tours outside of the city. You can also rent a bike and do your own thing, taking advantage of the Sun *ciclovía* when major roads, especially La Séptima, are closed to traffic. Second-hand books for sale or exchange.

Bullfighting
There are *corridas* on Sat and Sun during the season (Jan-Feb), and occasionally for the re of the year, at the municipally owned **Plaza de Santamaría**, near Parque Independencia. The brick bull ring was built in 1927 and has a capacity of 16,000. In season, the bulls weigh over 335 kg; out of season they are comparatively small (the local bullfight museum is at the bullring, door No 6). The **Corporación Taurina de Bogotá**, C 70A, No 6-24, T3341628, www.ctaurina.com, holds a summer festival every year in early Aug. Boxing matches are held here, too.

Football
Tickets for matches at El Campín stadium can be bought in advance at **Federación Colombiana de Fútbol**, Av 32, No 16-22, www.colfutbol.org. It is not normally necessary to book in advance, except for the local Santa Fe-Millonarios derby, and of course, internationals.

Hiking
Sal Si Puedes hiking group arranges walks every weekend and sometimes midweek on trails in Cundinamarca, and further afield at national holiday periods eg Semana Santa; very friendly, welcomes visitors. Hikes are graded for every ability, from 6 km to 4-day excursions of 70 km and more, camping overnight. The groups are often big (30-60),

ut after the preliminary warm-up exercises, and the *Sal Si Puedes* hymn, the regime relaxes and it is possible to stray from the main group. Reservations should be made and paid for a week or so in advance at Cra 7, No 17-01, office 640, T283 3765, open Mon-Thu 0900-1700, Fri 0900-1400. This is a very good way to see the national park areas in the Cordillera Oriental near Bogotá, eg Chingaza and Sumapaz. They also occasionally go at holiday times to the major tourist attractions of Colombia eg Tayrona, San Agustín, Leticia and Gorgona. **Corporación Clorofila Urbana**, Cra 49B, No 91-41, T616 8711, www.clorofilaurbana.org, offers similar walking opportunities with an emphasis on environmental awareness. **Confraternidad de Senderismo Ecológico El Respiro**, Transversal 48, No 96-48, T253 0884, is another group offering walks.

There are several other groups, good information on Fri in *El Tiempo* newspaper, *Eskape* section and in the monthly *Go Guía del Ocio* guide (has a small section in English and French).

Caminar por Colombia, Cra 7, No 22-31, of 226 B, T286 7487, caminarcolombia@hotmail.com, is a recommended operator offering walks around the capital every Sun, US$10 for small groups, includes transport and guide.

Horse riding
Cabalgatas Carpasos, Km 7 Vía La Calera, T368 7242, www.carpasos.com. About US$20 per person for a leisurely ride outside Bogotá for groups of 4-5. Horse riding at night too.

Rafting and kayaking
Fundación Al Verde Vivo, Calle 95 Nº 32-40 of 203, T218 3048, www.alverdevivo.org, organizes adventure water sports while trying to minimize environmental impact.

Rock climbing
La Gran Pared, Cra 7, No 50-02, T285 0903, www.granpared.com. Artificial rock-climbing wall in the centre of Bogotá. US$9.50 per hr including equipment.

Skydiving
Club de Paracaidismo Saint Michel, C 68 with Cra 68, T249 8923, www.skydivecolombia.com. 2-day courses with 3 jumps from US$275.

Tour operators
Aventure Colombia, Av Jiménez No 4-49, Of 204, T311-534 4554, www.aventure colombia.com. Specialize in classic (Caribbean coast, coffee region, the Andes) and alternative (Guajira, Sierra Nevada, Cocuy, Amazon) tours and expeditions across Colombia, focusing on trekking, eco and rural tourism. Their head office is in Cartagena (see page 154), but they have recently opened this branch in the capital. Highly recommended.
Colombia Quest, Cra 19 No 33-44, T704 3936, www.colombiaquest.com. Specializes in trips around Bogotá, especially around La

Candelaria and Zipaquirá. Also shopping and clubbing tours.

De Una Colombia Tours, Cra 26a, No 40-18, Apto 202, T368 1915, www.deunacolombia. com. Dutch-run tour agency with tailor-made trips throughout Colombia and an emphasis on introducing tourists to the country's people as well as landscapes. Particularly experienced in Los Nevados and Sierra Nevada del Cocuy.

Ecoguías, T347 5736 or T212 1423 (for the US), info@ecoguias.com. Colombian-British team specializing in eco-tourism, trekking, adventure sports and stays on *fincas*. Efficient and well organized.

See Colombia, T1800-5538701 (US/Canada), T+44-20-7101 9467 (UK), T8746102 (international), www.seecolombia.travel. Bogotá-based tour operator arranging tours across Colombia including Sierra Nevada del Cocuy, La Zona Cafetera and the Tatacoa Desert. Also does an exclusive 3-hr Pablo Escobar tour of Medellín from US$47 per person. Part of their profits are donated to the Río Urbano Foundation, working to clean up the Bogotá River. Recommended.

Travel agents
Local travel agents can often prove more economical for buying flights than dealing with the airlines direct.

Doble Vía, Carrera 11, No 77-20, T2112777. National and international flights. Best for fights to Leticia with **Copa Airlines**.

Vivir Volando, Cra 16, No 96-64, T601 4676, www.vivirvolando.com. Flights and packages to Pacific, Amazon and Caribbean coast. Strong links with **Satena**.

⊖ Transport

Bogotá *p48, maps p50, p56, p64 and p67*
Air
Since international and domestic flights use both the main **El Dorado** airport (T425 1000), currently being expanded, and the **Puente Aéreo**; you must check which terminal your flight will use.

There are a number of daily flights to most of Colombia's main cites including **Medellín**, **Cartagena**, **Cali**, **Barranquilla**, **Bucaramanga** and **Armenia** with Avianca Aires, Easyfly, Satena and Copa Airlines.

Also flights to **Pereira**, **Popayán**, **Leticia**, **Pasto**, **Quibdó**, **San Andrés** and more obscure destinations.

Local airline offices Copa Airlines, Cra 10, No 27-51, Local 165, Reservations T320 9292. **Aires**, Aeropuerto El Dorado, entrada 1 T413 9473, or at Cra 15, No 100-65, T294 0330. **Avianca**, C 19, No 4-37, Local 2, T342 6077, airport T4139862. **Satena**, Cra 10, No 26-21, of 210, T423 8500, former military airline, not always the best for comfort and delays. Easyfly, T414 8111.

International airline offices Air Canada, C 100 No 8A-49, Torre B piso 8, T296 6353. **Air France**, Cra 9A, No 99-07, Torre 1 p 5, T650 6000. **American**, C 71A, No 5-90, Local 101, T439 8022). **Continental**, Cra 7, No 71–21, Torre A, Oficina 2, T342 5279 or Cra 10, No 26-35, local 7, T01-800 944 0219. **Iberia**, Cra 19, No 85-11, T610 5066, airport T508 2525. **LAN**, C 100 No 8A-49, Torre B p 7, T01-800 956 4509. **Lufthansa**, C 100, No 8A-49, Torre B, piso 8, T296 6333. **Mexicana**, Av 15, No 114-36, Oficina 108, T215 2626. **Qantas**, C 116, No 9-35, piso 1, T213 2062. **TACA/LACSA**, C 113, No 7-21, Local 124, T01-800 951 8222 (toll free). Most airlines, local and international, have offices in both central and North Bogotá. Many international airline offices are closed on Sat and Sun.

Bus
Local Buses stop (in theory) by 'Paradero' boards but there are very few left and normally passengers flag buses down near street corners. Bus fares are from US$0.65 up, depending on length of route and time of day. Most buses have the day/night tariff advertised in the window. *Busetas* (small and green) charge a little more and can be dirty. There are some *ejecutivo* (red and white) routes with more comfortable seats, at

S$0.70. *Colectivos* are small vans, cramped ut faster, also US$0.70. To go north, pick ▸ne up at C 19/Cra 3, or any bus marked Jnicentro'; they follow Cra 7. Fares are a bit ▪igher at night and on holidays. The network an seem complicated and confusing, but ▪nost buses display the route on the front ▾vindow, indicating the last Calle or Carrera ▾hey are passing. People waiting for the ▸uses are also more than happy to help ✓ou to find the correct one.

Long-distance The long-distance bus terminal, **Terminal de Transportes**, is near Av Boyacá (Cra 72) between El Dorado (Av 26) and Av Centenario (C 13). There is also access from Cra 68. The exact address is C 33B, No 69-59, T423 3600, www.terminal detransporte.gov.co. The terminal is divided into modules serving the 4 points of the compass; each module has several bus companies serving similar destinations. If possible, buy tickets at the respective ticket office before travelling. It is possible to bargain with the various bus companies and reduce the price of a ticket. To get to the terminal take a bus marked 'Terminal terrestre' from the centre or a *buseta* on Cra 10. A taxi costs around US$5-6 from the centre, with a surcharge at night. As with the airports there is an effective system to stop drivers overcharging. Give your desired address at a kiosk, which will print out a slip with the address and price. Fares and journey times are given under destinations below. If you are travelling north, you can significantly cut down on the journey time by taking the **TransMilenio** to Portal del Norte, thus avoiding an arduous journey through Bogotá's traffic. **Velotax** *busetas* are slightly quicker and more expensive than ordinary buses, as are *colectivos*, which go to several long-distance destinations. The terminal is well organized and comfortable, but, as usual, watch out for thieves who are also well organized – the number of reports of baggage thefts there are increasing. Free self-service luggage trolleys are provided.

There are shops, restaurants and ATMs. There are also showers at the terminal (between Nos 3 and 4).

Modulo 4 also has a clinic giving vaccinations, open 0700 to 1900, reportedly now also free for non-nationals.

National long-distance: to **Armenia**, frequent with **Bolivariano**, **Magdalena** and **Expreso Palmira**, from US$17.50, 8-10 hrs; **Barranquilla**, frequent with **Brasilia**, 7 daily with **Copetran**, US$60-65, 20 hrs; **Bucaramanga**, hourly from 0500, every 30 mins from 0600, US$32, 9 hrs; **Buenaventura**, 1700, 1900 and 1930, US$22.50-24, 12 hrs; **Cali**, hourly 0530-2330, US$27.50, 10 hrs; **Cartagena**, only afternoon and evening departures, US$70, 18 hrs; **Cocuy**, 0500, 1830, 1900, 2000 and 2030, from US$17.50, 10 hrs; **Cúcuta**, hourly with **Berlinas**, US$42.50, 18 hrs; **Honda**, hourly 0400-2330 with **Rápido Tolima**, US$10, 4 hrs; **Ibagué**, hourly with **Autofusa** until 1900, US$10, 4½ hrs; **Ipiales**, 0945, 1230, 1430, 1730 and 2215 with **Bolivariano**, US$45, 24 hrs; **Manizales**, frequent with **Expreso Palmira** and **Bolivariano**, from US$17, 8 hrs; **Medellín**, hourly, many companies, US$25-30, 10 hrs; **Pasto**, 8 departures, US$37.50, 21 hrs; **Pereira**, hourly, from US$17, 8 hrs; **Popayán**, 7 departures, US$32.50, 14 hrs; **San Gil**, same times as Bucaramanga, US$33, 5 hrs; **Santa Marta**, afternoon and evening departures only, US$55, 16 hrs; **Tunja**, every 10 mins with Libertadors, US$7.50, 3-4 hrs; **Valledupar**, 1730 and 2330 with **Brasilia**, US$45, 16 hrs; **Villavicencio**, every 30 mins with Bolivariano, US$9, 2½ hrs.

International If going to **Venezuela**, it is better not to buy a through ticket to Caracas with **Berlinas de Fonce** as this does not guarantee a seat and is only valid for 2 Venezuelan companies; moreover no refunds are given in Cúcuta. Ideally, if you have time, make the journey to Cúcuta in 2 stages to enjoy the scenery to the full. Bus connections from San Antonio de Táchira in Venezuela to Caracas are good. There are buses from **Lima (Peru)** to **Caracas (Venezuela)** that travel through Ecuador run by **Transportes Ormeño** modelo 2 (blue), T410 7522. This thrice-weekly service is not recommended mainly because of the several days it takes and the unreliability of the timetable. The cost to **Lima** is about US$170, to **Quito**, US$83, to **Caracas**, US$61. Much better (and cheaper) is to do the trip in stages and enjoy the countries you are travelling through.

Car rental

Dollar Rent-a-Car, C 90, No 11A-09, T691 4700 and at airport, one of the cheapest. **Hertz**, at airport, T288 2636, and at Av 19, No 97-06, T327 6700.
Colombian Rent a Car, Autopista Norte 120-85, T214 5292, www.colombianrentacar.com.

Taxi

If you are short of time, have luggage or valuables, or at night, take a taxi. They are relatively cheap, there are many of them about and the service is generally good. If you take one on the street, try to pick one that looks in good condition. It should also be yellow and the driver's official ID card with photo should be visible; non official taxis are not recommended. At busy times, empty taxis flagged down on the street may refuse to take you to less popular destinations.

All official taxis are metered. The *taxímetro* (meter) registers units starting at 25 then calculates the time and distance travelled. The driver converts the total into pesos using a green fare table. If the conversion card is not displayed, the driver should show it to you. Check before taking your first taxi if there are any additional charges above what the meter/conversion card states eg: night charge or other surcharge; a list of legal charges should be posted in the taxi. Minimum fare is US$2.20 and a taxi from eg North Bogotá to the centre averages US$6.

Radio taxis are recommended for safety and reliability. When you call, the dispatcher gives you a cab number, write it down and confirm this when it arrives. There is a small charge but it is safer. Try these numbers: T288 8888; T311 1111; T411 1111; and T212 1212. Tipping is not customary, but is appreciated. If you are going to an address out of the city centre, it is helpful to know the area you are going to as well as the address, eg Chicó, Chapinero (ask at your hotel).

Train

Long-distance services were suspended in 1992. There are no passenger services at present from Bogotá **La Sabana** station at C 13 No 18-24, except a tourist steam train, which runs on Sat, Sun and holidays at 0830 calling at **Usaquén**, C 110, **Transversal 10**, in the north of the city at 0920, going north to **Zipaquirá**, 1130, and **Cajicá**, 1230, returning at 1640 and back to Bogotá Usaquén at 1515 and La Sabana at 1740. Adult US$19, child 2-10, US$11.50. Information, Turistrén Ltda, C 13, No 18-24, T3750557, www.turistren.com.co.

❶ Directory

Bogotá p48, maps p50, p56, p64 and p67
Banks
Banks are everywhere in Bogotá where there is commercial activity. Some head offices are grouped around the **Avianca** building at the corner of Plaza San Francisco, others have moved to North Bogotá on or near C 72.

The best way to obtain pesos in Bogotá is to use ATMs. Any other method will require your passport and, often, queues. Since it will probably require at least 2 or 3 attempts, either go downtown or in the north, where there are many banks. Unfortunately, there are no rules; there are countless ATMs accepting MasterCard, Visa and other cards; but machines may be down or out of cash, or just don't accept the cards stated. ATMs

so tend to give out a frustratingly small
mount of cash at a time (though you can
o back several times a day), resulting in
much money lost in transaction fees. Most
anks have a paltry COP300.000 (US$150)
maximum, though **Davivienda** (COP500/
IS$250) and **Bancolombia** (COP400/US$200)
re more generous. Those in more affluent
reas tend to dispense more.

Exchange: Emerald Trade Center,
Av Jiménez, Cra 5-43, Local 128, T2866181,
pen 0800-1800, accepts Thomas Cook TCs.
Titan, Cra 7, No 18-42, Local 116, T243 9384.
Cambios Country, C 72 No 7-64 p 12, and
t El Dorado airport, T413 8979. Several
ther city offices, good rates, speedy service.
Orotur, Cra 10, No 26-05 (below Hotel
Tequendama in pedestrian subway) is quick
and efficient, cash only, including sterling.
Cambios New York Money, in CC Andino,
Local 348, accepts sterling, efficient. Other
cambios on Av Jiménez de Quesada,
between Cras 6 and 11, and in the north of
the city. On Sun exchange is virtually
impossible except
at the airport. CC Hacienda Santa Bárbara
has several *cambios* but buying sterling can
be difficult. To replace lost Amex TCs,
American Express, Expreso Viajes y Turismo,
C 85, No 20-32, T593 4949 (has other
branches), open 0800-1900, Sat 0900-1400,
with full details, a police report of the loss
and preferably proof of purchase. They first
authorize cash advance on Amex cards and
then direct you to the appropriate bank
(**Banco Unión Colombia**).

Cultural centres

British Council, Cra 9, No 76-49, Piso 5,
T3259090, www.britishcouncil.org/colombia.
New modern centre, open Mon 1330-1900,
Tue-Fri 0700-1900, Sat 0830-1500, good TEFL
library, British newspapers. **Centro Colombo
Americano**, C 19, No 2-49, T3347640 or C 110,
No 15-36, T275 5052, also in CC Niza Bulevar,
T520 7888, www.colombobogota.edu.co.
English and Spanish courses, recommended.
Also in Medellín. **Alianza Colombo-Francesa**,

Cra 3, No 18-45, T341 1348 and several other
branches, www.alianzafrancesa.org.co.
Films in French, newspapers, library
monthly bulletin, etc. Other branches
in major cities across Colombia. **Goethe
Institut**, Cra 11A, No 93-52, T601 8600,
www.goethe.de/ins/co/bog/deindex.htm.

Embassies and consulates

Austria, Cra 9 No 73-44 p4, T326 3680
(emergencies) **Australia**, Cra 18, No 90-38,
T530 1046. **Belgium**, C 26, No 4A-45, piso 7,
T380 0370, bogota@diplobel.fed.be **Brazil**,
C 93, No 14-20, piso 8, T218 0800. **Canada**,
Cra 7, No 114-33, piso 14, T657 9800,
www.canadainternational.gc.ca **Cuba**, Cra 9,
No 92-54, T621 7054. **Ecuador**, C 89, No
13-07, T635 0322. **France**, Cra 11, No 93-12,
T638 1400, www.ambafrance-co.org.
Germany, Cra 69, No 25B-44, Piso 7,
T423 2600, www.bogota.diplo.de. **Italy**,
C 93B, No 9-92, T218 6680, www.ambbogota.
esteri.it. **Israel**, C 35, No 7-25, Piso 14, T327
7500. **Japan**, Cra 7, No 71-21, Torre B, piso 11,
T317 5001. **Netherlands**, Cra 13, No 93-40,
piso 5, T638 4200. Panama, C 92, No 7A-40,
T257 5067. **Spain**, C 92, No 12-68, T622 0090.
Sweden, C 72, No 5-83, piso 8, Edif Av Chile,
T325 6180, www.swedenabroad.com.
Switzerland, Cra 9, No 74-08, Of 101, T349
7230. **United Kingdom**, Cra 9, No 76-49,
piso 9, T326 8300, www.ukincolombia.fco.
gov.uk. **USA**, C 24, No 48-50, T315 0811,
http://bogota.usembassy.gov. **Venezuela**,
Cra 11, No 87-51, piso 5, T640 1213 (610 6622
visa information), 0830-1200. Visas can be
collected the following day 1200-1630.
Enquire by telephone before you go.

Immigration

DAS head office, Cra 28, No 17A-00, T408
8000, www.das.gov.co. Open Mon-Thu
0730-1600, Fri 0730-1500, or T153.
Cundinamarca office, C 58, No 10-51,
T5701077. DAS will not authorize
photocopies of passports; look
in Yellow Pages for notaries, who will.

Internet

Most hotels and hostels and many restaurants, bars and cafés are now Wi-Fi enabled and provide several computers for surfing the net. There are many internet cafés, charging US$1-2 per hr.

Listelnet Communications, Cra 3, No 15-47. Skype and heaphones. International calls. **Café Xanaledra**, Cra 4, No 12-78 Esquina. Skype and headphones as well as coffee, tea and cake. **Café del Cubo**, Cr 4, No 13-57, Mon-Sat 0900-2200. The tourist kiosk on Plaza Bolívar, Cra 8, No 9-83, has 3 computers. First 15 mins free. **Coffeemail**, CC Santa Bárbara. Mon-Sat 1030-2000, Sun 1400-1800. Helpful staff. US$1-2 per hr. **Foto and Internet Café**, Tequendama Hotel/Centro Internacional complex (2nd floor), loc 164, helpful, good service, Mon-Fri 0700-2000, Sat 0900-1600, US$0.90 per hr. **Web Café**, Diag 27, No 6-81, Mon-Fri 0900-2000, Sat 1000-1800.

Language courses

You need a student visa, not a tourist visa, to study. Some of the best Spanish courses are in the **Universidad Nacional**, T316 5000, www.unal.edu.co, about US$700, for 120 hrs, group discount available or **Universidad de los Andes**, T339 4949, www.uniandes.edu.co, US$300, 6 weeks, and **Pontificia Universidad Javeriana**, T320 8320 ext 4620, www.jave riana.edu.co. Good-value Spanish courses at the **Universidad Pedagógica**, C 72, No 11-86, T610 8080. Good reports. Language exchanges with students wishing to learn English are also popular. Enquire at Platypus hostel.

Medical services

Cruz Roja Nacional, Av 68, No 68B-31, T428 1111, T132 for emergencies, www.cruzrojabogota.org.co. Open 0830-1800, consultations/ inoculations US$12.50. **Fundación Santa Fe de Bogotá**, C 119, No 9-02, T629 0766, and **El Bosque**, C 134, No 12-55, T274 0577, are both modern, private hospitals, with good service For vaccinations, try **Clínica Marly**, C 50, No 9-67, T343 6600, www.marly.com.co.
Doctor Dr Paul Vaillancourt, Cra 11, No 94A-25, piso 4, T635 6312. English-speaking. **Dr Brigitte Scholz**, C 183, No 76-65, T670 4982.
Dentist Hyung Kuk Kim, Diagonal 86A, No 32-43, T616 1151, tmask10@hotmail.com English-speaking.
Chemists Farmacity, is a chain of new, well-stocked chemists open 24 hrs across the city. For 24-hr home deliveries in Bogotá, T530 0000, C 93A, No-13-41, off Parque de la 93, Cra 13, No 63A-67, among others.

Post

Main **Avianca** ticket office and **Deprisa** airmail office in basement of Ed Avianca, Cra 7, No 16-36, open Mon-Fri 0700-1900, Sat 0800-1500, closed Sun and holidays (poste restante Mon-Sat 0730-1800, letters kept for 1 month, US$1 per letter). Parcels by air are sent from here too. Also Cra 13 No 93-12 local 101; C 140 between Cra 19 y Autopista. Parcels by air, contact **Avianca**. **Adpostal**, Cra 7, No 27-54, www.adpostal. gov.co, handles international parcels.

Couriers Servientrega, C 64, No 89A-83, T018000-110 222 (international), T770 0410 (national). **Speedway**, C 64, No 90-67, T253 3305, open 0800-1800. **DHL**, C 19, No 4-29. **Fedex**, Cra 7, N 16-50, T2433315.

Telephone

Emergency Police 112 or 123 (from mobiles) Fire T119, **Ambulance** T132, Red Cross ambulance and traffic accidents T127. CAI Police T156.
International Calls can be made from several **Telecom** offices in centre of Bogotá (eg in the **Tequendama Hotel** complex, Cra 13, No 26-45, Mon-Sat 0800-1900); all close within 30 mins of 2000 and may be closed on holidays. Purchase of phone cards is recommended if you are using call boxes.

Around Bogotá

he buzz of Bogotá can sometimes be tempered by its chilly nights and frequent drizzle. But just a
~w hours away in most directions it can be pleasingly sunny and hot. Exiting northwest from the
ty, the road swiftly descends towards the Magdalena River valley and a string of pretty towns such
s Guaduas and Honda. To the southwest, on the edge of the Sabana de Bogotá, lies the
oud-forested Chicaque Parque Natural, a private nature reserve popular with hikers and horse
ders. Just before the road reaches the hot plains of the Magdalena River that lead to Neiva is
irardot, a popular weekend retreat for bogotanos nicknamed the 'swimming pool city'. Driving
ue north of Bogotá in the direction of Boyacá are two of the country's most impressive cultural
ophies. The Laguna de Guatavita was a lake prized by the Muisca and is believed to be the source
f the legend of El Dorado. A few kilometres beyond is the salt cathedral at Zipaquirá, a truly
we-inspiring monument to religious devotion. ▸▸ *For listings, see pages 87-88.*

Southwest to Parque Natural Chicaque

he Simón Bolívar Highway runs from Bogotá to Girardot, the former main riverport for
Bogotá, now a popular second-home destination thanks to its climate. Only small boats
an go upriver from here and it is known for the volume of swimming pools built by
weekending *bogotanos*. This 132-km stretch is extremely picturesque, running down the
mountains. About 20 km along this road from the centre of Bogotá is **Soacha**, now the
end of the built-up area of the city. A right fork here leads along a poor road to the Indumil
plant, 3 km after which there is a large sign for the **Parque Natural Chicaque**
① www.chicaque.com, T368 3114/244 1230, daily 0800-1700, US$12.50. Take a bus to
Soacha and ask for onward transport. The entry booth is 300 m down a track.

The park is a privately owned 300-ha estate of principally cloudforest between 2100 m
and 2700 m on the edge of *La Sabana de Bogotá*. The property, which has never been
developed, now has some 10 km of trails down and around 500 m of cliffs, with a
supplementary peak and an 80 m waterfall. It is a popular spot for walkers and riders at
weekends with good facilities for day visitors and a new Swiss-style *refugio* at the bottom
level, about one hour down the trail from the entrance. This provides meals and
accommodation for 70 or so costing US$27.50 a day including meals and other facilities
for day visitors. There is an abundance of birds, butterflies and a great natural diversity of
forest cover. The owner also reports frequent sightings of UFOs.

Bogotá to Honda → *For listings, see pages 87-88.*

La Sabana de Bogotá is dotted with white farms and groves of eucalyptus. The road to
Honda passes through two small towns; Fontibón and Madrid. **Facatativá** is 40 km from
Bogotá. Some 3 km from Facatativá, on the road to the west, is the park of **Piedras de Tunja**,
a natural rock amphitheatre with enormous stones, numerous indigenous pictographs and
an artificial lake. A further 71 km from Facatativá on the road to Honda, **Villeta** is a popular
weekend resort for bogotanos. It is a busy town at the centre of the *panela* (unrefined sugar
cane) industry, in a cattle-raising area. Not far away are the waterfalls of **Quebrada
Cune** ① 0800-1200, 1400-1800. The annual **National Panela Festival** is held during three
days in January and there is a Band Festival in mid-August. Look out for *Piedra de Bolívar*
(Bolívar's stone), on which is marked all the occasions when Bolívar passed through the town.

The legend of El Dorado

The Spanish came to South America with an insatiable thirst for gold. Nowhere was this more evident than in their search for El Dorado, a fruitless quest that drove them to explore the furthest reaches of the continent and was responsible for the deaths of thousands of indigenous locals and Spaniards alike.

The legend itself is based on an annual custom in which the Chibcha king was coated with gold dust and set adrift on a ceremonial raft. He would dive into

the lake and emerge cleansed of the gold. It was said that the lake also had precious offerings thrown in.

The lake was eventually identified as Guatavita, just north of Bogotá, and the story was verified by the discovery of a miniature raft made from gold wire that now holds pride of place in Bogotá's **Museo de Oro.**

Several attempts have been made to drain Lake Guatavita and many items recovered but never on the scale the Spanish imagined.

Midway between Villeta and Honda is **Guaduas**. Of the towns in the *tierra caliente* northwest of the capital, Guaduas preserves its colonial charm more than the others. Founded three times between 1572 and 1644, it was a stopover on the *camino real* between Bogotá and the river at Honda. Policarpa Salavarrieta, heroine of the Independence movement, was born here on 26 January 1796 (see box, page 85). There is a statue of her in the plaza and the **Casa de La Pola** ⓘ *free*, where she lived, is one block from the plaza and now an interesting museum. **Calle Real** is the best-preserved colonial street. The oldest house in town is the **Alcaldía** on Avenida José Antonio Galán. Simón Bolívar slept in the room on the second floor before leaving by river for Santa Marta. About 10 km outside the town is the **Salto de Versalles**, a lovely 45-m waterfall, now a National Monument. There is a public swimming pool in Guaduas and a Sunday market. The best local dish is *quesillos*.

Honda

On the west bank of the river, Honda is 32 km upstream from La Dorada. Founded in 1539, it's a pleasant old town with many colonial houses, including Colombia's oldest pharmacy, a lively indoor market and three museums. The streets are narrow and picturesque, and the town is surrounded by hills. Many of the colonial buildings are slowly and lovingly being restored to their former glory and a small group of expats has settled here, opening up new hotels and restaurants. Popular with visitors from much colder Bogotá, Honda, with an average temperature of 33°C, is gradually also being discovered by international travellers. **El Salto de Honda** (the rapids which separate the Lower from the Upper Magdalena) is just below the town. Honda is well known for its many bridges, some very old and rickety, spanning the Río Magdalena and Río Guali, at whose junction the town lies. In February the Magdalena rises and fishing is unusually good. People come from all over the region for the fishing and the festival of the Subienda, the fishing season. There is a row of good cheap restaurants across the Río Magdalena bridge in **Puerto Bogotá.**

The town has an interesting covered market, selling mostly fruit and vegetables but some *artesanías* too, in a grand old building next to the river. At the top of the town, up some steep cobbled streets, is the Parque Principal with a fine stone church, **El Alto**

Policicarpa Salavarrieta

María Policarpa Salavarrieta Ríos, affectionately known as 'La Pola', managed to pack a lot into her short life, although perhaps not as much as the popular *telenovela* about the heroine of the Colombian Independence movement would have you believe. The fifth of seven children, Policarpa is believed to have been born in Guadas, Cundinamarca in 1791, but even her given name is disputed, as her birth certificate has never been encountered. What is certain, however, is the date of her death. She was executed for high treason in Bogotá on 14 November 1817, after being caught by the Spanish Royalists. Working as a seamstress,

she infiltrated royalist homes in Bogotá and supplied information to the revolutionary forces fighting to free the country from Spanish rule. La Pola and six others, including her lover Alejo Sabaraín, were executed by firing squad in Bolívar Square and La Pola is now buried in La Candelaria, thanks to the intervention of two of her brothers, both Augustinian friars. Legends about her abound and in 2010 Colombian television created *La Pola – Amar La Hizo Libre* (La Pola – Love Set Her Free), based on her life in love and politics. It was a fresh, but fictionalized look, at one of the most intriguing figures of the Independence movement.

Rosario, and a statue dedicated to David Hughes Williams, an Englishman who became a popular town mayor.

Guatavita → *Colour map 2, C5.*

About 75 km from Bogotá, overlooking the lake is the small, modern town of Guatavita Nueva, which was built in colonial style when the old town of Guatavita was submerged by the reservoir. The original inhabitants were unwilling to stay in the new town, so it is now a weekend haunt for *bogotanos* and tourists. There is a cathedral, artisan workshops and two small museums; one devoted to the indigenous Muisca and the other to relics of the old Guatavita church, including a delightful Debain harmonium. The Sunday market is best in the morning, before *bogotanos* arrive. To get there, catch a bus from Bogotá.

Laguna de Guatavita (also called **Lago de Amor** by locals), is where the legend of El Dorado originated (see box, page 84). The lake is a quiet, beautiful place. You can walk right round it close to the water level in 1½ hours, or climb to the rim of the crater in several places. Opinions differ on whether the crater is volcanic or a meteorite impact, but from the rim at 3100 m there are extensive views over the varied countryside. Access to the park is only allowed with a permit obtained from the **Corporación Autónoma Regional de Cundinamarca (CAR)** ① *Cra 7, No 36-45, T3209000, www.car.gov.co, US$6.*

Getting there

Flota Aguila, at the bus terminal, US$3, two to three hours, hourly departures 0400-1600. You can walk (two to three hours) or ride (US$7 per horse) from Guatavita Nueva to the lake. An easier approach is from a point on the Sesquilé–Guatavita Nueva road (the bus driver will let you off) where there is a sign 'via Lago Guatavita'. There is a good campsite and places to eat nearby. From the main road to the lakeside the road is paved as far as a school, about half way. Follow the signs. This road and subsequent track can be driven in a good car to within 300 m of the lake, where there is a car park and good restaurant. Taxi tour from Bogotá costs around US$60 for a full day.

Zipaquirá → *For listings, see pages 87-88. Colour map 2, C5.*

ⓘ *Entry to the new cathedral is US$7.50, including 1¼-hr guided tour and film showing history of salt mining, car park US$2, daily 0900-1645 (last entry), Sun Mass at 1300 admission by ticket. The entrance to the cave is in hills about 20 mins' walk west of the town. There is an information centre and a museum at the site.*

A further 13 km beyond is Zipaquirá (commonly called Zipa), centre of a rich cattle-farming district, and famous for its rock salt mine (which has been exploited for centuries) and fabulous **salt cathedral**. This should not be missed, as it is a truly awe-inspiring sight. Salt has been mined here since the 15th century, long before the Spaniards came and established the town in 1606. Many kilometres of tunnels have been excavated since then. There was a shrine in the cave carved by the miners into the salt many years before the original cathedral started to take shape in 1950. It was dedicated in 1954 to Nuestra Señora del Rosario (patron saint of miners). Continuing deterioration made the cave unsafe and it was closed in 1990. A new salt cathedral was begun in 1991 and opened on 16 December 1995 by President Samper. It is 500 m from, and 58 m below, the old cathedral. There is a short section before the 14 stations of the cross. Each station has been sculptured by a different artist; at their centre is a cross 4 m high, subtly lit and imaginatively executed. This is followed by sections representing the choir, narthex, baptistry (with a natural water source) and sacristy. Finally, at the lowest point in the cave, 180 m below the surface, are the nave and the north and south aisles with huge pillars growing out of the salt and dominated by the central cross, 16 m high. All is discreetly illuminated and gives an austere impression.

The church in the attractive central plaza of town is also worth a visit for its stonework (despite its external appearance, it has a modern interior). The market on Tuesday is good for fruit and vegetables.

Nemocón → *Colour map 2, C5.*

Around 15 km northeast of Zipaquirá, at Nemocón, there are salt mines and a church, but the mines are now not operating and closed to visitors. However, there is a small but interesting **Museo de Sal** ⓘ *on the plaza, Tue-Sun 0900-1700, US$0.65*, which includes local history and the beginnings of the salt industry in the time of the Muisca people. The main salt mine is four blocks above the museum, with some bizarre lamp posts on the approach road.

For Sleeping and Eating price codes and other relevant information, see pages 23-28.

Sleeping

Honda *p84*
All accommodation is across the Gualí river in the newer part of Honda.
C Casa Belle Epoque, C 12, No 12A-21, Cuesta de San Francisco, T310-481 4090, www.casabelleepoque.com. A lovely old house with spacious, high-ceilinged rooms, all with bath and fan, beautiful roof terrace with jacuzzi, pool, free Wi-Fi, lots of antique, period touches. British-Colombian run, excellent breakfasts, advance booking preferred. Also arranges horse riding, boat and fishing trips. Recommended.
C-D Hotel Calle Real, Cra 11, No 14-40, T251 2260. The rooms are clean and there is a small swimming pool on the roof. Prices vary according to whether you want a/c or a fan. Parking available.
D Asturias Plaza, Cra 11, No 16-38, T251 3326. Large, rambling hotel near the bus terminal with swimming pool, private bathrooms and cable TV. The rooms are a little dusty but otherwise OK.
D Riviera Plaza, C 14, No 12-09, T312-893 7520. The French Riviera it is not but nonetheless it has modern, clean rooms around a large swimming pool. If you get the rooms at the end there are good views over the River Gualí and the colonial part of town.

Zipaquirá *p86*
B-C Cacique Real, Cra 6, No 2-36, T851 0209, www.hotelcaciquereal.com. Recently declared 'Patrimonio Cultural', this fine little hotel has a lovely courtyard with hanging baskets and good rooms with cable TV and hot water. There's Wi-Fi in the lobby and a car park.

D Casa Virrey, C 3, No 6-21, T852 3720, casavirreyorani@hotmail.com. New building with 36 clean, comfortable rooms and private bathrooms. Laundry service available.
E Torre Real, C 8, No 5-92, T851 1901. Light and airy rooms with large beds. Laundry service available.

Eating

Honda *p84*
There are many economical fish restaurants by Río Magdalena a short walk from town behind the bus station, serving fresh catch of the day, including **El Corralito de Tuky-Tuky**, Av Pacho María, Bahía 3.

Zipaquirá *p86*
¶¶ Parque Restaurante Funzipa, C 1A, No 9-99. Enormous ranch with beautiful garden and original ovens for cooking salt. Serves *parrillas* and *bandejas*.
¶ La Antigua, Cra 8, No 3-35. Cheap and cheerful *almuerzo ejecutivo* for US$3. There are several more similar options near the plaza.

Chía
¶¶¶ Andrés Carne de Res, C 3, No 11-56, www.andrescarnederes.com. Open Thu-Sun. This arty, rustic restaurant and bar has become an institution with great typical food, highly original decor, 'performers' to liven things up and free arts and crafts workshops for children. Now also has a branch in North Bogotá, but this is the original and best.

Activities and tours

Honda *p84*
Tours Honda Travel, C 9, No 21-30, T317-309 3633, offers boat trips up the Magdalena.

A popular walk is up to the **Cerro Cacao en Pelota**, one of the hills behind Honda. It takes 30 mins and affords good views of the Magdalena. From Puente Navarro, walk up Calle las Trampas up to Puente Quebrada Seca. Keep asking locals for directions, take lots of water and try to avoid the midday sun.

● Transport

Honda *p84*
Bus
As a junction point between Bogotá and Medellín, Honda is an ideal place to stop if you want to break up the long bus rides to these destinations. From **Bogotá** with **Velotax** and **Rápido**. To **Lima**, US$11, 4 hrs. To **Manizales** with Bolivariano, US$11, 4 hrs. **Rápido Tolima** run half-hourly buses to **La Dorada** (1 hr), and beyond, to **Puerto Boyacá** (3 hrs). To Medellín, 5 hrs, US$15. The Bogotá–Medellín highway currently being built will pass around the town.

Zipaquirá *p86*
Bus
The bus station is 15 mins' walk from the mines and cathedral. There are many buses to/from Bogotá: Cra 30 (Av Ciudad de Quito), marked *'Zipa'*, **Flota Alianza**, or others from the C 174 terminus of the **TransMilenio** in North Bogotá opposite Exito supermarket, US$2 each way, 1¼ hrs. Zipaquirá can be reached from **Tunja** by taking a Bogotá-bound bus and getting off at La Caro for connection to Zipaquirá, US$2.40. Note when arriving at C174 terminus from Zipaquirá you need to buy a TransMilenio bus ticket to leave the station. To avoid this, ask the driver to drop you off before the bus station.

Train
You can also reach Zipaquirá and some of the surrounding towns via train, see page 80.

Contents

92 Boyacá Department
  92 Tunja and around
  95 Villa de Leiva
  99 Chiquinquirá
  99 Ráquira and around
  99 Monasterio Desierto de
      la Calendaria
  99 Paipa and around
  100 Sogamoso
  100 Iza
  100 Lago de Tota
  101 Monguí
  102 Sierra Nevada del Cocuy
  104 Listings

111 Santander Department
  111 San Gil
  114 Barichara
  115 Guane
  116 Bucaramanga
  119 Girón
  119 Listings

**126 Norte de Santander
      Department**
  126 Pamplona
  128 Cúcuta
  130 Listings

Footprint features

  90 Don't miss ...
  101 How Lago de Tota was formed
  127 Simón Bolívar

Border crossing

Colombia–Venezuela
  129 Cúcuta–San Antonio

At a glance

⊜ **Getting around** Walking in town centres; buses, taxis and *colectivos* to explore outlying regions.

⊜ **Time required** 2-3 weeks to explore towns and villages. 1 week for trekking.

⊛ **Weather** Variable: cool in mountainous regions around Tunja and El Cocuy. Hotter as you head north to Santander.

⊗ **When not to go** Good all year.

★ **Don't miss ...**

1 Exploring Villa de Leiva and Barichara, pages 95 and 114.

2 Relaxing at Paipa or Iza hot springs, pages 99 and 100.

3 A stroll along Lago de Tota's Playa Blanca, page 100.

4 Trekking Sierra Nevada del Cocuy, page 102.

5 Whitewater rafting near San Gil, page 111.

6 Admiring the stunning landscape of the Chicamocha Canyon, pages 111, 113, 115 and 116.

Heading north from Bogotá towards Venezuela or the Caribbean coast, the road takes you on a historical journey to the heart of Colombia, passing through picturesque valleys, canyons and spectacular high mountain passes. Set on a high plateau is Tunja, capital of the Department of Boyacá. This was the seat of power of the indigenous Muisca and nearby Laguna Guatavita, is believed by many to be the source of the myth of El Dorado. The area also played its part in the liberation of Colombia from the Spanish, particularly at Puente de Boyacá where Simón Bolívar and his troops fought a decisive battle to wrest control of the country from the conquistadors. Boyacá is dotted with dozens of untouched colonial towns and villages, notably Villa de Leiva and Monguí. From the Andean foothills of Boyacá, the road swoops down to the turbulent Río Fonce and the start of the Department of Santander. Here too the Spanish colonial legacy is very much intact, particularly in the charming villages of Barichara, Guane and Girón. In recent years the area's natural resources, with countless tumbling rivers, caves and deep canyons, have made it the capital of Colombia's burgeoning adventure sports scene, centred around the pretty town of San Gil. From the Department capital of Bucaramanga, a road climbs northeast over moorland for more lessons in independence history around Pamplona and Cúcuta in Norte de Santander. Another road heads north towards the Sierra Nevada de Santa Marta and the Caribbean coast.

Boyacá Department

Boyacá is the cultural and historical heart of Colombia. This department of green valleys and colonial villages was the centre of the Muisca empire, whom the Spanish fought so vigorously to prize away their gold. The empire's capital was at Tunja, which at the time rivalled Bogotá in size and importance. Today, tourists mostly flock to nearby Villa de Leiva, which, with its whitewashed colonial mansions and cobbled streets, is becoming a popular weekend retreat for affluent bogotanos. But there are many more undiscovered gems. Villages such as Iza and Paipa with their thermal springs, and Monguí with its rich history and fresh mountain air, are therapy for both body and soul. In the northeast of the department is the Sierra Nevada de Cocuy, a mountain range of jagged ice peaks and breathtaking lakes to rival any in South America. ▸▸ For listings, see pages 104-110.

Tunja and around → *For listings, see pages 104-110. Colour map 2, B5. Phone code: 8. Population 160,000. Altitude 2800 m.*

Tunja, capital of Boyacá Department, is 137 km from Bogotá, in a cool dry mountainous area, on a platform that slopes down to the north and east to the valley of the Río Chulo. Ugly on the outside but with a pleasant centre and an interesting history, most travellers shun Tunja, probably as a result of impressions gained on arrival at its bus station. Tunja, however, is worth a peek, particularly to visit its impressive churches and museums. Moreover, it has very friendly people and good, cheap accommodation. When the Spaniards arrived in what is now Boyacá, Tunja was already an indigenous city, the seat of the Zipa, one of the two Muisca kings. He ruled over the northern part of the Muisca territories, the most populous and well-developed indigenous area of what is modern-day Colombia. It was refounded as a Spanish city by Gonzalo Suárez Rendón in 1539. The city formed an independent Junta in 1811, and Bolívar fought under its aegis during the Magdalena campaign of 1812. Six years later he fought the decisive battle of Boyacá, nearby. The climate is cool, with an average temperature of 12°C, due to the altitude.

Ins and outs

Getting there There are four routes that converge on Tunja, all busy and in good condition. The main road from Bogotá through to Bucaramanga and the Caribbean bears left at the northern outskirts of the town. Straight on, leads to Sogamoso, the Lago de Tota and Yopal and to the Sierras of Cocuy. West lies Villa de Leiva and Chiquinquirá. There are good bus services along all these roads; the bus station is near the main highway, which skirts the east side of town. There is no air service to Tunja and the railway no longer takes passengers.

Getting around From the bus station to the main square is a steep walk up, but the centre of the town and the main things to see are readily accessible from the Plaza de Bolívar.

Tourist office **Casa del Fundador** ① *Plaza de Bolívar, 742 3272, cultura.turismo@boyaca. gov.co*, is next to the cathedral; the website www.tunja.gov.co also has good information (Spanish only).

Sights

The **cathedral**, on the Plaza de Bolívar, has a Romanesque façade and right tower, with an unusual balustrade along the roof of the west front. It dates from the end of the 16th century. Inside, it is a mixture of styles, gothic and Moorish, with ornamented pillars and colonial paintings. There are several fine side chapels and a mausoleum honouring Gonzalo Suárez Rendón, founder of the city. The **Casa de la Cultura**, opposite the cathedral, also 16th century, is where Simón Bolívar stayed before the battle of Boyacá. Cultural events are held here from time to time. Also on Plaza Bolívar is the **Casa del Fundador Suárez Rendón** ① *Plaza de Bolívar (Cra 9 19-56, next door to the cathedral), daily 0830-1230, 1400-1800, US$0.70*, one of the few extant mansions of a Spanish conquistador in Colombia (1539-1543). See the attractive peaceful courtyard with a fine view of the countryside and the unique series of platteresque paintings on the ceilings.

Of the many colonial buildings, the most remarkable is the church of **Santo Domingo**, one block west of the plaza, a masterpiece begun in 1594, with its splendid interior covered with richly carved wood. There are several chapels in the side aisles, but the Chapel of Our Lady of Rosario, the work of Fray Pedro Bedón, glistens with gold and glass ornamentation and is one of the finest examples of the period in Colombia. Most of the churches, except the San Lázaro chapel, are open to visitors during the day, or at least at Mass times. Two blocks east of the plaza is another fine building, the **Santa Clara La Real chapel** (1580), with some fine wood carving in Moorish style particularly in the ceiling of

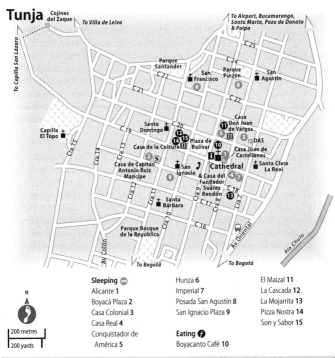

Tunja

Sleeping	Hunza **6**	El Maizal **11**
Alicante **1**	Imperial **7**	La Cascada **12**
Boyacá Plaza **2**	Posada San Agustín **8**	La Mojarrita **13**
Casa Colonial **3**	San Ignacio Plaza **9**	Pizza Nostra **14**
Casa Real **4**		Son y Sabor **15**
Conquistador de	**Eating**	
América **5**	Boyacanto Café **10**	

the single-nave chapel. There is fine ornamentation everywhere, interesting oil paintings and wall decorations revealed after restoration a few years back. This was the chapel to the Santa Clara convent, begun in 1574, probably the first to be established in Colombia. One of the nuns, Sister Josefa del Castillo y Guevara lived in a cell near the choir for over 50 years and was buried here. Some of her writings are exhibited in the museum into which part of the former convent has been converted. One block from the plaza, on Calle 20 with Carrera 9, is the house of the writer **Casa Don Juan de Vargas** ① *Tue-Fri 0900-1200, 1400-1700, Sat, Sun and holidays 0900-1200, 1400-1600, US$1 adults, US$0.50 children*, built 1590, has been restored as a museum of colonial Tunja, with many interesting exhibits relating to the city. Note the murals, gold candlesticks and particularly the fine ceiling of the upper floor.

One block south, on Calle 19, the **Casa Juan de Castellanos**, a chronicler and friend of Suárez Rendón, is another notable colonial building, much of it carefully restored and again contains some fine ceiling paintings, both religious and of flora and fauna. **Casa de Capitán Antonio Ruiz Mancipe** is now a bank, on Calle 18, but much of the original has been preserved or restored. Four blocks from the plaza, on Carrera 11, the church of **Santa Bárbara** dates from 1592 and also has much fine ornamentation and a *mudéjar* ceiling. The treasury has many valuable items of gold and silver, part donated by the mother of Charles V of Spain. The chapel of La Epístola is the best of several. In the nearby parish house are some notable religious objects, including silk embroidery from the 18th century.

A short walk further south, in **Parque Bosque de la República**, is the adobe wall against which three martyrs of the Independence were shot in 1816. The wall, and bullet holes, are protected by a glass screen. Ask the tourist police guarding these buildings for information: they are helpful and knowledgeable. The church and convent of **San Francisco** is another 16th-century construction notable for its white colonial façade, sculptures of San Francisco and Mary Magdalene, striated pillars and the gilded arch over the central retable. Also note the Altar de los Pelícanos, believed to have been brought from Quito, housed inside the chapel of the Virgin de las Angustias. The church of **San Ignacio** has an interesting embossed façade constructed by the Jesuits in the 17th century. It is now used for cultural presentations. The small **San Lázaro** chapel, dating from 1587, restored during the 18th century, has four semi-circular arches supporting an ornamental ceiling. At 2940 m it overlooks the town and is a fine viewpoint. **Note** Take advice before walking up there.

Around Tunja

There are two pre-Columbian sites to visit outside the city. The **Cojines del Zaque** (literally the cushions of the Zaque, who was the principal chief of the Muisca government) is a ritual site around a large rock, which has pillow-like features carved into it. It is thought that sacrifices to the Sun God and ritualistic sun-worship were carried out here. The **Pozo de Donato (Pozo de Hunzahúa)**, a short distance northeast out of town on the road to Paipa, was a well or pond also used for Muisca rituals. Legend had it that this included gold offerings. In the early days of colonization, a Spaniard by the name of Jerónimo Donato drained the pool looking for gold – which he did not find. The Pozo de Donato is in the grounds of the Universidad Pedagógica, which has done considerable archaeological work in the region. There is a small attractive park now around the pond.

Some 16 km south of Tunja on the main road from Bogotá, is the site of the **Battle of Boyacá** ① *daily 0800-1800, entrance free, or US$1.50 per car*, one of the most significant events in the history of Colombia. Overlooking the bridge at Boyacá is a large monument to Bolívar. Bolívar took Tunja on 6 August 1819, and next day his troops, fortified by a British Legion, the only professional soldiers among them, fought the Spaniards on the banks of the swollen Río Boyacá. With the loss of only 13 killed and 53 wounded they captured 1600 men and 39 officers. Only 50 men escaped back to Bogotá, and when these told their tale, the Viceroy Samao fled in such haste that he left behind him half a million pesos of the royal funds. There are several other monuments, an exhibition hall and restaurant at the site. Bus from Tunja, US$0.60, ask for 'El Puente'.

Villa de Leiva → For listings, see pages 104-110. Colour map 2, B5. Phone code: 8. Population 12,000 Altitude 2144 m.

About 40 km west through the mountains is the colonial town of Villa de Leiva (also spelt Leyva). This is one of Colombia's very special places. It is not on any important through route and there are no significant natural resources nearby to be exploited, so it has been left alone and now is prized by Colombians and visitors alike. The town dates back, like Tunja, to the early days of Spanish rule, but unlike Tunja, it has been declared a National Monument, so will not be modernized. It was founded by Hernán Suárez de Villalobos in 1572 by order of the first president of Nueva Granada, Andrés Díaz Venero de Leiva.

It has an enormous, undulating plaza which appears as though it has buckled under the weight of the thousands of feet that have walked across it down the years. At 14,000 sq m it is believed to be the largest cobbled square in South America. Almost the entire village is in pristine condition with whitewashed mansions with terracotta-tiled roofs and streets with cobbles large and uneven enough to twist an ankle.

Villa de Leiva and its surroundings are blessed with a bewildering mixture of topographies and climates. To the west the landscape is semi desert, typified by the reddish clay that is used to make bricks and terracotta tiles, and dotted with cacti. Fossils from the Jurassic and Cretaceous period are abundant. To the southeast, steep hills rise to *páramo* or moorland, sparse in vegetation. At the nearby Iguaque National Park it is mainly high cloudforest.

Ins and outs
Getting there To reach it from Bogotá, turn left at the Puente de Boyacá monument, and go through the small attractive town of **Samacá** which has a pretty plaza ornamented with bougainvillea arcades. The church has a bright white/yellow interior and a fine gilt retable. Alternatively, go through Tunja and out by the northwest corner of the town. The two roads join and you must turn right at Sáchica for the final 6 km to Villa de Leiva. Most of the public transport goes through Tunja. There is an alternative from Tunja, staying on the main road towards Bucaramanga, and after 34 km, turn left at Arcabuco. This is an unsurfaced road and rough in places but you will see fine scenery as it goes alongside the Iguaque National Sanctuary.

Getting around This is very much a place for walking around. Many of the streets are cobbled and such traffic as there is, travels at a snail's pace. If you want to visit the attractions outside Villa de Leiva, there are taxis that will take you.

Tourist information Oficina Municipal de Turismo ① *Cra 9, No 13-04 just off the plaza, open daily 0800-1800*, has some local maps, gives advice on cheaper accommodation. **Instituto von Humboldt** ① *Claustro de San Agustín, T732 0174, call before visiting*, is an excellent research and documentation centre for environmental studies. Publications sold. The websites www.villadeleyva-boyaca.gov.co and www.villaleyvanos.com also have good information.

Sights

Two colonial houses are particularly worth a visit. One is the house in which **Antonio Nariño** ① *Cra 9, No 10-39, free, Mon-Sat 0900-1800, Sun 0830-1700*, lived. He translated the *Rights of Man* into Spanish.

The second is the building known as the **Casa del Primer Congreso** ① *C 13/Cra 9, on the corner of the plaza, free, Tue-Fri 0900-1200, 1400-1700, Sat 0900-1200*, in which the first Convention of the United Provinces of New Granada was held. This is the seat of the local authority and the building is closed to the public when they are in session.

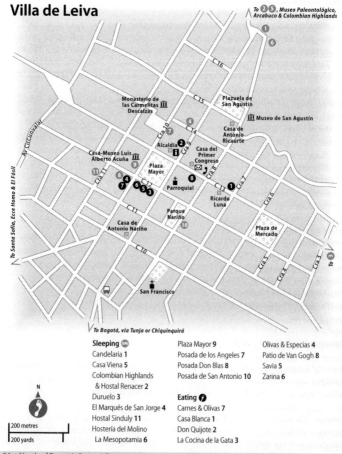

Villa de Leiva

To ② ⑤ , Museo Paleontológico, Arcabuco & Colombian Highlands

Sleeping 🛏
Candelaria 1
Casa Viena 5
Colombian Highlands
  & Hostal Renacer 2
Duruelo 3
El Marqués de San Jorge 4
Hostal Sinduly 11
Hostería del Molino
  La Mesopotamia 6

Plaza Mayor 9
Posada de los Angeles 7
Posada Don Blas 8
Posada de San Antonio 10

Eating 🍴
Carnes & Olivas 7
Casa Blanca 1
Don Quijote 2
La Cocina de la Gata 3

Olivas & Especias 4
Patio de Van Gogh 8
Savia 5
Zarina 6

200 metres
200 yards

Also worth a visit is the restored birthplace of the Independence hero **Antonio Ricaurte** ① *Cra 8/C 15, Wed-Fri 0900-1200, 1400-1700, Sat, Sun and holidays 0900-1300, 1400-1800, free, there is a statue of Ricaurte on Plazuela San Agustín.* Ricaurte was born in Villa de Leiva and died in 1814 at San Mateo, Venezuela, in a famous act of courageous self-sacrifice while fighting in Bolívar's army. The house has an attractive courtyard and garden.

On the Plaza Mayor the **Casa-Museo Luis Alberto Acuña** ① *US$1.10, daily 1000-1300, 1400-1800*, housing fascinating examples of Acuña's work, is well worth a visit.

The **Monasterio de las Carmelitas Descalzas** ① *C 14 and Cra 10, US$2, Sat-Sun and holidays 1000-1200, 1400-1700*, has one of the best museums of religious art in Colombia. The monastery also includes the **Convento** and the **Iglesia del Carmen** ① *open at Mass times: Mon-Fri 0700, Tue 0600, Sat 0700, 0900, 1100, Sun 0600, 0700, 1100*, a simple, dignified church with a large fine Lady Chapel, all worth a visit. The **Iglesia de San Agustín** is now being converted into a museum.

An interesting and well-displayed **palaeontological museum** ① *Cra 9 11-42, www.expovilla.com, US$2, Tue-Sat 0900-1200, 1400-1700, Sun and holidays 0900-1500*, has been opened 15 minutes' walk north of the town. It also has an old windmill, Molino de Losada, dating from the 16th century when Villa de Leyva was a leading wheat producer.

Around Villa de Leiva

The wide valley to the west of Villa de Leiva is rich in fossils; 5 km along the road to Santa Sofía you will see the road signs for **El Fósil** ① *daily 0900-1700, US$2*. The skeleton displayed is a Plesiosaur group reptile, possibly a small Kronosaurus, found here in 1977, and the museum was built around it. The second exhibit is a baby of the same group, complete with tail, found in 2000 and placed alongside. They were similar to dolphins with flippers and a fine set of teeth. The museum contains a wide selection of other Mesozoic and Cretaceous exhibits.

About 2 km along the road to Monquirá is **La Casa de Terracota** ① *www.casaterracota.com*, a house designed and belonging to Colombian architect Octavio Mendoza. This Gaudiesque construction, built entirely out of ceramic tiles extracted from the local area and worked directly onto the building, claims to be the largest such structure in the world, as well as being cheap, environmentally friendly and earthquake-proof. Almost everything is made from terracotta, including all the furniture, while there are fine examples of mosaics in the showers and clever use of light. There are workshops and ceramics courses being held here.

About 1 km further along this road, 4 km from Villa de Leiva, is the well-endowed archaeological site of the **Parque Arqueológico de Monquirá** ① *0900-1200, 1400-1700, closed Mon, US$2 with guide*, otherwise known as El Infiernito, where there are several huge carved phalluses (which make for popular photo opportunities!). This is one of the most important Muisca religious sites in the country and features the only solar observatory in Colombia as well as a *dolmen* burial site. The site was discovered by the Spanish who baulked at the enormous stone penises and proclaimed that the Muisca would be banished to hell, hence the name 'El Infiernito' (Little Hell). Much of it was destroyed and the stone used by local *campesinos* to build their homes. Some of it still remains, however, and was lovingly studied and maintained from the 1960s by archaeologist Eliecer Silva Célis, who passed away in 2007 at the age of 93.

About 1 km beyond El Infiernito is the **Fibas Jardín de Desierto** ① *Parque Ecológico, Espiritual y Educativo, T311-222 2399 (mob), free, meditation US$5.50 (with free plant), Wed-Sun 0800-1730, Mon and Tue by appointment*, run by former advertising executive

Jaime Rodríguez Roldán. As well as selling many varieties of cactus and other desert plants, the nursery aims to educate visitors in environmentally friendly practices. No fertilizers, even organic ones, are used in nurturing the plants. The centre also features two mazes, based on ancient indigenous designs, in which Jaime holds meditation exercises.

About 6 km beyond the Infiernito turning is a track on the left for the **Monastery of Ecce-Homo** ① *0900-1800, just knock on the door, closed Mon, US$1.50* (founded 1620); note the fossils in the floor at the entrance. The monastery has had a turbulent history. It was built by the Dominicans between 1650 and 1695, but a century later it was taken over by the military and the friars expelled. It was later abandoned until 1920 when it was reclaimed by the Dominicans, and some restoration was done. It has been repeatedly robbed since then, and some of the religious art is now in the Chiquinquirá museum for safe-keeping. What can be seen of the church, chapel and monastery is impressive, but the fabric and roof are in a poor state. There are buses from Villa de Leiva (0800-1615) going to Santa Sofía, US$1.75; it is 30 minutes to the crossing, then a 2-km walk to the monastery. A good daytrip is to take the bus to Ecce Homo and walk back to Villa de Leiva via El Fósil and El Infernito. Beyond Santa Sofía is **La Cueva de Hayal**, a cave set in beautiful scenery.

Some 12 km from Villa de Leiva on the road to Arcabuco, there is a right turn for the **Santuario de Fauna y Flora de Iguaque** ① *for non-nationals US$17.50, T732 0792*, a National Park. The entrance to the Park is 3 km from the junction. About 40 minutes' walk up the valley from the entrance is a tourist centre with accommodation for 48 and a restaurant with good food at reasonable prices and a fine view of the surrounding countryside. There are guided paths and a marked trail to Lake Iguaque, a steep walk of 2½ hours. The lake is central to Muisca mythology. The most likely day for a lift is Saturday, market day, but there is a daily bus at 0645 from Villa de Leiva that passes the junction for the Park at Casa de Piedra. It returns at 1230 and 1600. US$11.

The 6750-ha park is mainly high cloudforest of oak, fig and other temperate trees, much covered with epiphytes, lichens and bromeliads. There is also *páramo* (moorland) and a series of high-level lakes, formed in the last Ice Age, at over 3400 m, and the mountains rise to 3800 m. The height creates cloud and there is frequent rain, about 1700 mm a year, giving the park a deep green quality. At the visitor centre, **Furachiogua**, there is accommodation with seven shared rooms (capacity 48) with bunk beds or single beds, US$15.50 per person. There is also a campsite with showers and toilets and cooking facilities, US$2.70. **Colombian Highlands** in Villa de Leiva (see page 109), are recommended for organized tours to the park.

There are a number of expeditions to nearby waterfalls and bathing spots, including **Paso del Angel**, near Santa Sofía where the narrowest of natural bridges (less than a metre across) links two ridges with the 80-m **Guatoque waterfall** falling nearby. Some 10 km on the road to Alto de los Migueles is Cascada La Periquera which falls 15 m into the Río La Cebada and is surrounded by lush vegetation. On the road to Monquirá, 4 km from Villa de Leiva, are the **Pozos Azules**, a series of aquamarine natural pools, US$1. On the way to Santa Sofía is **Valle Escondido**, a verdant valley guarded by imposing mountains. Here there are various lodgings, including **El Arca Verde** ① *www.arcaverde.blogspot.com*, an eco-friendly *maloka*. It is possible to abseil down some of the valley's many canyons. **Colombian Highlands** (see page 109) can organize tours to these and other spots.

Chiquinquirá → *For listings, see pages 104-110. Colour map 2, B5. Phone code: 8.*
Population: 45,000. Altitude: 2580 m.

On the west side of the valley of the Río Suárez, 134 km from Bogotá and 80 km from Tunja, this is a busy market town for this large coffee and cattle region. In December thousands of pilgrims honour a painting of the Virgin whose fading colours were restored by the prayers of a woman, María Ramos. The picture is housed in the imposing Basílica, but the miracle took place in what is now the Iglesia de la Renovación. In 1816, when the town had enjoyed six years of Independence and was besieged by the Royalists, this painting was carried through the streets by Dominican priests from the famous monastery, to rally the people. The town fell, all the same. There are special celebrations at Easter and on 26 December, the anniversary of the miracle. The town is also known for making guitars.

Ráquira and around → *For listings, see pages 104-110. Colour map 2, B5.*

In the Chibcha language, Ráquira means 'city of pots' and with over 100 *artesanía* shops selling earthenware pottery in a village of just a dozen blocks, Ráquira is rightly considered the capital of Colombian handicrafts. Known for its ceramics, in recent years there has been an influx of cheap products from Ecuador, somewhat diluting its appeal. The village itself has been painted in an array of primary colours and has a picturesque plaza embellished with terracotta statues, including one of a local version of Belgium's Manneken-Pis and another of Jorge Veloza, inventor of the musical genre *carranga*, who was born here.

Monasterio Desierto de la Calendaria → *For listings, see pages 104-110. Colour map 2, B5.*
ⓘ *Daily 0900-1700, US$1.50 plus US$0.55 to Hermit's Cave.*
About 7 km from Ráquira is the beautiful 16th-century monastery of La Candelaria. In an otherwise dry area, the monastery is a small oasis, thanks to the water provided by the Río Guachaneco. It has a fine church, where the altar displays the painting of the Virgen de la Candelaria by Francisco del Pozo, dating from 1597. The painting was miraculously saved from burning and brought here by Augustinian monks, who founded the monastery in 1604 on the site of an indigenous altar. The anniversary of the painting is celebrated each 1 February in addition to 28 August, the saint's day of San Agustín.

The convent has two beautiful cloisters, one featuring a 170-year-old dwarf orange tree, the other virtually untouched since the 17th century. The monastery is an important location for novice Augustinian monks who come here on retreat for one year and are allowed no contact with their family during this time. A guided tour of the monastery includes a visit to the church, the cloisters, which are lined with anonymous 17th century paintings of the life of San Agustín and the catacomb-like Hermit's Cave, originally used by the local indigenous people but appropriated by the monks who built the monastery.

Paipa and around → *For listings, see pages 104-110. Colour map 2, B6.*
ⓘ *daily 0900-1800, US$18.50, children US$12.*
Along the road, 41 km northeast of Tunja is Paipa, noted for the Aguas Termales complex 3 km to the southeast. The baths and the neighbouring Lago Sochagota (boat trips

possible) are very popular with Colombians and increasingly so with foreign tourists. From Paipa there is a minibus service, US$3.50, a taxi costs US$22.50, or you can walk in 45 minutes. There are innumerable hotels (D-F) and restaurants on the main street of Paipa and on the approach road to the Aguas Termales, though hotels at the springs are more expensive. Paipa is a good place to buy carpets, hammocks and handicrafts.

Sogamoso → *For listings, see pages 104-110. Colour map 2, B6. Phone code: 8. Population: 90,000. Altitude: 2569 m.*

At Duitama, a town 15 km beyond Paipa known for basket weaving, turn right and follow the valley of the Río Chicamocha for Sogamoso, a large, mainly industrial town. This was an important Chibcha settlement, and the **Parque Arqueológico Suamox** ① *C 9A No 6-45, T770 3122, Tue-Sat 0900-1200, 1400-1700, Sun 0900-1500, US$1.75,* has been set up on the original site. A comprehensive museum describes their arts of mummification, statuary, and crafts, including gold-working. There's a *cafetería* near the entrance. Camping possible in the grass car park opposite, with permission.

Iza → *For listings, see pages 104-110. Colour map 2, B6. Phone code: 8. Population: 2081. Altitude: 2560.*

South of Sogamoso the road winds its way through a grassy valley backed by imposing pine-clad hills. After 15 minutes, the road reaches the colonial village of Iza. In Chibcha, Iza means 'place of healing', no doubt a reference to the thermal springs found outside the village. Not much happens in Iza but you could easily spend a week here soaking up its curative atmosphere. It has what could classify as the most beautiful Parque Principal in Colombia, its four corners guarded by arched yew trees intertwined with bougainvillea bushes. South of the village, lush water meadows shaded by the drooping fronds of willow trees, run down to the Río Iza. A path runs over a picturesque covered wooden bridge and joins the road leading to the hot springs 1 km away. On Sundays, the plaza is lined with stalls selling all types of sugary puddings.

Iza was founded on 12 February 1780 and today most of its inhabitants make a living from livestock, agriculture and wool spinning. There are several access points to the hot springs. The most popular is **Piscina Erika**, which has a good-sized concrete pool and a children's paddling pool fed by piping hot sulphurous water from the spring just above. Entrance US$3.30 with restaurant, changing rooms and showers. There are also two simple rooms for overnight stays (see Sleeping). Beyond Piscina Erika there is free access to natural pools, popular with locals at weekends. Unfortunately, these marshy pools are not well maintained and have been allowed to clog up with discarded rubbish.

There is good hiking around Iza, especially to Cascada El Encanto del Amor, a waterfall in the hills above the village. Ask at the Casa de la Cultura on the plaza or at Posada del Virrey Solis for directions.

Lago de Tota → *For listings, see pages 104-110. Colour map 2, B6.*

Beyond Iza the road rises sharply through pastures rich in wild flowers, passing through Cuitiva and the indigenous village of Tota. Here, the landscape changes to *páramo* or moorland, the graceful curves of its hills tinged with traces of purple, pink and red, before the road drops down to the steely blue waters of Lago de Tota. At 15 km long and 10 km wide, this is the largest natural lake in Colombia. The indigenous *campesinos* who

How Lago de Tota was formed

Many years ago an indigenous family was bequeathed a mysterious vessel of water by the gods. The gift was to be emptied to form a great lake. The husband and wife travelled over many lands looking for a suitable spot to create the lake. Their son and daughter did not understand their parents' obsession and decided to find out what was so special about this jar that they guarded so jealously.

They accidentally spilt the water, causing a disaster. As soon as it hit the ground the water swelled and flooded everything. The landscape changed. The boy, knowing he was the culprit, ran from his parents in fright. The girl ran to her mother and both were turned to stone, forming the two islands that today can be seen opposite Playa Blanca. The father tried to climb up to the moor above the lake but was overcome by the waters and turned into what is today known as the Potrero Peninsula.

populate its edges cultivate tidy patches of onions right up to the water's edge. There are reeds and algae all along the shore and few beaches, the notable exception being Playa Blanca, on the southwest corner of the lake, a beach of white sand with milky green water at its shallows, backed by pine-clad hills. The sight would not look out of place on the Caribbean, but at 3015 m, the water is cold. There is camping and a restaurant serving trout. At weekends Playa Blanca fills up with Colombians but is generally quiet otherwise.

Aquitania, on the eastern shore, is the principal town on the lake. There are plenty of food shops, and restaurants including, **Lucho** and **Pueblito Viejo**, together on the corner of the plaza, and a bright, restored church with modern stained-glass windows. Above the town is a hill (El Cumbre) with beautiful views. The road eventually does the round of the lake and heads back toward Sogamoso.

Monguí → *For listings, see pages 104-110. Colour map 2, B6.*

About 12 km northeast of Sogamoso is Monguí, once voted 'the most beautiful village in Boyacá'. The department has many contenders for this title but it would be difficult to build a case against this village with its large, cobbled plaza and whitewashed houses with doors and windows painted racing green and embellished with the occasional red. It has a magnificent **Basílica** ① *US$2.50, open only at weekends*, constructed by the Franciscans in the 17th century, which has many oil paintings including the *Virgin de Monguí*, donated by Philip II of Spain. The basilica has a very good museum, with exhibits that include the convent's original kitchen and dining room with 17th-century reliefs and a mummified cat found in the rafters of the building's ceiling.

Set high in the hills with sweeping views down towards Sogamoso in the valley below, this is a very pleasant place to stroll around, peaceful and quiet. It's not uncommon to see a horse or cow tethered outside the local bar while its owner chews the cud with his neighbour. It has good *artesanía* shops, selling woollen *ruanas* and leather products.

Don't miss the walk down Carrera 3 to the Calycanto Bridge, built by the Spanish out of stone cemented with clay, lime and bull's blood in order to bring large stones across the river to the church. At the top of Calle 4, to the right of the church, is the Plaza de Toros. If you feel energetic, take any path beyond the bull ring to a rock on which stands a shrine to the Virgin and Child, illuminated at night. From here there are tremendous views in all directions. A recommended excursion is east to the Páramo de Ocetá with particularly fine *frailejones* and giant wild lupins, a three-hour walk from Monguí.

Aside from traditional crafts, Monguí is one of the leading manufacturers of footballs. There are many football outlets in town, selling handmade balls.

Sierra Nevada del Cocuy → *For listings, see pages 104-110.*

① *Entry to the park US$17.50 for non-Colombians, payable at the park office (on the corner of the main plaza in Cocuy), where you can also obtain a map with the main walking paths.*

The Sierra Nevada del Cocuy is a mecca for hikers and climbers on high altitude in Colombia. This breathtaking mountain area in the national park is located in two departments, Boyacá and Santander and consists of two parallel north-south ranges about 30 km long, offering peaks of rare beauty, many lakes, big cliffs, waterfalls and literally thousands of *frailejón* plants. There are more than 22 snowy peaks, meeting the biggest mass of snow and ice in South America north of the equator. The snow-clad peaks range from 4900 m to 5330 m of the Ritacuba Blanco, which is the highest in the park. This park is simply THE place in Colombia for any high-altitude hiker or climber.

The park is accessible in the south from the small town of **El Cocuy** or further north from **Güicán**. Both towns are perfect starting or ending points for any hiking or climbing activity in the park. On the central square of El Cocuy you will find a miniature model of the mountain area. One of the most spectacular hikes in the park is walking from south to north (or vice versa), taking in a large part of what the park has to offer. It might seem to be an easy marked trail but it is highly recommend to go with a guide if you don't know the park as sudden changes in climate means visibility can unexpectedly drop to less than 10 m. You will need to know where to camp and where to get drinking water.

There is no accommodation in the park, so you will need to bring all equipment yourself. Basic food supply can be bought in El Cocuy or Güicán but otherwise you should bring your food from Bogotá. There is no need to bring ice axes or crampons, unless you are climbing Pan de Azúcar. Temperature can drop below 0°C during the nights as most campsites are around 4000 m. A number of treks and hikes are available. ▸▸ *See Activities and tours, page 109, for further information.*

Ins and outs

El Cocuy and Güicán can be reached by direct bus (early morning or late in the evening) from Bogota (10-12 hours) with **Paz del Río**, **Libertadores** and **Concorde** (US$17.50-30). Coming from Bucaramanga, switch buses in Capitanejo, although at the time of writing this road had been severely damaged by landslides and was not recommended. Around 0600 milk trucks leave the main plaza of El Cocuy. They can take you to the **Cabañas Guaicany** (the southern entrance of the park), **Finca la Esperanza** (for Laguna Grande de la Sierra) or to **Hacienda Ritacuba** from where it is about an hour's walk to get to the **Cabañas Kanwarra**. An Expreso (private transport) costs around US$34, which can be arranged at the main plaza in El Cocuy.

When to go

It is best to avoid the peak holiday periods (the last week in December, the first two weeks of January and Easter week) as campsites can get very busy during these times. Dry seasons are December to April and July to August but even in those months it can rain or be very foggy. There has been no problem with safety in recent years.

Sights

La Laguna de La Plaza is probably the most beautiful lake of all those in the Sierra Nevada del Cocuy, surrounded by the snow tops of **Pan de Azúcar** and **Toti** in the west and **Picos Negro** and **Blanco** in the east. Just below Pan de Azúcar you can see **Cerro El Diamante**, a pointy rock that might remind you of a real *diamante*. During sunrise, the colour of this rock can change from grey to yellow, gold, red and orange if you are lucky with the weather. **Laguna Grande de la Sierra** is surrounded by the tops of Pan de Azúcar, Toti, Portales, Concavo and Concavito and is a perfect spot as base camp to climb up to the summits of (one of) these peaks. **El Púlpito de Diablo** is an enormous, square rock with a shape of an altar at 5000 m. From El Púlpito you can continue to climb up to the top of **Pan de Azúcar** (5100 m) overlooking Laguna de la Plaza on one side and Laguna Grande de la Sierra on the other side. **Valle de los Cojines** is an enormous valley surrounded by snow tops and filled with *cojines* (pillow plants), typical of the region. **Ritacuba Blanco** is the highest mountain of all (5322 m) and is not too difficult to climb. The views at the top over

Sierra Nevada del Cocuy

the Valle de Cojines and many other parts of the park are just stunning. Mountain climbing with guide costs around US$75.

◉ **Boyacá Department listings** → *Phone code: 8.*

For Sleeping and Eating price codes and other relevant information, see pages 23-28.

● Sleeping

Tunja and around *p92, map p93*
AL Hunza, C 21A, No 10-66, T742 4111, www.hotelhunza.com. Tunja's largest hotel, the Hunza has fine views of the Iglesia San Francisco from its lobby. Its modern rooms are spacious, with Wi-Fi throughout, a swimming pool and Turkish bath and a restaurant.
A Boyacá Plaza, C 18, No 11-22, T740 1116/17, www.hotelboyacaplaza.com. This smart, modern hotel has comfortable rooms and includes breakfast and Wi-Fi connection in the price.
B San Ignacio Plaza, C 18, No 10-51, T743 7583, www.hotelsanignacioplaza.com. This hotel has a pretty colonial façade, though it's modern on the inside with bright, airy rooms. Also has a restaurant, parking and Wi-Fi.
C Alicante, Cra 8, No 19-15, T740 8073, www.hotelalicantetunja.com. With its minimalist design and a sunny patio fringed by varieties of cacti, this hotel is a bargain. The rooms are full of light and have cable TV, while there is Wi-Fi in reception and some of the rooms.
C Posada San Agustín, C 23, No 8-63, T743 0245. This beautiful colonial building on the Parque Pinzón is a bit of a gem, with comfortable rooms and a gorgeous balustraded courtyard painted olive green. The hotel is embellished with antiques and photographs of Tunja down the ages, while it also has Wi-Fi. Includes breakfast.
D Casa Colonial, Cra 8, No 20-40, T742 2169. This hotel has a nice, sunny patio and rooms with cable TV and en suite bathrooms – though they can be a bit dingy.
D Casa Real, C 19, No 7-65, T743 1764, www.hotelalicantetunja.com. Housed in

a beautiful colonial building, this hotel is a real bargain and could easily fetch 3 times the price. The rooms are comfortable and clean with private bathrooms and freshly varnished wooden floorboards. Some larger deluxe rooms. Sister hotel to **Alicante**. Highly recommended.
D Conquistador de América, C 20, No 8-92, T742 3534. The **Conquistador** has a lovely foyer with a bright skylight, and while the rooms are small they are clean and comfortable with en suite bathrooms, hot water and cable TV.
E Imperial, C 19, No 7-43, T742 3056. There's nothing outstanding about this small hotel but it does have clean rooms with cable TV, hot water and en suite bathrooms.

Villa de Leiva *p95, map p96*
Villa de Leiva is usually quiet on the early days of the week but fills up at weekends.
L-AL Plaza Mayor, Cra 10, No 12-31, T732 0425, www.hotelplazamayor.com.co. 28 rooms on 3 levels, right on the plaza, this worn brick building has a delightful octagonal courtyard with lemon trees and very comfortable rooms, plus Wi-Fi, parking and a good (expensive) restaurant.
AL Duruelo, Cra 3, No 12-88, T732 0222, www.duruelo.com.co. Villa de Leiva's most exclusive hotel, the building sits on a hill above the town, commanding views across the valley. The rooms are comfortable, though they perhaps could do with refurbishment but its biggest draw is the 4 swimming pools carved into the side of the hill and its spa and massage services.
AL Posada de San Antonio, Cra 8, No 11-80, T732 0583, www.hotellaposada desanantonio.com. With its thick adobe walls, colourful decor, enormous antique beds and location on the beautiful Parque Nariño, this hotel is a popular choice with

weekending *bogotanos*. The hotel also boasts a pool table and Wi-Fi in the lobby. Spa opening in 2011.

A Candelaria, C del Silencio 18, No 8-12, T732 0534, www.hotelcandelaria.villadeleyva.com.co. Located on the delightful cobbled Calle del Silencio, this refurbished colonial building has 9 rooms of monastic simplicity with thick, whitewashed walls and wooden beams. It also has a restaurant serving up international cuisine. Free tea, coffee, soft drinks, fruit basket and bottle of wine included.

A Hostería del Molino La Mesopotamia, C del Silencio, 15A-265, T732 0235, www.hosterialamesopotamia.villadeleyva.com.co. This former grain mill dates back to 1568, 4 years before Villa de Leiva was founded, and has retained much of its original lime and mud architecture in the house. It has delightful gardens with running rivulets of water fed by a spring, as well as a superb natural swimming pool. Non-guests can use the pool for US$2.50.

B El Marqués de San Jorge, C 14, No 9-20, T732 0240, www.elmarquesdesanjorge.com. This simple little place has rooms set around a courtyard and offers cable TV, Wi-Fi, parking and breakfast included.

C Posada de los Angeles, Cra 10, No 13-94, T732 0562, www.villaleyvanos.com. This *posada* has basic, clean rooms in a fine building 2 blocks from the plaza and a restaurant serving American breakfasts and pastas. Be sure to ask for a room overlooking the beautiful Iglesia del Carmen.

C-D Posada Don Blas, C 12, No 10-61, T732 0986. This sweet and simple little place is just 1 block away from the plaza and has small, clean rooms with private bathrooms and cable TV.

D-F Casa Viena, Cra 10 No 19-114, T732 0711, www.casaviena.com. New *hostal* run by Austrian Hans, who also runs **Casa Viena Cartagena**. 5 rooms, including 1 dorm, 3 private rooms and 1 larger private room with own bath and balcony overlooking the glorious mountain scenery. Internet access, herb garden, pizza oven and Wi-Fi. Hans makes good curries and also runs nearby Austrian bakery with artisan breads.

D-F Colombian Highlands and Hostal Renacer, Cra 9, No 11-02, T732 1201/ T311-308 3739 (mob), www.colombianhighlands.com. A 15-min walk from town, this hostel, belonging to English-speaking biologist Oscar Gilède, has some of the most comfortable private rooms you are likely to find in any Colombian backpackers' hostel. This country *finca* has turned the grounds of a former mine into an extensive garden and there are excellent facilities, including a kitchen, a wood-fired pizza oven, hammocks, bike hire, internet and dorms with bunk beds. Oscar also runs a tour agency offering a variety of trips including horse rental and adventure sports and has excellent information on the local area. Camping available, US$4.50 with own tent or US$8 for a tent and all equipment. Excellent for birdwatching, 75 species.

D-F Hostal Sinduly, Cra 11, No 11-77, T320-429 4050, noconadelsol@hotmail.com. Run by Austrian expat Manfred, this 10-bed hostel has 1 private room with bathroom and a couple of dorms in a colonial house 1 block from the plaza. There is use of kitchen and hot water, and Manfred also arranges trips to a *finca* he owns near the entrance to Iguaque National Park. English and German spoken.

Chiquinquirá *p99*
C El Gran, C 16 No 6-97, T726 3700. This hotel is central, secure and comfortable and includes breakfast. It has a good restaurant, laundry service and parking.
E Sarabita, C 16, 8-12, T726 2068. This business hotel has a pool, sauna (when working) and restaurant, all housed in a building declared a National Monument.
F Moyba, Cra 9, No 17-53, T726 2649, on the plaza. This hotel is a bit dingy, cheaper without private bathroom.

Ráquira and around *p99*
D Hostería Nemqueteba, T735 7016. This charming colonial house has a brightly painted patio brimming with bougainvillea as well as a swimming pool.
D Suaya, C del Comercio, T735 7029. 1 block from the plaza, this colonial building has brightly painted rooms with en suite bathrooms and hot water.
E La Candelaria, C 5, No 3-24, T735 7259. This basic hotel, 1 block from the plaza, has clean rooms with private bathrooms.

Monasterio Desierto de la Calendaria *p99*
Adjoining the monastery is a hotel, often used for spiritual retreats.
A Posada San Agustín, T621 0531, www.agustinosrecoletos.com.co. A 16th-century building set around a colourful cloister with flower beds and a water feature,

the rooms are simple but comfortable. There are 2 suites with jacuzzis as well as 2 saunas.

Paipa and around *p99*
AL Casona del Salitre, Vía Toca, Km 3, T785 1508, www.haciendadelsalitre.com. 5 mins' drive from town. A National Monument and a memorable place to stay near the baths and lake in a well-preserved hacienda where Simón Bolívar stayed before the Battle of Boyacá. Hot pools, spa, good restaurant, quiet, fireplace. Highly recommended.

Sogamoso *p100*
E Bochica, C 11, No 14-33, T770 7381. Good value, with comfortable rooms, hot water, TV, tourist info, and a restaurant.
E Valparaíso, C 11A, No 17-56, T771 6935. Near the bus station, this hotel has rooms with private bath and TV. Restaurant, sauna, and tourist information.

Iza *p100*
C Piscina Erika, Vereda Agua Caliente, T779 0038. Within the thermal springs, the complex has 2 simple but comfortable rooms with en suite bathrooms and access to the pool. Breakfast is included.
D Hotel Santa Isabel, T779 0038. Charming colonial building with rooms with beamed ceilings and private bathrooms. It has a restaurant serving *almuerzos* for US$2.70. The owners also run Piscina Erika.
D Posada del Virrey Solis, C 4A, No 4A-75, T779 0245. Just off the Parque Principal on a little plazoleta dominated by an enormous pine tree, this 180-year-old house, declared a National Monument, has baroque rooms full of religious paintings and iconography, old books and Egyptian statuettes. Breakfast, US$2.20, is served in an eccentric room full of ornate furnishings. The price of the room includes access to the thermal springs at Piscina Erika.

Lago de Tota *p100*
B Refugio Pozo Azul, 3 km beyond Camino Real, in a secluded bay on the lake, T619 3463

Bogotá), www.hotelrefugiopozoazul.com.
Also has cabins up to 6. With breakfast.
Suitable for children, comfortable,
watersport facilities, good food.
C Camino Real, Km 20 Vía Sogamoso
a Aquitania, T770 0684, on the lake.
Pleasant public rooms, colourful gardens,
boat slipway, boats for hire, restaurant,
sauna, tourist information.
E Residencia Venecia, C 8, No 144,
Aquitania. Clean, basic, reasonable.
Camping Playa Blanca, US$2.20 for
tent up to 5 people. US$4.40 for over 5.

Monguí *p101*
C El Portón de Ocetá, neat the plaza.
A beautiful large converted colonial house.
C La Casona, Cra 4, No 3-41, T782 498,
chopo11110@yahoo.es. This small hostel
has clean comfortable rooms with en suite
bathrooms behind a restaurant of the same
name. It has lovely views down into the
valley. Recommended.
D Hostal Calycanto, a pink house next
to the bridge with a lovely setting and
a restaurant. Best to book in advance.
F La Cabaña, chalet on road beyond
river (cross bridge, turn left). Basic but
comfortable. Cooks up food if forewarned.

Sierra Nevada del Cocuy *p102, map p103*
F pp Cabañas Guaicany, El Cocuy, at
the entrance of Valle de Lagunillas. With
shared bathroom. Great views of the
Ritacuba Blanco, the peaks of San Pablín
Sur and Norte and Concavo. Also possible
to camp and to hire horses and/or guide.
F pp Cabañas Kanwarra, El Cocuy, located
at the foot of Ritacuba Blanco. The perfect
starting point to climb Ritacuba Blanco or
to walk to Laguna Grande de los Verdes.
With shared bathroom.
F pp Hotel Casa Muñoz, El Cocuy, on the
main square. With private bathroom.
F pp Hotel Villa Real, El Cocuy. With
shared bathroom.
G pp Finca La Esperanza, El Cocuy, at
the entrance of Valle de Frailejones.

Convenient for the walk to Laguna
Grande de la Sierra. Simple rooms
with shared bathroom.

🍽 Eating

Tunja and around *p92, map p93*
🍽 **Boyacanto Café**, Cra 9, No 19-92,
www.boyacantocafe.com. This café
on the plaza principal has a sunny courtyard dominated by a large magnolia tree
and good coffees to boot.
🍽 **El Maizal**, Cra 9, No 20-30, T742 5876.
This restaurant has a good varied menu
of local specialities such as *mondongo*
and trout.
🍽 **La Cascada**, Pasaje Vargas (C 19A),
No 10-82, T744 5750. This large canteen
is a popular lunchtime venue with *almuerzos*
at US$2.45.
🍽 **La Mojarrita**, C 18, No 7-43, T743 8330.
This seafood restaurant is famous in Tunja
for its *mojarra* and *sancocho de pescado*.
🍽 **Pizza Nostra**, C 19, No 10-36, T740 2040.
Pizzas and lasagnas on a pedestrianized
street just off the main plaza.
🍽 **Son y Sabor**, Pasaje Vargas (C 19A),
No 10-71, T740 2970. This typical restaurant
has a good, varied menu serving rabbit and
trout as well as steaks.

Villa de Leiva *p95, map p96*
Villa de Leiva has dozens of good restaurants
with varied international and local menus.
Most, but not all, are concentrated in the
town's upmarket foodcourts, **Casa Quintero**
(on the plaza) and **La Guaca** (on C Caliente).
Bear in mind that many are closed Mon-Wed
or Mon-Thu.
🍽🍽 **Savia**, Cra 9, No 11-75, Casa Quintero,
T732 1778. Savia has an excellent range of
organic dishes of all kinds, such as chicken
in mango sauce.
🍽🍽 **Zarina**, Cra 9, No 11-75, Casa Quintero.
This small restaurant serves up excellent
Arabic and Oriental dishes as well as the
usual chicken and steak.

Don Quijote, La Guaca, C Caliente (Cra 9), Local No 12. This Spanish restaurant was the winner of Villa de Leiva's gastronomy prize in 2006 for its enormous leg of lamb cooked in its 400-year-old kitchen and it's still living off the reputation, with prices rising accordingly. There is also sangría and other Spanish fare.

La Cocina de la Gata, Casa Quintero, T732 1266. This pleasantly decorated fondue restaurant also serves chicken and steak.

Olivas & Especias, Cra 10, No 11-99, T732 1261. On the corner of the plaza, this restaurant serves pizzas and pastas in homely surroundings. Also worth a try is **Carnes & Olivas** (ⵜⵜⵜ), its prettier but pricier sister restaurant around the corner (also Cra 10).

Casa Blanca, C 13, No 7-06, T732 0821. This popular restaurant has been feeding locals for more than 20 years and serves up regional specialities such as *longaniza*.

Patio de Van Gogh, C 13, a block north of the main plaza. Coffee, desserts, ice cream and art in a pleasant patio setting.

Chiquinquirá *p99*
There are plenty of reasonable places to eat around and near Parque Julio Flores.

Ráquira and around *p99*
La Raquireñita, Cra 3, No 3-36, T735 7025. On the plaza, this lunchtime restaurant is brightly decorated with ceramic masks and other *artesanías* and serves up a mixture of fish, steak and chicken dishes.

Nemqueteba, C del Comercio, T735 7016. This restaurant belonging to the hotel of the same name serves up local trout as well as chicken and steak in pleasant surroundings.

Sogamoso *p100*
Susacá, Cra 16, No 11-35, T770 2587. One of the best restaurants near the centre, its specialities include trout. It has good *comida* with large portions.

Iza *p100*
There are a couple of restaurants on the Parque Principal.
M'c Jotas. A little hole-in-the-wall, run by a friendly couple who cook up steaks, chicken and burgers.

⊛ Festivals and events

Tunja and around *p92, map p93*
Late May-1st Sun in Jun The main local festival, culminating with the crowning of the 'queen' amid popular and cultural festivities. There is a special ceremony at the chapel of El Topo at this time.
Dec The week before Christmas there is a lively festival with local music, traditional dancing and fireworks.

Villa de Leiva *p95, map p96*
Jan-Feb There is an Astronomical festival, where telescopes are set up in the plaza principal for public use.
13-17 Jul Virgen del Carmen is celebrated each year.
Aug The International Kite Festival is held in the Plaza Mayor.
Nov Judges for the Festival de Gastronomía choose the best individual dish cooked up by the town's restaurant.
7 Dec A festival of light, with impressive firework displays, is held every year from this date.

⊙ Shopping

Tunja and around *p92, map p93*
The market is near the Plaza de Toros on the outskirts of town, open every day (good for *ruanas* and blankets). Fri is the main market day.
Tunjartesanal, Cra 9, No 19-56, T740 0655. In the Casa del Fundador, this shop has an excellent range of high quality regional handicrafts. Open Mon-Sun 0900-1800. Recommended.

Villa de Leiva *p95, map p96*

Shops in the plaza and the adjoining streets have an excellent selection of Colombian handicrafts and offer many bargains.

Market day is Sat, held in the Plaza del Mercado (not the Plaza Mayor).
Ricardo Luna, C 13, No 7-42, T732 0491. Good leather products.

Chiquinquirá *p99*

Many delightful toys are made locally. Along the south side of the Basilica are shops specializing in musical instruments.

▲ Activities and tours

Villa de Leiva *p95, map p96*
Horse riding
Mauricio Cortez, T311-807 4562. Hires horses and guides for US$7.50 per hr, minimum 1 hr.

Tour operators
Colombian Highlands, Cra 9, No 11-02, T732 1201, www.colombianhighlands.com. Biologist Oscar Gilède runs tours of the local area, as well as trips to local nature spots such as Iguaque National Park specifically geared towards botanists, ornithologists and enthusiasts of adventure sports such as abseiling and caving. His office on Carrera 9 is also an excellent source of information on the local area.
Zebra Trips, C Caliente, T311-870 1749. With its zebra-striped fleet of Land Rovers, this company provides a fun way to explore the desert area outside Villa de Leiva. 8 different tours, as well as bike hire and a gourmet outing.

Sierra Nevada del Cocuy *p102, map p103*
Aventure Colombia, based in Cartagena and Bogotá, www.aventurecolombia.com. French/Colombian-run tour agency with tailor-made trips throughout Colombia and an emphasis on trekking, eco and rural tourism. They run a 6-day trek in Sierra Nevada de Cocuy, taking in the Valle de Lagunillas – Púlpito del Diablo – Pan de Azúcar – Laguna de la Plaza costing US$950 per person. Price includes transport to/from Bogotá – El Cocuy/Guícán, park fees, accommodation, meals and a guide. A good level of physical fitness is required.

⊖ Transport

Tunja and around *p92, map p93*
Bus
The bus station is 400 m steeply downhill from the city centre. From Bogotá, with **Rápido Duitama, Libertadores** (comfortable and recommended), **Transportes Alianza** or **Copetran**, 3-3½ hrs, 4½-5 hrs weekends and holidays, US$8.50. To **Bucaramanga**, frequent services, 7 hrs, US$19. To **Villa de Leiva**, frequent services in *colectivo* or mini bus, US$3, 45-60 mins.

Villa de Leiva *p95, map p96*
Bus
The bus station is on Cra 9 between C 11 and C 12. To **Tunja**, 45-60 mins, US$3 with **Flota Reina, Coomultrasvilla, Cootax, Libertadores** or **Trans Alianza**, or microbus every 15 mins from 0530 to 1830.
To **Bogotá** via Tunja, takes 4 hrs, US$10, several companies, and via Zipaquirá and Chiquinquirá, US$10. To **Chiquinquirá**, 1 hr, US$3.30, hourly minibus. To **Ráquira** *busetas* leave infrequently, times change often, US$2.20, 30 mins taxi, US$15. To **Monquirá**, 1000 connects with bus to **Bucaramanga**, thus avoiding Tunja. To **Iguaque National Park entrance**, 50 mins, US$1.70 at 0700 and 1000.

Taxi
Taxi to outlying areas (including **Hostal Renacer**) US$2.50.

Chiquinquirá *p99*
Bus

To **Villa de Leiva**, 1¾ hrs, US$3.30, several daily. To **Tunja**, 3 hrs, US$6. To **Zipaquirá**, US$6. To **Bogotá**, 2½ hrs, US$5.50.

Ráquira and around *p99*   •
Bus

Buses leave **Villa de Leiva** at 0730, 0830, 1230 and 1630, 30 mins, US$2.20. The return journey is more complicated, with direct bus services at 0430 and 1230, also 1345, 1600 and 1730 by minibus. Otherwise change at **Ramera**.

Taxi

Round-trip taxis from **Villa de Leiva**, US$33.

Sogamoso *p100*
Bus

Bogotá, 4-4½ hrs, US$11.50; to **Tunja**, 1-2 hrs, US$5.50.

Iza *p100*
Bus

From Sogamoso with **Flota Alianzana**, US$2.20. If no buses from terminal in Sogamoso, take a taxi to Puente de Pesca, 5 or 6 blocks away, and catch from there.

Lago de Tota *p100*
Bus

From Sogamoso, US$2.80, 1½ hrs with **Flota Alianzana**. Buses leave every 1½ hrs, passing through Iza, Tota and on to **Aquitania**.

Monguí *p101*
Bus

Buses leave from the plaza. To **Sogamoso**, every 20 mins by *buseta*, US$1, 45 mins.

ⓘ Directory

Tunja and around *p92, map p93*
Banks Several banks in the C 20/Cra 10 area. **Internet** Coffenet, Cra 9, No 19-98, upstairs, US$2 per hr.

Villa de Leiva *p95, map p96*
Banks Banco Popular and Banco Agrario in the Plaza will give pesos against Visa, limited hours. There is a Visa ATM in the Plaza. **Internet** Redside, Cra 9, No 9-99. Skype, headphones and international calls. **Post** In Telecom building, C 13, No 8-26.

Iza *p100*
Telephone There is a Telecom with (pricey) international calls on the Parque Principal.

Santander Department

Tumbling rivers, green valleys and countless immaculately preserved colonial towns and villages – Santander has much to recommend it. Take away the tropical vegetation and you could almost imagine yourself in the mountains of southern Spain. With an established adventure-sports scene centred around the town of San Gil, this area of Colombia is becoming an increasingly popular destination for national and foreign visitors alike. What's more, it is also one of the cheapest parts of the country and you will get the chance to sample some of the regional culinary delicacies and stay in delightful colonial hotels without fear of breaking the bank. The village of Barichara was voted the most beautiful in Colombia and was declared a National Monument in 1975, while Girón, just a few kilometres from the industrial capital Bucaramanga, does not lag far behind. Bucaramanga is a modern city with a thriving nightlife and one of the best places for paragliding in the country. ▸▸ *For listings, see pages 119-125.*

San Gil → *For listing, see pages 119-125. Colour map 2, B6. Phone code: 7. Population: 33,000. Altitude: 1140 m.*

About 21 km northeast of Socorro, is San Gil, a colonial town with a good climate in the deep valley of the Río Fonce. San Gil is an important centre for adventure sports. The river systems of the Ríos Fonce and Chicamocha run through deep valleys and gorges in this part of Santander, providing the best rafting and canoeing in Colombia (see Activities and tours, page 124). With a broad range of hotels, San Gil is an excellent base from which to explore Santander's string of stunning colonial villages. There is a tourist office here: **Instituto Municipal de Turismo y Cultura** ① *C 15, No 14-66, T727 3529.*

Near the centre of the town by the river is the enchanting **Parque Gallineral** ① *daily, US$2, T724 0821, there are excellent guides, some English-speaking, be sure to tip generously as they are not paid by the park.* The park, created in 1919, covers 4 ha where the Quebrada Curití runs through a delta to the Río Fonce. It is named after the *chiminango* trees, which make up 80% of the trees in the park. These trees have a natural tendency to lean over and are therefore popular with roosting chickens (*gallinas*). There are streams everywhere to create a delightful botanical garden full of butterflies and birds. Notable are the heliconias and the huge *ceiba* near the *playa* where the canoes end their trip down the Río Fonce. Outstanding are the many fine trees covered with moss-like *tillandsia*, a bromeliad. There is a restaurant and a superb public natural swimming pool which uses water siphoned off from the Quebrada Curití.

In the centre, the **Parque Principal** has a fountain surrounded by huge *ceiba* and heliconia trees, and is very attractive when illuminated in the evening. Overlooking it is the **church**, which has interesting octagonal towers. There is a good view of the town from **La Gruta**, the shrine overlooking the town from the north (look for the cross).

Activities

San Gil is increasingly recognized as the centre of Colombia's burgeoning adventure-sports industry. There are a number of activities available in the surrounding countryside. There are many adventure companies in San Gil, some better equipped than others. See Activities and tours, page 124, for recommendations, or speak to Shaun at the **Macondo Guesthouse** for advice. For most activities wear good footwear, bring a hat and sunscreen.

About 20 km south of San Gil on the road to Duitama, is **Páramo** (with some accommodation eg **Páramo** in the Plaza Principal), one of the centres of activity sports (see above). About 30 km further on is **Charalá**, which has a plaza with a statue of **José Antonio Galán**, leader of the 1781 Comunero revolt. It also has an interesting church and Casa de la Cultura. Bus to San Gil, US$2.

Abseiling Known as rappelling in Colombia, abseiling down Juan Curi, a spectacular three-tier, 180-m waterfall, is a popular activity. A descent down one of the waterfall's 60-m cascades costs US$20 per person. The trip is best done in the mornings and should be pre-booked. It's also possible to cycle to the waterfalls, a trip of two hours.

The Juan Curi waterfall is also a popular hiking destination and has a lovely swimming spot at the base of one of the cascades. You can climb to the second of the three tiers using a number of ladders and ropes. From San Gil, take a bus (US$3.50 return) towards Charalá and ask to be dropped off at the waterfall. There are two approaches, passing through private *fincas*. You may have to pay a small fee for access, about US$2 (this entrance fee is included in the price if abseiling). A return taxi fare is US$20.

San Gil

To Pozo Azul

Public Swimming Pool
Football Stadium
Basketball Courts

Cra 5

Cra 6

University

Cra 7

To ① & Bella Isla (1 km)

Cra 8

Cathedral

Cra 9

Vera Cruz Supermarket

Parque Principal

To Bus Terminal, Tejo centre (3 km) & ⑥ (4 km)

To ② & Bella Isla (1 km)

Cajasán Supermarket

Cra 10

Bus Terminal Bucaramanga

Cra 11

Tourist Police

Park Gallineral

Local Bus Terminal (Barichara)

Cra 11

Cra 12

N

200 metres
200 yards

Sleeping		
Abril **1**	Sams VIP Hostel **9**	Gringo Mike's **3**
Bella Isla **2**	Santander Alemán **10**	Pizzería Pierrot **4**
La Hormiga **3**	Santander Alemán	Rogelia **5**
Macondo Hostel **4**	Terrace Vista **11**	Saludable Delicia **6**
Mansión del Parque **5**	Victoria **12**	Santa Lucía **7**
Mesón de Cuchicate **6**		
Panorama Plaza **7**	**Eating**	
Posada Familiar **8**	Donde Betty **1**	
	El Maná **2**	

Caving On the road to Barichara there are a series of caves known as La Antigua with saloons full of spiders and bats. A guided crawl through small tunnels of mud and water to underground waterfalls costs US$14. Near Paramo is Cueva del Indio, a cave full of stalactites, stalacmites and bats. You have to slide down a zip line into the dark mouth of the cave before wading through waist-level water. Cost is US$14. To get there, take a bus (US$2) from bus station in San Gil or taxi (US$17 return). Another exciting cave to explore is Cueva Vaca near Curití, tours US$12.50, two hours, transport to Curití US$1.75 by bus or US$6.50 by taxi. Pre-book all in San Gil.

Hiking The surrounding countryside has several old indigenous trails, known as the Lenguake or Camino Real, linking many of its beautiful villages. A popular 1½-hour walk is between the historic villages of Barichara and Guane (see under Barichara, below, for more details).

Horse riding Day trips to local swimming spots cost US$14 per person.

Kayaking Three-day beginners courses on the Río Fonce, including eskimo roll training in a local swimming pool, cost US$175. More experienced kayakers can make runs on different rivers with experienced guides.

Paragliding San Gil has two excellent locations for paragliding (known as *parapente*). The most spectacular location is over the Chicamocha Canyon and costs US$85, lasting between 30 minutes and one hour. The second is near Curití and lasts 20-30 minutes, costing US$30.

Rafting Blessed with three rivers in proximity to each other, San Gil can provide excellent rafting for people of all levels of experience.

The Río Fonce is the main river running through San Gil and is the best one for beginners with Grade II-III rapids. The trip begins 11 km from town and winds up in the centre of San Gil, opposite the Parque Gallineral. A trip costs US$15 with transport and safety equipment. It is best to wear sandals.

The Río Chicamocha has Grade I-IV rapids and travels through the spectacular Chicamocha Canyon. The journey starts 1½ hours from San Gil and costs US$75 with a minimum of four people, transport included.

For a more extreme experience, the Río Suárez has Class IV+ rapids. The 20-km trip lasts three hours and costs US$60 per person.

Swimming There are lots of good swimming holes on San Gil's rivers. A local favourite is the Pozo Azul, just outside town, popular on Sundays. The most spectacular option is Pescaderito, just outside Curití, which has a number of beautiful, clear pools. From the main square in Curiti, walk past the church four blocks and take the road leading out of town. A bus to Curití costs US$1.30. Alternatively, Parque Gallineral in San Gil has a spectacular swimming pool fed by water from the Río Fonce.

Other possible activities include bungee jumping from US$17.50, hydro speed US$20 and mountain biking US$10.

Barichara → *For listing, see pages 119-125. Colour map 2, B6. Phone code: 7. Population: 10,000 Altitude: 1300 m.*

From San Gil a direct paved road leads to Barichara, 22 km away. Often touted as the most beautiful small town in Colombia, it would be difficult to argue against this claim. Barichara is a lovely colonial town founded in 1741 and designated as a National Monument in 1975. There are several interpretations of this indigenous Guane name, the best is 'the place of rest with flowering trees'. It has a wonderfully peaceful, bohemian atmosphere, with white and green or blue paint everywhere and a lot of fine stonework. The walls of many buildings – whitewashed with doors and zócalos (the lower half of the building) painted green, blue or turquoise – are made with a technique called *tapia pisada*, which uses compacted mud mixed with water. The churches are constructed from the brown stone found all over Santander, and the streets are paved with it throughout. Fortune has been kind to Barichara; it is a prosperous little town, as can be seen by the number of boutique-style *artesanía* and clothes shops. This is very much a place to relax as an increasing number of Colombians find at weekends, mainly from Bucaramanga but also Bogotá. Artists congregate here too, but midweek it is quieter.

Barichara

Sleeping
Greengoes Guesthouse **1**
Corotá **2**
Hostal Misión Santa Bárbara **3**
La Mansión de Virginia **4**
La Posada de Pablo **5**
Los Tiestecitos **6**

Eating
Color de Hormiga **1**
El Compá **2**
La Puerta **3**

Sights

Among Barichara's places of historical interest, is the house of the former president, **Casa de Aquileo Parra Gómez**. If you wish to visit, ask the lady at the house next door who has the key. The **Casa de Cultura**, on the Parque Principal, has a small exhibition of local historical interest and archeological finds.

The **Catedral de la Inmaculada Concepción** is a fine colonial building, which sets the tone for the town. The façade and twin towers are strikingly illuminated at night. The interior is all in finished sandstone, with fluted columns, a carved wooden ceiling, gallery, cupola and a bright, gold-leaf *reredos*. There are three other interesting churches, **San Antonio** ① *Cra 4/C 5*, with a house for the elderly alongside, **Santa Bárbara** ① *C 6/Cra 11*, at the top of the town, **Jesús Resucitado** ① *C 3/Cra 7*, with the cemetery next to it – all with simple, even stark, interiors. There is a superb wide-ranging view from the *mirador* at the top of Carrera 10 across the Río Suárez to the Cordillera de los Cobardes, the last section of the Cordillera Oriental before the valley of the Magdalena. At the corner of the Carrera 10 and Calle 4, there is a **Piedra de Bolívar**, which shows the number of times the Liberator passed through the village.

You can walk to Barichara from Guane, or vice versa, along a delightful camino real, originally used by the indigenous Guane and later appropriated by the Spanish. The path still retains much of the original paving and most of what fell into disrepair has been restored. You will walk past lush green pastures full of grazing cows and goats and through orchards. It takes about two hours. It is best to leave in the early morning and to carry plenty of water and head protection as the sun can be punishingly hot at midday. There are a couple of *fincas* selling refreshments along the way. From Barichara, walk to the top of the town along Carrera 10 and continue downhill along the stone trail. From Guane, exit the plaza to the left of the church, walk uphill for two blocks and take a left; continue walking and you will eventually hit the path.

There is a more extensive, three-day walk to the villages of Barichara, Guane, Villanueva, Los Santos, and the ghost town of Jerico, involving a spectacular descent of the Chicamocha Canyon. There are various hostals to stay in on the way, and places to sample local food and drinks. Speak to Shaun at the Macondo Guesthouse in San Gil for more details.

Guane → *For listing, see pages 119-125. Colour map 2, B6.*

Much like Barichara, the tiny village of Guane, 9 km away by road, is a place seemingly lost in time. That the surrounding valley abounds in fossils only adds to this impression. Former capital of the pre-Columbian Guane culture, it has a beautiful plaza dominated by a **church** of simple but imposing design, with an interesting beamed and ornamented roof, fine wooden doors, a balcony at the west end and an elegant chapel to Santa Lucía to the left of the altar. In the plaza there is a monument, studded with fossils, dedicated to the last Guane chief, Guaneta, and several brilliant-orange acacia trees. Not much happens in Guane: you are as likely to see a donkey parked outside the local shop as a car.

There are many colonial houses and an excellent and surprisingly large **paleontological and architectural museum** ① *daily 0900-1200, 1400-1700 (times can be erratic), US$1.20*, housed in the Parroquia San Isidro on the plaza. It has an enormous collection of fossils found in the local area (which is constantly being added to), as well as woven Guane textiles and a mummified woman. Ask at the local shop if it is closed. A lady will take you on an informative if rather whirlwind tour.

North to Bucaramanga

North of San Gil on the main road to Bucaramanga is **Curití**, noted for handicrafts in fique (agave sisal). Mixed with cotton, it is used to make fabrics, shoes, bags and even building materials. You can see weaving at **Ecofibras** in the village. Near Curití are limestone caves. To visit, see under San Gil, above. About 28 km north of San Gil, a little off the road, is the picturesque village of **Aratoca**, with a colonial church. Near Aratoca you will notice the deep valley to the east of the road, the canyon of the **Río Chicamocha**. At one point in the next section, look for the place where the road takes to a narrow ridge with spectacular views on both sides as the river loops round to the southwest. The descent from the heights along the side of a steep cliff into the dry Río Chicamocha Canyon, with spectacular rock colours, is one of the most dramatic experiences of the trip to Cúcuta, but, if driving, this is a demanding and dangerous stretch. The deep valley of the river at this point is becoming an interesting place for canoeing and whitewater rafting, especially between Cepitá and Pescadero, which is where the main road crosses the river. There is a grandstand view of this section of the river from near Aratoca. See under San Gil, above, for sporting possibilities in this region. After crossing the river, the road ascends again to the plateau for the remaining few kilometers to Bucaramanga.

Between San Gil and Bucaramanga lies the recently opened **Parque Nacional Chicamocha** ① *C 44, No 35-27, San Pío, Bucaramanga, T657 4400, www.parque nacionaldelchicamocha.com, Tue-Fri 0900-1800, Sat-Sun 0800-1900, US$19, including cable car and park entrance, children US$10,* with a new visitor centre with panoramic views, activities, parking, snack bars and toilets and a 6.3-km cable car across the canyon. It has more of a theme park feel than an actual national park, but the views are splendid.

Bucaramanga → *For listing, see pages 119-125. Colour map 2, A6. Phone code: 7. Population: 539,000. Altitude: 960 m.*

Bucaramanga, 420 km from Bogotá, is the capital of Santander Department. A modern, industrial city with little remaining of its colonial past, it is nonetheless not without charm. It still has a small colonial area, some lovely parks and squares and fine dining and nightlife. It is also an important transport hub, connecting Bogotá with the main border with Venezuela, Cúcuta, and with the Caribbean coast. If you are heading to any of these destinations it is more than likely that you will have to make a stop in Bucaramanga. It stands on an uneven plateau sharply delimited by eroded slopes to the north and west, hills to the east and a ravine to the south. The city's great problem is space for expansion. The metropolitan area has grown rapidly because of the success of coffee, tobacco and staple crops.

The city was founded in 1622 by Paéz de Sotomayor but was little more than a village until the 19th century. Simón Bolívar established his campaign headquarters here in 1813, and lived here for some time in the **Casa de Bolívar** around 1828. Perú de la Croix, a French officer in Bolívar's army wrote his *Bucaramanga Diary* here, an interesting study of his leader. Gold was found in the hills and rivers nearby, hence the Río Oro to the southwest, which were worked until the end of the 19th century.

Ins and outs

Getting there The airport is at Palonegro, on three flattened hilltops on the other side of the ravine, south of the city. There are spectacular views on take-off and landing. Taxi from town US$15; *colectivo*, US$1. Buses are scarce despite the fact that some bus boards say 'Aeropuerto' (direction 'Girón/Lebrija' from Diagonal 15) At the time of writing major roadworks where slowing down all traffic to the airport, so leave yourself extra time. ➔ *For flight details, see Transport, page 125.*

The **bus terminal** is on the Girón road, with cafés, shops, a bank and showers. Taxi to centre, US$3.25; bus US$0.80. To the Magdalena at Barrancabermeja, 115 km; to Cúcuta, 198 km; to Bogotá, 420 km; to Santa Marta, 550 km, all paved.

Getting around Most taxis have meters; beware of overcharging from bus terminals. The minimum fare is US$1.80 and this should get you to most places within the city centre. When you get in the taxi make sure the driver switches the meter to '42', which is the code for the minimum fare. For longer journeys, taxis usually charge about US$10-15 per hour. Buses charge US$0.80.

Tourist office On Parque de los Niños, underneath the library, also inside, Instituto Municipal de Cultura, is **Oficina Asesora de Turismo** ⓘ *C 30, No 26-117, T6341132, Mon-Fri 0800-1200, 1400-1800, maps, etc.* **DAS** ⓘ *Cra 11, No 41-13, T633 9426.* **National Parks Office** ⓘ *Av Quebrada Seca 30-44, piso 1, T645 4868.*

Sights
The city can be divided into three sections, running west to east. The **Parque García Rovira** is the centre of the colonial area where you will find most of the museums and cultural centres.

The **Parque Santander** is the heart of the modern city and this is where most of the budget hotels can be found. Further east is the Zona Rosa, centred around Calle 33 and

Bucaramanga

Sleeping 🛏	Ruitoque 9	Los Tejaditos 16
Asturias 1		Mercagán 17
Balmoral 2	**Eating** 🍴	Tony's 18
Carolina 7	DiMarco 10	
Chicamocha 3	El Viejo Chiflas 11	**Bars & clubs** 🍸
Colonial Plaza 4	La 22 12	El Sombrero 20
El Pilar 5	La Carreta 13	Venado do Oro 19
Guane 6	La Pamplonesa 14	
Kasa Guane 8	Los Kioskos 15	

Carrera 33, where many of the city's better restaurants, bars and clubs are located. Bucaramanga is notable for its green spaces. There are a number of fine parks, including **Parque de Mejoras Públicas** ① *C 36/Cras 29-32*, with an open-air *concha acústica* (concert shell) for public performances, **Parque de los Niños** ① *C 30/Cra 26*, and **Parque Centenario**, from which buses used to leave before the new terminal was built. Other parks worth visiting are **Parque San Pío** ① *C 45, No 33*, with its many trees, and **Parque Las Palmas** ① *C 41, No 30*. Although Bucaramanga is blessed with numerous lovely parks and open spaces, note that not all of these are safe and muggings have been reported even in daylight in and around Parque Centenario and the small park at C33/Cra22.

There are several churches of interest. The **Catedral de la Sagrada Familia** ① *C 30/Cra 19*, overlooks the Parque Santander, a clean white Romanesque building with twin towers and statues of the Virgin and San José in between. The church of **San Pío** ① *C 45/Cra 36*, has several paintings by Oscar Rodríguez Naranjo, and the **Capilla de los Dolores** ① *C 35/Cra 10*, was the first chapel to be built in the town and is where the poet Aurelio Martínez Mutis was buried.

The **Museo de Arte Moderno** ① *C 37/Cra 26, US$0.50*, is a centre for art and culture with occasional film festivals. Just off Parque García Rovira, is **Casa de Bolívar** ① *T642 2542, Mon-Fri 0800-1200, 1400-1800, US$1, at C 37, No 12-15*, an interesting ethnographic and historical museum and a centre of research on Bolívar and his period.

Across the street is the **Casa de La Cultura** ① *C 37, No 12-46, Mon-Sat 0900-1800, US$1, T6302046*, in a fine colonial building with exhibitions, film showings and a local *artesanía* display. Also worth a visit is the **Museo Arqueológico Regional Guane** ① *in the Casa de Cultura 'Piedra del Sol', Cra 7, No 4-35, Floridablanca, T639 4537*, good collection of Guane culture artefacts and textiles.

Away from the centre, the **Club Campestre** is one of the most beautifully set in Latin America. There is an amusement park, **Parque El Lago**, in the suburb of Lagos, southwest of the city on the way to Floridablanca. On the way out of the city northeast (towards Pamplona) is the **Parque Morrorico**, well maintained with a fine view. There is a sculptured Saviour overlooking the park, a point of pilgrimage on Good Friday.

The suburb of **Floridablanca**, 8 km southwest, has the famous **Jardín Botánico Eloy Valenzuela** ① *Tue-Sun 0800-1100 and 1400-1700, US$0.25, children US$0.15*, also known as **El Paragüitas** gardens), belonging to the national tobacco agency. The Río Frío runs through the gardens, which have been recently reconstructed. To get there, take a bus (US$0.80) from Carrera 33, Bucaramanga, either 'Florida Villabel' which goes by the botanical gardens, or 'Florida Autopista' (continuation of Carrera 33) which goes direct to the square in Florida and you have to walk about 1 km, taxi from the centre, US$3.

Around Bucaramanga

Lebrija, 17 km to the west, is situated on an attractive plain, and **Rionegro**, is a coffee town 20 km to the north with the Laguna de Gálago and waterfalls close by. One fine waterfall is 30 minutes by bus from Rionegro to Los Llanos de Palma followed by a two-hour walk through citrus groves towards Bocas. Complete the walk along an old railway to the Bucaramanga–Rionegro road.

Piedecuesta, 18 km southeast of Bucaramanga, is where you can see cigars being hand made, as well as furniture carving and jute weaving. Cheap, hand-decorated *fique* rugs can be bought. There are frequent buses to all these towns from the city, or a taxi costs US$6. Corpus Christi processions in these towns in June are interesting. To get there, take bus from Carrera 22 (45 minutes).

The road (paved but narrow) runs east to Berlín, and then northeast, a very scenic ascent through cloudforest to the summit of the Eastern Cordillera and eventually on to Pamplona, about 130 km from Bucaramanga. **Berlín** is an ideal place to appreciate the grandeur of the Eastern Cordillera and the hardiness of the people who live on the *páramo*. The landscape is stark, barren and dramatic, much like the Scottish highlands. The village lies in a valley at 3100 m. The peaks surrounding it rise to 4350 m and the temperature is constantly around 10°C, although on the infrequent sunny days it may seem much warmer. There is a tourist complex with cabins and there are several basic eating places. Camping (challenging but rewarding) is possible with permission. At the highest point on the road between Bucaramanga and Berlín (3400 m) is a café where you can camp on the covered porch.

Girón → *For listing, see pages 119-125. Colour map 2, A6.*

Girón, a tobacco centre 9 km southwest of Bucaramanga on the Río de Oro, is a little gem of a colonial town. Far from the bustle of industrial Bucaramanga, at weekends it is filled with *bumangueses*, many of whom come for Mass at its beautiful church. In 1963 Girón was declared a National Monument: the buildings are well preserved and the town unspoilt by modernization. By the river are *tejo* courts and popular open-air restaurants with *cumbia* and *salsa* bands. In the square at weekends, sweets and *raspados* (crushed ice, rather like slush puppies) are sold, while children buy balloons and are wheeled about in miniature cars. Take the bus from Carrera 15 or 22 in Bucaramanga, US$0.80. A taxi costs US$4.50.

◉ Santander Department listings → *Phone code: 7.*

For Sleeping and Eating price codes and other relevant information, see pages 23-28.

◉ Sleeping

San Gil *p111, map p112*

A Bella Isla, north of town, Vía Javel San Pedro, T724 2972, www.bellaislaventura.com. On top of the hill looking out over town, Bella Isla has a beautiful setting in lovely grounds but nonetheless has the feel of a resort hotel that has seen better days. A 1960s building constructed over 4 levels, it does however cater for most needs with large rooms, many with a balcony for hanging a hammock, TV, tennis courts, a swimming pool and Wi-Fi. Breakfast is included in the price.
B-C Mansión del Parque, C 12, No 8-71 Esquina, T724 5662, www.hosteltrail.com/mansiondelparque. Occupying a colonial building on the corner of the Parque Principal, this is easily the most picturesque hotel in town. The rooms are large with antique furniture and there are internet facilities. Ask for one of the street-facing rooms, which have balconies for people-watching.
C Mesón de Cuchicute, Km 1 Vía San Gil–Socorro, T724 2041. On the western outskirts of town, **Mesón de Cuchicute** offers either *cabañas* or 2 up, 2 down rooms with balconies looking out onto one of the hotel's 2 enormous pools. With very comfortable beds, all the mod cons (TV, a/c, minibar, room service), jacuzzi, gym, restaurant and some nice details such as wash basins carved out of local Barichara stone, it represents good value for money.
C Posada Familiar, Cra 10, No 8-55, T724 8136. Small place with 6 rooms set around a sunny courtyard with a water piece and hanging plants. Rooms are clean and have TV, fan, Wi-Fi and private baths. Recommended.

C Victoria, Cra 11, No 10-40, T724 5955, www.baricharavive.com. Eccentrically decorated in garish colours which somehow seem to work, the Victoria has some bizarre ornaments, including fake knitted sunflowers in one room. Rooms open onto a long corridor-courtyard with a fountain. Some rooms with a/c or fan and even a DVD player but no hot water.

D Abril, C 8, No 10 Esquina, T724 8795, hotelabrilsangilss@yahoo.es. Strangely laid out with the reception area essentially in the car park but has clean rooms with antique beds (comfortable), hot water, Wi-Fi, fan, TV and a minibar.

D Panorama Plaza Hotel, Cra 10, No 13-17, T724 2170, panoramaplazahoteles@yahoo.es. Fine old building off the Parque Principal. Has a restaurant serving breakfasts and the occasional weekend lunch as well as Wi-Fi, though the double rooms have no windows. Prices tend to double during high season.

D-F La Hormiga, Cra 8 10-35, T724 8001, hormigahostel@gmail.com. New venture from Shaun from Macondo, this is more of a flashpackers' hideaway, with more private rooms, in addition to 2 dorms, TV room, nice garden with 2 kittens (at the time of writing at least) and a place to have BBQs. Recommended.

D-F Former Macondo Hostel (as yet to be named at the time of writing), C 12, No 7-26, T724 4463. This hostel, also run by Shaun (see **Macondo Hostel**, below) has a communal area decked out with hammocks, and an honesty system for drinks and internet. Board games, free coffee, free internet access and cheap, comfortable rooms – it has several bunks in dormitory rooms (**F**). There is now a 2nd building next door, with more private rooms.

D-F Macondo Hostel, Cra 8 10-35, www.macondohostel.com. Australian Shaun Clohesy has recently moved his long-standing hostel into a new, flasher building. There are more private rooms than before, in addition to 2 dorms, TV room, nice garden with 2 kittens (at the time of writing at least) and a place for BBQs. **Macondo**'s biggest asset is the wealth of information available on local activities and the chance to swap tales with the many backpackers who pass through. Recommended.

D-F Sam's VIP Hostel, Cra 10 12-33, T724 2746, www.samshostel.com. The poshest backpackers' hangout in San Gil, this hostel overlooking the main plaza has everything from rooms with private balconies to an outdoor rooftop pool and a bar that stays open until midnight. Recommended.

E San Carlos, Cra 11, No 11-25, T724 2542. Sweet little place set round an atrium. Has TV and private bath but some of the rooms have no windows.

E Santander Alemán, C 12, No 7-63, T724 2535, www.hostelsantanderaleman.com, and **Santander Alemán Terrace Vista**, Cra 10 15-07 esquina. 2 hostels run by the same couple. The latter is larger with a beautiful roof terrace for meals and beers. Several nice common areas, hammocks, internet access and book exchange. Emphasizes that it's Catholic and family-oriented, so not for the party crowd.

Barichara *p114, map p114*

A Hostal Misión Santa Bárbara, C 5, No 9-08, T726 7163 (or Bogotá T288 4949), www.hostalmisionsantabarbara.info. If you have the cash to splash this is the place to stay in town. Each room is individually decorated with great taste (1 even has stained-glass windows) and all open onto a delightful plant-filled courtyard. Has a good restaurant, spa, gym and a swimming pool.

B Coratá, Cra 7, No 4-08, T726 7110, www.baricharadigital.gov.co. This delightful colonial building has a beautiful balustraded terrace looking down onto a courtyard with an impressive *saucellaron* tree. TV, and hot water in private bathrooms. No fans or a/c but the high ceilings keep you cool.

B Greengoes Guesthouse, C 6 5-24, T316-237 6343, www.greengoestravel.com. New Colombian/US-run guesthouse, with

rooms, 2 doubles and 1 twin. Fabulous
garden with herbs, veg and chill-out spots.
In fact there's even a shower in the garden
if the day gets too hot. Backpacker discount,
bike hire and meals can be arranged.
Recommended.

C La Mansión de Virginia, C 8, No 7-26, T726
7170. Impeccable colonial house with rooms
set around a lovely courtyard. Has fine,
comfortable beds and private baths with hot
water. Breakfast included. Recommended.

C La Posada de Pablo 2, C 3, No 7-30,
T726 7719. One of several places belonging
to 'Pablo' in town. This one is next to the
Iglesia de Jesús Resucitado and a gorgeo
us park. Has TV and good beds. Try for rooms
10 or 11, which have exquisite views across
the rooftops to the cathedral. Another Pablo
is at Cra 7 3-50.

E Los Tiestecitos, Cra 5, No 7-62, T726 7224.
The only real budget option in town – but
it's a good one. Run by a couple of old ladies,
you almost have to fight your way through
a profusion of plants to reach your room.
Clean rooms, own bath and comfortable
beds. Also doubles as an *artesanías* shop
selling ceramics.

   Camping Just outside Barichara on
the road to San Gil is **La Chorrera**, a natural
swimming pool, T726 7422, US$0.30 to
bathe, US$1.60 to camp, meals by
arrangement, clean, attractive.

Guane *p115*
Guane has 2 delightful and economical
hostels to stay in, both highly recommended.
D Posada Mi Tierra Guane, Parque Principal,
opposite museum, T310-488 4378, hildaui@
hotmail.com. Run by a nice woman, this small
6-room hostel is comfortable and charming
with a pleasant courtyard and private
bathrooms. Some rooms have bunk beds.
D Shia Shue, C Real, T724 7753. Just off the
plaza. Fine, comfortable rooms with private
baths in a colonial house.

Bucaramanga *p116, map p117*
Since Bucaramanga has numerous
national conventions, it is sometimes
hard to find a room in more expensive
hotels, especially mid-week.

AL Chicamocha, C 34, No 31-24, T634 3000,
www.hotelchicamocha.com. Large hotel
near the Zona Rosa. Has a pool, sauna,
gym, spa and Wi-Fi throughout, as well as
2 restaurants and 2 bars.

A Guane, C 34, No 22-72, T634 7014,
www.hotelguane.com. Smart hotel with
large rooms that include reception areas. Has
a pool, gym and solarium. Breakfast included.

A-B Asturias, Cra 22, No 35-01, T635 1914,
www.ciudadbonita.com. Rooms are set
around a sunny atrium and vary in quality
Includes American breakfast in price and
has a pizza restaurant attached. Guests can
use next door swimming pool at La Ciudad
Bonita for free.

B El Pilar, C 34, No 24-09, T634 7207. Good
rooms and lots of extras: private parking,
an internet room, Wi-Fi, restaurant and
accident insurance. Cheaper with fan.

B Ruitoque, Cra 19, No 37-26, T633 4567,
www.hotelruitoque.com. From the outside
it may not be much to look at, but it's been
recently refurbished, has good-sized, clean
rooms with tiled bathrooms, a restaurant, Wi-Fi
and is just a block from Parque Santander.

D Balmoral, Cra 21/C 35, T630 3723. A good
budget option with clean rooms, cable TV,
internet room, hot water, bar and jacuzzi.
Also conveniently situated a block from
Parque Santander. Its downside is that
street-facing rooms are noisy while back
rooms have no windows and can be stuffy.

D Colonial Plaza, C 33, No 20-46, T645 4125.
It's certainly not colonial, but the rooms are
clean, it has hot water and Wi-Fi throughout.
Slightly cheaper with fan. Friendly place, but
take care in the nearby park even during the
day. Ask for a room at the back, away from
the street, as these are much quieter.

D Kasa Guane, C 49, No 28-21, T657 6960,
www.kasaguane.com. This backpackers'
hostel is the best budget option in town.

Owned by paragliding instructor Richi Mantilla of Colombia Paragliding, it's decorated with Guane culture artefacts and has several private rooms as well as dorms with bunks. Additional services include internet, a kitchen for use by guests, table games, a pool table and good information on the local area.

F Hotel Carolina, Cra 18, No 30-56, T680 2225. Good value at the price. Rooms are simple but clean and it offers laundry service. The area, nicknamed the Zona Roja, although somewhat improved can still be dangerous; be careful at night.

Girón p119

B-D Girón Chill Out, Cra 25, No 32-06, T646 1119, www.gironchillout.com. This Italian-owned hostel has 7 private rooms in a colonial house with high ceilings. As well as Wi-Fi, cable TV and use of a washing machine, there is also a kitchen for use by guests, though you might be tempted by the excellent restaurant serving Italian food with ingredients imported from the mother country, also owned by the hostel, on the corner of the same street.

D-E Hotel Las Nieves, C 30, No 25-71, T681 2951, www.hotellasnievesgiron.com. Colonial buidling on the main plaza, large rooms, TV and hot water. Street-facing rooms have balconies, Wi-Fi, good value restaurant. Much cheaper with fan.

🍴 Eating

San Gil p111, map p112

San Gil has a number of good eating options but it should be noted that here, as in much of this region, it is difficult to find places open in the evening.

The market on Cra 11 between C 13 and 14 is another great breakfast and lunch spot with lots of stalls selling fruit salads and juices. If you don't have a sweet tooth be sure to ask them to lay off the condensed milk and cheese on your salad.

Can get a bit chaotic at weekends, so watch your pockets.

♆♆ Gringo Mike's, C 12 No 8-40, T724 1695, US/British-run sandwich shop, with some lovely Mexican influences. Open evenings only Thu-Tue. Also runs bike tours (see page 124). Friendly staff and good nosh. Recommended.

♆ Donde Betty, Cra 9, C 12 esquina. Great little breakfast spot selling *arepas*, scrambled eggs and fruit juices. On the corner of the Parque Principal, hence an excellent place for people-watching, unless they bring the sun blinds right down to street level, which they frequently do in the afternoons.

♆ El Maná, C 10, No 9-49. It would be difficult to leave this restaurant without feeling a little bloated what with the many set menu courses you get for less than US$5. Try the chicken stuffed with ham and cheese. Open at lunchtime and evenings except Mon.

♆ Pizzería Pierrot, Cra 9, No 9-104. The best pizzas in town. Open in the evenings and does home delivery.

♆ Rogelia, Cra 10, No 8-08. Great little lunchtime place in a colonial building with large wooden beams. Serves local specialities such as *cabrito con pepitorio* and *carne oreada* (a bit like beef jerky). *Menú ejecutivo* US$3.

♆ Saludable Delicia, C 11, No 8-40. Excellent vegetarian restaurant with a wide choice of options including pumpkin soup, veggie burgers and *frijoles en salsa*. Also has many honey, nut and cereal products for sale. Closed Sat.

The **Centro Comercial Camino Real**, Cra 9 11-68 has several nice bars and eateries – **Santa Lucía** on the ground floor and **Habana** upstairs are 2 good places.

Barichara p114, map p114

♆♆ Color de Hormiga, C 8, No 8-44. If you visit only 1 restaurant in Santander it should be this one. Billing itself as 'atypical' food, **Color de Hormiga** specializes in all things ant; the *hormiga culona* is a large-winged ant often eaten as a snack in the region. Here, the chefs have taken this to another level with

...ne steaks or chicken served in ant sauce. What's more, the restaurant's setting – on a terrace with a pretty garden and views onto the town below – is a delight.

La Puerta, C 6 8-51, T7267649. Spanish cuisine. Book in advance. Dinner until 2030 or 2130 on Sat.

El Compá, C 5, No 4-48. Family-run restaurant serving typical regional food, including *sobrebarriga* and *arepa santandereana*.

Guane *p115*

There are 3 good restaurants on the plaza all serving typical regional food.

Guayubi, to the left of the museum as you face it. Goat is a bit of a speciality as is the *chicha de maíz*, a mild alcoholic drink made from corn masticated by the local women.

Bucaramanga *p116, map p117*

Try the *hormigas culonas* (large-bottomed black ants), a local delicacy mainly eaten during Holy Week (mostly sold in shops, but occasionally in restaurants and also sold on main highways in Santander at that time).

La Carreta, Cra 27, No 42-27. Established by local football legend Roberto Pablo Janiot nearly 50 years ago, this very swish colonial building has been tastefully restored. *Parrillas* and seafood can be enjoyed around a courtyard of sculpted gardens and water features.

Mercagán, C 45, No 33-47. The large photograph of a cow on the menu immediately tells you that this place is not for vegetarians. Steaks and hamburgers are the order of the day. Fine setting opposite the beautiful Parque San Pío.

DiMarco, C 28, No 54-21. Top-notch steaks in pleasant surroundings.

El Viejo Chiflas, Cra 33, No 34 esq. Good restaurant in the heart of the Zona Rosa. Try the *cabrito* (goat), a local speciality.

La 22, Cra 22, No 45-18. So popular is this local canteen that at weekends you will struggle to be seated. Paella and *sancocho* are some of their specialities. Also does a roaring trade in takeaways and home deliveries – very busy.

Los Kioskos, C 45, No 22-45. Los Kioskos consists of a series of thatched huts festooned with plants. Menu of regional food. There are often live *vallenato* bands to help you digest.

Los Tejaditos, C 34 27-82. Popular with locals, with a varied menu of meats, seafood, pastas and salads.

La Pamplonesa, C 35, No 18-29. Just off Parque Santander, this *panadería* does good breakfasts as well as sandwiches, cakes and fruit juices. For local sweets and delicacies, try Alba, Cra 10, No 41-01, a family-run *dulcería* more than 100 years old. It's so sweet you have to battle with a hive of bees that swarm around the shop.

Tony's, Cra 33A-67 Not satisfied with their enormous breakfasts and lunches, *bumangueses* like to fit in an extra meal in between known as *onces* (elevenses). Tony's caters for them all. Good *tamales* and *arepas*. Popular with families.

Bars and clubs

Bucaramanga *p116, map p117*

When they want to party, most *bumangueses* head for the Zona Rosa in the eastern end of town, where many bars and clubs will jostle for your attention. **El Venado de Oro**, **Garibaldi** and **El Sombrero**, on Cra 33, all have live mariachi bands. In fact Cra 33 between C 37 and 39 is known as **Calle de los Marachis**, but there is also plenty of other bars and music to be enjoyed. **Moe's Bar**, **Saxo** and **Joy's Gourmet** are all in the same street.

Festivals and events

Bucaramanga *p116, map p117*

Sep The annual international piano festival is held in the Auditorio Luis A Calvo at the Universidad Industrial de Santander, one of the finest concert halls in Colombia. The university is worth a visit for the beautiful grounds.

Mar Feria de Artesanías (Handicraft Fair) at the Centro de Exposiciones y Ferias (CENFER).

O Shopping

San Gil *p111, map p112*
Armando Palitos, Cra 11, No 9-44, T724 3345. Excellent selection of *artesanías*, ranging from furniture and plates to *bolsos de fique* (woven bags).

Baricha *p114, map p114*
Artes y Variedades, C 6, No 7-40. Lots of locally made handicrafts, including *sandalias de fique* (woven sandels).
Tierrarte, C 6, No 7-81. Fine leather products such as belts and bags, as well as beautiful jewellery. Credit cards accepted. Also has shops in San Gil and Bucaramanga.

Bucaramanga *p116, map p117*
Camping equipment
Acampemos, C 48, No 24-70, open Mon-Sat, last place in Colombia to get camping-gas cartridges before Venezuela.

Handicrafts
Try **Bosque**, near the Parque García Rovira, C 36, No 12-58, www.bosquedecoracion.com, or opposite the market in barrio Guarin, C 33A, No 33-23. Also try **Girón** (see below) and typical clothing upstairs in the food market, C 34 y Cras 15-16. Similar articles (*ruanas*, hats) in San Andresito.

▲ Activities and tours

San Gil *p111, map p112*
Adventure sports companies
Colombia Rafting Expeditions, Cra 10, No 7-83, T311-283 8647, www.colombiarafting.com. The best for rafting, with

International Rafting Federation-qualified guides. Also does hydrospeed.
Exploracion Colombia Guides, C 8, No 10-38, T723 8080, exploracol@hotmail.com. Offers paragliding, whitewater rafting, canyoning and caving.
Páramo Santander Extremo, Parque Principal, Cra 4 No 4-57, Páramo, T725 8944, www.paramosantanderextremo.com. Based in nearby Páramo, this company is best for abseiling and canyoning but also does caving, rafting and horse riding.

Cycling
Hire bikes for US$1 per hour from **El Ring**, C 7, No 10-14, T243189, or try at the **Macondo Guesthouse** (see Sleeping).
Gringo Mike's Bike Tours (see also Eating, above), www.gringomikes.net. Downhill mountain bike tours in the San Gil area, including a visit to goat farm or the Chicamocha Canyon.

Bucaramanga *p116, map p117*
There are opportunities for parapenting at the nearby Mesa del Ruitoque and over the Cañón de Chicamocha, to the south of the city. Good schools are **Las Aguilas**, Km 2 vía Mesa de Ruitoque, Floridablanca, T678 6257, www.voladerolasaguilas.com.co, and **Colombia Paragliding**, T312-432 6266, www.colombiaparagliding.com, which also has a hostel, where you can stay while you take lessons.

⊖ Transport

San Gil *p111, map p112*
Bus
Bus station 5 mins out of town by taxi on road to Tunja, the bus terminal for local destinations is on Cra 11 with C 15. To **Bogotá**, US$19. To **Bucaramanga**, US$6, 2½ hrs. To **Baricha** from C 12, US$1.90, 45 mins, every 30 mins, taxi US$5. To **Bucaramanga**, Cotransangil has regular

buses throughout the day, 2½ hrs. Sit on the right, or as these are mostly minibuses, in front next to the driver, for beautiful views of the Chicamocha Canyon. For Villa de Leiva leave for Tunja by 1400 to catch the last onward minibus.

Baricha *p114, map p114*
To **San Gil**, every 30 mins from early morning, **Cotransangil**, 45 mins, US$1.90. To **Guane**, frequent, US$0.85.

Bucaramanga *p116, map p117*
Air
To **Bogotá**, several flights a day with **Avianca** and **Aires**. To **Cúcuta** 2 daily with **Satena** and **Aires**. To **Medellín** 2 daily with **Satena** and 1 with **Aires**.
    Airlines offices **Avianca**, C 52 No 35A-10, T657 3888. **Aires**, Cra 34 No 42-29, T632 3938. **Satena**, C 36, No 15-56, T670 7087.

Bus
The bus station is several miles outside the town. You can book tickets to all destinations here. Call T637 1000, www.terminalbucara manga.com, and you will be connected to all relevant bus companies. To **Bogotá**, 8-11 hrs, US$30 (Pullman) with **Berlinas del Fonce** (C 53, No 20-40, T630 4468, www.berlinasdel fonce.com, or at bus terminal), at 0845, 1400, 1530, 1830, 2010, 2105, 2210 and 2245; with **Copetran**, www.copetran.com.co, US$25, frequent services day and night (this journey is uncomfortable, there are no relief stops, and it starts off hot and ends cold in the mountains, be prepared) To **Barranquilla**, 13 hrs, 1 departure daily 2100, US$55 with **Berlinas**. To **Cartagena**, US$42.50, 14 hrs, with **Copetran**, frequent services from 0800 until midnight, or 1 with **Berlinas** 2100, US$56, 12 hrs. To **Santa Marta**, 11 hrs, US$32.50, 0930, 2030 and 2200 with **Copetran** or **Berlinas** 2230. To **Valledupar**,

10 hrs, US$30 with **Copetran**, 9 a day.
To **El Banco** on the Río Magdalena, US$28, 7 hrs, several companies, direct or change at Aguachica, this journey should be made in daylight. To **Barrancabermeja**, 2 hrs, US$9, a scenic ride with 1 rest stop, this road is paved. Hourly buses to **San Gil**, 2½ hrs, US$10. To **Tunja**, 7½ hrs, US$40. To **Berlín**, US$6. To **Pamplona**, 3 a day, US$5 (Pullman), US$11.50 (Berlinas, 4 daily). To **Cúcuta**, 6 hrs, US$20.50 with Berlinas, 4 daily, *colectivo* US$22. The trip to Cúcuta is spectacular in the region of Berlín. Other companies with local services to nearby villages on back roads, eg the colourful folk art buses of **Flota Cáchira** (C 32, Cra 33-34), which go north and east.

❶ Directory

San Gil *p111, map p112*
Internet There are countless internet cafés dotted around the town. **Cofee em@il**, C 13, No 9-78, has Skype and headphones.

Bucaramanga *p116, map p117*
Banks HSBC, Cra 19, No 36-41. BBVA, C 35, No 18-02. **Bancafé**, C 35, No 16-20, Visa agents. **Bancolombia**, by Parque Santander, will cash Thomas Cook and Amex TCs, long queues (cheques and passports have to be photocopied). Many other banks, many with ATMs. **Internet** Setelco, Cra 27, No 19-15. Inter-Mega, Cra 29, No 32-58. **Colombia On Line**, C 13, No 29-16. There is free Wi-Fi in all of Bucaramanga's *parques* and in many of the shopping centres, but beware that not all parks are safe and exercise caution.
Money exchange Exprit, C 52, No 31-153, T657 7747. **Cambiamos**, Centro Comercial Cabecera, Level IV, local 104, Cra 35A con C 49. **Post** Servientrega, Cra 30 No 13A-18.

Norte de Santander Department

The border between Santander and Norte de Santander departments is at the high pass near Berlín. From there the Cordillera Oriental slowly reduces in height to become a ridge, now the border with Venezuela, ending at the peninsula of La Guajira and the Caribbean Sea. A spur however, turns northeast, crosses the border at the Tamá National Park to become the Sierra Nevada de Mérida, the highest mountains of Venezuela. The northeast of the department is down in the Maracaibo basin, the hottest place in South America. This border country with Venezuela was intimately linked with the Wars of Independence, and with Bolívar and Santander. Parts of Norte de Santander, particularly along the Venezuelan border, still have some guerrilla activity. Pamplona and Cúcuta are mostly safe but travellers should take advice before venturing into any other areas of the department. ➤➤ *For listings, see pages 130-133.*

Pamplona → *For listings, see pages 130-133. Colour map 2, A6. Phone code: 7. Population: 68,000. Altitude: 2200 m.*

Pamplona, set in a green valley and surrounded by mountains, is a more than worthwhile stopover between Bucaramanga and Cúcuta. It was founded in 1549 by Pedro de Orsúa and Ortún Velasco. During the colonial era it was as important as Bogotá. The Independence movement was started here in 1810 by Agueda Gallardo. It became important as a mining town but is now better known for its university – students make up almost 40% of the population. While an 1875 earthquake destroyed large sections of the town it still manages to retain a certain colonial atmosphere. At 2200 m, it can get cold, especially at night when a jumper or even a coat is required.

Tourist office Oficina de Turismo Pamplona ⓘ *C 5, No 6-45, T568 2880*, next to the *alcaldía*, off Plaza Central, is very helpful and friendly, and organizes tours into surrounding area and guides for hiking in hills.

Sights

The severe earthquake of 1875 played havoc with the monasteries and some of the churches. There is now a hotel on the site of the former San Agustín monastery, but it is still possible to visit the remains of the ex-monasteries of **San Francisco** and **Santo Domingo**. The **cathedral** is in the spacious **Plaza Central** (Plaza Agueda Gallardo), a massive building with five naves. It dates from the 17th century but has been damaged by earthquakes and rebuilt over the years. The **Iglesia del Humilladero**, adjoining the cemetery and also dating from the 17th century, is very picturesque and allows a fine view of the city. The sculpture *Cristo del Humilladero* came from Spain. In September, there is an annual festival celebrating the *Humilladero*.

Museo de Arte Religioso ⓘ *C 4/Cra 5, Mon-Fri 0800-1200, 1400-1800; Sat 0800-1200, US$0.50*, is a collection from the region and has paintings by many Colombians including Vázquez de Arce y Ceballos. The fine **Casa Colonial** ⓘ *C 6, No 2-56, Mon-Fri 0800-1200, 1400-1800, US$1*, is now an archaeological museum. It's a little gem, with artefacts from the Motilones and other indigenous communities still living in the north of the department.

Casa Anzoátegui ⓘ *Cra 6, No 7-48, Mon-Sat 0900-1200, 1400-1730, US$1*, is where one of Bolívar's generals, José Antonio Anzoátegui, died in 1819, at the age of 30, after the Battle of Boyacá. The state in northeast Venezuela is named after him. The restored

Simón Bolívar

Aside from Columbus, no single man has had a greater influence on South American history than Simón Bolívar. This Venezuelan aristocrat galvanized the many factions of the continent into a united army that succeeded in expelling the Spanish from present-day Colombia, Venezuela, Panama, Ecuador, Peru and Bolivia.

His campaign through the Departments of Norte de Santander, Santander and Boyacá remains one of his greatest achievements.

In May 1819, Bolívar marched into Colombia from Venezuela with a force of 2000 men, meeting with Santander's forces at Tame and proposing to cross the Andes by the rarely used route across the Páramo de Pisba, a barren, windswept section of the Cordillera Oriental, the lowest pass of which was over 3200 m.

There were many deaths and few of his 800 horses survived, but the audacious manoeuvre surprised the Spanish. The armies met near Paipa and Bolívar's troops inflicted a surprise defeat.

On 6 August, Bolívar marched into Tunja, but his route to the capital was blocked by the royalists at a bridge crossing the Río Boyacá, 16 km to the south. Despite the strength of their position, the Spanish were routed at the first attack and disintegrated. Over 1600 prisoners were taken and four days later, Bolívar entered Bogotá as the liberator of Colombia.

Two years later the First Congress of Gran Colombia met at Cúcuta on 6 May 1821. It was at this meeting that the plan to unite Venezuela, Colombia and Ecuador was ratified, the pinnacle of Bolívar's career.

colonial house is now a museum covering the Independence period. The **Museo de Arte Moderno** ⓘ *C 5 on the Parque Central, Mon-Sat 0900-0000, 1400-1730, Sun 1200-1400, US$0.80*, principally exhibits the paintings and sculptures of Eduardo Ramírez Villamizar of Pamplona, who died in 2004. The colonial building is a notable local example and was declared a National Monument in 1975. Next to the Iglesia del Humilladero is the **Museo de Fotografía Antigua de Toto** ⓘ *Cra 7, No 2-36, open 'whenever possible', free*. Toto was the local undertaker and a prolific artist. The exhibition consists of hundreds of photographs sent in by the citizens of Pamplona, some dating back to the early 20th century and makes for a fascinating archive of local history. Sadly, Toto passed away but the space is maintained by some of his ten sons.

Around Pamplona

Tamá National Park covers the point at which the Cordillera Oriental continues across into Venezuela, where there is also a national park. It is high, rising to the Páramo de Santa Isabel with several sections above 3400 m, and extending over 48,000 ha. Access is from Herrán. From here take the minor road to El Tabor, cross the Río Táchira into Venezuela and go south through Villa Paéz-Betanía to Palmazola, where you cross back into Colombia, with about 30 minutes to Orocué and the administrative centre of the park.

There is comparatively heavy rainfall (over 3000 mm per year on the lower slopes) which, combined with a wide range of altitudes, produces a full set of forest habitats from jungle to high temperate woodland and *páramo* (moorland), with a vast variety of flora and fauna, including anteaters, deer and spectacled bears. It is reported that a waterfall has recently been discovered in the park about 820 m high. If this proves to be true, this would place the falls as the third or fourth highest in the world. Pamplona is surrounded by a number of rivers and lakes, including Laguna de Cácota and Laguna Camagueta, all within an hour's drive. Trips to the villages of Pamplonita, famous for flower cultivation, and Mutiscua, renowned for its trout farms, are also easily organized from Pamplona. Ask at tourist office next to *alcaldía* for details.

Cúcuta → *For listings, see pages 130-133. Colour map 2, A6. Phone code: 7. Population: 918,000. Altitude: 325 m.*

Cúcuta, capital of the Department of Norte de Santander, is only 16 km from the Venezuelan frontier. For a border town, it is a surprisingly pleasant place to visit, with plenty of green spaces and a bustling but non-threatening centre. It was founded in 1733 by Juana Rangel, severely damaged by the earthquake in 1875, and then elegantly rebuilt, with the streets shaded by trees. Anyone spending more than five minutes here will appreciate this latter fact, for Cúcuta is one hot place: the mean temperature is 29°C. It also lays claim to being one of the few cities in the world with a street grid system that begins at 0, as in Avenida 0.

Cúcuta

Sleeping
Arizona Suites 1
Bolívar 2
Casa Blanca 3
Cavalier 4
Hotel de la Paz 5
Lady Di 6
Lord 7
República Bolivariana 8
Tonchalá 9

Eating
La Embajada Antioqueña 1
La Mazorca 2
Londero's Sur 3
Pinchos & Asados 4
Rodizio 5
Venezia 6

400 metres
400 yards

Border essentials: Colombia–Venezuela

Cúcuta–San Antonio

Colombian immigration Exit and entry formalities are handled at the DAS office in the white house before the international border bridge. DAS also has an office at the airport, which will deal with land travellers. If you do not obtain an exit stamp, you will be turned back by Venezuelan officials and the next time you enter Colombia, you will be fined. The DAS office in town is at Avenida Primera, No 28-53, T572 0033, and is open daily 0800-1130, 1400-1700. Take a bus from the city centre to Barrio San Rafael, southwards towards the road to Pamplona. Shared taxi from border US$3, will wait for formalities, then US$1 to bus station.

Entering Colombia by air All Colombian formalities can be undertaken at the airport. Visitors arriving by air may not need a visa: unfortunately, there are no local flights from Cúcuta to San Antonio or to Santo Domingo (San Cristóbal), the two nearby Venezuelan airports. In 2008, flights were suspended between San Antonio and Caracas and San Cristóbal and Caracas, but these have since reopened. Border relations vary frequently.

Entering Colombia by road You must obtain both a Venezuelan exit stamp and a Colombian entry stamp at the border. Without the former you will be sent back; without the latter you will have problems with police checks, banks and leaving the country. You can also be fined.

Leaving Colombia by private vehicle With all the right papers, the border crossing is easy and traffic normally flows smoothly.

Colombian customs Aduana office on the road to the airport (small sign); has a restaurant.

Entering Venezuela Passports must be stamped with an exit stamp at the white DAS building before the border crossing. If not you will have to return later to complete formalities. Expect very long queues. **Venezuelan consulate**, Avenida Camilo Daza con, Calle 7, T579 1954/579 1951, is open Monday-Friday 0800-1300. Car papers must be stamped at the SENIAT office in Venezuela.

Transport Bus to San Cristóbal, US$1.40 (**Bolivariano**), *colectivo* US$3; to San Antonio, taxi US$8, bus and *colectivo* from Calle 7, Avenida 4/5. From Cúcuta to or beyond, go to San Antonio or (better) San Cristóbal and change. On any form of transport which is crossing the border, make sure that the driver knows that you need to stop to obtain exit/entry stamps, etc.

Note There is a 30-minute time difference between Colombia and Venezuela.

Ins and outs

The **airport** is 5 km north of the centre, 15 minutes by taxi from the town and the border, US$4, US$10 at night, US$10 to border. Buses from Avenida 3 take rather longer. The notorious **bus station** is on Avenida 7 and Calle 0 (a really rough area). There is a private bus station belonging to Copetran on Avenida Camilo Daza, via Aeropuerto. Taxi from bus station to town centre, US$2.40. The new **Berlinas del Fonce** terminal is much safer; it is 2 km beyond the main terminal along continuation of Diagonal Santander. For more details, see page 132. **Note** Cúcuta and the surrounding area is a great centre for smuggling. Be careful.

Tourist information

Corporación Mixta de Promoción de Norte de Santander ① *C 10, No 0-30, Edif Roseta* T5718981, www.cucutaturistica.com, is helpful and has maps and brochures. Other maps are obtainable from Instituto Geográfico, Banco de la República building, in the main plaza.

Sights

The **Catedral de San José** ① *Av 5 between C 10/11*, is worth a visit. Note the oil painting by Salvador Moreno. The **Casa de la Cultura** ① *C 13, No 3-67*, also incorporates the **Museo del la Ciudad**, which covers the history of a city very much involved with the Independence movement. The **international bridge** between Colombia and Venezuela is southeast of the city. Just beyond it is San Antonio del Táchira, the first Venezuelan town, and 55 km on is San Cristóbal.

Around Cúcuta

Just short of the border is the small town of **Villa del Rosario**, where the Congress that agreed the constitution of Gran Colombia in the autumn of 1821 met. This was one of the high points of the career of Simón Bolívar. The actual spot where the documents were signed is now a park beside which is the **Templo del Congreso**, where the preliminary meetings took place. Formerly a church, it was severely damaged in the 1875 earthquake and only the dome has been reconstructed.

Also nearby is the **Casa de Santander** ① *daily 0800-1200 and 1400-1800*, where General Francisco de Paula Santander, to whom Bolívar entrusted the administration of the new Gran Colombia in 1821, was born in 1792 and spent his childhood. It became a National Monument in 1959 and a museum in 1971 dedicated to the period of the Independence campaigns and the contribution made then and later by General Santander.

◉ Norte de Santander Department listings → *Phone code: 7.*

For Sleeping and Eating price codes and other relevant information, see pages 23-28.

● Sleeping

Pamplona *p126*
Hotel accommodation may be hard to find at weekends, when Venezuelans visit the town.

Pamplona is famous for its bread: there's a *panadería* on practically every corner. Particularly well known are **Panadería Chávez**, Cra 6, No 7-36 and **Panadería Araque**. Try *pastel de horno*, *queso de hoja*, *pan de agua* or *cuca*, a kind of black ginger biscuit often topped with cheese. Pamplona even hosts a *cuca* festival in Sep/Oct each year.
A-B El Solar, C 5, No 8-10, T568 2010, www.elsolarhotel.com. Beautifully restored colonial building dating from 1776. Rooms upstairs are enormous and have their own kitchen and balconies looking onto the street. Rooms downstairs, without kitchen, are cheaper. Also has by far the best restaurant in town (see Eating, below).
B 1549 Hostal, C 8B, No 5-84, T568 0451, www.1549hostal.com. Another recent, lovingly restored colonial building. Rooms are light and airy and decorated with great taste by owners Ricardo and Kokis. Wi-Fi throughout. There is also a coffee bar and *panadería* in a large courtyard out back. Highly recommended.
B Cariongo, Cra 5/C 9, Plazuela Almeyda, T568 1515, www.cariongoplazahotel.com. A 1960s building that has seen better days, this was the best option in town until the opening of El Solar and 1549 Hostel. A newer annex out back has comfortable rooms and a garden with playground but lacks character. Wi-Fi in lobby.

-E Orsúa, C 5, No 5-67, T568 2470.
robably the best budget option in town.
rumbling but characterful building east
ide of plaza central. Friendly owner and
ood restaurant. Rooms are cheaper if
hey don't look onto plaza.

Imperial, Cra 5, No 5-36, T568 2571.
arge modern building on the plaza central
vith a youth hostel vibe. Rooms are a little
rubby but staff are friendly. Cable TV and
ot water.

Santa Clara, Cra 6, No 7-21, T568 4105.
lambling buidling in need of some tender
oving care but is easy on the eye in a
lilapidated sort of way and has hot
vater and a restaurant.

Cúcuta p128, map p128

-AL Tonchalá, C 10/Av 0, T575 6444,
www.hoteltonchala.com. A bit of an eyesore
rom the outside, the Tonchalá nevertheless
has friendly, professional staff and lots of
added extras including a large pool, a spa
and beauty parlour an internet room and
Wi-Fi throughout. Breakfast included in price.

AL Arizona Suites, Av 0, No 7-62, T573 1884,
www.hotelarizona-suites.com. Centrally
placed, the Arizona has all the mod cons
including Wi-Fi, safety boxes and a
restaurant serving Italian food.

AL-A Bolívar, Av Demetrio Mendoza, Barrio
San Luis, T576 0764, www.hotel-bolivar.com.
On the outskirts of town on the airport road,
the Bolívar is an old colonial building with
rooms in a series of modern bungalows set
around peaceful gardens and 2 swimming
pools. With a paddling pool and playground,
it's ideal for children.

A Casa Blanca, Av 6, No 14-55, T572 2888,
www.hotelcasablanca.com.co. The reception
area of the Casa Blanca looks kind of grand
with lots of glass and freshly painted white
walls. The back, where the rooms are, has
also had a recent facelift. The rooms are clean
and there is a large pool and a restaurant
serving regional and international food.
Only hot water in the suites, which are
more expensive.

B Lord, Av 7, No 10-58, T571 3609. On a
busy street lined with stalls and opposite
a shopping centre, the rooms are light
and airy and it offers parking and laundry
service. Cheaper with fan.

C Cavalier, Diagonal Santander C 6, No 1-28,
T583 0134. Basic but clean. Has a/c and offers
laundry service.

D Hotel de la Paz, C 6, No 3-48, T571 8002.
Rooms are basic but at this price this hotel
is recommended for having a pool and the
delicious La Embajada Antioqueña
restaurant next door (same address).

D Lady Di, Av 7, No 13-80, T583 1922. With
an enormous photo of Princess Diana above
the doorway, you know this hotel will be
kitsch but kind of fun. More photos feature
throughout. The rooms are clean but basic.

D República Bolivariana, Av 6, No 11-77,
T571 8099. Well placed near Parque
Santander, this hotel is dedicated to Simón
Bolívar and features lots of murals of the
Liberator. Rooms are cheaper with fan.

❶ Eating

Pamplona p126

¶¶ **Delicias del Mar**, C 6, No 7-60, T568 4558.
Popular lunchtime venue specializing in fish,
particularly *robalo* and trout.

¶¶ **El Portón Pamplonés**, C 5, No 7-83.
Specializes in locally caught trout and
other fish.

¶¶ **El Solar**, C 5, No 8-10 (see Sleeping).
By far the best in town. High-quality fare
served in the peaceful courtyard of this
colonial hotel. Try the side of pork in
honey. Highly recommended.

¶¶ **La Casona**, C 6, No 7-58, T568 3555.
Another local favourite serving meats
and seafood. Try the *paella valenciana*.

¶¶ **Piero's Pizza**, C 9 / Cra 5. Pizzas cooked
by an Italian family. Authentic.

¶ **Calle Real Restaurante**, Cra 6, No 7-60.
Family home that serves up a decent
lunchtime *menú ejecutivo*.

¶ El Arriero, C 6, No 7-18. Quirky little place serving basic fare.

Cúcuta *p128, map p128*
¶¶-¶¶ Rodizio, Av Libertadores, No 10-121, Malecon II Etapa, T575 0095. Boasts 13 different types of meat as well as seafood. Sometimes has live music.
¶¶ La Embajada Antioqueña, C 6, No 3-48, T5731874. Local and Antioquian food in a fine open-air setting.
¶¶ Londero's Sur, Av Libertadores, No 0E-60, T583 3335, Argentine grill serving *parrillas*, *empanadas*, ceviche and much more.
¶ La Mazorca, Av 4, No 9-67, T571 2833. More *comida criolla* served in a pleasant courtyard decorated with hanging baskets and Antioquian paraphernalia. *Menú ejecutivo* US$3.50.
¶ Pinchos & Asados, Av Libertadores, No 10-121, next to **Rodizio**, delightful setting on a terrace overlooking landscaped wooded gardens, delicious *brochettes*.
¶ Venezia, Condominio La Riviera, Av Libertadores, T575 0006. Oven-fired pizzas.
    Lots of fastfood outlets on the 3rd level of the spanking new Centro Comercial Ventura Plaza, C 10 y 11 Diagonal Santander.

⊛ Festivals and events

Pamplona *p126*
Easter The town's Easter celebrations are famous throughout Colombia, with processions, and cultural presentations.
4 Jul Pamplona was the first town in Colombia to declare Independence from the Spanish, a fact that is celebrated with bullfights, music concerts and art exhibitions.
14 Sep Dia del Señor del Humilladero is celebrated by *pamploneses*.
Oct Festival de la Cuca, local bakers compete to produce the tastiest ginger biscuit.
1 Nov Concerts and exhibitions are held to celebrate the foundation of the town.

⦿ Shopping

Pamplona *p126*
Pamplona is a great place to buy *ruanas*. There is a good indoor market 1 block west of the Plaza Central on C 6 (C del Mercado).

Cúcuta *p128, map p128*
Try C 10, Av 8 for leather boots and shoes.
Centro Comercial Ventura Plaza, C 10 y 11 Diagonal Santander, has plenty of international brand shops, as well as *artesanías*.
Cuchitríl, Av 3 No 9-89, has a selection of the better Colombian craftwork.
    Also try **Aquí Colombia**, C 10, No 1-46 or **Artesanías Franco**, Cra 7, No 5-10, Villa del Rosario.

⊖ Transport

Pamplona *p126*
Bus
To **Bogotá**, US$32.50, 13 hrs, 9 daily with Berlinas del Fonce. To **Cúcuta**, frequent, US$4-6, 2½ hrs. To **Bucaramanga**, frequent, US$11.50, 4-5 hrs, great views. To **Málaga** from plaza central, 5 daily from 0800, 6 hrs, US$5. To **Berlín**, US$5. Buy tickets only at the official office upstairs. Do not accept help from 'intermediaries'. You can also take *colectivos* or shared taxis to **Bucaramanga** (US$14) and **Cúcuta** (US$6.50), which usually cuts the journey by 1 hr and includes door-to-door pick up and delivery. Try **Cooptmotilon** on the north west corner of Plaza Central, C 5, T680 291.

Cúcuta *p128, map p128*
Air
There are only domestic flights from Cúcuta airport. For flights to Venezuelan destinations you must cross the border and fly from San Antonio airport. **Note** Do not buy 'airline tickets' from Cúcuta to Venezuelan destinations. All flights go from San Antonio. Flights to **Bogotá**, Aires has several daily, **Avianca** has 5 a day. To **Barranquilla**, 3 daily,

via Bogotá **Avianca**. To **Bucaramanga**, a day, **Aires**, also indirect flights with vianca. To **Medellín**, 2 daily, **Avianca** nd **Aires**.

Airline offices Avianca, Av 0, No 13-84, 571 6151 and at airport, T587 4884, www.avianca.com. **Aires**, Av 1E, No 18-12, os Caobos, T583 3941, www.aires.aero.

us

o **Bogotá**, hourly, 15-17 hrs, US$35, with erlinas del Fonce, 9 a day and US$30, 5 a ay with **Copetran**, both of whom have their wn terminals (see Ins and outs), making stops, 1 of which is **Bucaramanga**. There re frequent buses, even during the night f the bus you take arrives in the dark, sit n the bus station café until it is light).

o **Cartagena**, with Copetran, 4 a day at 500, 1400, 1600 and 1730, with Berlinas, a day, 1330, 16-19 hrs, US$50-70. To **Bucaramanga**, US$12.50, 6 hrs, with Copetrán and Berlinas del Fonce Pullman, ourly. There are good roads to **Caracas** (933 m direct or 1046 km via Mérida), and to **Maracaibo** (571 km). Bus to Caracas, 15 hrs, US$30, **Expreso Occidente**, or taxi *colectivo*.

Warning Travellers have been reporting or years that the bus station is overrun with hieves and con-men, who have tried every rick in the book. This is still true. You must ake great care, there is little or no police protection. On the 1st floor there is a tourist office for help and information and a café/snack bar where you can wait in comparative safety. Alternatively, go straight to a bus going in your direction, get on it, pay the driver and don't let your belongings out of your sight. Don't put your valuables in bus company 'safety boxes'. Make sure tickets are for buses that exist;

tickets do not need to be 'stamped for validity'. For San Cristóbal, only pay the driver of the vehicle, not at the offices upstairs in the bus station. If you are told, even by officials, that it is dangerous to go to your chosen destination, double check. If the worst happens, report the theft to the tourist police T572 3186 or the DAS office, T572 0053.

⊙ Directory

Pamplona *p126*
Banks Banco de Bogotá, on the plaza central, gives Visa cash advances. There are several ATMs nearby. **Internet** Miscelánea Shekina, Cra 6, No 8B-13. Internet La Séptima, Cra 7, No 3-62. **Post** Cra 6/C 6, in pedestrian passage. **Telephone** Telefónica Telecom, C 7 y Cra 5-79.

Cúcuta *p128, map p128*
Banks A good rate of exchange for pesos is to be had in Cúcuta, at the airport, or on the border. **Bancolombia** changes TCs. **Banco de Bogotá**, on Parque Santander, advances on Visa. Other options are Banco Davivienda, C 5 No 4-91 and BBVA, C 11 No 4-26 piso 2. There are money changers on the street all round the main plaza and many shops advertise the purchase and sale of bolivares. Change pesos into bolivares in Cúcuta or San Antonio as it is difficult to change them further into Venezuela. Similarly, do not take bolivares further into Colombia, change them here. There are also *casas de cambios*, Casa de Cambio Unidas, Av 5, No 11-39, L-3 CC. Cúcuta Plaza, El Bolívar de Oro, C 10, No 4-48.

Contents

138 Cartagena
138 Ins and outs
139 Background
140 Sights
147 Beaches
148 Listings

157 Around Cartagena
157 Volcán del Totumo
157 Islas del Rosario
158 South of Cartagena
164 Listings

170 Barranquilla
172 Listings

175 Santa Marta and around
176 Santa Marta
178 Around Santa Marta
180 Parque Nacional Tayrona
183 Ciudad Perdida
184 Sierra Nevada de Santa
    Marta
185 Listings

191 East to Venezuela
191 Riohacha
191 Santuario Los Flamencos
193 Valledupar
194 Guajira Peninsula
197 Listings

200 San Andrés and
    Providencia
201 San Andrés and around
203 Providencia
206 Listings

Footprint features

136 Don't miss ...
158 Mud volcanoes
181 Gabriel García Márquez
183 The Lost City
193 Música tropical
195 Hammocks
205 The black crabs of Providencia

Border crossing

Colombia–Venezuela
196 Maicao

At a glance

◉ **Getting around** Walking in city centre. Buses and taxis between cities.

◉ **Time required** 2-3 weeks to explore Cartagena, Santa Marta and other regions.

◗ **Weather** Hot all year round; more rain Aug-Nov.

✖ **When not to go** Very crowded during Christmas and Easter periods but most festivals occur during this time.

★ Don't miss ...

1 Watching the sun set from the ramparts of Cartagena, page 147.

2 Enjoying the Caribbean in Islas de Rosario and San Bernardo, page 157.

3 Experiencing Semana Santa at Mompós, page 159.

4 Wallowing in the mud volcanoes of Arboletes, page 161.

5 Trekking through the rainforest to Ciudad Perdida, page 184.

6 Learning about Wayúu culture in La Guajira, page 194.

To San Andrés & Providencia archipelago

N

50 km
50 miles

Gulf of Venezuela

Nazareth
Parque Nacional Macuira

Taroa
Punta Gallinas
Bahía Portete
Peninsula de la Guajira
Cabo de la Vela
Uribia
Manaure
Riohacha
Maicao
GUAJIRA

VENEZUELA

Santuario de Fauna y Flora Los Flamencos
Camarones
Palomino
Minca Ciudad Perdida
Sierra Nevada de Santa Marta
Valledupar
Parque Nacional Tayrona
Santa Marta
Rodadero
Ciénaga
Aracataca
Bosconia
CESAR
El Burro

NORTE DE SANTANDER
Cúcuta
San Alberto

Barranquilla
Soledad
Tasajera
Calamar
El Banco
Mompós
Talameque
BOLÍVAR

Puerto Colombia
La Boquilla
ATLÁNTICO
MAGDALENA
Río Magdalena

Cartagena
Barú
Islas del Rosario
Islas de San Bernardo
San Onofre
Tolú
Coveñas
Toluviejo
Sincelejo
SUCRE
Lorica
Montería
CÓRDOBA

Caribbean Sea

Arboletes
Turbo
Golfo de Urabá
Acandí
Capurganá

PANAMA

ANTIOQUIA

eaching the lowlands of Colombia's Caribbean coast you enter nother world. Steamy, colourful and lively, the entire area pulses to he rhythms of the omnipresent *vallenato*. *Costeños* may be looked own on by their more sombre countrymen, intimating that they ack the same sophistication and work ethic, but they certainly know ow to enjoy themselves. There are almost endless fiestas and the arranquilla carnival is held here, often cited as second only to Rio or colour and size and it's also much less commercial.

Aside from drinking and dancing, there is also fine architecture nd an impressive literary legacy, particularly in Cartagena, the merald in the crown of Colombia. This stunning colonial city is ositively bursting with colour and history and offers fine food, a vely nightlife and various sparkling coral islands within easy reach.

South from Cartagena is Mompós, a colonial town where the locks seem to have stopped somewhere back in the early 20th entury. Its main claim to fame is one of the best Easter festivals n the world. Up the Gulf of Urabá, on the way to Panama are the villages of Acandí, Capurganá and Sapzurro, unreachable by road nd boasting a wild shoreline of coral reefs and the virgin jungles of the Darién.

Travel east along the coast and you'll reach Santa Marta, Colombia's oldest city and gateway to the spectacular Tayrona National Park. Rising up from the shores is the Sierra Nevada de Santa Marta, the highest coastal mountain range in the world, and one of the few places that can boast tropical beaches and snow-capped mountains within 20 miles of each other. The Sierra Nevada was home to the indigenous Tayrona and a visit to one of their recently discovered cities, Ciudad Perdida, must come high on anyone's list of Latin American adventures.

Beyond Santa Marta is the arid landscape of the Guajira Peninsula, home to the indigenous Wayúu, enormous flocks of flamingos and the ethereal Cabo de la Vela, where turquoise waters lap against a desert shoreline.

Cartagena

→ *Colour map 1, B2. Phone code 5. Population: 1,200,000.*
Cartagena is one of the hottest, most vibrant and beautiful cities in South America, combining as does superb weather, a sparkling stretch of the Caribbean and an abundance of tropical fruit. Nuggets of history can be found around every corner and in every palm-shaded courtyard of th *most romantic of places. With exquisitely preserved colonial mansions, excellent museums and fin* *dining, it's a place not to be missed.* ▶ *For listings, see pages 148-156.*

Ins and outs

Getting there

Rafael Núñez airport is 1.5 km from the city in the Crespo district and it can be reache by local buses from Monumento India Catalina, in the northeast corner of the inner wa and along Avenida Blas de Lezo. There are two *casas de cambio*, one in the internation terminal and one in the domestic (T656 4943, Monday-Friday 0830-2030, Saturda 0830-1700 and Sunday 0830-2100). It cashes Amex TCs but not Bank of America an better rates are available in town. For tourist information, ask at the travel agent's office on the upper level. There is also a good self-service restaurant. A bus from the airport t Plaza San Francisco costs between US$0.70 and US$0.90, depending on whether the bu is air-conditioned. A taxi to the centre is US$7.50 (official price). Buses and taxis for th return trip can be found on Avenida Blas de Lezo close to Puerta del Reloj. Buses can b very crowded and if you have a lot of luggage, a taxi is recommended.

The **bus terminal** is 30 minutes away from town on the road to Barranquilla, a taxi cost US$7.50, or you can take the city buses to the 'Terminal de Transportes', from between US$0.70 and US$0.90. Agree your taxi fare before you get in.

Undoubtedly the best way to arrive is by sea and a description of the approach is given below, under Background. Regular lines are at present non-existent, but what is possible is detailed under Transport, on page 155. Cartagena is, however, popular for cruise ship and those who have their own sea transport: around 345,000 passengers pass through the docks each year. Equally, many tourists take trips to the offshore islands.

Getting around

Local buses are crowded, slow and ramshackle but also colourful, cheap and a good way to see the locals. As usual in Latin America, do watch your belongings. **Taxis** are also quite cheap and more convenient. There are no metres, journeys are calculated by zones, each zone costing about US$1.40, though the minimum fare is US$3. Thus Bocagrande to Centro, two zones, is US$3. It is quite common to ask other people waiting if they would like to share, but, in any case, always agree the fare with the driver before getting in. By arrangement, taxis will wait for you if visiting more remote places. Fares go up at night.

Best time to visit

The climate varies little during the year. Temperatures rise marginally when there is more frequent rain (August-November), and there can be flooding. Freak weather is very unusual, but almost all of Colombia suffered from unusually long and heavy rains during 2010, with some of the coast severely affected, although not Cartagena itself. Fiestas are taken seriously in Cartagena, and if you want a quiet time you might want to avoid certain mes of the year. If you want to join in, be sure to plan in advance or be prepared to struggle for accommodation and expect higher prices. ➤➤ *For further information, see festivals and events, page 153.*

Tourist information

Turismo Cartagena de Indias ⓘ *www.turismocartagenadeindias.com,* has 5 offices; the main one is in the **Plaza de la Aduana** ⓘ *T660 1583, Mon-Sat 0900-1300 and 1400-1800, Sun 0900-1700,* with very helpful and knowledgeable staff, and there are kiosks in Plaza de los Coches, Plaza de San Pedro Claver, at the airport and along the Muelle Turístico where the day-trip and excursion boats leave from. The Colombian Tourist Board, **Proexport** ⓘ *C 28, No 13A-15, p35, T560 0100, www.colombia.travel,* is another useful source of information.

Security

Carry your passport, or a photocopy, at all times. Failure to present it on police request can result in imprisonment and fines. Generally, the central areas are safe and friendly (although Getsemaní is less secure), but should you require the police, there is a station in Barrio Manga. Beware of drug pushers on the beaches, pickpockets in crowded areas and bag/camera snatchers on quiet Sunday mornings. At the bus station, do not be pressurized into a hotel recommendation different from your own choice.

Background

The full name of Cartagena is Cartagena de Indias, a name that is quite frequently used and a reminder that the early Spanish navigators believed they had reached the Far East. It was founded by Pedro de Heredia on 13 January 1533. The core of the city was built by the Spaniards on an island separated from the mainland by marshes and lagoons close to a prominent hill, a perfect place for a harbour and, more important at the time, easy to defend against attack. Furthermore, it was close to the mouth of the Río Magdalena, the route to the interior of the continent. In 1650, the Spaniards built a connection to the river, 145 km long, known as the **Canal del Dique**, to allow free access for ships from the upriver ports. This waterway has been used on and off ever since, was updated in the early 19th century and it is still used, mainly by barges, today.

The great Bay of Cartagena, 15 km long and 5 km wide is protected by several low, sandy islands. There were then two approaches to it, Bocagrande, at the northern end of Tierrabomba island – this was the direct entry from the Caribbean – and Bocachica, a narrow channel to the south of the island. Bocagrande was blocked by an underwater wall after Admiral Vernon's attack in 1741, thus leaving only one, easily protected, entrance to the approach to the harbour. The old walled city lies at the north end of the Bahía de Cartagena.

Cartagena declared its Independence from Spain in 1811. A year later Bolívar used the city as a jumping-off point for his Magdalena campaign. After heroic resistance, Cartagena was retaken by the royalists under General Pablo Morillo in 1815. It was finally freed by the patriots in 1821.

Cartagena today

Although Cartagena is Colombia's fifth largest city, the short-term visitor will not be aware of the size of the place. Beyond and behind the old walled city, Bocagrande and

Manga, is a large sprawling conurbation that stretches 10 km to the southeast. People have been moving in to add to the pressure on the poorer neighbourhoods as everywhere else in this part of the world, but Cartagena is a long way from the more heavily populated parts of highland Colombia, to the city's advantage.

Sights

The city's fortifications

Cartagena was one of the storage points for merchandise from Spain and for treasure collected from the Americas to be sent back. A series of forts protecting the approaches from the sea, and the formidable walls built around the city, made it almost impregnable.

Entering the **Bahía de Cartagena** by sea through Bocachica, the island of Tierrabomba is to the left. At the southern tip of Tierrabomba is the fortress of **San Fernando**. Opposite it, right on the end of Barú island, is the **Fuerte San José**. The two forts were once linked by heavy chains to prevent surprise attacks by pirates. Barú island is separated from the mainland only by the Canal del Dique. In recent years, the city has been expanding down the coast opposite Tierrabomba and settlements can be seen as you approach the entrance to the inner harbour of Cartagena, protected by another two forts, **San José de Manzanillo** on the mainland and the **Fuerte Castillo Grande** on the tip of **Bocagrande**, now the main beach resort of the city.

In the centre of the harbour is the statue of the Virgin with the port installations to the right on Manga Island. There is a very good view of the harbour, cruise boats and port activity from the end of Calle 6/Carrera 14, Bocagrande, though access to Castillo Grande itself is restricted. Manga Island is now an important suburb of the city. At its northern end a bridge, **Puente Román**, connects it with the old city. This approach to the city was defended by three forts: **San Sebastián del Pastelillo** built between 1558 and 1567 (the Club de Pesca has it now) at the northwestern tip of Manga Island; the fortress of **San Lorenzo** near the city itself; and the very powerful **Castillo San Felipe de Barajas** ① *open daily 0800-1800, US$7.50*, inland on San Lázaro hill, 41 m above sea-level, to the east of the city.

The first fortifications on the site were built in 1536 though the main constructions began in 1639 and it was finished by 1657. It is the largest Spanish fort built in the Americas. Under the huge structure is a network of tunnels cut into the rock, lined with living rooms and offices. Some are open and illuminated, a flashlight will be handy in the others; visitors pass through these and on to the top of the fortress. Good footwear is advisable in the damp, sloping tunnels. Baron de Pointis, the French pirate, stormed and took it, but Admiral Vernon failed to reach it. In the **Almacén de Pólvora** (Gunpowder store), there is an interesting 1996 reproduction of Vernon's map of the abortive attempt to take the city in 1741. On the statue of Don Blas de Lezo below the fortress, don't miss the plaque displaying the medal prematurely struck celebrating Vernon's 'victory'.

Yet another fort, **La Tenaza**, protected the northern point of the walled city from a direct attack from the open sea. The huge encircling walls were started early in the 17th century and finished by 1735. They were on average 12 m high and 17 m thick, with six gates. Besides barracks, they contained a water reservoir.

Around the old city

The old walled city was in two sections, outer and inner. Much of the wall between the two disappeared some years ago. Nearly all the houses are of one or two storeys. In the outer city, the artisan classes lived in the one-storey houses of **Getsemaní** where many olonial buildings survive. Today, there is a concentration of hotels and restaurants here. nmediately adjoining is the modern downtown sector, known as **La Matuna**, where endors crowd the pavements and alleys between the modern commercial buildings. everal middle range hotels are in this district, between Avenidas Venezuela and Lemaitre.

In the **inner** city, the houses in **El Centro** were originally occupied by the high officials nd nobility. **San Diego** (the northern end of the inner city) was where the middle classes ved: the clerks, merchants, priests and military. Today, the streets of the inner city are elatively uncrowded; upmarket hotels and restaurants are sprinkled throughout the area.

Just under a kilometre from the old city, along a seafront boulevard, **Bocagrande** is a pit of land crowded with hotel and apartment towers. Thousands of visitors flock to he beach with its accompanying resort atmosphere, fast-food outlets, shops – and lirty seawater. See Beaches, page 147.

The old city streets are narrow. Each block has a different name, a source of confusion, ut don't worry: the thing to do is to wander aimlessly, savouring the street scenes, and llow the great sights to catch you by surprise. However, if you do want to know what you re looking at, the maps are marked with numerals for the places of outstanding interest. Most of the 'great houses' can be visited. Churches are generally open to the public at 1800, some for most of the day. Weekends and holidays are the best time for photography when traffic is minimal. What follows is a walking route for the sights of the old city which you can pick up and leave wherever you wish. Note that the numbers below refer to the circled numbers on the Historical Centre map.

Outer city

The **Puente Román** (1) is the bridge which leads from Manga Island, with its shipping terminals, into Getsemaní, characterized by its *casas bajas* (low houses). The chapel of **San Roque** (2), early 17th century, is near the end of Calle Media Luna, and the hospital of Espíritu Santo. Just across the Playa Pedregal (3) is the Laguna de San Lázaro and the **Puente Heredia**, on the other side of which is the Castillo San Felipe de Barajas, see above. In an interesting plaza, is the church of **La Santísima Trinidad** (4), built 1643 but not consecrated until 1839, now gently crumbling. West of the church, at No 10 Calle Guerrero, lived Pedro Romero, who set the revolution of 1811 going by coming out into the street shouting 'Long Live Liberty'. His statue can be seen outside La Santísima Trinidad. Along Calle Larga (5), Calle 25, is the monastery of **San Francisco**. The church was built in 1590 after the pirate Martin Côte had destroyed an earlier church built in 1559. The first Inquisitors lodged at the monastery. From its courtyard a crowd surged into the streets claiming Independence from Spain on 11 November 1811. The main part of the monastery has now been turned into business premises – take a look at the cloister garden as you pass by. Handicrafts are sold in the grounds of the monastery, good value, fixed prices, and, at the back, is the Centro Comercial Getsemaní, a busy shopping centre. On the corner of Calle Larga, formerly part of the Franciscan complex, is the **Iglesia de la Tercera Orden**, a busy church with a fine wooden roof of unusual design and some brightly painted niche figures. The church and monastery front on to the Avenida del Mercado on the other side of which is the **Centro Internacional de Convenciones** (6). It holds gatherings of up to 4000 people and is frequently used now for local and international conventions. It was built in 1972 on the site of the old colourful market, now banished to the interior part of the city. Although the severe fort-like structure is more or less in keeping with the surrounding historic walls and bastions, not everyone believes this is an improvement. When not in use, ask for a guide to show you around.

Cartagena historical centre

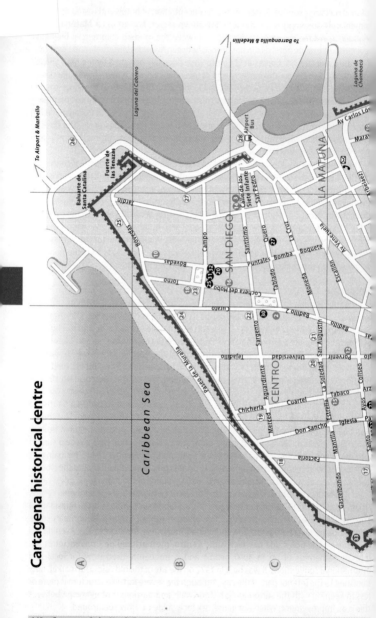

Caribbean Sea

To Airport & Marbello

Baluarte de Santa Catalina

Fuerte de las Tenazas

Laguna del Cabrero

To Barranquilla & Medellín

Laguna de Chambacú

Airport Bus

LA MATUNA

SAN DIEGO

CENTRO

Av Venezuela

Av Carlos Ló...

Calle de los, Siete Infante

San Pedro

Santísimo

Quero

La Cruz

Puntales Bomba Boquete

Moneda

Tablado

Badillo 2

San Augustín

Porvenir

La Soledad

Universidad

Cuartel

Tabaco

Estrella

Iglesia

Don Sancho

Mantilla

Gastelbondo

Factoria

Chichería

Merced

Aguardiente

Sargento

Tejadillo

Cochera del Hobo

Bóvedas

Torno

Campo

Jardín

Bóvedas

Paseo de la Muralla

To Castillo San Felipe, La Popa & Bus Terminal

Laguna de San Lázaro

Playa Pedregal

Espíritu Santo

Guerrero

Pozo

San Antonio

San Juan

Sirpe

Media Luna

Andrés

Centen...

Parque del Centenario

Plaza de la Independencia

GETSEMANÍ

Larga

Arsenal

Av del Mercado

Paseo de los Mártires

Playa de Barahona

Bahía de las Ánimas

Muelle de los Pegasos

To 22 & Isla Manga

To Bocagrande

N

100 metres
100 yards

Av Blaz de Lezo

...bernador

Inquisición

Vicaría

Damas

Ricaurte Santo Do...

Av Santander

Upsalena

San Juan de Dios

Habanos

D

E

F

○ See text for key to numbering

Sleeping
Casa de Pestagua 1 D1
Casa La Fe 2 C2
Casa Marco Polo 3 C3
Casa Viena 4 D4
El Marqués 5 D1
El Viajero 12 D2

El Viajero Hostel 14 C3
Familiar 6 D4
Holiday 7 D4
Hostal Baluarte 8 D4
Hostal La Casona 9 D4
Hostal San Diego 10 B3
Hostal Santa Clara 18 B3

Hostal Santo
Domingo 11 D1
La Passion 15 D2
Las Tres Banderas 16 B3
Marlin 13 D4
Monterrey 17 D3
Villa Colonial 19 D4

Eating
Balkoon 20 B3
Bistro 21 D2
Café Havana 34 D4
Café Lunático 29 D4
Club de Pesca 22 F4
Donde Olano 23 D1

El Coroncoro 24 D4
Juan del Mar 25 B3
La Casa de Socorro 26 F4
La Cocina de Pepina 28 E3
La Mulata 27 C3
Pizza en el parque 30 C2
Portal de los Dulces 36 D2

Santa Lucía 37 D1
Teriyaki 31 B3
Zebra 32 B3

Bars & clubs
Café del Mar 33 D1
Casa de la Cerveza 35 F4

Donde Fidel 38 D2
Mister Babilla 39 E3
Quiebra Canto 40 D3
Studio 54 41 E3
Tu Candela 42 D2

Immediately to the north is **Plaza de la Independencia**, with the landscaped **Parque del Centenario** alongside. At right angles to the plaza runs the **Paseo de los Mártires** flanked by the busts of nine patriots executed in the square on 24 February 1816 by the royalist Pablo Morillo after he had retaken the city.

Inner City

At the western end of the Paseo is a tall clock tower, Torre del Reloj, often used as the symbol of Cartagena. To the left is the **Muelle de los Pegasos** (Muelle Turístico) from where the tourist boats leave. Under the clock tower is the **Puerta del Reloj** and the three arches are the principal entrance to the inner walled city. Inside is the **Plaza de los Coches (7)**. As with almost all the plazas of Cartagena, arcades here offer refuge from the tropical sun. At one time, this plaza was the slave market, and later, it was from here that carriages (*coches*) could be hired for local journeys. On the west side of this plaza is the **Portal de los Dulces**, a favourite meeting place and where you can still buy all manner of local sweets and delicacies. It also has a number of good bars, often quite buzzing even during the day. **Plaza de la Aduana (8)**, with a statue of Columbus in the centre and the **Casa de la Aduana** along the wall, originally the tax office and now part of the city administration as the **Palacio Municipal**. Opposite is the **Casa del Premio Real** which was the residence of the representative of the Spanish King. In the corner of the wall is the **Museo de Arte Moderno** ⓘ *Mon-Sat 0900-1200, 1500-1800, US$3.50*, a collection of the work of modern Colombian artists. There is a museum shop.

Past the museum is the **Convento de San Pedro Claver (9)** ⓘ *Mon-Fri 0800-1730, Sat 0800-1600 US$3.50*, and the church and monastery of the same name, built by Jesuits in 1603 and later dedicated to San Pedro Claver, a monk in the monastery, who died in 1654 and was canonized 235 years later. He was called *El Esclavo de los Esclavos*, or *El Apóstol de los Negros*: he used to beg from door to door for money to give to the black slaves brought to the city. His body is in an illuminated glass coffin set in the high marble altar, and his cell and the balcony from which he kept watch for slave ships are shown to visitors. There are brightly coloured birds in the small monastery garden. Several upstairs rooms form a museum, with many interesting items linked or unrelated to Pedro Claver. In the pottery room, for example, is the chair used by the Pope on his visit to Cartagena in 1986. In another room there are several old maps, one of which shows the Caribbean maritime boundaries of Colombia, topical in that disputes with Nicaragua over San Andrés still persist in 2011, despite an international court ruling in favour of Colombia.

Following the wall round, it is well worthwhile climbing up the **Baluarte San Francisco Javier (10)** for a good view of the city and the Caribbean. There is a **Museo Naval del Caribe** ⓘ *Tue-Sun 1000-1700, US$3*, with maps, models and displays of armaments, near the Baluarte. On the corner of Calle Ricaurte is the convent of **Santa Teresa (11)**, founded in 1609 by a rich benefactor as a convent for Carmelite nuns. It had various uses subsequently, as a prison, a military barracks, a school and in the 1970s, was occupied by the police. It was recently purchased by the Banco Central as a heritage investment and has now been converted into a hotel. It is possible to visit the public areas of the hotel and admire the tasteful work of restoration. There is a great view from the roof.

El Bodegón de la Candelaria (12) ⓘ *C Las Damas No 64*, was an elegant colonial residence. It has been faithfully restored and there is some fine panelling and period furniture to see. It is now a restaurant specializing in good seafood. A small shrine in one of the rooms marks the place where the Virgin appeared to a priest who was living there at the time. One block away is **Plaza de Bolívar (13)** with an equestrian statue of the iberator in the centre. Formerly it was the Plaza de la Inquisición, with the Palacio de la Inquisición (see below), on its west side. The gardens of the plaza were given a face-lift in 2000 and is now an attractive corner of Cartagena.

On the opposite side of the Plaza de Bolívar to the Palacio de la Inquisición is the **Museo del Oro Zenú (14)** ① *Tue-Sat 1000-1300, 1500-1800 free.* Gold and pottery are very well displayed. Specially featured is the Zenú area to the south of Cartagena in the marshlands of the Sinú, San Jorge and Magdalena rivers, which is flooded by the river waters six to eight months of the year. Early drainage systems are featured, as is the advanced level of weaving techniques using the *cañafleche* and other fresh water reeds. This area was densely populated between the second and 10th centuries during which time the gold working skills of the people were developed to the high level that can still be seen today at Mompós, at the northern edge of the Zenú region.

The **Palacio de La Inquisición (15)** ① *Mon-Sat 0800-1800, Sun 1000-1600, US$6*, is on the other side of the Plaza Bolívar. The jurisdiction of this tribunal extended to Venezuela and Panama, and at least 800 were sentenced to death here. There is a small window overlooking the plaza where the public were informed of the sentences. The Palacio houses a modest historical museum, though some of the exhibits are in poor condition. Of special interest are the model of Cartagena in 1808, copies of Alexander Von Humboldt's maps showing the link he discovered between the Orinoco and Amazon rivers (*Canal de Casiquiare*) and of the Maypures rapids on the Orinoco – note that the longitude lines on the maps are west of Paris not Greenwich. The main attraction is the grisly collection of torture instruments. Historical books are on sale at the entrance.

The **Cathedral (16)**, in the northeast corner of Plaza de Bolívar, begun in 1575, was partially destroyed by Francis Drake. Reconstruction was finished by 1612. Great alterations were made between 1912 and 1923. It has a severe exterior, with a fine doorway, and a simply decorated interior. See the gilded 18th-century altar, the Carrara marble pulpit and the elegant arcades which sustain the central nave. Although established in 1610, the present building dates from 1706 with modifications up to 1770. The stone entrance with its coats of arms is well preserved and the ornate wooden door is very notable. The whole building, with its balconies, cloisters and patios, is a fine example of colonial baroque.

Across the street is the **Palacio de la Proclamación** named for the declaration of Independence of the State of Cartagena in November 1811. Before that it was the local Governor's residence, and later where Simón Bolívar stayed in 1826. The building was restored in 1950. The adjacent plaza has interesting local art and sculpture on display daily in high season.

The church and monastery of **Santo Domingo (17)**, built 1570 to 1579 is now a seminary. The old monastery was replaced by the present one in the 17th century. Inside, a miracle-making image of Christ, carved towards the end of the 16th century, is set on a baroque 19th-century altar. This is a most interesting neighbourhood, where very little has changed since the 16th century. In Calle Santo Domingo, No 33-29, is one of the great patrician houses of Cartagena, the **Casa de los Condes de Pestagua**, until recently the Colegio del Sagrado Corazón de Jesús, now a boutique hotel (see page 149). It has a fine colonnaded courtyard, marble floors and magnificent palm trees in the centre garden. Beside the church is the **Plaza de Santo Domingo**, one of the favourite corners of Cartagena, with popular restaurants, bars and cafés. A sculpture by Fernando Botero *La Gorda* is in the Plaza.

North of Santo Domingo at Calle de la Factoría 36-57 is the magnificent **Casa del Marqués de Valdehoyos (18)**, originally owned by the Marqués, who had the lucrative licences to import slaves and flour. The fine woodcarving is some of the best in Cartagena and the ceilings, chandeliers, wooden arches and balustrading are unique. The views of the city from the fine upper floor balconies are also recommended. Sadly it's been closed for renovations for well over a year and a half and still wasn't open to the public at the time of writing.

A short walk north is the plaza, church and convent of **La Merced (19)**, founded 1618. The convent, a prison during Morillo's reign of terror, is now occupied by a private university (Jorge Tadeo Lozano), and its church has become the **Teatro Heredia**, which has been beautifully restored.

Two blocks east is Calle de la Universidad, at the end of which is the monastery of **San Agustín (20)**, built in 1580, currently the Universidad de Cartagena. From its chapel, now occupied by a printing press, the pirate Baron de Pointis stole a 500-pound silver sepulchre. It was returned by the King of France but the citizens melted it down to pay their troops during the siege by Morillo in 1815.

One block along Calle de San Agustín is **La Casa Museo de Simón Bolívar (21)**, a collection of memorabilia in the first Cartagena house he stayed in, now the **Biblioteca Bartolomé Calvo** owned by the Banco de la República.

One block along Badillo (Carrera 7) is the church of **Santo Toribio de Mongrovejo (22)** ① *opens for Mass Mon-Fri 0630, 1200, 1815, Sat 0630, 1200, 1800 and Sun 0800, 1000, 1800, 1900, closed at other times.* Building began in 1729. In 1741, during Admiral Vernon's siege, a cannon ball fell into the church during Mass and lodged in one of the central columns; the ball is now in a recess in the west wall. The font of Carrara marble in the Sacristy is a masterpiece. There is a beautiful carved ceiling (*mudéjar* style) above the main altar with a rear lighted figure of Christ.

The church and monastery of **Santa Clara de Assisi (23)** is close by. It was built 1617-1621, and has been spectacularly restored. It is now a hotel, but this is one you must see. Behind the hotel is the orange **Casa de Gabriel García Márquez (24)**, the most famous living Colombian author, on the corner of Calle del Curato.

Beyond the Santa Clara is the **Plaza de Las Bóvedas (25)**. Towards the sea, before Las Bóvedas, you will see a bank (*espiga*) leading to a jetty used in colonial times when the water came up to the walls, as shown on the 1808 map displayed in the **Palacio de la Inquisición**. All the land below the walls has since been reclaimed, with sports fields, recreational areas and the Avenida Santander/Paseo de la Muralla, a busy bypass to the city. The walls of Las Bóvedas, built 1799, are 12 m high and from 15- to 18-m thick. At the base of the wall are 23 dungeons, now containing tourist shops. Both an illuminated underground passage and a drawbridge lead from Las Bóvedas to the fortress of La Tenaza, which guarded the approach to the city from the coast to the northeast.

Casa de Núñez (26) ① *Mon-Sat 0800-1200, 1400-1800, US$0.50, there is also a monument to the 1886 constitution in the small park beside the lagoon,* just outside the walls of La Tenaza in El Cabrero district was the home of Rafael Núñez, four-time president of Colombia. He established the constitution of 1886 and wrote the national anthem. His grandiose marble tomb is in the delightful small **Ermita El Cabrero** church opposite.

Back along the lagoon is the old **Plaza de Toros (27)**, bull ring. It is an interesting wooden building but now abandoned and in a dangerous state. It cannot be visited.

Closer to the centre, where the main road leads into the city, is a roundabout, in the centre of which is the monument to **La India Catalina (28)**, Pedro de Heredia's indigenous interpreter in the early days of the Spanish conquest. A miniature of this statue is given to the winner of the annual Cartagena film festival – a Colombian 'Oscar'.

The ramparts

In addition to being a spectacular feature of Cartagena, the city walls make a great walk and are an excellent way to visit many of the attractions inside. A good place to start is the **Baluarte San Francisco Javier (10)** from where, with a few ups and downs, it is continuous to **La India Catalina (28)**. From this point, there are two further sections along the lagoons to the **Puente Román (1)**. The final section along the Calle del Arsenal can be completed through the **Playa de Barahona**, a bayside park, which is busy at weekends. The entire walk takes about 1½ hours, although if you take a camera it can take considerably longer. It is a spectacular walk in the morning around 0600 and equally at sunset. At many points you can drop down to see the sights detailed above in the tour of the old city.

Three of Cartagena's sights are off our map. Two of them, the Fortress of San Fernando and the Castillo San Felipe de Barajas, across the **Puente Heredia (3)** have been described above. The third is **Convento La Popa, on La Popa hill** ⓘ *daily 0845-1730, US$3.50, children and students US$2, guides available*, nearly 150 m high, from where there is a fine view of the harbour and the city. It is not recommended to walk up on your own; either take a guided tour or take a public bus to Teatro Miramar at the foot of the hill (US$0.50), then bargain for a taxi up, about US$7 return. If driving, take Carrera 21 off Avenida Pedro de Heredia, and follow the winding road to the top. The Augustinian church and monastery of Santa Cruz (Convento La Popa), and restored ruins of the convent dating from 1608 can be found here. In the church is the beautiful little image with a golden crown of the Virgin of La Candelaria, reputed as a deliverer from plague and a protector against pirates. The statue was blessed by the Pope on his visit in 1986. The Virgin's day is 2 February and for nine days before the feast thousands of people go up the hill by car, on foot, or on horseback. On the day itself people carry lighted candles as they go up the hill. There is an attractive bougainvillea-covered cloister with a well in the centre, and a museum with illuminated manuscripts, old maps, music books, relics and an image of the *Cabro de Oro* (golden goat) found by the Augustinians on the site, presumed to be an object of veneration of the indigenous people who previously inhabited the area. The name was bestowed on the hill because of an imagined likeness to a ship's poop deck.

Beaches

Take a bus south from the Puerta del Reloj, taxi US$2.50, or walk to **Bocagrande**, where the beaches can be dirty in parts and often crowded. You will also be constantly hassled. The sea is a little dirty, though better if you go as far as the Hilton at the end of the peninsula.

Marbella beach is an alternative, just north of Las Bóvedas. This is the locals' beach, and therefore quieter than Bocagrande during the week and good for swimming, though subject at times to dangerous currents.

The **Bocachica** beach, on Tierrabomba island, is also none too clean and you may be hassled here too. Boats leave for Bocachica from Muelle Turístico. The departure point is the two-storey glass building halfway along, which also has some tourist information. The round trip can take up to two hours each way and costs about US$2.50 with the regular service, more if with private boats. *Ferry Dancing*, about half the price of the faster, luxury boats, carries dancing passengers. Boats taking in Bocachica and the San Fernando fortress include *Alcatraz*, which runs a daily trip from the Muelle Turístico. Alternatively, you can cross from Bocagrande, *lanchas* leave from near the Hilton Hotel and go to Punta Arena beach on Tierrabomba.

Boats to the Islas del Rosario (see page 157) may stop at the San Fernando fortress on Tierrabomba island and **Playa Blanca** on the Isla de Barú for one hour. You can bargain with the boatman to collect you later. Take food and water since these are expensive on the island. Barú, a long thin island, has mostly fine white-sand beaches which are slowly being exploited by upmarket hotel complexes that will hopefully respect this fragile environment. The stopping place for tourist boats from Cartagena is Playa Blanca which is crowded in the mornings, but peaceful after the tour boats have left at around 1400. There have been reports of people drinking alcohol and then renting jetskis at Playa Blanca; keep your wits about you when swimming or snorkelling, as safety measures aren't always complied with.

Another alternative is to catch a fishing boat from the Mercado Bazurto (a short distance beyond *La Popa*) to Playa Blanca, leaving around 0830, US$10-12 one way, and take another one back when you choose, although this might not be on the same day and they only leave when full. Note that this is not a legal practice and sometimes there are police checks. Many consider this to be the best beach in the region, with stretches of white sand and shady palm groves. There are several simple and cheap places to stay here and **Mama Root** is highly recommended. Other places include **Hugo's Place**, which has a campsite, restaurant and hires hammocks with mosquito nets, and El Paraíso. The **Wintenberg Camp** has good *cabañas*. Remember to take water, as there is little on the island. You can also reach Playa Blanca by taking the bus to Pasacaballo, crossing the Canal del Dique by canoe and continuing by truck or jeep to the beach. If walking, allow 2½ hours in all. If staying the night at Playa Blanca in *cabañas* or tents, beware of ferocious sandflies. A *cabaña* will typically cost about US$12 per night. **Note** Pay for boat trips on board if possible, and be certain that you and the operator understand what you are paying for.

The little fishing village of **La Boquilla**, northeast of Cartagena, is near the end of a sandy promontory between the Ciénaga de Tesca and the Caribbean, about 20 minutes past the airport. There is a camping area with an attractive pool surrounded by palm trees and parrots, entrance US$2. There is a good beach nearby, El Paraíso, which is busy at weekends with people dancing, but quiet during the week, and where you can get good fish dishes. Visit the mangrove swamps nearby to see the birds.

◉ Cartagena listings → Phone code: 5.

For Sleeping and Eating price codes and other relevant information, see pages 23-28.

● Sleeping

Hotel prices rise for the high season, Nov-Mar, and Jun-Jul. From 15 Dec to 31 Jan they can rise by as much as 50% on Bocagrande beach; in town you will find not find much below **D**. Hotels tend to be heavily booked right through to Mar.

Around the old city *p140, map p142*
Getsemaní and La Matuna
Many cheap hotels on C Media Luna used to be brothels, but the area has cleaned up

its act and now has lots of good budget options and new eateries.

AL Monterrey, Paseo de los Mártires, Cra 8B, No 25-103, T650 3030, www.hotel monterrey.com.co. Just outside the old city walls and with a view onto the Puerta del Reloj, this hotel has rooms in simple colours with balconies, TV and hot water. It also has a sunroof with a jacuzzi and access to internet.

C-D Hostal Baluarte, Media Luna, No 10-81, T664 2208. A family-run, converted colonial house with a fine courtyard shaded by a mango tree and wrought-iron furniture, rocking chairs and hammocks in which to relax. Can arrange tours to the Islas

del Rosario and has laundry service.
Rooms a little small.
D Casa Villa Colonial, C de la Media
Luna No 10-89, T664 5421, www.casavilla
colonial.com. Set around a lovely courtyard,
this is a family-run hotel with a/c, TV, free
internet in the lobby and breakfast available
for a charge. Also has a sister hotel, **Hotel
Villa Colonial** in C de las Maravillas.
D Hostal La Casona, C Tripita y Media,
Cra 10, No 31-32, T/F664 1301, www.la
casonahostel.com. Has a breezy central
courtyard and rooms with private bath.
Laundry service provided.
D Hotel Marlin, C de la Media Luna, No 10-35,
T664 3507, www.hotelmarlincartagena.com.
Aquatic-themed hostel run by a friendly
Colombian. Has fine balcony looking onto
the busy C de la Media Luna. Laundry service,
free coffee, internet access, lockers, tours
and bus tickets organized. Breakfast
included. Recommended.
D-E Holiday, C de la Media Luna, No 10-47,
T664 0948, www.hostelholidaycaribe.com.
Rooms and dorms open on to a corridor
patio with potted plants and tables. There's
a small kitchen and a good information
board. Internet access and free coffee.
E Casa Viena, C San Andrés, No 30-53, T664
6242, www.casaviena.com. A hub of information on activities in Cartagena, this hostel in
Getsemaní is very popular with backpackers.
Offers internet access, use of a kitchen,
washing machine, a TV room and very cheap
dormitories. Bustling and busy, good value.

E Familiar, C del Guerrero, No 29-66, off
Media Luna, T664 2464. Fresh and bright,
family-run hotel with rooms set around a
colonnaded patio. Has a good noticeboard
full of information, a laundry service and
use of a kitchen. Friendly and recommended.

El Centro and San Diego
LL Casa de Pestagua, C Santo Domingo,
No 33-63, T664 9510, www.casapestagua.
com. Formerly home to the Conde de
Pestagua, this historic house has been
restored by architect Alvaro Barrera Herrera
with great care. From the street it opens up
into a magnificent colonnaded courtyard
lined with enormous palm trees. Beyond
is a swimming pool and spa, and on the
top floor a sun terrace with jacuzzi and
sea views. Also has Wi-Fi.
LL El Marqués, C Nuestra Señora del Carmen,
No 33-41, T664 7800, www.elmarqueshotel
boutique.com. Another house belonging to
the Pestagua family. The central courtyard,
dominated by a large crumbling wall of
draping ivy, features giant birdcages,
hanging bells and large palm trees. The
rooms are crisp, white and have Wi-Fi and
iPod docks. Recent additions to the hotel
include a Peruvian restaurant, a wine
cellar and spa. Exquisite.
LL La Passion, C Estanco del Tabaco, No
35-81, T664 8605, www.lapassionhotel.com.
In the heart of the old city, this grand building
brings the concept of the Marrakech
boutique hotel to Latin America. Its French

owners have trawled the globe in search of exquisite furnishings. A mixture of colonial and Republican-era architecture, **La Passion** has cathedral-like rooms that provide modern, elegant and discreet comfort in the shape of plasma TVs, Wi-Fi and MP3 players. Breakfast is included in the price and served on the sublime roof terrace, next to the swimming pool. Also offers spa treatments including different massage and boat trips to nearby Islas del Rosario. Highly recommended.

LL Santa Clara, Calle del Torno, No 39-29, T650 4700, www.sofitel.com. The French Sofitel group own their magnificently restored early 17th-century convent on the enchanting Plaza de San Diego. Rooms, however, are in a modern annex and most have a balcony looking onto a large swimming pool, invariably with views of the sea. Has 2 restaurants, a bar and a spa.

L-AL Casa La Fe, Parque Fernández de Madrid, C 2a de Badillo, No 36-125, T664 0306, www.casalafe.com. A Republican-era house (c1930) on the delightful Parque Fernández de Madrid, the 14 en suite bedrooms of Casa La Fe have been restored by a British-Colombian team. It has a pool-jacuzzi on the roof and other services such as Wi-Fi, free bicycle use, and free breakfast served in a leafy patio. Organizes tours.

A Casa Marco Polo, C de los Siete Infantes, No 9-89, T316-874 9478, cantolindo1@ hotmail.com. Private rooms in a 450-year-old colonial mansion belonging to a local *cumbia* musician. 2 rooms, 1 cheaper (**B**), have a/c, cable TV and share a roof terrace with stunning views of Barrio San Diego. Breakfast included and limited use of kitchen possible. Highly recommended.

A Hostal San Diego, C de las Bóvedas, No 39-120, T660 1433, www.hostal sandiego.com. Near the delightful Plaza San Diego, this colonial building with its salmon pink exterior has modern rooms which open out onto a tiled courtyard. A/c and Wi-Fi.

A Las Tres Banderas, C Cochera de Hobo, No 38-66, T660 0160, www.hotel3 banderas.com. Another hotel in the

bohemian district of San Diego, this old building is split over 2 breezy courtyards with water features. All rooms have a safe and come with breakfast included. Free internet access. Also offers massage treatments.

B Hostal Santo Domingo, C Santo Domingo, No 33-46, T664 2268, hsantodomingopiret@ yahoo.es. If you are looking for a budget option in the old town, this is one of your best bets. Rooms are simple but clean and open up on to a sunny patio. Breakfast is included, there is a laundry service, free Wi-Fi and the gate is usually locked, so security is good.

B Hotel El Viajero, C del Porvenir, No 35-68, piso 2, T664 3289, hotelviajero664@ hotmail.com, www.hotelelviajero.com. Ideally located in the centre of the old town, this 2nd floor hostel is more practical than attractive. Organizes tours, has a/c, TV, Wi-Fi and access to a kitchen.

C-E El Viajero Hostel, C de los Siete Infantes 9-45, T660 2598, www.elviajerohostels.com. New spacious hostel with private rooms and dorms. A/c in every room, breakfast included, free Wi-Fi and bar. Busy and popular, but a bit noisy.

Beaches *p147*
Bocagrande
LL Capilla del Mar, Cra 1 No 8-12, T018000-510077 or 650 1500, www.capilla delmar.com. Resort hotel across the road from the beach, with swimming pool on top floor and 3 restaurants serving seafood and *parrillas*.

LL Hotel Caribe, Cra 1, No 2-87, T650 1160, www.hotelcaribe.com. Enormous Caribbean-style hotel with 2 newer annexes, a/c, beautiful grounds and a swimming pool in the expensive restaurant. Has several bars overlooking the sea.

L Hotel Almirante, Av San Martín, C 6 esq, T655 4700, www.hotelesestelar.com. Popular with affluent Colombian tourists, this high-rise hotel has 250 rooms and all the usual resort facilities, including a half moon-shaped pool on the top floor with good views out over the beaches.

AL-A Bahía, Cra 4 with C 4, T665 0316, www.hotelbahiacartagena.com. Has the feel of a 1950s hotel. Discreet, quiet, with fine pool and restaurant.

AL-A Hotel Charlotte, Av San Martín, No 7-126, T665 9201, www.hotelescharlotte. com. Stylishly designed in cool whites. Has a pool, and Wi-Fi in the lobby. Smart restaurant serves up Italian food. Recommended.

AL-A Playa Club, Av San Martín, No 4-87, T665 0552, www.hotelplayaclubcartagena. com. Some of the rooms are painted in lurid colours but are otherwise fine and it has an inviting pool and direct access to the beach. TV, a/c and breakfast included.

B Casa Grande, Av del Malecón, No 9-128, T665 6806. Yellow and blue house set back from the beach with spacious rooms off a tranquil garden at the back. Recommended.

B-C Leonela, Cra 3, 7-142, T665 4761, www.hostaleonela.com. A very helpful and friendly couple have run this hotel for more than 30 years. Has a family atmosphere and a small restaurant serving breakfast. Also has money exchange.

C Ibatama, Av San Martín 7-46, T665 1127, hotelesibatamactg@yahoo.com. Has a pleasant terrace looking out over 1 of the principal streets, with a/c and TV, though the rooms are quite small and few have windows.

C Mary, No 6-53, T6652833. Basic rooms but pleasant and friendly. A/c or fan.

🍴 Eating

At cafés try *patacón*, a round flat 'cake' made of green banana, mashed and baked; also from street stalls in Parque del Centenario in the early morning. At restaurants ask for *sancocho* the local soup of the day of vegetables and fish or meat. Also try *obleas* for a snack, biscuits with jam, cream cheese or caramel fudge (*arequipe*), and *buñuelos*, deep-fried cheese dough balls. Fruit juices are fresh, tasty and cheap in Cartagena: a good place is on the Paseo de los Pegasos

(Av Blas de Lezo) from the many stalls alongside the boats.

The city's fortifications p140

🍴 **Club de Pesca**, San Sebastián de Pastelillo fort, Manga Island, T660 4594, www.clubde pesca.com. Wonderful setting, perhaps the most famous fish and seafood restaurant in Cartagena, though expensive. Warmly recommended.

Around the old city p140, map p142
Getsemaní and La Matuna

With spiralling property prices Getsemaní is undergoing the same gentrification treatment as Centro and San Diego, evidenced by an increasing number of smart restaurants that have opened up in the area.

🍴🍴 **La Casa de Socorro**, C Larga, No 8B-112, T664 4658. This seafood restaurant is popular with locals and does very good *bandejas de pescado* and *arroz con camarones*. Take note that there are 2 rival restaurants of the same name on the same street. This one is the original and better. Friendly and recommended.

🍴🍴 **La Cocina de Pepina**, Callejón Vargas, No 9A-6. A new restaurant serving Colombian Caribbean cuisine, run by established chef and cookbook author María Josefina Yances Guerra.

🍴 **Café Havana**, C de la Media Luna y C del Guerrero, www.cafehavanacartagena.com. A fantastic Cuban bar and restaurant, which feels like it has been transported from Havana brick by brick. The walls are festooned with black-and-white portraits of Cuban salsa stars and it has live bands playing most nights. Note that it doesn't take credit cards. Highly recommended.

🍴 **Café Lunático**, C Media Luna 10-89 (next door to **Hostal Baluarte**). Interesting café with fresh juices, local and Indian dishes. Also sells weavings and blankets.

🍴 **El Coroncoro**, C Tripita y Media, No 31-28. More typical of the area, very popular at lunchtime with locals. It's atmospheric and offers *menús del día* from US$3.

El Centro and San Diego

Plaza San Diego has several good restaurants serving up a variety of international cuisines.

ŤŤŤŤ Santa Lucía, C Santo Domingo 3-30, piso 2. Lovely Argentine-style parrilla restaurant overlooking bustling Plaza Santo Domingo. Steaks to die for and generous portions. Highly recommended.

ŤŤŤ-ŤŤ Donde Olano, C Santo Domingo with Inquisición. Art deco restaurant serving French and Creole cuisine in a cosy atmosphere Try their fantastic seafood platter, Tentaciones de Zeus. Well worth the price.

ŤŤ Juan del Mar, Plaza San Diego, No 8-18. Offers 2 restaurants in 1: inside serves expensive seafood while outside cooks up fine, thin-based pizzas, though you are likely to be harassed by street hawkers.

ŤŤ Teriyaki, Plaza San Diego, No 8-28. Next to Zebra, serves sushi and Thai food in smart surroundings.

ŤŤ Zebra, Plaza San Diego, No 8-34. Café with wide selection of coffees, hot sandwiches and African dishes.

ŤŤ-Ť Bistro, C de los Ayos, No 4-46. German-run restaurant with a relaxed atmosphere. Sofas, music, European menu at reasonable prices. Has a German bakery and tasty food. Closed Sun. Recommended.

ŤŤ-Ť La Mulata, C Quero, No 9-58. A popular lunchtime venue with locals, you get a selection of set menu dishes. Try the excellent seafood casserole and coconut lemonade. Has Wi-Fi.

Ť Balkoon, C de Tumbamuertos, No 38-85, Piso 2. Small restaurant overlooking the Plaza de San Diego. Great views and nice atmosphere.

Ť Pizza en el parque, C 2a de Badillo, No 36-153. This small kiosk serves up delicious pizzas with some interesting flavours (pear and apple) which you can munch on while enjoying the delightful atmosphere of Parque Fernández Madrid.

The beaches *p147*

There are good fish dishes in La Boquilla.

Bocagrande

ŤŤ Carbón de Palo, Av San Martín, No 6-40. Steak heaven, cooked on an outdoor *parrilla*.

ŤŤ Restaurante Arabe, Cra 3A, No 8-83, T665 4365. Upmarket Arab restaurant serving tagines, etc. A/c, indoor seating or pleasant outdoor garden.

Ť Jeno's, Av San Martín, No 7-162. Eat in or take away pizza.

Ť Juan Valdez Café, Av San Martín, No 7-17, Starbucks-style chain serving various types of coffee and sandwiches. Has Wi-Fi.

Ť La Fonda Antioqueña, Cra 2, No 6-164. Traditional Colombian, nice atmosphere.

Ť Ranchería's, Av 1A, No 8-86. Serves seafood and meats in thatched huts just off the beach. *Menú del día*, US$8.

◑ Bars and clubs

Cartagena boasts a lively dance scene and the atmosphere in the city after dark is addictive. Any one of the cafés next to the Santo Domingo church is a great place for a drink.

Around the old city *p140*

Many of the hotels have evening entertainment and can arrange *chiva* tours, usually with free drinks and live music on the bus.

There are good local nightclubs in Bocagrande eg **La Escollera**, Cra 1, next to El Pueblito shopping centre, with other places nearby including spontaneous musical groups on or near the beach most evenings.

Most places don't get going until after 2400, though the Cuban bar **Donde Fidel**, on Portal de los Dulces, and **Café Havana**, on C de la Media Luna in Getsemaní start a little earlier and are highly recommended if you want to hear Cuban salsa. The former is open daytime and the atmosphere is good even early on. C del Arsenal host the majority of Cartagena's clubs and you will likely wind up there if you are really giving the city's nightlife a go. Most bars play crossover music.

Café del Mar, on Baluarte de Santo Domingo, El Centro. The place to go at sundown, where surrounded by ancient canons you can watch the sun set over the bay. Highly recommended, but very popular. Get here early to get a seat for the sundowners.

Casa de la Cerveza, at the end of C del Arsenal. Low sofas peppered around the battlements.

Mister Babilla, C del Arsenal. The most popular and exclusive bar. Take something warm with you – they really like to blast the a/c here.

Quiebra Canto, C Media Luna at Parque Centenario, next to **Hotel Monterrey**, Getsemaní. The best place for salsa. Nice atmosphere, free admission.

Tu Candela, Portal de los Dulces, next door to Donde Fidel Open from 2000.

Gay bars

Studio 54, C Larga, No 24, Getsemaní.

⊕ Entertainment

Cartagena *p138, map p142*

Cinema

There are many cinemas in Cartagena. In Bocagrande there is one in the **Centro Commercial Bocagrande**. Others are in the **Centro Comercial Paseo de la Castellana** on Av Pedro de Heredia and in **Centro Comercial La Plazuela** in the same area. **Teatro Heredia**, has been beautifully restored.

Dance

El Colegio del Cuerpo, C Larga, No 10-27, T664 3184, www.elcolegiodelcuerpo.org. A classical dance studio that works with children from Cartagena's slums. They perform internationally and occasionally in Cartagena.

⊛ Festivals and events

Cartagena *p138, map p142*

End-Jan Hay Festival Cartagena, www.hay festival.com. Franchise of the famous literary festival in the UK, takes place at the end of the month, with internationally renowned writers.

Jan-Feb La Candelaria (Candelmas).

Feb-Mar International Film Festival, Beluarte San Francisco, C San Juan de Dios, T660 1701/2, www.ficcifestival.com. The longest running festival of its kind in Latin America. Although mainly Spanish American films are featured, the US, Canada and European countries are represented in the week-long showings.

1 Jun celebrations commemorating the Foundation of Cartagena.

Nov Independencia. In the 2nd week of the month, to celebrate the Independence of Cartagena. People in masks and fancy dress dance in the streets. There are beauty contests, battles of flowers and general mayhem.

Dec Caribbean Music Festival. Groups from all over the Caribbean region and beyond perform salsa, reggae, etc.

○ Shopping

Cartagena *p138, map p142*

There is a good selection of *artesanías* at **Compendium** on Plaza Bolívar. **Galería Cano** (www.galeriacano.com.co), next to the Gold Museum has excellent reproductions of pre-Columbian designs. Pricey antiques can be bought in C Santo Domingo and there are a number of jewellery shops near Plaza de Bolívar in Centro, which specialize in emeralds. Beware of 'Cuban cigars' sold on the street; **Habanos**, C San Juan de Dios, has a wide selection but in general you will pay less in Bogotá.

The handicraft shops in the Plaza de las Bóvedas (**25**) have the best selection in town but tend to be expensive – cruise ship passengers are brought here. Woollen *blusas* are good value; try the **Tropicano** in

Pierino Gallo building in Bocagrande. Also in this building are reputable jewellery shops.
Abaco, C de la Iglesia with C Mantilla, No 3-86, www.abacolibros.com. A bookshop, which is a popular hangout for local writers and poets. Delightful atmosphere and a café serving juices and snacks.
Centro Comercial Getsemaní, C Larga between San Juan and Plaza de la Independencia. A large shopping centre. Good *artesanías* in the grounds of the convent.
H Stern, Pierino Gallo shopping centre and at the **Hilton Hotel**. Jewellery shop.
Instituto Geográfico Agustín Codazzi, C 34, No 3A-31, Edificio Inurbe, www.igac.gov.co. Maps.
Librería Nacional, C 2 (Badillo), No 36-27, T664 1448,www.librerianacional.com. Bookshop.
Magali París, Av Venezuela y C del Boquete. A supermarket, with a/c and cafeteria.
Santo Domingo, C Santo Domingo, No 3-34. Recommended for jewellery.
Upalema, C San Juan de Dios, No 3-99. A good selection of handicrafts.

Markets
The main market is to the southeast of the old city near La Popa off Av Pedro de Heredia (**Mercado Bazurto**). Good bargains in the **La Matuna** market, open daily including Sun.

▲ Activities and tours

Cartagena *p138, map p142*
Diving
La Tortuga Dive Shop, Edif Marina del Rey, C 1 2-23, Local 4, Av del Retorno, Bocagrande, T665 6995, www.tortugadive.com. A mini-course with 2 dives costs US$105. A faster boat, which allows trips to Isla Barú as well as Los Rosarios.
Diving Planet, C Estanco del Aguardiente, No 5-94, T664 2171, www.divingplanet.org.

PADI open certificate course, PADI e-learning, snorkelling trips, English spoken. Associated hotel in Cartagena, **Puertas de Cartagena**, www.hotelpuertasdecartagena.com.

Football
Estadio de Futbol Pedro de Heredia, Villa Olímpica, south of the city. Games are infrequent. Seats for matches cost between US$5 and US$13.50.

Horse-drawn carriage rides
Horse-drawn carriages can be hired for for a trip around the walled city from Puerta del Reloj, about US$16 for up to 4 people. Or from opposite Hotel El Dorado, Av San Martín, in Bocagrande, to ride into town at night (romantic but a rather short ride).

Tour operators
Aventure Colombia, C del Santísimo, No 8-55, T664 8500, T314-588 2378 (mob), www.aventurecolombia.com. The only tour organizer of its kind in Cartagena, Frenchman Mathieu Perrot-Bohringer and his Colombian wife Angélica specialize in alternative tours across Colombia, focusing on trekking, eco-tourism and rural tourism. They aim to practice responsible tourism, working (wherever possible) with local and indigenous groups. For further information on boat trips they organize, see Transport, page 155. Highly recommended.
Ocean & Land, Cra 2, No 4-15, Edificio Antillas, Bocagrande, T665 7772, oceanland tours@yahoo.com. Organizes city tours, rumbas in *chivas* and other local activities.

Yachting
Club Náutico, Av Miramar No 19-50, on Manga Island across the Puente Román, T660 4863, www.clubnauticocartagena.com. Good for opportunities to charter, crew or for finding a lift to other parts of the Caribbean.

⊖ Transport

Cartagena *p138, map p142*

Air
Direct flights daily to major Colombian cities and to smaller places in the north of the country. International flights direct daily to Miami and Panama. From Dec to Mar flights can be overbooked, so best to turn up at the airport early. Daily flights to all main cities and international destinations.

Airline offices Copa Air, Cra 6, No 8-116 (Bocagrande), T6650428; **Avianca**, C del Arzobispado, No 34-52, T6641729, also in Bocagrande, C 7, No 7-17, L 7, T665 5727 and at the airport; **CC Invercredito**, Local 18, T664 9077, Mon-Fri 0800-1800, Sat 0900-1300.

Bus
Colectivos for **Barranquilla** leave from C 70, Barrio Crespo every 2 hrs and cost US$14 and are a good option as they do a centre-to-centre service. There is a regular bus to **Barranquilla**, every 15 mins, 2-3 hrs, US$8, Berlinas del Fonce; Brasilia; Concorde; La Costeña.To **Medellín**, 665 km, approximately 1 every hour starting from 0530, 13-16 hrs, US$60, Brasilia; Copetran; Rápido Ochoa (slightly cheaper, recommended), book early (2 days in advance at holiday times). The road is now paved throughout, but in poor condition. To **Santa Marta**, 1 every hour, 4 hrs, US$13.50, Berlinas del Fonce; Brasilia; La Costeña.

To **Bogotá** via Barranquilla and Bucaramanga, 16 a day, 21-28 hrs (depending on number of check-points), US$75, with Berlinas del Fonce (3 a day); Brasilia; Concorde; Copetran; Rápido Ochoa. To **Magangué** on the *Magdalena*, US$12, 4 hrs with Brasilia. To **Mompós**, 0700, 12 hrs including ferry crossing from Magangué, US$17, Unitransco. To **Riohacha**, US$22. Bus to **Maicao** on Venezuelan frontier, every hour 0500-1200, 2 in the evening, 12 hrs, US$27, with Brasilia.

Car hire
Several of the bigger hotels have car rental company offices in their foyers, such as Hotel Bahía, Bocagrande, C 14, No 3-59, local 1. There are several car rental companies in Edif Torremolinos, Av San Martín: **International Car Rentals**, T665 5399; **National**, T665 3336; **Rentacars**, T665 2852. At the airport, try **Platinum** on 2nd floor, T666 4112.

Sea
Intermittent boats go from Cartagena to **Porvenir** in the San Blas Islands (Panama); the journey takes about 2 days and the 1-way fare is US$450-500 per person, including food and 3 nights touring the San Blas archipelago. The sailboats will normally end in **San Blas** from where you can continue your journey by air or overland to Panama City. The skippers will help with immigration paperwork.

There are 3 boats that provide a regular service between Cartagena and San Blas. Highly recommended is **Stella Luna**, T312-681 7833 (Colombia) or T507-6768 6121 (Panama), captained by Hernando Higuera, a key figure in establishing Cartagena's sailing club, who has strong friendships with many of the indigenous Cuna of San Blas. Also try: **Tango**, run by French skipper David, T314-558 8945 (mob) or German captain Guido, T316-243 6324 (mob), who also owns a backpackers' hostel in Panama. Take your time before choosing a boat. Some captains are irresponsible and unreliable. The journey is cramped and you do not want to make it with a captain you do not get on with.

Aventure Colombia, T314-588 2378 (mob), www.aventurecolombia.com, can provide reliable information on trustworthy boats and skippers. Also organize 8-day tours to San Blas via the Islas del Rosario, Islas de San Bernardo and Sapzurro in the Darién, costing about US$800 per person, including food.

Also try noticeboards at backpacker hotels such as Hotel Casa Viena or ask around at the Yacht Club (Club Nautico). In Panama, the only reliable information is in Porvenir.

Taking a vehicle It is possible to ship a car from Cartagena to Panama. 3 companies that can arrange shipment of vehicles to Panama are: **Agencia Internacional Ltda**, Cra 2, No 9-145, Edif Nautilus, Bocagrande, T664 7539, agents for King Ocean Services, 11000 NW 29 St, Suite 201, Doral, FL, T305-591 7595, serving Cartagena, Panama and Miami; **Hermann Schwyn**, Edif Chambacu Business Center, Piso 6, PO Box 1626, T650 3610, www.schwyn.com; **Mundinaves**, Edif City Bank, oficinas 13F y 13G, T664 4188, www.mundinaves.com.

Note On the street, do not be tempted by offers of jobs or passages aboard ship. Jobs should have full documentation from the Seamen's Union office and passages should only be bought at a recognized shipping agency.

● Directory

Cartagena *p138, map p142*
Banks There are many ATMs, the most convenient are in the Plaza de la Aduana, where there are **BBVA, Bancolombia, Davivienda** and **Santander** offices. In Bocagrande a number of banks can be found around Av San Martín with C 8. If you are changing TCs make sure you have your passport with you or you will probably be charged the 3% tax applicable to residents, or you may not be able to exchange the cheques at all. Never change money on the street in any circumstances. There are *cambios* in the arcade at Torre Reloj and adjoining streets which change Amex TCs; **Cambiamos**, Cra 2, No 1-100, Edif Seguros Bolívar, Bocagrande, T665 1600; **Comisiones Las Bovedas**, C del Colegio, No 34-53, T664 1692; **Comisiones Royal**, Cra 2, No 5-52, Centro Comercial Michel Center, Bocagrande,

T655 1556; **Western Union**, Av Venezuela, No 8A-87, Edif City Bank. **Embassies and consulates** Austria, Cra 13 Edif Chambacu Business Centre, piso 6, T650 3617; **Belgium**, Edif Viña del Mar Cra 6 6-57, Bocagrande, T655 0187, www.diplomatie.belgium.be; **Canada**, Cra 3, No 8-129, Of 1103, T665 5838; **Germany**, Diagonal 21 53-25 piso 2 T669 4041; **Sweden**, Av El Pastelillo 24-134, Isla Manga, T660 4594; **USA**, Cra 3, No 36-37, C de la Factoría, Centro, T660 0415; **Venezuela**, Cra 3, No 8-129, Edif Centro Ejecutivo, piso 14, T665 0382, Bocagrande, open to 1500, possible to get a visa the same day (US$30), you will need an onward ticket and 2 photos, but ensure you get a full visa not a 72 hrs' transit unless that is all you need.
Immigration DAS, just beyond Castillo San Felipe, Cra 20B, No 29-18, Plaza de la Ermita (Pie de la Popa), T656 3007, helpful. DAS passport office is in C Gastelbondo, near the ramparts. Get free visa extensions here.
Internet Camilina, C de Coliseo, No 5-52, T664 6866; **Conexion San Diego**, C de las Bóvedas, No 39-120, T664 2382; **Game Over**, C San Andrés, No 30-47. **Language** The Nueva Lengua School, www.nuevalengua. com, offers courses ranging from half-day schedules to a scheme that arranges volunteer jobs. There are even Spanish courses combined with dance, music, adventure, kite-surfing or diving. **Laundry** Chalet Suizo, C de la Media Luna, No 10-36, also email, information and tours arranged.
Medical services There is a recompression chamber at the naval hospital, Bocagrande; **Hospital Bocagrande**, C 5/Cra 6, Bocagrande, T655 0962, www.hospitalbocagrande.com.co.
Post In Centro, for airmail is at the Avianca office near the cathedral, Mon-Fri 0800-1830, Sat 0800-1500, and Av Lemaitre, La Matuna; **Adpostal**, C 34, La Matuna; **Deprisa**, C 33, No 8-20, La Matuna; **Envia Colvanes**, Av Principal del Bosque Diag 21, No 49-70. Next to **Adpostal**; long-distance phones behind this building.

Around Cartagena

Cartagena is surrounded on almost all sides by water and travellers will be drawn to the city's sparkling Caribbean coast. Islas del Rosario and Islas San Bernardo are glistening examples of what a tropical paradise should look like, and for those on a budget there is Playa Blanca on the Barú Peninsula. To the northeast of Cartagena, the coastline is characterized by ciénagas (mangrove swamps), such as the Ciénaga La Caimanera, which provide plenty of opportunities to observe the wildlife that subsists in these remarkable ecosystems. A few kilometres further on is the Volcán del Totumo, an extraordinary crater-like mud hole where bathers can wallow before washing off in the nearby ciénaga. ▶▶ For listings, see pages 164-169.

Volcán del Totumo

Along the coast north of Cartagena, at La Boquilla, is the Ciénaga la Caimanera, a labyrinth of mangrove swamps full of wildlife. Canoe trips can be made to explore these (motorboats are not allowed). Local guides cost US$10 per person, and they will catch oysters for you to eat. Further north is **Galerazamba**, there is no accommodation but good local food. Nearby are the clay baths of **Volcán del Totumo** ① *entry to the cone US$2.50 adults, US$1.75 children, the unusual experience will cost you US$2 and you wash off in the nearby Ciénaga*, in beautiful surroundings. Climb up steep steps to the lip of the 20-m-high crater and slip into the grey cauldron of mud, about 10 m across, at a comfortable temperature and reputed to be over 500 m deep. Massages are available for a small extra fee. You can catch a bus from Cartagena to Galerazamba at the Mercado Popular, Carerra 2 with Calle 16 (US$1.50, two hours), ask to be dropped off at Lomo Arena where the bus turns off to Galerazamba. Walk along the main road for 2 km to a right turn signposted to Volcán del Totumo which is 1.5 km along a poor road. Hitching is possible. Taking a tour from Cartagena will cost more but will save a lot of time. **Aventure Colombia** ① *C del Santísimo, No 8-55, Cartagena, T664 8500 or T314-588 2378 (mob), www.aventurecolombia.com*, organizes tours to the volcano for US$28, including transport and lunch at La Boquilla or Playa de Manzanillo. A tour of both the volcano and the mangroves is US$42.

Islas del Rosario → For listings, see pages 164-169.

The National Park of Corales del Rosario and San Bernardo embraces the archipelago of Rosario (a group of 30 coral islets, 45 km southwest of the Bay of Cartagena) and the mangrove coast of the long island of Barú to its furthest tip. **Isla Grande** and some of the smaller islets are easily accessible by day trippers and those who wish to stay in one of the hotels. Permits are needed for the rest, entrance fee US$6. These picture-postcard islands, low lying and densely vegetated, with narrow strips of fine sand beaches, form part of a coral reef. **Rosario** (the largest and best conserved) and **Tesoro** both have small lakes, some of which connect to the sea, and many of the smaller islets are privately owned. There is an profusion of aquatic and birdlife here and the **San Martín de Pajarales Aquarium (Oceanario)** ① *US$10*, is worth visiting. Look out for the huge catfish but note that the price of entry is not included in boat fares. The island has access to some of the best coral reefs in the archipelago and diving and snorkelling are available. The **Hotel El Caribe** in Bocagrande (see page 150) offers scuba lessons in its pool followed by diving at its resort on Isla Grande, for US$230 and upwards.▶▶ *For further diving information, see Activities and tours, page 168.*

Mud volcanoes

The Caribbean coast is peppered with several geological curiosities popularly known as 'mud volcanoes'. These large mud pools are believed to be the result of underground oil and gas deposits, which combine with water, forcing the mud to ooze to the surface. Often they form conical mounds, hence the name. Many of these pools can be found between the Gulf of Urabá and Santa Marta. Turbo has several in its proximity (Rodosalín, El Alto de Mulatos and Caucal), as does San Pedro de Urabá. The Volcán de Totumo is a popular day trip from Cartagena, but the pick of the bunch is Arboletes, where an enormous 30-m-wide lake has formed a stone's throw from the beach.

Wallowing in the grey-black mud is a strange experience. It's impossible to sink and attempts to swim are about as worthwhile as trying to battle your way across a vat of treacle. When you have had enough, clamber out and join the line of mud-caked figures waddling down to the Caribbean for a wash and a swim. The stuff is reportedly an excellent exfoliant and does wonders for the skin and hair.

Travel agencies and the hotels offer excursions from the Muelle Turístico, leaving 0700-0900 and returning 1600-1700, costing from around US$45, lunch included; free if staying at one of the hotels. Overnight trips can be arranged through agencies, but they are overpriced. Note that there is an additional 'port tax' of US$6 payable at the entrance to the Muelle or on the boat. Book in advance. For five or more, try hiring your own boat for the day and bargain your price. This way you get to see what you want in the time available. The tour boats leave you with plenty of time with the beach vendors. For the cheapest rates, buy tickets from the boat owners (make sure they are the boat owners!) at the dockside, but they may already be booked up. **Aventure Colombia** (see above) organizes sailboat tours of the islands.

If you wish to enjoy the islands at your leisure there are several hotels to stay in. Recommended is **Isla del Pirata**, which has a number of simple, comfortable *cabañas* and where fresh fish and lobster are served for lunch and dinner. On neighbouring Isla Grande is **San Pedro de Majagua**, owned by Hotel Santa Clara in Cartagena. Snorkelling and diving organizers **Cultura del Mar** also have an ecohotel here, where you can sleep in hammocks or beds, with cooking provided by a local family. ▸▸ *For further information, see Sleeping, page 164.*

South of Cartagena → *For listings, see pages 164-169.*

Just a few years ago, the area south of Cartagena was a no-go zone. The road between Cartagena and Medellín was the scene of frequent kidnappings by guerrillas who would perform raids on passing traffic and quickly abscond into the region's network of densely vegetated hills. Today it's a different story, and locals no longer sweat before making what was once a perilous journey. However, a word of warning: this area is still very much active in drug trafficking. Towns such as Sincelejo and Montería are fine to pass through but we advise against staying there too long. It is now considered reasonably safe to travel at night between Cartagena and Medellín.

The improvement in security also means that this area, rich in culture and natural wonders, has opened up to tourism. Southwest of Cartagena, on an island in the middle f the imperious Magadalena, is the equally regal town of Mompós (also spelt Mompóx).)ue south is Tolú, gateway to the coral islands of San Bernardo (also part of the Corales de tosario and San Bernardo National Park), while further along the coast is Arboletes,)cation of the largest mud volcano in the area. Further still is Turbo, a rough frontier town rom where boats can be caught to the emerald green coastline of the Darién.

Mompós → *Colour map 1, B3. Phone code: 5. Population 41,585.*

ns and outs To reach Mompós from Cartagena there are three options: a direct bus eaves at 0700, US$17 (negotiable). Alternatively, take a bus to Magangue, a *chalupa* motorized canoe), US$3.50, followed by *colectivo* from La Bodega, US$4 per person. astly, a *colectivo* direct from your hotel will cost US$33, call T312-622 5946 (mob). The **Secretaría de Turismo Municipio de Mompós** ① *Calle Real del Medio, Palacio de San Carlos, T685 5919, Mon-Fri 0700-1200 and 1400-1700.* ▸▸ *For further information, see Transport, page 168.*

Sights Thanks to a geographical anomaly, Mompós (officially known as Santa Cruz de Mompós) retains much the same atmosphere you might have experienced visiting this sleepy town in the early 20th century. The grand old Magdalena River splits in two just before Mompós. When the town was founded in 1537, the Mompós branch of the river was the main tributary and it became a major staging port for travellers and merchandise going to the interior. But at the beginning of the 20th century it silted up with mud and became

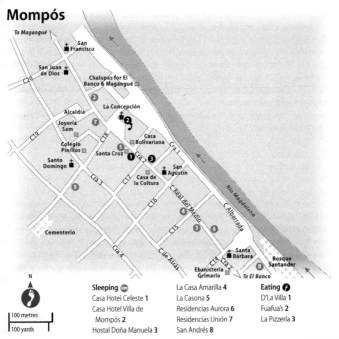

Mompós

N
100 metres
100 yards

Sleeping
Casa Hotel Celeste 1
Casa Hotel Villa de
  Mompós 2
Hostal Doña Manuela 3

La Casa Amarilla 4
La Casona 5
Residencias Aurora 6
Residencias Unión 7
San Andrés 8

Eating
D'La Villa 1
Fuafua's 2
La Pizzería 3

unnavigable for large boats, so traffic was diverted to the Brazo de Lobo. As a result Mompós became a backwater and it has remained practically untouched ever since.

In 1995 UNESCO declared it a World Heritage Site for the quality of its colonial architecture and its fine churches, and it was the setting for the film adaptation of Gabriel García Márquez's *Chronicle of a Death Foretold (1987)*.

Today, in the evenings, as the soporific heat begins to lessen and the bats start to swoop from the eaves of the whitewashed houses, locals carry their rocking chairs out onto the streets to chat with neighbours and watch the world go by. Cars are rare here; the main forms of transport are bicycle, moped, auto-rickshaw – or on foot.

Mompós is still a difficult place to reach – while direct buses are possible, most journeys include a combination of bus, motorized canoe and car. But plans are afoot to improve transport connections. Hopefully, these changes won't detract from its languid charm.

The churches demonstrate the colonial origins of the town; five of the six are close to the centre. The church of **San Francisco** is probably the oldest, dating from the end of the 16th century, with an interesting interior. **Santa Bárbara**, on Calle 14 by the river, has a unique octagonal Moorish tower and balcony. **San Juan de Dios, La Concepción, Santo Domingo** and **San Agustín** are all worth visiting. You may have to ask around for the key to see inside, they are not normally open except during Mass. Among the old buildings are the Casa de Gobierno, once a home of the Jesuits and now the **Alcaldía**, and the **Colegio Pinillos**. The cemetery is of considerable historical interest. Try to visit it on the Wednesday of Semana Santa when it is illuminated by thousands of candles lit by the locals to honour the dead. The town is well known in Colombia for hand-worked gold and silver jewellery, especially filigree, as well as its wicker rocking chairs.

Mompós was particularly dear to Simón Bolívar, as it was the site of one of the greatest victories in his campaign to expel the Spanish from South America. "If to Caracas I owe my life, then to Mompós I owe my glory," he said. He stayed in what is now called the **Casa Bolivariana**, which houses memorabilia of his times and also has some religious art exhibits. The **Casa de la Cultura** is a particularly interesting colonial building and home of the local Academy of History.

Ferocious mosquitoes and the odd bat are a nuisance after dusk; take insect repellent and wear long sleeves.

Tolú → *Colour map 1, B2. Phone code: 5.*

Tolú, 35 km northwest of Sincelejo, on the coast, is a fast developing holiday town popular with Colombians and, increasingly, foreign tourists attracted by visits to the offshore islands and diving. Along the *malecón* (promenade), there are plenty of bars and restaurants. A distinctive feature of the town are the bicycle rickshaws armed with loud soundsystems blasting out vallenato, salsa and reggaeton. The rickshaw drivers spend much of their time trying to outdo each other with the volume of their music. Tolú can also be reached more directly from Cartagena, through **San Onofre**, then, after 46 km from San Onofre, turn right for Tolú. Continue straight on from Toluviejo for 20 km to Sincelejo.

A good boat trip from Tolú is to the beautiful beaches of Múcura island or Titipán (**D** *cabañas*) in the **Islas de San Bernardo**, about US$25, 45 minutes. Trips to the mangrove lagoons are also recommended. **Club Náutico Mundo Marino**, run daily boats to San Bernardo Islands at 0830, returning at 1230, which cost US$25 return trip. Isla Múcura has a number of shacks serving seafood, including excellent barbecued lobster. The beach is of fine white sand with beautiful, clear water. Unfortunately, with several launches converging n the island at the same time, it can get crowded and the number of beach vendors can detract from the beauty of the place. There is a charge for everything, including sitting at table. To enjoy the islands at your leisure, it is better to stay overnight. It's also possible to reach the island from Cartagena, if you have a reservation at Punta Faro (one hour 45 minutes by boat, transfer included in the cost of accommodation. ▸▸ *For further information, see Sleeping and Activities and tours, pages 164 and 168.*

There are, perhaps surprisingly, good beaches at **Coveñas**, 20 km further southwest, the terminal of the oil pipeline from the oilfields in the Venezuelan border area. Coveñas is essentially a 5-km-long stretch of road peppered with *cabañas* and hotels. During high season (Easter, Christmas-mid January, June and July) it is very popular with Colombians eager to hit the beach and party. To get there, take a bus or *colectivo* from Tolú.

Further along the coast, turning right 18 km southwest of Coveñas at Lorica is **San Bernardo del Viento** from where launches can be arranged to **Isla Fuerte**, an unspoilt coral island with fine beaches and simple places to stay. It's a good place to dive, but there are very limited facilities on the island. Enquire at travel agencies in Medellín and elsewhere for inclusive trips or negotiate in San Bernardo.

Arboletes

Southwest of Tolú is the unremarkable town of Arboletes which nonetheless has an extraordinary attraction: the largest mud volcano in the area. Dipping into this swimming pool-sized mud bath is a surreal experience – like swimming in treacle. It's also very good for your skin. You can wash the mud off with a dip in the sea by walking down to the beach 100 m below. Arboletes is also a convenient stopover on the way to Turbo and the Darién coast.

The **Volcán de Lodo** is a 15-minute walk from town on the road to Montería or a two-minute taxi ride (US$5.50 return – the driver will wait for you while you bathe). A mototaxi costs US$1. There is a small restaurant and changing rooms (US$ 0.30), plus a locker room (US$1 per bag) and showers (US$0.50).

Turbo

At the mouth of the Gulf of Urabá is the port of Turbo, a hot, rough, frontier community with a lawless feel about it. It is a centre for banana cultivation. There is little reason to stop here except to catch a boat to Capurganá and the Panamanian border.

The Darién Gap

The Darién Gap has long held a special place in travellers' lore as the ultimate adventure – and with reason. This thin stretch of land, just 50 km wide and 160 km long, which links Central and South America, has some of the densest tropical jungle in the world – so dense that to date neither the Panamanians nor the Colombians have succeeded in building a road across. There are no roads of any kind, the only inland routes are by boat or on foot. At present, the Pan-American Highway from Canada to Tierra del Fuego in Chile stops at Yaviza in Panama, 60 km short of the frontier, and begins again 27 km west of Barranquillita, well into Colombia. The Darién is home to an incredible profusion of flora and fauna, as well as indigenous tribes who rarely see foreigners.

The trek across the Darién is held in high regard by adventurers but we strongly advise against it, not simply because it is easy and fatal to get lost, but also because bona fide travellers are not welcome (indigenous communities still living in Darién have never truly accepted trekkers passing through) and this area still has a heavy guerrilla presence. The

Colombian government's successes against the FARC have pushed them to the extreme of the country, where they have retreated to lick their wounds. Those trafficking drugs from South to North America have found the density of the jungle a useful protection for running consignments. Both FARC and ELN guerrilla groups have infiltrated the region and paramilitaries regard this as a threat to their land. As a result this has become a violent war zone, virtually deserted now by police and the military, and it is a hostile environment for any tourist. As recently as 2008 there were reports of kidnappings in the Darién. For the moment only the foolhardy will attempt the land crossing. However, the Caribbean coastline, heavily patrolled by Colombian and Panamanian forces, is safe, though you should exercise caution if venturing into the forest beyond.

Acandí
Acandí is a small fishing village on the Caribbean side of the Darién. It has a spectacular forest-fringed bay with turquoise waters. In April, thousands of leatherback turtles come here to lay their eggs. There are several cheap *residencias* to stay in. There are several flights a week from Medellín with **Aerolínea de Antioquia** (www.ada-aero.com) (US$120 one way).

Capurganá
For many years, Capurganá and neighbouring Sapzurro have been one of the best kept secrets in Colombia. In this most isolated of Colombia's corners, a glistening, untouched shoreline of crystal waters and coral reefs backs onto quiet little villages where, at night, if you listen carefully, you can hear the howler monkeys calling to each other in the jungle-clad hills behind.

Capurganá has developed into a resort popular with affluent Colombians and is increasingly visited by foreigners, despite it being somewhat difficult or expensive to get to. Until fairly recently it was an important point for smuggling drugs through to Panama, with heavy guerrilla activity. But a strong army presence has put an end to that and it is now considered a safe place to visit. It is a quiet place: there are no cars and just two motorbikes. Taxi rides are provided by horse and carts, and someone has had the ingenious idea of attaching modified plastic seats.

There are two beaches in the village. La Caleta is at the northern end, beyond the pontoon, and is protected by a barrier reef, has golden sand and is the best for swimming. There are a couple of restaurants and several hotels and *cabañas* here. Playa de los Pescadores, south of the village, is fringed by palm and almond trees but has disappointing grey sand and is more pebbly. Ask the fishermen about fishing trips from here (US$ 15-20 in rowing boats).

Around Capurganá
Several half- and full-day trips can be made by launch boat to neighbouring beaches. Aguacate is a beautiful bay with clear, aquamarine water and a small beach. There is a rocky promontory with a blowhole and what locals call '*La Piscina*', a natural jacuzzi amongst the rocks which you can lower yourself into using a rope. There is also a small restaurant serving fried fish for US$7. Aguacate has good snorkelling, but Playa Soledad is perhaps the most attractive beach in the area and was recently used as the location for a Colombian reality TV programme. The beach is white sand and fringed by palms.

A return trip by launch boat costs US$11 per person, minimum five people. You can also walk to Aguacate, 1½ hours along the coast, though not to Playa Soledad. Note that it can be difficult to obtain a return by launch if you walk.

Another trip is to Sapzurro, a few kilometres north (see below). Capurganá Tours organizes day trips to the San Blas archipelago in Panama, possibly some of the most beautiful islands in the Caribbean and launches stop at the island of Caledonia (US$55-60 per person with a minimum of 28 people).

There is excellent diving and snorkelling around Capurganá. You are likely to see nurse sharks, moray eels, spotted eagle rays, trumpetfish, jewfish, barracuda and hawksbill turtles, among other species, as well as large brain and elkhorn coral. Several of the hotels organize diving and the independent dive centre, **Dive and Green**, near the jetty is recommended.

A delightful half-day excursion is to **El Cielo** ① *entry US$2*, a small waterfall in the jungle. You can walk there in 40 minutes through beautiful primary jungle. Take flip flops or waterproof boots, as you will have to cross a stream several times and it is muddy. Take the path to the left of the airport and keep asking for directions as it is easy to get lost. Just before the waterfall there is a small restaurant serving *patacones* and drinks. There is a swimming hole with a zip wire. Alternatively, you can hire horses to take you there (US$7).

Another horse-riding trip is to El Valle de Los Ríos, a valley in the jungle with several crystalline rivers and beautiful waterfalls. The primary forest in this area is rich in wildlife; you might see, among other animals, sloths, howler monkeys, toucans, parrots, fishing eagles and several types of lizard and iguana. You should take a guide for this. The trip includes lunch at a *ranchería*. For more details, enquire at **Capurganá Tours** in town, by the jetty, or at the football pitch (*cancha de futbol*) in the village centre.

Sapzurro

Sapzurro is a quiet little village in the Darién and the last outpost before Panama and Central America. Set in a shallow, horseshoe-shaped bay dotted with coral reefs, little happens in this village of less than 1000 inhabitants. There are no roads, let alone cars. The houses of this tiny village are linked by intersecting pathways bursting with tropical flowers. It has a couple of excellent little hostels and some good restaurants serving up home-cooked seafood. The bay is excellent for snorkelling, with a couple of underwater caves to explore.

You can make a day trip to the small village of **La Miel** over the border in Panama by walking up the forested hill behind the village. This could qualify as the most relaxed border crossing in the world. The Colombian and Panamanian immigration offiers share a hut and copy each other's notes. Be sure to take your passport; if only going to La Miel they won't stamp it but they will take your details. There are breathtaking views of Panama and back into Sapzurro at the border crossing on the brow of the hill.

La Miel has a gorgeous white-sand beach with beautiful, clear waters and a coral reef. The snorkelling is relatively good though a little low on fauna. There are a couple of shacks selling beer and food. Try the sea snails in coconut sauce. You can arrange for a launch to pick you up and take you back to Sapzurro or Capurganá.

For Sleeping and Eating price codes and other relevant information, see pages 23-28.

● Sleeping

Islas del Rosario *p157*
AL Isla del Pirata, book through **Hotel Isla Pirata**, C 6 No 2-26, Bocagrande, T665 2952, www.hotelislapirata.com. 12 comfortable *cabañas* with activities that include diving, snorkelling, canoeing and petanque. Fresh fish and lobster are served for lunch and dinner. Prices include transport to the island, food and non-guided activities. Highly recommended.

Isla Grande
AL San Pedro de Majagua, book at Calle del Torno, No 39-29, T650 4460, www.hotelmajagua.com. Everything from a 'pillow menu' to Egyptian cotton bed sheets, this is a lovely, luxurious place for utter relaxation.

Mompós *p159, map p159*
Almost all of the hotels in Mompós are located on C Real del Medio, the main thoroughfare through town which boasts beautifully preserved whitewashed houses with enormous iron grills. Note that most hotels in Mompós double in price over Semana Santa and other festival periods.
A Hostal Doña Manuela, C Real del Medio (Cra 2), 17-41, T685 5621/5142, hostal mompox@turiscolombia.com. A charming hotel converted from the largest colonial house in town, centred around a courtyard with an extraordinary banyan tree. The rooms are spacious and fresh, while its swimming pool at the back provides welcome respite from the soporific heat. With an art gallery and jewellery shop and its central position, it is often at the hub of the action. Accepts credit cards.
B-C Residencias Aurora, Cra 2, No 15-65, T685 5723. Dishevelled but with character. Some shared baths, big ceilings, kitchen available, security could be an issue.

C Casa Hotel Celeste, C Real del Medio (Cra 2), No 14-174, T685 6875. Decorated with old photographs and fake oil paintings, this hotel is just the right side of chintzy. Rooms are a little small.
C Casa Hotel Villa de Mompós, 500 m east of Parque Bolívar, Cra 2 No 14-108, T685 5208. Charming family-run hotel, decorated with antique bric-a-brac. Internet access US$1 per hr. Can also arrange rooms for families during festival periods.
C Hacienda San Ignacio, a few kilometres out of town on the road to Talaigua. This modern hacienda, built on land belonging to Jesuit priests may offer welcome respite from the sometimes oppressive heat of Mompós. Rooms are clean and simple, it has a swimming pool and offers horse riding. It is managed by **Hostal Doña Manuela** (see above); ask there for details.
C La Casona, Cra 2, No 18-58, T685 5307, eusedeal@yahoo.es. Fine colonial building with delightful courtyards and plants. Has a billiard table, TV, a/c, laundry service and internet access. Just pips the rest of them for atmosphere.
C San Andrés, Cra 2, No 18-23, T855 886. Another fine, restored colonial building. The patio has parrots and aquariums. Rooms have TV and bathroom. Has own water and electricity supply (useful during power cuts). Can arrange guides for local area.
C-F La Casa Amarilla, C 13 No 1-05, T685 6326, www.lacasaamarillamompos.com. 1 block up from Iglesia Santa Bárbara on the riverfront, this backpackers' hostel has 6 luxury rooms with a/c, bath and cable TV, 3 economic rooms with bath and fan (**C-D**), and an a/c dorm (**E-F** pp), beautifully decorated. The hostel boasts 2 living rooms equipped with TV and DVD player, a book exchange and an information board while at the end of the garden there is an open-plan kitchen for guests' use. Thanks to his other job as a travel journalist, English owner Richard McColl is an excellent source of information on Colombia.

Residencias Unión, C 18, No 3-43, T685
723. The only hotel in Mompós in a modern
building. The rooms are cheap but a little dark
and likely to be noisy during festivities as hotel
is near the action. No double beds available.

Tolú p160

Alcira, Av La Playa, No 21-151, T288 5016,
alcirahotel@yahoo.com. On the promenade,
has a breezy courtyard and lots of balconies
with rocking chairs. Has a/c, laundry service,
parking, restaurant and Wi-Fi. Breakfast included.
Playamar, Av La Playa, No 22-22, T286
0587, playamar@yahoo.es. Large, white
building on the *malecón* with beautiful
lemon trees outside. Has all the mod cons,
including Wi-Fi, a/c, minibar, parking and TV.
Has a small restaurant serving breakfast.
C-D pp Estado Natural Ecolodge, 7 km
from San Bernardo del Viento, T301-442 2438,
www.estado-natural.com. Rustic cabins on
a beach, composting toilets and other
sustainable practices, meals not included,
cabins have kitchen, activities include
birdwatching, windsurfing, trips to Isla
Fuerte, riding and guided tours.
D Altamar, Cra 3, No 17-36, T288 5421. Bright
rooms opening onto an open-air corridor.
Has its own water and electricity supply.
Prices more than double in high season.
D Darimar, C 17, No 1-60, T288 5153. Just
off the beach front with small but clean
rooms, private bathrooms, TV and parking.
Friendly staff.
D Mar Adentro, Av La Playa, No 11-36,
T286 0079. Hotel belonging to tour agency
of same name. Nice, clean rooms with private
bathrooms. Rooms are cheaper (**E**) with fan.
E El Turista, Av La Playa, No 11-20, T288
5145. The cheapest option in town and
good value for money. On the promenade,
next to all the tour agencies.
E Los Angeles, C 17, No 1-23, T300-600
6107. Right on beach with TV, fan and
private bathrooms, though the rooms are
crammed with as many beds as possible.
E Villa Babilla, C 20, No 3-40, Barrio el
Cangrejo, T288 6124, www.villababilla

hostel.com. Easily the best option in Tolú.
Colombian/German couple Alex and Laffie
have built a quiet little haven of simple,
brightly painted rooms with a thatched
cabaña as a TV area and lots of hammocks.
Alex is a good source of information on
activities in local area.

Isla Múcura
LL Punta Faro, Isla Múcura, Islas San
Bernardo, T318-323 2323, www.punta
faro.com. Low-key luxury resort with 45
rooms in gorgeous setting by the sea, inside
Corales del Rosario y San Bernardo National
Park. Price includes all meals, buffet-style,
and return boat transfer from Cartagena
(boats leave once a day in high season
and Mon and Fri only in low season, so
make sure you catch it). Massage treatments,
hammocks on the beach, eco walks around
the island and a good sustainability policy.
Highly recommended.

Coveñas
A Villa Melissa, T288 0249, www.hotelvilla
melissa.com. Large apartments on the beach
each with their own balcony, a/c and TV.
Also has a swimming pool.
D Cabañas del Morrosquillo, Km 9 Vía
Tolú, T280 0341. Not the prettiest concrete
structures you have ever seen but have
comfortable beds and fan. On a good,
quiet stretch of beach.

Arboletes p161
E Ganadero, C Principal, T820 0086. Basic
but clean rooms. Has a pleasant reception
area under a thatched hut and a restaurant
serving basic fare for US$3.50.
E La Floresta, C Principal, T820 0034. Opposite
Ganadero, this small hotel has simple rooms
with private bathrooms. It's best to ask for a
street-facing room if you want a window.

Turbo p161
C Castilla de Oro, C 100, No 14-07,
T827 2185. The best option in town, has a/c,
safety box, minibar, a good restaurant and

a swimming pool. Modern building with reliable water and electricity. Friendly staff.

C Hotel 2000, C 101, No 12-115, T827 2333. Next to bus terminal, rooms with TV and private bathrooms. Almost half the price if you choose a room with fan only.

C Simona del Mar, Km 13 Vía Turbo, T824 3729, www.simonadelmar.com. Turbo is not a safe place in which to walk around at night, so this is a better, safer option for sleeping. A few kilometres outside town, this hotel has a number of *cabañas* in a tranquil setting and near the beach. Has good restaurant. The beach is nice enough, although like everywhere on this stretch of the coast, the sea is a muddy brown due to its proximity to the Gulf of Urabá. A taxi to and from Turbo is US$11. You can also ask *colectivos* to drop you there.

C-D Playa Mar, Av de la Playa, T827 2205. Good, but somewhat run down with a restaurant. Has a/c, TV and is cheaper with fan.

Acandí *p162*

C pp Al Vaivén de Hamacas, San Francisco, T321-643 1171, http://alvaivenreserva.blog spot.com. Price is half board, cheaper without bath, Colombian food, a resort accessible by boat from Turbo (leaves between 0830 and 0900, between 1200 and 1230) or Capurganá (0730, 1 hr), with trekking and horse riding on the beach or in the jungle, boat tours, kayak tours to nearby islands, fishing and river bathing, English spoken.

Capurganá *p162*

Accomodation and food are generally more expensive than in other parts of Colombia but it is possible to find reasonably cheap hostels and restaurants.

LL Almar, enquire through offices in Medellín, T436 6262, www.almar.com.co. Luxury wooden *cabañas* amongst manicured gardens and right on the beach. Has Turkish bath, spa, jacuzzi and a pool.

AL Tacaruna Lodge, T361 7809 (Medellín), www.hotelesdecostaacosta.com. *Cabañas* around a garden pool. All meals included.

A Playa de Capurganá, T276 4260 (Medellín T094-824 3914 (Capurganá), www.jardin botanicodarien.com/condominio.htm. Set in tropical gardens, this breezy wooden house has comfortable rooms with private bathrooms and a fine veranda with hammocks from which to look out to sea, as well as a great swimming pool right on the beach. The price includes a home-cooked breakfast and dinner. Recommended.

B HostalMarlin Hostal, T824 3611, capurgana marlin@yahoo.es. The best mid-range option in town. A beautiful wooden chalet on Playa de los Pescadores with good rooms, private bathrooms and a patio with a mango tree and lots of plants and songbirds. Has a good restaurant serving excellent fish. There are also bunks (**F**) available.

C Cabaña Darius, T314-622 5638, www.dariuscapurgana.es.tl. In the grounds of Playa de Capurganá, this little place is excellent value for money with simple, comfortable rooms in a wooden chalet set amongst acres of exquisite tropical gardens. Large balconies with hammocks. Rooms have fan, private bathroom and breakfast is included.

D Hostal Capurganá, C del Comercio, T316-743 3863. Comfortable, clean rooms with private bathrooms. Has a pleasant patio and is well situated on the main street, next to the jetty. Recommended.

D Luz de Oriente, T824 3719, luzdeoriente 999@hotmail.com. Right on the jetty, each of the rooms is named after a *Lord of the Rings* character. Rooms are a bit cramped with too many beds. Has a beautiful restaurant serving average food.

E Los Delfines, T682 8788. A few blocks back from the jetty, rooms are very basic but there are pretty balconies with hammocks, a restaurant and TV.

Private houses There are several private homes for hire, including:
Cabaña de los Alemanes, a simple self-catering bungalow with a thatched hut

or slinging hammocks and a small plunge pool. The *cabaña* is in a prime position, right in the waterfront – the sea laps against the edge of the garden. Sleeps 8 in bunks and single beds for US$150 per night. Enquire at **Dive and Green**, page 168, for more details.

Sapzurro *p163*

C Hostería Zingara, Camino La Miel, T313-673 3291. Pretty much the last building before you get to Panama, *Zingara* has 2 lovely *cabañas* with gorgeous views over the bay. The owners have a herb and vegetable garden and sell home-made chutneys. This also doubles up as the village pharmacy.

D-E Paraíso Sapzurro, T824 4115/T313-685 9862, www.paraiso-sapzurro-colombia.com. Right on the beach at the southern end of the village, this has a number of *cabañas*, a little more basic than *Zingara*'s, run by a charismatic Chilean. Has an excellent thatched ranch full of hammocks for relaxing. Also has space for camping. Ask for El Chileno and you will be directed here when you arrive. Higher price includes half-board.

🍴 Eating

Mompós *p159, map p159*

Good bakeries on C 18 and Cra 3 for coffee, cakes and snacks. A selection of fast food kiosks can be found at the Plaza Santo Domingo, next to the church.

¶¶¶ Restaurante Doña Manuela, part of the hostel of the same name (see Sleeping), probably the best restaurant in town (though pricey with it), fish is particularly good, try the *bagre momposino*.

¶¶ Fuafua's, on Parque Bolívar, T684 0609. Serves *comida corriente*, worth going to if just to experience its grand old dilapidated dining hall looking out over the square.

¶¶ La Pizzería, opposite San Agustín Church. Good pizzas in a lovely setting.

¶ D'La Villa, C 18, No 2-49, T685 8793. For those tired of chicken and steak this bakery/

ice cream parlour also serves up a selection of crêpes.

¶ La Parcela, a few kilometers out of town opposite the airport, open only on Sun. Momposinos go here to sit under the shade of mango trees and eat *sancocho* and *ajiaco* while listening to *vallenato*.

Tolú *p160*

¶ La 15, Av La Playa, No 15 esquina. Good quality steaks with swift service. Recommended.

¶ La Atarraya, C 15, No 1-38. Cheap fast food. Burgers, pizza and hotdogs.

¶ La Red, Av La Playa, No 20. Decorated with all things aquatic, including fishing nets, star fish, turtle shells, oars and model boats. Serves cheap but good seafood, steaks, burgers and hotdogs. Friendly staff.

¶ Punto B, C 15, No 2-02. Cheap and cheerful restaurant and *panadería* serving the usual Colombian fare. *menú del día*, US$ 3.

Capurganá *p162*

¶¶¶ Donde Josefina, Playa La Caleta, T316-779 7760. Josefina cooks exquisite seafood, served to you under a shady tree on the beach. Try the lobster cooked in garlic and coconut sauce.

¶ El Patacón, C del Comercio. Serves good, simple seafood.

¶ Luz de Oriente, on the jetty. Lovely looking restaurant decorated with lots of hanging shells, though the food is a bit bland.

¶ Pizzería Mi Ciclo, T314-789 1826. This isn't a restaurant as much as a lovely woman who will cook remarkably good pizzas from an oven in her bedsit and bring out a table and chairs for you to eat them on. Ask around for her on the C del Comercio, near Capurganá Tours.

Sapzurro *p163*

¶ La Negra, C Principal. Serves home-cooked seafood.

🎭 Entertainment

Mompós *p159, map p159*
There are a number of bars and discos along the riverfront, among the best of which is the bohemian **Luna de Mompox**.

🛍 Shopping

Mompós *p159, map p159*
Mompós is famous for its filigree gold and silver jewellery and its wicker rocking chairs. You can visit workshops to see how they are made.

Jewellery
Joyería Sam, C 18A No 2B, T685 5829. Fine selection of beautifully worked gold and silver earrings, bracelets and brooches.
Santa Cruz, Cra 2, No 20-132, T685 6371, tallersantacruz@yahoo.com.

Rocking chairs
Ebanistería Grimarlo, Cra 2, No 13-29, T685 5313.
Muebles Momposinos, Cra 2, opposite Monumento del Sagrado Corazón, T685 5349.

🛶 Activities and events

Islas del Rosario *p157*
Diving
Cultura del Mar, Getsemaní C del Pozo, No 25-95, Cartagena, T664 9312. Offices in Cartagena, organizes snorkelling and diving, and various tours of the coral reefs and mangroves of the islands.
Excursiones Roberto Lemaitre, C 6 No 2-26, Edificio Granada, local 2, Bocagrande, T665 5622 (owner of **Club Isla del Pirata**). They have the best boats and are near the top end of the price range but **Yates Alcatraz** is more economical; enquire at the quay.

Tolú *p160*
Tour operators
Club Náutico Mar Adentro, Av La Playa, No 11-36, T286 0079, www.clubnauticomaradentro.com. A good agency.

Capurganá *p162*
Diving
Dive and Green, near the jetty, T682 8825, www.diveandgreen.com. The only dive centre in town that does PADI. Has a 27 ft boat with 200 horsepower. Excursions to San Blas. English spoken.

Tour operators
Capurganá Tours, C del Comercio, T316 4823665, www.capurganatours.net. Organizes walking tours with knowledgeable guides to nearby beaches and into the jungle as well as horse riding, diving and birdwatching. Trips to San Blas islands in Panama arranged i sufficient people. Can assist in booking flights from Puerto Obaldía to Panama City. English spoken. Highly recommended.

🚍 Transport

Mompós *p159, map p159*
Bus
To **Cartagena** there are 3 options: with Unitransco, direct, US$17 (negotiable), bus leaves at 0600 from outside Iglesia Santa Barbara; or *colectivo* to La Bodega, US$4 per person, *chalupa* (motorized canoe) US$3.50, and finally bus to Magangué. **Asotranstax** runs a door-to-door *colectivo* service between Mompós and Santa Marta, US$30; and Mompós and Valledupar. To **Medellín**, taxi to La Bodega, then *chalupa* to Magangué and finally bus with **Brasilia** or **Rápido Ochoa**, 10 hrs, US$45. Alternatively, take a bus to Santa Ana via Aracataca and Bosconia, then a *chalupa* to Talaigua, and finally a *colectivo*.

Unitransco has direct service to **Barranquilla**, leaving at 0600. To **Bogotá**, Copetran and Omega have services leaving from El Banco (4WD trip from Mompós) at

500, US$27-39. To **Bucaramanga**, Copetran bus leaves El Banco at 1000. Return journey leaves Bucaramanga at 1000.

olú *p160*
us
rasilia has buses every hour to **Cartagena** between 0715 and 1730. 12 a day to **Medellín** with Brasilia and Rápido Ochoa, S$40, via Montería except at night. **Bogotá**, a day, US$55. To **Barranquilla**, **Santa Marta** and **Riohacha**, 5 a day, US$33. For ucaramanga you must change at Sincelejo, a day, US$55. To **Valledupar**, 1 a day, hanging at Sincelejo, US$25.

urbo *p161*
ea
aunches for **Acandí**, **Capurganá** and apzurro leave daily at 0800, US$25 and ake 3 hrs. It's a spectacular journey that ugs the Caribbean shoreline of the Darién. As passengers begin to embark you will otice a rush for seats at the back. You re well advised to join in the scrum as he journey is bumpy and can be painful n seats at the front. **Note** There is a 10 kg mit on baggage, excess is US$0.50 per kg. Between mid-Dec and the end of Feb the sea becomes very choppy and dangerous. We advise you not to make this journey during this period.

Capurganá *p162*
Air
1 flight daily to **Medellín** with Aerolínea de Antioquia (ADA), US$300-350 return. Twin Otter biplanes with 16 passenger capacity. Be sure to book ahead. Baggage limit of 10 kg. Excess is US$2 per kg. You may be asked to allow your baggage to follow on a later plane if seriously overweight.

Sea
There's a launch to **Turbo**, daily, leaving at 0800, US$25. Be sure to get a seat at the back as the 3-hr ride is bumpy and can be excruciatingly uncomfortable at the front.

There are daily launches to **Puerto Obaldía** in Panama, US$20 (leaving at about 0700). From here it's possible to catch an **Air Panamá** flight to **Panama City** on Sun, Tue or Thu, cost US$63, www.flyairpanama.com. Essential to book in advance. It is possible to catch a further launch from Puerto Obaldía to **Mulatupo**, US$20, and from there to **Colón**, US$66.

Sapzurro *p163*
You can walk to **Capurganá** in 4 hrs, a beautiful hike along the coastline through jungle rich in wildlife.

Sea
Launches to **Capurganá** cost US$3, 30 mins. Launches leave from Puerto Obaldía or La Miel to **Panama**. Launch to Puerto Obaldía 45 mins, US$15.

⊙ Directory

Tolú *p160*
Banks There are several banks with cash-points on Parque Principal. **Internet** Cyber Blue, C 15, No 2, headphones and camera.

Arboletes *p161*
Banks There is a Banco Agrario in the Parque Principal, though it doesn't have a cashpoint.

Capurganá *p162*
Banks There are no banks in Capurganá. It's best to bring sufficient cash with you though **Capurganá Tours** will exchange cash on credit cards for a 6.5% commission. **Internet** Capurganá Tours, with Skype and headphones. **Immigration** DAS office, on the waterfront next to the police station, between the jetty and Playa de los Pescadores, Mon-Fri 0800-1500, Sat, Sun and holidays 0900-1600, T311-746 6234. If leaving for Panama you must get your passport stamped here. For entry into Panama you'll need proof of US$600 in the bank and a yellow fever certificate.

Barranquilla

→ *Colour map 1, A2. Phone code: 5. Population: 1,148,000.*

Barranquilla, Colombia's fourth city, lies on the western bank of the Río Magdalena, about 18 k *from its mouth. It's a seaport (though less busy than Cartagena or Santa Marta), as well as a riv* *port, and a modern industrial city with a polluted but colourful central area near the river. First a* *foremost, however, Barranquilla is famed for its Carnival, reputed to be second only to Rio de Janei* *in terms of size and far less commercialized. In 2003 UNESCO declared it a "masterpiece of the or* *and intangible heritage of humanity". Pre-carnival parades and dances last through January un* *an edict that everyone must party is read out. Carnival itself lasts from Saturday, with the Batalla* *las Flores, through the Gran Parada on Sunday, to the funeral of Joselito Carnaval on Tuesday. T* *same families have been participating for generations, keeping the traditions of the costumes a* *dances intact. Prepare for three days of intense revelry and dancing with very friendly an* *enthusiastic crowds, spectacular floats, processions, parades and beauty queens. The main actic* *takes place along Calle 17, Carrera 44 and Vía 40.* ▸▸ *For listings, see pages 172-174.*

Ins and outs

Getting there and around **Ernesto Cortissoz airport** is 10 km from the city. A city bu from the airport to town costs US$0.35 (US$0.40 on Sunday). Only take buses marke 'centro', you can catch them 200 m from the airport on the right. A taxi to town costs US$ (taxis do not have meters, so agree on the fare in advance). The main **bus terminal** south of the city near the Circunvalación. Some bus companies have offices around Call 34 and Carrera 45. If arriving into Barranquilla by boat and shipping your car, allow tw

Barranquilla maps
1 Barranquilla centre, page 170
2 Barranquilla – El Prado, page 171

Sleeping 🛏
Girasol **3**
Horizonte **4**
Hotel del Mar **2**
San Francisco **5**

Eating 🍴
Pescadero El Centro **1**

...ys to complete all the paperwork you'll need to retrieve your car from the port. Taxis for ...ips within town cost US$1.60. ▶ *For more information, see Transport, page 174.*

...ourist information Tourist information is available at the main hotels, at the **tourist** ...fice ⓘ *C40 No 36-135, Edif La Aduana, T351 0415*, and from the **tourist police** ⓘ *Cra 43, No ...7-53, T340 9903.*

...ights

...he city is surrounded by a continuous ring road called the 'Vía Cuarenta' from the north ...long the river to the centre; 'Avenida Boyacá' to the bridge (Puente Pumarejo), which ...rosses the Río Magdalena for Santa Marta; and 'Circunvalación' round the south and ...est of the city. The long bridge over the Río Magdalena gives a fine view of Barranquilla ...nd the river.

...In the centre the principal boulevard is **Paseo Bolívar** leading to **Parque Simón** ...olívar. Two blocks south is a handsome church, **San Nicolás**, formerly the cathedral, in ...laza San Nicolás, the central square, and before it stands a small statue of Columbus. ...he more recent **Catedral Metropolitana** ⓘ *Cra 45, No 53-120*, is opposite Parque la Paz. ...here is an impressive statue of Christ inside by the Colombian sculptor, Arenas ...etancourt. Further along is the small **Museo Antropológico** ⓘ *C 68, No 53-45*, which has

2 Barranquilla – El Prado

➡ **Barranquilla maps**
1 Barranquilla centre, page 170
2 **Barranquilla – El Prado, page 171**

Sleeping 🛏
Barranquilla Plaza **1**
Bulevard 58 **3**
El Prado **2**
Majestic **4**

Eating 🍴
Don Pepe **1**
Jardines de Confucio **2**
La Fonda Antioqueña **3**
La Pizza Loca **4**

Los Helechos **5**

Bars & clubs 🍸
Froggs Leggs **6**
Henry's **7**

a big physical relief map on the front lawn, and the **Museo Romántico** ① *Cra 5 No 59-199*, which covers the history of Barranquilla, including the establishment of a services and radio in Colombia, with an interesting section on the local Carnival and replica of 'Camellón Abello', an old street of Barranquilla.

The commercial and shopping districts are round the Paseo Bolívar, a few blocks north the old cathedral, and in Avenida Murillo. The colourful and vivid **market** is between Pase Bolívar and the river, the so-called Zona Negra on a branch of the Río Magdalena. Nearb **Barranquilla Zoo** ① *Calle 77/Carrera 68*, is one of the biggest and best maintained zoos the country, however many of the animals (some rarely seen in captivity) are kept in sma cages. To get there, take bus 'Boston/Boston' or 'Caldes/Recreo'. There are good parks to th northwest of the centre, including **Parque Tomás Suri Salcedo** on Calle 72. Stretching bac into the northwestern heights overlooking the city are the modern suburbs of **El Prad** Altos del Prado, Golf and Ciudad Jardín, where you'll find the **El Prado Hotel**.

There is a full range of services including commercial and shopping centres, and bank between Bulevar Norte and Avenida Olaya Herrera towards the Country Club. There ar five stadiums in the city, a big covered coliseum for sports, two for football, and the other cater for basketball and baseball. The metropolitan stadium is on Avenida Murillo, outsid the city where it meets the south stretch of the Circunvalación.

Around Barranquilla

Regular buses from Paseo Bolívar and the church at Calle 33/Carrera 41 go to th attractive bathing resort of **Puerto Colombia**, 19 km, with its pier built around 1900. Thi was formerly the ocean port of Barranquilla, connected by a railway. The beach is clear and sandy, though the water is a bit muddy. Nearby are the beaches of **Salgar**, and nort of Barranquilla is **Las Flores** (2 km from the mouth of the Río Magdalena at Bocas de Ceniza), both good places for seafood.

South along the west bank of the Magdalena, 5 km from the city, is the old colonia town of **Soledad**. The cathedral and the old narrow streets around it are worth seeing A further 25 km south is **Santo Tomás**, known for its Good Friday flagellants who symbolically whip themselves as an Easter penance. There are also street theatre presentations at this time. The small town of Palmar de Varela is a little further along the same road, which continues on to Calamar.

◉ Barranquilla listings → *Phone code: 5.*

For Sleeping and Eating price codes and other relevant information, see pages 23-28.

◉ Sleeping

Barranquilla *p170, maps p170 and p171*
Hotel prices tend to double during Carnival. Watch out for thieves in downtown hotels.
L-AL El Prado, Cra 54, No 70-10, T369 7777, www.hotelelpradosa.com. A landmark in Barranquilla, this enormous hotel with 200 rooms has been around since 1930 and still retains some of its old-fashioned service.

It has a fantastic pool shaded by palm trees, various restaurants, tennis courts and a gym.
AL Barranquilla Plaza, Cra 51B, No 79-246, T361 0333, www.hbp.com.co. A deluxe hotel popular with Colombian businessmen, it's worth visiting just for the 360° view of the city from its 26th-floor restaurant. It has all the other amenities you would expect of a hotel of this standard, including gym, spa, sauna and Wi-Fi.
A Hotel Majestic, Cra 53, No 54-41, T349 1010, www.hotelmajesticcolombia.com. An oasis of calm from the bustle of Barranquilla,

Majestic has a fine pool and large, fresh rooms as well as a restaurant serving the usual fish and meat dishes and sandwiches.
Hotel Bulevard 58, Cra 58, No 70-41, 368 0810, www.hotelbulevard58.com. It has a 1980s feel about it even though it was apparently only converted from a residential home in the 1990s. Breakfast is included, and it has a pool, and Wi-Fi available in all rooms.
Hotel San Francisco, C 43, No 43-128, 351 5532, www.sfcol.com/barranquilla. With modern, bright, clean rooms and a courtyard full of songbirds, this is a good, safe bet. It also offers laundry, a restaurant and internet services,
Hotel Girasol, C 44, No 44-103, T379 3191, www.elhotelgirasol.com. It's clean, safe and has a restaurant and Wi-Fi in all rooms, but it doesn't offer much in terms of character.
Hotel del Mar, C 42, No 35-57, T341 3703. Popular with locals, this is probably the best option for those on a budget. The rooms are clean and bright, the service friendly and the food in its restaurant cheap. Good value.
Horizonte, Cra 44, No 44-35, T341 7925. Dingy and dark but just about passes.

🍴 Eating

Barranquilla *p170, maps p170 and p171*
In Barranquilla you'll find places to suit all tastes and budgets. There are Lebanese restaurants with belly-dancers, Chinese restaurants and pizzerías. The best selection is on C 70 from **Hotel El Prado** towards Cra 42. At C 70 y 44B you'll find several *estaderos*, bars with snacks and verandas.
Jardines de Confucio, Cra 54, No 75-44. Classy Chinese restaurant with a large menu and a good atmosphere.
Don Pepe, Cra 53, No 53-90, T349 1062. Opposite the **Hotel Majestic**, it has a breezy patio serving up *comida santandereana*.
La Fonda Antioqueña, Cra 52, No 70-73, T360 0573. Just across the road from **Los Helechos** and serving the same fare, but it has a fine patio with draping flowers.

La Pizza Loca, Cra 53, No 70-97, also at C 84, No 50-36. Pizzería.
Los Helechos, Cra 52, No 70-70, T356 7493. Around the corner from **Hotel El Prado**, this popular restaurant serves up typical *comida antioqueña*, including *sancochos* and *ajiacos*, in a good atmosphere.
Pescadero del Centro, Cra 44, No 42-43. A favourite, seving local seafood.

🍷 Bars and clubs

Barranquilla *p170, maps p170 and p171*
Froggs Leggs, C 93, No 43-122. Popular bar, good atmosphere. Open Thu-Sun.
Henry's Bar, C 80, No 53-18, Local 25. Open daily from 1600, until late. Popular US-style bar, with pizzería downstairs.

🎭 Entertainment

Barranquilla *p170, maps p170 and p171*
Theatre
Teatro Amira de la Rosa. This is one of the most modern theatres in Colombia, and it offers a full range of stage presentations, concerts, ballets, art exhibitions, etc. These run throughout the year.

🎉 Festivals and events

Barranquilla *p170, maps p170 and p171*
Jan/Feb Carnival, tickets for the spectator stands are sold in major restaurants and bars, eg **Froggs Leggs** (see Bars and clubs, above). La Casa de Carnaval, Carrera 54, No 49B-39, T379 6625, www.carnavaldebarranquilla.org, is the official office and the best place to get information. Carnival is a long-standing tradition in Barranquilla, lasting for the 4 days before Ash Wed, comparable to the carnivals of Rio de Janeiro and Trinidad. There are parades, floats, street dancing, beauty contests and general mayhem. As always on such occasions, take special care of your valuables.

O Shopping

Barranquilla *p170, maps p170 and p171*
Bookshop
Librería Nacional, CC Buenavista, Cra 53,
No 98-99 esq, local 225. Has a small selection
of English books.

Markets
San Andrecito, or 'Tourist Market', Vía 40.
Where smuggled goods are sold at very
competitive prices. Picturesque and
reasonably safe. Any taxi driver will take
you there.

Shopping centres
Centro Comercial Buenavista, Cra 53,
C 98. Has a good selection of shops,
cinemas and fast food outlets.

▲ Activities and tours

Barranquilla *p170, maps p170 and p171*
Tour operators
Aviatur, Cra 54, No 72-96, Edificio Miss
Universo, local 3, T361 6000,
www.aviatur.com.co. Organize tours to
Parque Tayrona and other destinations.

⊖ Transport

Barranquilla *p170, maps p170 and p171*
Air
The bus to the airport (marked 'Malambo')
leaves from Cra 44, goes up C 32 to C 38,
and then C 30 to the airport.
   Daily flights to **Bogotá**, **Cartagena**,
Medellín, **Bucaramanga**, **Montería** and
Valledupar. International flights to **Aruba**,
Curaçao, **Miami** and **Panama City**.
   Airline offices Avianca, Cra 56
No 75-155, local 102, T353 4989.

Bus
To **Santa Marta**, about 2 hrs, US$7.50,
Pullman (less in non-a/c, Coolibertador),
also direct to Santa Marta's Rodadero beach.
To **Valledupar**, Copetran, 7 a day, 5-6 hrs,
US$12.50. To **Montería** direct, 7-8 hrs, US$11.
To **Medellín**, 16 hrs, US$40, **Pullman**. To
Bucaramanga, frequent, 9 hrs, US$37.50
with Copetran (a/c, 1st class). To **Bogotá**, 5 a
day, 20 hrs, US$40, direct with Copetran.
To **Caucasia**, 8-11 hrs, US$17. To **Maicao**,
every 30 mins from 0100-1200, 6 hrs, S$15,
Brasilia and Copetran. To **Cartagena**, 2 hrs
by *colectivo* US$7, 2½-3 hrs, US$4.50 with
Transportes Cartagena; frequent, US$6 with
Copetran; Brasilia Van Tours minibus, from
their downtown offices and the bus terminals.

Taxi
Avianca, C 72, No 57-79, T353 4691.
   To **Cartagena**, US$15 per person,
leaves when full.

❶ Directory

Barranquilla *p170, maps p170 and p171*
Banks There are a number of banks,
including **Bancolombia** and **Banco de
Bogotá**. ATMs are also readily available. For
currency exchange, **El Cairo**, C 76, No 48-30,
T360 6433, and at C 34, No 43-177; **Paseo
Bolívar**, T379 9441, TCs, euros, dollars but
not sterling, Mon-Fri and Sat 0900-1200.
Embassies and consulates Germany,
Cra 52 No 76-167 Of 216 (CC Atlantic Center),
T353 2078; **Netherlands**, C 77B, No 57-141,
of 806, T368 8387; **USA**, C 77B, No 57-141,
of 511, T353 2001 (visas obtainable only in
Bogotá); **Venezuela**, Edif Bancafé, Cra 52,
No 69-96, p 3, T368 2228, 0800-1500, visa
issued same day, but you must be there by
0915 with photo and US$30 cash; proof of
onward travel may be required.
Internet Chatnet, Cra 54, No 72-111, local 3.
Post Plaza Bolívar. **Security** DAS, C 54,
No 41-133, T371 7500; **Tourist police**, Cra 43,
No 47-53, T351 0415, T340 9903.

Santa Marta and around

→ Colour map 1, A3. Phone code: 5. Population: 385,000.

Santa Marta, the capital of Magdalena Department, is the third Caribbean port, 96 km east of Barranquilla. Unlike Cartagena, it is no colonial beauty but what it lacks in architecture it makes up for in character and bustle, and the Samarios are some of the most welcoming and gregarious people you will find anywhere in Colombia. The area around Santa Marta has much to offer, including a number of beaches. Head west to the family resort of Rodadero, or north to the former fishing village of Taganga. Backpackers love Taganga's lazy charm, it's a convenient stopping point en route to Tayrona and a good place to organize treks to Ciudad Perdida in the Sierra Nevada de Santa Marta. Southeast is Ciénaga de Santa Marta, 4000 sq km of wetlands with all types of waterbirds, and from here you can reach Aracataca, birthplace of Colombia's most famous writer, Gabriel García Márquez, and believed to be the inspiration for the village of Macondo which features in several of his books, including One Hundred Years of Solitude.

When leaving Santa Marta, most travellers will make a beeline for Tayrona National Park and its wild coastline of golden sands, secluded coves and tropical jungle. But there are other options. If the heat of the coast becomes too much, the rural village of Minca in the foothills of the Sierra Nevada, will provide welcome respite. ›› *For listings, see pages 185-190.*

Ins and outs

Getting there The **airport**, Simón Bolívar, is 20 km south of city. A bus to town costs US$0.60 and a taxi to Santa Marta is US$10, or US$4 to Rodadero. If you arrive by bus, beware of taxi drivers who take you to a hotel of their choice, not yours. The **bus terminal** is southeast of the city, towards Rodadero, and a minibus to the centre of Santa Marta costs US$0.30, a taxi US$2.00. To Rodadero a taxi is US$4.

Although cruise ships from various places (eg USA, Puerto Rico, Panama and even Europe) visit Santa Marta from time to time, it is difficult to find a passage here from overseas. Without a *carnet de passages*, it can take up to four working days to get a car out of the port, but it is usually well guarded and it is unlikely that anything will be stolen. ›› *For further information, see Essentials, page 17.*

Getting around Local bus services from Santa Marta to Rodadero cost US$0.60 (this is a flat fee all the way to the airport), and a taxi is US$4. Many of the buses coming from Barranquilla and Cartagena stop at Rodadero on their way to Santa Marta.

Tourist information The **tourist office** ⓘ *Alcaldía Distrital de Santa Marta, C 14 No 2-49, T438 2777, turismo@santamarta.gov.co.* A useful website is www.santamartaturistica.org.

Climate This area is relatively humid but the on-shore winds moderate the temperature much of the time. February and March are pleasant months to visit.

Security The north end of town near the port and beyond the old railway station are dangerous and travellers are advised not to go there alone, as it's rife with drugs and prostitution is common. South of Rodadero beach has also been reported unsafe. Beware of jungle tours, or boat trips to the islands sold by street touts.

Background

This part of the South American coastline was visited in the early years of the 16th century by the new Spanish settlers from Venezuela. At this time, many indigenous groups were living on and near the coast, and were trading with each other and with communities further inland. The dominant group were the Tayrona.

Santa Marta was the first town created in Colombia by the conquistadors, in 1525. The founder, Rodrigo de Bastidas, chose it for its sheltered harbour and its proximity to the Río Magdelena and therefore its access to the hinterland. Also, the *indígenas* represented a potential labour force and he had not failed to notice the presence of gold in their ornaments.

Within a few years, the Spanish settlement was consolidated and permanent buildings appeared (see the Casa de la Aduana, below). Things did not go well, however. The *indígenas* did not 'collaborate' and there was continual friction amongst the Spaniards, all of whom were expecting instant riches. Bastidas' successor, Rodrigo Alvarez Palomino attempted to subdue the *indígenas* by force, with great loss of life and little success. The *indígenas* that survived took to the hills and their successors, the Kogi, are still there today.

By the middle of the 16th century, a new threat had appeared. Encouraged and often financed by Spain's enemies (England, France and Holland), pirates realized that rich pickings were to be had, not only from shipping, but also by attacking coastal settlements. The first raid took place around 1544, captained by the French pirate Robert Waal with three ships and 1000 men. He was followed by many of the famous sea-dogs – the brothers Côte, Drake and Hawkins – who all ransacked the city in spite of the forts built on a small island at the entrance to the bay and on the mainland. Before the end of the century more than 20 attacks were recorded and the pillage continued until as late as 1779, the townsfolk living in constant fear. Cartagena, meanwhile, became the main base for the conquistadors and much was invested in its defences. Santa Marta was never fortified in the same way and declined in importance as a result, something that accounts for a certain lack of colonial heritage here. Over the years caches of treasure have been unearthed in old walls and floors – grim testimonies to the men and women of those troubled times who did not survive to claim them.

Two important names connect Santa Marta with the history of Colombia. Gonzalo Jiménez de Quesada began the expedition here that led him up the Río Magdalena and into the highlands to found Santa Fe de Bogotá in 1538, and it was here that Simón Bolívar, his dream of Gran Colombia shattered, came to die. Almost penniless, he was given hospitality at the *quinta* of San Pedro Alejandrino, see below. He died there on 17 December 1830, at the age of 47.

Santa Marta → *For listings, see pages 185-190.*

Orientation

Santa Marta lies at the mouth of the Río Manzanares, one of the many rivers that drain the Sierra Nevada de Santa Marta, on a deep bay with high shelving cliffs at each end. The city's fine promenade offers good views of the bay and is lined with restaurants, accommodation and nightlife, though none of a very high quality. At the southern end, where the main traffic turns inland on Calle 22, is a striking sculpture dedicated to the indigenous heritage of the region, La Herencía Tairona. The main commercial area and banks are on Carrera 5 and Calle 15.

he centre of Santa Marta is the pleasant and leafy Plaza Bolívar, which leads down to the
each. It is complete with statues of Bolívar and Santander, and a bandstand. On the
orth side is the **Casa de la Aduana/Museo de Oro** ① *C 14/Cra 2*, which became the
ustom House when Santa Marta was declared a free port in 1776. Previously it belonged
o the Church and was used as the residence of the Chief Justice of the Inquisition.

Santa Marta

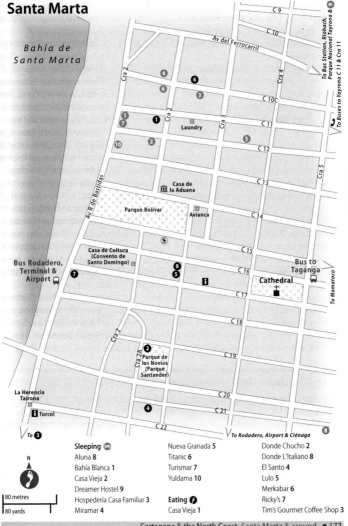

Sleeping	Nueva Granada 5	Donde Chucho 2
Aluna 8	Titanic 6	Donde L'Italiano 8
Bahía Blanca 1	Turismar 7	El Santo 4
Casa Vieja 2	Yuldama 10	Lulo 5
Dreamer Hostel 9		Merkabar 6
Hospedería Casa Familiar 3	**Eating**	Ricky's 7
Miramar 4	Casa Vieja 1	Tim's Gourmet Coffee Shop 3

The house dates from 1531 and was probably the first built of brick and stone in Colombia. An upstairs garret, added in 1730, offers an excellent view of the city and the bay. Simón Bolívar stayed here briefly in December 1830 and he lay in state on the second floor from 17 December to the 20 December before being moved to the cathedral. The Custom House now displays an excellent archaeological collection, with four rooms of exhibits mainly dedicated to the indigenous Tayrona. Especially interesting is the model of Ciudad Perdida, the most important of the Tayrona cities. At the time of writing Casa de la Aduana was closed for conservation work, but it's still worth checking out its exterior. The **Museo de Oro (Gold Museum)** ① *usually contained within the building, has been moved to the library of Banco de la República next door, during the conservation work, Mon-Fri, 0830-1800, Sat 0900-1300, free*, with a number of pre-Columbian gold artefacts held in the vault.

Quinta de San Pedro Alejandrino ① *daily 0930-1700 (high season 0930-1800) US$5, discounts for students and children*, an early 17th-century villa, is 5 km southeast of the city and dedicated to sugar cane production. This is where Simón Bolívar lived out his last days and the simple room in which he died, with a few of his personal belongings, can be visited. Other paintings and memorabilia of the period are on display in the villa, and a contemporary art gallery featuring works by artists from Venezuela to Bolivia (the countries associated with Bolívar's life), and an exhibition hall have been built on the property. The estate and gardens, with some ancient cedars, *samanes*, dignified formal statues and monuments, can be visited. It is an impressive memorial to the man most revered by Colombians. To get there take a bus or *colectivo* from the waterfront, Carrera 1C, to Mamatoca and ask to be dropped off at the Quinta (US$0.60).

The original building on the site of the **cathedral** ① *Cra 4, C 16/17, open for Mass daily at 0600 and 1800 (more frequently on Sun), and you may find it open at 1000*, was completed a few years after the founding of the city and was probably the first church of Colombia as proclaimed by the inscription on the west front. The present building is mainly 17th century with many additions and modifications, hence the mixture of styles. There are interesting shrines along the aisles, a fine barrel roof and chandeliers, and a grey Italian marble altar decorated with red and brown, the whole giving a light, airy and dignified impression. Notable is the monument to Rodrigo de Bastidas, founder of the city, to the left of the main entrance and the inscription by the altar steps commemorating the period when Bolívar's remains rested here from his death in 1830 to 1842 when they were transferred to the Pantheon in Caracas. The **Convento de Santo Domingo** ① *Cra 2, No 16-44*, now serves as a cultural centre and houses a library.

Around Santa Marta → For listings, see pages 185-190.

There are rocky headlands and beaches in the bays and coves all along this coast, surrounded by hills, green meadows and shady trees. The largest sandy bay is that of Santa Marta, with Punta Betín, a promontory, protecting the harbour to the north and a headland to the south on top of which are the ruins of an early defensive fort, Castillo San Fernando. The rugged Isla El Morro lies 3 km off Santa Marta and is topped by a lighthouse. Because of the proximity of the port and the city, the beach is not recommended for bathing. There is marine ecosystem research science centre, run by Colombian and German universities near the end of Punta Betín.

In addition to those listed below, there are more beaches in the bays near the Cabo and Isla de la Aguja. Villa Concha has a nice beach, popular with the locals at the weekends nd a good day trip during the week. The bay is surrounded by tree-covered hills and here are a number of restaurants nearby. ▶▶ *For further information on nearby beaches, see ayrona National Park, page 180.*

Rodadero and around

Rodadero beach, 4 km southwest of Santa Marta, is one of the best along this coast. It is part of the municipality of **Gaira**, a small town 2 km away, alongside the main road, on the Río Gaira which flows into the Caribbean at the southern end of Rodadero beach. The main part of the beach has high rise hotels of all standards, but it is attractive, tree lined, relatively clean and pleasant for bathing. Behind the promenade are the restaurants, cheaper accommodation and services. Nearby are a number of holiday flats and other holiday centres operated by public and social entities. Rodadero is a popular destination for family holidays. There is a waterpark popular with kids and families at the southern end of the main beach (0900-1700, US$6). **Fondo de Promoción Turística** ① *C 10, No 3-10, T/F422 7548*, can provide local information and advice on hotels.

Launches leave Rodadero beach for the 10-minute trip to the **Aquarium**, north along the coast at Inca Inca Bay, where you'll find sharks, seals and many colourful fish of the Caribbean. The aquarium is linked to a small museum housing relics from Spanish galleons sunk by pirates, and a collection of coral and seashells. The boats leave from the beach at the end of Calle 12 every hour from 0800, the aquarium opens from 0900 and the last boat back leaves at 1630. Admission is US$7.50 and US$5 for children. **Coomarsertur** ① *T422 6208*, on the south end of the beach organizes boats US$5 per person (minimum four people) or US$4 per person (more than four people). From the aquarium, you can

Around Santa Marta

walk (10 minutes) to the Playa Blanca and swim in less crowded conditions tha
elsewhere. There is also food available at this beach.

Taganga and around
Close to Santa Marta is the former fishing village (most people now make a living fror
tourism) and beach of **Taganga**, 15-20 minutes away by minibus (US$0.50) or taxi (US$4
Set in a tranquil semi-circular bay surrounded by scorched hills dotted with cacti, Tagang
attracts its fair share of backpackers and is fast changing from sleepy fishing village to mor
of a party resort. The swimming is good, especially on Playa Grande, 25 minutes' walk roun
the coast, but do not leave your belongings unattended. Taganga is even more popular a
weekends. Boat trips along the coast for fishing, and to the many bays and beaches are ru
by **Hotel La Ballena Azul** and by a syndicate of boatmen along the beach.

Half an hour north of Taganga is Isla de la Aguja, a good fishing zone, and nearer i
Playa Granate, with excellent places to snorkel and dive around the coral reefs, althougl
lately the reefs have been showing signs of bleaching.

Ciénaga de Santa Marta
The paved coast road to Santa Marta from Barranquilla passes salt pans and skirts the
Ciénaga de Santa Marta, where all types of waterbirds, plants and animals may be seen
Cutting off the access to the sea to build the coast road caused an ecological disaster, bu
a National Environment Programme has been working to restore the area. There are
several villages built on stilts in the lake. On the east shore of the lagoon is **Ciénaga**
famous for *cumbia* music.

Aracataca
Aracataca, 60 km south of Ciénaga and 7 km before Fundación, is the birthplace of Gabriel
García Márquez. It was fictionalized as Macondo in some of his novels, notably in *One
Hundred Years of Solitude*. His home is now a modest museum 1½ blocks from the plaza,
ask for directions. There are *residencias*, try **Hospedaje El Porvenir**, and a restaurant, but it
is better to stay in Fundación. In 2007 a new train was inaugurated, **El Tren Amarillo de
Macondo**, between Santa Marta and Aracataca. García Márquez himself, with a large
entourage, joined the first run on 30 May 2007; however, a regular service has yet to come
into operation.

Parque Nacional Tayrona → *For listings, see pages 185-190. Colour map 1, A3.*

The beaches of Tayrona National Park are what you would expect of a tropical paradise;
thick jungle teeming with wildlife spills over onto golden sand beaches with pounding surf
and there are small, secluded bays, excellent for swimming and sunbathing. There is
something of the prehistoric about Tayrona. Squint your eyes and with a little imagination
the flocks of pelicans that glide overhead become pterodactyls, the bright-tailed lizards
that scurry underfoot as you walk through the forest paths reminders of their extinct
cousins and the enormous boulders that stand guard over the beaches look like they have
been there since the beginning of time. However, time and tourism have caught up with
Tayrona and it is becoming increasingly popular. Prices have rocketed in the past 10 years
and there is now a steady stream of visitors, especially during national holidays. If you want
to enjoy this corner of paradise in isolation then you might consider avoiding the busier
periods of Semana Santa, July, August and December to January.

Gabriel García Márquez

More than any other Colombian, Gabriel García Márquez, or Gabo as he is affectionately known, has shaped the outside world's understanding of Colombian culture. His books champion the genre of magical realism where the real and the fantastical blur so naturally that it is difficult to discern where one ends and the other begins.

But is this what life in Colombia is really like? Schoolteachers-turned-dictators who fashion a town's children into an oppressive army, a woman so beautiful she causes the death of anyone who courts her and a child born with his eyes open because he has been weeping in his mother's womb seem improbable, especially to sceptical Western sensibilities. Yet many of the places, events and characters are based on real life. Macondo, a place which features in so many of his stories, is modelled on his town of birth, Aracataca. Cartagena is easily recognizable as the unnamed port that is the setting for *Love in the Time of Cholera*, while Fermina Daza and Florentino Ariza's love affair is based on his own parents' marriage. Events in *Chronicle of a Death Foretold* and *The Story of a Shipwrecked Sailor* were inspired by real life stories lifted from newspaper articles.

"Owing to his hands-on experience in journalism, García Márquez is, of all the great living authors, the one who is closest to everyday reality", wrote the American literary critic Gene H Bell-Villada, and who can challenge Gabo's interpretation of the truth when Colombia has produced real life characters such as Pablo Escobar? Where else in the world are there villages that host donkey beauty contests or elect a mayor who dresses up as a superhero? Sometimes Colombian reality is stranger than Gabo's fiction.

The park is named after the Tayrona (also spelt Tairona) culture, one of the most important of pre-colonial Colombia. It extends from north of Taganga for some 85 km of rugged coastline much of it fringed with coral reefs. You will see monkeys, iguanas and maybe snakes.

Ins and outs

Getting there To get to the park entrance, take a minibus from the **market** ⓘ *Cra 11/ C 11*, in Santa Marta. The services are frequent and start from 0700, with the last minibus back at 1730 or later, but double check. The journey will take 45 minutes and cost about US$2. Alternatively, go to the Riohacha road police checkpoint (taxi US$1 or bus to Mamatoca) and catch any bus there going towards Riohacha. Private minivan can also be organized at hotels or with tour operators, approximately US$6 per person depending on number of passengers.

Park information Entry to the park is US$17.50 per person, US$3 for a motorcycle, US$4.50 for a car. Open 0800-1700. If you arrive before 0800, you may be able to pay at the car park at Cañaveral. Visitors normally stay overnight and hotels can help with arranging tours. Normally, you are advised to book accommodation before going, especially at holiday times. However, in the past few years, the park has been closed for safety, water shortages, local staffing and other reasons, only to be reopened after a short break. Unfortunately, this has given rise to confusion and contradiction. The best place for information is Santa Marta, and hopefully you will find that the park is open when you wish to visit. Information can also be found on the **Colombian Tourist Board – Proexport** website, www.colombia.travel.

Hiking boots may be useful and there are sometimes bloodsucking insects to contend with. There are by now food and water stands available in the park, or you can take your own food and water, but no valuables as robbery has been a problem. You can hire horses to carry you and your luggage from Cañaveral to Arrecifes (US$8) and El Cabo de San Juan (US$18). Littering was a big problem in the past, but there are now camouflaged litter bins along all the main trails and around the campsites. In the wet, the paths are very slippery. There is no need to take guides, who charge US$20 or more per person, for a day trip.

Out of high season the park is relatively empty and you will usually find beaches with barely a soul on them. But beware, during holiday periods, especially during Semana Santa, the visitor numbers can increase fivefold.

Around the park

There are various places where there is access to the bays and beaches by road, including an unsurfaced road from the eastern edge of Santa Marta at Bastidas north 5 km to the beach at Villa Concha (see below). On towards Riohacha beyond Bonda there is a road in poor condition to Bahía Gayraca and Neguange (where indigenous peoples had an important settlement to exploit marine salt resources), to a point near Ancón Cinto. You can reach Negangue beach by *colectivo* from Santa Marta. Enquire also for transport to Villa Concha. Alternatively, take a boat from Taganga.

The normal entry to the park is further on, turning off the main road at El Zaino, 35 km from Santa Marta and at the eastern end of the park. From there, a road leads within the park 4 km to the administrative and visitor centre with car park at **Cañaveral**, about one hour's walk into the park from the gate. About 40 minutes west of Cañaveral on foot is **Arrecifes**, from where it is a 45-minute walk to El Cabo de San Juan, then up inland along a stream (La Boquita) 1½ hours on a clear path to the archaeological site of **Pueblito**. A guided tour around the site is free, but check at the entry if it is available. There are many other smaller Tayrona settlements in the park area and relics abound. At Pueblito there are indigenous people; do not photograph them without permission. From Pueblito you can either return to Cañaveral, or continue for a pleasant two-hour walk to Calabazo on the Santa Marta–Riohacha road. A circuit of Santa Marta, Cañaveral, Arrecifes, Pueblito, Calabazo, Santa Marta in one day is arduous, needing an early start.

Bathing is not recommended near Cañaveral or Arrecifes as there is often heavy pounding surf and the currents are treacherous. About 5 km east of Cañaveral are splendid, deserted sandy beaches. You have to walk there, but take care as the park borders marijuana-growing areas. The beach at **Villa Concha** is one of the most beautiful beaches of the area, with camping and several places to eat. Beyond Arrecifes (the sea can be dangerous on this beach) near **Cabo de San Juan** is La Piscina, a beautiful, safe natural swimming pool, excellent for snorkelling. Other safe bathing beaches can be found further along the shore but the going is difficult.

East from Tayrona

Approximately 3 km beyond Cañaveral and Guachaca along the coast is **Los Angeles** ⓘ *Km 33.5 on the Santa Marta–Riohacha road*, a camping site which offers access to fine empty beaches, excellent for surfing, at a fraction of the cost of a stay in Tayrona. Charming owner Nohemi Ramos hires out hammocks or tents for around US$10 (less if

The Lost City

From the first day we set out on the trail toward the mysterious Colombian Lost City, until day six when the remarkable adventure into the heart of the sierra came to an end, I was blown away by the crystal-clear rivers that cascaded down from the upper reaches of the mountains and treated us to amazing natural swimming pools, beautiful waterfalls and a much welcomed respite after hours of hiking amidst the endless jungle landscape. There are 18 or so river crossings en route to the Lost City, river pools to swim in each day and 1300 stone steps to climb at the very end of the third day that take you above the gorgeous river valleys to the high ridges blanketed in green. While the site alone is impressive, and its mysterious history and late discovery only add to its splendour, the surrounding mountain peaks dominate the endless landscape. What else lies undiscovered and hidden among such wild, rugged and beautiful terrain?

Despite the unsettling events in 2003, when eight foreigners were kidnapped along the Lost City trail, the region is currently considered safe and is heavily patrolled by the Colombian Army. The site is guarded day and night by about 40 friendly soldiers who pass their two month assignment on site by asking visitors for cigarettes in exchange for odd looking nuts that they have picked up off the jungle floor. They will also obligingly pose for photos, which they seem to enjoy more than anything else.

There is more than one option when it comes to choosing a route, some a little more difficult and with longer days, but the rewards will outweigh the fatigue. Starting and finishing the hike in different places will give you the chance to see more of the remote landscape and travel to less visited parts of this unique mountain range. For more information on trekking, see page 184.

Craig Weigand

---

you bring your own) and can cook up simple meals of freshly caught fish. She also offers guided tours of Tayrona, Pueblito and other local sights (for Spanish speakers, and she can put you in touch with English-speaking guides).

A 10-minute walk west from Los Angeles brings you to the mouth of the Río Piedras, the border of Tayrona Park, where you can bathe in the company of egrets and enjoy sights to rival any of those seen in the park. The paved coastal road continues from Tayrona and crosses into Guajira Department at Palomino, 80 km from Santa Marta, which has a fine beach and cheap *cabañas* as accommodation; 72 km from Palomino is Los Camarones and the entry to Santuario Los Flamencos, 25 km short of Riohacha.

Ciudad Perdida → For listings, see pages 185-190. Colour map 1, A3.

Ciudad Perdida (Lost City) is the third of the triumvirate of 'must-sees' on Colombia's Caribbean coast (the other two being Cartagena and Tayrona). The six-day trek is right up there with the Inca Trail in Peru and Roraima in Venezuela, as one of the classic South American adventures and is a truly memorable experience.

Don't forget that Ciudad Perdida is in a national park: it is strictly forbidden to damage trees and collect flowers or insects. Note also that there are over 1200 steps to climb when you get there.

The site

Discovered as recently as 1975, Cuidad Perdida was founded near the Río Buritaca between 500 and 700 AD and was surely the most important centre of the Tayrona culture. It stands at 1100 m on the steep slopes of Cerro Corea, which lies in the northern part of the Sierra Nevada de Santa Marta. The site, known as Teyuna to the indigenous locals, covers 400 ha and consists of a complex system of buildings, paved footpaths, flights of steps and perimetrical walls, which link a series of terraces and platforms, on which were built cult centres, residences and warehouses. Juan Mayr's book, *The Sierra Nevada of Santa Marta* (Mayr y Cabal, Bogotá), deals beautifully with Ciudad Perdida.

Trekking

Five or six-day trips can be organized by the tourist office and Turcol in Santa Marta (see page 189). Price should include transport, mules and porters, guide and food, but double check that you don't need to pay extra for porters. It is three days there, one day (two nights) at the site, and two days back. The route goes beyond Parque Tayrona on the road to Riohacha, then past Guachaca turning inland to the roadhead at El Mamey. The climb broadly follows the Río Buritaca, and apart from crossing a number of streams, is uphill all the way. Ciudad Perdida is on a steep slope overlooking Río Buritaca.

Ask at hotels in Santa Marta (eg **Hotel Miramar**) or Taganga, or at the Santa Marta market for alternative tours. If you are prepared to shop around, and cook and carry your supplies and belongings, a tour could cost you less. Under no circumstances should you deal with unauthorized guides, check with the tourist office if in doubt, and try to get views of the quality of guides from travellers who have already done the trip.

You will need to take a tent or a hammock and mosquito net (on organized tours these may be supplied by the guide), a good repellent, sleeping bag, warm clothing for the night, torch, plastic bags to keep everything dry, and strong, quick-drying footwear. Small gifts for the indigenous children are appreciated.

Be prepared for heavy rain – the northern slopes of the Sierra Nevada have an average rainfall of over 4000 mm per year. Check conditions, especially information on river crossings, and ensure you have adequate food, a water bottle and water purifying tablets before you start. Try to leave no rubbish behind and encourage the guides to ensure no one else does. Going on your own is discouraged and dangerous. Route finding is very difficult and unwelcoming *indígenas*, paramilitaries and drug traders increase the hazards. Properly organized groups appear to be safe.

Sierra Nevada de Santa Marta → *For listings, see pages 185-190.*

Minca

ⓘ *Catch a bus from C 11 with Cra 11 in Santa Marta (30 mins, US$1.50). A taxi will cost US$10.*

If the heat of the coast becomes too much then a stay up in Minca is a refreshing alternative. Some 20 km from Santa Marta in the foothills of the Sierra Nevada, this small village, surrounded by coffee *fincas* and begonia plantations, is becoming increasingly popular and offers several cheap and truly charming places to stay. Horse riding, birdwatching and tours further into the Sierra Nevada can be arranged from here.

About 45 minutes walk beyond the village is **El Pozo Azul**, a local swimming spot under a waterfall, popular at weekends but almost always empty during the week, well worth a visit. El Pozo Azul was a sacred indigenous site where purification rituals were performed and on occasion it is still used by the Kogi of the Sierra Nevada.

San Lorenzo

Beyond Minca, the partly paved road rises steeply to San Lorenzo which is surrounded by a forest of palm trees. On the way to San Lorenzo is **La Victoria**, a large coffee *finca* which offers tours to demonstrate the coffee-making process. It is possible to stay in *cabañas* run by the park authorities near San Lorenzo. **Aventure Colombia** organizes tours with guides, transportation, food and lodging to this section of the park.

◉ Santa Marta and around listings → *Phone code: 5.*

For Sleeping and Eating price codes and other relevant information, see pages 23-28.

◉ Sleeping

Santa Marta *p176, map p177*
Av Rodrigo de Bastidas (Cra 1) has several seafront holiday hotels while **Cra 2** and connecting *calles* have many budget *residencias*. For groups of 4 or more, consider short-let apartments. All hotels near the beach can be noisy, especially at weekends.

B Hotel Bahía Blanca, Cra 1, 11-12, T423 6411. Slightly impersonal, but with a pleasant patio serving breakfast. Right near the beach and all the action.

B Yuldama, Cra 1, No 12-19, on the seafront, T421 0063, www.hotelyuldama.com. Modern but a bit sterile, with clean rooms, a/c, cable TV, Wi-Fi and safe provided.

C Hotel Casa Vieja, C 12, No 1-58, T431 1606, www.hotelcasavieja.com. Has a Spanish feel about it with white tiling and simple, clean rooms and a/c. Prices cheaper with fan. Friendly staff and a pleasant restaurant serving delicious Colombian food.

C Nueva Granada, C 12, No 3-17, T421 1337, www.hotelnuevagranada.com. This charming old building in the historic quarter has a peaceful courtyard and a yacuzzi pool. Breakfast is served in the pleasant patio, they have bikes for guests to borrow and offer welcome drinks, airport transfers, a medical service and free calls to the US and Canada. The pick of the bunch. Highly recommended.

D Turismar, Cra 1a, No 11-41, T421 2408. A good option for a dorm but individual rooms are dark and spartan. Beachside, with pleasant courtyard and newly opened restaurant.

D-E Aluna, C 21 5-72, T432 4916, www.aluna hotel.com. Irish-run, pleasant, large hostel with private rooms and a dorm with roof terrace. Kitchen, laundry service, Wi-Fi, new café and a good noticeboard. Recommended.

E Hospedería Casa Familiar, C 10C, No 2-14, T421 1697, www.hospederia casafamiliar. freeservers.com. An extremely friendly and helpful family run this hostel. Offers rooms with a private bath and fan, dorms and space for hammocks. Pleasant roof terrace and kitchen available. Has its own dive shop and organizes trips to Tayrona and Ciudad Perdida. Recommended.

F Dreamer Hostel, Cra 51, No 26D, 161 Los Trupillos, Mamatoco, T300-251 6534, www.thedreamerhostel.com. Newish hostel, opened in Dec 2009, just 5 mins from the bus station.

F Hotel Titanic, C 10C, No 1C-68, T421 1947. Opposite the **Miramar**, offering similar rooms with own bath, fan and cable TV. Clean but a little dark.

F Miramar, C 10C, No 1C-59, T423 3276. Its reputation as the ultimate backpackers' hotel precedes it. Basic but cheap rooms, a good restaurant serving delicious fruit juices, has a number of computers and Wi-Fi, and organizes tours to Tayrona Park and Ciudad Perdida.

Rodadero *p179*
L Tamacá, Cra 2, No 11A-98, T422 7016, www.tamaca.com. Resort-style hotel with fine pool, casino, large reception area and direct access to beach. All rooms have balcony with sea view, hot water, Wi-Fi and a safe but are a little sterile. Half- and full-board also available.

AL Hotel La Sierra, Cra 1, No 9-47, T422 7960, www.hotelasierra.com. Fine hotel with pleasant terrace set back from beach, rooms with balcony and Wi-Fi. Recommended.

A-B El Rodadero, C 11, No 1-29, T422 8323, www.hopertour.com. Stylish, modern building with a touch of art deco. Excellent pool, rooms with fine views of the beach and breakfast and dinner included.

C Hotel Bariloche, C 13, No 2-59, 500 m from the beach, T422 8692, hotelbariloche77@hotmail.com. Leafy, tiled courtyard with fountain. Rooms are clean but a little musty.

C Hotel Nashama, C 13, No 2-41, T422 5794. Clean but unspectacular rooms, with a/c and TV. There is a restaurant and they offer discounts for groups.

C Tucuraca, Cra 2, No 12-43, 2 mins' walk from the beach, T422 7493, hoteltucuraca@yahoo.com. Rooms are clean with cable TV and a/c or fan, but lacking character. Wi-Fi available. For groups of 4 or more, ask for apartments.

Taganga p179

A La Ballena Azul, Cra 1, No 18-01, T421 9009, www.hotelballenaazul.com. Right on the beach, this stylish hotel offers friendly service, a fine restaurant and a terrace bar. Decorated in cool blues and whites, rooms open onto a central atrium with hanging bougainvillea and a palm tree. If you are prepared to spend a little more this is easily the best option in town. Rooms with fan or a/c, breakfast included, Wi-Fi available.

B Bahía Taganga, C 4 No 1B-35, T421 9049, www.bahiataganga.com. If you want to get away from the backpacker crowd and can't afford **La Ballena Azul**, then this is your place. Up on a hill at the north end of the bay it has commanding views over the village and is tastefully decorated with clean rooms. Friendly owner.

D Techos Azules, Sector Dunkarinca, Cabaña 1-100, T421 9141, www.techosazules.com. Off the road leading into town, this hostel is a collection of *cabañas* with good views over the bay. Offers internet, free coffee and a laundry service.

D-E Bayview Hostel, Cra 4, No 17B-57, T421 9560, www.bayviewhostel.com. With a technicolour façade, it offers pleasant rooms with balconies or cheaper dorms with bunk beds. There's a kitchen, BBQ area, 2 lounges with DVD player and rocking chairs, and Wi-Fi.

D-E Casa Blanca, Cra 1, No 18-161, at the southern end of the beach, www.casablancahosteltaganga.com. Crumbling but has character. Each room has a balcony with hammock and the roof terrace is a fine place to pass the evening drinking beer with fellow guests.

D-E Casa de Felipe, Cra 5A, No 19-13, 500 m from beach behind football field, T421 9101, www.lacasadefelipe.com. The true backpackers' choice. Has a shady garden of bougainvillea, cacti and hammocks, its own kitchen and Wi-Fi. Some dorms available.

D-F pp Divanga B&B, C 12, No 4-07, T421 9092, and also **Casa Divanga** C 11 No 3-05, T421 9217, www.divanga.com. French-owned hostels, doubles with private bath or 3-person dorm, includes great breakfast, comfortable, 5-mins' walk from beach, nice views, attentive service, lovely atmosphere, good pool, HI affiliated, Wi-Fi, internet. Recommended.

E Hotel Pelikan, Cra 2, No 17-04, T421 9057. Has character and offers rooms with fan and private bath. Laundry service available.

E-F Hostal Moramar, Cra 4, No-17B-83, T421 9202, www.hostalmoramar.com. 2 blocks up from beach opposite football pitch. Simple, quiet rooms with bath and fan, bright, airy, patio, laundry, attentive owners, welcoming.

Parque Nacional Tayrona p180

Thatched 'eco' cabañas (**LL**) are available in the park, they are circular cabins built in the style of indigenous *bohíos*, which hold 2-6 people. These cost at least US$300 in high season for 2-4 people, US$240 in low season, and the price includes breakfast, cable TV, phone, safe and hot water. There is also a spa offering various massages and treatments. The eco refers more to proximity to nature than any strict environmental policy, although they do recycle. Great views over sea and jungle and a good restaurant.

Park accommodation in Arrecifes and Cañaveral is managed by Aviatur, C 15, No 3-20, T421 3848, reservasparques@aviatur.com.co, T01-900-331 2222/01-382 1616, or Bogotá, T381 7111. National parks office: C 17, No 4-06, Santa Marta, T421 1732.

Camping Campsite US$15 for a 5-person tent, or US$4 for a hammock. There are facilities, but only a tiny shop, take all supplies or eat in the restaurant. An attractive site but plenty of mosquitoes. Beware of falling coconuts and omnivorous donkeys.

Arrecifes
LL Yuluca, Arrecifes beach. Huts with TV, safe, minibar, fan and ultra sonic insect repellent. US$225 for 2-4 people in high season; US$170 in low season.

Camping Yuluca (see above) charges around US$3 for a tent, US$8 for a hammock, and offers fresh water showers and toilets, very clean. There is a good restaurant, though bringing your own food is recommended, as it is expensive.

Cabo de San Juan
Camping On the path to Pueblito, there is a campsite at this beautiful double bay divided by a thin strip of sand and a large rock, where there is excellent bathing. There is also a small restaurant and hammocks for hire (US$13 in high season or US$10 in low season); there are 2 cabañas built on the rock that divides the 2 bays (US$50 in high season or US$43 in low season); pitching your own tent will set you back US$7, while hiring a tent for 2 persons costs US$19. There are other camping and hammock places en route. There is nowhere to stay at Pueblito.

Minca *p184*
C Sierra's Sound, C Principal, T421 9993, www.sierrasound.es.tl. With a veranda overlooking a rocky river, pasta home-made by its Italian owner, hot water, TV and organized tours into the Sierra Nevada, this is perhaps the most sophisticated place to stay in Minca.

D La Casona, on the hill to the right as you enter the village, T421 9958, lacasona@colombiaexotic.com. With commanding views of the valley below, this is a converted convent with a wraparound veranda. The art is by the owner, a sculptor from Bogotá, who runs the hostel with his family. Magical.

D Sans Souci, T421 9968, sanssouciminca@yahoo.com. Rambling house in beautiful garden of bamboo and exotic flowers. German owner Chris provides rooms in the house or separate apartments. Has rustic swimming pool, football pitch, kitchen and the option of a discount in exchange for gardening services. Stunning views.

● Eating

Santa Marta *p176, map p177*
₶₶₶-₶₶ El Santo, C 21 2A-52. Gorgeous Argentine food with happy hour 1700-2000, 2x1 *mojitos*.

₶₶ Donde Chucho, C 19 2-17. A little expensive but well situated in the corner of Parque Santander (Parque de los Novios). Serves seafood and pasta.

₶₶ Donde l'Italiano, next door to Lulo, serves up tasty Italian fare at reasonable prices. Generous portions. Recommended.

₶₶ Ricky's, Cra 1a, No 17-05. Beachside restaurant serving international food, including Chinese. Reasonably priced.

₶ Lulo, Cra 3 16-34, www.lulocafebar.com. Cosy café and bar in the pedestrianized part of Cra 3. Organic coffee, fresh juices and gourmet *arepas*.

₶ Merkabar, C 10C, No 2-11. Pastas, great pancakes, good juices and specializes in seafood. Also open early for good breakfasts. Family-run, good value and provides tourist information. Recommended.

₶ Restaurante Casa Vieja, C 12, No 1-58. Part of the hotel, see Sleeping. Serves delicious *comida criolla*.

₶ Tim's Gourmet Coffee Shop, Cra 1A 23-57, behind the marina, www.timsgourmetcoffee.com. Colombian/Canadian-run café open 7 days a week 0700-2000, serving great coffee, crêpes and sandwiches, fresh fruit juices and Canadian desserts. Has Wi-Fi. Recommended.

Rodadero *p179*
There are fast-food restaurants and very good juice kiosks along the seafront. Cra 2 between C 7 and 8 has a food court, serving everything from pizzas and Mexican, to Colombian grilled meats (*asados*) and there is a Chinese next door. The same stretch also has a number of bars and discos.

¶ **El Banano**, Cra 2, No 7-38. Good meat dishes and light meals, try their *carne asada con maduro* (banana) *y queso crema*, delicious. Recommended.

¶ **El Pibe**, C 6, No 1-26. Argentine-run restaurant, serving steaks.

Taganga *p179*
Fresh fish is available along the beach and good pancakes can be found at the crêperie at the **Hotel La Ballena Azul**.

¶ **Bitácora**, Cra 4, No 17-03, just off the beach. Serves seafood, pastas, burgers, steaks and salads.

¶ **Donde Juanita**, Cra 1, No 17-1. Serves fine home-cooked food, including fish and meat. Very cheap, with good vegetarian options.

¶ **Yiu Nu Sagu**, C 12, No 1-08. Beachside pizzeria, large helpings.

🍸 Bars and clubs

Santa Marta *p176, map p177*
Santa Marta is a party town with many new clubs, discos and bars opening every week. The website www.samarios.com, is an excellent resource for finding out what's going on at night.

Barrio Samario, C 17 No 3-36, between Cra 3 and 4 (on same road as **La Puerta**). A popular bar playing local music.

La Puerta, C 17 No 2-29, between Cra 3 and 4. Excellent bar and atmosphere in a colonial house. Highly recommended.

Rodadero *p179*
There are many bars and nightclubs here.
Burukuka, Vía al Edif Cascadas del Rodadero, T301-374 6620, www.burukuka.com. Steak bar looking out over Rodadero beach.
La Escollera, Cra 4 and C 5, No 4-107, www.la-escollera.com. Huge club under an open straw roof. Concerts are also staged here.

Taganga *p179*
El Garaje, C 8 No 2-127 with Cra 3, T421 9003. Plays hip hop and other forms of electronic music. Starts late, finishes late.
Mojito Net, C 14, No 1B-61. Open 0800-0200, happy hour 1400-2100. Live music, open-mic sessions, wine, cocktails, food and internet.

⊕ Festivals and events

Santa Marta *p176, map p177*
Jul Festival Patronal de Santa Marta. Celebrates the founding of the city with parades and musical performances.
Jul Fiestas del Mar Aquatic events and a beauty contest.
Sep International Caribbean Theatre Festival. Contributions from many of the Caribbean countries.

⊙ Shopping

Santa Marta *p176, map p177*
Look around for small artefacts and figurines in the indigenous tradition, sometimes sold on the beach. Best if you can find the artists who live in and around Santa Marta.

Craft shops
The **market** is at C 11/Cra 11, just off Av del Ferrocarril and has stalls with excellent selections of hammocks. There are several good handicraft shops on **Parque Bolívar**. **Artesanías La 15**, C15 with Cra 9, T310 730 9606, good selection of typical handicrafts; **Artesanías Sisa**, Cra 4, No 16-42 on the Plaza Catedral, T421 4510, local handicrafts

including bags, hammocks and sombreros; **José Pertuz**, C 38, up the hill beyond Cra 17.

Shopping malls
El Barco, C 13, No 5-26; **El Emporio**, C 12 No 8-105.

▲ Activities and tours

Santa Marta *p176, map p177*
For guided trips to Quinta San Pedro Alejandrino and other local points of interest, ask at your hotel, travel agencies or the tourist office. Similarly, if you wish to visit the Marine Centre at Punta Betín you will need a boat or a permit to pass through the port area, so ask for guidance. For trips to Tayrona National Park, Ciudad Perdida and the Sierra Nevada, see under the relevant destination. Coach tours also go to Aracataca and Ciénaga de Santa Marta from Santa Marta.

Tour operators
Aviatur, C 15, No 3-20, T421 3848. Good service.
New Frontiers Adventures, Calle 27, No 1C-74 (close to Playa los Cocos), T317-648 6786. www.colombia.newfrontiersadventures.com. Arranges trips with English-speaking guides to the Ciudad Perdida, Tayrona National Park and Guajira.
Nohemi Ramos, Tierra Mar Aire, C 15, No 2-60, T421 5161. Amex agent and full tourist travel agent.

Sendero Tairona, Cra 3, No 18-46, T422 9505, clubsenderotayrona@gmail.com. A hiking club, offers trips into Tayrona Park and the Sierra Nevada from US$130, which includes transport, food, guides and accommodation.
Turcol, Cra 1C, No 20-15, T/F421 2256, www.buritaca2000.com. Arranges trips and provides a guide service.

Rodadero *p179*
Diving shops
Caribbean Divers, Cra 1, No 5-113, Local 1, Edif Rodamar, T422 0878, www.caribbean diverscol.com. Offers PADI and NAUI qualifications. A mini course costs US$90.

Taganga *p179*
Diving shops
There are various dive shops in Taganga.
Aquantis, B&B and Diving, C 18, No 1-39, T316-818 4285, www.aquantisdive center.com. Belgian-run, PADI-certified, passionate team, PADI course US$275. Recommended.
Oceano Scuba, Cra 2, No 17-46, T421 9004, www.oceanoscuba.com.co. PADI courses, 2, 3 and 4 days from US$70.
Octopus Diving Center, C 15, No 1B-14, T317-327 7570, www.octopusdivecenter taganga.com. PADI, NAUI and BIS courses. Night and wreck dives offered. English spoken.
Poseidon Dive Center, C 18, No 1-69, T421 9224, www.poseidondivecenter.com. PADI courses at all levels and the only place

on the Colombian Caribbean coast to offer an instructor course. Offers a tourist package with no sales tax. German owner, with English and Croatian spoken. Own pool for beginners, also has rooms to rent. **Tayrona Dive Center**, Cra 2, No 18A-22, T318-305 9589, www.tayronadivecenter.com. Mini course with 2 dives is US$77.

Parque Nacional Tayrona *p180*
Ecoturt come highly recommended for guided tours of Pueblito and other parts of the park. Speak to Nohemi Ramos or Jarven Rodríguez, T316-373 8846, ecoturt@ latinmail.com. Some English spoken.

Ciudad Perdida *p183*
Expotur Eco, C 18 No 2A-07, T421 9493, www.expotur-eco.com. Community tourism and Ciudad Perdida treks from US$250 for 6 days.
Magic Tour Taganga, T421 9429/5820, www.magictourstaganga.com. Offices in Santa Marta and Taganga. Work closely with **La Ballena Azul**.

⊖ Transport

Santa Marta *p176, map p177*
Air
There are daily flights to **Bogotá** and **Medellín**, as well as connections to other cities. During the tourist season get to the airport early and book well ahead (the same goes for bus reservations). Facilities at the airport are sparse, no exchange or internet, but a reasonable restaurant on the ground floor.

    Airline offices Avianca, Cra 2A No 14-17, Edif de los Bancos, Local 105, T421 4958, T432 0106 at airport; Centro Comercial Prado Plaza, Cra 4, No 26-40, T431 2020; and at C 7, Cra 3 esq, Edif Los Andes, Rodadero T422 7211.

Bus
To **Barranquilla**, 7 daily, 2 hrs, US$5.50, Brasilia, 3 daily with Copetran, US$10. To **Medellín**, 6 daily, 15 hrs, US$52, **Brasilia** or Copetran. To **Bogotá**, 7 daily, 16 hrs, US$45, Brasilia or Copetran. To **Cartagena**, 5 hrs, US$12.50, **Copetran**. To **Riohacha**, 3 hrs, US$8.50. Frequent buses to **Maicao**, 4-5 hrs, US$12.50 for a/c or cheaper for buses without. **Brasilia** runs a bus through to **Maracaibo**, daily, US$28. To **Bucaramanga**, 9 hrs, US$35, **Brasilia** or Copetran. To **Mompós** there's a door to door *colectivo* service, US$30 with Asotranstax, C 23, No 4-27.

Sea
Although cruise ships stop here, it is difficult to find onward passage.

⊕ Directory

Santa Marta *p176, map p177*
Banks Most banks and ATMs are in Plaza Bolívar eg **Banco Occidente**, good rates for MasterCard. There are plenty of cash machines. For currency exchange, 3rd block of C 14, many others on this street. In Rodadero, Apto 201, Cra 1, No 9-23. Santa Marta is a good place to exchange pesos into Venezuelan bolivares. **Emergencies** Police, T112. **Immigration** DAS Office, Cra 8, No 26A-15, T421 4917. **Internet** Tama Café, C16 with Cra 13, open 0800-1230 and 1400-1830, sells delicious food too. **Laundry** Several laundry services in C 11 between Cra 3 and Cra 2. **Telephone** Good rates in Cra 5 corner with C 11.

Rodadero *p179*
Banks For currency exchange, Apto 201, Cra 1, No 9-23.

Taganga *p179*
Internet Playanet, Cra 1, No 15-9, T421 9296, also sells credit for mobile phones.

East to Venezuela

Along the coast from Santa Marta the lush vegetation of the foothills of the Sierra Nevada gives way to flat expanses of scorched earth where only a scrub-like tree known as trupillo and the cactus survive. The change in landscape marks the beginning of the Guajira Peninsula, home to the Wayúu. It is also the northernmost tip of South America and it certainly feels like the end of the world; an arid and unforgiving terrain which nonetheless offers a home to vast flocks of flamingos and other birds and a chance to mingle with one of Colombia's best-preserved indigenous cultures. Riohacha may be a departmental capital but it feels more like a sleepy fishing village, though it livens up considerably at the weekend and on public holidays. Musichi and Manaure with their flocks of flamingos and salt works will be of interest to nature lovers and Cabo de la Vela with its turquoise waters that lap against a desert landscape is a sight to behold. If you have the time and energy then Parque Natural Nacional Macuira, an oasis of tropical green sprouting out of the semi desert, and Punta Gallinas, the northernmost point of the continent, will cap off a trip into this strange and sometimes ethereal land. The difficulties in transport only add to the sense of adventure this peninsula presents. ▶ For listings, see pages 197-199.

Riohacha → For listings, see pages 197-199. Colour map 1, A5. Population: 169,000

Riohacha, 160 km east of Santa Marta, is capital of La Guajira Department. Formerly a port, today it has the ambience of a provincial fishing town. The city was founded in 1545 by Nicolás Federmann. One of Riohacha's resources of those days was oyster beds, and the pearls were valuable enough to tempt Drake to sack it. Pearling almost ceased during the 18th century and the town was all but abandoned. José Prudencia Padilla, who was born here, was in command of the Republican fleet that defeated the Spaniards in the Battle of Lago Maracaibo in 1823. He is buried in the **cathedral**, and there is a statue in the central park which bears his name. *Riohacha y Los Indios Guajiros*, by Henri Candelier, a Frenchman's account of a journey to the area 100 years ago, has very interesting depictions of the life of the Wayúu.

The **José Prudencio Padilla Airport** is south of the town towards Tomarrazón and the main **bus terminal** is on Calle 15 (Avenida El Progreso)/Carrera 11. There are good white-sand beaches lined with coconut palms and a long wooden pier in the centre. Also two bustling markets, the old market in town and a newer one further out, are worth a visit. At weekends Riohacha fills up, with bars and music springing up all over the place. The sea is clean, despite the dark silt stirred up by the waves and it is a good place to take stock before pushing through into the more remote areas of La Guajira. There is a tourist office, **Dirección de Turismo de Guajira** ⓘ *Cra 7/C 1, Av La Marina, T727 1015*, which is well organized.

Santuario Los Flamencos → Colour map 1, A5.

ⓘ *US$17 entry fee for non-nationals.*

The Santuario de Fauna y Flora Los Flamencos is 7000 ha of saline vegetation including mangroves and lagoons. There are several small, and two large, saline lagoons (Laguna Grande and Laguna de Navío Quebrado), separated from the Caribbean by sand bars. The latter is near **Camarones** (take a *colectivo* from the roundabout between the water tower and bus station in Riohacha, US$2.50), which is just off the main road. A swift boat ride

(US$0.25) takes you to the park entrance. Some 3 km beyond Camarones lies 'La Playa', a popular beach to which some *colectivos* continue at weekends. The two large lagoons are fed by several intermittent streams which form deltas at the south point of the lakes and are noted for the many colonies of flamingos, some of which are there all year, others gather between November and May, during the wet season when some fresh water enters the lagoons. The birds are believed to migrate to and from the Dutch Antilles, Venezuela and Florida. There is also plenty of other birdlife throughout the year.

Across **Laguna de Navío Quebrado** is a warden's hut on the sand bar, ask to be ferried across by local fishermen or the park guards who are very helpful. There is a visitor centre and some basic and rather pricey accommodation, *cabañas* (**C-D**) and hammocks (**F**). Beware that it gets very windy and sleeping in hammocks can be uncomfortable. Camping is permitted near the centre. Take plenty of water if walking. The locals survive, after the failure of the crustaceans in the lagoons, on tourism and ocean fishing. There are several bars/restaurants and two shops on the beach, but food is expensive.

Riohacha

Sleeping	Internacional 4	Eating
Arenas 3	Majayura 8	El Malecón 1
Almirante Padilla 1	Tunebo 5	La Tinaja 2
Arimaca 2	Yalconia del Mar 6	Yoto Express 3
Castillo del Mar 7		

Música tropical

No country in South America has a greater variety of musical genres than Colombia, and nowhere is music more abundant than in the fertile breeding grounds of the North Coast. The diversity of musical expression comes from a mixture of African, indigenous and European influences.

On the coast, *música tropical* is an umbrella term used to encompass the many hybrids that have arisen over the years. Most popular among these is *vallenato*, a form of music which originated with farmers around Valledupar and which primarily uses the accordion, *guacharaca* (a tube, made from the trunk of a small palm tree, with ridges carved into it, which when scraped with a fork produces a beat) and the *caja vallenata* (a cylindrical drum brought over by African slaves) as its instruments.

Vallenato is the current favourite but it has its roots in a more ancient genre,

cumbia. *Cumbia* began as a courtship dance practiced among the slave population – it is believed to derive from Guinean *cumbe* – and later mixed with European and indigenous instruments, such as the guitar, the accordion and the *gaita*, a type of flute used by the *indígenas* of the Sierra Nevada de Santa Marta. *Cumbia* is celebrated for bringing together Colombia's three main ethnic groups and it was used as an expression of resistance during the campaign for Independence from the Spanish. *Cumbia* has many other derivatives, such as *porro*, *gaita*, *fandango* and *bullerengue*.

The newest genre to emerge is *champeta*. This is the most African of the genres, it takes its influence from *soukous* and *compas*, and is characterized by very sensual dancing. It gained popularity among the black population of Cartagena and San Basilio de Palenque in the 1980s.

Valledupar → *For listings, see pages 197-199. Colour map 1, B4. Phone code: 5. Population 354,000.*

South of Riohacha on an alternative road to Maicao and the Venezuelan border is **Cuestecita** (Hotel Turismo), where you can turn southwest to **Barrancas**, with one of the largest coal mines in the world, **El Cerrejón**ⓘ *T595 5554, cerrejonvisitas@cerrejon.com, for information about pre-arranged visits to the mine.* Continuing on this road, which takes you either round the Sierra Nevada to Barranquilla and Santa Marta via Fundación (see above) or south to Bucaramanga, you come to **Valledupar**, capital of César Department.

The Alfonso López Pumarejo **airport** is on the southern outskirts of the city, 3 km from the centre, and a short walk from the bus terminal. A taxi to the centre will cost US$3. The **bus terminal**ⓘ *Av Salguero (Cra 7A) No 44-156, is 3 km down the road to Robles and Maicao.*

One of the few old buildings in the town, which was founded in the middle of the 16th century, is the **Iglesia La Concepción** which overlooks the central plaza named after a past president, Alfonso López Pumarejo. Nearby is a fine balconied colonial façade of the **Casa del Maestre Pavejeau**, and there is an interesting display of indigenous cultures in the **Casa de la Cultura**ⓘ *Cra 6, No 16A-24, T572 3271.* Valledupar claims to be the home of the *vallenato* music. Each April (26-30), *El Festival de la Leyenda Vallenata* draws thousands of visitors. There are *casas de cambio* on Calle 16. There's a **tourist office**ⓘ *in Gobernación, Cra 12, No 16-120, T574 8230.*

Beyond Riohacha to the east is the arid and sparsely inhabited Guajira Peninsula, with its magnificent sunsets. The indigenous peoples here, the Wayúu, collect *dividivi* (pods from a strangely wind-bent tree, the *Caesalpina coriaria*, which are mainly used for tanning), tend goats and fish. Increasingly, thanks to government schemes, they are also involved in tourism. Look out for the coloured robes worn by the women.

Ins and outs

To visit the peninsula you can book a tour with one of the many tour companies in Riohacha (see Activities and tours, page 198). Alternatively, you can catch a ride in a *carrito*, a taxi shared with three others, on the paved road to Uribia or Manaure (one hour 30 minutes, US$7) and from there on dirt tracks to Cabo de la Vela (two to three hours).

Manaure and around

Manaure is known for its salt flats southwest of the town. Hundreds of workers dig the salt and collect it in wheelbarrows, a bizarre sight against the glaring white background. If you walk along the beach for an hour, past the salt works, there are several lagoons where flamingos gather. Around 14 km from Manaure in this direction is **Musichi**, an important haunt of the flamingo, sometimes out of the wet season. Note that they may be on the other side of the lagoon and difficult to see. You can hire a moto-taxi in Manaure that will take you towards Musichi to see the flamingos.

From Manaure there are early morning busetas to **Uribia** (30 minutes, US$1-2), and from there to Maicao, another hour. In Uribia, known as the indigenous capital of Colombia, you can buy authentic local handicrafts by asking around, but the town really doesn't have much to its name. It's also full of Venezuelan contraband and has a rough and ready feel to it. There is a **Wayúu festival** here annually in May, and *alijunas* (white people) are welcome, but ask permission before taking photographs. You can get *camionetas* from Uribia to **Cabo de la Vela** (about three hours once everyone has been dropped off at their various *rancherías*, US$5-7.50; *busetas* run until 1400, few on Sunday; all transport leaves from the market). The drive is spectacular with the final few kilometres involving a bumpy ride across a shimmering, dried-out salt lake that generates mirages. Cabo de la Vela is where the Wayúu believe their souls go after death, and is known as Jepirra. In recent years tourism has really taken off and there are now more hostels in Cabo de la Vela than in Riohacha itself, all of them following the two-mile bay. The barren landscape of shrubs and cacti only serves to accentuate the colour of the water, which glimmers in a dozen shades of aquamarine. There are various excursions from Cabo de la Vela, to Pilón de Azúcar mountain, with lovely views of the sea, nearby beach and also a lighthouse, on a different bay. The beach is beautiful and don't forget to look up at night for spectacular starry skies.

Getting to Cabo de la Vela independently is a time-consuming and at times uncomfortable experience, particularly during or immediately after, the wet season, although it can be done. It is far easier (but more expensive) to book a tour from Riohacha.

Hammocks

There's no better way to enjoy Colombia's beaches than to relax in a hammock, and there are abundant conveniently located palm trees to use as supports. Plenty of places hire them out but for true comfort it's best to buy your own.

The hammocks developed by the Wayúu are made up of intricately woven threads of cotton that form a crocheted net. These are known as *chinchorros* and they are larger than the average hammock, with wrap-around sides serving as a blanket and they often feature elaborate tassels. The other most common style uses brightly coloured woven cotton or wool to form a large stretch of material.

San Jacinto, a couple of hours south of Cartagena, is the capital of Colombia's hammock industry and the best place to find a bargain, but the market in Santa Marta also has a good selection. For *chinchorros*, the best places are the market in Riohacha and Uribia's handicraft shops in La Guajira.

Macuira National Park

① *Free entry. Registration and 30-min compulsory induction at Nazareth park office, guides US$20.*

Towards the northeast tip of the Guajira Peninsula is the Serranía de Macuira, named after the Makui people, ancestors of the Wayúu. The 25,000-ha park is entirely within the Wayúu reservation. It consists of a range of hills over 500 m, with microclimates of their own creating an oasis of tropical forest in the semi-desert. The highest point is **Cerro Palúa**, 865 m, and two other peaks are over 750 m. Moisture comes mainly from the northeast, which forms clouds in the evening that disperse in the early morning. The average temperature is 29°C and there is 450 mm of mist/rain providing water for the streams that disappear into the sand once they reach the plains. Macuira's remoteness gives it interesting flora and fauna and notable wildlife includes the cardinal bird and 15 species of snake, including coral snakes. There are also Wayúu settlements little affected by outsiders, where the indigenous people cultivate cashew nuts, coconuts and plantains, as well as collecting dividivi pods. The rangers are all locals and are very friendly. A recommended walk in the park is a visit to the 40-m-high **El Chorro** waterfall, a delightful lush, green area.

Beyond Macuira is **Punta Gallinas**, the northernmost point in South America and a spectacular location. Nearby is **Taroa**, where sand dunes drop directly into the sea – perfect for a swim, but beware the waves are powerful here and the currents can be strong. Spending a few days exploring this area is a remarkable and rewarding experience. The landscape, usually arid and desolate, turns a bright shade of green after the rainy season and there are gorgeous bays for swimming and chilling. It's also the perfect place for getting closer to Wayúu culture and traditions.

Ins and outs To reach the Parque Natural Nacional Macuira you must travel northeast from Uribia along the mineral railway, then either round the coast past Bahía Portete, or direct across the semi-desert, to Nazareth on the east side of the park. There are no tourist facilities anywhere nearby and no public transport, though trucks may take you from the Bahía Portete area to **Nazareth** (six to eight hours), if you can find one. Nazareth is a Wayúu village where you can stay the night. Food and local guides are available. The best way to visit is to contract your own jeep and guide; **Kaí Eco Travel** ① *T717 7173, www.kaieco travel.com*, run by a network of indigenous families, is recommended. A full tour of the

Border essentials: Colombia–Venezuela

Maicao
Note that there is no Venezuelan consul in Maicao. If you need a visa, get it in Cartagena or Riohacha. Entering Venezuela, a transit visa will only suffice if you have a confirmed onward ticket to a third country within three days.

Transport *Colectivos*, known as *por puestos* in Venezuela, run from Maicao to Maracaibo, US$10 per person, or there is an infrequent microbus, US$3.50. There are very few buses to Venezuela after 1200. **Brasilia** bus company has its own security compound, non-passengers are not allowed in. You can change money, buy bus tickets and food before your journey. *Por puestos* wait here for passengers to Maracaibo; it is a very easy transfer.

Paraguachon
If travelling by *por puesto* make sure the driver stops at the Colombian entry post. If not you will have to return later to complete formalities. With all the right papers, border crossing is easy.

Transport Minibuses or *busetas* can be caught from the terminal de Maracaibo (T0261-723 9084) to Maicao for US$13, but they only run from 0400 to 0800. *Carritos*, taxis shared with three other passengers, continue to leave Maracaibo until 1500 (US$18 per person).

peninsula, with visits to Cabo de la Vela, Parque Natural Nacional Macuira and Punta Gallinas costs US$540 per person for 8 days, including transport, accommodation and food, US$350 not including the national park or US$95 for two days. Beyond Cabo de la Vela we strongly advise you take a tour (see page 198) as there is no public transport, little Spanish is spoken and the locals aren't always welcoming. This is also a semi-self governing zone, replete with Venezuelan contraband. **Eco-Guías** in Bogotá and **Aventure Colombia** in Cartagena also arrange trips here from time to time.

Note The Guajira Peninsula is not a place to travel alone, parties of three or more are recommended. If going in your own transport, check the situation before setting out. The roads can be in very bad condition, mostly dirt tracks and these can become impassable around the wet season. When the road is bad Punta Gallinas is only reached by boat from near Cabo de la Vela, two to three hours, often choppy and very wet. Also remember it is hot, it is easy to get lost, there is little mobile cover and very little water. Locals, including police, are very helpful in giving lifts.

Maicao → *Phone code: 5. Colour map 1, A5. Population: 103,000.*
The paved Caribbean coastal highway, continues from Riohacha inland to Maicao, 78 km, close to the Venezuelan border. Now that there are no flights from Barranquilla to Maracaibo, taxi or bus to Maicao and *colectivo* to Maracaibo is the most practical route. There is a new bus terminal to the east of town.

Maicao is full of Venezuelan contraband, and is still at the centre of the drugs trade. It has a real Wild West feel to it. Most commercial premises close before 1500, and after 1600 the streets are unsafe, though in recent years security has improved somewhat.

For Sleeping and Eating price codes and other relevant information, see pages 23-28.

● Sleeping

Riohacha *p191, map p192*

A Arimaca, C 1, No 8-75, T727 3481, www.hotelarimaca.com. Impressive high tower with clean, light and spacious rooms, some with reception room, all with balconies and magnificent sea views. There is a fine swimming pool on 2nd floor, a good restaurant and buffet breakfast is included.
A Hotel Majayura, Cra 10 1-40, T728 8666, majayurasol@hotmail.com. New hotel centrally located near the beach. Restaurant, internet access, a/c, minibar and buffet breakfast included.
B Hotel Arenas, Cra 5, No 1-25, T727 5424, www.guajirahotelarenas.com. Clean rooms if a little dark, with cable TV and a/c. Helpful staff and near the beach.
D Tunebo, Cra 10, No 12A-02, T728 8174, marytunebo@hotmail.com. A few blocks from the action, but very friendly staff. Near the old market. Also organizes tours. Recommended.
D-E Castillo del Mar, C 9A 15-352, T727 5043, www.hotelcastillodelmarriohacha,com. Pleasant hotel by the sea, a bit rough around the edges, but very reasonably priced. Large rooms with a/c or fan. Recommended.
E Almirante Padilla, Cra 6/C 3a, T727 2328. Crumbling but with character, has an inviting patio and a restaurant with cheap *almuerzo*. It's clean, friendly, large and very central. Some rooms with a/c (**D**).
E Internacional, Cra 7, No 13-37, T727 3483. Down an alleyway off the old market, friendly with a pleasant restaurant on the patio. Free iced water. Recommended.
E Yalconia del Mar, Cra 7, No 11-26, T727 3487. Private bath, clean, safe, friendly, helpful, halfway between beach and bus station.

Valledupar *p192*

B Vajamar, Cra 7, No 16A-30, T574 3939, www.hotelvajamar.com. With breakfast, pool and expensive food.
E Hotel/Restaurant Nutibara, C19, No 9-19, T574 3225. Rooms with a/c, reakfast included.
E-F Provincia Hostel, C 16A No 5-25, T580 0558, www.provinciavalledupar.com. New hostel with both dorms and private rooms. There are plenty of chilling spots including hammocks, patio and common rooms. BBQ area, free bikes to borrow and eco-tours of the area.
F Residencia El Triunfo, C 19, No 9-31. Small rooms with fan, clean and with bath.

Manaure and around *p193*
Manaure

D Palaaima, Cr 6, No 7-25, T717 8195. Comfortable, cool rooms with a/c or fan, helpful. There are always Wayúu locals hanging around the hotel who are eager to talk about their culture and traditions.

Uribia

There are several cheaper options (**G**), somewhat on the grottier side.
D Hotel Juyasirain, C 14A 9-06, T717 7284. The only slightly more upmarket hotel in Uribia. Large, light and airy with a patio restaurant.

Cabo de la Vela

Along the coast, ask anyone and you will probably be able to get fried fish, coconut rice and a place to sling a hammock (US$7). There are now some 60 hostels along the beach, all offering roughly the same set-up for the same cost. Try **Playa Bonita** (rooms **D**, hammocks **E**) in the main cluster of houses and shops or **Pujurú** (rooms **D**, hammocks **E**) further up the beach towards Pilón de Azúcar.

Punta Gallinas
F Luz Mila. A lonely, but friendly little hostel and restaurant run by the Wayúu and where

Kai Eco Travel (see below) has a base for their tours. Recommended.

Maicao *p195*

B Hotel Maicao Internacional, C 12, No 10-90, T726 7184. Good rooms with a/c, friendly staff and a rooftop swimming pool and bar. A good option in Maicao.
B Maicao Plaza, C 10, No 10-28, T726 6597. Clean and spacious, this hotel offers a/c, cable TV, and en suite bathrooms with cold water.
C Los Medanos, Cra 10, No 11-25, T726 8822. This hotel has clean, large rooms, though they are a bit dark. Extras include a/c, cable TV, minibar, a restaurant and a disco. Its private bathrooms have cold water only.
D El Dorado, Cra 10, No 12-45, T726 7242. A little dilapidated, but it has a/c, TV and a good water supply.

🍴 Eating

Riohacha *p191, map p192*
Many ice cream and juice bars, and small *asados*, serving large, cheap selections of barbecued meat can be found at the western end of the seafront and there is also a row of picturesque, brightly painted huts serving ceviche and fresh seafood. The eastern end has more restaurants for sit-down meals.
¶¶ El Malecón, C 1, No 3-43. Good selection of seafood and meats served in a palm-thatched barn looking out to sea. There is music and dancing in the evenings. A good place for people-watching.
¶¶ La Tinaja, C 1, 4-59. Excellent seafood in light, breezy restaurant. Try the *Delicias de la casa* rice dish, tasty and substantial. Recommended.
¶ Yoto Express, C 1, 3-42. Economic restaurant serving sandwiches and some Mexican specialities.

Manaure and around *p193*
Cabo de la Vela
¶¶-¶ El Caracol. Expensive but good, serving catch of the day (try the *langostina al ajillo*).

Valledupar *p192*
¶ Hotel/Restaurant Nutibara, next door to **Residencia El Triunfo**. Cheap meals, excellent fruit juices.

⊛ Festivals and events

Riohacha *p191, map p192*
Mar Festival Francisco el Hombre.
Vallenato festival.

Valledupar *p192*
Apr Festival de la Leyenda Vallenata, www.festivalvallenato.com. One of the most important music festivals in Colombia.

⊙ Shopping

Riohacha *p191, map p192*
Good hammocks sold in the market.
The best place for buying local items is **La Casa de la Manta Guajira**, Cra 6/C 12. Be prepared to bargain.

▲ Activities and tours

Riohacha *p191, map p192*
Tour operators
Guajira Viva, C 3, No 5-08, loc 1, T727 0607. 5-day tours to Alta Guajira, Cabo de la Vela, Santuario de Fauna y Flora los Flamencos.
Lucho Freyle, T728 2885, T312-647 1434 (mob). Wayúu guide in Riohacha, jeep tours around La Guajira and Cabo de la Vela.
Operadora Turística Wayúu, C 1A, No 4-35, T311-400 7985 (mob). Wayúu-run and can be found on the seafront. Sells beautiful, colourful Wayúu *mochilas*. Organizes tours to *rancherías* and Cabo de la Vela.
Kaí Eco Travel, based at Hotel Castillo del Mar, C 9A 15-352, T717 7173, T311-436 2830 (mob), www.kaiecotravel.com. Run by a network of Wayúu families, organizes tours to Cabo de la Vela, Parque Natural Nacional Macuira, Punta Gallinas, the northernmost

point of South America, costs from US$95 for 2 days, to US$540 for 8 days per person, including transport, accommodation and food. Highly recommended.

Uribia
Kaishi, T311-429 6315, T316-429 6315 (mob). Speak to Andrés Orozco, this company organizes jeep tours around La Guajira.

⊜ Transport

Riohacha p191, map p192
Early morning is best for travel, transport is scarce in the afternoon.
Air
1 flight a day **Bogotá**, **Avianca**; where connections to other cities can be made. Flights to **Aruba** Tue and Sat.

Bus
It is best to travel from Riohacha in a luxury bus, in the early morning, as these are less likely to be stopped and searched for contraband. **Brasilia** runs Pullman buses to **Maicao**, every 30 mins from 0630-1700, US$5.50.
Brasilia also has buses to **Santa Marta** ($US8.50, 3 hrs) and **Cartagena** every 30 mins. No direct buses to **Cabo de la Vela**: travel to **Uribia** and wait for a jeep (leaves when full). It's a long and uncomfortable journey. Some *colectivos* for Uribia and the northeast leave from the new market, 2 km southeast on the Valledupar road.

Taxi
Coopcaribe Taxis travel throughout the region and can be picked up almost anywhere in town, especially close to the old market area near the Hotel Internacional or outside Drogas La Rebaja. Daily to **Uribia**, 1½ hrs, US$7; **Manaure**, 1¾ hrs, US$8. They leave when full (4 people), be prepared to pay slightly more if there are no travellers.
Colectivos for the Flamingo Sanctuary leave from the large roundabout between the market and bus station, US$2.50.

Valledupar p192
Air
There are flights to **Bogotá** and **Barranquilla** with **Aires**.

Bus
To **Barranquilla**, 5-6 hrs, US$12.50; **Bucaramanga**, 8 hrs US$30, 7 a day with Copetran; **Santa Marta**, 4½ hrs, US$11; **Cartagena**, US$13 with Expreso Brasilia, US$20, 6 a day with Copetran.

Maicao p195
Bus
Brasilia has a service every 30 mins from 0630-1700 to **Riohacha**, US$5.50, **Copetrán** has 3 a day, US$5; **Santa Marta**, 3 hrs, US$12.50; **Barranquilla**, 4-5 hrs, US$15; **Cartagena**, 6 hrs, US$20.
2 daily to **Bogotá** at 0930 and 1430 with Copetran, US$50; to **Medellín**, 3 daily, 0915, 1330, 1615, US$77. Regular service to **Barranquilla**, US$15-22.

⊙ Directory

Riohacha p191, map p192
Banks Most are on Parque Almirante. Banco de Colombia, Cra 7, between C 2/3, for Visa, Mon-Fri, 0800-1800, Sat, 0900-1200. Banco de Bogotá, Cra 9/C 3, Mon-Fri 0800-1200 and 1400-1600 **Embassies and consulates** Venezuela, Cra 7, No 3-08, p7-B, T727 4076, F727 3967, Mon-Thu 0900-1300, Fri 0900-1500, if you need a visa, you should check all requirements for your nationality before arriving at this consulate. Travellers report it is easier to get a Venezuelan visa in Barranquilla.
Immigration DAS Office (immigration) C 5 y Cra 5, open 0800-1200, 1400-1800. **Internet and telephone** On Parque Almirante. **Post** C 2, Cra 6/7.

Valledupar p192
Banks You can change money at *casas de cambio* on Calle 16.

San Andrés and Providencia

San Andrés and Providencia are destinations most Colombians dream about visiting at least once in their lifetime. Closer to Nicaragua than to the Colombian mainland – there is a running dispute between the two countries over sovereignty – these Caribbean islands have what locals have dubbed 'the sea of seven colours', though it often seems like more. The waters around the archipelago play host to a variety of marine life, and the clarity of the sea makes this one of the best diving destinations in the Caribbean. In 2000, UNESCO declared the archipelago a World Biosphere Reserve, christened The Seaflower. At 32 km in length, the Old McBean Lagoon barrier reef of Providencia is the third largest in the world. ▸▸ *For listings, see pages 206-209.*

Background

San Andrés and Providencia share a coastline rich in coral reefs, white-sand cays and water of extraordinary colours, but are in fact very different. San Andrés, the larger island, is a popular mass tourism destination, replete with resort hotels and discos. Providencia has quietly observed its big sister's development, decided it does not want to follow the same path, and has put in place certain restrictions to halt the encroachment of package tourism.

The original inhabitants are mostly the descendants of Jamaican slaves brought over by English pirates such as Henry Morgan, and with the arrival of English, Dutch, French and Spanish settlers over the years this has led to an extraordinary genealogical mix. Today, especially in San Andrés, much of the original culture has been diluted and about 50% of the population is now made up of immigrants from mainland Colombia. The remainder are locals and there are Lebanese and Turkish communities too. Immigration is less pronounced in Providencia.

San Andrés and Providencia are famous in Colombia for their different styles of music including the local form of calypso, soca, reggae and church music, as well as schottische, quadrille, polka and mazurka, the musical legacies of the various European communities that settled here. A number of good local groups perform on the islands and in Colombia. Concerts are held at the **Old Coliseum** every Saturda at 2100 in the high season. There is a cultural centre at Punta Hansa in San Andrés town.

After Colombus spotted the islands on his fourth trip to the Caribbean, their early colonial history was dominated by the conflicts between Spain and England, though the Dutch occupied Providencia for some years. English Puritans arrived on Providencia from Bermuda and England in 1629 and later moved to San Andrés. The English left in 1641, but Creole English remained the dominant language until recent times and is still widely spoken. Surnames such as Whittaker, Hooker, Archbold, Robinson, Howard and Newell are also common. Providencia later became a pirate colony, shared between the Dutch and the English before it was taken back by the Spanish and assigned to the Vice Royalty of New Granada (modern-day Colombia) in 1803. In 1818 French Corsair Louis-Michel Aury successfully invaded Providencia and declared it part of the United States of Argentina and Chile, using it to capture Spanish cargo to bolster the burgeoning Latin American Independence movement. Finally, in 1822 San Andrés, Providencia and Santa Catalina were incorporated into the newly independent state of Gran Colombia.

The islands are 770 km north of continental Colombia, 849 km southwest of Jamaica, and 240 km east of Nicaragua. This proximity has led Nicaragua to claim them from Colombia in the past. Three battleships patrol San Andrés to guard against any invasion by the Nicaraguans.

an Andrés, a coral island, is 11 km long, rising at its highest to 120 m. The town, commercial centre, major hotel sector and airport are at the northern end. A good view of he town can be seen from **El Cliff**. San Andrés is a popular, safe and local holiday estination for Colombians.

ns and outs

etting there A cheap way to visit San Andrés is by taking a charter flight from Bogotá or nother major city for a weekend or a week, with accommodation and food included. See he newspapers, which usually have supplements on Wednesday or Thursday. Standards f hotel and restaurant packages can vary greatly. You may wish to go for a cheap airfare nd choose where to stay on arrival. The airport is 15 minutes' walk from town. Buses to he centre and San Luis go from across the road. A taxi is US$5.50, a *colectivo* US$0.70.

Cruise ships and tours go to San Andrés but there are no other official passenger services by sea. ▸▸ *See Transport, page 209.*

Getting around Buses run every 15 minutes on the eastern side of the island, US$0.30, and more often at night and during the holidays. Taxis around the island cost US$11, but in town fares double after 2200.

Bicycles are easy to hire but are usually in poor condition, so choose your own bike and check all parts thoroughly. Motorbikes and golf buggies are also easy to hire.

Tourist information Staff at the **tourist office** ① *at the airport, Circunvalar Av Newball, Edif Coral Palace, www.sanandres. gov.co/turismo, Mon-Fri 0800-1200, 1400-1800*, are helpful and English is spoken. They can also provide maps and hotel lists. On arrival in San Andrés, you must buy a tourist card, US$9, which is also valid for Providencia so don't lose it. You must also have an onward or return ticket.

Sights

Besides the beautiful cays and beaches on the eastern side, see **Hoyo Soplador** (South End), a geyser-like hole through which the sea spouts into the air when the wind is in the right direction. The west coast is less spoilt, but there are no beaches on this side. Instead there is **El**

ⓘ San Andrés Island

Punta Norte
Johnny Cay
Bahía Sardinas
Punta Hansa
San Andrés
Roca del Pescador ①
Punta Paraíso
Bahía de San Andrés

Caribbean Sea

Baptist Church
Bahía Baja
Seaquarium — La Loma (104m) ②
El Acuario
La Laguna
Haynes Cay ①
Cueva de Morgan
Rocky Cay

San Luis
El Cove
Bahía Sonora

N

1 km
1 miles

Monte Derecho
La Piscinita ③

Sleeping 🛏
Casa Harb 1
Sunset 3
Súper Decameron
Marazul 2

Eating 🍴
Bibi's Place 1

Hoyo Soplador
Punta Sur

➡ San Andrés maps
1 San Andrés island, page 201
2 San Andrés town, page 202

Cove (The Cove), the island's deepest anchorage, and **Cueva de Morgan** (Morgan's Cave reputed hiding place for pirate's treasure, which is penetrated by the sea through a underwater passage. Next to Cueva de Morgan is a **pirate museum** ① *entry US$1*, wit exhibitions telling the history of the coconut, lots of paraphernalia salvaged from wreck around the island and a replica pirate ship. The museum is run by Jimmy Gordon, autho of *Legado de Piratas*, who has extensive knowledge of the island's history. About 1 km south from Cueva de Morgan is **West View** ① *daily 0900-1700, entry US$1.10 includin bread to feed the fish*, an excellent place to see marine life as the sea is very clear. There is small jetty with a diving board and slide, and you can hire Aqua Nauta equipment (US$5 for 30 minutes), old-fashioned diving equipment with oxygen piped through a tube to helmet. There is a small restaurant opposite the entrance.

At El Cove, you can continue round the coast, or cross the centre of the island back t town over **La Loma**. This is the highest point on the island and nearby is **La Laguna**, freshwater lake 30 m deep, home to many birds and surrounded by palm and mang trees. On the town side of La Loma is the first **Baptist Church** to be built on the island (1847), acting as a beacon to shipping. The church has a Sunday service from 1000-130 with gospel singing. If you take a turning just before the church you will reach th **Mirador Escalona**, a lookout point on someone's unfinished roof (US$1), from which there are spectacular views of the island. In the centre of the island you will find some lif as it was before San Andrés became a tourist destination, with clapboard houses anc traditional music.

Around San Andrés

Boats leave from San Andrés in the morning for El Acuario and Haynes Cay, and continue to Johnny Cay (frequently spelt Jhonny) in the afternoon, which has a white beach anc parties all day Sunday (US$16.60 return). **El Acuario** has crystalline water and is a gooc place to snorkel, and see eagle and manta rays. You can wade across the water to **Haynes Cay** where there is good food and a reggae bar at **Bibi's Place**. These are popular tours; i you want to avoid the crowds a good option is to hire a private boat (US$110 for the day)

② **San Andrés town**

To West Coast

Boats t Johnny C

Av Colombia

Aeropuerto Sesquicentenario

Av de la Playa

Av Aeropuerto

SAM   Avia (Airn

Cra 6

Coliseo

Carrera 5

Av Las Américas

Banco d Repúbl

El Cliff

Boyacá

Av New

To Port, Customs, San Luis & Loma Alta

N

Not to scale

Sleeping		
Decameron Boutique	Hernando Henry **2**	Posada d'Lulu **7**
Los Delfines **3**	Lord Pierre **4**	Posada Doña Rosa **8**
	Mediterráneo **6**	Portobelo **9**

and do the tour in reverse. Boats for the cays leave from Tonino's Marina between 0930 and 1030, returning at 1530, or from Muelle Casa de la Cultura on Avenida Newell.

Apart from those already mentioned, other cays and islets in the archipelago are **Bolívar**, **Albuquerque**, **Algodón** (included in the Sunrise Park development in San Andrés), **Rocky**, the **Grunt**, **Serrana**, **Serranilla** and **Quitasueño**. On San Andrés the beaches are in town and on the eastern coast. Perhaps the best is at **San Luis** and **Bahía Sonora** (Sound Bay).

Diving

Diving off San Andrés is very good; the depth varies from 3-30 m, visibility from 30-60 m. There are three types of site: walls of seaweed and minor coral reefs, large groups of different types of coral, and underwater plateaux with much marine life. It is possible to dive in 70% of the insular platform. The **Pared Azul** (Blue Wall) is excellent for deep-water diving. **Black Coral Net** and **Morgam's Sponge** are other good sites. ▸▸ *For further information, see Activities and tours, page 208.*

Providencia → *For listings, see pages 205-209. Colour map 1, inset. Phone code: 8.*

Providencia, also called **Old Providence**, 80 km to the north-northeast of San Andrés, is 7 km long and 3.5 km wide. The island is more mountainous and considerably more verdant than San Andrés, rising to 360 m, due to its volcanic origin and is much older. There are waterfalls, and the land drops steeply into the sea in places.

Providencia is striving to retain its cultural identity. Hotels must be constructed in the typical clapboard style of the island and cannot be built higher than two storeys, while mainland operators cannot manage them directly; they must work in partnership with local owners. Only locals are allowed to buy property on the island and outsiders can stay no longer than six months at a time.

Ins and outs

Getting there Visitors can arrive by air from San Andrés (20 minutes) or by sea on launches and boats that ferry goods over to Providencia. Beware that the sea can be choppy on this trip.

> **San Andrés maps**
> 1 San Andrés island, page 201
> 2 San Andrés town, page 202

Getting around *Chivas* circle the island at more or less regular intervals, the standard fare is US$1.60. *Colectivos* can also be found on the island and charge much the same.

Tourist office In Palacio de la Alcaldía, T514 8054, alcalde@providencia.gov.co.

Around the island

Day tours are arranged through hotels around the island, stopping typically at Cayo Cangrejo to swim and snorkel, they cost about US$17. Snorkelling equipment can be hired and diving trips arranged: the best places are Aguadulce and South West Bay.

Eating ⑦
Guillos Café **11**
La Fonda Antioqueña **12**

Margherita e Carbonara **13**
Niko's **14**

In 1996 part of the east coast and offshore reefs and coral islands were declared National Park (**Parque Nacional Natural Old Providence – McBean Lagoon**). The lan⋯ position includes Iron Wood Hill (150 m), mainly small trees but including cocksp⋯ (*Acacia colinsii*) which has large conical-shaped needles, home to a species of an⋯ (*Pseudo-myrmex ferruginea*) with a very painful sting. There are superb views from⋯ **Casabaja** (Bottom House) or **Aguamansa** (Smooth Water), a climb to the summit will tak⋯ about one hour, and with a guide will cost US$13.80. You will see relics of the fortification⋯ built on the island during its disputed ownership.

Horse riding is available, and boat trips can be made to neighbouring islands such a⋯ **Santa Catalina**, an old pirate lair separated from Providencia by a channel cut for thei⋯ better defence. To the northeast is **Cayo Cangrejo** (Crab Cay), a beautiful place fo⋯ swimming and snorkelling, and **Cayos Tres Hermanos** (Three Brothers Cays). Boat trip⋯

Providencia

The black crabs of Providencia

With the arrival of the first rains between April and June, Providencia is the scene a spectacular natural phenomenon. Each night during the wet season thousands of black crabs (*Gecarcinus lateralis*) descend from the forests of High Hill and release their eggs in the waters between South West Bay and Freshwater, wriggling their abdomens in the surf to deposit their eggs. The hatchlings are born in the sea and return to the hills one month later.

During the migration the road that encircles the island is closed to traffic, thus allowing the crabs free access to the beaches without the risk of being run over. Coralina, the government's environmental agency on the archipelago, has banned the capture and eating of crabs during the breeding season and anyone caught disobeying the ban risks a heavy fine equivalent to three months of the minimum wage.

Many of the islanders make a living from crab fishing but during this time hunters turn protectors as they are employed as enforcers of the ban, thus ensuring that Providencia's black crab population will continue to thrive.

eave from 1000-1500 and cost about US$17 per person, with a two hour lunch in South West Bay. Santa Catalina is joined to the main island by a 100-m wooden bridge, known as the **Puente de los Amantes** (Lovers' Bridge). On the west side of Santa Catalina are the ruins of an old fort, built by the English to defend their pirate colony. Formerly known as Fort Warwick, it was rechristened **Fuerte de la Libertad** after the island was taken back by the Spanish in the 17th century. The fort still has the original canons and it is rumoured that there is a secret cave which was used by Henry Morgan to escape to the sea below (most probably untrue). Beyond the fort is a fine beach, excellent for snorkelling, with caves with air chambers and lots of starfish. Further still is a rock formation called **Morgan's Head**; seen from the side it looks like a man's profile. The path beyond Morgan's Head leads through thick forest to the top of the mountain and an abandoned house formerly belonging to a drug trafficker.

The beaches

Bahía Manzanillo (Manchineel Bay) is named after the manzanillo trees found on its edges (the fruit is like a miniature apple, sweet smelling but with an acid taste – and dangerous; do not eat), and is the largest, most attractive and least developed, with a couple of restaurants, including **Roland's Reggae bar** (see page 207). **Bahía del Suroeste** (South West Bay) is fringed by almond trees, palms and has bottle green water, and on Saturday afternoons the local boys put on bareback horse races. **Bahía Agua Dulce** (Freshwater Bay) has a small strip of beach and the sea laps at the fronts of the many hotels in this small bay. Two smaller beaches are **Alan's Bay**, between Aguadulce and San Felipe, which is very secluded and seldom visited, and **Playa del Fuerte**, underneath the fort on Santa Catalina, which has excellent snorkelling and lots of starfish.

For Sleeping and Eating price codes and other relevant information, see pages 23-28.

⊖ Sleeping

San Andrés *p201, maps p201 and p202*

LL Casa Harb, C 11, No 10-83, La Rocosa, T512 6348, www.casaharb.com. Just outside town, this boutique hotel takes its inspiration from the Far East and is the most stylish location on the island. Each room is individually decorated with antique furniture. The baths, made of solid granite, are enormous. A former family home, this mansion has a an infinity pool and offers home-cooked meals.

LL Hotel Súper Decameron Marazul, Km 2 Vía San Luis, T513 2600, www.decameron.com. This enormous all-inclusive resort hotel sits on the southern end of town on the way to San Luis. It has a private beach, pool, 3 restaurants and a disco.

L Lord Pierre, Av Colombia, No 1B-106, T512 7541, www.lordpierre.com. While it may boast a magnificent pier on the tip of the *malecón*, this is a hotel that needs a rehaul. Rooms are large but a little dated, with heavy furniture.

AL Decameron Boutique Los Delfines, Av Colombia, No 1B-86, T512 7816, www.decameron.com. Another hotel in the **Decameron** chain, this one achieves some individuality. The rooms are particularly comfortable, all painted a cool white and set around a fine pool. There is also a restaurant on a jetty, under which large schools of fish congregate for feeding.

A Portobelo, Av Colombia, No 5A-69, T512 7008, www.portobelohotel.com. Occupies a couple of buildings on the western end of the *malecón*. Rooms have large beds, a/c and cable TV. Breakfast included.

A Sunset Hotel, Carretera Circunvalar Km 13, T513 0433, sunsetsai@hotmail.com. On the western side of the island, this is the perfect place to stay if you want to do some serious diving – or just want to escape the crowds. It has bright, fresh rooms with high ceilings, all set around a saltwater swimming pool. With a restaurant serving a mixture of international and regional food in a typical clapboard house and a dive shop next door, this is one of the best places to unwind in San Andrés.

B-C Hernando Henry, Av Las Américas, No 4-84, T512 3416. At the back of town, this hotel has shoddy but passable rooms. TV and laundry service. Rooms are significantly cheaper with fan.

C La Posada D'Lulú, Av Antioquia, No 2-28, T512 2919, www.descansorural.com. This brightly coloured hostel with its clean and comfortable rooms is one of the best mid-range options in town. There are 2 apartments to rent for longer stays and an excellent restaurant serving home cooked food for US$3. Recommended.

C Posada Doña Rosa, Av Las Américas con Aeropuerto, T512 3649, www.posada rosa.blogspot.com. A 2-min walk from the airport, this is a reasonable and economical option. It has clean rooms with private bathrooms and a small patio with potted plants. There is a kitchen and TV room, and it's a short walk from the beach. Also has 2 apartments to rent.

D Mediterráneo, Av Colón, T512 6722. Noisy, crumbling building near the beach. Rooms just about pass for cleanliness. TV and fridge provided.

Private houses

D pp Red Crab, Av Circunvalar, San Luis, T513 0314, www.arriendos.biz/RedCrab.html. A villa on the beach with 4 independent apartments, each with a capacity of up to 6 people. Price includes use of a swimming pool and the services of a housekeeper.

Camping

You can camp on Hayes Caye for US$100 per person (includes transport, food and drinks), but you must ask the Port Authority for permission through **Bibi's Place** (see Eating, below).

rovidencia *p203, map p204*
here are several rooms available for rent at
affordable prices in local houses or *posadas
nativas*. Try **Captain 'Hippie'**, T514 8548/
311-485 4805 (mob), who offers home-
cooked food and lodging in his house (**E** pp).
AL-A Cabañas Miss Elma, Aguadulce,
T514 8229, philhuffington@yahoo.es. Wood-
panelled *cabañas* with terraces, right on the
beach. Large rooms, some with reception
rooms and baby cots. Cable TV and a/c.
A Hotel Sirius South, South West Bay, T514
8213, www.siriushotel.net. Large, colourful
house set back from the beach, run by a
Swiss family. The rooms are large and light,
some have balconies with hammocks.
Kitchen available for guests. Prices negotiable.
A Posada del Mar, Aguadulce, T514 8168,
posadadelmar@latinmail.com. Pink and
purple clapboard house with comfortable
rooms, each with a terrace and hammock
looking onto the bay. The sea laps at the
edge of the garden. Has cable TV, a/c,
minibar and hot water. Recommended.
B Cabañas Miss Mary, South West Bay,
T514 8206. On the beach at South West Bay,
Miss Mary has clean, comfortable rooms with
cable TV and hot water. Breakfast is included.
C Hotel Old Providence, Santa Isabel,
T514 8691. Above supermarket **Erika**,
rooms are basic but clean and have a/c,
cable TV, fridge and private bathroom.

Camping
Roland's Reggae bar, Playa Manzanillo,
T514 8417, rolandsbeach@hotmail.com.
Hires tents for camping (**F**).

🍴 Eating

San Andrés *p201, maps p201 and p202*
🍴 **Bibi's Place**, Haynes Caye, T513 3767,
caritoortega@hotmail.com. Reggae bar and
restaurant on cay next to **El Acuario** serving
seafood, including crab and lobster. Organizes
full moon parties and civil and rasta weddings.

🍴 **Margherita e Carbonara**, Av Colombia,
opposite the Lord Pierre Hotel. Italian-owned
restaurant decorated with photographs from
Italian films. Good pizzas.
🍴 **Niko's**, Av Colombia, No 1-93. Bills itself
as a seafood restaurant though its steaks are
actually better. Lovely setting by the water.
🍴 **Guillos Café**, Av Peatonal next to **Portobelo
Hotel**. Fast-food restaurant serving sandwiches and burgers, as well as local specialities.
🍴 **La Fonda Antioqueña**, Av La Playa, No 1-16.
On the main beach in San Andrés town, this
paisa restaurant serves good, cheap food.

Providencia *p203, map p204*
Local specialities include crab soup and
rondón, a mix of fish, conch, yucca and
dumplings, cooked in coconut milk. Corn
ice cream is also popular – it tastes a little
like vanilla but a little sweeter. Breadfruit,
a grapefruit-sized fruit with a taste similar
to potato, is the archipelago's official fruit.
🍴 **Caribbean Place** (Donde Martín),
Aguadulce. *Bogoteño* chef Martín Quintero
arrived for a brief stay in 1989 and has never
left. He uses local ingredients. Specialities
include lobster in crab sauce, fillet of fish
in ginger and corn ice cream.
🍴 **Roland's Reggae Bar**, Playa Manzanillo,
T514 8417, rolandsbeach@hotmail.com.
Roland is a legend on the island, as are the
parties at his bar-restaurant on Manzanillo
Beach. The menu is mainly seafood, with
fried fish and ceviches.
🍴 **Pizza's Place**, Aguadulce. Basic pizzas
and pastas.

❀ Festivals and events

San Andrés *p201, maps p201 and p202*
Jun Jardín del Caribe. A folkloric festival.
20 Jul Independence.
Dec Rainbow Festival. Reggae and
calypso music.

Providencia *p203, map p204*
Jun Carnival.

▲ Activities and tours

San Andrés *p201, maps p201 and p202*
From Toninos Marina there are boat trips to the nearby cays, US$17 with lunch included.

Canopying
Canopy La Loma, Vía La Loma-Barrack, T314-447 9868 (mob). Has a site at the top of the hill in San Andrés. 3 'flights' over the trees at heights of 450 m, 300 m and 200 m above sea level with spectacular views out to sea and costs US$17. Safety precautions and equipment are good.

Diving
Banda Dive Shop, Hotel Lord Pierre, Local 104, T512 2507, www.bandadiveshop.com. PADI qualified, mini-courses from US$83. Fast boat and good equipment.
Sharky Dive Shop, Carretera Circunvalar Km 13, T512 0651, www.sharkydive shop.com. Next to **Sunset Hotel**, Sharky's has good equipment and excellent, English-speaking guides. PADI qualifications and a beginners' course held in the Sunset Hotel's saltwater swimming pool.

Fishing
Cooperativa Lancheros, on the beach in San Andrés town. Can arrange fishing trips. Windsurfing and sunfish sailing rental and lessons are also available from **Bar Boat**, on the road to San Luis (opposite the naval base), 1000-1800 daily (also has floating bar, English and German spoken), and **Windsurf Spot**, Hotel Isleño; waterskiing at **Water Spot**, Hotel Aquarium, and **Jet Sky**.

Watersports and boat trips
Snorkelling equipment can be hired for US$10.
Centro Comercial New Point Plaza, No 234, T512 8787. Morning boats to El Acuario Cay, off Haynes Cay. The trip takes 20 mins and costs US$16 return. You watch the colourful fish wearing mask and sandals as protection against sea-urchins. They also run the *Nautilus*, a glass hull semi-submarine, US$17.

Cooperativa Lancheros, on the beach in San Andrés town. Can arrange windsurfing, jet skiing and kite surfing.
Also try **Windsurf Spot**, Hotel El Isleño, Av Colombia, No 5-117; and **Water Spot**, Decameron Aquarium, Av Colombia, No 1-19, www.decameron.com.

Providencia *p203, map p204*
Diving
Recommended diving spots on the Old McBean Lagoon reef are **Manta's Place**, a good place to see manta rays; **Felipe's Place** where there is a submerged figure of Christ; and **Stairway to Heaven**, which has a large wall of coral and big fish.
Felipe Diving, Cabañas El Recreo, Aguadulce, T514 8775, www.felipediving.com. Mini-courses from US$80, also rents snorkel equipment. Owner Felipe Cabeza even has a diving spot on the reef named after him. Warmly recommended.
Sirius Diving, South West Bay, T514 8213, www.siriusdivecenter.com. PADI qualifications, mini-course US$100.

Snorkelling and boat trips
Recommended snorkelling sites include the waters around Santa Catalina, where there are many caves to explore as well as **Morgan's Head** and lots of starfish; **Hippie's Place**, which has a little bit of everything; and **El Faro** (The Lighthouse), the end of the reef before it drops into deep sea, some 14 km from Providencia.
Valentina Tours, T514 8548. Lemus Walter, aka Captain 'Hippie', organizes snorkelling, and boat trips (US$17 per person) to the outlying cays and reefs. He has a section of the reef named after him. He charges US$140 for a day's hire of the boat.

Tour operators
Body Contact, Aguadulce, T514 8283. Owner Jennifer Archbold organizes excursions, fishing and hiking trips, currency exchange, accommodation, and more. Recommended.

Walking

There is a good walk over Manchineel Hill, between Bottom House (Casa Baja) and South West Bay, 1.5 km through tropical forest, with fine views of the sea; many types of bird can seen, along with iguanas and blue lizards. Guided tours depart twice a day at 0900 and 1500 from Bottom House. Enquire at **Body Contact**, see Tour operators, above, or **Coralina**, T514 9003.

Transport

San Andrés *p201, maps p201 and p202*
Air Flights to **Bogotá**, **Cali**, **Medellín** and **Cartagena** with AeroRepública; Avianca; Satena; and Searca (booked through Decameron). Copa runs 1 flight daily to **Panama City**. To **Providencia** 2 times a day with Satena and Searca. Bookable only in San Andrés.

Boat Cargo ships are not supposed to carry passengers to the mainland, but many do. It's possible to catch a ride on one of the cargo boats to **Providencia** 3 times a week. The journey takes 7-8 hrs and is uncomfortable. Normal price is US$22. They usually leave at 2200, arriving in the early morning. *Miss Isabel*, *Doña Olga* and *Razíman* are 3 boats that make the trip regularly. Speak directly to the captain at the port in San Andrés, or enquire at the Port Authority (*Capitanía del Puerto*) in San Luis. Any other offer of tickets on ships from San Andrés, or of a job on a ship, may be a con. The sea crossing to **Cartagena** takes 3-4 days, depending on the weather.

Vehicle and bicycle hire

Motorbikes are easy to hire, as are golf buggies. Cars can be hired for US$22 for 2 hrs, US$65 for a day. Passport may be required as deposit.

Bikes are a popular way of getting around on the island and are easy to hire, eg opposite **Los Delfines Hotel** on Av Colombia, US$2 per hr or US$7 per day.

Providencia *p203, map p204*
Vehicle and bicycle hire
Mopeds can be hired for US$27 per day from many of the hotels (eg **Posada del Mar** in Aguadulce) and golf buggies are a lso available for US$83 per day.

Directory

San Andrés *p201, maps p201 and p202*
Banks Banks close 1200-1400. Banco de Bogotá, will advance pesos on a Visa card. Banco Occidente, for MasterCard. ATMs available in town and at the airport (Davivenda, in the lobby at the foot of the stairs). Some shops and most hotels will change US$ cash; it's impossible to change TCs at weekends. **Titan casa de cambio**, inside CC Leda, Av de las Américas, open Mon-Fri, and Sat, 0830-1200, changes TCs, US$ and euro. **Immigration** DAS, right next to airport, T512 7182/T512 5540. **Internet and telephone** Bistronet, Av Colón, Edif Bread Fruit, Local 105, headphones and Skype, also, international calls; Varieteam Shop, Av Providencia, Centro Comercial Leda, Local 111, head-phones and Skype, photocopying, fax and scanner, CDs and DVDs sold. **Post** Deprisa at the airport and Av Colón, Edif Salazar.

Providencia *p203, map p204*
Banks Banco de Bogotá, Santa Isabel, Mon-Thu 0800-1130, 1400-1600, Fri 0800-1130, 1400-1630, exchanges cash; and Banco Agrario, Santa Isabel, exchanges cash. An ATM is tucked away just before the Lover's Bridge, on the road to Santa Catalina. Exchange rates from shops and hotels are poor. **Emergencies** Police: T2. **Internet** Bodycom, in CC Newball, next to super-market Hamilton. **Medical services** Ambulance, T514 8016 at hospital; Medical emergencies, T11. **Telephone** Telecom in Santa Isabel (centre), Mon-Sat 0800-2200; Sun 0900-1230, 1400-1900.

Contents

214 Medellín
214 Ins and outs
215 Background
218 Sights
226 Around the city
227 Listings

237 Around Medellín
237 East of Medellín
South of Medellín
242 North of Medellín
242 Santa Fe de Antioquia
and around
244 Listings

248 Department of Chocó
248 Quibdó
248 Along the Pacific Coast
250 Listings

252 La Zona Cafetera
252 Manizales
256 Around Manizales
257 Marmato
259 Parque Nacional
Los Nevados
261 Santa Rosa de Cabal
and around
261 Pereira
264 Around Pereira
264 Pereira to Armenia
265 Salento
266 Valle de Cocora
267 Nevado del Tolima
267 Armenia
269 Parque Nacional
del Café
269 Ibagué and around
269 Cartago
270 Listings

Footprint features

212 Don't miss ...
218 Pablo Escobar
222 Fernando Botero
223 Tango in Medellín
230 Gastronomic Medellín
234 The Metrocable
240 Discovering Reserva Natural
Cañón del Río Claro
245 Love hotels
255 Staying on a coffee finca
257 The legends of Marmato

Northwest Colombia

At a glance

◉ **Getting around** Metro or taxi in Medellín; buses between towns in rest of region. Car hire recommended for exploring coffee *fincas* of Zona Cafetera.
◉ **Time required** 3-4 days in Medellín; 1-2 weeks to explore villages and towns of Antioquia; 1 week to explore Zona Cafetera; 3-4 days trekking in Los Nevados.
☼ **Weather** Spring-like all year round. Prone to more rain (and land/mudslides on roads) Mar-May and Sep-Nov.
✖ **When not to go** Good all year.

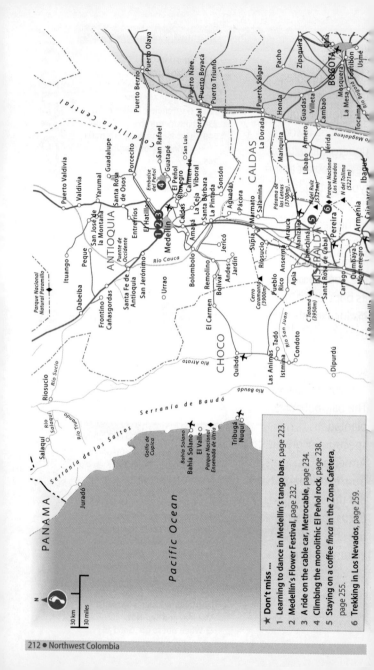

Pacific Ocean

PANAMA

Golfo de
Cupica

Serranía de los Saltos

Serranía de Baudó

N

30 km
30 miles

★ Don't miss ...

1 Learning to dance in Medellín's tango bars, page 223.
2 Medellín's Flower Festival, page 232.
3 A ride on the cable car, Metrocable, page 234.
4 Climbing the monolithic El Peñol rock, page 238.
5 Staying on a coffee finca in the Zona Cafetera, page 255.
6 Trekking in Los Nevados, page 259.

CORDILLERA CENTRAL

ANTIOQUIA

CALDAS

CHOCÓ

RISERALDA

BOGOTÁ

The people of Antioquia have made this corner of Colombia the country's industrial heartland and *paisas*, as people from here are known, are enterprising, business-savvy individuals, known for their pride in their distinctive accent, gregarious nature and generous hospitality. Their boundless optimism has seen Medellín, for so long associated with Pablo Escobar and his drug cartel, undergo an extraordinary transformation into a city buzzing with new ideas, art and culture. Outside of Medellín there are delightful typical villages such as Santa Fe de Antioquia, unique in character, that locals will tell you are pure *paisa*.

The department of Chocó could not be more different. This area's relentless rainfall and dense jungles have hampered attempts to build any significant roads and as a result, it is one of the poorest places economically but one of the richest culturally. Its population is proud of its African heritage, reflected in their distinctive music. Travellers should take advice before going, but Bahía Solano and Nuquí are relatively safe and boast some of the most beautiful, untouched beaches in Colombia and a chance to see one of the great whale migrations.

The Zona Cafetera is Colombia's main coffee-producing region. The bamboo forests, babbling brooks, banana groves and coffee plantations that make up its landscape create a bewildering spectrum of greens. The three main cities – Manizales, Pereira and Armenia – are relatively new and their susceptibility to damage from earthquakes has left them lacking in architectural charm. But the surrounding countryside is brimming with delightful *fincas* and pretty villages. Moreover, the icy peaks of Los Nevados, the eerie wax palms of the Valle de Cocora, or the incredible volume of birdlife at the Río Blanco reserve make this an excellent destination for nature lovers.

Medellín

→ *Colour map 2, B3. Phone code: 4. Population: 2,636,000 (city). Altitude: 1495 m.*

Medellín, capital of Antioquia Department, is a dynamic, contemporary city, considered by many to be the engine of Colombia. Previously the home and headquarters of notorious drug-trafficker Pablo Escobar, Medellín has since shaken off its association with drugs and violence in what is one of the most remarkable turnarounds in Latin America. Medellín is now a fresh, vibrant and prosperous city known for its progressive social politics, art, culture and partying. It is one of the main industrial cities of Colombia, and paisas are known for their canny business sense as well as the pride they take in their city. In the centre, the new has driven out much of the old and few colonial buildings remain. However, large new buildings must, by law, incorporate modern works of art which, together with plazas and parks that feature monuments and sculptures, make for an interesting walking tour. Music, arts and gastronomy festivals attract many visitors and the flower festival, the Desfile de Silleteros, in August, is the most spectacular parade in Colombia. Known as 'The City of Eternal Spring', Medellín has a pleasant, temperate climate; warm during the day and cool in the evening.
▶▶ *For listings, see pages 227-236.*

Ins and outs

Getting there
Air The **José María Córdova international airport** (sometimes called Rionegro airport), is 28 km from Medellín by the new highway, and 9 km from Rionegro. A taxi to town is US$25, but can sometimes be bargained down to US$20, *buseta* to centre, US$5, frequent service 0400-2100, taking about one hour to the small road (Carrera 50A/Calle 53) next to **Hotel Botero Plaza**. To Rionegro from the airport is US$0.20 bus, US$8 taxi.

There is also the **Enrique Olaya Herrera metropolitan airport** in the city, where some internal flights arrive. Taxis between the airports are US$27. From Enrique Olaya Herrera to the centre or El Poblado, US$2.50.

Bus Long-distance buses arrive either at **Terminal del Norte** or **Terminal del Sur**. A taxi from either costs US$2.70 to the centre, or there are local buses and the metro.

Getting around
The best way to get around the city is by metro, which serves the three main sectors of Medellín: centre, south and west. It is efficient and safe. A single ticket, US$0.75, is valid for the Metrocable as well. The town bus services are marginally cheaper but slower. There are plenty of taxis.

Orientation
Medellín is set in the comparatively narrow Aburrá valley surrounded by high mountain barriers of the Cordillera Central in nearly all directions. The built-up metropolitan area now extends from Copacabana in the north to Sabaneta in the south, more than 25 km.

The city is centred around the old and new cathedrals, the former on Parque Berrío and the latter overlooking Parque de Bolívar. The main commercial area is three blocks away on Carrera 46, with shopping and hotels throughout the area. Some streets have been pedestrianized.

In the south, El Poblado has become an upmarket commercial and residential area and many companies have moved their headquarters there from the centre. The best hotels and restaurants are in or near El Poblado. The area around Parque Lleras, known as the Zona Rosa, is where most of the bars and nightclubs are situated.

Also favoured is the area west of the centre between Cerro El Volador and the Universidad Pontificia Bolivariana. Around Carrera 70 and Calle 44 are busy commercial and entertainment sectors with many new hotels, shopping centres and the huge **Atanasio Girardot** sports stadium nearby.

A new feature of Medellín is the pedestrianization in the centre. Pasaje Junín (Carrera 49, dug up for resurfacing at the time of writing) is now closed to traffic from Parque de Bolívar to Parque San Antonio (Calle 46). This gives walkers pleasant relief from traffic in the busy heart of the city. If driving out of Medellín, check routes carefully before leaving. There are few signs and information from officials and petrol stations is often less than clear.

In listings, pages 227-236, we give the Calle (C) and Carrera (Cra) numbers for easy reference. Unlike most other Colombian cities, most central streets are named, and locally these are normally used. Refer to the maps which show both numbers and names. Particularly important are: Carrera 46, part of the inner ring road, which has several names but is known popularly as 'Avenida Oriental'; Carrera 80/Carrera 81/Diagonal 79, the outer ring road to the west, which is called 'La Ochenta' throughout; Calle 51/ 52, east of the centre is 'La Playa'; and Calle 33, which crosses the Río Medellín to become Calle 37, is still called 'La Treinta y Tres'.

For your first general view of the city, take the metro. Most of the track in the centre is elevated, none of it is underground and you can ride the whole system on one ticket for US$0.75.

Tourist information

Oficina de Turismo de Medellín ⓘ *C 41, No 35-80, oficina 302, T2616060*. For information on the city, helpful staff. **Information booth (Burbuja informativa)** ⓘ *Plaza Botero, Cra 51 52A-48, www.conexionciudad.com, Mon-Fri 0900-1900, Sat 0900-1800, Sun 1000-1300, 1400-1700*, has very helpful staff. Also has an email response service in Spanish, English and French, burbujainformativa@comfenalcoantioquia.com. There's another **tourist office** ⓘ *C 57, 45-12, T254 0800*. There are tourist booths at both airports and the bus stations.

Best time to visit

Medellín's climate is generally warm and pleasant though it is often cloudy and rain can come at any time over the Cauca valley from Chocó, which is only 100 km to the west. The city's festivals draw many visitors from the rest of Colombia and abroad and the *paisas* know how to have a good time. ▸▸ *For details, see Festivals and events, page 231*.

Safety

Travellers should take the same safety precautions as they would in any large city, particularly at night. Medellín is, nevertheless, a friendly place. For all police services: T112.

Background

Though the Valle de Aburrá was discovered early on by the Spaniards (1541), there were few settlements here until early in the 17th century. The founding of the town is thought to be in 1616 as 'San Lorenzo de Aburrá', on the site of what is now El Poblado. It was given the official title of town (*villa*) in 1675 by Queen Mariana of Austria and named after Don Pedro Portocarrero y Luna, Count of Medellín, who achieved this recognition of the town by Spain. It was declared a city in 1813 and in 1826 it became the capital of Antioquia, by which time the city had become established around the **Basílica de La Candelaria** (now known as the Old Cathedral), which was built at the end of the 17th century.

1 Medellín

Sleeping
Florida **1**
Hostal Medellín **2**
Lukas **3**
Palm Tree Hostal **4**
Parque 70 **5**
Plaza 70 **6**
Villa Real **7**

Eating
La Margarita No 2 **2**
Opera Pizza **3**
¡Orale ! **4**

500 metres
500 yards

The industrialization of Medellín followed the coffee boom. The first looms arrived in 1902 and the textile industry has remained an integral part of Medellín to this day, being a major source of export. Other major local industries are brick-making, leather goods and plastics. There has been limited immigration from overseas since the original settlement, but the natural growth in population has been extraordinary. Recently, the city has

To Santa Elena & Airport

To Las Palmas & Airport

➡ **Medellín maps**
1 **Medellín, page 216**
2 Medellín centre, page 220
3 El Poblado, page 225
4 Medellín metro, page 235

Teatro Pablo
Tobón Uribe

BUENOS
AIRES

C 51
C 50
C 49
Cra 29
Cra 35
Cra 32
Cra 30ª

Morro El
Salvador

Variante Las Palmas

C 32

Variante Las Palmas

Cra 25

Ⓜ Alpujarra

Variante Las Palmas

Exposiciones Ⓜ

Cra 45
Cra 43A
C 29

Cra 43F

Av El Poblado

C 24

3

Cerro
Nutibara

Ⓜ Industriales

Cra 52

Cra 48

Río Medellín

Plaza del 🏛 San José
Poblado

EL POBLADO

C 10

C 30
C 29
C 33
C 35
C 36
C 20

Parque
Zoológico
Santa Fe

SANTA
FE

Ⓜ Poblado

Autopista Sur

To Envigado

MALIBU

Cra 66B

Terminal
del Sur

Olaya Herrera
Airport

C 10
Cra 65

Cra 52
C 4
C 2
C 15
C 22

CRISTO
REY

To Cali

Cra 73
C 78

Cra 70

GRANADA

Pomodoro **5**

Bars & clubs 🍸
Trilogía **7**

Pablo Escobar

Not since the assassination of presidential candidate Jorge Eliécer Gaitán has a man had such a powerful hold over Colombia.

Pablo Emilio Escobar Gaviria, one of the world's most notorious outlaws, was born in 1949 into a middle-class family in the Antioquian town of Rionegro. Rumour has it he began his criminal career stealing tombstones and selling them on. He progressed to car crime and then muscled his way into the drug business, eventually becoming the head of the most powerful drug cartel in the world.

Escobar developed a reputation for casual, lethal violence, often kidnapping his enemies and holding them for ransom. His trademark technique for dealing with the authorities became known as *plata o plomo* (cash or lead); any judge or official who refused his bribes was shot.

By the mid-1980s his drug organization was so lucrative that he owned 19 residences in Medellín alone, each with its own heliport, as well as boats, planes, banks and properties throughout the world. In 1989, Forbes magazine listed him as the 7th richest man on the planet, estimating that the Medellín cartel was pulling in US$30 billion a year.

Despite his brutal methods, he was incredibly popular. A master at manipulating public opinion, he actively cultivated an image as the '*paisa* Robin Hood', raising money to build roads and put up electricity lines, build roller-skating rinks, football pitches and even a housing development for the poor, known as Barrio Pablo Escobar.

At the height of his popularity he ran and was voted into Congress. But his forays into public life also brought attention to his nefarious activities and after the assassination of presidential candidate Luis Carlos Galán (in which he is believed to have been involved), President César Gaviria ordered his arrest. He went on the run for several years, using a string of hideouts in Medellín and Antioquia before he eventually tired and negotiated very favourable terms of surrender.

continued to expand at a great pace, a manifestation of which is the fine metro, giving easy communication across the city.

Sights

Central Medellín

The focus of the city is the **Plaza de las Esculturas** (also known as Plaza Botero), Calle 52 y Carrera 52, which has 23 sculptures donated by Fernando Botero, Colombia's leading contemporary artist, as well as two fountains designed by him. Botero made these sculptures to be touched and his sensuous pieces depicting rotund characters certainly invite this. On the north side of the plaza is **El Palacio de la Cultura Rafael Uribe**, an extraordinary Gothic building, built by Belgian architect Agustín Goovaerts between 1929 and 1937. It was formerly the governor's office and is now a cultural centre and art gallery (free entry). Opposite is the **Museo de Antioquia** ① *Cra 52, No 52-53 (metro stop: Parque Berrío), T251 3636, open Mon, Wed-Fri 0930-1700, Sat and holidays 1000-1600, US$2.50, students US$1.50*. It has contemporary pictures and sculptures, including the best collection of works by Botero, and a room of paintings of Francisco Antonio Cano. There's an auditorium, film shows, etc, as well as a good gift shop selling clothes by up-and-coming Colombian fashion designers and postcards and *molas* (colourful, painted fabrics). Three blocks away, the **Parque de Berrío** is bounded on

Escobar was allowed to design and have constructed a luxurious prison on a hill outside Medellín, known as La Catedral. It had a football pitch and gym and the rooms were like hotel suites, with jacuzzis, giant TVs and bars. He hosted lavish parties, while he came and went as he pleased, often attending football matches in Medellín, his motor-cade accompanied by a police escort that blocked traffic to ensure smooth passage.

Eventually the government decided to transfer him to a 'real' prison but in the resulting siege of La Catedral, Escobar slipped through the cordon of an entire army battalion and went on the run for a further 18 months.

In the meantime a vigilante group known as Los Pepes (Los Perseguidos por Pablo Escobar – People Persecuted by Pablo Escobar), believed to be funded by his rivals, the Cali Cartel and to be colluding with the government, began a campaign in which 300 of his business associates were assassinated, severely hampering his cash flow. He was eventually tracked down and shot by special forces in December 1993 while attempting to escape across the rooftops of a Medellín suburb.

During his three-decade career he is believed to have been responsible for the death of more than 4000 people, including 30 judges and 457 policemen, while he is also charged as being the single figure who most developed Colombia's reputation as nation synonymous with drugs, kidnappings and pitiless violence. Today, the Pablo Escobar tour is becoming one of the most popular in Medellín, taking in his family home, the house where he was shot, as well as his final resting place. Morbid tourism perhaps, but it gives greater insights into the life and death of one of the most influential men in Colombia's history. For tour information, see under Bogotá Tour operators, page 77.

one side by the **Señora de La Candelaria** church. The original building on this site dated from the latter part of the 17th century. The present church was finished around 1767 and became the original cathedral of the city, consecrated in 1776, with the towers built five years later and the cupola in 1860. The clock was donated by Tyrell Moore (see below) in 1890. It remained the city's cathedral until 1931 and has a fine flat-roofed nave and interesting altar gilding by local artisans dedicated to the patron saint of Medellín.

Overlooking Parque Berrío is **Museo Filatélico** ① *4th floor of Banco de la República building, C 50, No 50-21, T5767402, Mon-Fri 0800-1130, 1400-1745, metro stop: Parque Berrío*, with an interesting stamp collection and special displays connected with postal services. There is also a music room with concerts on video in the afternoons.

Parque de Bolívar, four blocks away, is dominated by the new **Catedral Metropolitano**, one of the largest (sun-dried) brick structures in the world, built between 1875 and 1931. It is also claimed to be the largest cathedral in South America. It is impressive inside, with marble used only for the pulpit, the altar canopy and some statuary around the nave. The Spanish stained-glass windows are a good example of the period. There are several paintings of Gregorio Vázquez de Arce. There is a plaque in the square to Tyrell Moore, the Englishman who dedicated the land to the city for the park, in the centre of which is a statue of Bolívar. On the first Saturday of the month there is a craft market known as the **Mercado de San Alejo** in Parque de Bolívar.

The oldest church in the centre of Medellín is believed to be the **Iglesia de la Veracruz**, originally started in 1682 by early Spanish settlers. It was only finally completed around the end of the 18th century. Pablo Chávez was commissioned to decorate the interior and the main altar was brought directly from Spain. It has an attractive *calicanto*-style façade. In the square outside, there is a statue of Atanasio Girardot, a hero of the War of Independence.

② Medellín centre

Sleeping		Eating
Botero Plaza 1	Nutibara 4	1,2,3... Cazuelas 5
Gran 2		Café Botero 6

Further south, the **Iglesia de San Benito** was also founded about 1685 but its present baroque style dates from 1802. Another old foundation is the **Iglesia de San José** begun in the 17th century but modified several times up to 1903, the last work done by the Nicaraguan architect Félix Pereira. It houses the oldest painting in Medellín – of San Lorenzo, the first patron saint of Medellín. The painting of San José is by Carlos Hefritter.

➡ **Medellín maps**
1 Medellín, page 216
2 **Medellín centre, page 220**
3 El Poblado, page 225
4 Medellín metro, page 235

Deli Lunch **8**
Hacienda Real **7**
Hato Viejo **9**

Fonda Parque Boívar **10**
Salon de Té Astor **11**
Versalles **12**

Bars & clubs
La Boa **13**
Guanábano **14**

Fernando Botero

If you visit Medellín, you'll be hard pushed to miss the enormous sculptures adorning several parts of the city, including one of the main squares, known as Plaza Botero. These imposing works were created by local-born Fernando Botero, one of Latin America's best-known sculptors and artists. Botero, who has spent many years living abroad, donated these works to the city of Medellín, perhaps, one might guess, because he found them too difficult to pack on his departure. His striking rotund figures tower impressively over the viewers, disproportionately large, bulbous and voluptuous, in Botero's own characteristic style. Despite first leaving the country in 1952, Botero returns to his roots every year, spending a month in his native Colombia. Now mostly based in Paris, his works have been exhibited worldwide from Tokyo and New York, to Mexico City and Athens. He is one of the most celebrated Colombians of all time.

Three other churches are worth a visit. **San Ignacio**, a Franciscan church in Plaza San Ignacio, begun in 1793, has a colonial interior with a barrel vaulted central nave and a splendid red and gold altar. It was later taken over by the Jesuits forming part of the original group of buildings of the Universidad de Antioquia: this complex includes the auditorium (*paraninfo*) of the university, which was declared a National Monument in 1982 and over a period of eight years was tastefully renovated and reopened in 1997; there is a great view of the city from the top of the tower. The two others are **San Juan de Dios**, in colonial style, and **San Antonio,** designed by Benjamín Machiantonio and built between 1884 and 1902. It was inspired by San Antonio de Padua, a 13th-century Venetian church. This church has one of the biggest domes in the country.

The city's main business area is **Villanueva**, named after the nunnery which has now been converted into a commercial centre. It is interesting for its blend of old and modern architecture, including many skyscrapers. To the north across Calle 58, is El Prado section, originally a *finca* named La Polka, where there were many fine old houses, most of which have been replaced or are in decay. Some, however, have been restored and the area attracts artists and musicians. There are many sculptures in the city (see below). One collection not to be missed is of the works of **Fernando Botero** in **Parque San Antonio** ① *between C 44/46 and Cra 46*, including the *Torso Masculino* (which complements the female version in Parque Berrío), *La Mujer Inclinada* and the *El Pájaro de Paz (Bird of Peace)*, which was severely damaged by a guerrilla bomb in 1996. At the request of the sculptor, it has been left unrepaired as a symbol of the futility of violence. A new *Bird of Peace* has been placed alongside to make the point yet more dramatic. There is a garden beyond the plaza with the sculptures and a useful footbridge to cross the busy Calle 44 (San Juan).

On the other side of the metro is the **Palacio Cultural** ① *Cra 52, C 48*, designed by Agustín Goovaerts in the Romantic style. Built in 1925, it is now a commercial centre, recognisable by its brass-coloured domes, stylishly renovated with sweeping marble staircases and spacious hallways. Government of the city and department is now conducted from **La Alpujarra** administrative centre, a nine-block area from Calle 44/Carrera 52. Within the complex is the fine old Medellín railway station building designed in 1914 by Enrique Olarte.

Also in the centre is **Casa Museo Maestro Pedro Nel Gómez** ① *Cra 51B, No 85-24 (metro station: Universidad), T233 2633, free, Mon-Fri 0900-1200, 1400-1700, Sat 0900-1400,*

Tango in Medellín

Tango may have originated in the *barrios* of Buenos Aires and Montevideo but it has been adopted in Medellín as one of its own.

How tango arrived in Medellín is unclear but by 1919 it is evident that it was gaining widespread popularity. A short story written by local poet Ciro Mendía references tango star Carlos Gardel's *Mi Noche Triste* in a tale that revolves around a fallen woman who is assassinated by her jealous lover in the red-light district of the city.

By 1922, North American record companies such as RCA Victor and Columbia had picked up on tango's increasing popularity and began to distribute tango songs for the Colombian market, while tango films featuring Argentine starlets such as Libertad Lamarque drew large crowds to the city's cinemas. In Medellín, tango was concentrated around the working-class barrio of Guayaquil, where cantinas and cafés played songs by Argentine stars.

It was after the tragic death of Carlos Gardel in 1935 in a plane accident at Medellín's Olaya Herrera airport that tango really took off. The death in their city of its biggest star crystallized tango's connection with the local imagination and during the 1940s, 50s and 60s, tango gained increasing clout as a form of music intrinsic to Medellín's distinctive culture.

By the 1950s Medellín was hosting large-scale tango concerts with many of Argentina's biggest tango stars coming to perform and even settle in the city.

Today, tango culture is still strong in Medellín. Bars such as Salón Málaga and La Boa (where the novel *Aire de Tango* was written) are popular venues for tango aficionados, while the city hosts monthly *Tangovías*, in which entire streets are given over to tango dancing events. Each June, the Festival de Tango takes place with over 60 events, including dance competitions and concerts.

may be closed during school holidays, house of the Colombian painter and sculptor (1899-1984) with many of his artworks, and a specialist library. **Archivo Histórico de Antioquia** ⓘ *Cra 51, No 52-03, T251 8461*, is a research library for the department with over 30,000 volumes.

Of the modern buildings, the **Edificio Coltejer** deserves a mention. It is the tallest building in Medellín (35 floors) and was built as the headquarters of the **Compañía Colombiana de Tejidos**, thus symbolizing the importance of textiles to the city. It is in the form of a needle with the 'eye' clearly visible near the top. The building contains offices, a commercial centre, two cinemas and various other public facilities for cultural events.

An unusual attraction is the **Punto Cero** (Point Zero), an elegant steel double arch with a pendulum marking the 'centre of the city'. It was the initial idea of students at the neighbouring Universidad Nacional. It straddles the river where it is crossed by Calle 67.

The **Edificio Inteligente** ⓘ *C 43, No 58-01*, was completed in 1996. All the main public services in Medellín concentrate their administrative operations here in a highly energy-efficient building. Nearby is the **Parque de los Pies Descalzos** (Barefoot Park) ⓘ *C 42B, No 55-40*, an excellent example of urban planning. It is designed to encourage local workers to relax during their lunch break and, as the name suggests, sand pits, fountains, a Zen garden and a bamboo forest actively promote strolling about shoeless. It has several restaurants and internet cafés, as well as the **Museo Interactivo EPM**

ⓘ *www.fundacionepm.org.co, closed to the public until end 2011, when it will reopen a Museo del Agua.*

One of the city's more unusual sights is the **Cementerio San Pedro** ⓘ *Cra 51, No 68-68, T212 0951, www.cementeriosanpedro.org.co, near the Hospital metro station, daily 0730-1800*. Built in 1828, it has the dubious honour of being the resting place of many notorious drug dealers, guerrillas and the like, as well as of the richest families of Medellín. One particularly elaborate tomb is reserved for the Muñoz family who were some of Pablo Escobar's most ruthless *sicarios* (assassins). Up until 2004 this had *mariachi* music playing from speakers but these were later removed. Also of note is the tomb of Jorge Isaacs, celebrated author of the romantic novel *María*. Even for Latin America, some of the tombs are spectacular, and the small chapel has some of the most colourful stained glass in Antioquia. It also houses some unique sculptures such as *Dolor de Madre*, depicting the anguish of a mother losing a young son, a replica of Michelangelo's *La Pietà*. Each month during the full moon there are nocturnal tours of the cemetery with violin music, dancing and storytelling.

South of the Río Medellín, in the Suramericano district, is the **Museo de Arte Moderno** ⓘ *Cra 64B, No 51-54, T230 2622, Mon-Fri 1000-1900, Sat 1030-1700, US$1.80*. It has a small collection of paintings, collages, photographs etc. Particularly good paintings by Débora Arango. Foreign films daily except Wednesday. There is also a coffee shop.

Nearby is the **Biblioteca Pública Piloto para América Latina** ⓘ *Cra 64, No 50-32, T230 2422, Mon-Fri 0830-1900, Sat 0900-1800*. This is one of the best public libraries in the country, set up by UNESCO and the Colombian government in 1952. There is also art and photo exhibitions, authors reading their own work, and foreign films. There are several branches in Medellín and it has links to the **Biblioteca Luis Angel Arango** in Bogotá.

North of the centre

Joaquín Antonio Uribe botanical gardens ⓘ *Cra 52, No 73-298, T244 5500, www.botanico medellin.org, gardens daily, 0800-1700 (last entry, closes at 1800), free at time of writing, but a fee may be added; the public entrance is at Cra 52/C 78 about 300 m away from metro station Universidad*, was formerly the **Finca Edén** turned into a garden by the owner, the botanist, Joaquín Antonio Uribe. It was rescued from developers in 1972 and converted into a public garden with 5500 species of plants and trees. There is a lake with various lilies on display – a cool and restful place. In March there is an international orchid show in the gardens in a covered exhibition area and Medellín's gastronomy festival in August has also been hosted here. There are two restaurants, one pricey and one more economical with nice views of the gardens. Also facilities for children, a library and an open-air auditorium.

Opposite the botanical gardens is the **Parque Explora** ⓘ *Cra 52, No 73-75, T516 8300, www.parqueexplora.org, Tue-Fri 0830-1730 (ticket office closes 1600), Sat, Sun and holidays 1000-1830 (ticket office closes at 1700), US$4.50 to US$8 depending on how many rooms you plan to see, full tour approximately 6-8 hrs*, a science and technology museum. With 20,000 sq m of more than 300 interactive scientific puzzles and games, this is fun for adults and heaven for kids. It has four state-of-the-art rooms, each of which take one to two hours to explore. **Territorios Digitales** features the latest technological advances. You can make your own radio or TV programme, find out about stop-motion animation and play around with shadow photography. In **Colombia Geodiversa** you can learn all about seismic activity and the forces of nature in the earthquake and tornado simulators. The **Conexión de la Vida** room has enormous leaves plucked from the Amazon as well as a large display of insects. You can also simulate a race with a cheetah or an elephant. In ísica Viva lots of interactive games teach you about how birds sing and how fish swim. There is also a 3D cinema. One of the highlights of a visit to Medellín.

Nearby is the **Parque Norte J Emilio Valderrama** ① *Cra 55, No 76-115 (metro station: Universidad), www.parquenorte.gov.co, Tue-Fri 1000-1630, Sat, Sun and holidays 1000-1730, entry to park US$2.50, different attractions and funfair from US$3.50,* a recreational park with a lake and children's playground.

Next to it is the old railway station **El Bosque**, now restored and converted into a recreation centre for the elderly. Also in this area is the **Planetario** ① *Cra 52, No 71-117, T527 2222, Tue-Fri 0930, 1100 and 1505, Sat and Sun, 1100, 1430, 1600 and 1730,* with a 300-seat projection room, an auditorium for 200, library and exhibition hall.

The **Parque Zoológico Santa Fe** ① *Cra 52, No 20-63, T235 1326, www.zoologico santafe.com, daily 0900-1700, US$4, children half price, take the metro to Industriales, cross the river and walk along Cra 52 about 10 mins,* mainly houses South American animals and birds and is concerned with the protection of threatened local species including the spectacled bear and the Andean condor. There are special exhibits of Caribbean fauna and a butterfly section. Within the complex is the **Museo Santa Fe** with exhibition halls including displays of furniture and pictures of Medellín's past, including the Antioquia railway and the construction of La Quiebra Tunnel (additional charge US$0.50).

El Poblado

➡ **Medellín maps**
1 Medellín, page 216
2 Medellín centre, page 220
3 **El Poblado, page 225**
4 Medellín metro, page 235

500 metres
500 yards

Sleeping 🛏
Black Sheep Hostal 1
Casa Kiwi 2
Dann Carlton 3
Geo Hostel 7
Global Hostel 4
La Habana Vieja 5
Park 10 6

Pitstop Hostel 8
Tiger Paw Hostel 9

Eating 🍴
Bagels & Brunch 1
Basílica 2
Donde Paco 3
Le Bon 4

Thaico 6
Tony Roma's 7
Triada 5

Bars & clubs 🍸
Blue Bar 9

South of the centre: El Poblado

Museo El Castillo ① *C 9 Sur, No 32-269, T266 0900, Mon-Fri 0900-1130, 1400-1730, Sa 0900-1100, free,* formerly a landowner's home, constructed in 1930 in neo-Gothic style has interesting collection of paintings, sculptures, porcelain and furniture. The house is set in beautiful grounds. There is also a 250-seat concert hall. Take a bus to Loma de los Balsos, El Poblado, then walk 1 km up the hill until you see the road lined with pine trees to the right.

The church **Iglesia San José** is on the central park of Poblado in the south of the city, where the Spanish first settled in the Aburrá valley in 1616. The present church is the third on the site, in which the architect Agustín Goovaerts was involved. There are commemorative plaques in the park.

West of the centre

Museo Etnográfico Miguel Angel Builes ① *Cra 81, No 52B-120, T264 2299 www.yarumal.org, Mon-Fri, 0800-1200, 1400-1700, Sat 0830-1200, free but voluntary contributions appreciated,* was originally founded in 1963 in Yarumal, Antioquia by missionaries and moved to Medellín in 1972. It has an extensive collection of artefacts from indigenous cultures, two floors dedicated to Colombia, one to other Andean countries including Peru and Bolivia and another floor to Africa. There are models of indigenous houses in a fine building with a library and bookshop.

Take the metro to Floresta and walk along Carrera 81 (about 10 minutes). The **Museo de la Madre Laura** ① *Cra 92, No 34D-21, T252 3017, Tue-Fri 0800-1200, 1400-1700,* has a good collection of indigenous costumes and crafts from Colombia, Ecuador and Guatemala collected by a community of missionary nuns.

Around the city

You will notice three prominent hills within the Aburrá valley. They are first, **Cerro Nutibara** (across the river from Industriales station), where there is an outdoor stage for open-air concerts, sculpture park (the idea of former President Belisario Betancur), with exhibits from other Latin American countries, a miniature Antioquian village (known as Pueblito Paisa), souvenir shops and restaurants. There is a statue of Chief Nutibara near the village. Every month, on the night of the full moon, there is a party here with music, dancing, food stalls, tango show, etc, organized by the Department of Sports and Recreation. To get there, take a 301 bus from Carrera 43/Calle 54, which takes you to the bottom of the hill with 1.5 km to walk, or a taxi from Industriales or Exposiciones metro stations to the village, approximately US$2.50. Second is **Cerro El Volador** (seen as the metro turns between Universidad and Caribe stations), tree-covered and the site of an important indigenous burial ground. And third is **Morro El Salvador** (to the east of Alpujarra station), with a cross and statue on top designed by Arturo Longas in 1950. This hill and its small public park have been absorbed into building developments and is not recommended for visits on foot.

No visit to Medellín would be complete without a ride on the Metrocable, one of the city's proudest achievements. There are now three lines, **J** from San Javier to La Aurora, **K**, serving the areas on the mountain slopes up to Santo Domingo Savio, and **Línea L** from Santo Domingo, further up the mountains to Arví. Take the metro north to Acevedo and transfer to the cable-car line up to Santo Domingo Savio, formerly one of the city's most dangerous and crime-riddled barrios. You can now walk around the neighbourhood perfectly safely (although it's best not to flash your cash or expensive cameras). The new library, **Parque Biblioteca de España**, a short walk down from the metro station, opened by the King and Queen of Spain in March 2007 is worth a look. Designed by Colombian architect Giancarlo Massanti it has seven floors with 14,000 donated books and 108 computers. All this in what was once one of the most feared areas of Medellín (see box, page 234).

Medellín listings → *Phone code: 4.*

For Sleeping and Eating price codes and other relevant information, see pages 23-28.

Sleeping

Central Medellín *p218, map p220*
Medellín has transformed beyond recognition in the last decade and one of the changes is that much of the accommodation has moved out of the centre. Many of the cheaper hostels in this part of town are now *acostaderos* or pay-by-the-hour brothels with questionable security that we advise you to avoid. The area west of Plaza Botero, especially Calle 55 is increasingly seedy with down-and-outs, drug addicts, prostitutes and homeless people. It has an edgy feel also during the day.
A Botero Plaza, Cra 50A, No 53-45, T511 2155, www.hotelboteroplaza.com. Just 1 min's walk from Parque Botero, this hotel is also convenient as it is on the same street where the *busetas* leave for the airport. It has clean rooms, an internet café, sauna, gym and Turkish bath but is also located in a slightly seedy area that can be dangerous at night.
A Gran, C 54, No 45-92, T513 4455, www.granhotel.com.co. A 1970s structure often used for business conventions, the **Gran** is just 5 blocks from Parque de Las Esculturas. It has a swimming pool, room service, free internet, parking and a restaurant serving steak, fish and pastas. Nominally cheaper if paying by cash.
A Nutibara, C 52A, No 50-46, T511 5111, www.hotelnutibara.com. The grand old lady of Medellín, the Nutibara was the city's first major hotel, built in 1945. Its best days

may be behind it, but it retains a certain art deco charm and has all modern amenities, including a pool, sauna, Turkish bath, an internet room, Wi-Fi in the lobby and a new lobby bar.

South of the centre: El Poblado
p226, map p225
L Dann Carlton, Cra 43A, No 7-50, Av El Poblado, T444 5151, www.danncarlton.com. Enormous block of brick that towers over Av El Poblado, the Dann Carlton has all the usual amenities, including a pool, spa, sauna, beauty parlour and Wi-Fi throughout. Features include a computer in every room and a revolving restaurant on the top floor. **Aviatur** office on the premises.
L Park 10, Cra 36B No 11-12, T310 6060, www.hotelpark10.com.co. In a quiet and green corner of El Poblado, the **Park 10** has a cultured air with wooden floorboards and smartly dressed bellboys. All rooms have a reception area and safes. It also has a sauna, gym, Wi-Fi and the travel agency **Aviatur** in the same building.
A La Habana Vieja, C 10 Sur, No 43A – 7, T321 2557, www.hotellahabanavieja.com. Tucked away just off Av Poblado, this is about the only colonial hotel you will find in Medellín. Has TV, minibar and balconies for rooms on 2nd floor. Breakfast included.
B Global Hostel, Cra 35, No 7-58, T311 5418, www.globalhostelcolombia.com. In a city that has a poor selection of mid-range hotels, this is an excellent option. The owners have gone for a minimalist, boutique look and generally succeed. Close to the Zona Rosa, with breakfast included and Wi-Fi throughout.

B-E Hostel Casa Blanca, Transversal 5A, No 45-256, T586 5149, www.hostelcasa blanca.es.tl. Large private rooms as well as a 5-bed dorm and a 15-bed dorm (**E**), storage, kitchen, laundry, free Wi-Fi. Spanish classes once a week. Close to the Zona Rosa.

C Geo Hostel, Cra 35 8A-58, T311 7150, www.geohostel.com. Pleasant, light and airy new hostel near la Zona Rosa. Private rooms or dorms (**E**) available. Internet, kitchen and laundry, disabled access and a small shop selling arty, crafty things.

C-D Tiger Paw, Cra 36, No 10-49, T311 6079, www.tigerpawhostel.com. A variety of rooms and dorms (**E-F**), US-owned, free internet and Wi-Fi, laundry service, tourist packages, sports bar and lots of activities.

D The Black Sheep Hostal, Transversal 5a, No 45-133, T311 1589 or T317-518 1369 (mob), www.blacksheepmedellin.com. Run by New Zealander Kelvin, **The Black Sheep** is another very comfortable backpackers' hostel on the site of an ex-hospital. Internet or Wi-Fi, a kitchen, Spanish classes and a Sun BBQ, it is a great place to unwind and plot excursions around Antioquia. Kelvin also writes an excellent blog on his website, full of invaluable information on the rest of Colombia. Bunks in dorms (**F**) also available. Quieter private rooms at the back. Recommended.

D Casa Kiwi, Cra 36, No 7-10, T268 2668, www.casakiwihostel.com. A maze of living areas, games rooms and outdoor patios, Casa Kiwi is one of the most comfortable backpackers' hostels in Colombia. The rooms are tastefully decorated while a couple of dorm rooms with bunks (**F**) provide an economical alternative. Has Wi-Fi, several computers, a pool table, DVD collection and is just a couple of blocks from the bars and restaurants of Parque Lleras. There's also a roof terrace with pool, hammocks and a brand new bar, Recommended.

D-F Pitstop Hostel, Cra 43E No 5-110, T352 1176, www.pitstophostel.com. The biggest hostel in Colombia, with swimming pool, Irish bar, steam room, gym, pool table and a huge outdoor area. Tours and events organized.

West of the centre *p226, map p216*

Cra 70, next to metro Estadio, is replete with hotels, all of a similar standard and with similar prices. There are also a number of eateries lining the same road.

B Florida, Cra 70, No 44B-38, T260 4900, www.hotelfloridamedellin.com. Standard hotel on Carrera 70. Has internet room, Wi-Fi, laundry service, car park and restaurant. Some rooms lack windows.

B Lukas, Cra 70, No 44A-28, T260 1761, www.lukashotel.com. Clean and crisp rooms with all the necessary amenities, including safe, a/c, cable TV, mini bar, an internet room and Wi-Fi throughout. Breakfast included.

B Parque 70, C 46B, No 69A-11, T260 3339, www.hotelparque70.com. Good little mid-

ange hotel in a quiet cul-de-sac off Cra 70.
Clean rooms with minibar, stereo, TV and Wi-
i. Just 1 block from the Estadio metro station.
C Hotel Villa Real, Cra 70 45E-153, T414
905, www.hotelvillarealmedellin.com.
Comfortable, modern hotel with a/c, TV,
telephone for local calls and private bath.
C Plaza 70, Cra 70, No 45E-117, T412 3266.
This functional hotel has clean but dark and
small rooms with cable TV. Wi-Fi.
D Palm Tree Hostal, Cra 67, No 48D-63, T260
2805, www.palmtreemedellin.com. Another
backpackers' hostel which ticks all the boxes
in terms of facilities, including a kitchen,
Wi-Fi, TV and DVD room, bike hire, book
exchange and hammocks. Private and
dormitory rooms (**F**) available. Friendly.
D-F Hostal Medellín, Cra 65, No 48-144,
www.hostalmedellin.com. Spacious hostel
run by a German and Colombian couple,
popular with bikers for its large garage.
Has a fine little garden with a hammock,
pool table and organizes tours to Guatapé
and Santa Fe de Antioquia.

🍴 Eating

Central Medellín p218, map p220

🍴 Café Botero, Cra 52, No 52-43 Esquina.
Excellent lunchtime venue next to the Museo
de Antioquia. Fish, fine steaks and delicious
puddings. Recommended.
🍴 Hacienda Real, Cra 49 59-98 (next door to
Salón de Té Astor). Pleasant restaurant with
balcony seating, overlooking Pasaje Junín.
🍴 Hato Viejo, Cra 47, No 2-17, 2nd floor.
Overlooking Av La Playa, Hato Viejo serves
typical dishes such as *ajiaco*, *sudao* and
mondongo as well as the usual steaks and fish.
🍴 Versalles, Pasaje Junín (currently being
dug up), No 53-59. Argentine-run restaurant,
famous in Medellín for being the epicentre
of the Colombian nihilism movement of the
1960s. *Parrillas*, pastas and pizzas in a room
filled with photographs of renowned Latin
American philosophers. Tasty food in
atmospheric setting.

🍴🍴 1,2,3… Cazuelas, CC Unión, Cra 49,
No 52-107, local 219. Fast food *cazuelas* in
what was once the Union Club, Medellín's
most exclusive social club.
🍴🍴 Salón de Té Astor, Cra 49, No 52-84.
Excellent pastries, a delightful traditional tea
house, famous throughout Colombia for its
chocolate delicacies. Try the *besitos de negro*.
Lasagna, sandwiches and salads also served.
🍴 Deli Lunch, CC Plaza Orquídeas, Cra 49,
No 52-81, local 9915. Creole food at
economical prices. *Menú ejecutivo* US$4.
Several similar places nearby.
🍴 Fonda Parque Bolívar, C 55, No 47-27.
Just off the Parque Bolívar, this popular
lunchtime venue is festooned with
antiques. *Menú ejecutivo* US$3.

El Poblado p226, map p225

The area around Parque Lleras is positively
heaving with bars and restaurants, with
more springing up each year. Below is just
a selection, mostly long-runners with a
good track record, but there are many
others to try out from Mexican to sushi.
🍴🍴🍴 Basílica, Cra 38, No 8A-42, Thick Argentine
steaks, sushi and Peruvian dishes on an open
terrace on Parque Lleras.
🍴🍴🍴 Tony Roma's, Cra 43, No 7-50. Revolving
restaurant on top of the **Hotel Dann Carlton**,
serving ribs and steak. Worth visiting just for
the view.
🍴🍴🍴 Triada, Cra 38, No 8-08. Enormous
restaurant/bar/club in the heart of the
Zona Rosa. Huge steaks, sushi, salads and
Tex Mex are the order of the day. It even
has a bell on each table for calling the waiter.
Good atmosphere with open terrace.
🍴🍴 Thaico, C 9, No 37-40. Good Thai food
with fresh ingredients. A popular spot for
watching televised sports (or just people
strolling through Parque Lleras).
🍴 Le Bon, C 9, No 39-09. French café serving
omelettes, pancakes, fruit salads and coffees
and teas from around the world.
🍴 Donde Paco, Cra 35, No 8A-80.
Economical Colombian or Oriental
food in a good atmosphere.

Gastronomic Medellín

Of Colombia's three main cities, Bogotá, Cali and Medellín, it is Medellín that has arguably succeeded in turning itself into the gastronomic centre of Colombia – hotly contested by the other two, to be sure. Colombia has yet to gain a reputation as a gourmet destination, but the days when you were presented with the sole option of rice, meat and an *arepa* are long gone, at least in the cities.

Many of Medellín's best restaurants are centred around Parque Lleras in El Poblado district and the place is buzzing any evening of the week. Anything from Thai, Mexican, Peruvian or Italian can be found here, but Medellín is also the place to try some traditional Colombian fare. The *bandeja paisa* is *the* regional dish to sample, containing everything from sausages, pork crackling, rice, beans, avocado, *arepa*, black pudding and more. Try to finish it all and it'll leave you positively groaning.

Chains such as J&C Delicias are taking the humble *arepa* to new heights and Medellín also hosts a food festival, *Otro Sabor*, the last weekend of August for three days.

♯ **Bagels & Brunch**, C9, No 38-26. 0% fat free boasts the slogan of this breakfast venue, but it's a hearty start to the day all the same with stuffed bagels, omelettes, pancakes with maple syrup and fruit smoothies.

West of the centre *p226, map p216*
♯♯♯ **La Margarita No 2**, Cra 70, No 45E-11. Antioquian dishes in a pleasant atmosphere – *bandeja paisa* and *cazuelas*.
♯ **Opera Pizza**, C 42, No 70-22. *Paisas* swear these are the best pizzas in town. Italian-owned restaurant with a wood-fired oven. Recommended.
♯ **¡Orale!**, C 41, No 70-138. Excellent little Mexican canteen with tables on the street. Burritos, tacos and fajitas. Recommended.
♯ **Pomodoro**, C 42, No 71-24. This little Italian restaurant serves lots of different pastas and sauces at reasonable prices. *Menú ejecutivo* good value.

🎵 Bars and clubs

Medellín *p214, maps p216, p220 and p225*
In the **centre**, the area around the Parque de Los Periodistas attracts a more bohemian crowd with goths, punks, and students. Be careful how you go, however, as this area is considerably seedier than the upmarket Zona Rosa. Try **La Boa**, C 53, No 43-59, which has been around for more than 40 years and is famous for its tango and jazz. The book *Aire de Tango* by Manuel Mejía Vallejo was written here. It claims to be the only bar in Medellín where there has never been a fight! Also try **Guanábano**, Cra 43, No 53-21, which has an atmosphere reminiscent of the edgier parts of East London or East Berlin, lots of Rolling Stones album covers decorate the walls of an old building with a *caña brava* roof.

In the **south**, the best are in the centre of El Poblado, in what is commonly known as the Zona Rosa, around Parque Lleras. Try **Blue bar**, C 10, No 40-20. Open Thu-Sat, plays rock and Colombian music. Also **Red bar** opposite is worth checking out. **Triada**, Cra 38, No 8-08, is another popular spot with a bar and disco upstairs.

Between the centre and El Poblado, in Barrio San Diego, **Trilogía**, Cra 43G No 24-08, T262 6375, attracts an older crowd and has live cover bands playing a mix of rock and Colombian music. Arrive before 2230 on Fri and Sat.

In **west** Medellín, you will find plenty of bars along Cra 70 and the adjacent streets.

If the prices and plastic people of the Zona Rosa get too much, an alternative

fter-hours location is **Sabaneta**, 11 km
rom the centre of Medellín. This suburb
as an attractive plaza and fills up in the
venings with a mixed crowd of young and
ld. The best way to get there is by taxi,
US$6 from El Poblado. Try **El Viejo John**,
Cra 45, No 70 Sur-42, a popular local spot
with strings of chorizo hanging from the
ceiling; they also serve *bandeja paisa* and
other typical dishes. Alternatively there's
onda Sitio Viejo, C 70 Sur, No 44-33,
another bar full of character, this time with
a jumble of photographs of every church in
Medellín. Or you could opt for **La Herrería**,
Cra 45, No 70 Sur-24, which is crammed to
the ceiling with pictures of local characters,
Mexican sombreros, horse saddles and
banana bunches, this bar also serves popcorn
and fruit salad to accompany your drinks.

🔆 Entertainment

Medellín *p214, maps p216, p220 and p225*
Cinema
The shopping centres **CC Oviedo**, Cra 43A,
No 6 Sur-15, T321 6116, **CC Unicentro**, Cra 66B,
No 34A-76, T265 1116, **Parque Comercial El
Tesoro**, Cra 25A, No 1A Sur-45, T321 1010, and
CC Los Molinos, C 30A, No 82A-26, T238 3505
all have multiplexes showing the latest
releases. Free foreign/cultural films at
Universidad de Antioquia, or **Universidad de
Medellín**. The **Centro Colombo Americano**,
Cra 45, No 53-24, T513 4444, shows foreign
arthouse films, check the local press.

Music
Monthly concerts by the **Antioquia
Symphony Orchestra** in the **Teatro
Metropolitano** (see below). Band concerts
and other entertainments in the Parque de
Bolívar every Sun.
    Universidad de Medellín theatre has
monthly tango shows. Tango also at **Vos
Tango**, C 34, No 66A-13, opposite the **Super
Ley** supermarket in Unicentro, T265 3428,
US$5. There is a museum, **Museo Casa**

Gardeliana, Cra 45, No 76-50, T212 0968,
www.museocasagardeliana.org, commemorating tango legend Carlos Gardel who died
in a plane crash in Medellín in 1935, and an
annual **Festival Internacional de Tango** in
Jun. **Salón Málaga**, Cra 51, No 45-80, T231
2658, is one of Medellín's oldest tango bars
(its 50th anniversary was in 2008). Owner
Gustavo Arteaga is considered one of the
principal collectors of tango in Colombia.
Tangovía is a general term for occasions
when streets, especially in Barrio Manrique,
are closed to traffic for tango dancing.
Cra 45 (Av Carlos Gardel), leads north east
into the centre of Barrio Manrique and is
normally the centre of activity. Enquire at
the **Oficina de Turismo**, T261 6060 when
the next fiesta will be, usually 1 per month.

Theatre
Teatro Metropolitano, C 41, No 57-30,
T232 2858, www.teatrometropolitano.com.
A modern-style brick building close to the
river, 1600 capacity, symphony concerts,
opera, ballet, tango shows, etc.
Teatro Pablo Tobón Uribe, Cra 40, No 51-24,
T239 7500, www.teatropablotobon.com.
Traditional theatrical presentations, 880
capacity. There are many other theatres of
all types in the centre and barrios of the city.
See local press for details.

🎉 Festivals and events

Medellín *p214, maps p216, p220 and p225*
Easter Semana Santa (Holy Week) has
special Easter religious parades.
Jul International Poetry Festival, held
annually, on Cerro Nutibara in the open-air
Carlos Vieco. For information, see
www.festivaldepoesiademedellin.org.
17-26 Jul Feria de Artesanías, handicrafts
of all kinds from all over the country, held
in the Atanasio Girardot stadium complex.
Jul Colombiamoda, Colombia's largest
fashion and designer fair.

Aug Feria de las Flores/Desfile de Silleteros (flower fair), held annually in the 1st half of the month, for several days ending on the Sat with parades and music. The parade goes from Cra 55 across the Puente Colombia to the Atanasio Girardot Stadium. The flowers are grown at Santa Elena in the Parque Ecológico de Piedras Blancas, 14 km from Medellín (bus from Plaza Las Flores). It has been growing in popularity since 1957. A horse *Cabalgata* is a special feature – in 2006, 8223 riders took part, taking 4 hrs to pass by: a Guinness World Record.
End of Aug, Otro Sabor gastronomy festival, 3 days, usually held in the lovely setting of the botanical gardens.
2nd Sat in Sep Amor y Amistad, in true *paisa* style, this equivalent of St Valentine's day lasts for a whole week!
Dec Christmas starts with a fantasy parade and dancing on Dec 7 to coincide with the switching on of the Christmas lights.

O Shopping

Medellín *p214, maps p216, p220 and p225*
Handicrafts
Try the *artesanía* shops on the top of Cerro Nutibara, or **Salvarte in CC Oviedo**, Almacén de Turantioquia in the Plaza Mayor.

Markets
There is a small handicrafts market at C 52 near Cra 46 with many hippy stalls.
Mercado San Alejo, Parque Bolívar, first Sat of every month except Jan, 0800-1800. Before Christmas, it is there Sat and Sun with handicrafts on sale at good prices. Good shopping generally around Parque Bolívar.

Textiles
Many of the textile mills have discount-clothing departments attached offering good bargains. Ask at your hotel for more info.
Aluzia Correas y Cinturones, Cra 55 No 29B-62 (also in Bogotá), for an incredible selection of belts.

Shopping centres
Centros Comerciales are in all the main areas of the city, of which the most notable are: **Sandiego**, C 34/Cra 43; **Camino Real**, Cra 47/ C 52; **Villanueva**, C 50/Cra 49; **Oviedo**, Cra 43A/ C 6 Sur; **Monterrey**, Cra 48/C 10 (computers and technology); **Junin La Candelaria**, Cra 49/C 50; **Unicentro**, Cra 66B/ C 34A; **El Diamante**, C 51/Cra 73; **Obelisco**, Cra 74/C 48; **El Tesoro** at Cra 25A/C 1A Sur.

Bookshops
Librería Continental, Cra 50/C 52; **Librería Científica**, C 51, No 49-52, T231 4974. Large selection, some foreign books, has another 4 branches, www.libreriacientifica.com.co; **La Anticuaria**, C 49, No 47-59, T511 4969. Antique and second-hand books, including in English, helpful; **Centro Colombo Americano**, Cra 45, No 53-24, T513 4444, www.colombo world.com. Good selection of books in English for sale (including Footprint).

Maps
Virtually nothing in the bookshops. Good map of the city centre from the **Oficina de Turismo** (see page 215). Local and national maps from **Instituto Geográfico Agustín Codazzi** in Fundación Ferrocarril building, Cra 52, No 42-43, T381 0561, Mon-Fri 0800-1600, office in the basement.

▲▲ Activities and tours

Medellín *p214, maps p216, p220 and p225*
Bullfighting
At the bullring of La Macarena, C 44A/Cra 63, T260 7193, in Jan and Feb; cheapest US$8.50, usually fully booked.

Dance lessons
Academia Dance, Cra 46, No 7-9, T266 1522. Salsa lessons. **Black Sheep Hostal** guests get a 10% discount. Individual classes US$6. Good reports.

alón Malaga, Cra 51, No 45-80, T231 2658.
This is one of Medellín's oldest tango bars.
It celebrated its 50th anniversary in 2008.

Spanish classes

Eafit University, Cra 49, No 7 Sur 50, T261
6500, www.eafit.edu.co. US$445 for 38 hrs,
2 hrs a day for 4 weeks, popular, well-
organized Spanish courses, good reports.
Medellín Spanish School (part of **Black
Sheep Hostal**), Transversal 5A, No 45-133,
T311 1589, Spanish classes from US$6 per hr
in a group, US$10 individual class.

Sports complex

Estadio Atanasio Girardot, Cra 73, C 48. This
sports complex was enlarged in 1978 for the
Pan American games and has facilities for
over 50 sports including football, baseball,
Olympic swimming pool, velodrome, etc.
It is next to the Estadio metro station.

Tour operators

Destino Colombia, C 50, No 65-42, Centro
Comecial Contemporáneo, Local 225, T260
6868, www.destinocolombia.com. Tours to
nearby attractions in Antioquia and nationwide. Very well-informed English-speaking
guides. Can also arrange flights. Very helpful.
Recommended.

Trekking

Instituto de Deportes y Recreación (Inder),
T369 9000, www.inder.gov.co. Walking tours
around Medellín on Sun, T576 0780.

⊖ Transport

Medellín *p214, maps p216, p220, p225 and
p235*

Air

Note There are 2 airports, when leaving
by air, make sure you go to the correct one.

The international airport **Aeropuerto
José María Córdova**, 28 km from Medellín
(40 mins from the city centre), T562 2828,
has a **Presto** restaurant, shops, Telecom

with email and fax service. There's no left
luggage, but the tourist office may oblige.
It is reached by the toll road or by 2 other
routes, 1 of which enters the city along
Variante Las Palmas through the south of
the city. This is normally used by *busetas*
and you can be dropped at a convenient
point for transport to hotels in El Poblado.

From **Aeropuerto José María Cordova**
(sometimes called **Rionegro** airport) there
are frequent flights to **Bogotá**, 25 mins with
Avianca, or **Aires**. To **Cali**, 1 hr, **Avianca** and
Aires both requiring a change in Bogotá. To
Barranquilla, **Bucaramanga**, **Cartagena**,
1hr, 1 daily, **Avianca**.

The smaller, more central **Aeropuerto
Enrique Olaya Herrera**, T365 6100, is 10 mins
by taxi from the centre. National flights only
to **Bogotá**, several a day with **Satena**, also
with **easyfly** (sometimes via Armenia,
cheapest). To **Cali**, with Satena. To **Quibdó**,
with **easyfly** or **Aerolíneas de Antioquia**
(ADA). To **Bucaramanga**, with Satena. To
Acandí and **Capurganá**, 1 a day with ADA.

There are non-scheduled charter flights to
coastal resorts eg San Andrés, and elsewhere,
check with travel agents. To get the best
price, shop around. Special offers can mean
substantial savings. With difficulties on the
road network from time to time, air services
have become more comprehensive.

Airline offices Aerolíneas de Antioquia,
C 10, No 35-32, T444 4232 or at Olaya Herrera
airport. **Aires**, Cra 65A, No 13-157, T365 6100.
Avianca, Cra 43A, No 1A Sur-108, T266 8789
and at both airports. **Copa Air**, C 5AN, No 39-
141, Edif Centro de Trabajo Corfin Torre 4,
T268 4500. **Satena**, Olaya Herrera airport, or
C 9, No 41-56, T266 2185.

Bus

Local Slow because of the volume of traffic,
but many are smart and comfortable.
Colectivos operate on certain main routes,
US$0.75-0.80.
Long distance For buses going north
and east, **Terminal del Norte** is at Cra 64

The Metrocable

Medellín's cable car, the Metrocable, has become one of the symbols of this city's remarkable renaissance. It is the first cable car in the world designed primarily as a public transport system. Its success as a tool for social change has made it a popular tourist attraction.

The Metrocable connects the *comuna nororiental* (northeastern community), a slum full of brick and corrugated-iron shack communities constructed haphazardly on the side of the hill, with the metro station at Acevedo. During the 1980s and 1990s this was one of the most notorious slums in Latin America, the *zona de cultivo,* or cultivation area, for drug trafficker Pablo Escobar's army of *sicarios* (assassins).

In terms of transportation, it was a difficult place to leave. Narrow streets clogged with traffic meant that it could take someone up to two hours to get into town by bus. Back in the 1990s the area was highly segregated, with sectors at war with each other. For example, the bridge between the communities of La Francia and Andalucía was a no-go area. Today, residents walk freely between the two neighbourhoods over what has been rechristened the 'Bridge of Reconciliation'.

Part of the local government's drive to propagate 'participatory democracy', the Metrocable's aim is to allow the city's very poorest to take an active role in society and to 'de-ghettoize' the area. Commuting time has been reduced to 45 minutes, allowing easier access for those looking for employment in the centre, and it has significantly improved congestion in the area. Most importantly, it has restored a sense of pride to the community.

The Metrocable is just one cog in a movement that has allowed the people of this neighbourhood to reclaim public space from criminals. Other initiatives include public libraries such as the recently opened **Biblioteca de España**, which brings books, computers and spaces for social and artistic activities to one of Latin America's most deprived communities.

The success is measurable. Violent deaths in the neighbourhood have fallen from 6349 in 1994 to 373 in 2005, while individual living space has grown from less than half a square metre to between two and three square metres per person.

The cable car's success is being replicated across Colombia and the region. A second line was inaugurated in 2008 to link La Aurora district with San Javier metro station, and a third recently opened from from Santo Domingo Savio as far as Arví, near Lake Guarne. There is even talk of building a connection with the airport in Rionegro. Elsewhere in Colombia, the villages of Guatape near El Peñol and San Agustín in Huila have expressed an interest in building their own systems while Caracas, Venezuela already has one under construction.

(Autopista del Norte) y Transversal 78 (full address Cra 64C, No 78-58), T230 8514, about 3 km north of the centre, with shops, cafés, left luggage, Visa/MasterCard ATMs and other facilities. It is well policed and quite safe, though best not to tempt fate. Metro stop: Caribe. A taxi to or from the centre about US$2.70-US$4.40.

To **Bogotá**, 9-12 hrs, US$27.50, every 40 mins or so, with 5 companies. To **Cartagena**, Brasilia, Rápido Ochoa, or Copetran, 15 hrs, US$44-53, road paved throughout but poor. To **Santa Marta**, 18 hrs, US$53-58. To **Sincelejo**, 9½ hrs, US$37. To **Arboletes**, Rápido Ochoa, US$34, 12 hrs. To **Turbo**, US$27 with **Gómez** (the best), 14 hrs. To **Santa Fe de Antioquia**, 1½ hrs, US$4.25

with Rápido Ochoa **Sotrauraba** or **Gómez Hernández**. To **Magangué**, US$46.50, with **Rápido Ochoa** or **Brasilia**.

The **Terminal del Sur**, Cra 65, No 8B-91, is alongside the Enrique Olaya Herrera airport. There are similar services to those of Terminal del Norte. To get there, take a bus

4 Medellín Metro

➡ **Medellín maps**
1 Medellín, page 216
2 Medellín centre, page 220
3 El Poblado, page 225
4 **Medellín metro, page 235**

No 143 marked 'Terminal del Sur' from C 51 (in front of the Banco Popular) along Cra 46 or the metro to Poblado on Línea A, from where you will probably need a taxi for the remaining 1.5 km to the bus station. Frequent buses to **Manizales**, 5-7 hrs US$16, frequent services, first 0430, last 1930 with **Empresa Arauca**, also **Flota Ospina** US$17.50, faster service in minivans. To **Pereira**, 6-8 hrs, US$14 by **Flota Occidental Pullman** or **Empresa Arauca** first 0630, last 1500. Many buses to **Cali**, eg **Flota Magdalena**, US$20, 10 hrs. To **Popayán**, US$33.50, 12 hrs, **Expreso Bolivariano** at 1430, 1700 and 2315. To **Ipiales**, US$47.50, 22 hrs and to Pasto, US$47.50, 18 hrs (both same times as to Popayán) **Expreso Bolivariano**. To **Quibdó**, 11-13 hrs, US$33, 4 daily with **Rápido Ochoa**. To **El Retiro**, US$2.50, with **Sotra Retiro**. To **La Ceja**, US$3.50, every 20 mins, 0600-2000, with **Transportes Unidas La Ceja**. To **Jardín**, 4-5 hrs, US$9, 3 daily with **Rápido Ochoa** or **Transportes Suroeste**.

Car
Car hire Milano, C 10 No 43B-80, T448 7778, www.milanocar.com. Hertz, Cra 43A, No 1A Sur-69 of 101, T319 1010. Also offices and vehicles at International airport. If driving in Medellín, check if there are any restricted routes (eg car-sharing, bus lanes, rush-hour restrictions) that apply to hire cars.

Metro
The metro has 2 lines: **Línea A** from Niquía to Itagüí; and **Línea B** from San Javier to San Antonio, where they intersect, which connect up with 3 cable car lines, **Línea K**, **Línea J** and **Línea L**. 1 journey (anywhere on the system) US$0.75. The system operates 0430-2300 on weekdays, 0500-2230 Sun and holidays.

Taxis
Taxis have meters, make sure they are used, minimum charge US$2.50. Radio taxis include **Flota Bernal**, T361 6464 and **Taxi Andaluz**, T444 5555.

❶ Directory

Medellín *p214, maps p216, p220 and p225*
Banks Opening hours 0800-1130 and 1400 to 1600. Most banks in the business zones have ATMs. Many accept international cards. **Bancolombia**, in El Poblado, cash against MasterCard, Amex, good rates for TCs and cash. Many banks open late and on Sat. Main hotels will cash TCs for residents when banks are closed, but at less favourable rates. Most *casas de cambio* are found in the shopping malls, eg **CC El Tesoro**. **Cultural centres Centro Colombo Americano**, Cra 45, No 53-24, T513 4444, www.colomboworld.com. English classes, library, bookshop (including Footprint Handbooks), daily films, gallery for monthly exhibitions, very helpful. **Alianza Francesa**, Cra 49, No 44-94, Local 258, T576 0780, www.alianzafrancesa.org.co, near San Antonio church. **Biblioteca Público Piloto**, library. **Embassies and consulates** Austria, Cra 43A, No 7-50, Of 701, T312 1289. **Belgium**, Diagonal 75B, No 2A-120, Of 309, T341 6060. **Brazil**, C 29D, No 55-91, T265 7565. **Chile**, Cra 48, No 12 Sur-70, Edif El Crucero Of 808, T313 2209. **Ecuador**, C 50, No 52-22, Edif Banco de Caldas Of 603, T266 5433, **France**, Cra 65, No 35-71, Itagüí. T373 4771. **Germany**, Cra 43F, No 17-419, T262 1756. **Italy**, C 31, No 43A-172, T262 1823. **Mexico**, C 36, No 66A-70. T351 4812. **Netherlands**, C 52, No 51A-23, Of 401-402. T514 0756 **Panama**, C 10, No 42-45, Of 233, T312 4590. **Peru**, Cra 43A, No 16A Sur-38, Of 601, T313 6075. **Spain**, C 7D, No 43A-99, Of 410 T352 3451. **Sweden**, C 16A Sur, No 30-53 T311 9983. **Switzerland**, C6 Sur, No 43A-96, Of 802. T311 3314. **UK**, Cra 42 No 53-26, T377

9966. **Venezuela**, C 32B, No 69-59, T351 1614 Note the Venezuelan consul will not issue visas. **Immigration** DAS, C 19, No 80A-40 in Belén La Gloria section, T3415710 and at main airport. **Internet** There are plenty of internet cafés in El Poblado, travellers' hostels and most shopping centres. **Language** Eafit University, www.eafit.edu.co, has popular 4-week courses with 2 hrs of lessons a day, from US$445. The **Black Sheep Hostal** www.spanishinmedellin.com, offers 1-on-1 lessons. **Media** The local daily newspaper is **El Colombiano**, www.elcolombiano.com. There is also a weekly **El Mundo**, www.el mundo.com. 2 TV stations are **Telemedellín** and **Teleantioquia**. **Medical services** Hospital General de Medellín, Cra 48, No 32-102. T384 7300, www.hgm.gov.co. Hospital Pablo Tobón Uribe, C78B, No 69-240, T445 9000, www.hptu.org.co. Hospital Universitario San Vicente de Paul, C64, No 51D-154, T444 1333, www.elhospital. org.co. **Clínica Soma**, C 51, No 45-93 T576 8400, www.soma.com.co. **Clínica Medellín**, C 53, No 46-38, T356 8585, or C 7 No 39-290, El Poblado, T311 2800, www.clinicamedellin. com. **Clínica Las Américas**, Diagonal 75B, No 2A-120, Of 309 CC Plazoleta Las Américas, T341 6060, www.pmamericas.com. **Clínica Oftalmológica de Antioquia**, Av Las Vegas Cra 48, No 19A-40, T444 0090, www.clofan.com. **Clínica Oftalmológica Laureles**, Transversal 74C, No 1-23, T411 1000. **Police** Local police T112. **Post** Main Deprisa office, C 10, No 56-06, Mon-Fri 0730-2100, Sat, 0730-1800. Also Cra 46, No 52-36 and in all Exito super-markets. **Telephone** Telecom Cra 48, No 54-62, on Parque Bolívar, for international telephones and fax.

Around Medellín

By the time they reach Antioquia, the Andes have almost petered out, yet their foothills can still reach heights of up to 3000 m. This gives the rolling green countryside around Medellín an agreeable temperate climate in which all types of flowers and fruit thrive, and the typical villages of the region make for popular daytrips from the departmental capital. One such excursion is known as the Circuito del Oriente and involves a tour through typical paisa villages such as El Retiro, La Ceja and Río Negro. Further on is the network of artificial lakes known as the Embalse del Peñol, towered over by an extraordinary granite rock that bears an uncanny resemblance to Río de Janeiro's Sugar Loaf Mountain. On the shores of the lake is Guatapé, a sleepy town that livens up at weekends.

Further east still, as the road drops down towards the Río Magdalena, temperate turns to tropical and hidden in the jungle is the Río Claro Nature Reserve, where a crystalline river with a marble bed has cut a path through an enormous rock, creating a 150-m canyon. Just a few kilometres on is Hacienda Napoles, former home of drug baron Pablo Escobar, now a theme park with pretensions to be the new Jurassic Park. Due south is the beginning of coffee country. Enchanting villages such as Jardín, Jericó and Andes are seldom visited, a just reward for the intrepid traveller. Santa Fe de Antioquia, to the north, was once the departmental capital, but fortunately for architecture lovers it was eclipsed by Medellín, allowing it to take on a new role as Antioquia's very own time vacuum. ▶▶ For listings, see pages 244-247.

East of Medellín → For listings, see pages 244-247.

Climbing east out of the valley of Medellín, the landscape becomes increasingly more attractive with carefully cultivated hills bursting with an abundance of coffee, tomatoes, corn and beans. This is Antioquia's breadbasket and its many colonial towns are a popular weekend excursion for Medellín's well-heeled. The **Circuito de Oriente** includes the towns of El Retiro, La Ceja and Rionegro and passes through some of the most expensive property in Colombia, including that of former Colombian president Alvaro Uribe.

El Retiro → *Colour map 2, B3, Phone code: 4. Altitude: 2175 m. Population: 17,900.*

El Retiro, 33 km from Medellín, is a quiet colonial town with a fine plaza dominated by a 100-year-old ceiba tree. The pretty church, **Nuestra Señora del Rosario**, built in 1774, has an interesting stained-glass dome. There is an even older adobe mud chapel, the Capilla de San José, where a document to free local slaves, the first in South America, was signed in 1813. The **Fiesta de los Negritos** is held in late December to mark the event. El Retiro is also known for its furniture-making and you can have almost anything copied here.

Beyond El Retiro is the pretty town of **La Ceja**, which has an attractive church dedicated to Nuestra Señora de Chiquinquirá. The main industry in town is flower-growing and a local flower festival is held annually in December. Any of the surrounding hills offer excellent views of the area, one of the best known is **Cerro Capiro**. The **Circuito de Oriente** continues its loop through several pretty colonial towns including **Carmen de Viboral**, known for its pottery; there are several factories north of the market place.

Five kilometres from Medellín airport in a delightful valley is **Rionegro**. The Casa de Convención and the cathedral are worth a visit. There are colourful processions in Easter Week. There are various hotels (**C-F**) and many places to eat in and near the plaza.

Near Rionegro on the road southwest to El Retiro is **La Fe** reservoir, with a fine public park, **Parque de los Salados**, popular at weekends for aquatic sports amid pine forests.

El Peñol and around → Colour map 2, B3. Phone code: 4. Population: 16,150. Altitude: 2250 m.

At Rionegro, the western circuit loops back towards Medellín, but beyond, and not to be missed, is El Peñol, an extraordinary, 200-m-high, bullet-shaped granite rock, which towers above a countryside of interlocking artificial lakes known as the Embalse de Peñol. A spiral staircase has been built into a crack from the base to the summit. You can climb the 649 steps to the top in 30 minutes, where there are impressive views across the aquamarine lakes, as well as several tourist stalls and a snack bar. On the side of the rock you will notice the letters GI carved in white. This was originally meant to spell 'GUATAPE', an effort by residents of that town to claim it as their own and a view that is vociferously rejected by the residents of El Peñol. The painters were caught in the act and prosecuted though the graffiti is yet to be removed. Entrance fee US$5, or US$6 with full day parking.

The original town of El (Viejo) Peñol was founded in 1714 on an indigenous site known as Sacatín. In 1978, however, it was submerged in water when the reservoir was created. El Peñol Nuevo, built to replace it about 1 km from the original site is of little interest although it does have a strange-looking church modelled on the rock. If you walk down to the lake you can still see the spire of the original church sticking out of the water.

Guatapé

An entirely more agreeable place to stay in is Guatapé, 3 km beyond the rock, a pretty lakeside town with brightly coloured colonial houses and a pleasant plaza with a white and red Greco-Roman church, the **Parroquia Nuestra Señora del Carmen**. If you look closely you will notice a mistake on the church clock: the Roman numeral for '4' has been executed incorrectly.

At the weekend Guatapé transforms with the volume of visitors from Medellín and the *malecón* (promenade) along the lake shore tends to fill up with pleasure boats blasting out music. There is also a zip wire (known as 'canopy') across a section of the lake. During the week it's a quiet town with several economical accommodation options.

Aside from the rock and the pleasure boats, Guatapé is known for its *zócalos*, the brightly painted skirting boards that adorn many of the houses. While originally a Spanish import, Guatapé is unique in that the residents have chosen to embellish theirs with intricate sculptures depicting local families and political events. **Calle de los Recuerdos**, a couple of blocks from the main plaza, has the best examples of these fascinating public works of art.

Guatapé has two convents nearby. One is a Benedictine monastery, which holds Eucharistic services with Gregorian chanting every Sunday at 1100. **Las Adornadas del Divino Paráclito**, a convent 6 km away, holds 24-hour vigils. The nuns produce and sell honey and royal jelly. You can visit both by taking a mototaxi from the Parque Principal. **Note** There are no banks in Guatapé; the nearest bank with a cashpoint is at El Peñol.

Reserva Natural Cañón del Río Claro

ⓘ *www.rioclaroelrefugio.com, free.*

The Medellín–Bogotá road eventually descends into hot tropical forest before it meets the Río Magdalena at Puerto Triunfo. About three hours' drive and 152 km from Medellín is Reserva Natural Cañón del Río Claro, one of Colombia's first national parks, founded in 1970 by local landowner Juan Guillermo Garcés. A 450-ha conservation area based around a 150-m-deep limestone canyon, the park has spectacular walks along jungle paths following a crystal-clear river with a marble bed. There are several caves that show the geological history of the area and a couple of sandy beaches. The reserve is noted for its incredible biodiversity with over 50 new species of plant discovered and more than 370 different species of bird identified since its foundation.

Around Medellín

Discovering Reserva Natural Cañón del Río Claro

Before the main Bogotá–Medellín trunk road was completed, this majestic 150-m-deep limestone canyon was known only to jaguars and other animals of the forest.

Eduardo Betancourt, a *campesino* from a nearby *finca*, first discovered the gorge in 1964. Tracking a jaguar that had been killing his livestock, it took him six weeks to follow it back to the canyon. The animal eventually escaped him but not before leading him to the site, which locals refused to enter, believing it to be bewitched.

He returned home empty-handed but told his landowner Juan Guillermo Garcés about the canyon. Garcés was fascinated but nothing was done for a further six years until in 1970 a government engineer spotted it from a helicopter while searching for a suitable place to build a bridge across the river for the new road.

Garcés was inspired to see it for himself, so he set out with his brother and Betancourt. It took them two days to hack through the jungle and they had to enter the canyon itself by pulling themselves upriver on a raft.

They remained at the site for several months, building shelters in the caves under the steep walls of the canyon, and the diversity of species Garcés discovered during his stay inspired him to develop it into a private nature reserve to ensure its protection.

Fears that the building of the road would threaten the site were confirmed when 1500 visitors came on the first weekend of the completion of its construction. The canyon had gained some fame because journalists coming to stake out the nearby Hacienda Nápoles belonging to Pablo Escobar had made reports about this special place.

Garcés decided that it would be impossible to keep people away and that the best way of protecting the canyon was to develop a sustainable tourism reserve. He named it 'El Refugio', in memory of its former role as a jaguar refuge.

Doradal

About 15 km beyond Río Claro is Doradal, which has several hotels and restaurants alongside the busy Medellín–Bogotá trunk road but has an attractive plaza with palm trees and a beautiful church if you venture into the town proper. It is a convenient place to stay for visits to both the Río Claro Nature Reserve and Hacienda Nápoles.

Ins and outs Buses from the Terminal del Norte in Medellín to Doradal take three hours and cost US$14.

Hacienda Nápoles

ⓘ *www.haciendanapoles.com, US$12-16.*

About 20 km beyond Río Claro is Hacienda Nápoles, former country retreat of the notorious drug baron Pablo Escobar, now a theme park with a wildlife reserve full of exotic animals. Hacienda Nápoles was notorious throughout Colombia for the private zoo that Escobar put together and opened up for free to the public. Many of the animals – along with huge quantities of drugs – were flown into the estate's private runway which with a length of 1280 m can land a Boeing 747. As the war between Escobar and the Colombian government escalated in the late 1980s, the estate was abandoned and was pillaged for secret stashes of money and drugs. It was repossessed by the government in

1989 and many of the animals died or were stolen. Some even escaped; it is believed that two of the hippos are now roaming free in the Magdalena river.

The nature reserve part of the estate is home to a herd of hippos – including 'El Viejo', who was part of Escobar's collection – as well as water buffalo, ostriches, llamas, wild cats, monkeys and a butterfly sanctuary. In a slightly surreal turn, there is a collection of life-size dinosaur models, rebuilt by the same model makers who built similar replicas for Escobar. You enter the reserve through gates with lettering uncannily similar to that used for the film of Jurassic Park.

It is also possible to visit Escobar's old house, left in a state of disrepair, with holes in the swimming pool where bounty hunters excavated for buried treasure. The house, especially Escobar's bedroom, is remarkably small considering analysis by Forbes magazine placed Escobar as the seventh richest man in the world in his heyday. Other attractions include a Coliseum, used by Escobar as his private bullring, which now holds cultural events and exhibitions, and the runway.

There are two luxury hotels, a hacienda hotel and a camping zone available within the grounds themselves, as well as several hotel options in nearby Doradal (see Sleeping, page 244).

South of Medellín → *For listings, see pages 244-247.*

Santa Bárbara (altitude 1857 m) is 57 km south of Medellín on the main road via the town of Caldas, with stunning views of coffee, banana and sugar plantations, orange-tiled roofs and folds of hills, in every direction. There are hotels and restaurants on the main plaza; the bus from Medellín costs US$1.20. A further 26 km is **La Pintada** (camping; hotels **F-G**). Here the road crosses the Río Cauca, then splits. To the left is the particularly attractive road through Aguadas, Pácora and Salamina, all perched on mountain ridges, to Manizales.

Alternatively, from La Pintada, the main road goes up the Cauca valley through **Riosucio**, a delightful town with fine views, a large church and many restaurants and shops. At Anserma the road turns east to Manizales via Arauca. There is beautiful country on the west side of the Río Cauca.

Shortly after Caldas, a road to the right (west) descends through Amagá to cross the Cauca at Bolombolo. From here, several attractive towns can be visited. **Jericó** is an interesting Antioquian town with a large cathedral, several other churches, two museums and a good view from Morro El Salvador. **Andes** is a busy coffee-buying centre, several places to stay and to eat, all on Carrera 50/51, with pretty waterfalls nearby.

Jardín is 16 km southeast of Andes. This pretty Antioquian village is surrounded by cultivated hills and trout farms. The plaza is full of flowering shrubs and trees. It was founded in 1863 on the site of an indigenous settlement (of the Embera-Katío group), who worked the naturally iodized salt in the river there. There is still a reservation of the Cristianías community in the locality. It is a delightful place with an attractive fountain in the plaza full of flowering shrubs and trees, living up to its name. The neo-Gothic church, **Templo Parroquial de la Inmaculada Concepción**, has a fine façade built of dark, dressed stone and is a National Monument. It has an elegant, striking altar of Italian marble and an eight-pointed star in the ceiling of the apse. There is a delightful festival (Fiesta de las Rosas) in January. The small museum in the **Casa Cultura** has paintings and local artefacts, and a bank that accepts Visa cards.

North of Medellín

The main road north from Medellín leads to Cartagena, 665 km. About 21 km north is **Santa Rosa de Osos**, 2550 m, founded in 1636 and with several surviving colonial buildings including the Humildad chapel. There are sculptures by Rodrigo Arenas Betancur and Marco Tobón Mejía. About 15 km southwest from Santa Rosa is **Entrerríos**, between the Río Grande and the Río Chico in attractive steep country, somewhat extravagantly called the 'Switzerland of Colombia'. The fishing is said to be good. Nearby there is a 75-m *peñón*, El Monolito, which has proven to be of archaeological interest.

About 25 km north of Santa Rosa, a road to the west leads to **San José de la Montaña**, 2550 m, in the Páramo de Santa Inés, with cloudforest, caverns and waterfalls. Over the gorge of Río Cauca, 75 km beyond, the rough road climbs again to **Ituango**, 1550 m, a town with simple accommodation, banks, pharmacies and a supermarket.

From Ituango, rural transport is available to Badillo in the **Parque Nacional Natural Paramillo**, 460,000 ha of forest from the plains of the Río Sinú and the Río San Jorge to the headwaters of both rivers. There is *páramo* (moorland) over 3000 m, the highest point is 3960 m, and a wide range of flora and fauna to see; caiman and turtles in the lower areas, monkeys and many varieties of trees and birds at all levels.

The main road then climbs over to **Yarumal**, 122 km from Medellín, a friendly town in a cold mountain climate with fine views from Parroquia La Merced. There is a museum of religious art in the town hall and an interesting chapel, **Capilla de San Luis**, nearby. There is a natural bridge 1 km from the town and several *peñoles* in the neighbourhood. There are many *hosterías* on the main plaza and Calle Caliente. A further high pass, **Alto de Ventanas** follows, then a drop to **Valdivia**, 159 km from Medellín. There are a number of good walking and riding trails here including to the gorges of **Quebrada Valdivia** and **Quebrada El Oro** and two waterfalls, **Cascadas de Santa Inez** and **Chorros Blancos**. There are *residencias* (**D-E**) for staying the night, on the main road and several restaurants.

Santa Fe de Antioquia and around → *For listings, see pages 244-247. Colour map 2, B3.*
Phone code: 4. Population: 23,000. Altitude: 530 m.

About 78 km northwest of Medellín is Santa Fe de Antioquia, or Santa Fe as it is frequently called. It was founded as a gold mining town by Mariscal Jorge Robledo in 1541, the first in the area, and still retains its colonial atmosphere, with interesting Christmas and New Year fiestas. For a time in the 19th century it was the capital of the department, and retains much of its grandeur and character, little affected by the changing times since then. It has some beautiful colonial mansions with wooden balconies and narrow cobbled streets. The plaza mayor is particularly attractive with an imposing cathedral and *artesanía* stalls selling tamarind products, nuts, honey and dried fruits. Its preservation was assured when it was given National Monument status in 1960.

The bus station is on the road to Turbo at the north end of Carreras 9 and 10.

Sights

The **Catedral Metropolitana** is on the site of the first modest church in the town, built in the late-16th century. A second church was completed in 1673, with three naves and other embellishments, including chapels, added in the next 100 years. This in turn, was replaced in 1799 and the present building consecrated in 1837. It has an imposing white and coloured stone/brick façade (a style called *calicanto* seen in a number of local buildings) overlooking the main plaza. There is a fine 17th-century Christ figure as the centrepiece of the high altar, and a notable Last Supper sculpture from the 18th century. The shrine, with embossed-silver ornamentation, was the work of local artists, but unhappily, several fine gold pieces, also of local workmanship, were stolen from the Treasury in 1986. The tower was used as a prison in times past.

The **Plaza Mayor** is dominated by the fountain, which has been supplying water to the town for 450 years and has a bronze statue of Juan del Corral, the President of Antioquia during its few years of Independence between 1813 and 1826.

The **Iglesia de Santa Bárbara** ① *Cra 8 y C 11*, is also on the site of at least one previous building, which was passed to the Jesuits in 1728. They found it too small, and the present three-nave church was finished by Juan Pablo Pérez de Rublas at the end of the 18th century. The broad west front, also in *calicanto* style as are the interior walls and arches, is crowned with turrets and bells. An interesting woodcarving of the Virgin is enshrined in the Altar of San Blas, which is the oldest altar in Santa Fe. The font, in rococo style, is also older than the building.

Santa Fe de Antioquia

The church of **Jesús Nazareno** is another classical-style building, this one from the 19th century, and it's notable for the wood sculptures of Jesus on the cross and the representation of the Crown of Thorns. The church of **Nuestra Señora de Chiquinquirá** is across the José María Martínez Pardo square from the **Hotel Mariscal Robledo**, whose statue stands in the centre. The present church was built in the late 19th century on the site of a 17th-century Franciscan temple. An old painting of the Virgin of Chiquinquirá is built into the modern marble altar. This church too was used in the past as a prison. On the south side of the square is the **Palacio Arzobispal**, in Republican style, well worth a look inside. Opposite is a music school, further evidence of the cultural life of the town.

The Museo Juan del Corral has been incorporated into the **Museo de Arte Religioso** ① *Calle 11, next to the Iglesia de Santa Bárbara, open weekends and holidays, 1000-1700*, which contains an interesting collection of historical items, paintings, gold objects, etc from colonial and more recent times. There are many fine colonial houses in the town, take a look inside where you can. Typical of the *calicanto* style are the **Casa de la Cultura**, and **La Casa Negra** (the birthplace of Fernando Gómez Martínez).

Sleeping 🛏
Alejo 1
Caserón Plaza 2
Guaracú 3
Hostal Tenerife 4

Hostería de la Plaza
Menor 5
Hostal Plaza Mayor 6
Las Carnes del Tío 7
Mariscal Robledo 8

Eating 🍴
Don Roberto 9
La Comedia 10
Macías 11
Napoli Pizzaría 12

Around Santa Fe de Antioquia

A trip to the **Puente de Occidente** is well worthwhile. It is about 3 km downstream from the main (new) bridge and about 6 km from the centre of Santa Fe. You can walk, drive or take a taxi. Hitching is difficult as there is little traffic. Leave the town northeast on Carrera 9, cross the main Turbo road, and follow the signs to the 'Coliseo'. The paved road winds through the suburbs of the town, then drops down steeply through dry scrub to the river. The fine slender suspension bridge across the Cauca was designed and constructed by José María Villa, who studied in the USA, between 1887 and 1895 (and declared a National Monument in 1978). It is single track with wooden cross slats, 300 m long. Small vehicles are allowed to cross the bridge but are not encouraged; have a look – you will see why very few do so.

◉ Around Medellín listings → *Phone code: 4.*

For Sleeping and Eating price codes and other relevant information, see pages 23-28.

◉ Sleeping

El Retiro *p237*

B El Gran Chaparral, Km 2 Vía La Fe, T541 2451. Just outside El Retiro, this beautiful horse ranch and trout farm has fine rooms in a converted stable. The horses across the yard are not for hire but alternative ones can be arranged on request. There is a large pond full of rainbow trout for fishing and a restaurant serving enormous Angus beef steaks or fish while horses are paraded past hungry diners. Rooms have cable TV and hot water.

C El Zaguán, C 21, No 22-08, T541 2534, hotelzaguan@gmail.com. Modern brick building with 6 large, very clean rooms. Has a rooftop with good views of the town and a small bar showing occasional films. Laundry service, TV and hot water.

E Casa Campesina, Cra 20, No 22-43, T541 0692. This slightly run-down establishment near the Parque Principal has an extraordinary pulley system for opening the front door. Despite being a bit shabby it has good beds and several dorms.

Guatapé *p238*

B Hotel Guatatur, C 31, No 31-04, T861 1212, www.hotelguatatur.com. Newish hotel in modern building just off the *parque*. Crisp, airy rooms with large windows and comfortable beds. The suites have lovely elevated jacuzzis with good views out to the lake. Restaurant, plasma-screen TV, minibar, room service. Breakfast included.

D El Descanso del Arriero, C 30, No 28-82, T861 0878. An *arriero* is a mule driver and this pleasant hostel has a suitably rustic feel. It has good, clean rooms with private bath and hot water, some with a view to the church.

E La Florida, Cra 30, No 29-47, T861 0600. On the main plaza above the bar of the same name. Simple but clean rooms. Rooms for hire in houses (**E**) can be found through calling the local tourist office on T861 0555 ext 30 or T312-873 0302 (mob).

Reserva Natural Cañón del Río Claro *p238*

A-B El Refugio, T268 8855 (Medellín), www.rioclaroelrefugio.com. Swiss Family Robinson-style wooden structures perched high above the river. All rooms have a balcony open to the elements and include all meals. There is also a small hostel (**D**) at the entrance to the reserve, with rooms with private bath, as well as a campsite (**F**). El Refugio also organizes rafting expeditions, Grade I and II, more scenic than adventure sport. There is a series of zip wires (known in Colombia as 'canopy') which zigzag across the canyon and you can hire rubber rings to float down the river on.

Doradal *p240*

A Doradal Mediterráneo, Aldea Doradal, T834 2129, http://hoteldoradalmediterraneo.blogspot.com. **Aldea Doradal**, a small

Love hotels

Every town has one but they are not what they seem. Colombia's motels are not cheap hotels for the weary motorist, but rather love hotels – convenient hideouts for lovers sneaking off for some alone-time that provide rates by the hour and the ultimate in discreet service.

You can recognize them by their suggestive nomenclature – names such as 'Hotel Seed' or 'Passion Hotel' – and by their lurid paintjobs, a mixture of electric blues or Pepto Bismol pinks, like sorry cast-offs from Miami's South Beach. Most have drive-in garages so that customers never have to show their faces at reception. Inside, a revolving dumb waiter allows the client to receive food, drinks, condoms and sex toys without ever having to meet the staff face-to-face.

Some have jacuzzis, mirrored ceilings and pornography on TV, while others have special Saturday-night discounts.

Who goes there? Mainly teenagers and twenty-year-olds still living at home, but also adulterous couples and, of course, prostitutes with their clients. Colombia is a highly sexualized nation but also a predominantly Catholic country with strict moral codes. Motels are a convenient way of satisfying these conflicting desires and standards. You can measure how traditional a town is by the number of motels it has. For example, Armenia, in the heart of coffee country, has so many on its outskirts that the area has been nicknamed the Bermuda Triangle – no doubt because it's an easy place in which to lose yourself in passion.

---

community a couple of kilometres from Doradal could be a theme park nightmare. The whole village has been modelled on a Greek town, complete with whitewashed houses and narrow, windy streets. Somehow it works, partly due to the fact that locals have bought properties and injected some life into the place. The hotel, at the top of the village, has airy, a/c rooms with tiled bathrooms, a swimming pool and jacuzzi and Wi-Fi. Breakfast included.

B El Lago, 200 m east of Doradal on main road, T834 2126. *Cabañas* with a/c and private bathrooms and a fine pool, though a little noisy with all the traffic.

E Hotel Yahaya, on the Bogotá–Medellín road, T834 2177, www.hotelyahaya.com. On the main road but has clean, comfortable rooms with fan, TV, private bathroom and balcony as well as a good swimming pool. Has a restaurant serving typical dishes.

South of Medellín p241

A Hacienda Balandú, Vía Jardín Río Sucio, 800 m from town, T845 6850. Comfortable

rooms, pool, gardens, lake, spa, sports, good restaurant.

Santa Fe de Antioquia *p242, map p243*

A Guaracú, C 10, No 8-36, T853 1097. Gorgeous colonial mansion with a restaurant set around a courtyard full of mango trees and palms. Beautiful antique furniture, gramophones, cameras and pistols interspersed throughout the building. There is even a large pet tortoise that wanders around the corridors. Rooms are very comfortable with TV and stereo. If not a guest you can pay for a *día de sol*, US$20, which includes lunch and a towel for relaxing by the delicious swimming pool.

A Hostal Tenerife, Cra 8, No 9-50, T853 2261. This beautifully decorated colonial house has 7 rooms, each equipped with a/c, cable TV, and a minibar. There's free use of house bikes, internet access and a gorgeous pool in one of the courtyards. Breakfast is included in the price. Recommended.

A Mariscal Robledo, C 10, No 9-70, T853 1563, www.hotelmariscalrobledo.com.

Former home of José María Martínez Pardo, former governor of Antioquia, this colonial mansion has a large swimming pool and commanding views across the valley. Staff can organize horse-riding trips and guided tours of the town.

B Caserón Plaza, Plaza Mayor, C 9, No 9-41, T853 2040, www.hotelcaseronplaza.com.co. Large colonial building on the main plaza, decorated with African carvings and potted plants. Comfortable rooms, some with balconies looking onto large pool. Has a fine sun deck with fantastic views across the valley. Internet room, Wi-Fi, bike hire, a/c and can arrange guides for local tours.

B Hostería de la Plaza Menor, C 9A, No 13-21, T853 1133, www.hosteriadelaplaza menor.com. Tucked away round the corner from the Plaza Menor, this hotel has 26 comfortable rooms and offers a swimming pool, Turkish bath, gym and a children's playground. A *día de sol* costs US$15.

C Las Carnes del Tío, C 10, No 7-22, T853 3385. A restaurant that also offers some good rooms with vaulted ceilings and enormous bathrooms. Some dorms and shared baths.

D Hostal Plaza Mayor, Parque Principal, T853 3448. Right on the main square, this is a popular choice with backpackers. There are hammocks, a small pool and a small *cabaña* with bunk beds (**E**). The owner also has a Mexican ranch outside town where he will take guests for a BBQ.

E Alejo, C 9, No 10-56, T853 1091. Well placed at just 1 block from the Parque Principal, it has small and basic but clean rooms with their own TV and bathroom. Has a restaurant serving cheap food.

🍴 Eating

El Retiro *p237*
In addition to **El Gran Chaparral** (see Sleeping), there are several good places to eat on the Parque Principal, where there is also an ATM.
🍴 **Fonda de los Recuerdos**, T541 1605, at the entrance to town on the main road to

Medellín, more antique junkyard than restaurant, which plays old boleros, tango and 1940s ballads and is reportedly a favourite with local politicians (there is a photograph of President Alvaro Uribe with eccentric owner Chepe on the wall).

Guatapé *p238*
There are several places to eat on the Parque Principal. Trout is a local speciality.

Doradal *p240*
🍴 **Asados del Camino**, on main road at entrance to Doradal. *Bandeja paisa*, burgers and hotdogs in a large ranch.

Santa Fe de Antioquia *p242, map p243*
🍴 **Guaracu**, C 10, No 8-36, in the hotel of the same name (see Sleeping). The speciality is fish, especially trout. A *día de sol* includes a set menu lunch, use of the swimming pool 0900-1700 and a towel, and costs US$17.
🍴 **Don Roberto**, C 10, No 7-37. In a large colonial building with a swimming pool out the back, this restaurant has a simple menu of typical dishes such as *bandeja paisa* and *sancocho de bagre* as well as fast food. Delicious juices: try the *guandolo* – bitter orange with brown sugar. For use of the pool all day: US$4.50.
🍴 **La Comedia**, C 11, No 8-03. On the corner of Parque Santa Bárbara, this restaurant has a novel concept: you can buy any of the furniture or utensils you use while you eat, all of which are made by *artesanos* from Barichara. Jazz music and exhibitions of work by local artists give it a Bohemian atmosphere. Colombian and international arthouse films are shown every Thu evening, projected either in the bar or in the *parque*.
🍴 **Las Carnes del Tío**, C 10, No 7-22. Steaks and fish in the sunny courtyard of a fine colonial building.
🍴 **Macías**, Parque Principal. This small restaurant has been serving locals for over 35 years, so it must be doing something right. The menu is a mixture of regional and national dishes.

† Napoli Pizzería, Cra 9, N0 10-61.
Cheap and cheerful pizza by the slice.

✪ Festivals and events

Santa Fe de Antioquia *p242, map p243*
Mar/Apr Holy Week is a major celebration
here, and is followed by another week of
festivities between the 2nd and 3rd Sun
of Easter when there are many children's
parades. This is known as **Semana Santica**.
11 Aug Antioquian Independence
is celebrated.
Early/mid-Dec Film festival for 5 days,
www.festicineantioquia.com.
22-31 Dec Fiesta de los Diablitos, with
folk dancing, parades, bullfights, etc.

○ Shopping

Santa Fe de Antioquia *p242, map p243*
Artesanías Antiguedades, Cra 10,
No 10-71. Antique clocks, locks, cameras
and typewriters as well as beautiful pâpier
maché figurines.
Guarnielería, C 10, No 7-66. Leather products,
especially *carriel paisa*, a man's handbag
replete with secret pockets for hiding your
gun, now often used by women too.
Joyería Leydi, C 10, No 8-58. Excellent
filigree gold jewellery.

▲▲ Activities and tours

El Retiro *p237*
Club Hípico Los Malos, Cra Santander,
No 18-07, T541 0436. Hire horses from US$22
per day with optional *burroteca* (a donkey
with a music sound system attached).

Santa Fe de Antioquia *p242, map p243*
Gimnasio Life, C 10, No 7-09, T853 4177.
Only in Santa Fe can you get a gym housed in
the courtyard of a beautiful colonial building.
Exercise bikes and weights. US$2 for a half day.
For horse-riding excursions around
local countryside, try **Carlos López
Correa** T853 1148/T311 352 5213).

⊖ Transport

South of Medellín *p241*
Bus From **Medellín** (Terminal Sur), 4-5 hrs.

Santa Fe de Antioquia *p242, map p243*
Bus To **Medellín** US$5 (Sotraurabá), 1 hr,
US$4.25 with **Rápido Ochoa**, 5 a day.
Colectivos, US$7. To **Turbo**, US$20, 8 hrs,
every 2 hrs or so.

❶ Directory

Santa Fe de Antioquia *p242, map p243*
Internet Comunícate sin límites, C 9,
No 9-33 (Parque Principal). Internet and
fax services.

Department of Chocó

Undoubtedly one of the rainiest and most biodiverse locations on the planet, the Pacific coast of Colombia's Chocó region is overlooked and undervisited. Fearing tales of kidnapping and guerrilla activity in this region, tourists are understandably quick to avoid this region of Colombia; but the security situation has been improving and with a little research and some good faith there are several parts of Pacific Chocó that are no longer out of bounds. For the most part it is recommended that you check in with the local authorities to find out what might be going on here before visiting.

Stretching like a ribbon for 400 km between t he Cordillera Occidental and the Pacific coast, from Panama to Valle del Cauca, Chocó is one of Colombia's least-developed and most beautiful departments. In the northern three-quarters of the department, the mountain ranges of the Serranía de Los Saltos and Serranía del Baudó rise directly from the ocean to reach a height of about 500 m. The scenery of pristine rainforest descending the mountain slopes to the sea is spectacular.
➤➤ *For listings, see pages 250-251.*

Ins and outs

The easiest and most convenient way to get to the coast is to fly from Medellín or Bogotá via Quibdó to either Nuquí or Bahía Solano. **Satena** (www.satena.com) and **Aires** (www.aires.aero) both cover the routes. **Aerolínea de Antioquia** (www.ada-aero.com) also flies from Medellín. You can travel overland from Medellín with **Rápido Ochoa** but the journey is arduous and not recommended.

Quibdó ➤ *For listings, see pages 250-251. Colour map 2, B2. Phone code: 4. Population: 162,000. Altitude: 50 m.*

Quibdó, the capital of the department, is an unlovely and underwhelming city on the frontline where the few Western faces you are likely to see are aid workers or delegates from Médecins Sans Frontières. There is little to keep you here save for the unstoppable partying during the city's fiestas and the warmth and curiosity of the locals regarding your choice of tourist destination. The San Pacho festival (20 September-4 October, www.sanpacho.com) has parades and a San Francisco de Asís procession. There is an interesting mural in the cathedral. Hordes of birds fly in to roost at dusk and there are magnificent sunsets, which locals watch from the waterfront promenade, El Malecón.

Quibdó is the jumping-off point for most military operations in this stretch of the country and it is not uncommon to see brigades of soldiers returning war weary from the jungle here while the new batch ready themselves for their next outing.

Travelling on from Quibdó you are strongly recommended to fly to Nuquí or Bahía Solano, it is not safe to travel beyond the city by road. In July 2008 a dozen or so Colombians travelling the Atrato River from Quibdó to the coast were kidnapped by the FARC guerrillas. They have since been released.

Along the Pacific coast ➤ *For listings, see pages 250-251.*

Nuquí ➤ *Colour map 2, B1.*

Nuquí town has very little to offer the visitor aside from a serviceable runway and some poorly stocked shops. It is to the north and south of the town where the real attractions lie in the form of award-winning ecolodges. ➤➤ *For further information, see Sleeping, page 250.*

El Valle → *Colour map 2, B1.*

ⓘ *Visitors to Nuquí have to pay a US$2.50 tourism tax.*

Some 50 km north of Nuquí along the coast, El Valle has the best bathing and surfing beaches in the area. With tourism development there has been a decline in friendliness. **El Almejal**, north of town, is the best beach and has *cabañas*. The entrance to El Valle's harbour is very tricky at ebb tide and many boats have been swept onto the rocks here. As yet there is no access for regular vehicles. If hiring boats privately, check carefully before accepting offers. Make sure there are life jackets for any sea journeys. Solomon and his son Absolom are recommended.

A local product is *borojo* marmalade, made from a local fruit tasting like tamarind. Guides are available for tours by canoe up the Río Baudó, and to other places of interest along the coast. El Nativo has been recommended. A beautiful isolated beach, **El Tigre** can be visited by boat, or a three hour walk. Near El Valle, the **Fundación Natura** have a Tortugario, known as **Estación Septiembre** ⓘ *www.natura.org.co*, where they protect turtle eggs from predators in season. Visits are possible.

Parque Nacional Ensenada de Utria → *Colour map 2, B1.*

ⓘ *Entry is US$1.50 with a US$2 embarkation/disembarkation charge.*

Between Nuquí and El Valle is Parque Nacional Natural Ensenada de Utria. This 54,000-ha Park was created in 1987 to preserve several unique aquatic and terrestrial habitats. Steep, heavily forested mountains come down to the ocean to create dramatic scenery. Day trips may be arranged from El Valle, Nuquí, or Bahía Solano and special permits are sometimes granted for longer stays by the national parks office in Bogotá. A (free) permit must be obtained from a national parks office. The ranger welcomes volunteers to help in clearing rubbish from the beaches and other tasks (also best arranged in advance from Bogotá).

Getting there Boats hired from El Valle take one hour and cost approximately US$16 return, from Nuquí 1½ hours, US$24. Boats will not leave when the sea is too rough, which may be for several days. The launch that runs from Nuquí to El Valle can sometimes (depending on tides) leave you at Playa Blanca, a small, privately owned island near the park boundary. Here Sr Salomón Caizamo has a simple restaurant, but the food is good and he rents space, US$2 for up to five hammocks (a nice spot). There is good snorkelling and fishing. The park headquarters are five minutes away by motorboat and you can generally hitch a ride with fishermen or park employees. There are also a road and trail leading through the jungle from El Valle to the head of the inlet (9 km, four to five hours, can be very muddy), but you must arrange for a boat to pick you up as it is not possible to reach the park headquarters on foot.

The park is named after a large inlet (*ensenada*) at its centre, which is home to two varieties of whales, corals, needlefish, and many other aquatic species. This is one of the best places on the west coast of South America to see humpback whales migrating from late July to mid-October. Motorboats are not allowed past the park headquarters, located halfway up the inlet, and the area is best appreciated if you paddle through in a canoe (try to rent or borrow). The surrounding hillsides are covered with pristine rainforest and there are several magnificent white-sand beaches.

At the park headquarters and visitor centre there are maps, good information and a display of whale bones and other exhibits, plus a small restaurant. There are several well-marked trails. There is simple but comfortable accommodation for about 15 people in a guest house at US$6 per night and an outdoor kitchen with a wood stove, meals US$3, but camping is prohibited. Fresh fish can sometimes be purchased, but all other provisions should be brought from town. Mosquito nets are essential for protection against insects and vampire bats. Across the inlet from the headquarters is a private research station run by **Fundación Natura** as a base for biologists.

Bahía Solano → *Colour map 2, B1.*

Bahía Solano should be a much bigger tourist destination than it is given its levels of security and infrastructure. During the annual migration of the humpback whales – their breaching can be seen from the shore – the town in overrun with holidaymakers from Medellín. Outside of this period Bahía Solano is a functional fishing town with a side trade in collecting discarded keys of cocaine on their way north. This industry is so lucrative to local fishermen, who stand to earn a lifetime's pay in one swoop, that it has become a principal activity and at times this fishing village is often bereft of fish! Diving to a scuttled Naval Ship, hiking to waterfalls, sports fishing and visiting neighbouring beaches are just some of the attractions that can be enjoyed here. Drop in to the **Hotel Balboa Plaza**, you can't miss it as the only three-storey building in town, a folly and luxury pad built by Pablo Escobar falling into disrepair.

⊙ Department of Chocó listings

For Sleeping and Eating price codes and other relevant information, see pages 23-28.

⊜ Sleeping

Quibdó *p248*
Quibdó is not overwhelmed with decent places to stay, but centrally located and safe is the **Hotel Malecón**, T671 4662.

Nuquí *p248*
The **Piedra Piedra** (T318-285 5656, www.piedrapiedra.com), **Pijiba Lodge** (T574-474 5221, www.pijibalodge.com), and **Morromico** (T578-521 4172, www.morro mico.com) are environmentally aware, award-winning and design-oriented locations that can organize fishing trips, surfing outings and kayak rental. Communication is scant out here so it is imperative to book ahead through the main offices in Medellín as the staff will be providing you with 3 sumptuous meals and will need to stock up in advance.

In 2007, several Colombians and 1 Norwegian were kidnapped from the Morromico lodge by FARC guerrillas. It is believed that a ransom was paid that resulted in the captives being liberated.

El Valle *p249*
Several large but simple tourist complexes at El Almejal with rooms and cabins (**D-E** range), as well as bars and restaurants (deserted on weekdays off-season).
L Las Gaviotas Centro Vacacional, T341 3806 (Medellín). Cabins, good facilities.
AL Cabañas El Almejal, T230 6060 (Medellín), www.almejal.com.co. Cabins with private bath, the best, clean, friendly, full board. Price depends on the package arranged, eg 3 nights/4 days, US$200.
C El Morro, full board, **D** with breakfast.
F Cabinas Villa Maga, between El Valle and El Almejal. Friendly, safe, family-run.

There is other accommodation in **E** and **F** categories, for example **Carmen Lucía** or **Nativo y Rosa**. Ask around.

Bahía Solano *p249*
Mapara Crab Hotel Bahía Solano, www.maparacrab.com, T573-154 887679. Run by the affable and knowledgeable Nancy and Enrique Ramírez, this is a small, comfortable family enterprise offering private rooms with fan and breakfast. Enrique is a master sports fisherman and diving enthusiast.

🍴 Eating

Nuquí *p248*
Several small restaurants on the road to the airport serving mostly fish. Shops are well stocked with basic goods, prices somewhat higher than in Quibdó.

Bahía Solano *p250*
Good food at **Las Delicias** and at the restaurant run by Señora Ayde near the **Balboa** hotel.

🚍 Transport

Quibdó *p248*
Air To **Medellín**, Aires and Avianca daily flights, US$40-60. To **Bogotá**, Aires 1 daily; to **Bahía Solano** and **Nuquí**, daily, **Satena**. Enquire about other non-scheduled flights at holiday times.
Boat From Buenaventura up the Río San Juan to **Istmina** and on by road; infrequent services. Irregular cargo service down the Río Atrato to **Turbo** and **Cartagena** takes passengers. Cost to Turbo US$26, food included; to/from Cartagena US$40-55, 4 days, take drinking water. Deal directly with boatmen. Also 20-seater power boats, 7 hrs to Turbo, about US$30. The lower Atrato was a very dangerous area in 2000 (guerrillas, kidnappings, drug running). Much caution and detailed advance enquiry are strongly recommended.
Bus Rápido Ochoa to **Medellín** via El Carmen and Bolívar, 3 daily, 10-12 hrs, US$32 luxury coach, cheaper by regular bus. Transportes Arauca to **Manizale**s via Tadó, Pueblo Rico, La Virginia and Pereira, Tue, Thu, Sat, Sun at 0600, 14-17 hrs, US$16. **Flota Occidental** along same route to Pereira, daily at 0700, 8-10 hrs, US$15. Occasional buses to **Cali**, US$22 otherwise change at La Virginia. To **Bogotá**, US$27. Local service to **Santa Cecilia** and **Tadó**.

Nuquí *p248*
Air To **Quibdó**, Satena, 20 mins; to **Medellín** and Avianca, US$70, 50 mins.

All flights on Mon, Wed, Fri, and Sun only, return same day. Some extra flights Christmas and Easter time.
Road Construction is continuing on a road from Las Animas to Nuquí, which will eventually connect the port planned for Tribugá with the interior. It is presently a strenuous 3-day trek along a jungle trail, through several indigenous villages, to Nuquí.
Sea There are launches south to **Arusi** (Mon, Wed, Fri) and north to **El Valle**, and a new twin-engined boat, the *Magdalena*, Mon, Wed and Fri calling at **Jurubidá**, US$4, **La Esperanza**, US$4, and **El Valle**, US$8, returning Tue, Thu and Sat, as well as occasional coastal vessels (small fuel barges) to **Buenaventura**, cost to Buenaventura about US$40. Sea taxis will take you to beaches and villages along the coast.

El Valle *p249*
Jeep A road runs 18 km from El Valle to Bahía Solano (passes by the airport before town). Jeeps leave every morning, 1-hr ride, US$2.50, tickets can be purchased 1 day in advance.

Bahía Solano *p250*
Air To **Medellín**, daily flights with Satena, 4 a week with SAM, US$65. To **Quibdó**, daily with Satena, US$35. Reconfirm return flights and arrive early when leaving.
Sea Some coastal cargo vessels north to **Juradó** and south to **Buenaventura**, eg M/V Fronteras, US$45, including food, 36 hrs, cramped bunks.

ℹ️ Directory

Quibdó *p248*
Banks Banco de Bogotá, cash against Visa, other banks do not change money. Restaurant El Paisa, Farmacia Mercedes, and a few shopkeepers sometimes change US$ cash, but rates are poor. Best to buy pesos in larger centres before arriving.
Immigration DAS office C 29, Cra 4. No entry or exit stamps.

La Zona Cafetera

The three departmental capitals of La Zona Cafetera are in a north-south line, Manizales (Caldas) in the north, Pereira (Risaralda) 50 km away in the centre and Armenia (Quindío) a similar distance to the south, flanked to the east by the massif of Los Nevados. Because of the altitude, the climate is very agreeable and the road and transport facilities are good. There is much to see and enjoy and this is an excellent part of Colombia to visit with good services in the three cities. Much of the local transport in this region is by chiva (literally 'goat'), which are old, simple, brightly coloured buses, and jeeps, often called by the historic name 'Willys', also ancient but lovingly maintained. You will see that this area would be much the poorer without them.

All three can be reached from Bogotá by a road (309 km) passing through Facatativá and Honda and then over the Páramo de las Letras pass (3700 m, the highest main road pass in Colombia), or through Girardot to Ibagué and over the high crest of the Quindío pass (3250 m).
▸▸ *For listings, see pages 270-282.*

Manizales → *For listings, see pages 270-282. Colour map 2, C3. Phone code: 6. Population: 414,000. Altitude: 2153 m.*

Manizales is a comparatively new city, founded in 1848 by a group of settlers from Antioquia looking for a peaceful place at a time of civil disturbances further north. As a result, Manizales has the feel of a late 19th-century city with 'Republic-period' architecture and a fierce pride in Los Fundadores, the founders of the city. However, this area is unstable geologically and was struck by severe earthquakes in 1875 and 1879 only to be followed by fires that swept through the city in 1925 and especially 1926, severely damaging the centre. The city is now dominated by its enormous cathedral, not unreasonably of reinforced concrete, and still to be finished. Two previous cathedrals on the site were destroyed and even this one suffered during an earthquake in 1979. Yet another threat to the city is the Nevado del Ruiz volcano seen to the southeast, which erupted in November 1985, but most of the damage done was to communities on the side away from Manizales.

Ins and outs

Getting there **La Nubia** airport is 8 km to the southeast overlooking the city. Buses to the centre US$1, taxi US$4. There are several daily flights from Bogotá, Cali and Medellín with **Avianca**, **Aires** and **Aerolínea de Antioquia** (ADA), though due to the altitude and humidity, services can sometimes be delayed by fog. The bus terminal has moved to Cra 43 No 65-100, T878 7858, www.terminaldemanizales.com and is connected to the popular area of El Cable, also known as la Zona Rosa, by a new cablecar, opened some 18 months ago (US$0.75 per journey, one midway stop at Betania). Alternatively a taxi to the centre costs US$2.50 and to El Cable US$3-3.50. There are good roads and comfortable bus services from the main cities of Colombia. From Bogotá and the east the Cordillera Central must be crossed. The most direct route via Honda crosses at 3700 m. Alternatively, via Girardot and Pereira, the pass is lower at 3250 m. Both are long winding climbs and descents. The three main cities of the coffee region are currently being connected via the newly built Autopista del Café highway, cutting journey times. This is a toll road.

Getting around The centre of Manizales is pleasant and convenient for walking, though narrow streets can create traffic problems. An added attraction is the extensive views over the local countryside. The key thoroughfare is Carrera 23, which runs the full length of the city, also called Avenida Santander in the east. Lined with shops and eateries, it's busy any day of the week. Moreover, it is the road to La Nubia airport, Honda and Bogotá. East of the centre, also centred around Carrera 23, is **El Cable**, near one of the pylons that made up the old cable car route and also the new cable car from the bus station. It's the city's Zona Rosa and has the best restaurants and bars. Further east again is **Barrio Milán**, another popular night time area.

Tourist information

There are three **city tourist information points** in Manizales, one at the bus terminal, one in El Cable (**Fondo de Información Turística** ① *Cra 22 corner with C 31, open 0700-1900 daily*) and one in Chipre at the Monumento de los Colonizadores, as well as the main department tourist information in Plaza Bolívar. The website www.culturayturismo manizales.gov.co is useful. For Los Nevados and other national parks, try **Unidad de Parques Nacionales** ① *C 76B, No 18-14, T886 4104*.

Sights

The city was founded on a narrow saddle that falls away sharply to the north, west and south into adjacent valleys. Expansion has been to the east, along precipitous ridges between the Río Chinchiná and Quebrada Olivares using every available piece of flat land. Villages in the valleys are gradually being absorbed by the city. Although a spectacular site for the visitor, the terrain causes significant travel difficulties, often due to landslides during the rainy season. The climate is extremely humid (average temperature is 17°C, and

Manizales

N

200 metres
200 yards

Sleeping
Basecamp **3**
Bolívar Plaza **1**
Carretero **4**
Escorial **5**
Estelar Las Colinas **6**

Manzinales Hostel **8**
Mountain House **7**
Pitstop **13**
Roma Plaza **9**
Regine's **10**
Tama Internacional **11**

Varuna **12**

Eating
Frisby **1**
Pollos Asados Mario **2**

the annual rainfall is 3500 mm), encouraging prodigious growth in the area around the city including the flowers that line the highways to the suburbs north and south. Frequently the city is covered in cloud but when it is clear, there are brilliant views in every direction. With luck, you may see the snows of the Nevados to the southeast. The best months of the year are from mid-December through to early March. The city looks down on the small town of Villa María, 'the village of flowers', now almost a suburb. Due to the earthquakes and fires, much of the architecture is predominantly modern with high-rise office and apartment blocks. Traditional 19th-century architectural styles are still seen in the suburbs and the older sections of the city.

The centre of the city is the **Plaza de Bolívar** with two ceramic murals by Guillermo Botero and a central plinth on which stands an extraordinary bronze statue of Bolívar Condor (1991) by Rodrigo Arenas Betancur, which depicts Bolívar as a condor, his head dismembered from his body and protruding into the plaza. On the north side of the plaza is the departmental government building, **La Gobernación**, an imposing example of neo-colonial architecture, built in 1926 around a central garden patio. The building was declared a National Monument in 1984.

Opposite is the **cathedral**, a new building constructed after the fires of 1925 and 1926 mainly of reinforced concrete, neo-gothic in style, with an elegant spire over 100 m high. It was designed and built by Italian architects between 1928 and 1939, although some work still continues, including strengthening the cupola. It now has four towers, one each dedicated to saints Inés, Francis, Mark and Paul. Inside look for the fine decorated altar cover with a suspended cross above, the wooden choir stalls and colourful stained-glass windows including a fine rose window at the west end. There is also a simple but elegant marble font to the left of the west door. One-hour tours including a climb up the cathedral tower take place Thursday to Sunday, US$3.50.

Nearby, the **Banco de la República** ⓘ *Cra 23, No 23-06, Mon-Fri 0900-1200, 1400-1800, free*, has a gold and anthropology museum, a good reference library, records and videos.

The **Iglesia de la Inmaculada Concepción** ⓘ *Cra 22/C 30*, overlooking **Parque Caldas**, is again in neo-Gothic style with cedarwood pillars, roof arching inside and stained-glass windows. It was built 1903-1921. **Iglesia de los Agustinos** ⓘ *Cra 18, near the bus station*, has a colonial-style façade and many spires around the building.

The **bull-ring** ⓘ *Av Centenario*, built around 1950, is an impressive copy of the traditional Moorish style, based on the one in Córdoba, Spain. It holds 20,000 people. Bullfights take place in late January, early Febuary, tickets US$8-27 depending on whether they are in *sol* or *sombra*. There are also fights in June and July with young bulls with no kills. The **University of Manizales** ⓘ *off Cra 23 at C 40*, is housed in a fine building (originally the railway station) of considerable historic interest. **Universidad de Caldas** ⓘ *C 65 No 26-10, www.ucaldas.edu.co, Mon-Fri 0830-1200, 1415-1800 (take a 'Fátima' bus to the University)*, has a natural history museum with a good selection of butterflies, moths and birds. The **Centro de Museos** ⓘ *Cra 23, No 58-65, T886 2720, Mon-Fri, 0830-1200, 1415-1600*, also part of Caldas University, has an art gallery and exhibitions on geology and archaeology. **The Teatro de los Fundadores** ⓘ *Cra 23/C 33*, at the eastern entrance to the city centre is a good example of local architecture. This is well worth a visit with some fine murals and metal sculptures in the foyer and upper floors, including works by Guillermo Botero (see below).

La Galería del Arte ⓘ *Av Santander (Cra 23) at C 55*, which has exhibitions and sale of works by local artists. Further out on the road to Bogotá at Calle 65, you will see the tower of the Manizales terminal of the aerial cableway that went 75 km to Mariquita from 1922

Staying on a coffee finca

The severe coffee crisis that hit the world in 1992 has to some extent continued to this day, adversely affecting the coffee regions of Caldas, Risaralda and Quindío.

Colombia, with its emphasis on quality over quantity, is one of the nations that has been left struggling. Coffee growers in the region have been forced to diversify into other crops. In 1994, Quindío's tourism board, emulating the success of Spain's countryside haciendas, proposed to the region's *finca* owners an alternative source of income, and the idea of opening up coffee farms to tourism was born.

From stately post-colonial Antioquian mansions to some pretty primitive accommodation, no two *fincas* are the same. Some still produce their own coffee – and offer tours where you can learn about the process of coffee-growing – while others have retired that part of the business altogether and give guests the chance to relax, lounge around pools and appreciate the incredible richness of flora and fauna of the region.

Below are a few recommended *fincas*.

L Hacienda San José, see page 272, simply breathtaking.
AL Hacienda Bambusa, see page 274, an enchanting traditional hacienda.
A Finca Villa Nora, see page 275, a working coffee farm.
A-B El Delirio, see page 275, a beautiful, traditional *finca*.
A-B Hacienda Guayabal, see page 272, one of the best places to do a coffee tour.
B-E Hacienda Venecia, see page 271, beautiful and friendly working coffee farm with good coffee tour.
C El Carriel, see page 275, runs an excellent coffee tour.

For further details, visit www.clubhaciendasdelcafe.com.

---

till the 1960s carrying coffee, thus avoiding the difficult grind up to the Alto de Las Letras pass (3700 m) and down the other side. From Mariquita the coffee was taken by road and rail to the Río Magdalena for shipment and export.

Chipre is a suburb in the northwest of the city and has, in its centre, the **Nuestra Señora del Rosario church**, which is a replica of the previous city cathedral. Along Avenida 12 de Octubre, the west side is an open park with magnificent views over coffee country down towards the Río Cauca. Across to the east are views of the city. It is much frequented by locals at weekends. Stalls along promenade sell *obleas*, large wheat wafers, served with *arequipe* and coconut and well worth a try. The large water tower, known as **El Tanque** is a local landmark. At the end of the avenue, is an impressive sculpture, the **Monumento a los Colonizadores** ① *daily 1000-1830, free*, interestingly made from keys collected locally and melted down. There is also a **tourist information point** here.

Excursions

Visits to coffee farms in the area are warmly recommended. They are often included in local tours arranged by agencies or through hotels. You will also see the spectacular local countryside. For staying on coffee farms, see box, above. For visits to Los Nevados National Park, see page 259.

About 8 km from Manizales is the **Parque Ecológico Río Blanco**, a 4343-ha protected cloudforest, considered by the World Wildlife Fund the best place for birdwatching in Colombia. To date, 335 species of bird have been identified, including 33 species of hummingbird. There are also 350 species of butterfly as well as 40 types of orchid and mammals such as spectacled bears, ocelots and the white-tailed deer. Some of the rarer birds that can be seen include a sub species of the rusty-faced parrot, the royal woodpecker and four types of toucan. The park is owned by **Aguas de Manizales** ① *T886 7777*, which manages the water from the Río Blanco, providing Manizales with 35% of its drinking water, believed to be some of the purest in the world.

There are several hikes of between 20 minutes and eight hours as well as a rangers' hut where 22 species of hummingbird come to feed, managed by the **Fundación Ecológica Gabriel Arango Restrepo** ① *www.fundegar.com*, which conducts scientific flora and fauna investigation in the park with the support of WWF.

Before the area was turned into a reserve it was inhabited by campesino farming families. These have been allowed to stay and have been trained as rangers.

Entry is free but you must take a guide (recommended tip US$9 per group) and you must get permission from Aguas de Manizales – ask for the Oficina de Recursos Naturales. Birdwatchers, photographers and hikers can stay at the **Fundación Ecológica Gabriel Arango Restrepo's rangers' hut** ① *contact Technical Director Sergio Ocampo, T886 7777, ext 1164, sergiofundegar@gmail.com*. There are basic dormitories with bunk beds, US$17 per person, food US$12.50.

North of Manizales

The Pan-American highway runs north from Manizales to Medellín through some picturesque countryside dotted with small villages perched on the fertile montainsides of the Cordillera Occidental. As the road crosses the Río Cauca it reaches a fork: you can take the left turn to Supía and Río Sucio, or turn right to Medellín via Marmato.

Supía → *Colour map 2, B3. Phone code: 6. Population: 30,000. Altitude: 1183 m.*

With its backdrop of resplendent rolling green hills and an agreeable temperate climate, the small town of Supía, 77 km from Manizales, is worth a visit. It has a picturesque Parque Principal with palms and *ceiba* trees covered in Spanish Moss or *tillandsia*, as well as several attractive bird houses. A mixture of colonial and modern architecture, the town has an impressive church with two imposing towers.

It is known throughout the region for its *colación*, a sweet delicacy made from sugar cane; the **Feria de Colación** is celebrated every two years around the end of June/ beginning of July.

It is an excellent place for hiking in the hills. A particularly interesting trip is to Marmato, a town where gold is still mined as it was during the time of the Spanish conquistadors (see below), which can be reached by walking over the mountain or by *chiva* or jeep via a spectacular unpaved road.

There is an interesting little museum displaying religious artefacts at the back of the church, where there is also useful tourist information on the surrounding area.

The legends of Marmato

Known as the 'cradle of Colombian gold', it is believed that gold has been mined in Marmato for more than 500 years. When Sebastián de Belalcázar and Jorge Robledo arrived with their Spanish conquistadors in 1536 they found the local indigenous Cartamas already mining the mountain and fashioning beautiful *huacas* out of its gold.

Belalcázar and Robledo promptly disappeared (taking the Cartamas' bounty with them) but marched back in 1539 bringing black slaves from Cartagena to work the mines. Word spread about the fortune under the mountain and shortly afterwards German mercenaries, who joined the Spanish hunt for El Dorado, arrived. They built their own mines in San Juan, a village just up the mountain from Marmato. In the 19th century, the British arrived on the invitation of the Colombian government, which used Marmato as collateral to secure funding for its fight for Independence against the Spanish.

Marmato is a place steeped in myth, legend and superstition. Witches are said to live in the hills above; a cross at the mountain's peak is meant to ward off flying witches. These witches are beautiful, rumour has it, and have the power to entrance any man. In former times, the locals say they persuaded the foreign gold prospectors who came to Marmato to drink from the enchanted waters of the Cascabel spring. This was supposed to make them fall in love with the women of Marmato and never want to leave.

The slaves brought in by the Spanish to work the mines had their own distinct culture. Legend has it that they practised a sacred ritual under an ancient *ceiba* tree in which they formed a ring around the most beautiful slave girl and made her drink the blood of a sacrificial goat while she undressed. The local Catholic priest, shocked by the practice, denounced the slaves as devil worshippers and cursed them. The *ceiba* tree is believed to have fallen away in a landslide following the priest's damnation.

This is not the only example of divine intervention. The 16th-century **Iglesia de Santa Bárbara** has collapsed and been rebuilt several times, some say because the town priest cursed the village for of its penchant for heavy drinking and prostitution; there is a belief in Marmato that the more you drink, the more gold you will find. The curses appear to continue to this day: in 2006 the town plaza and *alcaldía* were buried under a landslide. Luckily, no-one was killed.

Marmato has continued in its mining tradition to the present day and many of the techniques used are little different to those used 400 years ago.

Marmato → *For listings, see pages 270-282. Colour map 2, B3. Phone code: 6. Altitude: 1350 m.*

Situated on top of a mountain, up an unpaved road, some 7 km off the Manizales–Medellín highway and 80 km from Medellín, is Marmato, a village with a colourful history steeped in myths and legends. Since the 16th century, Marmato has been the focus of foreign exploitation by the Spanish, German and English because of its gold mines. Today local gold prospectors dynamite and excavate the mountain much in the same way they would have done 400 years ago. The locals still tell stories of witches, curses and ancient religious practices carried out by the black slaves who were brought to Marmato to extract gold for their foreign masters (see box, above, for more details).

Marmato is something of a paradox. While some of its houses have retained their traditional *tapia pisada* architecture and afford spectacular views down into the valley below; other parts are not so picturesque but are nonetheless fascinating to behold. Entire chunks of the mountain have been gouged out in the pursuit of gold, or have fallen away in frequent landslides; in 2006 the Plaza Mayor and the *alcaldía* were buried under tons of mud which at the time of writing had yet to be cleared. Buckets full of gold ore extracted from the mines zip up and down on wires that criss-cross the valley, while lorries trundle through its steep, narrow streets.

Marmato has a reputation for heavy drinking and philandering. The **Feria de Oro**, in late October, is a raucous event involving the consumption of copious quantities of beer and *aguardiente*. On Friday afternoons, busloads of prostitutes are shuttled in to satisfy the miners' needs.

Sights

The most interesting sights are above the village. Walk past the church and its square, along the main street. Beyond a row of shops there is a narrow cobbled street to the left. Keep climbing past the primary school and you will reach the secondary school where they will hire out helmets and Wellington boots (essential if you are going to visit one of the mines).

Beyond the school you will reach the main plaza and *alcaldía* (currently abandoned). Here there are spectacular views down into the village and the valley below, and some interesting murals depicting the legends of Marmato.

Exiting the plaza to the right you will notice several abandoned houses. Step inside to see how these homes incorporated former mines built by the Germans – some were used as kitchens or pantries. If you continue walking along a narrow path – be mindful how you go as this path is prone to landslides – you will reach a viewpoint from which you can see a stream running down a muddy gully. This is the source of the **Aguita de Cascabel**, a spring whose water the witches of Marmato fed to unsuspecting foreigners to make them fall in love with the village and its women. It is said that once someone has drunk from its waters they will never leave Marmato. From here, looking further down, beyond a former water mill, you can also see several stone buildings pegged to the side of the hill opposite. These were prison cells used to punish slaves.

From the plaza's lookout point, down below to your left you will notice a colonial building with a small park. This is the **Parque de los Mineros**, which houses a small library and several ingenious statues – a miner, a witch and a slave girl – made from miners' tools and nuts and bolts. It also has the original bell that was used to call the slaves to work, although someone has stolen the clapper! You can reach the park by leaving the plaza opposite the Alcaldía and turning right beyond a group of buildings.

In these buildings there is a small silver studio where the workers will sell pieces of silver at reasonable prices. Retracing your footsteps from the Parque de los Mineros, past the silver studios you will reach a small gold mine, owned by the town mayor. Here there are several pulley systems bringing down gold ore from mines further up. You can observe how the crushed rock is siphoned off with water to separate the gold. You can ask one of the miners to take you into the mine. The miners can provide head torches. There is no charge but a tip of US$5 would be appreciated. Health and safety is not a priority in Marmato. The mines are narrow, muddy and there is little oxygen. Do not enter if you suffer from claustrophobia. This is a working mine; you are likely to hear dynamite blasts in other parts of the mountain. You enter at your own risk.

① *Entry to the park is US$28.50 for non-Colombians, including compulsory guide.*
Los Nevados are a compact range of volcanic peaks in central Colombia and the nearest and most accessible mountains to Bogotá. This is a park with all the savage beauty associated with mountains, dormant volcanoes, hot springs and recent memories of tragic eruptions. The park is home to three huge volcanoes: **Nevado del Ruiz**, **Nevado de**

Los Nevados National Park

Santa Isabel and Nevado del Tolima and a further three high peaks without snowcover, Paramillo del Cisne, Paramillo de Santa Rosa and Paramillo del Quindío. The highest of all, Nevado del Ruiz (5321 m) erupted in 1985, completely destroying the village of Armero under a mud stream. In total the eruption killed more than 25,000 people. At the time of writing Nevado del Ruiz was again displaying seismic activity and it was not possible to climb to the summit, or even the viewpoint at 5100 m. Nevado del Tolima is also still active but hasn't shown major changes in activity recently The high-altitude volcano vegetation with *frailejones* up to 12 m, the volcanic lakes and the active volcanoes are all absolutely worth visiting.

The three volcanoes can normally be climbed and there are several treks within the park. The longest and toughest trek is from south (Ibagué) to north (Manizales) in the park in six days. From Manizales you can take a 4WD up to Laguna del Otún, but deeper into the park it is hard to find any trails at all and you may not hike independently, but have to hire a guide who knows the area well. Two shorter day-treks can be organized on the spot at the visitor's centre at El Cisne – the three-hour El Cisne–Mirador Laguna Verde (US$25) walk and the eight-hour Santa Isabel glacier walk (US$65). ▸▸ *For further information, see Activities and tours, page 279.*

Sights

Nevado del Ruiz is the highest of the three volcanoes. From Manizales it is normally easy to climb to 5100 m (after being dropped by car at 4800 m, but this was closed at the time of writing), which is a popular day tour, but with a special permit and gear it is also possible to climb to the top (5321 m), provided seismic conditions are favourable. On peak days, the easier climb may be very crowded. **Laguna Verde Encantado** is a beautiful green lake between Paramillo el Cisne and **Nevado de Santa Isabel**. Nevado de Santa Isabel is the lowest of the three volcanoes and inactive. At the summit (5000 m) there is an amazing view (weather permitting), with Nevado del Ruiz to the north and Nevado del Tolima to the south. **Laguna del Otún** is the biggest lake of the park and full of trout, fishing gear is available to rent. It is also one of the base camps to climb up Nevado de Santa Isabel. **Laguna Leona** was another large lake, but it has almost completely dried up. It sits at the feet of **Paramillo de Quindío**, which used to be the source of the lake. **Valle del Placer** is a big valley covered with *frailejón* plants. **El Rancho** (2600 m) is an area of hot springs and is a good place to start and end any attempt to climb **Nevado del Tolima**. Nevado del Tolima is the most beautiful but also the toughest summit in the park. From El Rancho it is a long climb to the summit (5215 m). The crater is spectacular; a walk around it in the snow is impressive. There are several routes to climb to the top but some are only for experienced climbers, otherwise it is recommended to go with a guide with good equipment.

Ins and outs

From Manizales it is possible to access the park by car. The main route is from the road between Manizales and Bogotá. At La Esperanza you take the right fork, then it is 17 km to the main park entrance/office. From this point you must enter the park with an official guide. If you don't come with an organized group you will have to pick and pay the guide at the entrance office. It is also possible to enter the park by car from the Termales del Otoño. By foot or on horse you can enter the park from Santa Rosa, Pereira (following Río Otún), Salento (Valle de Cocora) and Ibagué (following Río Combeima).

When to go

For trout fishing the season is April to August. The dry seasons are January to February and June to September, but even in those months it can rain for days or be very foggy. There has been no problems with safety in recent years.

Santa Rosa de Cabal and around → *Colour map 2, C3.*

Some 22 km southwest of Manizales is **Chinchiná**, one of the main coffee-producing towns in Colombia. The surrounding hills are carpeted with coffee bushes and on roasting days the smell of coffee hangs in the air. Just outside the town (taxi US$3.30) is the **Hacienda Guayabal**, a coffee *finca* owned by the Londoño family since 1959. This is one of the best places to observe the growing and production process (see box, page 255). Halfway to Pereira, 15 km from Chinchiná, is Santa Rosa de Cabal, from where several thermal pools can be reached, including **Termales de Santa Rosa/Los Arbeláez** ① *0800-2400, US$8*. A 9-km unpaved road from Santa Rosa leads to the hot baths (early morning *chiva* or taxi, US$9 to entrance). They are surrounded by forests, with waterfalls. It's packed at the weekend.

Pereira → *For listings, see pages 270-282. Colour map 2, C3. Phone code: 6. Population: 806,000. Altitude: 1411 m.*

Capital of Risaralda Department, 56 km southwest of Manizales, Pereira, stands within sight of the *Nevados* of the Cordillera Central. Pereira is situated on a small plateau, bounded to the south by the Río Consota and to the north, the Río Otún, about 140 m below. Beyond the Otún is **Dosquebrados**, an industrial town, now virtually part of the city, and dramatically linked by a viaduct. Pereira is the largest city in this part of Colombia and acts as the centre of the Zona Cafetera with the appropriate range of official and commercial institutions and services. It has a very pleasant climate, though the green countryside around indicates a regular rainfall, usually short, sharp showers. Apart from coffee and cattle, there is a wide variety of local agricultural produce and you will notice the high quality of the food available here. Unfortunately this is an active seismic zone and earthquakes periodically damage Pereira. In 1995 significant damage was done to some buildings in the centre and again in January 1999 it was affected by the serious quake that devastated Armenia. The city has also grown rapidly and suffers from the attendant ills of high unemployment, petty crime and prostitution in some areas.

Getting there

Air The airport is 5 km west of the city. Daily flights from Bogotá, Cali, Ibagué and Medellín. Less frequent to other cities.

Road The bus terminal is 12 blocks south of the centre. Main roads are good in the Zona Cafetera, particularly the new Autopista del Café from Manizales to Armenia and beyond. Frequent bus services from the main cities of Colombia. The direct road via Armenia to Ibagué, Giradot and Bogotá goes over La Línea pass (3250 m).

Getting around

The city is centred around Plaza de Bolívar and most points of interest are within walking distance. The centre is safe (subject to the usual common sense precautions) but the semi-derelict area between Carrera 10 and 12 is not a place to linger. The same applies to the streets heading east, starting with Calle 14. Local taxi and bus services, including the recent addition, the Megabus, www.megabus.gov.co, modelled on the TransMilenio in Bogotá, are of good quality.

Tourist information

Centro Cultural Lucy Tejada ⓘ *Cra 10 No 6-16, T311 6544, Mon-Fri 0800-1200 and 1400-1800, www.pereiraculturayturismo.gov.co.* **Corporación Autónoma Regional de Risaralda (Carder)** ⓘ *Av de las Américas and C 46 No 46-40, T311 6511, www.carder.gov.co* has information but does not deal with park permits. Contact **Aviatur** ⓘ *Av 30 de Agosto No 34-38 L1/15, T326 3630, www.aviatur.com*, for park permits. **Turiscafé** ⓘ *www.turiscafe.net*, for good information on coffee farms in Risaralda.

Background

A settlement was established here around 1541 by Mariscal Jorge Robledo but around 1700 it was moved to the present site of Cartago on Río La Vieja after continuing difficulties with a tribe of indigenous Quimbaya. Francisco Pereira from Cartago set out to re-establish a town here in the 19th century but died before achieving his objective

Sleeping 🛏	Condina 1	San Simón 9	Eating 🍴
Cataluña 3	Hotel de Pereira 6	Soratama 8	El Apertivo Paisa 12
Colonial 5	Royal 7	Sweet Home 4	El Gran Sazón 9

Remigio Antonio Cañarte, a priest and friend of Pereira, with a group of settlers, succeeded in 1863 and named the town after him.

Sights

The central square is the **Plaza de Bolívar**, noted for its *El Bolívar Desnudo*, a striking sculpture of the nude general on horseback by Rodrigo Arenas Betancur to commemorate the city's centenary in 1963. It caused a stir when unveiled, and brought a whole new meaning to the term 'liberator', but it is now accepted with pride by the local citizens. Enthusiasts of Arenas Betancur can find three of his other works in the city, *Monumento a los Fundadores* on Avenida Circunvalar/Calle 13, *El Prometeo*, in Universidad Tecnológica de Pereira (South on Calle 14), and *Cristo Sin Cruz* in the **Capilla de Fátima**, Avenida 30 de Agosto/Calle 49, towards the airport. There are many other examples of public art on display; look for works by Jaime Mejía Jaramillo and Leonidas Méndez. There is an interesting bronze of Benito Juárez, Mexico's first president of indigenous origins, on Avenida 30 de Agosto. Also in Plaza de Bolívar is the **cathedral**, unimpressive from the outside but with an interesting and elegant interior. After the 1999 earthquake extensive restoration work was carried out, uncovering the original wooden interior, which has been left bare. There are also fine chandeliers down the central nave, two large mosaics depicting baptism and the eucharist and a fine dome with roof paintings. Also interesting are the two Lady Chapels and the stained-glass windows.

There are three other parks with their churches. The **Parque del Lago Uribe Uribe** is the most picturesque with an artificial lake and a fountain illuminated at night. **Parque Gaitán** and **Parque La Libertad** (with its striking mosaic by Lucy Tejada) are also worth a visit. Opposite the **Meliá Pereira** hotel is the **Templo Nuestra Señora del Carmen**, a Gothic-style church with a dull grey concrete finish outside but inside it has some good sculptures and stained glass.

Two early 20th-century houses of architectural interest are **Casa de Luis Carlos González** ① *Cra 6, No 21-62*, and **Casa Carrera** ① *Cra 7, No 15-58*. Both have been declared National Monuments. The impressive road bridge over the Río Otún connecting Pereira with Dosquebrados, is known as **El Viaducto César Gaviria Trujillo**. It was built by Colombian, German and US contractors to Italian designs.

An interesting old Spanish service is to be found in the centre of Pereira; *Los Escribanos*. These scribes help locals with

To Manizales
To Manizales

DOSQUEBRADAS

A POPA

Viaducto Gaviria Trujillo

Parque La Libertad

Cra 8
Cra 10
Cra 12

Avenida del Ferrocarril

Nuestra Señora del Carmen

Monumento a Los Fundadores cross

Av Circunvalar

Av Ricaurte

14

N

1 km
1 mile

Food Alley 2
La Jarra 1
Mediterráneo 14

legal documents and filling in official forms, working on the street with their typewriters. They are found, in office hours, on Calle 19 by the post office.

Some way from the city centre, but worth a visit, is the small **Museo del Oro Quimbaya** ① *Av 30 de Agosto, No 35-08, free*, which features many Quimbaya pottery and gold items including three exquisite 2-cm-high face masks. Alongside is a library and a music auditorium with a daily programme of classical music. On the campus of Universidad Tecnológica de Pereira, the **botanical garden** ① *T321 2523, www.utp.edu.co, US$2.50 including 2-hr tour, Mon-Fri 0800-1700, Sat, Sun and holidays 0900-1700; you must book visits in advance and use a guide*, is good for birdwatching and has bamboo forests and two-hour nature walks.

Around Pereira → *For listings, see pages 270-282.*

Northwest of Pereira, 30 km towards the Río Cauca, is **Marsella**, and the **Alexander von Humboldt Gardens**, a carefully maintained botanical display with cobbled paths and bamboo bridges. Just outside the town is the **Ecohotel Los Lagos** ① *T368 5298, www.ecohotelloslagos.com*, previously a gold mine, then a coffee hacienda, and now restored as a hotel (**B**) and nature park with lakes.

Parque Ucumari
① *Park office T325 4781, open daily for good information.*
From Pereira it is possible to visit the beautiful Parque Ucumari. If you're just visiting for the day and not staying overnight, entrance is free. It's one of the few places where the Andean spectacled bear survives. From Pereria, a *chiva* leaves daily (0900, 1500, more frequently during high season) with **Transporte Florida** from Calle 12, No 9-40 to the village of **El Cedral**. From El Cedral it is a two or 2½-hour walk to **La Pastora**, the park visitor centre and refuge. There is excellent camping, US$2.50 per person or US$8.50 at a refuge, meals extra. From La Pastora it is a steep, rocky one- to two-day hike to **Laguna de Otún** through beautiful scenery of changing vegetation. The **Otún Quimbaya Flora and Fauna Sanctuary** forms a biological corridor between Ucumari and Los Nevados; it protects the last remaining area of Andean tropical forest in Risaralda. There are marked paths as well as *cabaña* accommodation, camping and meals available.

Pereira to Armenia

Along the road from Pereira to Armenia are some pleasant places to eat, art galleries and craft centres. This is the heart of the Zona Cafetera. The coffee grows here up to about 2000 m, above which is forest providing some communities with wood products as a livelihood. One such place is **Filandia**, a pleasant village 7 km off the main road, which has excellent examples of *paisa* architecture with doorways, windows and balconies painted in primary colours. Unhappily, fire destroyed a corner of the town near the central plaza in 1996, but the unusual grey and white **Iglesia de la Inmaculada Concepción**, dating from 1892, was not harmed.

Founded in 1878 by colonizers from Antioquia it is rumoured that its name was supposed to be a reference to the Nordic country Finland (Finlandia in Spanish), but this was misspelt as Filandia. The village was used for the popular local *telenovela* – TV soap – called *Café con Aroma de Mujer*. Baskets for coffee picking and many other uses are made here. Because it is higher than the land to the east, there are splendid views of the evados, especially dramatic if the weather is unsettled, and if there has been a recent storm, you may well see snow on the mountains well below the normal permanent snowline of about 4800 m. A **mirador** ① *1000-2100, US$1.60*, has been constructed recently next to the cemetery, 1 km from the Parque Principal, a bit of an architectural disaster made from mangrove wood imported from San Bernardo del Viento, but which nonetheless has expansive views of Pereira, Armenia, Cartago and Quimbaya.

There are frequent buses from Pereira and Armenia, though none direct from Salento; take a bus to Pereira and change at Las Cruces on the main Pereira–Armenia highway.

Salento → *For listings, see pages 270-282. Phone code: 6. Population: 9400 Altitude: 1985 m.*

Well into the foothills of the Cordillera and on a promontory above the valleys that leads up to the Nevado de Tolima and Paramillo de Quindío, is the little town of Salento. The oldest settlement in Quindío, established on 5 January 1842 as the epicentre of the Antioquian colonization of the region, this used to be a sleepy village, but tourism has really taken off in recent years. The days when you could hear a dog's bark resonate across the valley and the greatest obstacle to a good night's sleep was an overenthusiastic cockerel are long gone. Although much busier than before, Salento is still a charming place, which has retained its village feel, even though there are now plenty of hostels, shops, bars and restaurants to choose from and it's firmly on the backpacker trail. It has some of the best examples of bahareque architecture of any town in the coffee region. On a clear day – especially in the mornings – you can see the snowy peaks of Los Nevados. It's also prone to a lot of rain, as evidenced by the

Salento

Sleeping 🛏
Balcones del Ayer **1**
Casa Alto del Coronel **2**
Hostal Ciudad
 de Segorbe **3**
Las Palmas **4**
Plantation House **5**
Posada del Angel **6**
Posada del Café **7**
Tralala Hostel **8**

Eating 🍴
Café Jesús Martín
 Bedoya **1**
El Rincón Campestre **3**
El Rincón de Lucy **2**

N
Not to scale

abundance of crops and flowers grown in the region, and it often has low-lying cloud that drape over the mountains like loosely flung scarves.

The main plaza is especially impressive with a curious grey and white church, **Nuestra Señora del Carmen**, which sets off the nature of the rest of the square's architecture.

From the plaza, a walk up the Calle Real (Carrera 6), which has further beautiful examples of post-colonial architecture, the street leads to a 250-step climb, with the 14 stations of the cross to measure your progress, to an outstanding viewpoint overlooking the upper reaches of the Quindío and Cardenas rivers known as the Cocora valley. A military guard is usually stationed at the top. To the west many kilometres of the Cordillera Occidental can be seen. This is some of the finest countryside and mountain views in Colombia. It is a popular weekend resort for Colombians for walking, riding and trekking but quieter during the week. The local fiestas are held in the first week of January.

Tourist information **Alcaldía de Salento** ① *Parque Principal, T759 3183.* Tour operator Ecoaventuras Cocorá Extremo ① *C6 4-34, T313 263804. www.ecoaventurascocora extremo.com, open daily 0800-2000,* also offers free tourist information as well as their own tours and sell an excellent map of the area for US$3. **Plantation House** is another excellent resource for information.

Valle de Cocora

Above Salento is the Cocora valley, part of the upper reaches of the Río Quindío. This fertile valley has an enchanting landscape of pines and eucalyptus towered over by the famous wax palms, Colombia's national tree. It makes for an extraordinary sight, the palms looming over the valley like sentinels on guard. With the crystal-clear waters of the Río Quindío, rich in freshwater trout, dissecting the valley, this beautiful spot has some breathtaking walks.

Getting there The centre of the valley (known as 'Cocorá') is 12 km up from Salento along a rough track. Jeeps from Salento's plaza take about 35 minutes (US$1.50, Monday-Friday 0610, 0730, 0930, 1130, 1600; last return 1700; Saturday-Sunday, 10 departures, last return 1800). Jeeps also leave when there are eight people waiting or someone willing to pay for eight people.

It is possible to hire a jeep (one way 24,000 pesos or 3000 pesos per person, whichever is the greater). You can arrange with the driver to collect you (same price).

About 5 km beyond Cocora is the **Acaime Natural Reserve**, at 2770 m, a 2½-hour walk, with a visitor centre, ponies for hire, accommodation for 20, US$5.50 per person, and a small restaurant. This is the most important wax palm zone in Colombia, one of the reasons for the many varieties of humming birds, parrots, toucans and other wild life that can be seen feeding on the fruit of the palm.

A little before Acaime is **Finca La Montaña**, the end of the vehicular track, where there is a nursery for the wax palm. It is overlooked by Morro Gacho (see below). Jeeps take 20 minutes from Cocora, and the remaining 2 km to Acaime is a steep walk down across the infant Río Quindío and up the other side; approximately one hour.

Above Acaime there are many trails into the high mountains. Day trips include **Cerro Morro Gacho**, 3450 m and **Alto El Español**, 3600 m, both steep walks through the forest of the Natural Reserve. The trip to **Paramillo del Quindío**, 4700 m, one of the principal mountains of Los Nevados, takes three to four days, via **Finca Argentina** (3400 m, private *finca*, camping) and a total of 12 hours' ascent from Cocora to the top. This is an exposed rocky summit but not technically difficult. There are the remnants of a crater on the summit and climbers occasionally pitch their tents here on the grey/yellow sand. There are other *fincas*/camping sites that can be used on this trip.

Nevado del Tolima

The ascent of Nevado del Tolima (5221 m), normally takes three days up, staying at **Finca Primavera** (3680 m), and a two-day descent. This area is known as the Valley of the Lost as it is easy to wander off the track. It is best to call ahead to Finca Primavera and request a guide (US$8-14) to shepherd you through this section. Again there are variants, including camping at **Laguna El Encanto** midway between Tolima and Quindío, from which both can be climbed. You will need snow equipment for Tolima, ice axe and crampons recommended, but this too is not difficult.

The whole upland area is subject to wide temperature changes during the day depending on cloud cover and very cold nights. Route finding in this featureless country can be especially difficult in mist and guides are strongly recommended.

Details of what is available, prearranging places to stay, guides, transport, etc can be found in Salento. Guides cost around US$50 per day, mules US$25 per day.

Armenia

→ For listings, see pages 270-282. Colour map 2, C3. Phone code: 6. Population: 324,500. Altitude 1838 m.

Armenia, capital of Quindío Department, was named in memory of the massacres that took place in Armenia by Turkish Ottomans in the 19th century. Armenia, Colombia also has a tragic recent past. It has been affected by some of the worst earthquakes in the area, with that of January 1999 being particularly devastating. Most buildings in the centre of the city were damaged; about 30% were destroyed.

In spite of this, Armenia is a busy place, more so than both Pereira and Manizales. The Rodrigo Arenas Betancur **Monumento al Esfuerzo** in the Plaza de Bolívar poignantly portrays the present attitude of the local population. New construction is of high quality and hotels and restaurants are fresh and comfortable.

Armenia

To ❷❶❷❸❹❺❻❾,
Museo Quimbaya & Pereira

Parque Sucré

San Francisco

Plaza de Mercado

To Calarcá & Bogotá

Cathedral

Plaza de Bolívar

Parque Cafetero

To ❾ ❿, Bus Station (7 blocks) & Airport

To Cali

Parque Uribe Uribe

N

200 metres
200 yards

Sleeping
Armenia 2
Bolívar Plaza 3
Café Real 5
Centenario 6
Finca Los Alamos 9
Hacienda Bambusa 10

Imperial 7
Zuldemayda 8

Eating
Anis 1
Café Quindío 2
Donde Nelson 3
El Rancho Argentino 4
Keizaki 5
La Fogata 6
La Fonda Antioqueña 7
La Puerta Quindiana 8
Natural Food Plaza 9

The surrounding Quindío countryside is a major coffee zone, and the slopes of the Cordillera here are home to the wax palm (see under Salento, page 265). Armenia, founded in 1889, suffers when international coffee prices fall and they have been low since the mid-1990s, but this is an enterprising sector of Colombia and you will see many new and different agricultural crops and activities developing. One of particular interest is the opening of many fine *fincas* to visitors for holidays; see box, page 255.

Ins and outs

Getting there To Bogotá, several flights daily with **Avianca**, **easyfly** and **Aires**. **Aires** and **easyfly** also fly to Medellín. Comprehensive bus services run to Armenia from major Colombian cities. The bus station is at Carrera 20, Calle 35, south of the city. www.terminalarmenia.com.

Getting around The interesting part of the city is within walking distance of the Plaza de Bolívar. There are important attractions in Quindío outside the city for which buses, taxis, tours or your own transport will be required.

Tourist information

Fondo Mixto de Promoción del Quindío ① *C 20, No 13-22, T741 7700, www.turismo cafeyquindio.com*. **Corporación Autónoma Regional de Quindío (CRQ)** ① *C 19N, No 19-55, T746 0600, www.crq.gov.co*, for information on parks and natural reserves. Also Corporación de Cultura y Turismo ① *Centro Administrativo Municipal CAM, p 4, T741 2991, www.armeniainolvidable.com*. For maps and information, **Instituto Geográfico Agustín Codazzi** ① *Cra 17, No 19-29, piso 2, www.igac.gov.co, open Mon-Fri 0730-1130, 1400-1630*.

Sights

The central square, **Plaza de Bolívar**, has a fountain and two bronze sculptures, a conventional Bolívar by Roberto Henau Buritacá, and a fine example of Rodrigo Arenas Betancur's work, the *Monumento al Esfuerzo*. The plaza has lost many of the surrounding buildings including part of the Quindío administration building (services relocated to the outskirts of the city). The striking modern **cathedral** was badly damaged but has been faithfully restored to its former triangular shape. Inside, the nave continues the form and leaves a light airy feeling, accentuated by the fine modern stained glass. There is also an impressive bronze figure of Christ. Well worth a visit. Also of interest is the **San Francisco church**, with some notable stained-glass windows that overlook the market, covering four blocks in the centre of the city. There are many stalls of local *artesanía*, basket work is a local speciality, good prices. **Parque Sucre** is a colourful square with an ancient *ceiba* tree and a bust of Marshal Ayacucho. To the south in the oldest part of the city is **Parque Uribe Uribe** where concerts are held from time to time. Carrera 14, from Plaza Bolívar to Parque Sucre, has been pedestrianized.

Museo del Oro Quimbaya ① *Av Bolívar, C 40 Norte 80, Tue-Sun, 1000-1700, free*, is worthwhile. In the north of the city, **Parque de la Vida** has bamboo structures, waterfalls and a lakeside theatre.

Parque Nacional del Café

Some 12 km northwest of Armenia is **Montenegro** (for Sleeping, see page 275) near which is the **Parque Nacional del Café** ① *1 km from Pueblo Tapao, T741 7417, www.parquenacionaldelcafe.com, in high season, daily 0900-1800, low season, Wed-Sun and public holidays, 0930-1800, general entrance, US$10, or US$17.50-25 for extra activities and rides, parking US$1; take a bus or colectivo (US$0.45) from Armenia to Montenegro and then a jeep marked 'Parque' (US$0.25) or taxi (US$2) to the entrance.* There are restaurants, a Juan Valdez coffee shop, a botanical garden, ecological walks, a Quimbaya cemetery, a tower with a fine view and an interesting museum which covers all aspects of coffee. A cableway links to a children's theme park (rollercoasters, water rides, etc).

Beyond Montenegro is **Quimbaya**, known for its **Festival of Light** (Fiesta de Velas y Faroles) in December each year. About 7 km away is the **Parque Nacional de la Cultura Agropecuaria (PANACA)** ① *T01-800 012 3999, Tue-Sun 0900-1800, US$17-26.50*, an educational theme park, with many varieties of horses (and a very good show/display), cattle and other animals. A good family outing.

Ibagué and around → *For listings, see pages 270-282. Colour map 2, C3. Phone code: 8.*
Population: 421,000. Altitude: 1248 m.

Ibagué, capital of Tolima Department, lies at the foot of the Quindío mountains. Parts of the town are old: see the **Colegio de San Simón** and the market (good *tamales*). The **Parque Centenario** is pleasant and there is a famous **Conservatory of Music**. Try the local alcoholic drink called *mistela*. **Tourist office** ① *Cra 3 between C 10 and 11, p 2, T262 5264, turismotolima@tolima.gov.co.*

Just outside town, on the Armenia road, a dirt road leads up the Río Combeima to El Silencio and the slopes of the Nevado del Tolima, the southernmost Nevado in the Parque Nacional Los Nevados. The climb to the summit (5221 m) takes two to three days', camping at least one night over 4000 m, ice equipment necessary. For safety reasons, it is recommended to visit the Nevado del Tolima only from Ibagué and not Manizales. A *lechero* (milk truck) leaves Ibagué marketplace for El Silencio between 0630 and 0730, US$2.50, two hours. A guide in Ibagué is **Maklin Muñoz** ① *Cra 1, No 5-24, T261 5865, 300-675 6216 (mob).*

Quindío Pass, 3350 m (known as La Línea after the power lines that cross the mountains) is on the Armenia–Ibagué road (105 km), across the Cordillera Central. On the east side of the Pass is **Cajamarca**, a friendly town in a beautiful setting at 1900 m. There's accommodation at **Residencia Central** (F) and **Nevado**, both on the same street. **Bar El Globo** is on the corner of the main plaza serves excellent coffee. Interesting market on Sunday.

Cartago → *For listings, see pages 270-282. Colour map 2, C3. Altitude: 920 m.*

From Pereira and Armenia roads run west to Cartago, at the northern end of the rich Cauca Valley, which stretches south for about 240 km but is little more than 30 km wide. The Pan-American highway goes south along this valley to Cali and Popayán, at the southern limit of the valley proper. There it mounts the high plateau between the Western and Central Cordilleras and goes through Ecuador.

Founded in 1540, Cartago, 25 km southwest of Pereira, still has some colonial buildings, particularly the very fine **Casa del Virrey** ① *C 13, No 4-29*, and the **cathedral**. Cartago is noted for its fine embroidered textiles.

⏱ La Zona Cafetera listings → *Phone code: 6 (unless otherwise indicated).*

For Sleeping and Eating price codes and other relevant information, see pages 23-28.

● Sleeping

Manizales *p252, map p253*

In Jan, during the Feria de Manizales, hotel prices are considerably increased.
AL Hotel Estelar Las Colinas, Cra 22, No 20-20, T884 2009, www.hotelesestelar.com. Part of the Estelar chain of hotels, Las Colinas has large rooms with cable TV and Wi-Fi. It also has a sauna. Rates almost 50% lower at weekends.
A Hotel Carretero, C 23, No 35A-31, T887 9190, www.hotelcarretero.com. Well placed, halfway between the centre and El Cable, the Carretero has a smart, glassy lobby and large, comfortable rooms. Breakfast is included in the price and it has Wi-Fi throughout as well as a sauna. Can also organize car hire.
A Hotel Escorial, C 21, No 21-11, T884 7696, www.hotelesmanizales.com. Smart hotel with good, clean rooms, including a junior suite and some 5-bedded rooms. Extra services include Wi-Fi, parking, cable TV and a restaurant serving local and international food. Breakfast is included in the price.
B Bolívar Plaza, C 22, No 22-40, T884 7777, bolivarplaza@hotmail.com. Just round the corner from Plaza Bolívar and the cathedral, this hotel has cable TV, Wi-Fi, laundry service and a restaurant.
B Roma Plaza, C 21, No 22-30, T884 7037, www.hotelesmanizales.com. Around the corner from the Bolívar Plaza with simple, clean rooms, cable TV, Wi-Fi, free local calls and breakfast included.
D Tama Internacional, C 23, No 22-43, T884 2124. Cavernous, Republican-era building off Plaza Bolívar with a popular

restaurant. Rooms are a little small and dark, but breakfast is included.

El Cable (Zona Rosa) and around
A Regine's Hotel, C 65A, No 23B-113, T887 5360, www.regineshotel.com. Located in a quiet suburban street behind El Cable, Regine's has good, clean rooms and computers for internet access, Wi-Fi, cable TV and laundry service. The free breakfast can be served in a small garden out the back where there are also some smaller, cheaper rooms. Lovely views and room 1 has a nice balcony. An excellent mid-range option. Recommended.
A Varuna, C 62, No 23C-18, T881 1122, www.varunahotel.com. The newest hotel in town, has a slick, minimal look and a good restaurant, Tabil, serving international food. The rooms are large and comfortable with hydro massage showers and Wi-Fi throughout. Recommended.
D-F Basecamp, Cra 23 32-20, T882 1699, www.basecamphostel.com. Perfectly situated new hostel, 2 mins' walk from the new cablecar station connecting the bus terminal with El Cable, American/Colombian run. Excellent facilities including personal kitchen lockers to store food, a rooftop terrace and bar with extensive views of Manizales and the surrounding countryside. The American owner has many years' experience of organizing volcano tours in Guatemala and runs unusual tours to Los Nevados nearby. Recommended.
D-F Manizales Hostel, C 66 23B-91, T887 0871, www.manizaleshostel.com. A sister hostel to **Mountain House** (see below), this is a recently opened Belgian/Colombian-run hostel, which offers a good introduction to Manizales and the region at check-in, including a 'What to do

Manizales' info sheet. There are dorms and private rooms, a nice patio for socializing, kitchen, internet (US$1 per hr) and Wi-Fi. Friendly and recommended.

D-F Mountain House, C 66, No 23B-137, T887 4736, www.mountainhouse manizales.com. One of few backpacker options in town, **Mountain House** is a suburban home with 5 private rooms and several 4-6 bed dorms with bunks. It has a pool table and a terraced garden with a BBQ, also offers use of a kitchen and access to an internet-enabled computer. There is Wi-Fi throughout, a cosy TV room, laundry service and the price includes breakfast of eggs on toast, free tea and coffee.

D-F Pitstop, C65 23B-19, T887 3797, www.pitstophostelmanizales.com. Irish-run, lively hostel, with 2 branches in Medellín. Offers everything you'd expect from a good hostel with added facilities, such as jacuzzi, TV room, Spanish lessons and an Irish bar open to the public. Rooms near the main road/above the bar can be a bit noisy.

Around Manizales p256

A Hacienda Normandia, Km 4 Antigua vía al Nevado, T310-202 0864. Beautifully kept hacienda with period furniture, on the way to Los Nevados National Park. A tranquil haven with manicured gardens and gorgeous views. Meals can be arranged, as well as horse riding, coffee tours and visits to the national park. Recommended.

B-E Hacienda Venecia, 3.5 km off the Chinchiná autopista, T320-636 5719, www.haciendavenecia.com. Delightful 4th-generation coffee *finca* with 2 different types of accommodation – guesthouse with private or shared rooms, or staying in the main *finca* itself, both include breakfast and have pools. Beautiful location and surroundings, attentive, English-speaking hosts, lunch and dinners can be arranged, as well as a number of tours. Highly recommended.

Supía p256

D El Diablito, C 18, No 6-10, T856 0504, www.fincahoteldiablito.com. A few blocks outside town, next to the bullring, this family-run *finca* has a large garden full of fruit trees and a lake with fish and turtles. It has good, comfortable rooms with cable TV and fans as well as a *cabaña* next to a swimming pool.

D Hotel Plazazul, Cra 9, No 34-15, T856 0176. This hotel is excellent value with very comfortable beds with crisp white sheets. It has a roof terrace with hammocks, a BBQ and great views of the hills as well as 2 computers for internet access. The suites, a little more expensive, have enormous jacuzzis.

D Hotel Premium Biss, Av Guayabal (Cra 10) No 29-65, T311-631 7032, www.hotelpremiumbiss.com. Another good-value new hotel with very clean rooms with a/c and cable TV. You pay a little more (**C**) for rooms with windows that look out onto the street.

F Hostal Santa Ana, C 34, No 6-28, T312-816 0661. This hostel, 1 block behind the Parque Principal, is very basic but has friendly staff and is housed in a beautiful colonial building.

Marmato p257

There is no accommodation available in Marmato but nearby Supía has several excellent options (see above).

Parque Nacional Los Nevados p259, map p259

A pp Cabañas el Cisne, comfortable, or camp outside (**G** pp). From here it is easy to reach Laguna Verde Encantada.

Camping Besides the Cabañas el Cisne and camping nearby there is no accommodation inside the park, so you will need to bring all equipment yourself. Temperature can drop below 0°C at night as most of the park lies above 3800 m.

Santa Rosa de Cabal *p261*

A Hotel Termales de Santa Rosa de Cabal, attached to the hot springs, T364 5500, www.termales.com.co. Comfortable, chalet style, with restaurant.

A-B Hacienda Guayabal, Km 3 Vía Chinchiná–Santa Rosa, T850 7831, www. haciendaguayabal.com. Working coffee *finca* 30 mins outside Manizales. Set in 64 ha of gorgeous rolling fields brimming with coffee plants well as a botanist's note- book full of flowers and trees. One of the best places to do a coffee tour in the region, guests can stay at the Londoño family home in private bedrooms or dorms. The price includes accommodation, 3 excellent home-cooked meals, a fine swimming pool and the tour. Coffee is free, of course (see box, page 255).

Pereira *p261, map p262*

L Hacienda San José, Entrada 16 cadena El Tigre, Km 4 Vía Pereira–Cerritos, T313 2612, www.haciendahotelsanjose.com. Breakfast included. One of the oldest houses in the region, this *bahereque* hacienda built by Franciso Mejía Jaramillo in 1888 is simply breathtaking. Today it is run as a hotel and almost all of the features have been pain-stakingly preserved. Popular activities include horse riding through sugarcane, coffee and livestock fields and visits to one of the largest bamboo reserves in the region and a trapiche where you can see how *panela*, unrefined sugarcane, is processed (see box, page 255).

L Hotel de Pereira, Cra 13N, No 15-73, T311 3333, www.hoteldepereira.com. Pereira's grandest hotel with a spacious lobby and excellent service. Well located 3 blocks from the centre, it has good rooms with plasma TVs, Wi-Fi and a great pool. It has a travel agency within the building and a sauna, gym and Turkish bath. Discounts available at weekends.

AL San Simón, C 19 7-41, T333 4595, www.hotelsansimon.com. One of the most central hotels available, with a cool, suave and trendy look. Healthy food served in sleek restaurant.

AL Soratama, Cra 7, No 19-20, T335 8650, www.hotelsoratama.com. Recently refurbished hotel on the Plaza Bolívar with helpful staff and lots of services available, including parking, free local calls, Wi-Fi, massage therapist, new spa and an internet room. Breakfast included. Discounts available at the weekend.

B Hotel Condina, C 18 6-26, T333 4484, www.hotelcondina.com. New hotel with a/c or fan, Wi-Fi, minibar, and TV. Price includes breakfast and parking.

C Hotel Cataluña, C 19, No 8-61, T335 4527. The Cataluña has clean and airy rooms with balconies and private bathrooms with hot water. Brand new plasma-screen TVs and a popular restaurant serving fixed meals for US$2.50, it's good value for money.

C Hotel Colonial, C 17, No 5-50, T333 7206, www.hotelcolonialpereira.blogspot.com. Hotel with clean rooms and good security, though none have windows.

D Hotel Royal, C 16, No 5-78, T335 2501, hotelroyal@yahoo.com. Near the Plaza Bolívar, this hotel has clean, basic rooms with cable TV.

D-F Sweet Home, Cra 11 44-30, T345 4453, www.sweethomehostel.com. Pereira's only backpackers' hostel. Slightly out of town, but worth the trek. 3 dorms, 1 private room, use of kitchen, Wi-Fi, hot water and all-day breakfast. Handy for the airport. Recommended.

Around Armenia *p264*

AL-A Castilla Casa de Huéspedes, Km 10 Vía Pereira–Cerritos, T01800-123470, www.loshotelesconencanto.com. Beautiful colonial hotel with pool and gardens. Wi-Fi available.

Pereira to Armenia *p264*

B-D La Posada del Compadre, Cra 6, No 8-06, Filandia, T313 33597, www.laposada delcompadre.com. This beautifully preserved *paisa* building has several good rooms of variable price depending on size and a gorgeous terrace with fine views out toward alento. All rooms have en suite bathrooms that jar a bit with the rest of the architecture. Cable TV and breakfast included. Recommended.

C Hostal Tibouchina, C 6, No 5-05, T758 2646, Filandia. Fine old hostel on the corner of the plaza with a beautiful gallery looking out on the street. Comfortable, wooden panelled rooms with private bathrooms, cable TV and breakfast included.

D-F Cabaña del Recuerdo, Km 5 Vía Filandia–Montenegro, T311-628 5149, reservaselrecuerdo@hotmail.com. A few kilometres outside Filandia, this chalet on a Colombian family's *finca* is surrounded by banana and coffee plantations. It has a swimming pool, ping pong table and great walks in a *guadua* bamboo forest with a swimming hole in its midst. Free pick up from Filandia with enough forewarning.

Salento *p265, map p265*

B Casa Alto del Coronel, Cra 2, corner of C 7, T759 3760, www.casahotelaltodel coronel.com. Obscured by bushes of bougainvillea, this *bahareque* house has beautifully kept gardens and a summer house with fine views over the town and surrounding area. The 4 rooms are good if a bit heavy on the floral wallpaper. Breakfast is included. Also possible to rent the whole house for larger parties.

B Posada del Café, Cra 6, No 3-08, T759 3012, www.laposadadelcafe.webs.com. This traditional house has rooms set around a beautiful garden brimming with flowers. The rooms are nicely decorated and there is a larger family room for 5. Friendly, English-speaking owner. Recommended.

C Balcones del Ayer, C 6, No 5-40, T759 3273. Great position half a block from the plaza, recently expanded with improved rooms and facilities. Most rooms have balconies with lovely views, private bath, hot water, parking and cable TV. Friendly and family-run with good restaurant attached. Recommended.

C Posada del Angel, C 6, No 7-47, T759 3507. Sweet little place with clean rooms and great balcony with fine views. Cheaper midweek (**D**).

C-E Hostal Ciudad de Segorbe, C 5 4-06, T320-283 6973, www.hostalciudadde segorbe.com. Friendly hostel not far from the main square. Rooms all have private bathrooms, including the spacious dorm. Music, TV and reading room, breakfast included and there is 1 room with disability access. Recommended.

D-E Las Palmas, C 6, No 3-02, T759 3065. This small, traditional hostel has 8 comfortable rooms with en suite bathrooms and hot water. With a kitchen available and cable TV as well as a roof terrace with a table and chairs it represents good value for money. Internet available 30 mins at a time.

D-F Camping Monteroca, Km 4 Vía Pereira–Salento, T315-413 6862 (mob), www.campingmonteroca.com. Sitting at the bottom of the hill next to the Río Quindío, Camping Monteroca offers something a little different. Owner Jorge has run the site for 12 years and knows the area, its history and wildlife well. The place is well maintained with clean bathrooms, showers, a communal cooking area and TV lounge. There is an eclectic museum filled with fossils and meteorites as well as a room dedicated to Simón Bolívar, who is reported to have stayed a night there. There's also a serpentarium. While the normal campsite, housing 200, is fine, what makes this place special are the themed cabins. Among others, you can sleep in your own jungle tree house, a safari cabin or step into the Hippie Hilton, going back to the 60s, where the 'welcome cocktail' reputedly is something 'more smoky'. Both this and the American cabin, have waterbeds and there is a jacuzzi nearby. All cabins offer good privacy, a stove and hot showers.

D-F The Plantation House, C 7, No 1-04, T316-285 2603, www.theplantationhouse salento.com. The pioneer among the backpackers' hostel, now has 2 houses, a number of private bedrooms and several dorms with bunks. This traditional *bahareque* house has fine views, they rent out bikes and there is free internet in reception (1 computer). English owners Tim and his Colombian wife, Cris, have the best information in town on the local area and also have a coffee plantation to which they offer tours. Pick up from airports can be arranged for a fee with advanced warning. Recommended.

D-F Tralala Hostel, Cra 7 6-45, T314-850 5543, www.hosteltralalasalento.com. New, Dutch-run hostel with dormitories, as well as 3 private rooms (one with bathroom), 2 kitchens, laundry service, hot water and Wi-Fi. Cosy DVD/reading room, great views, Wellington boot hire. Recommended.

Valle de Cocora p264

B Las Palmas de Cocora, Km 10 Vía al Valle de Cocora, T310-455 6070, www.laspalmasdecocora.com. Wooden, 2-storey chalet with comforable rooms. Each of the 2 rooms has space for more, with various bunk beds, but they will rent to couples if you want. Also has a restaurant serving trout (¶). Horses for hire (US$5.50 per hr, guide US$5.50 per hr).

C-E Bosques de Cocora, Km 11 Vía Cocora, T312-721 5087,www.bosquesdecocora.com. Offers accommodation at nearby *finca*, as well as camping next to the restaurant. Hires out tents, mattresses, sheets, blankets and pillows. Shower facilities and free coffee and hot chocolate offered. Good restaurant. Try the *canelazo* to warm up – *agua de panela* with cinnamon.

E Finca San José, Km 11 Vía Cocora, T310-0227 5091 (Mariela Pérez in Armenia). **Finca San José** is a 100-year-old farm, which sits above the hamlet of Cocora. With basic but characterful rooms and a delightful veranda with shuttered windows opening up onto spectacular vistas, this is an excellent place to stay while hiking the hills of the Cocora Valley.

Armenia p267, map p267

AL Armenia, Av Bolívar, No 8N-67, T746 0099, www.armeniahotelsa.com. Impressive

hotel in the northern part of Armenia. It has a cavernous lobby and enormous rooms with beds made from *guadua* bamboo as well as all the usual services expected from an international hotel – sauna, gym, swimming pool, Wi-Fi and a restaurant with Chilean and Argentine wines. Opposite is the Parque de la Vida, a verdant space with waterfalls. Discounts available at weekends. English spoken.

AL Hacienda Bambusa, vía El Caimo–Portugalito Km 93, T311-506 9915, www.haciendabambusa.com. Not strictly a coffee *finca* – this enchanting traditional hacienda sits hidden in a labyrinth of banana plantations – but the 160 ha are so beautiful that visitors are unlikely to be bothered by such details. This is very much a place to relax but there are plenty of activities for the restless, including canopying in a bamboo forest, horse riding, birdwatching or simply relaxing by the majestic pool. Has cable TV, restaurant and free pick up from airport or bus station (see box, page 255).

A Bolívar Plaza, C 21, No 14-17, T741 0083, www.bolivarplaza.com. Just off the Plaza Bolívar, this hotel's rooms are a bit dark and musty, though they do have large beds. It also has parking, Wi-Fi and an internet room, free local calls and breakfast included.

A Centenario, C 21, No 18-20, T744 3143, www.hotelcentenario.com. Modern hotel with airy, bright rooms and attentive staff. Has Wi-Fi throughout and a small internet room as well as cable TV, parking and breakfast included.

A Finca Los Alamos, Km 3 Vía nueva al Caimo, T746 6129, www.fincalosalamosquindio.com. Traditional house with simple, tasteful rooms and a large veranda. Set in landscaped gardens surrounded by banana plantations and with a good pool, the only downside is its proximity to a major road.

A Zuldemayda, C 20, No 15-38, T741 0580, hzuldemayda@telecom.com.co. Popular business hotel with facilities such as Wi-Fi, internet room and parking. Breakfast included.

Café Real, Cra 18, No 21-32, T744 3055, www.hotelcafereal.com. Modern hotel with bright but slightly pokey rooms. Has sauna, gym, Turkish bath and jacuzzi, Wi-Fi and breakfast included in the price.

Café Plaza, Cra 18, No 18-09, T741 1500, hotelcafeplaza@hotmail.com. Near the Plaza Bolívar, this hotel is a little noisy but has simple but clean rooms with en suite bathrooms, cable TV and breakfast included.

E Imperial, C 21, No 17-43, T744 9151. This hotel has basic but clean rooms with cable TV and good security. No hot water, however.

F Alferez, Cra 17, No 17-47, T7443 4096. Hotel with very basic rooms but nonetheless secure and with TV and laundry service.

Parque Nacional del Café *p269*
Montenegro

A Hotel del Campo, Km 7 contiguo a Panaca, T741 5222, www.hoteldelcampo.com.co. Set on the lip of a steep valley surrounded by banana, yucca and alfalfa plantations, this hotel is ideally located just 500 m from the Panaca park. It has good rooms with interesting bathrooms and a kidney-shaped pool. It has Wi-Fi in reception and a restaurant.

A-B Casa de Campo El Delirio, Km 1 Vía Montenegro–Parque del Café, T744 9955, casadelirio@hotmail.com. This beautiful, traditional *finca* has been restored with immaculate taste with original mahogany furniture, wrought-iron beds and black-and-white photographs of bullfighters. It's a perfect place to unwind, boasting a pool, large gardens with a coffee plantation at the bottom and delicious home-cooked food (see box, page 255).

Quimbaya

A Finca Villa Nora, vereda La Granja, Km 1 Carretera Antigua vía Quimbaya–Montenegro, T741 5472, www.quindiofinca villanora.com. The rooms all have the same fittings as they would have when Antioquian settlers built it in the 19th century and its spacious veranda is decorated with original

Quimbaya artefacts. It has an excellent kitchen serving up home-cooked food and a pleasant pool for relaxing after a tour of its working coffee farm. Also has Wi-Fi (see box, page 255).

B Hostería Mi Monaco, Km 7 Vía Armenia–Pueblo Tapao, T310-374 5643, www.mimonaco.net. On the side of a hill with a bamboo copse that plunges down to a stream, **Mi Monaco** has comfortable rooms with crisp, white sheets in a traditional 60-year-old *bahareque* house. With a good pool, jacuzzi, and professional mountain bike guides, it's an excellent place to relax.

C El Carriel, Km 1 Vía Quimbaya–Filandia, T746 3612, elcarriel@hotmail.com. This is an excellent option if you are looking for an economic way to stay on a working coffee *finca*. The rooms are simple but comfortable with private bathrooms and hot water and a good little restaurant, all in a traditional house. There's an excellent coffee tour in which you are encouraged to pick coffee grains and follow the whole coffee-making process from plant to cup (see box, page 255).

Ibagué and around *p269*

A Ambalá, C 11, No 2-60, T2613888, www.hotelambala.com. Business hotel, includes breakfast, and has rooms with TV, a pool, sauna, parking, and a restaurant.

F Sandremo, C 16, No 2-88, T8-261 3339. Rooms with fan and TV.

Cartago *p269*

Many hotels in area around bus terminals (Cra 9) and railway station (Cra 9 y C 6).

C Don Gregorio, Cra 5, No 9-59, T211 5111, www.hoteldongregorio.net. Rooms with a/c (cheaper with fan). Also has pool, sauna and includes breakfast.

F Río Pul, Diag 3, No 2-142, T211 0623. Rooms with fan, private bathroom and TV. Recommended.

❶ Eating

Manizales *p252, map p253*
Apart from the hotels, the best restaurants are on or near Cra 23 in **El Cable** (**La Zona Rosa**) and **Barrio Milán** the east part of the city.
️️️️-️️️ Bologninis, C 77 21-116.
Italo-Argentine restaurant with good pasta, good steak and good wines.
️️️ Spago, C 59 24A-10 Local 1. Tasty Italian food and a good variety of pastas.
️️️ Valentino, Cra 23 63-128. Gourmet dining with artisan chocolates for dessert. Turns into a late-night spot with excellent cocktails, open until 0200.
️️️-️ El Zaguán Paisa, Cra 23 31-27 (almost directly opposite the new cablecar station). You enter this cosy, reasonably priced restaurant through a long bamboo corridor (hence the name). Typical Caldense dishes, *bandeja paisa* and a set lunch menu for US$2.50.
️ Benigno, C 63 23C-68. European-style deli with many Colombian twists.
️ Don Juaco Snaks, C 65A, No 23A-44. Sandwiches and burgers as well as typical dishes such as *ajiaco* and *mondongo*.
️ La Ricura, C 62 24-38 and Cra 23 63-122A. The best spot for breakfast *buñuelos* and fresh juices, with 2 outlets.
️ Las Cuatro Estaciones, C 65, No 23A-32. Good selection of pastas and pizzas. Be sure to order big as helping can be a bit small.
️ Il Forno, Cra 23, No 73-86. Italian restaurant in pleasant surroundings serving pastas, pizzas and salads. Good vegetarian options.
️ Juan Valdez, Cra 23, No 64-55. Part of the ubiquitous coffee chain, this one is in a good position next to the old cablecar line, has free Wi-Fi.
️ Pollos Asados Mario, C23 Cra 22 (corner). Traditional Colombian *asadero* with the best rotisserie chicken in downtown. Also does burgers and steaks.
️ Frisby, Cra 23 23-01. Colombian chain of fried chicken, a la Kentucky and other meat dishes.

Supía *p256*
There are several good places to eat on the Parque Principal.
️ La Casona, Cra 6, No 33-36, good *bandejas* in pleasant surroundings.
La Cabaña de los Dulces, Cra 9, No 30-38. Sample some of the town's varieties of sweets such as *colación* and *blanqueados*.

Marmato *p257*
There is a small restaurant in the plaza opposite the church, serving whatever is available.

Santa Rosa de Cabal and around *p261*
️️️ Punta de Anca, on the Autopista de Café, 3 km from Chinchiná. Worth the trip for the excellent cuts of meat and a hearty *bandeja paisa*.

Pereira *p261, map p262*
️️️ Mediterráneo, Av Circunvalar, No 4-47. Steaks, seafood, fondus and crêpes in a relaxed atmosphere on an open terrace.
️️️-️ Pasaje de la Alcaldía, is a narrow alleyway next to the Alcaldía with a number of cheap eating options including French, Italian, Colombian and a few cafés.
️ Delight, Cra 16, No 4B-35. Popular upmarket canteen serving *sancocho*, *sobrebarriga* and other typical dishes.
️ El Aperitivo Paisa, C 17, No 7-62. Typical regional food served on a 2nd-floor terrace decorated with antiques.
️ El Gran Sazón, Cra 5, No 16-52. Cheap-as-chips canteen serving typical dishes for just over US$2.
️ La Jarra, Cra 7 18-12. Fresh fruit juice place with simple snacks. The juices are served *con ñapa* – ie with an extra top-up free of charge – and there are 2 more outlets of this popular juice bar in the centre.

Salento *p265, map p265*
Salento has an increasing variety of restaurants. Make sure you try the local speciality, trout.

Balcones del Ayer, C 6 5-40 (see Sleeping). Hotel restaurant specializing in trout and meat dishes. Family-run and friendly and is the only restaurant in Salento with disability access.

El Rincón Campestre, Mirador de Salento. Just outside Salento, at the top of the lookout point, this restaurant is a treat. Although specializing in trout, they also do excellent meat, which makes a nice change.

Café Jesús Martín Bedoya, Cra 6 6-14. Excellent little café with their own coffee from Señor Bedoya's father's *finca* (see also tours, page 279).

El Rincón de Lucy, Cra 6 4-02. Lovely little eatery with good breakfasts and economical dishes typical of the region.

Armenia *p267, map p267*

Café Quindío, Cra 19, No 33N-41. Gourmet coffee shop and restaurant, serving recipes such as chicken or steak in coffee sauce as well as international dishes (Thai, French, Italian). This popular café next to Parque de la Vida also sells coffee products from its own farm and even has a school where you can learn about all aspects of coffee. The menu includes 29 varieties of coffee.

El Rancho Argentino, Av Bolívar, No 13N-57. Another popular restaurant in the fashionable northern part of Armenia, this restaurant serves mainly *parrillas* but pastas too.

Keizaki, Cra 13, No 8N-39. Relatively new restaurant serving sushi and other Asian dishes. There are several other good restaurants on the same block.

La Fogata, Cra 13, No 14N-47. One of Armenia's most popular high-end restaurants, La Fogata serves all sorts of cuts of thick, juicy steaks as well as pork chops and typical dishes like *ajiaco*.

Anis, C 10N, No 13-94. This excellent little restaurant has a varied menu cooked to a high standard and with good presentation. The steaks are thick and cooked to perfection while it also offers salads, sandwiches, crêpes and other

brunch options. It has a pleasant sunny patio with a wood-fired oven and even makes its own pasta. Recommended.

Donde Nelson, Cra 13 with C 15. Family-run hole-in-the-wall, popular with locals, serving *almuerzo ejecutivo* for US$3.50.

La Fonda Antioqueña, Cra 13, No 18-59. Pleasant *paisa* restaurant on a 2nd floor gallery festooned with antiques. Serves the usual dishes such as *bandeja paisa*, etc. Open till 1900.

La Puerta Quindiana, C 17, No 15-40. This restaurant serves cheap *comida corriente* for US$3 with dishes such as *sancocho* a speciality, as well as good fruit juices.

Natural Food Plaza, Cra 14, No 18N-40. Vegetarian restaurant with a varied menu that includes veggie burgers, crêpes, salads, Mexican, *tamales* and fruit juices. Also has a wholefood shop. A lunchtime *menú ejecutivo* is US$3.75.

Ibagué and around *p269*

El Fogón Antioqueño, Cra 6, No 26-03. Good local dishes.

La Vieja Enramada, Cra 8, No 15-03. Local and international dishes.

Bars and clubs

Manizales *p252, map p253*

Most night clubs have a cover charge of between US$2.50 and US$5 per person, some include a few free drinks. Most clubs don't get going until 2300 or later. Manizales' Zona Rosa is in **El Cable**, which is centred around the old cable car station on Cra 23.

For a more rough-and-ready Colombian experience, the area of **Alta Tablazo** is worth a visit (best reached by taxi US$4). This is where many locals gather at the weekends for a beer, a dance and very occasionally a brawl. The views around here are also stunning with Manizales lit up below – beware of steep *quebradas* nearby and go easy on the fire water.

El Cable

Bar La Plaza, Cra 23B 64-80, local 1. Playing pop and rock, this bar also does deli platters and substantial (2 litres) jugs of sangría. Open Mon-Thu until 0100, Fri and Sat until 0200.

Juan Sebastián Bar (JSB), Cra 23 63-66. Plays jazz, blues, Brazilian and Cuban rhythms. Open Mon-Sat 1900-0200. Good margaritas and dry martinis.

Salsoteca Yare, Cra 23 62-57, www.yaresalsoteca.com. New salsa club, no cover charge. Open Thu 2100-0100 and Fri 2100-0200.

Barrio Milán

The 2nd nightlife area, a little smaller and a taxi ride from Cable Plaza, is Barrio Milán. All bars are open until late.

Bar Aguila, the biggest bar in Milán and very popular with students. Open Thu-Sat and plays mostly Latin music. It's mostly outside, so bring a coat.

Bar Babylon Cocktail, C 77, No 17-55, at the top end of Milán. Small, local video bar playing a mix of western and Latin music, owner Adolfo speaks a little English.

Son de Milan, a *salsateca*.

⊕ Entertainment

Manizales *p252, map p253*
Cinema
Cable Plaza Cinema in El Cable has all the latest releases but few films in English.
Centro Cultural y Convenciones los Fundadores, Cra 22 with C 33, www.cclos fundadores.com, has an interesting carved-wood mural by Guillermo Botero, who also has murals in the Club Manizales, Hotel Las Colinas. Events held here and at other locations during Jazz and Theatre Festival in Sep/Oct.
Universidad Nacional, free films on Tue and Thu.

Pereira *p261, map p262*
Cinema
Several cinema complexes within 2 blocks of Plaza de Bolívar.

Theatre
Teatro Comfamiliar, Cra 5/C 22, www.comfamiliar.com, cultural activities.
Teatro Municipal Santiago Londoño, Centro Comercial Fiducentro, Av 30 de Agosto/C 19, T335 7724, major stage productions.

⊛ Festivals and events

Manizales *p252, map p253*
Early Jan Feria de Manizales, includes a coffee festival, bullfights, beauty pageants and folk dancing as well as general partying.

Pereira *p261, map p262*
Aug Fiestas de la Cosecha (Harvest Festival).
Late Oct Feria Gastronómica (Food Fair).

Ibagué and around *p269*
Jun The National Folklore Festival.
24 Jun San Juan; and **29 Jun** San Pedro y San Pablo, both commemorated by the departments of Tolima and Huila with bullfights, fireworks, and music.
Dec Biannual choral festivals.

⊙ Shopping

Manizales *p252, map p253*
Cable Plaza Av Santander Cra 23 No 65-11, www.cableplaza.com.co, in El Cable for more expensive shops or **Centro Comercial de Parque Caldas**, Cra 22 No 29-29, for cheaper shopping.

▲ Activities and tours

Manizales *p252, map p253*

Colombia57, local office number ++(57)
6 886 8050 or 0800-078 9157 (UK freephone),
ex-pats Simon Locke, Russell Coleman,
Brendan Rayment and team organize tailor-
made trips for individuals or groups around
the coffee zone and the rest of Colombia.
Well-organized, thoroughly researched with
a commitment to sustainability and quality.
Highly recommended.

O.X. Expeditions, based at Basecamp Hostel
(see page 270) www.oxexpeditions.com are
just starting up a series of adventure and
activity tours around Los Nevados national
park and in other areas of Colombia.
The manager has years of volcano tours
experience from Guatemala. Also does
bike tours.

Marmato *p257*

Marmato is not a village geared towards
tourism. There is little infrastructure and
it is a difficult place to reach. The locals,
however, are friendly and helpful.
Colombia57, see above, can arrange tours
to Marmato from Manizales, providing
transport and knowledgeable local guides.

Parque Nacional Los Nevados *p258*

De Una, based in Bogotá, www.deuna
colombia.com. Organize several treks.

Pereira *p261, map p262*

D'p@seo, Cra 13, No 13-69, piso 2, T334 9883,
www.dpaseo.com. Opposite **Hotel Pereira**.
Arranges weekend trips to Los Nevados, trips
on Río la Vieja. Mon-Sat 0800-1200, 1400-1900.

Salento and around *p265, map p265*

Aldea del Artesano, book through Alejandro,
T320-782 9128, aldeadelartesano@ gmail.com.
This community of 19 families of artisans live
on the outskirts of Salento in 4 large houses,
each family practising a number of crafts. The
community project has only recently started
offering courses in a number of different crafts

on a 1-hr, half-day or full-day basis. You can try
your hand at bamboo craft, candle-making,
gardening, jewellery-making and much more.
If you opt for a full-day course, lunch, cooked in
the outdoor community kitchen, is included.
There is also a small outlet to buy some of the
handicrafts – **Xue Arte y Luz**, run by the
inspiring Janneth. Highly recommended.

Ecoaventuras Cocóra Extremo, C6 4-34,
T313-263804. www.ecoaventurascocora
extremo.com. Tours of the area and
extreme sports.

Jesús Bedoya, Cra 6, No 6-14 (coffee shop),
T316-620 7760, www.cafejesusmartin.com.
1-hr tours of local coffee roasting factory,
Mon-Wed any time between 0800-1000,
but tours can also be arranged at other times,
US$10, fun and informative. Also 4- to 5-hr
tours taking in a visit to a coffee *finca* in
Quimbaya, tour of the plantation with full
explanation of the coffee-making process
and coffee and a brownie in the Salento
coffee shop (see page 277) US$45,
minimum 3 participants. Recommended.

Valle de Cocora, Marino Toro Ospina,
matoros432@hotmail.es. Organizes tours,
walks and horse riding in Valle de Cocora,
where he works daily 0800-1800. He is
particularly good on historic information
about the area and the park.

Armenia *p267, map p267*

Balsaje Los Remansos, Cra 7, No 17-08,
Apto 201, Quimbaya, T752 3937. Organizes
balsaje excursions (punting down rivers on
bamboo rafts) on the Río la Vieja.

Millenium Turs, C 19, No 32, N-11, Apto 402,
T749 6036, milleniumturs@hotmail.com.
Does tours of the coffee region as well
as walks into hills behind Armenia. Can
arrange stays on coffee *fincas*. English,
German, French, Italian and Japanese
spoken. Recommended.

Territorio Aventura, Cra 14, No 14N-6,
Edif Acuarium, local 1, T749 3352,
www.territorioaventura.com.co. Organizes
rafting, kayaking, parapenting, horse riding
and zip wiring in local area.

⊖ Transport

Manizales *p252, map p253*
Air
Manizales has a small airport, La Nubia, 7 km east of the centre. To **Bogotá**, 50 mins, from US$70, with **Avianca**, or **Aires**. To **Medellín**, 30 mins if direct, US$50-125, with **Aires** (via Bogotá) or **ADA**.

 Airline offices Avianca, Hotel Las Colinas, Cra 22, No 20-20, Local1, T883 2237. **Aires** Centre: Cra 23, No 60-26, local 3, T881 2324.

Bus
The terminal has moved to Cra 43 No 65-100, T878 7858, www,terminaldemanizales.com. There is a new, direct cablecar system from the station up to the area of El Cable (US$0.75 per journey, 10 mins). To **Medellín**, 14 a day from 0430 to 2000, 6 hrs, US$17 with **Arauca**; by *kia* (7-seater mini van, faster) with **Flota Ospina**, 4½ hrs, US$17.50. To **Bogotá**, Expreso Bolivariano, US$25, 9 hrs, every hour 0600-2300. To **Honda**, US$14, Expreso Bolivariano. **Cali** with Ruana Azul, 6 hrs, US$17, every hour between 0400-2100; by *kia*, 4½ hrs, US$18, 10 a day 0630-1830 **Pereira**, with Expreso Palmira or Arauca, 2 hrs, US$4.40, half hourly, or in *kia* (Flota Ospina), every hr 0600-1800, 1½ hrs. **Armenia**, 3 hrs, US$8, with Expreso Palmira, hourly 0600-1800. To **Ibague**, 5 hrs, US$13, with **Expreso Palmira**. To **Buenaventura**, 7 hrs, US$15, with Ruana Azul at 0730 and 0930. To **Marmato**, 2 hrs, US$7, with Flota Occidental at 1200, 1500 and 1800. To **Supía**, 1½ hrs, US$5.50; in *colectivo*, US$7 with connections every 40 mins to Marmato. For Cartagena, Santa Marta and Turbo change at Medellín.

Car
To **Medellín**, see above. Manizales–Honda–Bogotá: all paved. The road climbs to 3700 m, with most superb scenery.

Car hire Thrifty Car Rental, in Hotel Carretero, Cra 23, No 35A-31, T8847047, www.thriftycolombia.com.

Marmato *p257*
Bus
From Manizales, 3 buses a day with **Flota Occidental** at 0615, 0830 and 1600, US$7, 2½ hrs. Return buses to Manizales leave at 1200, 1500 and 1600. To **Supía**, *chivas* and Willys jeeps take the high road over the mountain via San Juan. Alternatively, you can walk to Supía via the high road in 5 hrs.

Pereira *p261, map p262*
Air
Matecaña airport is 5 km to the west of the city with good services including 2 banks with ATMs and a Telecom office with long-distance facilities. To **Bogotá**, around 15 a day, Aires and Avianca. To **Medellín**, 4 most days, Aires. To **Cali**, frequent via Bogotá, Aires. To **Ibagué**, frequent via Medellín, Aires. Flights also to **Bucaramanga** and the **north coast**, Aires, local airlines to the **Chocó**.

 Airline offices Copa Air, C 20 No 8-68, T01-800 011 2600, Mon-Fri 0800-1800, Sat 0830-1200. Satena, Aeropuerto Matecaña Local 27, T314 2774, satenapei@epm.net.co. Avianca, Cra 10, No 17-55, Edif Torre Central, L 301 and at the airport.

Bus
The terminal is 1.5 km south of city centre, C 17, No 23-157, www.terminalpereira.com; stores luggage. To **Armenia**, 1 hr, every 20 mins from 0600, US$3.30, a beautiful trip. To **Cali**, US$10.50, 4½-5 hrs, *colectivo* by day, bus by night with Expreso Trejos, same price. To **Medellín**, 6-8 hrs, every hour, US$17 with Bolivariano or Expreso Trejos. To/from **Bogotá**, US$10-12, 7 hrs (route is via Girardot, Ibagué – both cities bypassed – and Armenia), every hour 0630-2330 with Bolivariano. To **Buenaventura**, 3 a day with Expreso Trejos at 0730, 0930, 1130, US$17. To **Quibdó**, US$18 at 0500 and 0600. To **Salento** with Flota Alcalá 3 times a day

0650, 1320 and 1620 or take any bus towards Armenia and get off at Ciscaria/entrada Salento (US$2.50 40 mins) and change to a minibus to Salento (US$0.75).

Car
Car rental Hertz, Muelle Nacional, Suite 8, 2nd N, Matacaña airport, T314 2678, www.hertz.com; RentaCar, Av 30 de agosto, No 30-30, Local 25, Centro Comercial Los Puntos, T329 1155, www.rentacarpereira.com.

Salento p265, map p265
Microbuses (Cootranscir) to **Armenia** every 20 mins, US$1.60, 50 mins, taxi US$7; to **Pereira** Mon-Fri only 0750, 1450 and1750 , US$2.50, 1 hr; to **Medellín** colectivos 0400, 0930 and 1100 daily, US$14, 5 hrs. Salento – Valle de Cocóra, Mon-Fri 0610, 0730, 0930, 1130, 1600. Last return 1700. Sat-Sun, 10 departures, last return 1800.

Armenia p267, map p267
Air
Airport El Edén, 13 km from city, taxi 15 mins US$7.50. Scheduled direct flights only to: **Bogotá**, frequent, Aires, and **Medellín**, 3 daily, Aires. Also Easyfly and Avianca.
 Airline offices Avianca, C 21, No 13-23, L 4, T741 4842 and at the airport, T747 9911.

Bus
Terminal 15 blocks from centre at Cra 19/C 35 (C 35 No 20-68), www.terminalarmenia.com. To **Bogotá**, 7-9 hrs, US$23, hourly until 2230. To **Cali**, 3-4 hrs, more than hourly, US$8.50. To **Medellín**, 6-7 hrs, hourly, US$19.50. To **Popayán**, 5-6 hrs, 7 a day from 0800 to 1700, US$17. To **Ipiales**, 14 hrs, at 1530 and 1830 with Bolivariano, US$30. To **Pasto**, 12 hrs, at 1820 and 2320 with Flota Magdalena, US$25. To **Manizales**, 3-4 hrs, more than hourly, US$9. To **Neiva**, 6-7 hrs, 7 a day with Coomotor or Cootranshuila from 1000-2200, US$19.50. To **Pitalito/San Agustín**, 10 hrs, at 1900, 2030 and 2230 with Coomotor or Cootranshuila, US$27. To **Buenaventura**,

5-6 hrs, at 0640, 0840, 1040 and 1400 with Expreso Trejos, US$14.50. To **Cartagena**, 20-22 hrs, at 2130 with Copetran, US$72. To **Bucaramanga**, 12-13 hrs, at 1730 with Coomotor, US$40.

Ibagué and around p269
Air
Daily Aires flights to **Bogotá**, **Cali** and **Medellín** and **Pereira**.

Bus
Terminal is between Cras 1-2 and C 19-20. Tourist police at terminal helpful. Frequent services to **Bogotá**, US$8, 4 hrs. To **Neiva**, US$8-9, 3 hrs, and many other places.

Cartago p269
Air
easyfly has daily flights to **Bogotá**.

Bus
To **Cali**, US$7, 3½ hrs. To **Armenia**, US$2, 2½-3 hrs. To **Pereira**, US$1.50, 45 mins. To **Medellín**, US$12, 7 hrs.

O Directory

Manizales p252, map p253
Banks Davivienda, Cra 23, No 22-04, T884 2217, Centro, or Cra 23, No 63-22, local 56, T885 2038. Bancolombia, Cra 22, No 20-55, T8783660, or C 66, No 22-56, T881 6065. HSBC, Cra 23, No 56-42, T885 7054. **Embassies and consulates** Germany, via al Magdalena, No 74-71, 10th floor, T887 2928. Italy, Edif 7 Banco de Bogotá, Of 501, T883 1935. Spain, C 36, no 22-22, T884 5960. **Immigration** DAS, C 53, No 25A-35, T881 0600 ext 153. **Internet** El Cable, Cra 23, No 63-82. Skype, headphones, international calls, fax and photocopying services. **Post** Barrio Milán: Cra 23, No 73-90, piso 1, T886 8819; Centro: Cra 22, C 27 esquina T882 6166; El Cable: Edif Torres Panorama, local 15, T885 6900.

Pereira *p261, map p262*
Banks Many banks in the centre. *Casas de cambio* change cash and some exchange TCs but check at what time of day: several around Cra 9/C 18. **Internet/telephone** Cybernet, C 19, No 7-49. Lots of computers, has Skype and headphones. Also does international calls. **Post** For airmail, Avianca, C 19, No 6-28, T335 5297. Adpostal, C 19, No 9-75, T334 1239.

Salento *p265, map p265*
Internet/telephone Real.Net, Cra 6, No 4-24. Skype and headphones. International calls. **Language** Marcia Pozos, T311-241 0727, marciapozos@ yahoo.com, is a qualified **Universidad Nacional** Spanish teacher and has the ringing endorsement of having taught the staff of the British embassy in Bogotá.

Armenia *p267, map p267*
Internet/telephone Cabinas del Café, Cra 18, No 19-34. Internet Jota y Efe, Cra 18, No 21 Esq, Local 3. **Post** Avianca, Cra 14, no 19-38.

Contents

286 Cauca Valley
  286 Cali
  292 North of Cali
  293 South of Cali
  293 West of Cali
  294 Buenaventura
  295 Around Buenaventura
  296 Listings

**304 Popayán and
       Tierradentro**
  304 Popayán
  307 Tierradentro
  308 Neiva
  309 Desierto de Tatacoa
  310 Parque Nacional Puracé
  312 Listings

317 San Agustín and around
  317 Ins and outs
  318 Parque Arqueológico
  320 South of San Agustín
  320 Listings

323 Far south
  323 Pasto
  326 Pasto to the coast
  328 South to Ecuador
  330 Listings

Footprint features

284 Don't miss ...
290 Salsa
294 The brujitas of San Cipriano
311 Spa Tourism
327 Las Lajas

Border crossings

Colombia–Ecuador
329 Tumaco–San Lorenzo
329 Ipiales–Rumichaca

Southern Colombia

At a glance

◐ **Getting around** MIO, taxi or bus in Cali; walking in town centres. Intercity buses around region.
◐ **Time required** 2-3 days in Cali; 2-3 weeks for the rest of the region.
◑ **Weather** Hot in Cali and surrounding area; warm but cooler at night in Popayán, San Agustín and Tierradentro; cooler still in mountainous regions approaching the Ecuadorian border.
✕ **When not to go** Good all year round.

★ Don't miss ...

1 Dancing in Cali's *salsatecas*, page 290.

2 Riding a *brujita* to San Cipriano, pages 293 and 294.

3 Admiring Tierradentro and San Agustín, pages 307 and 317.

4 A night in the Tatacoa desert, page 309.

5 Puracé National Park's sulphur pools, page 310.

6 The neo-Gothic Las Lajas sanctuary, page 327.

7 The Carnaval de los Blancos y Negros in Pasto, page 331.

Much of Southern Colombia is characterized by the three mountain ranges that eventually join up to form the high Andes, South America's spine. The people of this region have adapted to the physical obstacles these mountains present, while inaccessibility has kept at bay the cultural dilution that comes with modern advancements. The sensual city of Cali has branded itself as the capital of salsa music and sits in the tropical, sugar cane-rich plains of the Valle del Cauca. To the west lies the port of Buenaventura, gateway to the Pacific coast and its many isolated beaches and islands, most notable of which is Isla Gorgona. The Pan-American Highway continues south to the city of Popayán, known for its dazzling white colonial buildings and its solemn Easter processions, second in size only to Seville in Spain. Hidden in the mountains east of Popayán are the mysterious archaeological sites of Tierradentro and San Agustín, while next to the Magdalena river lies the geographical anomaly that is the Tatacoa Desert.

From Popayán, the Cordillera Occidental reaches ever higher as it rises up to the highland towns of Pasto and Ipiales, ideal places to observe indigenous ways of life. Before crossing into Ecuador, the extraordinary Gothic cathedral that straddles a gorge at Las Lajas is worth a visit.

Cauca Valley

South from Pereira and Armenia the Pan-American Highway drops to the hot, sugar-rich Valle del Cauca, a narrow strip of flat plains abundant in wheat, pineapple, livestock and sugar cane, flanked on either side by the slender fingers of two mountain ranges, the Cordillera Occidental and the Cordillera Central. Capital of the valley is Cali, a sweltering, sexy city and self-appointed capital of salsa music, known for its beautiful women. The road continues south onto Popayán and eventually to Ecuador, while from Cali a road and railway, the latter mostly used for cargo, run west high over mountains down to the port of Buenaventura, the largest settlement on the Pacific coast.
▶▶ *For listings, see pages 296-303.*

Cali → *For listings, see pages 296-303. Colour map 3, A3. Phone code: 2. Population: 2,732,000. Altitude: 1030 m.*

Cali may be second to Bogotá and Medellín in terms of size, but this vibrant, prosperous city is very much número uno when it comes to partying. Cali has proclaimed itself salsa capital of the world, and few would dispute that. The sensuous, tropical rhythms are ubiquitous, seemingly seeping out of every pore of the city. Cali's other major claim, rather more contentious, is that it boasts the most beautiful women in Colombia.

Ins and outs

Alfonso Bonilla Aragón airport is 20 km to the northeast of Cali. The best way to the city is by minibus, which you will find at the far end of the pick-up road outside arrivals. They will take you to the bus terminal (ground floor), on the edge of the centre, every 10 minutes from 0500 to 2100. It takes approximately 30 minutes, US$2. From here taxis are relatively cheap to any destination in the city (currently US$3-4 due to detours for major roadworks throughout the city; fares should come down once completed). Alternatively, take a taxi from the airport, US$25, 30 minutes. The minibuses to the airport, marked 'Aeropuerto', leave from the second floor of the bus terminal. There are direct flights to Cali from Mexico, Panama and several cities in the USA. The **bus terminal** ① *C 30N, No 2AN-29, www.terminalcali.com*, is a 25-minute walk from the centre following the river along Avenida 2N (leave terminal by the taxi stands, take first right, go under railway and follow river to centre, or go through tunnel, marked 'túnel' from the terminal itself). Hotel information available, left luggage US$1.20 per item for 12 hours, good food at terminal. Bus information, T668 3655. *Casa de cambio*, cash only, and ATMs. Showers on second level (US$2.15). Buses between the bus station and the centre, US$0.40.

Getting around The centre of the city is comparatively small – most places of interest to the visitor are within comfortable walking distance. Transport by bus or taxi is tedious because of the density of the traffic, particularly as there were major roadworks at the time of writing, that look set to take their time. The city has the MIO metro system, opened March 2009, with north–south and west–east trunk routes and some pre-trunk routes, US$2 per journey, you can prepay at stations. Cali's taxis have meters (make sure that these are used) and can be flagged in the street, or ordered by telephone. Some also have helpful translations of common phrases on display in Spanish and English. Radio taxis include **Taxis Libres** ① *T444 4444*, and **Taxis Valcali** ① *T442 2630*. Local buses cost US$0.40-70.

Best time to visit There is little climate variation during the year, average temperatures stay around 25°C. It is hot and humid at midday but a strong breeze that blows up in the afternoon makes the evenings cool and pleasant. Rain can come at more or less any time but Cali is shielded from the heavy rainfalls of the Pacific coast by the Cordillera Occidental.

Orientation Cali is bounded on the west by the Cordillera and to the east by the marshy plains of the Río Cauca. Through the centre of the city runs the Río Cali, a tributary of the Cauca, with grass and exotic trees on its banks. North of the river, all streets have the suffix 'N', and Carreras become Avenidas. The city extends southwards 15 km from the Río Cali. Near the southern end a new area is building up around Carrera 100 with the large Unicentro shopping mall and the residential community of Ciudad Jardín.

Safety In the early 1990s Cali achieved international notoriety through the success of its drug cartel. Known as the 'Gentlemen of Cali', thanks to their high society background, the Rodríguez Orejuela brothers and their associate José Santacruz Londoño profited from Pablo Escobar's war with the government, rising to supersede his Medellín organization. But in 1995, six of the seven heads were arrested and in 2006 the Rodríguez Orejuela brothers were extradited to the United States, effectively bringing an end to the era of the drug-trafficking cartel in Colombia. Although still associated with drug and anti-drug operations, the atmosphere in Cali is quite relaxed. Violent crime is still a problem in the city's barrios but less of a threat in more affluent areas. However, carry your passport (or photocopy) at all times and be prepared for police checks. At night, do not walk east or south of Calle 15 and Carrera 10. Do not change money on the street under any circumstances and avoid all people who approach, offering to sell. Take advice on where and where not to go.

Tourist offices Secretaría de Cultura y Turismo ① *Cra 5, No 6-05, sala 102, T885 6173, www.cali.gov.co, by appointment only.* **Punto de Información Turística** ① *Cra 4 C 6 esq, Mon-Fri 0800-1200 and 1400-1700, Sat 0800-1300,* housed inside the large red-brick Cultural Centre has good information. The centre also has free exhibitions in the hallways. See also **www.caliescali.com** for news, chat, entertainment, music and tourist information on *La Guía.* **National Parks Office** ① *C 29N, No 6N-43, Santa Mónica, T667 6041,* for information on Los Farallones de Cali and other parks, very helpful. Also **Fundación Farallones** ① *Jamundi, Valle – Km 1, 5 vía Potrerito, www.fundacionfarallones.org,* on the same subject. For information on the many privately owned nature reserves in this part of Colombia, enquire at **Asociación Red Colombiana de Reservas Naturales de la Sociedad Civil** ① *C 2A, No 26-103, T558 5046, www.resnatur.org.co.* Ask for maps of Cali at these tourist offices. None are very accurate. Try at **Instituto Geográfico Agustín Codazzi (IGAC)** ① *Cra 6, No 13-56, T881 1351, www.igac.gov.co.* They have the best maps although they are probably out of date.

Background
After the collapse of the Incas in 1533, Sebastián de Belalcázar left Pizarro's army in Peru and came north, founding Quito in 1534. He established Popayán and Cali in 1536, then intending to continue northwards and establish other new settlements, but around Cali he encountered stiff resistance from the indigenous locals, which delayed him for several years so that others founded Antioquia and Bogotá. The first site of the city was

beside the Río Lili near the present Ciudad Universitaria and Ciudad Jardín but it was moved north to the present location in 1539. Cali remained a dependency of Popayán and was dominated by Quito for 250 years, as north–south communications along the line of the *cordillera* are so much easier than across the mountain ranges. Indeed, until 1900, Cali was a leisurely colonial town. Then the railway came, and Cali became a rapidly expanding industrial complex serving the whole of southern Colombia. The railway has since been eclipsed by road and air links but today Cali is economically closely tied with the rest of Colombia.

Cali

Sleeping 🛌
Boutique San Antonio **1** *C1*
Calidad House **3** *A4*
Casa Republicana **4** *D2*
Don Jaime **6** *B4*
Dragonfly **7** *A4*
El Hotel **10** *C2*

Four Points **8** *B4*
Hostal Iguana **9** *A4*
Hotel del Puente **5** *C2*
Intercontinental **11** *C1*
La Casa Café **13** *C1*
Obelisco **14** *B1*
Pelican Larry Hostel **12** *B5*

Posada de San Antonio
16 *C1*
Sartor **17** *A4*
Torre de Cali **18** *C4*
Tostaky **2** *C1*
Vizcaya Real **19** *B4*

The capital of Valle del Cauca Department is set in an exceptionally rich agricultural area producing sugar, cotton, rice, coffee and cattle, and acts as the southern capital of Colombia. It sits on the main route north from Ecuador along the Río Cauca and controls the passage to the only important port of Colombia's Pacific coast, Buenaventura. Thanks to the port and the sugar industry, many Afro-Caribbeans and other groups of people came to the valley and now contribute to the city's wealth and entertainment. It was originally named Santiago de Cali, a name often officially used today. It has tropical climate, but with a freshness that encourages economic as well as cultural activity, producing 20% of the country's GNP.

Eating 🍴
Alicante 1 A4
Archie's Pizza 3 B3
Bahareque 2 C1
Carambolo 5 B3
D'Toluca 4 B4
El Solar 6 B4
Granada Faro 7 B4
La Colina 9 C1
La Tartine 10 B1
Ojo de Perro Azul 12 C1
Pampero 13 A4
Rosa Mezcal 8 C1
Solsticio 14 B3
Taisu 16 B4
Tortelli 17 B1

Bars & clubs 🍸
Blues Brothers 18 A6
Forum 19 A6
Kukara Makura 20 A6
Tin Tin Deo 21 D1
Zaperoco 22 B4

Salsa

Salsa may have its roots in Cuba and have developed its sound in the Latin *barrios* of New York, but the people of Cali cheekily claim it's in their city that it has found its true home. It can be heard everywhere – on radios, in taxis, bars and nightclubs. So all-pervasive is its reach that it can be said that this horn-led music with its complex, syncopated beats has, literally, become part of the rhythm of everyday life.

Local groups such as Orquesta Guayacán, Grupo Niche and Jairo Varela have helped develop a distinctive sound, which is mirrored on the dance-floor by a style that is characterized by an upright upper body and intricate movements of the feet.

'No salsa, no dates', say the locals and at the weekend, sexual attraction is measured by moves on the dancefloors of Juanchito's enormous *salsatecas*. But salsa purists also head for traditional salsa bars nearer the centre such as Zaperoco where the dancing is the most important thing.

Sights in the centre

Among the most interesting buildings in Cali are the church and monastery of **San Francisco** ⓘ *Cra 6, C 9/10*. The brick church originates from 1757 and was structurally renovated inside in the 19th century and most recently in 1926. It has a fine ceiling and many 17th- and 18th-century images, carvings and paintings. The altar came from Spain. A second church in the complex is the **Capilla de la Inmaculada**, with a long nave, well lit *reredos* and gold-headed columns. The adjoining 18th-century monastery has a splendidly proportioned domed bell tower in the mudéjar style known as the *Torre Mudéjar*. On the opposite side of the square is the imposing 20-floor **Gobernación** building.

Cali's oldest church, **La Merced** ⓘ *Cra 4, No 6-117, T880 4737*, dates from 1545 and was constructed on the symbolic site of the founding of the city nine years earlier. It is in the classical style with a fine altar. It has been well restored by the Banco Popular. The adjoining convent houses two museums: **Museo de Arte Colonial** (which includes the church), a collection of 16th- and 17th-century paintings, and the **Museo Arqueológico** ⓘ *Cra 4, No 6-59, T8813229, Mon-Sat 0900-1245, 1345-1800, US$2,50*. This houses a good pre-Columbian pottery collection highlighting Calima and other Southwest Colombia cultures. By the well in the courtyard is a replica of a Tierradentro tomb.

Opposite La Merced is the **Casa Arzobispal** ⓘ *Cra 4, No 6-76*. This is one of the earliest buildings of Cali and the only surviving two-storied house of the period. Bolívar stayed here in 1822.

Nearby, in the Banco de la República building, is the **Museo Calima (Museo de Oro)** ⓘ *C 7, No 4-69, Tue-Fri 0900-1700, Sat 1000-1700, free*. This is another of the national gold museums, of the usual high standard and well worth a visit. In addition to pre-Columbian gold work, well presented, with some exquisite tiny items magnified, it has an excellent pottery collection. There is a music room and library in the basement and exhibition halls.

Another church the visitor cannot fail to notice is **La Ermita** ⓘ *by the river at Cra 1, C 12/13*. The original church was built here in 1602, but was totally destroyed by the 1925 earthquake. It was rebuilt between 1926 and 1942 with funds from public subscription, with Cologne cathedral in mind. There is a fine marble altar and the painting *El Señor de la Caña* reflecting the local importance of sugar cane, one of the few items that survived the earthquake. The neo-Gothic blue and white exterior is striking. In the pleasant plaza in front of the church you can sit next to lifesize figures of notable *caleños* of the past, including Joaquín de Caycedo and Jorge Isaacs. Across the street is an example of the older architecture of the city, the ornate Colombia de Tabaco building.

The city's centre is the **Plaza de Caicedo**, with a statue of one of the Independence leaders, Joaquín de Caycedo y Cuero. Facing the square is the **Catedral Metropolitana**, a large three-aisle church, with a clerestory, elaborate aisle niches and stained-glass windows. The original church on the site dated from around 1539, the present building is mid-19th century. The **Palacio Nacional** is on the eastern side of the plaza, a French neoclassical style building (1933), now the city archive.

Cross the river by the delightful, pedestrianized **Puente Ortiz**, built in the 1840s, two blocks from the Plaza de Caicedo, to the **Paseo Bolívar**, alongside the Centro Administrativo Municipal (CAM) and the main post office. On the Paseo, are a bronze statue of *El Libertador* and a sculpture honouring Jorge Isaacs, the romantic 19th-century novelist, depicting the characters of his novel *María*.

A special feature of the centre of Cali is the ribbon of green along the river, lined with exotic and ancient trees that always give a freshness to the heat of the day. Several sculptures were commissioned in the late 1990s, now in position along the river: look out for the *María Mulatta* a black bird seen everywhere along the coasts of Colombia and the splendid bronze *El Gato del Río* by Hernando Tejada, inaugurated in 1996. Also notable are the tall palms of Plaza Caicedo and the trees of the San Antonio park overlooking the west of the city. Cali prides itself on its trees. Several are marked out for conservation, for example, the huge *ceiba* on Avenida 4N at Calle 10, by the viaduct.

Sights outside the centre

Along the river from the city centre is the **Museo de Arte Moderno La Tertulia** ① *Av Colombia, No 5-105 Oeste, Tue-Sat 0900-1300, 1500-1900, Sun 1500-1900, US$2.50*, has exhibitions of South American art, including local, modern works.

To the west of the city, a popular morning 'run' is up the hill to the 18th-century church of **San Antonio** on the Colina de San Antonio, built around 1747. It is a favourite place for weddings. There are some attractive colonial-style houses on the way and pleasant parkland at the top with fine views of the city, though partly obstructed by high-rise buildings.

For a full view of the city, you can take a taxi to the **Monumento Las Tres Cruces**, at 1450 m, to the northwest of the city, a traditional pilgrimage site in Holy Week, or go to the huge **Monumento Cristo Rey**, at 1470 m above San Antonio to the west of the city. This statue can be seen for 50 km across the Río Cauca. It is also worthwhile going up the skyscraper Torre de Cali for a view of the city, but you may have to buy an expensive meal as well.

Zoológico de Cali ① *Cra 2A Oeste/C 14, entrance on the south bank of the Río Cali about 3 km upstream from the centre, T892 7474, www.zoologicodecali.com.co, daily 0900-1700, US$5 adults, US$3.50 children*, interesting and well organized collection of all types of South American animals, birds and reptiles. It makes very good use of the river as it enters the city. There is a small aquarium and an 'ant' auditorium.

The orchid garden, **Orchideorama** ① *Av 2N, No 48-10, T664 3256, www.caliorquideas.com, free, closed Sun*, is worth seeing. Major international show annually in mid-November.

A popular family park is **Acuaparque de la Caña** ① *Cra 8, No 39-01, El Troncal (about 4 km from the centre), T438 4812, daily 1000-1700 (pool) or 0900-1800 (park), adults US$6,* *children US$4.50*, with family entertainment including sports, swimming, riding and children's diversions. Also has a small sugarcane museum.

North of Cali→ *For listings, see pages 296-303.*

Buga, some 73 km north of Cali, has been firmly on the radar of most Colombians for decades and attracts large numbers of national visitors a year to its cathedral, Basílica del Señor de los Milagros, a pilgrimage site. Slowly but surely it's beginning to attract more foreign visitors with its first hostel recently opened. The pleasant town with its imposing

Around Cali

cathedral is surrounded by beautiful countryside and day excursions can be arranged to visit several nearby nature reserves including Bosque de Yotoco and Laguna de Sonso. The area is perfect for hiking or biking with plenty of picturesque waterfalls and natural swimming pools to cool off in the often hot climate.

South of Cali

From Cali it is 135 km south to Popayán. The road crosses the Río Cauca, then rejoins the main east bank route south at Villa Rica. About 17 km along the main road is **Santander**, an attractive town with a colonial chapel, Capilla de Dominguillo, worth a visit. Ceramics and *fique* handicrafts are sold here.

West of Cali → *For listings, see pages 296-303.*

To the west of Cali is the northeast/southwest line of the Cordillera Occidental, which rises here to over 4000 m. A large section of this area and down to 200 m on the Pacific side is the Farallones de Cali National Park (see below). North of this are the road and rail links to Buenaventura. Along the main road (toll) there is much heavy traffic to Colombia's main Pacific port. There are however places to stop, eg San Cipriano and Córdoba, both near the railway, where you can rent small *cabañas* in the forest, swim in the rivers and visit the rainforest. Busy at weekends and holidays but quiet otherwise. The railway is being refurbished for freight transport.

Parque Nacional Farallones

ⓘ *Entrance to the park, US$3, www.fundacionfarallones.org, restricted access at the time of writing, permit necessary.*

Both the toll and ordinary roads out of Cali and Buenaventura give beautiful views of mountains and jungle, and from the old road you can reach the Farallones National Park. Take the dirt road south from the plaza in El Queremal, at 1460 m, about an hour from Cali, 3½ hours from Buenaventura. At El Queremal, a pleasant local mountain village. Alternatively, take the road southwest out of Cali, or *colectivo* (one hour), to Pance. From Pance there is a path, about 30 minutes, to the environmental centre at the entrance to the park at El Topacio. There is good walking and bathing in the park and peaks to climb, one of which is the Pico de Loro, a steep slippery scramble for 2½ hours, but worth it for the views and the sound of the swooping birds. Busy at weekends, camping possible at US$6 for five people a night at El Topacio or at Quebrada Honda, near the Río Pance. You will need a permit from the national parks office in Cali. It is best to go with a guide.

San Cipriano

If the expression 'the journey is the destination' had been coined about one specific place then San Cipriano, 20 km before Buenaventura, would be it. Sat in steaming jungle next to a shallow river, San Cipriano is only accessible by the railway line between Cali and Buenaventura, mostly used for cargo, but there's now also a passenger tourist train for this journey (see Transport, page 302). To compensate for the lack of roads to their village the locals have come up with an ingenious transport system to ferry people to and fro, see box, page 294. You can get a bus from Cali to Córdoba, from where rail cars, man-powered or motorbike-powered (US$2.50, only pay for the return leg when returning), go to the village in beautiful scenery.

Brujitas of San Cipriano

What do you do when there's no road to your village and trains trundle by every now and then? For the villagers of San Cipriano the answer was obvious: make your own train, or something vaguely resembling one. They came up with an innovative system consisting of carts mounted on the line that use large poles to punt them along. The whole effect resembles a witch riding a broomstick, hence the name. Lately, they have started using motorbikes strapped onto the trolleys. The back wheel sits on the line and powers the cart along like a motorbike with a sidecar.

There's little in terms of a braking system; the 10-minute descent through thick jungle to the village can be hairy and if the train comes along it's a desperate scramble to get the cart off the line, but there's no doubting that in the case of San Cipriano the journey is the destination.

On arrival at the village you will have to pay US$1 at the Fundación San Cipriano office to enter the reserve. Enquire here about guides for walks in the forest, including one to a waterfall, La Cascada Veinteadora. Most houses near the river hire out inflatable rubber rings for floating down the river, US$2.70. Take insect repellent.

The village and its environs were declared a national reserve in 1979, and Fundación San Cipriano has 8564 ha of protected forest, through which runs the San Cipriano river. It is noted for the rich variety of animal life which can be seen and heard, which includes spectacled bears, spider monkeys, toucans and several varieties of hummingbird.

San Cipriano was founded in the 18th century as a base for hunting, tree felling and gold panning. Today, most people live off tourism or work at the local water works.

Buenaventura → *For listings, see pages 296-303. Colour map 3, A2. Phone code: 2. Population: 324,000.*

Colombia's only important port on the Pacific is Buenaventura, 145 km by road from Cali over a pass in the Western Cordillera. The commercial centre is now entirely paved and has some impressive buildings, but the rest of the town is poor, with unpaved streets lined with wooden shacks. It is more expensive than Cali and it is difficult to eat cheaply or well. On a hill near the centre is the **cathedral** and a good view of the town can be seen from the nearby **El Mirador** Edificio del Café. There is a festive atmosphere every night. **Warning** This town is one of Colombia's main drug- and people-trafficking centres and has severe poverty; this has led to high levels of violent crime and homicide. You are advised to avoid walking about at night and to stick within a couple of blocks of the seafront.

Buenaventura was founded in 1540, but not on its present site. It now stands on the island of Cascajal, 16 km at the end of the Bay of Buenaventura. The port handles 80% of Colombia's coffee exports, and 60% of the nation's total exports, including sugar and frozen shrimp. South of the town a swampy coast stretches as far as Tumaco (see page 327). To the north lies the deeply jungled Chocó Department, with abundant wildlife and some good beaches.

Ins and outs

Getting there The **bus terminal** is at Carrera 5/Calle 7. It is 560 km by sea from Panama, 708 km by road from Bogotá. From Cali, the new road climbs 12 km to Saladito, a fresh 10°C cooler than the city. Many *caleños* enjoy the roadside restaurants, especially at weekends in this sector. The highest point is reached at Km 18 where the old road turns off left through El Queremal to Buenaventura. Dagua (828 m), 46 km from Cali, is in a semi-arid pineapple-growing zone, a good place for refreshments. Here the railway comes alongside the road, both following the Río Dagua to the coast. Further down, tropical forests are continuous with several places to stop and bathe on the way.

Climate Mean temperature, 27°C. It rains nearly every day, particularly at night; the average annual rainfall is 7400 mm (relative humidity 88%). There are some problems with malaria.

Tourist information Enquire at **Embarcaciones Asturias** ⓘ *Muelle Turístico, T240 4048*, about trips around Buenaventura. **Cámara de Comercio** nearby is also helpful.

Around Buenaventura → *For listings, see pages 296-303.*

North of Buenaventura is the beautiful coastline of the Bahía de Málaga, part of the new Uramba Bahía Málaga national park, with rocky promontories sagging under the weight of thick tropical vegetation. Squadrons of pelicans patrol its glassy green waters and from a boat you will catch glimpses of some inviting golden sand beaches. These are all accessible from **Juanchaco**, one hour on a lancha from Buenaventura. Juanchaco has cheap accommodation and restaurants but its beach is polluted and its streets muddy. **Ladrilleros** is just around the headland and has much better beaches, albeit a bit grey, backed by picturesque cliffs and with many sea caves and freshwater falls to explore. The village itself is quiet and pretty with rickety clapboard houses and dirt tracks for streets.

Bahía Málaga → *Colour map 3, A2.*

Now part of the latest national park to open in Colombia, in 2010, the bay of Bahía Málaga boasts the greatest plant biodiversity on the planet – 265 species per hectare. Just as impressive is the number of animals: there are 60 species of amphibian, 114 reptiles, 148 types of fish and over 400 species of bird. Some 3500 people subsist primarily as fishing communities on its various islands. In its eastern corner is the waterfall **Las Sierpes**, which falls 65 m directly into the sea. The bay also has some fine beaches, including **Playa Dorada** (golden sand), **Juan de Dios** (white sand) and **Chucheros**, which has a waterfall falling onto the beach, creating a freshwater pool. All these are accessible by *lancha* from Buenaventura or Juanchaco.

Partly because of the richness of the water in this region, this is the location of spectacular dolphin and humpback whale sightings, as the whales migrate south with their calves from July to early October each year. There are also all kinds of sea birds to see including pelicans, and frigate birds. A good place is near the Isla Palma, an island off Juanchaco owned by the Colombian Navy. A number of tours are on offer, see page 301.

Another worthwhile activity near Ladrilleros is a tour round the inland sea canals. This network of tidal mangrove rivers, consisting of 90% fresh water, winds its way through thick jungle with encroaching vines. A tour in canoe of motorboat (US$14) includes a visit to a swimming hole fed by a waterfall. Enquire at **Eco-Guías**, page 301, for more details.

Isla Gorgona → *Colour map 3, A1.*

ⓘ *Visits to the island are managed and run by Aviatur, T01-900-331 2222, or 01-382 1616, www.concesionesparquesnaturales.com. Accommodation per couple ranges from US$86 to US$311 depending on type. All visitors must have a permit before arriving at the island, obtainable from Aviatur. It is recommended to book accommodation and boat tickets well in advance during high season. Entrance fee US$17.50 for foreigners. Currently there are 2 ways of getting to the island. One way is via the town of Guapi flying with Satena from Cali or Popayán, from which there are launches to the island, 1½ hrs. Alternatively, launches can be contracted from Buenaventura, a journey of 4 hrs to Gorgona, US$130.*

Until 1984 the island of Gorgona was Colombia's high-security prison (a sort of Alcatraz). The prison is derelict but some parts can still be clearly seen. Convicts were dissuaded from escaping by the poisonous snakes on the island (after whom Francisco Pizarro named the island) and the sharks patrolling the 46 km to the mainland (both snakes and sharks are still there). The national park boasts many unspoilt, deserted sandy beaches. From the paths you can see monkeys, iguanas and a wealth of flora and fauna. (Rubber boots are provided and recommended.) There is an abundance of birds (pelicans, cormorants, geese, herons) that use the island as a migration stopover. Snorkelling and diving are rewarding, equipment can be hired (but take your own if possible), there are many exotic fish and turtles to be seen. Killer whales visit the area from July to September.

Embarcaciones Asturias ⓘ *offices at the Muelle Turístico in Buenaventura, T240 4048, barcoasturias@hotmail.com*, offer a weekend package leaving Buenaventura on a Friday at 1900 and returning Monday, US$290 per person, including accommodation on boat, food, permit and snorkelling equipment.

Isla Malpelo

Declared a UNESCO site in 2006, Isla Mapelo is located 506 km from Buenaventura in the Pacific and is an acclaimed birdwatching haven with great diving opportunities. The island is considered to be one of the world's best places to observe hammerhead sharks in great numbers. Boats leave from Buenaventura, a 36-hour bumpy voyage. There are no places to stay on the island and camping is not allowed. Contact **national parks office** ⓘ *T243 2009*, in Bogotá, for more information. **Embarcaciones Asturias** in Buenaventura offers an eight-day tour, including transport and accommodation for US$1650. There is no entry fee to the island.

◉ Cauca Valley listings → *Phone code: 2.*

For Sleeping and Eating price codes and other relevant information, see pages 23-28.

◉ Sleeping

Cali *p286, map p288*

LL Intercontinental, Av Colombia, No 2-72, T684 7000, www.intercontinental.com. The most expensive hotel in town, recently refurbished with new spa, the Intercontinental has all the services you would expect with a half-size Olympic pool, sauna, Turkish bath, large rooms with plasma TVs and a 24-hr casino. Additionally, it is well placed on the edge of San Antonio. Prices drop at weekends.

L Hotel Boutique San Antonio, Cra 6 2-51, T524 6364, www.hotelboutiquesan antonio.com. Charming, new hotel with 10 sound-proofed rooms, HD TVs, own security system and free Wi-Fi.

A-B Obelisco, Av Colombia, No 4 Oeste-39, T893 3019, www.hotelobeliscocali.com. One of Cali's traditional upmarket hotels,

the Obelisco is sorely in need of a facelift.
It does, however, have a pool and sauna
and Wi-Fi in its pizzeria.

B Casa Republicana, C 7, No 6-74, T896
0949, www.hotelcasarepublicana.com.
Gorgeous Republican-era building with a
lovely courtyard full of large plants. Has good
rooms with cable TV, Wi-Fi and a good
restaurant serving lunch for US$3.50 and
dinner for US$5. Can be noisy early mornings
when stallholders set up outside, but friendly
and welcoming. Recommended.

C Posada de San Antonio, Cra 5, No 3-37,
T893 7413, www.posadadesanantonio.com.
With rooms set around a couple of sunny, leafy
patios and decorated with Calima indigenous
artefacts, this *bahareque* building dating back
to 1906 represents good value for money.
Use of internet, Wi-Fi and 3 different breakfast
menus to choose from only add to that
feeling. 10 % discount for Footprint readers.

D El Hotel, C 9 3-13, T888 1011, www.elhotel
cali.com. Brand new hotel in the centre,
which with Wi-Fi and American breakfast
included in the price provides very good
value for money. There is a bar and
business centre. Recommended.

D Hotel del Puente, C 5, No 4-36, T893 8484.
A little noisy and lacking some basic things
such as loo seats but it's well situated on the
edge of San Antonio.

D-F La Casa Café, Cra 6, No 2-13, T893 7011,
www.lacasacafecali.blogspot.com. Nice
backpackers' hostel/cultural café/house of
coffee in San Antonio. The hostel has simple
rooms with high ceilings and wooden floorboards while the café plans to host cultural
evenings, including talks and laid-back music
evenings. There is a kitchen and DVD room.

E-F Tostaky, Cra 10, No 1-76, T893 0651,
www.cafetostaky.blogspot.com. Situated at
the bottom of San Antonio park, this sweet
backpackers' hostel with 13 rooms, run by a
French/Colombian team, has airy rooms
above a café open only to guests, serving
French breakfasts and snacks. Facilities include
use of a kitchen, a TV room with DVDs and hot
water in shared bathrooms. Recommended.

Barrio Granada and around

L Four Points, C 18 Norte, No 4N-08, T685
9999, www.fourpointssheraton.com. Slick
hotel with lots of steel, glass and brick with
a swimming pool, gym, Wi-Fi and à la carte
restaurant. It's recently been refurbished.

AL Vizcaya Real, C 20 Norte, No 5AN-30,
T683 1000, www.hotelvizcayareal.com.
Located on a palm-lined avenue, with good
facilities, including a small pool, gym, Turkish
bath and an internet room, the beds are a bit
short. Free airport transfers included in price.

A Don Jaime, Av 6 Norte, No 15N-25, T667
2828, www.hoteldonjaime.com. Large but
dated hotel on the noisy Av 6 with a/c, cable
TV, Wi-Fi and breakfast included. Restaurant
and terrace bar in bustling Av 6 Norte.

A Torre de Cali, Av de las Américas, No 18N-
26, T683 3535, www.glhhoteles.com. From its
imposing 41-floor tower, the Torre de Cali has
one of the best views in town. The rooms
are large with big TVs and it's been recently
refurbished. There are significant discounts
at weekends.

C Dragonfly, Av 9 Norte, No 21N-30, T667
6186, www.dragonflycali.com. Located in
a beautiful, slightly dilapidated art deco
building, this hotel has Wi-Fi, a TV room and
a good swimming pool. Breakfast is included
and there is a restaurant opening soon.
Look for the door bell by the postbox near
the gate to enter.

C Sartor, Av 8 Norte, No 20-50, T668 6482,
hotelsartor@yahoo.com. The rooms are
basic and have hot water en suite
bathrooms but small beds. Has Wi-Fi,
cable TV and laundry service.

D-E Pelican Larry, C 20 Norte, No 6AN-44,
Barrio Granada, T392 1407, www.pelican
larrycali.com. Rooms with and without bath,
F in dorms. Close to Zona Rosa (Barrio
Granada) restaurants and bars, 15 mins'
walk from bus terminal, hot water,
laundry and internet extra, kitchen,
Sun night BBQ, Spanish lessons arranged,
TV room, helpful staff.

D-F Calidad House, C 17 Norte, No 9AN-39,
T661 2338, www.calidadhouse.com. English-

owned hostel with dorms, kitchen, BBQ, and a sunny patio. Excellent when the owner is in residence.

D-F Hostal Iguana, Av 9 Norte, No 22N-46, T313-768 6024, www.iguana.com.co. Spread over 2 pleasant suburban houses on the edge of the fashionable Barrio Granada, this has long been Cali's best-known backpacker's hostel. Several private rooms, some with en suite bathrooms, a kitchen, garden, TV room with DVDs, Wi-Fi, free coffee, Spanish and salsa classes (first hour free) and great local information. Run by Urs from Switzerland.

North of Cali *p292, map p292*
E-F Buga Hostel and Holy Water Ale Café, Cra 13 4-83, Buga, T236 7752, www.bugahostel.com. New German/Colombian-run hostel with their own microbrewery and the Holy Water Ale Café (www.holywaterale.com). Dorm beds and a private room with balcony. Rooftop terrace with lovely views. They can organize tours of the area. Recommended.

San Cipriano *p293*
Accommodation in San Cipriano is about as basic as it gets, though there is running water and electricity.
E Cabañas Carvajal, T320-644 8241. Simple *cabañas*. near the river.
E Hotel David, towards the end of the village, T312-815 4051. Run by the lovely Luz Mari and her family. She has basic rooms including a chalet above her restaurant with clean showers and fan provided. She also guarantees that if you get bitten by mosquitoes during the night she won't charge!

Buenaventura *p294*
AL Hotel Estelar Estación, C 2, No 1A-08, T243 4070, www.hotelesestelar.com. With its white neoclassical façade, the 80-year-old Estación gleams in comparison to the rest of Buenaventura. Smartly dressed bellboys and sculpted gardens add to the old world charm. Also with a large swimming pool, sauna, cable TV and a restaurant serving *criollo* food. Be sure to ask for a room in the old part of the hotel, which has more character. There are healthy discounts available, especially at weekends. The hotel can also organize whale-watching trips to the nearby Bahía de Málaga.

D Los Delfines, C 1, No 5A-03, T241 5449, hotellosdelfines@mibuenaventura.com. 4 blocks up the hill from the *muelle*, this hotel is good value with clean rooms, a/c, cable TV, private bathrooms and a breezy terrace.

D Titanic, C 1, No 2A-55, T241 2046. Handily located about a block from the *muelle turístico*, this hotel has clean rooms with en suite bathrooms and beds with crisp, white sheets. Its 6th-floor restaurant has great sea views and serves *almuerzos* at US$3.80, as well as à la carte options. Cable TV, a safe in each room and an internet salon make it a good option if you get stuck in Buenaventura.

Around Buenaventura *p295*
Ladrilleros
A-B Cabañas Reserva Aguamarina, T311-728 3213, www.reservaaguamarina.com. Colourful wooden *cabañas* set amongst lush tropical gardens. Fan, cable TV and en suite bathrooms. 2 meals included in price. Owner John Janio also runs Eco-guías, which organizes whale-watching tours (from US$17) and other activities.

B Palma Real, T310-820 0026, www.hotelpalmarealcolombia.com. Up on a cliff, this hotel affords spectacular glimpses of the sea through a canopy of trees. It has a good pool and jacuzzi and private access down a jungle path to the beach below. The rooms, in a clapboard house, are a bit small and the walls a little flimsy, but there are 2 meals at its restaurant thrown into the price.

D Doña Francia, T246 0373. This little place has a couple of good, clean rooms with fan and a shared bath. Ask at the restaurant of the same name around the corner.

🍴 Eating

Cali p286, map p288

Cali has a good restaurant scene. In the centre, the areas of El Peñón, and San Antonio, have an excellent selection of restaurants serving all types of international food. In the north, the sheer volume of eateries in Granada, particularly on Calles 14N and 15N, makes for some difficult dining dilemmas.

₩₩₩ **La Tartine**, C 3 Oeste, No 1-74, T893 6617. Classic French-owned restaurant serving delicacies such as snails and *chateaubriand* in eccentric surroundings.

₩₩₩ **Tortelli**, C 3 Oeste, No 3-15, T893 3227. Little Italian restaurant serving home-made pasta.

₩₩ **Rosa Mezcal**, C 2 No 4-63, T893 6597. Restaurant with traditional dishes and live mariachi bands Thu-Sat. Happy hour 1700-1900.

₩ **Bahareque**, C 2, No 4-52. This laid-back restaurant has a hint of a lounge feel about it. Ultra-friendly owners Marly and José are a wealth of information on the local music and dance scene. It serves typical Colombian food as well as salads. Lunch menu for US$3.

₩ **La Colina**, C 3, No 10-35. This restaurant serves what according to one traveller are the best pizzas he had eaten in Central or South America.

₩ **Ojo de Perro Azul**, Cra 9, No 1-27. Bright bohemian hangout with cards, dominoes, chess – the place to chat, eat and drink. Serves mostly *picadas* and *tostadas* but has a few traditional Colombian mains on the menu. The funky animal-print furniture is mostly fake but at least one zebra died to decorate the floor.

Barrio Granada and around

₩₩₩ **Carambolo**, C 14 9N-18/28, T667 5656, www.carambolocali.com. Excellent themed restaurant with Latin and Mediterranean dishes. Friendly and recommended.

₩₩₩ **El Solar**, C 15 Norte, No 9N-62, T653 4628. With a great atmosphere created by an open-air gravel patio shaded by trees, and a varied international menu of Asian, Italian and Mexican cuisines, a popular *caleño* choice.

₩₩₩ **Granada Faro**, Av 9 Norte, No 15AN-02, T667 4625, www.granadafaro.com. Another Cali culinary fixture, the Granada Faro serves Mediterranean-Peruvian fusion.

₩₩₩ **Solsticio**, Av 9N No 13-76, T661 2951. Colombian and world food in pleasant setting. Occasionally live music in the evenings.

₩₩₩-₩₩ **Archie's Pizza**, Av 9N No 14N-22, www.archiespizza.com. Quite simply the best pizzas in Cali. Part of a gourmet pizza chain. Pricey, but worth it.

₩₩ **Pampero**, C 21N, No 9-17, T661 3117, www.pamperoparrillaargentina.com. Pitch perfect Argentine steaks on pleasant terrace with good service. Recommended.

₩₩ **Taisu**, C 16N, No 8N-74, T661 2281. Taisu serves a variety of Asian cuisines, including sushi, *teppanyaki* and various stir-fried dishes.

₩ **D'Toluca**, C 17N, No 8N-36, T661 8390. Good little Mexican restaurant serving fajitas, tacos and burritos at reasonable prices.

Buenaventura p294

Most hotels have their own restaurant, otherwise there are several cheap joints along the promenade.

🌙 Bars and clubs

Cali p286, map p288

Cali is legendary for its nightlife and especially so for its *salsatecas* – salsa-playing discos. The most popular with *caleños* can be found on Av 6 Norte where there are dozens of venues to choose from, although the real salsa purists would direct you to **Zaperoco**, Av 5N, No 16-46, www.zaperocobar.com. An alternative is **Tin Tin Deo**, C 5, No 38-71, T514 1537, which attracts a liberal crowd of students and teachers and is more forgiving on salsa beginners. But it's not just salsa, there's bars playing rock, jazz, blues and electronic music as well.

Escondité Nightclub Tequendama, Cra 37, Calle 5-14, Barrio Estadio. Crossover music.

Sometimes stays open (illegally) on Sat nights until 0400 if enough people are there. Reasonably priced.

Forum, C 25N, No 5-68. Electronic music.
Talberts Pub and Bourbon St, C 17N and Cra 8N, Barrio Granada. English- and American-themed bars, owned by same person. English music generally. Good live bands on Fri, and good atmosphere in general.

Bars in town close by 0300, after which many people head to Barrio Juanchito and its range of salsa bars and discos, including huge, hi-tech *salsatecas* (eg the popular Don José). It is worth visiting just to watch couples dancing salsa and to join in, if you dare. Go with locals and couples; groups of foreign male tourists might have a hard time getting in. Most advisable to take a registered radio taxi there and back; 15-min ride out of Cali, across the bridge over the Río Cauca.

Entertainment

Cali *p286, map p288*
Cinema
Centro Cultural Colombo-Americano (see page 303 for contact details). Films are shown on Wed nights.
Alianza Colombo-Francesa, Av 6N, No 21-34, also shows films on Fri nights.
Museo La Tertulia, also shows good films.

Theatre
Teatro Aire Libre Los Cristales, Cra 14A Oeste, No 6-00, T558 2009. All kinds of musical and artistic presentations.
Teatro Experimental, C 7, No 8-63, T884 3820. Theatre productions most weekends by resident company.
Teatro Jorge Isaacs, Cra 3, No 12-28, T889 9322. Neoclassical 1930s building declared a National Monument in 1984. Puts on jazz and pop music events as well as comedy nights.
Teatro La Máscara, Cra 10, No 3-40, T893 6640, www.lamascaracali.blogspot.com.

Feminist theatre ensemble putting on alternative productions.
Teatro Municipal, Cra 5, No 6-64, T684 3578, www.cali.gov.co/teatromunicipal. Opened in 1918, hosts major cultural activities including opera, ballet and weekly classical concerts and is also home to the Cali Symphony orchestra.

Festivals and events

Cali *p286, map p288*
25 Dec to 3 Jan Feria Internacional de Cali, centred at Plaza Cañaveralejo on C 5 but engulfing the whole city, with bullfights, horse parades, masquerade balls, sporting contests and salsa competitions everywhere with groups coming from all over the world.
Jun Feria Artesanal at Parque Panamericano, C 5, handicrafts and excellent leather goods.
Aug The Festival de Música del Pacífico Petronio Álvarez champions music from Colombia's Pacific coast. Recommended.
Sep The AjazzGo festival, www.ajazzgo festival.com, with international artists.
Sep Festival Internacional de Arte (painting, sculpture, theatre, music, etc).

Shopping

Cali *p286, map p288*
Artesanías Pacandé, Av 6N, No 17A-53. Typical regional handicrafts.
Centro Artesanal Parque La Loma de la Cruz, C 5 entre Cra 15 y 16. Permanent handicraft market, nice setting and pleasant neighbourhood, safe, cafés around the park. Open 1130-2030.
Cerámicas Palomar, Cra 12 with C 2-41. Good pottery.
La Caleñita, Cra 24, No 8-53, www.lacalenita.com. Good selection of typical handicrafts.
Librería Nacional, Cra 5, No 11-50, www.librerianacional.com, almost next to the cathedral on Plaza de Caicedo. Bookshop

with a café, as do most branches elsewhere in the city. Also at the airport and in all major shopping centres. Bookstalls on the sidewalk on Cra 10 near C 10.

Platería Ramírez, many outlets, www.plateriaramirez.com, including CC Unicentro. Good selection of jewellery, lessons offered in jewellery making.

▲ Activites and tours

Cali *p286, map p288*

Bullring
The new, bullring, the **Plaza de Toros Cañaveralejo**, is 5 km from the city centre along C 5. Bullfights take place at the end of Dec, beginning of Jan.

Cycling
Ciclovía On Sun 0700-1400, C 9 is closed from north to south to allow people to cycle, run and exercise on the roadway.
Bicicletas Todo Terreno, C 5, No 57-54, T552 1579, also at Av 8AN, No 17-33, T661 2456, bltcolombia@emcali.net.co. Cycle shop, hires mountain bikes and organizes tours in the local area.

Dance classes
Academia El Manicero, Cra 39 No 9-56, piso 2, T513 0231. Classes for individuals or groups. Prof Ximena Castillo, T316-707 8885 (mob) is also recommended for 1-on-1 classes. Also enquire at **Hostal Iguana**, see page 298.

Diving
Contact **Rafael Lozano**, T313-767 6099 (mob), for diving trips to Isla Gorgona and Malpelo. Speaks English, lots of experience and very responsible. Recommended.
Casco Antiguo Diving Centre, Cra 34, No 3-89 (Parque del Perro), cascoantiguo@ telesat.com.co. PADI certified.

Football
Cali's 2 major football teams, América de Cali and Deportivo Cali both play at the **Pascual Guerrero Stadium**, which holds 50,000 people.

Parapenting
Speak to **Rob Ottomani**, T314-678 7972. German and English spoken.

Tour operators
Aviatur, Cra 5, No 8-12, T889 3121, www.aviatur.com. For tours to Isla Gorgona, and other services.
Kaffe Erde, Av 4N, No 4N-79, T661 5475, www.kaffeeerde.com. From the backpackers' hostel of the same name, organizes tours in the local area.
Panturismo, C 18N, No 8-27, T668 2255, www.panturismo.com.co and other branches, including at airport, T666 3021. Organizes all-inclusive trips to Gorgona.
Vela, Cra 4, No 8-64, local 104, T889 0760. Student travel agency, cheap tickets. Recommended.

Yoga
Hostal Iguana (see Sleeping) organizes yoga weekends.

Around Buenaventura *p295*
Eco-Guías, T313-750 6430 (mob), www.reservaaguamarina.com, can organize whale watching and boat trips, as well as diving, snorkelling and kayaking excursions.
Hotel Estación, Buenaventura, run tours mid/late Jul to end Sep, hopefully for whale sighting: 3 nights/4 days, including all meals and boat trip, US$264 per person.

⊖ Transport

Cali p286, map p288
Air
Alfonso Bonilla Aragón airport, 20 km from city, T442 2624, has banks, including Banco Popular, and ATMs near domestic departures/arrivals. The **Telecom** office with international telephone facilities, is near international departures, as is the tax-exemption office. Internet is available. Frequent services to **Bogotá**, **Medellín**, **Cartagena**, **Ipiales** and other Colombian cities with **Satena** and **Avianca**. International flights to **Miami**, **New York**, **Ecuador** and **Panama**.

Airline offices Copa Air, C 26N, No 6N-16, Aires, C 22N, No 4N-22, T660 4777. **American**, Hotel Intercontinental, Av Colombia, No 2-72, Local 6. Avianca, Av 6N, No 23N-05, T660 7822 or Cra 6, No 11-42, T682 5012. Satena, C 8, No 5-19, T885 7709. TAME, Cra 4, No 12-41, of 118, Edif Seguros Bolívar. For Cali–Quito flights.

Bus
The bus terminal is at C 30N, No 2AN-29, 25 mins' walk from the centre following the river along Av 2N and about 15 mins from Barrio Granada. Bus information at www.terminalcali.com. There are 3 floors – ground floor has most of the shops, restaurants and services, including hotel information and left luggage US$1.20 per item for 12 hrs. *Casa de cambio* (cash only), banks and ATMs. The 2nd floor has showers (US$2.15) and also most of the ticket offices for long-distance buses, while the 3rd floor has taxis and more bus company ticket offices. There are plenty of local buses between the bus station and the centre, which charge US$0.40. Taxi from centre to bus station, US$3-4. A tunnel connects the terminal with C 25, from where it's cheaper to get a taxi to the centre, avoiding a detour around the terminal.

Busetas (**Velotax** and others) charge 50% more than buses but save time; *taxi-colectivos* are about 2½ times bus

prices and even quicker. To **Popayán**, US$6, 2½-3 hrs, also *colectivos*, US$10. To **Pasto**, US$15, 8-9 hrs. To **Ipiales** (direct), US$22.50, 12 hrs; to **San Agustín**, 9 hrs, US$14-16. To **Cartago**, 3½ hrs, US$4. To **Armenia**, US$13. To **Ibagué**, US$18.50, 6-7 hrs. To **Manizales**, US$17.50, 7 hrs. To **Medellín**, US$23, 8-10 hrs. To **Bogotá**, 10-15 hrs,, US$30 (sit on the left of the bus). To **Buenaventura**, 3 hrs with Expreso Palmira, US$8.

Train
The **Tren Turístico Café y Azúcar**, Estación del Ferrocarril, Av Vásquez Cobo No 23N-47, T620 2326, www.trenturisticocafeyazucar. com.co, operates several different routes from Cali, including to San Cipriano, Buga and Buenaventura, mostly at weekends. Prices start from US$12.50 and usually include lunch and some excursions.

Car
Car rental Hertz, Av Colombia No 2-72 (Hotel Intercontinental), T892 0437, also office at airport, T666 3283. **Colombia Rent a Car**, Av 8, No 16N-50, Of 1. **National**, C 5, No 39-36, T524 4432, aiport, T666 3016.

Taxi
Ensure that meters are used. Prices are posted in the window: minimum fare is US$2. On Sun and holidays and at night an extra charge is made.

Buenaventura p294
Air
Flights to **Cali** and **Bogotá**.

Bus
The toll road to Cali is fully paved; the toll is about US$1.30 for cars and US$0.30 for *moto* The ordinary road is not paved. To **Cali** there are plenty of buses, US$8.50, 4 hrs; *colectivos* also run at 30-min intervals to Cali.

Sea
Cargo boats to **Nuquí** and **Bahía Solano** are slow, intermittent and uncomfortable. They

leave from the Puente del Piñal. 1 or 2 boats leave a week, stopping at Nuquí, 18 hrs, and going on to Bahía Solano, 24 hrs from Buenaventura, US$55 1 way.

🛈 Directory

Cali *p286, map p288*
Banks Davivienda, C 11, No 8-03 (Centro) or Av 6N, No 22-08 (norte). Banco de Bogotá, Cra 4, No 11-55 (Plaza Caycedo, Centro) or Av 8N, No 20-67. **Bancolombia**, Cra 5, No 10-79 (Plaza Caycedo, Centro) or C15N, No 6N-56, piso 2. Citibank, Av 5N, No 23AN-41, piso 3. HSBC, Av 6N, No 25N-11. Banco Agrario, C11, No 5-28. Many other banks and ATMs in main commercial areas. **Casas de Cambio** Cambiamos, C 5 No 50-103, of 103. Giros y Financias (Western Union), Av 6N, No 30N-67. Casa de Cambios Titán, C 11, No 4-42, www.titan.com.co. **Cultural centres** Alianza Colombo Francesa, Av 6N, No 21-34A, T661 3431, www.alianzafrancesa.org.co. Centro Cultural Colombo-Americano, C 13N, No 8-45, T687 5800, www.colombo americano.edu.co. All give language classes, show films and have other events, enquire for programme. Centro Cultural de Cali, Cra 5, No 6-05, T885 8855. Centro Cultural Comfandi, C 8, No 6-23, T334 0000.
Embassies and consulates France, Av 3N, No 8N-24, Of 405, T883 5904. Germany, C 1B, No 66B-29, Barrio El Refugio, T323 4435. Switzerland, Av 4N, No 3-33, T653 4793 (same building as Pensión Stein). UK, C 22N, No 6-42, Of 401, Edif Centro Granada, T667 7725, britishcali@uniweb.net.co, Mon-Fri 0900-1230. **Immigration** DAS office Av 3AN, No 50-20, T664 3809/10.
Internet Unimegas, Av 6, No 17A-57, T660 3853. Has Skype and headphones. Cosmonet, Av 6N, No 17N-65, T653 5228. Skype and headphones, scanning and photocopying, as well as international calls.
Laundry Lavaprisa, Av 8N, No 12-08.
Media 2 local daily newspapers are *La Nación*, www.lanacion.com.co, and *El País*, www.elpais.com.co. **Medical services** Cíinica del Occidente, C 18N, No 5-34. Centro Médico Imbanaco, Cra 38A, No 5A-100, www.imbanaco.com. Clínica Fundación Valle de Lili, Cra 98, No 18-49, www.valledellili.org. Clínica Oftalmológica de Cali, C 47S, No 8C-94, www.clinicaofta.com. Optician Optica Alemana, Av 6N, No 21-51, www.optica-alemana-cali.com. **Post** Adpostal, for national service, C 10, No 6-25; Deprisa, for international service, C 9, No 4-45. **Telecom** C 10, No 6-25.

Buenaventura *p294*
Banks Banco Popular, Cra 2, No 2-37, changes US$ cash TCs. Bancolombia, C 1A, No 3-55, cash against Visa. Banco del Occidente, Cra 2, No 2-39, cash against Mastercard. Western Union, C 1, No 3-97, Of 205, T242 2766. **Immigration** DAS near Avianca post office, T2419592. **Internet** Ciber P@cifico, C 1, No 2-11. Internet and local phone calls. **Post** Avianca, C 8, No 26-05. **Telecom** C 3/Cra 3.

Popayán and Tierradentro

South of Cali is Popayán, one of the country's oldest Spanish settlements, which gleams like a beacon in the crisp sunshine of the Cordillera Central's mountain air. Its colonial centre may have suffered severe damage after an earthquake hit the region in March 1983, but an extensive restoration programme has left little sign of the tragedy and the city's dazzling white buildings appear much as they would have to the Spanish sugar plantation owners who first came here to escape the heat of the Cauca Valley. Popayán has a cultured air about it, no doubt aided by its large student population. Maybe there is something in the water, as it has produced more Colombian presidents than any other city, while over the years it has also been home to many notable painters, writers and composers. Its famously austere Semana Santa celebrations are second in size only to those of Seville in Spain.

To the Spanish, Popayán was a strategic link between Lima and Quito, in the south and Bogotá and Cartagena, further north. For today's traveller, the city makes a convenient jumping-off point for visiting the remote archaeological sites of Tierradentro and San Agustín, the indigenous market at Silvia, or a break from the heat and partying in Cali.
➤➤ *For listings, see pages 312-317.*

Popayán → *For listings, see pages 312-317.* Colour map 3, B3. Phone code: 2. Population: 258,650. Altitude: 1760 m.

The city of Popayán has managed to retain its colonial character, which is remarkable given that it was partially destroyed by the March 1983 earthquake and extensively restored. Many of the streets are cobbled and the two-storey buildings are in rococo Andalusian style, with beautiful old monasteries and cloisters of pure Spanish classic architecture.

Ins and outs

Getting there The **airport** is 20 minutes' walk from the centre. Popayán's **bus terminal** is near the airport, 15 minutes' walk from the centre (taxi US$1.75 daytime or US$2 at night). Luggage can be stored safely (receipt given); there is a charge to use the toilets. From the bus station, walk up Carrera 11 and take a left at Calle 4 to reach the centre. Take care if you cross any of the bridges over the river going north, especially at night.

Tourist office There is a recently established office on the Parque Principal with a reasonable selection of maps and brochures. **Punto de Información Turística** (known as PIT), next door to the **Cámara de Comercio de Cauca, Cultura y Turismo** ① *Cra 7, No 4-36, T824 3625, www.cccauca.org.co.*

Background

Popayán was founded by Sebastián de Belalcázar, Francisco Pizarro's lieutenant, in 1536, in the valley of the Pubenza, a peaceful landscape of palm, bamboo, and the sharp-leaved agave. The early settlers, after establishing their sugar estates in the hot, damp Cauca valley, retreated to Popayán to live, for the city is high enough to give it a delightful climate. After the conquest of the indigenous Pijao, Popayán became the regional seat of government, subject until 1717 to the Audiencia of Quito, and later to the Audiencia of Bogotá. Popayán has given no fewer than eleven presidents to the Republic. The scientist Francisco José de Caldas was born here in 1771. It was he who discovered how to determine altitude by variation in the boiling point of water, and it was to him that Mutis (of the famous *Expedición Botánica*) entrusted the directorship of the newly founded Observatory at Bogotá. He was a passionate partisan of Independence, and was executed in 1815 during Morillo's 'Reign of Terror'.

Today, Popayán is the capital of the Department of Cauca. To north, south and east the broken green plain is bounded by mountains. To the southeast rises the cone of the Volcán Puracé (4650 m). The Río Molino runs through the town, a tributary of the Río Cauca, which rises near Puracé and flows past Popayán a few kilometres to the north.

Sights

ⓘ *Museums are closed on Mon.*

The **cathedral** ⓘ *C 5/Cra 6*, built around 1900, is the third on the site and it was beautifully restored after the 1983 earthquake. It has a fine marble Madonna sculpture behind the altar by Buenaventura Malagón.

San Agustín ⓘ *C 7/Cra 6*, is notable for the gilt altar piece and the unusual statue of Christ kneeling on the globe. **Santo Domingo** ⓘ *C 4/Cra 5*, has some fine wood carvings, now used by the Universidad del Cauca whose building next door on Carrera 5, is worth a visit. **La Ermita** ⓘ *C 5/Cra 2*, on the site of the first chapel established by Sebastián de Belalcázar, dates from the 16th century. **La Encarnación** ⓘ *C 5/Cra 5*, dates from 1764 and has a fine retable, is also used for religious music festivals. **San Francisco** ⓘ *C 4/Cra 9*,

Popayán

Sleeping
Casa Familiar El Descanso 1
Casa Familiar Turística 2
Colonial 4
Dann Monasterio 9
Hostel Trail Guesthouse 3
La Casona del Virrey 5
La Plazuela 6
Los Balcones 7
Los Portales 8

Pass Home 10

Eating
Capriccio Café 3
El Muro 1
Italiano 5
Jengibre 2
Juan Valdez 6
Kanda Vegetarian 9
La Viña 8

Madeira Café 10
Tequila's Mexican 13
Verde y Mostaza 7
Wipala Café 14

Bars & clubs
El Sotareño 4
Iguana Afro-Club 11
Tijuana 12

100 metres
100 yards

dating from about 1775, has been frequently damaged by earthquakes and is now partly restored, note the fascinating figures on the pulpit stairs. **El Carmen** ⓘ *C 4/Cra 3*, is a monastery church constructed about 1730 with *mudéjar* influences.

Museo de Historia Natural ⓘ *Cra 2, No 1A-25, daily 0900-1200 and 1400-1700, US$1.50, children US$1*, has good displays of archaeological and geological items with sections on insects (particularly good on butterflies), reptiles, mammals and birds. Other museums are **Museo Negret** ⓘ *C 5, No 10-23, open 0800-1200, free*, with works, photographs and furniture of Negret, **Museo Guillermo Valencia** ⓘ *Cra 6, No 2-69, 0900-1200 and 1400-1800, free*, birthplace of the poet, and **Museo Casa Mosquera** ⓘ *C 3, No 5-14, open 0800-1200 and 1400-1800, free*, where General Tomás Cipriano de Mosquera lived, four times President of Colombia. A small collection of indigenous artefacts is held in **Banco de la República** ⓘ *Cra 6, No 2-28*. There is also a **Museum of Religious Art** ⓘ *C 4 No 4-56, T824 2759, open Mon-Fri 0900-1230, 1400-1800, Sat 0900-1400, US$2.50*.

Walk to **Belén chapel** ⓘ *C 4/Cra 0*, with a fine view of the city, seeing the statues en route, and then continue to **El Cerro de las Tres Cruces**, if you have the energy, and on to the equestrian statue of Belalcázar on the **Morro de Tulcán**, which overlooks the city. This hill is the site of a pre-Columbian pyramid. Next to El Morro is **Rincón Payanés**, also known as El Pueblito Patojo, which has scale models of the town's landmarks and a number of handicraft stalls and cafes. Although the area is reasonably safe around the Belén chapel at Mass times, take care of your belongings at quiet times and don't flash your camera.

A fine arched bridge built in 1868, **Puente del Humilladero** crosses the Río Molino at Carrera 6. Public presentations and concerts are given in the gardens below. It is said that Bolívar marched over the nearby **Puente Chiquito**, built in 1713.

Around Popayán

The little town of **Silvia** lies in a high valley northeast of Popayán. The local Guambianos wear their typical blue and fuchsia costumes, and are very gregarious and friendly. You can watch them spinning and weaving their textiles. The Tuesday market seems to be full of indigenous Otavalo from Ecuador and their goods – more expensive than in Otavalo. The market is at its best between 0600 and 0830. There's not much to buy, but it's very colourful. There are several indigenous settlements in the hills around Silvia, a typical one to visit is **La Campana**, 45 minutes on the bus, 2½ hours' walk downhill back to Silvia. It is not safe to park cars in the street at night in Silvia. There is a small **Museo de Artsesanías** ⓘ *Cra 2, No 14-19*, with exhibits of local crafts, past and present. Tourist information is 1½ blocks up from the *plazuela* on the right-hand side. There are beautiful places to walk and ride around Silvia.

About 25 km from Popayán, on the road to San Agustín, is **Coconuco**, a particularly beautiful spot, surrounded by green hills and cascading waterfalls. The village is famous for its hot springs and you can get a jeep for US$3.50 or a moto-taxi for US$1 from the centre to the hot springs. **Aguas Hirviendas** ⓘ *US$1.50*, just outside the village, has several concrete pools, one of which has water hot enough to boil an egg in five minutes. Open 24 hours, this is a popular spot at weekends but quiet during the week. Mondays some of the pools are shut for cleaning. Further up the valley is **Aguas Tibias** ⓘ *US$4*, whose waters are warm rather than hot. These pools, run by an indigenous family, have a rather more rustic feel to them and include a waterslide and therapeutic mud bath.

You can reach Coconuco by bus from Popayán, one hour, US$2, buses leave 0600-1800, every 30 minutes. From there you can walk to either of the springs or catch a jeep or mototaxi. Buses to San Agustín pass by both sites.

On the Popayán – Pasto highway Km 6 (take any Pasto bus and ask to get dropped off near La Bomba de Bohío) lies the scenic health and spiritual centre **Vida Sana** ① *T311 6059766, open Sun-Fri, treatments from US$10, book in advance*, open to the public for a variety of treatments. This isn't a spa as such, but more of a rustic health centre with lovely surroundings. It's possible to stay overnight and meals can be included in a package. Eco walks also available in the area.

Further along the same highway, Swiss/Colombian-run coffee *finca* **Alas y Raíces**, is worth a visit for the lovely scenery and coffee tour (see Activities and tours, page 315).

A great trip to do is the five-day circuit known as the **Southern Loop**, taking in San Agustín, Tierradentro, the Tatacoa desert and more. Enquire at Hosteltrail in Popayán for information (see page 312).

Tierradentro → *For listings, see pages 312-317. Colour map 3, B4.*

Tierradentro is one of Colombia's great pre-Columbian attractions. Scattered throughout the area are man-made burial caves painted with red, black and white geometric patterns. Some are shallow, others up to 8 m deep. The surrounding hills are spectacular, and there are many small indigenous villages to explore (get exact directions before setting out). For many years the unforgiving mountains of this region were a FARC stronghold, which stunted any kind of tourism development. Today, the guerrilla presence is no more, the number of visitors steadily increasing.

Try to go to Tierradentro for a week and just walk in the hills. The people are very friendly, and you can stop and ask at almost any house to buy *guarapo*, a local slightly fermented sugarcane drink. It's great to sit and talk, enjoying the hospitality, as well as the spectacular night skies. If you don't have that much time, do try to stay at least two days.

Indigenous Páez can be seen on market days at **Inzá** (Saturday) and **Belalcázar** (Saturday); both start at 0600. An excellent guide to the Páez and their culture is *Valores Culturales de Tierradentro* by Mauricio Puerta Restrepo, published by the Instituto Colombiano de Antropología (available at the Gold Museum in Bogotá).

Ins and outs

Getting there The road from Popayán to Tierradentro is extremely rough, but this is compensated for by the beautiful scenery; 67 km beyond Totoró is **Inzá**. There are several stone statues in the new plaza. About 9 km beyond Inzá is the Cruce de Pisimbalá, sometimes known as the Cruce de San Andrés or simply El Cruce, where a road turns off to **San Andrés de Pisimbalá** (4 km), the village at the far end of the Tierradentro Park.

Tierradentro

Tourist information The **Casa de Cultura**, in a building just as you enter the village, has good information. Helpful, they can organize guides to local indigenous villages.

Sights

Tierradentro museum ① *0800-1800, but may close at lunchtime and the entry ticket is valid for the museum and all sites, US$7.50.* Before reaching Pisimbalá, you pass the Tierradentro Museum. The well-maintained museum is in two parts, an archaeological section including a model of the Tierradentro region with details of the sites and what has been found. The second floor is dedicated to an overview of the Páez and their culture, past and present. This is all very well worth visiting before going to the sites and the staff are very helpful also with local information.

At **San Andrés de Pisimbalá**, about 2 km beyond and up the hill from the museum, there is a unique and beautiful **colonial missionary church** with a thatched roof, dating back to the 17th century. This is a charming village, peaceful and friendly. Around the cobbled square, the locals lay their coffee to dry on the grass outside their chocolate box houses, while chickens wander in and out of the church and swallows dive between its eaves.

Tierradentro Archaeological Park

At the archway directly opposite the museum, or at Pisimbalá village, you can hire horses (US$2 an hour; make sure they are in good condition) – or you can walk – to the burial caves. There are four cave sites – Segovia, El Duende, Alto de San Andrés and El Aguacate. The main caves are lit, but a torch (your own or one borrowed from the park administration) is advisable.

At Segovia (15 minutes' walk up behind the museum across the river), the guard is very informative (Spanish only) and turns lights on in the main tombs. Segovia has around 30 tombs, five of which are lit: Nos 9, 10 and 12 are best decorated; Nos 8 and 28 are also impressive. Check if photography is permitted. Some 15 minutes up the hill beyond Segovia is El Duende (two of the four tombs are very good). From El Duende continue directly up to a rough road descending to Pisimbalá (40 minutes). El Tablón, with eight stone statues, is just off the road 20-30 minutes' walk down. El Alto de San Andrés is 20 minutes from Pisimbalá (Nos 1 and 5 tombs the best – the guard is very helpful). From the back of El Alto it's 1½ hours up and down hills, with a final long climb to El Aguacate. Only one tomb is maintained although there may be 30 more. The views from El Aguacate are superb. You can continue to the museum.

Some say it's better to do this section starting from the museum. Either way, it is a splendid walk. The whole area is good for birdwatching. For a longer hike, ask about the Páez reserve at Tumbichutzwe, a strenuous three- to four-day walk, or less on horseback. When walking between the sites, take a hat and plenty of water. It gets crowded at Easter. Women are advised not to wander around this area alone at night.

Neiva → *For listings, see pages 312-317. Colour map 3, A5. Phone code: 8. Population: 352,900.*

Capital of the Department of Huila, Neiva is a hot, modern city on the east bank of the Río Magdalena. Surrounded by arid cattle plains, the snow-capped Nevado del Huila (5365 m) looms large to the west. It has a series of pleasant plazas and hosts the Festival Folclórico y Reinado Nacional del Bambuco for 11 days in late June/early July, which incorporates the fiestas de San Juan and San Pedro. A raucous affair, it involves Bambuco dancing competitions and various parades in which bikini-clad beauty queens float downriver on boats and up to 5000 (often) drunken women ride horses through the streets. It culminates in the crowning of a Bambuco queen.

Neiva was founded in 1539 when Belalcázar came across from Popayán on his quest for El Dorado. By the riverside a monument by Rodrigo Arenas Betancur has been erected to commemorate the struggles in the fight for Independence from the Spanish. The cathedral was destroyed in an earthquake in 1967.

Around Neiva

A 30-minute drive south from Neiva is the pretty little town of Rivera, famous for its thermal springs. At the weekend it livens up with plenty of activity around its picturesque plaza and it's a popular destination for locals wishing to escape the heat of Neiva.

The springs are 5 km north of the town. There are several options but the most popular, **Termales de Rivera** ⓘ *US$6.50, open until midnight at weekends*, are set around exuberant tropical gardens and have two restaurants, changing rooms and lockers, a cold swimming pool to cool down and an excellent waterslide. The complex has several (**A**) rooms onsite. A tuk-tuk or taxi from town is US$2.80. There are several hotels in town (**C-D**).

Desierto de Tatacoa → *For listings, see pages 312-317.*

Driving through the lush plains and mountains of Huila it might be difficult to imagine that a desert sits just around the corner. But just 50 km north of Neiva is the Tatacoa desert, a 370-sq-km area of scrub and surreal rock formations dotted with candelabra and prickly pear cacti. Named after a snake that used to thrive in its unforgiving conditions, it is wedged between two mountain ranges that absorb the region's rainfall, starving it of moisture.

It presented a challenging obstacle to the Spanish conquistador Juan Alonso on his quest for El Dorado. He was following the Magdalena river and looking for a route to Popayán when he stumbled across the desert, which he subsequently named El Valle de las Tristezas (The Valley of Sorrows). In 1550 he founded a town on the site on the desert's edge and named it San Juan de Nepomuceno. It was later razed to the ground by the indigenous locals but was rebuilt by Diego de Ospina y Medinilla in 1562 and renamed **Villavieja**. The town played an important role in the 1000-Day War at the turn of the 20th century when a battle between the Liberals and Conservatives was fought nearby.

Villavieja has a particularly charming Parque Principal, surrounded on all sides by 18th-century colonial buildings and with a replica of a Megatherium, an elephant-sized sloth that existed here in the Pleistocene epoch, in the centre. The **Capilla de Santa Bárbara** was built by Jesuit priests in 1630, making it the oldest church in Hulia. It was recently restored, although the local priest keeps it under lock and key and it is difficult to gain access. Next to the church is the **Palaeontological Museum** ⓘ *US$2.70*, with displays of fossils of armadillos, turtles and crocodiles found in the desert, mainly from the Miocene period. Also worth visiting is the railway station, decommissioned since 1975, a reminder of Villavieja's former role as an important staging post on the Bogotá-Neiva line.

The **desert** itself begins 10 km outside Villavieja. On top of a small incline some 15 minutes' drive from Villavieja is the **Observatorio Astronómico de la Tatacoa** ⓘ *www.tatacoa-astronomia.com*, run by stellar enthusiast Javier Fernando Rua. Tatacoa's clear skies and almost non-existent light pollution make it perhaps the best place in Colombia for star gazing and Javier gives an excellent talk every evening at 1830 on the observatory roof, with telescopes and a laser to point out individual constellations, US$2.70 per person. Camping is permitted next to the observatory. Javier hires tents or bring your own.

Opposite the observatory is a viewpoint looking out over **El Cuzco**, a labyrinthine landscape of ochre red hillocks and plateaux that would not look out of place in a Star Trek episode, and where pop star Shakira filmed one of her early music videos. You can walk down into the miniature valley; it is particularly spectacular at sundown.

Some 8 km beyond El Cuzco, is **Los Hoyos** with similar topography only the earth is grey here. Enterprising locals have built a **swimming pool** ① *entry US$1.65 (pay at the estadero)*, amongst the rock formations, fed by water from a natural spring.

Parque Nacional Puracé → *Colour map 3, B3.*

① *Standard entrance fee to the park is US$9.50 (for the Termales at San Juan or climbing the volcanoes).*

The national park contains Volcán Puracé (4646 m), Pan de Azúcar (4670 m) with its permanently snow-covered peak, and the line of nine craters known as the Volcanes los Coconucos. A strenuous two-day hike can be made around the summits. The park also encompasses the sources of four of Colombia's greatest rivers: the Magdalena, Cauca, Caquetá and Patía. Virtually all the park is over 3000 m and covers an area of 86,600 ha. The Andean condor is being reintroduced into the wild here from Californian zoos, and there are many other birds to be seen. The park's fauna include the spectacled bear and mountain tapir. **Pilimbalá** is a good base from which to explore the northern end of the park, where there are Páez settlements. Although much of the park is *páramo*, there are also many species of orchid to be found. For those who do not wish to make the strenuous climb up Volcán Puracé there are many waterfalls, lakes and some technicolour sulphur pools to visit further down.

Ins and outs

All these places beyond Puracé village can be reached by any bus from Popayán to La Plata or Garzón. The last bus returning to Popayán in daylight leaves the visitor centre at about 1700. The bus service can be erratic so be prepared to spend a cold night at 3000 m. The park is open all week, but reduced service on Monday. From Popayán a road crosses the Cordillera Central to Garzón on the paved highway south of Neiva. At Km 18 from Popayán, the road turning up to the right (south) leads to Coconuco (see page 306) and San Agustín (see page 317).

Around the park

The valley road climbs to the small town of **Puracé**, at Km 12 (30 km from Popayán), which has several old buildings. Behind the school a path leads for 500 m to Chorrera de las Monjas waterfalls on the Río Vinagre, notable for the milky white water due to concentrations of sulphur and other minerals. At Km 22, look for the spectacular San Francisco waterfall on the opposite side of the valley. At Km 23 is the turning right to Puracé sulphur mines (6 km) which can be visited by applying to **Industrias Puracé SA** ① *C 4, No 7-32 Popayán*, or, better still, through the Popayán tourist office. About 1 km along this road is a turning left leading in 1.5 km to **Pilimbalá** in the Puracé National Park. There are several buses daily to Puracé from Popayán, the last returning about 1730. At Pilimbalá saloon cars will struggle up the last stretch to the centre, but it is an easy 2.5-km walk from Km 23.

The walk to the **Cascada de San Nicolás** from Pilimbalá is recommended. Turn right when you see the abandoned cabin and continue steadily uphill through very muddy

Spa tourism

If you're looking to be pampered on a five-star luxury spa break, Colombia isn't quite the place ... yet. However, the country makes the most of its natural spas – hot springs, thermal waters, mud volcanoes – sometimes in a rather rustic fashion, sometimes with more flair. Rather than focusing on luxury and pampering, the emphasis tends to be on health benefits and relaxation, bringing spa travel back to its roots, to a time when the whole point was to cure ailments and 'take the waters'. There are treatments and indulgence to be enjoyed, but in an altogether more understated environment. You can roll in the mud at Arboletes mud volcano, then wash off in the Caribbean; spend a few days enjoying the thermal waters at the hot springs of Paipa and Iza, northeast of Bogotá, or at Coconuco outside Popayán, further south. The options are endless; make the most of them before they are transformed into sleek luxury resorts.

terrain, rubber boots advisable. The waterfall is spectacular, take care on the slippery overhanging rocks. At Km 37, the visitor centre has a good geology/ethnology museum. The rangers are very helpful and will allow you to stay there. The centre has picnic shelters, a good restaurant (rainbow trout a speciality) and three *cabañas* that hold eight, US\$13. There is a shared (cold water) bathroom and a small fireplace. Camping costs US\$2 per person. Sleeping bags or warm clothing is recommended to supplement bedding provided. There's also a good scale model of the park.

Half an hour's walk past the visitor centre on the road to La Plata are the Termales de San Juan. The toxic, sulphurous gases released by these hot pools means that swimming is not advisable but a walkway allows for a tour through the colourful mosses and algae surrounding the bubbling, multi-coloured pools and along the milky white streams that run off them. There's a basic place to eat where the bus stops and a cabin with information about the national park. Buses are not regular but up until 1700 there should be something every hour or so. Hitching a lift for around US\$1 should also be possible.

Climbing Volcán Puracé

The hike to the summit is demanding; loose ash makes foothold difficult. Avoid getting down wind of the fumaroles, and do not be tempted to climb down into the crater. Although the best weather is reported to be December to March and July to August, this massif creates its own climate, and high winds, rain and sub-zero temperatures can come in quickly at any time. A marked trail goes from behind the park office and eventually joins the road leading to a set of telecommunications antennae. These installations are no longer guarded by the military **but the area around them is mined; don't take shortcuts.** The summit is about one hour beyond the military buildings. Start early; the total time from Pilimbalá is at least four hours up and 2½ down, and you may need to take shelter if there is a sudden storm. Rangers will not allow you to start after 1200. An alternative route is from the sulphur mine (at 3000 m), or driving, with permission, to the military base. It is also possible to walk round the crater (30 minutes). Rope and crampons are useful above the snowline if you want to continue to Pan de Azúcar and the Coconucos. For this trek, high-altitude camping and mountaineering equipment are required and a guide is strongly recommended. A descent over the *páramo* to Paletará on the Popayán–San Agustín road is also possible.

Continuing on the main road to La Plata, at Km 31 there is a viewpoint for Laguna Rafael, at Km 35 the **Cascada de Bedón** (also chemically charged water) and at Km 37 the entrance to the most northerly part of the Puracé National Park where there is another park centre (see above).

◉ Popayán and Tierradentro listings

For Sleeping and Eating price codes and other relevant information, see pages 23-28.

◉ Sleeping

Popayán *p304, map p305*
Hotel prices include taxes, but are subject to a 100% or more increase in some cases for Holy Week and festivals, eg 5-6 Jan.
L Hotel Dann Monasterio, C 4, No 10-14, T824 2191, hdannmo@tvoconectado.com. Run by the ubiquitous Dann group, this 17th-century Franciscan monastery, with its cobbled courtyards and fountains, emanates tranquillity. The rooms are comfortable and it has a swimming pool and sauna. Staff can be a bit snooty.
A La Plazuela, C 5, No 8-13, T824 1084, www.hotellaplazuela.com.co. Located opposite the Iglesia San José, this beautiful colonial building has good-sized rooms with antique furniture set around a colonnaded, cobbled courtyard. There is Wi-Fi throughout the building, cable TV and breakfast included.
B Los Balcones, Cra 7, No 2-75, T824 2030, www.hotellosbalconespopayan.com. Los Balcones is a mixed bag. It has some enormous rooms, including one in the attic with stained glass skylights, while others are small. Ancient TVs and antique furniture give it a certain charm while Wi-Fi and a free internet room are the hotel's concession to modernity.
C La Casona del Virrey, C 4, No 5-78, T824 0836, hotellacasonadelvirrey@hotmail.com. Most hotels in Popayán are beautiful colonial buildings but la Casona del Virrey is a cut above the rest. It has a gorgeous spiral staircase leading up to rooms that look down on a cobbled courtyard. Many of the rooms have wooden floorboards and original

wainscot panelling. Modern services include Wi-Fi. Recently opened a disco, **Club Corona**, Thu-Sat, so perhaps best avoided if looking for a tranquil stay.
C Los Portales, C 5, No 10-125, T821 0139, www.losportaleshotel.com. This sweet little hotel has rooms set around 3 leafy, sunny courtyards with water features. It also has cable TV and an internet room. Discounts for longer stays.
D Hotel Colonial, C 5, No 10-94, T831 7848, hotelcolonial@hotmail.es. This hotel has clean – if a little dark – rooms with comfortable beds. It has a restaurant serving home-cooked food, cable TV, hot water, Wi-Fi, safe and free local calls.
D-F Pass Home, C 5, No 10-114, T316-448 9513 (mob), hotelpasshome@gmail.com. Friendly hotel with a relaxing atmosphere, has private rooms or dorms for 4 with private bathrooms, hot water, cable TV and Wi-Fi. Use of kitchen, free laundry service with a 3-day stay, can arrange pick-up from airport or bus terminal for a charge. Recommended.
E Casa Familiar El Descanso, Cra 5, No 2-41, T2-824 0029. This family house has been a popular backpackers' choice for many years. With lots of plants and antiques, it is a peaceful place of just 5 rooms and 3 shared bathrooms. The owners speak German and English and will happily share their local knowledge.
E Casa Familiar Turística, Cra 5, No 2-07, T2-824 4853. Another popular backpackers' choice, this little place has simple rooms with incredibly high ceilings. It has good notice boards with information and messages from other travellers.
E-F HostelTrail Guesthouse, Cra 11, No 4-16, T314-696 0805 (mob), www.hosteltrail.com. This excellent,

backpackers' hostel is efficiently run by Scottish couple Tony and Kim. The rooms are comfortable and clean (most with shared bathroom) and have Wi-Fi access, while there are cheap dorms with bunks, good communal areas, a kitchen, DVD room, book sale and lockers. Tony and Kim have extensive knowledge of the local area and also do a good bike tour to the thermal springs at Coconuco.

Tierradentro *p307, map p307*

E Residencias Pisimbalá, near the museum, T311-612 4645 (mob). The Pisimbalá has rooms with private bathrooms and hot water as well as the cheaper option of shared cold-water bathrooms. It has a good little restaurant, while camping costs around US$1.50 per person.
E-F Hospedaje Ricabet, near the museum, T312-795 4636 (mob). This little *hospedaje* has a bright courtyard bursting with colourful flowers and clean rooms and en suite bathrooms with hot water. Rooms with a shared bath are a little cheaper.
F El Cauchito, in the village. This family home has 3 basic rooms and friendly service. Shared bathrooms and there is no hot water.
F El Viajero, in the village, another family home with a friendly owner, the rooms are basic but clean and the shower is *al clima*. Food available on request.
F Hospedaje Luzerna, next to the museum. Run by a lovely old couple, this little place has clean, basic rooms and very good hot showers (with 30 mins' forewarning).
F Los Llanos, 100 m past the church. Pleasant colonial building with clean, basic rooms and a colourful courtyard.
F-G La Portada, bamboo building at jeep/bus stop in village. Basic rooms, popular.

Neiva *p308*

A Hotel Neiva Plaza, C 7, No 4-62, T871 0806, www.hotelneivaplaza.com. Neiva's traditional smart hotel for more than 50 years, the **Plaza** has good, comfortable rooms, a restaurant and a swimming pool.

D Andino, C 9, No 5-82, T871 0184. This centrally located hotel's rooms are a little small and dark but nonetheless clean and with cable TV.
E Tayronas, C 8, No 3-46, T871 3038. You'll be greeted by the smell of incense and a reception covered in pre-Columbian artefacts as you enter this hotel, which has dark, small rooms with en suite bathrooms.

Desierto de Tatacoa *p309*
Villavieja

E La Portada al Sol, T313-217 2983 (mob). This *posada*, built on the site of a Jesuit *finca* on the edge of town, has simple rooms with fan and private bathroom. Food can be prepared on request.
E-F La Casona, C 3, No 3-60, T8-879 7636, hostellacasonavillavieja@yahoo.es. This gorgeous old building on the Parque Principal once had Simón Bolívar stay the night and has a shady backyard full of well-presented tables. Its monasterial rooms are crammed with beds but the owner won't fill them up if you ask for privacy. Recommended.
F Residencia Geraldo Calderón. This little place has a couple of very basic rooms with shared bathrooms in the backyard of a colonial house.

The desert
Camping at the observatory is US$5.50 for a 2-person tent, less if you bring your own. There are showers and good food prepared with forewarning.
There are also several *posadas nativas*, run by local families. Enquire at the **Asociación de Operadores Turísticos** on the Parque Principal, T314-315 2067 (mob). You can also call the *posadas* direct. Try: **Elvira Cleves**, T312-559 8576 (mob), who can also arrange stays with her mother **Doña Rosalia**. At Los Hoyos, **Señora Ofanda Sott**, T311-536 5027 (mob).

🍴 Eating

Popayán *p304, map p305*

Popayán has a tradition of good food. In 2005 the city was named a UNESCO City of Gastronomy. Local specialities include *tamales de pipián*.

🍴 **Lochería La Viña**, C 4, No 7-07, T824 0602. Open 24 hrs a day, this *parrillada* restaurant has an enormous selection of juicy, Argentine-style steaks accompanied by good salads, fries and rice.

🍴-🍴 **Kanda**, vegetarian restaurant. Good lunchtime spot with vegetarian and vegan options.

🍴-🍴 **Restaurante Italiano**, C 4, No 8-83, T824 0607. This Swiss-run restaurant has been serving an excellent selection of pastas, pizzas, crêpes and fondues since 1995 with much love and attention. Recommended.

🍴-🍴 **Tequila's**, C 5 No 9-25. Mexican-run cantina with great Mexican food, reasonably priced. Also good cocktails. Recommended.

🍴 **El Muro**, Cra 8, No 4-11, T824 0539. This little place serves vegetarian US$2.50 *almuerzos* with daily menus ranging from quinoa salad to pizzas and veggie burgers. At night it converts into a dimly lit bar.

🍴 **Jengibre**, Cra 7, No 2-71, T820 5456. Good breakfast venue and the restaurant opposite with the same name (Cra 7 2-38) is serving *almuerzos* for US$4 as well as à la carte options.

🍴 **Verde y Mostaza**, Cra 4 con C 4 esquina. Popular with students, this little restaurant serves up cheap fast food such as crêpes, pizzas and burgers.

Cafés

Popayán has a thriving café culture, with many of them located in gorgeous colonial buildings.

Capriccio, C 5, No 5-63. Popular with the locals, this café has excellent hot drinks, some with potent shots added, as well as brownies and ice creams.

Juan Valdez, Cra 7, No 4-36 to 49. Part of the ubiquitous chain, this one is housed in

a beautiful courtyard with 4 enormous palm trees. Large selection of coffees and merchandise on sale. Has Wi-Fi.

Madeira Café, C 3 esq con Cra 5. Good selection of coffees, milkshakes, brownies, fruit juices and cheesecakes.

Wipala, Cra 2 2-38. Art and café in lovely surroundings.

Tierradentro *p307, map p307*

🍴 **La Portada**, on the edge of the village. *Almuerzos* for US$2.50.

🍴 **Pisimbalá**, near the museum. Good, cheap food. Recommended.

Neiva *p308*

🍴 **Carbonara**, C 9, No 6-41. Cheap *almuerzos* served on a pleasant terrace. Next door is an internet café.

🍴 **Confucio**, Cra 6, No 9-34. Popular Chinese restaurant.

🍴 **Frutería y Heladería Alaska**, Cra 6, No 8-40. This little fruit and ice cream spot does delicious fruit salads, though be sure to inform them if you don't want ice cream with your breakfast fruit salad.

🍴 **La Casona**, Cra 4, No 12-37, T8-872 1454. This restaurant serves up cheap *almuerzos* in the smart courtyard of an old house. A la carte dishes include baby beef and catfish.

🍴 **Yoga Inbound**, C 9, No 5-74, T9-871 7895. Indian-influenced vegetarian restaurant serving lunchtime buffets, US$2.70, consisting of soups, salads and soya products.

🍸 Bars and clubs

Popayán *p304, map p305*

El Sotareño, C 6, No 8-05. Run by an old couple from San Agustín this eccentric bar plays old tango LPs from the 1940s and 50s as well as *bolero* and *ranchero* music.

Iguana Afro-Club, C 4, No 9-67. Good music, jazz, salsa, friendly owner.

Tijuana, Cra 9, No 4-68. Mix of music, popular.

⊛ Festivals and events

Popayán *p304, map p305*
5 Jan Día de los Negros; and
6 Jan Día de los Blancos; both are
like those at Pasto, but a lot less wet.
Mar/Apr Semana Santa (Holy Week).
The processions, every night until Good Fri
are spectacular; the city is very crowded. The
children's processions in the following week
are easier to see. The children assume all the
roles of the official processions to the delight
of parents and onlookers. During Holy Week
the Museo de Arte Religioso opens up its
vaults and displays several large emeralds,
including one the size of an avocado. Also
during Semana Santa there is an international sacred music festival, founded in
1964. Orchestras and groups from many
countries have participated in the past.
At the same time there are presentations
at Santander de Quilichao on the main road
halfway between Popayán and Cali.

⊙ Shopping

Popayán *p304, map p305*
During the week, the open markets are
interesting. For handicrafts, there are lots of
stands at Rincón Payanés, next to El Morro.
Bolívar market, C 1N, Cra 5. Best in the early
morning – local foods such as *pipián*, *tamales*
and *empanadas*.
The Mercado Esmeralda, on C 5 and
Autopista, west of the centre. A little bigger
and also worth a visit.

▲ Activities and tours

Popayán *p304, map p305*
Tour operators
Aviatur, C 4, No 8-69, T2-820 8674. For Isla
Gorgona and Malpelo.
Luna Paz Tours, C 8, No 7-61, T315-513 9593
(mob). Organizes tours to Tierradentro as well
as further afield destinations in Colombia.

Tour of coffee *finca* **Alas y Raíces**,
Swiss/Colombian-run, T320-742 3470,
manuela.ruegg@gmail.com. US$60 for 4
people, price includes transportation from
Popayán (leaves 0930) to *finca*, plantation
tour and typical lunch. Also possible to visit
waterfalls nearby and see the coffee-toasting
and grinding process. The *finca* has limited
accommodation (**D** – price includes
breakfast and dinner). Recommended.

Tierradentro *p307, map p307*
Cayo Oidos Galindo, T310-229 2971 (mob),
based in La Plata, spent 15 years working with
archaeologists from Banco de la República
unearthing many of Tierradentro's tombs.
Organizes tours of Tierradentro and surrounding villages with accommodation and food
provided. Can arrange English-speaking
guides. Recommended.

Desierto de Tatacoa *p309*
**The Asociación de Operadores Turísticos
de La Tatacoa**, T314-315 2067/T311-499
2512 (mob), on the Parque Principal, can
arrange guides, transport and accommodation in the desert. Alternatively, contact
astronomer and manager of the observatory
Javier Fernando Rua, T879 7585/T310-465
6765 (mob), who can make arrangements
with local guides and transport.

⊖ Transport

Popayán *p304, map p305*
Air To **Bogotá** with **Avianca** (Cra 7, No 5-77)
and **Satena** (Cra 9, No 4-14), daily. To **Guapi**,
3 times a week with **Satena**.

Bus To **Bogotá**, Expreso Bolivariano,
US$32.50, 1900 and 2000, 12-16 hrs, also
Flota Magdalena and Velotax. To **Cali**, US$6,
2½-3 hrs, or **Velotax** microbus, US$11,
colectivos leave from the main plaza. To **Pasto**,
US$12.50- 14.50, 4-6 hrs, spectacular scenery
(sit on right). To **Ipiales**, Expreso Bolivariano,
US$15.50, 7-8 hrs, runs every hour but many

buses arrive full from Cali, book in advance. To **San Agustín**, Cootranslaboyana, 7-8 hrs, US$14, 4 a day, **Cootranshuila** or La Gaitana, 5 a day until 1500, US$14, 6-8 hrs. Sit on the left for the best views. To **Tierradentro** (Cruce de Pisimbalá, also known as Cruce de San Andrés or San Andrés de Pisimbalá), 4 daily 0430- 1300, US$9, 4-6 hrs continues to La Plata. To **La Plata**, US$11, 5 hrs, with Cootranshuila also Sotracauca. To **Puracé**, Cootranshuila and Sotracauca 5 a day, US$4.50-6, 2-2 ½ hrs.

Taxi No metres; normal price within city is US$1.75.

Warning Avoid travelling by night between Popayán and San Agustín, the roads have been reported dangerous in the past. Additionally, they are in very bad condition. Also we have received many reports of theft, recently and in the past, on the buses between these towns; do not trust 'helpfuls' and do not put bags on the luggage rack.

Around Popayán *p306*
Bus To **Silvia**, from **Popayán**, daily Coomotorista and Belalcázar, several *busetas* in the morning (US$2.50-3, 90 mins).

Tierradentro *p307, map p307*
Bus To **La Plata**, buses leave from San Andrés, passing by the museum at 0500, 0600 and 0800. Otherwise, you must go to El Cruce. From La Plata, *colectivos* leave when full for **Tierradentro**, US$4.40 per person, with Cootransplateño and others. From Popayán daily 0430, 0800, 1030 and 1300, US$9, 4-6 hrs to **Cruce Pisimbalá**. Best to take early buses, as afternoon buses will leave you at the Cruce in the dark. Walk uphill (about 2 km, 30 mins) to the museum and on, 20 mins, to the village. If you want to go to Silvia, take this bus route and change to a *colectivo* (US$1.50) at Totoró. Buses and *camionetas* from the Cruce to **La Plata** (en route to San Agustín, see below) US$4.50, 4-5 hrs or more frequent *colectivo* jeeps,

US$6. If you cannot get a direct Cruce–La Plata bus, take one going to **Páez** (Belalcázar) (US$1.50), alight at Guadualejo, 17 km east of Inzá, from where there is a more frequent service to La Plata.

Neiva *p308*
Air Several flights daily with **Avianca** or Aires, 1 hr.

Bus To **Bogotá**, 5½ hrs, US$15, with Bolivariano (5 a day) or Coomotor. To **Rivera**, *colectivo*, US$1.50, 25 mins. To **Villavieja**, *colectivo*, 30 mins, To **La Plata**, 2 hrs, US$5.50, *colectivo*.

Desierto de Tatacoa *p309*
To **Neiva**, US$4, 1 hr, from the Parque Principal in Villavieja or from the terminal in Neiva. To the **desert**, transport is expensive, US$11 per person as far as El Cuzco, 15 mins. The walk takes 1 hr but bear in mind that temperatures can reach up to 49°C so be sure to take lots of water, a hat, and sun cream. To **Bogotá**, take a *colectivo* to Neiva and transfer there. Alternatively, it's possible to cross the Río Magdalena in a motorized canoe, US$1.10. Walk past the cemetery down to the river and shout if there is no-one there as they might be waiting on the other side. From the far side of the river it's a 1.5-km walk to the town of Aipe from where it is possible to hail down buses, US$11, on the main Neiva–Bogotá highway, about 250 m from the Parque Principal. From the river, follow the path until you reach the edge of town and walk up C 5 past the *parque*. A taxi from the centre of Aipe to the main road, US$2 (recommended).

❻ Directory

Popayán *p304, map p305*
Language classes The HostelTrail Guesthouse organizes Spanish lessons with graduates from the Universidad del Cauca, US$5 per hr. Also language exchanges with students of English.

Around Popayán *p306*

Silvia

Banks Banco Cooperativo, Cra 6, Banco del Estado, and others will change TCs. Some, eg Banco Popular, C 4, No 5-48, will give cash advances against Visa cards or Banco del Occidente against MasterCard. Banco de Bogotá, C 4, No 6-44. **Davivienda**, Cra 9, No 00, gives largest withdrawals, 500,000 pesos at a time. **Bancolombia**, Cra 6, No 4-49. **Titan**, good rates offered, Cra 7, No 6-40, T2-824 4659, inside CC Luis Martínez, Mon-Fri 0800-1200, 1400-1700, Sat 0830-1200. They also offer an international money transfer

service. There are other *cambios*, but their rates are poor. **Internet** Cafeto Internet, Cr 9, No 5-42, T2-824 3400. Good value, open late. **Post** Correos de Colombia/Adpostal, C 14, No 2-56, T2-824 4564. **Security** DAS, C 4, No 10B-66, T2-823 1889 ext 108. **Telephone** Telecom, Cra 4 y C 3; closes 2000. You can make international calls for less than 3 mins.

Tierradentro *p307, map p307*

Telephone There are no landlines in Tierradentro at present but mobile phones work and locals will sell you *minutos*.

San Agustín and around

→ *Phone code: 8. Colour map 3, B3. Population: 30,000. Altitude: 1700 m.*

Famed for its mysterious pre-Columbian stone figures of men, animals and gods, the little town of San Agustín is also an opportunity to enjoy the rural landscape of Colombia at its finest. The largest collection of religious monuments and megalithic sculptures in South America, the statues uncovered in this wild, spectacular countryside were hewn from stone between 3300 BC and the arrival of the Spanish. Little is known about the culture that produced them, further adding to their mystery. Many of the figures have been moved to an archaeological park just outside the town but you can also visit some which remain in their original locations, ensconced in rolling green hills rich in colourful, sub-tropical flowers and tumbling brooks. Here, the Río Magdalena is at its angriest, kicking and screaming into life as it begins its journey through the heart of Colombia towards the Caribbean coast. ►► *For listings, see pages 320-322.*

Ins and outs

Tourist information

There are several tour agencies portraying themselves as 'tourist offices'. While they may well give out useful advice, some of this will be clouded by contracts they hold with various hotels and other operators around town. For impartial advice visit the **Oficina Municipal de Turismo** on the Plaza Cívica or the tourist police at the police station just nearby, **Oficina de Policía de Turismo** ① *C 3, No 11-86*. For cultural information there is a **Casa de Cultura** ① *Cra 3, No 3-61*.

Climate

The rainy season is April to June/July, but since the weather often comes up from the Amazon basin to the southeast, it can rain at any time of year, hence the beautiful green landscape; the driest months are November to March. The days are warm but sweaters are needed in the evenings; average temperature 18°C.

Recommended reading

The best books on the subject are *Exploraciones Arqueológicas en San Agustín*, by Luis Duque Gómez (Bogotá, 1966, 500 pages) or *San Agustín, Reseña Arqueológica*, by the same author (1963, 112 pages); a leaflet in English is obtainable from tourist offices. The Colombian Institute of Archaeology has published a booklet (English/Spanish) on San Agustín and Tierradentro; it may be available at museums in San Agustín and San Andrés.

Warning Beware of 'guides' and touts who approach you in the street. Have nothing to do with anyone offering drugs, pre-Columbian objects, gold, emeralds or other precious minerals for sale. Enquire about safety before walking to the more distant monuments.

Parque Arqueológico

① *Daily 0800-1800, last entrance 1600, museum closes at 1600. Entrance to the park and museum is US$5, entrance to Alto de los Idolos is US$5. It is also possible to buy a combined entry ticket for both, for US$8. There are refreshment stands at 'Fuente' and on the way up to Lavapatas.*

The nearest archaeological sites are in the Parque Arqueológico, which includes the **Bosque de las Estatuas**. The park, which was declared a World Heritage Site by UNESCO in 1995, is about 2.5 km from San Agustín, less than 1 km from the **Hotel Osoguaico**. The statues in the park are in situ, though some have been set up on end and fenced in. Those in the Bosque de las Estatuas have been moved and rearranged, and linked by gravel footpaths.

Apart from the distinctive statues, the most notable features of the San Agustín site are the **Mesitas** (barrows) consisting of large vertical stone slabs, standing in circular enclosures about 25 m in diameter. These were probably originally roofed over with statues set inside and out. There is some doubt if they were primarily in places of ceremony or tombs. There are four Mesitas, Mesita D is beside the museum area near the entrance to the park, you will visit B, A and C following the trail. Beyond Mesita C are the carved rocks in and around the stream at the **Fuente de Lavapatas** in the park, where the water runs through carved channels. The park authorities have reduced the water flow to the Fuente as there was considerable damage being caused by too much water. It is, however, now easier to see the engravings on the rocks. The **Alto de Lavapatas**, above the Fuente, has an extensive view.

Within the park children sell various things including *guama* fruit, which comes in a large pea-like pod. They have a refreshing moist flavour, but do not eat the black seeds!

There is also a **museum** ① *daily 0800-1600*, in the park, which contains pottery and artefacts and a good scale model of the local sites giving an excellent idea of the topography of the area.

You can get a very good idea of the park, the Bosque and the museum in the course of three hours' walking, or add in El Tablón and La Chaquira (see below) for a full day. The whole site leaves an unforgettable impression, from the strength and strangeness of the statues, and the great beauty of the rolling green landscape.

In the town is the **Museo Arqueológico Julio César Cubillos** ① *Cra 11, No 3-61, open Mon-Fri 0800-1200, 1300-1730*, with a good library, videos in Spanish and English, and light refreshments.

Archaeological sites

El Tablón (five sculptures brought together under a bamboo roof) is reached up Carrera 14, over the brow of the hill and 250 m to a marked track to the right, then down to the left. Continue down the path, muddy in wet weather, ford a stream and follow signs to the Río Magdalena canyon. **La Chaquira** (figures carved on rocks) is dramatically set halfway down to the river. Walking time round trip from San Agustín is two hours. Plenty of houses offer refreshments as far as El Tablón. There are many pleasant paths to follow in this area, ask locally for ideas.

Continue along the road from San Agustín for the site of **La Pelota**, where two painted statues were found in 1984. It's a three-hour return trip, six hours if you include El Tablón and La Chaquira, 15 km in all. Archaeological discoveries in 1984/1986 include some unique polychromed sculptures at **El Purutal** near La Pelota and a series of at least 30 stones carved with animals and other designs in high relief. These are known as **Los Petroglifos** and can be found on the right bank of the Río Magdalena, near the **Estrecho** (narrows) to which jeeps run.

Also part of the UNESCO site is **Alto de los Idolos**, about 10 km by horse or on foot (0800-1630, US$5 or US$8 if combined with park and museum entrance). It's a lovely, if strenuous, walk, steep in places, via **Puente de la Chaquira**. Here on a hill overlooking San Agustín are more and different statues known as *vigilantes*, each guarding a burial mound (one is an unusual rat totem). The few excavated have disclosed large stone sarcophagi, some covered by stone slabs bearing a sculpted likeness of the inmate (the site is open until 1630).

Alto de los Idolos can also be reached from **San José de Isnos** (5 km northeast) 27 km by road from San Agustín. The road passes the **Salto del Mortiño**, a 170 m fall about 7 km before Isnos, 500 m off the road. Isnos' market day is Saturday.

About 6 km north of Isnos is **Alto de las Piedras**, which has a few interesting tombs and monoliths, including the famous 'Doble Yo'. Only slightly less remarkable than the statues are the orchids growing nearby. Bordones is 8 km further on. Turn left at end of the village and there is (500 m) parking for the **Salto de Bordones** falls.

Tours around San Agustín

Horse hire You are strongly advised to hire horses for trips around San Agustín through hotels. The centre for horses (**Asociación de Acompañantes y Alquiladores de Caballos** ⓘ *along C 5 on the road to the park*, costs about US$11.65 per hour, per rider. If you require a guide, you must add the hire cost of his horse. **Pacho**, T311-827 7972 (mob) and **Abuy**, T311-453 3959 (mob) come highly recommended as guides and are contactable through El Maco or La Casa de Nelly. There are fixed tariffs for 20 or so standard trips.

Vehicle tours Jeeps may be hired for between four to five people. Prices vary according to the number of sites to be visited, but the daily rate is about US$16.50 per person with a minimum of four people. Try bargaining for a lower price.

Guides There are countless guides in town offering tours of the various sites. Some give a better service than others. Enquire at your hotel or at the tourist office for advice. Some recommended names are **Marino Bravo**, T313-221 4006 (speaks good English), **Gloria**, T312-440 2010 and **Carlos Bolaños**, T311-459 5753.

South of San Agustín

Southeast of San Agustín is the little town of **Pitalito**. It has little to offer the tourist except that it is here that the brightly painted, imaginative ceramics are made that are often used in tourist advertisements for southern Colombia. Most notable are the extravagantly decorated *chivas*, the ubiquitous country buses of the region. Many other items are produced, a delightful art form expressing a popular culture.

South of Pitalito is the **Cueva de los Guácharos National Park** ⓘ *entry US$16.50 for foreigners; accommodation (when available), US$5 per night per person; permission to visit the park must be obtained from the National Parks Office, Cra 4, No 4-21, Pitalito*. Between December and June swarms of oilbirds (*guácharos*) may be seen; they are nocturnal, with a unique radar-location system. The reserve also contains many of the unusual and spectacular cock-of-the-rock (a type of bird). The rangers are particularly friendly, providing tours and basic accommodation. The 9000-ha park extends to the crest of the Cordillera Oriental, here rising to over 3000 m. It is mostly rain and cloudforest with an abundance of wildlife, but inaccessible. The main interest centres on the valley of the Río Suárez, a tributary of the Magdalena, which here flows through limestone caves and gorges. There are three caves to visit, **Cueva Chiquita** near the entrance, **Cueva del Indio**, 740 m long with interesting calcium formations, and further upstream, the **Cueva de los Guácharos** with a natural bridge over the river. To reach the park, take a bus to **Palestina**, US$1.20, one hour, and then walk for six hours along an eroded, muddy path. Another unpaved road from Pitalito goes southwest to Mocoa through remote jungle, crossing the Río Caquetá 25 km before Mocoa. This is a faster way to get to Ecuador. Until recently security was poor on this route due to strong guerrilla and drugtrafficking presence but lately it has improved, though the road still suffers from many landslides and accidents.

◉ San Agustín and around listings → *Phone code: 8.*

For Sleeping and Eating price codes and other relevant information, see pages 23-28.

● Sleeping

San Agustín *p317*

B Yalconia, Vía al Parque Arqueológico, T837 3013, hotelyalconia@hotmail.com. The only mid-range hotel in town, the Yalconia is a modern building with cleanish rooms, although some of the paintwork is starting to deteriorate.

D Hacienda Anacaona, Vía al Estrecho, T311-231 7128, www.anacaona-colombia.com. This traditional *finca* has comfortable, spacious rooms and a colourful garden with fine views into the hills as well as a restaurant serving typical regional food such as trout and *sancocho*.

D-E Casa de Nelly, Km 2 Vía Parque Archeológico por Vereda La Estrella, T310-215 9067 (mob), www.hosteltrail.com/hotelcasade nelly. On top of the hill on the road to the archaeological park, this lovely old house has colourful rooms and *cabañas* set in a gorgeous garden bursting with subtropical flowers and bushes. There's a kitchen serving home cooked pastas and pizzas as well as a thatched kiosk with hammocks for taking in the atmosphere.

D-E El Jardín, Cra 11, No 4-10, T837 3455, www.hosteltrail.com/eljardin. In town, this colonial house has a colourful patio decorated with hanging baskets, snake skins and animal pelts as well as a couple of chirpy songbirds. The rooms are simple but clean and it has a restaurant. There are also dorms (**E**).

E Casa del Sol Naciente, 1 km from the village along Cra 13, T311-587 6464, www. refugioecologicocasadelsolnaciente.com. This rustic retreat has a several *cabañas*, including

2 that must have one of the most spectacular views in Colombia, looking down into a gorge with the raging Magdalena river racing along the bottom. With a vegetable and herb garden and an open air bath, this is a place for nature lovers, though it's best not to opt for a room in the main house, which is a little dark. There is also camping from US$2.50 per person in the gardens and US$3 near the canyon.

€ El Maco, 1 km from town, 400 m past Piscina Las Moyas, T837 3437, www.elmaco.ch. Swiss-owned, working organic farm with colourful gardens, rustic, peaceful, cosy cabins, also teepee, welcoming, basic kitchen facilities, internet, laundry service, very good restaurant (reserve in advance), excellent local information; see **Chaska Tours**, below. Recommended.

€ La Casa de François, T314-358 2930 (mob), 200 m via El Tablón (Cra 13), www.lacasade francois.com. Just outside town, this French-run hostel has private rooms with bathrooms as well as dorms set in 2 ha of gardens blooming with orchids and other flowers. There's a kitchen that's free to use or there's a varied menu available of home-made food for US$2.70, as well as crêpes and home-baked bread. Other pluses include bike and horse hire and Wi-Fi.

Camping Next to Yalconia is Camping San Agustín, US$1.60 per person with own tent, US$5.50 to hire tent, clean, pleasant, safe (guards), showers, toilets, lights, laundry service, horse hire.

Eating

San Agustín *p317*
Tap water in San Agustín is not safe to drink.
Brahama, C 5, No 15-11, T301-417 1077 (mob). This small restaurant serves up the usual Colombian fare as well as some good vegetarian options.
Donde Richard, C 5, No 23-45, T312-432 399. On the outskirts of town, this is one of the better restaurants in San Agustín, with excellent quality steak, chicken and fish

dishes cooked in agreeable surroundings and accompanied by soups and salads.
℉ El Fogón, C 5, No 14-30, T837-3431. Festooned with local trinkets and antiques, El Fogón does à la carte and *comidas corrientes*, including fish, steaks, and *patacón*.
℉ El Maco, T8373437. It's a healthy 1-km walk from town but **El Maco** serves some of the best food in San Agustín, including excellent Thai curries and pastas as well as organic options. Recommended.
℉ La Rana Verde, Cra 11, No 2-26, T314-267 8123 (mob). Good little lunchtime venue serving fixed-menu meals for US$2.20.
℉ Surabhi, C 5, No 14-09, T313-345 7519 (mob). Surabhi serves up tasty regional specialities. *Almuerzos* cost US$2.20.

Festivals and events

San Agustín *p317*
Mid-Jul (not a fixed date) **Fiesta of Santa María del Carmen** is held in San Agustín.
24 Jun Festival in San Juan, with horse races and dances.
29 Jun Festival in San Pedro, with horse races, dances, fancy dress, competitions and other events.
1st week of Oct La Semana Cultural Integrada is celebrated in the Casa de Cultura, with many folklore events from all parts of the country.
End Oct/beginning Nov Feria de San Agustín, with livestock shows and horse displays.

Shopping

San Agustín *p317*
Leather goods are beautiful and priced reasonably. Many local shops make boots to your own design (double-check the price beforehand). C 5, No 14-25 is a good place for handicrafts by local leatherworker Angélica.

▲ Activities and tours

San Agustín *p317*

Chaska Tours, T837 3437, www.chaska tours.net. Run by Swiss René Suter (who also owns the hostel **El Maco**), this agency organizes tours around San Agustín as well as to Tierradentro, Puracé and the Tatacoa desert. English and German spoken. Recommended.

Magdalena Rafting, C 5 No 16-04, T311-271 5333, www.magdalenarafting.com. French-run adventure sports company specializing in whitewater rafting (all grades of rapids and experience available, from US$22.50 per person), as well as kayaking and caving.

Pacho, T311-827 7972, pachitocampesinito @yahoo.es, is a very good horse-riding guide. As well as to the various archaeological sites he also does tours to Lago Magdalena, the source of the Río Magdalena, US$27 for guidance plus US$20 per person.

Piscina Municipal, behind the **Yalconia**. A clean swimming pool, with water fed from a natural spring, busy at weekends, US$1 per day.

⊖ Transport

San Agustín *p317*
Bus

To **Bogotá** by *buseta* (**Taxis Verdes**, C 17, No 69D-54, T411 1152 (Bogotá), www.taxis verdes.net, 0500, 0700 and 1900 direct, US$23, 9 hrs or by bus **Coomotor**, C 3, No 10-71), 3 a day, buses US$26-29. From Bogotá, **Taxis Verdes**, 0300, 9 hrs, US$21.50. **Coomotor**, 3 a day at 0700, 2100 and 2330 10-12 hrs, US$26-29 (depending on type of bus). More frequent services from Bogotá to **Pitalito** with Coomotor or **Cootranshuila**, 8 hrs, US$23-27 from which *colectivos* leave for San Agustín, US$2.70, 45 mins. To **Neiva**, 6 buses a day, including

Coomotor and Cootranshuila, 6 hrs, US$12.50. To **Pitalito** 1½ hrs, US$4-5 by *colectivo*, or any bus to Neiva. To **Popayán**, services at 0600, 0900, 1100, 1400, and 1630 with **Cootranshuila**, US$14. You may have to take a *colectivo* to Km 5 on Popayán–Pitalito road and catch a bus from there. To **Tierradentro**, take early transport to Pitalito (US$2.70), 1 direct bus with **Cootransmayo** at 0630 otherwise *colectivo* or taxi. From Pitalito there are direct buses at 1000 and 1400 to **La Plata** (US$8.30), finally *colectivo* to **Tierradentro** (US$4.40). If you miss the connection to La Plata at Pitalito do the same route but go via Garzón (this road is in much better condition) and take a *colectivo* from La Plata. To **Pasto via Mocoa**, 11 hrs, take a bus or *colectivo* to Pitalito, where there are buses or Kia's (**Pony Express**) to Mocoa, US$11. From Mocoa to Pasto, US$19. There is also transport from here to Laguna Cocha. This is a far quicker route to Pasto than going via Popayán and relatively safe from guerrilla activity but take advice before going. Do not travel at night, there have been reports of thefts and hijackings, and bear in mind that this road is prone to landslides and traffic accidents.

Note Bus times change constantly. Enquire at bus station or hotel before setting out.

❶ Directory

San Agustín *p317*

Banks Travellers are advised to change TCs before arriving in San Agustín; enquire at the travel office and the small shop opposite the police station who may exchange cash. **Caja Agraria**, C 4/Cra 13, and **Ultrahuilca Redeban**, Cra 3, No 12-7, will give cash advances against Visa card. **Almacén de Todo**, opposite the town hall, will cash TCs but at a bad rate. **Internet** Connections are slow in San Agustín. **Galería Café**, C 3 is one option.

Far south

From Popayán to Ecuador, the Pan-American highway travels through arguably the most spectacular scenery in Colombia, at first dipping into humid agricultural land before rising again as it nears the highland city of Pasto. It is a forever engaging ride as the landscape becomes increasingly dramatic; at times the road follows in the shadow of the Western Cordillera, as waves of small hills roll out towards its edges like crumpled sheets on an unmade bed. Beyond Pasto it is even more impressive as the road snakes its way ever upward, clinging to the edges of steep escarpments painstakingly planted with maize, peas and wheat, over deep gorges that plunge down to raging rivers. The area is dominated by volcanoes, some of them active, especially those that overlook the border town of Ipiales. Near Pasto is Laguna La Cocha, which has a national park well worth visiting on the Isla de Corota. Just outside Ipiales is the extraordinary Gothic church of Las Lajas that straddles a deep gorge and is a magnet for miracle-seekers and pilgrims. To the west it's a long ride down to the Pacific coast at Tumaco where salt marshes and mangroves have created a distinct ecosystem. On the way, the private nature reserve of La Planada has a unique population of native birds and a conservation programme of special interest to ecologists.
➡➡ *For listings, see pages 330-332.*

Pasto → *For listings, see pages 330-332. Colour map 3, B2. Phone code: 2. Population: 400,000. Altitude: 2534 m.*

The capital of the Department of Nariño stands upon a high plateau in the southwest, 88 km from Ecuador. Pasto (full name San Juan de Pasto), is overlooked from the west by Galeras Volcano (when not in cloud) and to the east by green hills not yet suburbanized by the city, and enjoys a very attractive setting. Surrounded by hills and swirling clouds, it still retains some of its colonial character, but has not been helped by several serious earthquakes in the meantime. A little unfairly, the people of Pasto have a reputation throughout the rest of Colombia as being very stupid and are the butt of many jokes. What is fair to say is that they are extremely friendly.

Ins and outs

The **airport** is at Cano, 35 km north of Pasto; by *colectivo* (beautiful drive), 45 minutes. US$2.40 or US$13.50 by taxi. There are no currency-exchange facilities, but the shop will change US dollar bills at a poor rate. All interurban buses leave from the new **terminal** ⓘ *Cra 6, C 16, 4 km from the centre*. To get there by taxi, US$2 or take city bus No 4 from the centre.

The **tourist office** ⓘ *just off the main plaza, C 18, No 25-25, T723 4962, www.turismonarino.gov.co, open Mon-Fri 0800-1200 and 1400-1800, closed Sat-Sun*, is friendly and helpful and will advise on money changing.

Background

The city was founded in 1539 by Lorenzo de Aldana, who came up from Quito, and it is therefore one of the oldest cities of Colombia. During the Wars of Independence, it was a stronghold of the Royalists and the last town to fall into the hands of the patriots. Simón Bolívar directed the bloodiest battle of the Independence War against the forces of Basilio García on 7 April 1822. His headquarters was nearby in Bomboná. Then the people of

Nariño Department wanted to join Ecuador when that country split off from Gran Colombia in 1830, but were prevented by Colombian troops. Today Pasto is a centre for the agricultural and cattle industries of the region. Pasto varnish (*barniz*) is mixed locally, to embellish the strikingly colourful local wooden bowls.

Pasto

Sleeping 🛏

Canchalá 1
Casa Madrigal 2
Chambú Plaza 3
Don Saúl 4
Fernando Plaza 5
Galerías 6
Koala Inn 7
Loft 8
María Belén 9
Metropol 10
Morasurco 11

Eating 🍴

El Gastronom' 1
Guadalquivir Café 2
Inca Cuy 3
Loto Verde 4
Parrilla Chipichape 5
Picantería Ipiales 6

Sights

A legacy of colonial times is the considerable number of churches. The **cathedral** is a large but not distinguished building, sombre in its appearance and austere inside. **San Juan Bautista** church (St John the Baptist) is the oldest in Pasto, though the finely decorated building dates from 1669, a replacement for the original of 1539 after damage by earthquakes. The church of **Cristo Rey** ① *C 20, No 24-64, near the centre*, has a striking yellow stone west front with octagonal angelic turrets. **La Merced** ① *C 18 y Cra 22*, has rich decoration and gold ornamentation.

The **Museo de Oro del Banco de la República** ① *C 19, No 21-27, T7215777, Tue-Sat 1000-1700, free*, has a small well-displayed collection of pre-Columbian pieces from the cultures of south Colombia, a library and auditorium. Another museum in the city centre is the **Museo Alfonso Zambrano** ① *C 20, No 29-78*, which houses a private collection of indigenous and colonial, especially *quiteño* (from Quito), and period arts. Alfonso Zambrano was a renowned local woodcarver. The **Museo Maridíaz** ① *C 18, No 32A-39*, is mainly concerned with religious art and relics from the region.

From the church of **Santiago Apóstol** ① *Cra 23 y C 13*, there is a good view of the green mountains beyond the city. Four blocks to the north are the green tiled domes of the church of **San Felipe** ① *C 12 y Cra 27*, opposite the monastery of the **Inmaculada Concepción**. The interior courtyard of the **municipal building** ① *corner of C 19 y Cra 24, on the main plaza*, has two tiers of colonnaded balconies.

Volcán Galeras

The Galeras volcano (4276 m), quiescent since 1934, began erupting again in 1989 and again in 2005 and 2010. Check at the tourist office whether it is possible to climb on the mountain – it has been officially closed since 1995. A road climbs up the mountain to a ranger station and police post at 3700 m where you will be stopped. From there, a rough road goes to the summit near which there is a TV relay station. It is reported that this area is now mined to discourage unauthorized visitors, at least one of whom has died as a result. The volcano itself has claimed several victims including a British geologist, Geoffrey Brown, who died in 1993 when the volcano erupted just as he was setting up equipment to measure gravity changes which, it is hoped, will help eventually to predict volcanic activity.

On the north side of the volcano lies the village of **Sandoná** where Panama hats are made. They can be seen lying in the streets in the process of being finished. Sandoná market day is Saturday. There are frequently buses daily, 1½ hours, US$2. There are good walks on the lower slopes through Catambuco and Jongovito (where bricks are made).

Laguna La Cocha

About 25 km east of Pasto, on the road to Mocoa is **Laguna La Cocha**, 2760 m, the largest lake in South Colombia (sometimes called Lago Guamuez). It is 14 km long and 4.5 km wide. Near the north end of the lake is the Santuario de Fauna y Flora **Isla de la Corota** nature reserve (10 minutes by boat from the **Hotel Sindamanoy**). This is the smallest protected area administered by the Colombian National Parks service and can be visited in a day. The island was the ritual centre for Quillacinga and Mocoa cultures for several centuries. There is now a small chapel near where you land on the island. There is a research unit and an interesting information centre and a marked path to see the many varieties of trees, small mammals and birds of the island. There are good viewing points of the lake, which is also surrounded by forested mountains. A (free) pass to visit the island is needed.

Around the lake are 15 or 20 private nature reserves run by a local association to protect prime forest areas and the páramo of the Guamuez river, part of the Putumayo river system. Several of these reserves have trails for visitors. Take *botas pantomeras* (rubber boots) and wet-weather clothing if you plan to hike. Average temperature at the lake is 12°C. For information on reserves around Laguna La Cocha, contact **Asociación para el Desarrollo Campesino** ⓘ *C 10, No 36-28, Pasto, T231 022.*

By the lake, 3 km from the main road, is the C Chalet Guamuez (T721 9308, www.chaletguamuez.com), recommended, with chalets, boats and jeep trips. Try also C Hotel Sindamanoy (T721 8222, www.hotelsindamanoy.com), chalet-style, government-run, good views, and tent camping allowed with manager's permission. There are also cheap and friendly places to stay in and near **El Encano** (sometimes shown on maps as 'El Encanto'), with many restaurants serving trout.

Beyond El Encano there is a steep climb over the Sierra, where a large statue of the Virgin marks the entry into the Putumayo. The road then descends steeply to Sibundoy, Mocoa and Puerto Asís. For many years this has been guerrilla territory and a drug growing and processing area. It is also the centre of the government-led coca eradication programme. While security has improved markedly in this area, we advise anybody to err on the side of caution and refrain from visiting this part of Colombia.

Pasto to the coast

The 250 km road west from Pasto to Tumaco is paved, but is subject to landslides – check in Pasto. It leaves the Pan-Americana 40 km south of Pasto at El Pedregal, passing the brick factories of the high plains of the Cordillera Occidental. At **Túquerres** (3050 m), the Thursday market is good for ponchos. A short distance beyond Túquerres is a track to the right which leads in 2½ hours up to the Corponariño cabin where you can stay the night and then a further 1½ hours to the spectacular **Laguna Verde** fed by sulphur springs. The lake is in the large crater of Volcán Azufral (4070 m), still intermittently active – beware of fumaroles. For information on walking and climbing in this area, enquire in Túquerres.

The road continues to El Espino (no hotels) where it divides, left 36 km to Ipiales, and right to Tumaco. About 90 km from Túquerres, before the town of Ricaurte, is the village of **Chucunez**.

Reserva Natural La Planada → *Colour map 3, B1.*

A dirt road branches south here, and after crossing the river climbs for 7 km to **Reserva Natural La Planada**, a private 3200-ha nature reserve created in 1982 by Fundación FES La Planada. This patch of dense cloudforest on a unique flat-topped mountain is home to a wide variety of flora and fauna and believed to have one of the highest concentrations of native bird species in South America.

The foundation has initiated a programme reintroducing the spectacled bear to the reserve. There are also many orchids and bromeliads to be seen from the nature trails. Day visitors are welcome but camping is prohibited. Check at the tourist office on whether it is safe to climb on the mountain and whether you need a permit. The visitor centre has maps and details of nature trails. There is accommodation on site, comfortable cabins, hot water, with three meals US$12.50 per day. For further information contact **Reserva Natural La Planada** ⓘ *T927-753396/97, fesplan@col2.tele com.com.co.* Fundación FES has published a fine illustrated book on the reserve, US$25, proceeds help conservation.

Las Lajas

In 1754 María Mueces de Quiñonez was travelling from the village of Potosí to Ipiales with her deaf-mute daughter Rosa when she stopped to rest by a cave next to the Guaitara river. Rosa escaped her clutches and ran into the cave. Some moments later she emerged and spoke for the first time in her life, saying: "Mother, look at the *mestiza* over there holding a boy in her arms". María did not look in the cave but grabbed Rosa and continued on her way. When in Ipiales, she recounted what had happened, though no one took what she said seriously.

A few days later, Rosa disappeared from home. María guessed that her daughter must have gone to the cave. Rosa had often said that the Lady was calling her. María ran to Las Lajas and found her daughter in front of a lady and playing with a child. María fell to her knees before the Virgin Mary and Baby Jesus.

From that day, she and Rosa often went to the cave to place wild flowers and candles in the cracks in the rocks.

One day Rosa fell gravely ill and died. A distraught María decided to take her daughter's body to Las Lajas to ask the Lady to restore Rosa to life.

The Virgin resurrected Rosa and María returned home brimming with joy. Crowds began to visit the cave, curious about what had happened. They discovered a picture of the mysterious Lady on the wall of the grotto that is still there to this day.

That same year Fray Gabriel Villafuerte returned to the cave and built a straw church and as more pilgrims visited the miraculous spot, a new cathedral was planned on the other side of the river. The first stone was laid in 1899 and the extraordinary Gothic Revival structure was finally finished in 1949.

Today it is a popular destination for religious believers from all parts of Latin America and is commonly described as "topographically the most beautiful in the world, in religious terms the most visited in the Americas and architecturally the most audacious and original in Colombia".

Tumaco → *Colour map 3, B1. Phone code: 2. Population: 169,000.*

Tumaco isn't exactly the most appealing of places. It suffers from high unemployment, poor living conditions, poor roads and has problems with water and electricity supplies. To make matters worse, it is in one of the world's rainiest areas, and the yearly average temperature is about 30°C. The movement of the tides governs most of the activities in the area, especially transport. The northern part of the town is built on stilts out over the sea (safe to visit only in daylight). A natural arch on the main beach, north of the town and port, is reputed to be the hiding place of Henry Morgan's treasure. Swimming is not recommended from the town's beaches, which are polluted; stalls provide refreshment on the beach. Swimming is safe, however, at El Morro beach, north of the town, only on the incoming tide (the outgoing tide uncovers poisonous rays).

The area is noted for the archaeological finds associated with the Tumaco culture. Ask for Pacho Cantin at El Morro Beach who will guide you through the caves. The coastal area around Tumaco is mangrove swamp, with many rivers and inlets on which lie hundreds of villages and settlements; negotiate with boatmen for a visit to the swamps or the beautiful island tourist resort of **Boca Grande**. There are several places to stay in the F category. There are water taxis north up the coast, across the bay to Salahonda and beyond. **Warning** This area is known for its coca plantations. Take advice before visiting.

Passing through deep valleys and a spectacular gorge, buses on the paved Pan-American Highway cover the 84 km from Pasto to Ipiales in 1½ to two hours. The road crosses the spectacular gorge of the Río Guáitara at 1750 m, near El Pedregal, where *choclo* (corn) is cooked in many forms by the roadside.

Ipiales → *Colour map 3, C2. Phone code: 2. Population: 109,000. Altitude: 2898 m.*

Ipiales, 'the city of the three volcanoes', stands close to Colombia's main border crossing with Ecuador and is famous for its colourful Friday morning indigenous market. The **Catedral Bodas de Plata** is worth visiting. There is a small museum, set up by Banco de la República. **San Luis airport** is 6.5 km out of town. Buses to most destinations leave from a new terminal at Carrera 3 with Calle 6. It has good facilities with a 24-hour left-luggage facility (US$1.10 per item) and toilets (US$0.27). Most buses leave from here but **Bolivariano** and **Transipiales** have kiosks at the border and will collect passengers from here for main destinations further into Colombia.

The city's main attraction, 7 km east on a paved road, is the **Sanctuary of the Virgin of Las Lajas** ① *US$0.55, Mass at the church Mon-Fri 0600, 0700, 0900, 1100, 1500 and 1700, Sun every hour 0600-1200, 1500-1700*, which was declared a National Monument in 1984. Seen from the approach road, looking down into the canyon, the sanctuary is a magnificent executed architectural vision, set on a bridge over the Río Guáitara. It is very heavily ornamented in the Gothic style. The altar is set into the rock face of the canyon where the Virgin Mary appeared in 1754. This forms one end of the sanctuary with the façade facing a wide plaza that completes the bridge over the canyon. There are walks to nearby shrines in dramatic scenery. It is a 10- to 15-minute walk down to the sanctuary from the village along a path lined with plaques giving thanks for miracles rendered by the virgin as well as a statue of Manuel de Rivera, a blind man cured by the virgin who walked through Ecuador begging for alms as thanks. He raised 388 pesos and 7 reales. Pilgrims come from all over Colombia and Ecuador (very crowded at Easter) and the sanctuary must be second only to Lourdes in the number of miracles claimed for it, although the church only recognizes one. In the vaults of the church is an interesting museum telling the history of the construction of the church as well as religious artefacts and some interesting taxidermy – a 'two-headed' and an 'eight-legged' sheep, presumably examples of further miracles but clumsily stitched together from many animals.

There are several basic hotels and a small number of restaurants at Las Lajas. You may also stay at the convent, simple but cheerful. Try local guinea pig (*cuy*) and boiled potatoes for lunch (or guinea-pig betting in the central plaza may be more to your taste).

Getting there Ipiales town buses going 'near the Sanctuary' leave you 2.5 km short. Take a *colectivo* from outside the bus station, US$1 per person, taxi, US$6 return (it's about a 1½ hours' walk, 7 km).

Border essentials: Colombia–Ecuador

Tumaco–San Lorenzo

It is possible to travel to Ecuador by boat. Part of the trip is by river, which is very beautiful, and part on the open sea, which can be very rough; a plastic sheet to cover your belongings is essential. Take suncream.

Colombian immigration DAS C23, Manzana 10, Casa16, Barrio Pradomar, T727 2010; obtain a stamp for leaving Colombia here; office open weekdays only. Visas for Ecuador (if required) should be obtained in Cali or Pasto. Entry stamps for Ecuador must be obtained in the coastal towns.

Entering Colombia from Tumaco You will have to go to Ipiales to obtain the entry stamp. Apparently the 24/48 hours 'unofficial' entry is not a problem, but do not obtain any Colombian stamps in your passport before presentation to DAS in Ipiales. DAS in Pasto is not authorized to give entry stamps for overland or sea crossings, and the DAS office in Tumaco seems to be only semi-official.

Ipiales–Rumichaca

Ipiales is 2 km from the Rumichaca bridge across the Río Carchi into Ecuador. The frontier post stands beside a natural bridge, on a concrete bridge, where customs and passport examinations take place from 0600 to 2100.

Colombian immigration and customs All Colombian offices are in one complex: DAS (immigration, exit stamp given here), customs, INTRA (Deptartment of Transportation, car papers stamped here; if leaving Colombia you must show your vehicle entry permit) and ICA (Dept of Agriculture for plant and animal quarantine). There is also a restaurant, Telecom for long-distance phone calls, clean bathrooms (ask for key, charge) and ample parking.

Ecuadorean immigration and customs The Ecuadorean side is older and more chaotic than the modern Colombian complex, but adequate. There is a modern Andinatel office for phone calls. Ask for 90 days on entering Ecuador if you need it, otherwise you will be given 30 days. You are not allowed to cross to Ipiales for the day without having your passport stamped. Both Ecuadorean exit stamp and Colombian entry stamp are required. Although no one will stop you at the border, you risk serious consequences in Colombia if you are caught without your documents 'in order'.

Crossing by private vehicle The vehicle is supposed to be fumigated against diseases that affect coffee plants, at the ICA office; the certificate must be presented in El Pedregal, 40 km beyond Ipiales on the road to Pasto. (This fumigation process is not always carried out.) You can buy insurance for your car in Colombia at Banco Agrario, in the plaza. In addition, car owners must present title deeds to the vehicle with a photocopy, and the vehicle's chassis and engine number.

Ecuadorean consulate In the DAS complex (Cra 7 No 14-10 esq C 14 piso 3); weekdays 0900-1230, 1430-1700.

Exchange There are many moneychangers near the bridge on both sides. Travellers report better rates on the Colombian side, but check all calculations.

Transport From Ipiales to the border, *colectivo* from Calle 14/Carrera 11, wait till all seats are full, US$0.80. From border to Tulcán (Parque Ayora near the cemetery six blocks from the centre) US$0.75, to Tulcán bus station, US$1. Taxi to or from border, US$3.50. From Ipiales airport to the border by taxi, about US$6.50.

For Sleeping and Eating price codes and other relevant information, see pages 23-28.

● Sleeping

Pasto *p323, map p324*

AL Morasurco, Cra 40/Av de los Estudiantes with C 20, T731 3250. Located on the northern outskirts of town, Pasto's most expensive hotel has rooms with large beds, cable TV, Wi-Fi, parking and a Turkish bath.

A Don Saúl, C 17, N0 23-52, T722 4480, www.hoteldonsaul.com. This hotel stays close to its Jordanian owners' roots with murals depicting Arabic scenes and a restaurant serving Middle Eastern food. It has very large beds, a sauna, Turkish bath, cable TV and Wi-Fi, while breakfast is included in the price.

A Hotel Galerías, Cra 26, No 18-71, p 3, T723 7390, www.hotel-galerias.com. Situated in the town's main shopping centre, the *Galerías* has good-sized rooms as well as Wi-Fi, parking and a good restaurant with a typical Colombian menu.

A Loft Hotel, C 18, N0 22-33, T722 6733, www.lofthotelpasto.com. Comfortable hotel with minimalist decor and extras such as Wi-Fi, an internet room, and a spa. Sleek and stylish.

A-B Fernando Plaza, C 20, No 21B-16, T729 1432, www.hotelfernandoplaza.com. Smart, newish hotel with lots of good details such as beds with orthopaedic mattresses and stereos and Wi-Fi in every room. It also has a restaurant serving steak and seafood.

B Casa Madrigal, Cra 26, No 15-37, T723 4592, www.hotelcasamadrigal.blogspot.com. This hotel has spacious rooms with good beds and cable TV, parking, a restaurant, Wi-Fi and breakfast included.

D Chambu Plaza, Cra 20, No 17 esq, No 16-14, T721 3129, www.hotelchambuplaza.net. This hotel has clean, basic rooms and good extras, such as Wi-Fi, an internet room, parking and a restaurant serving *menú del día*, as well as friendly staff.

E Canchalá, C 17, No 20A-38, T721 3965. This hotel has clean but small rooms with private bathrooms and but its position on a busy street makes it a little noisy.

E Koala Inn, C 18, No 22-37, T722 1101. This creaky hostel is the best backpackers' option in town. It has an enormous central atrium, large, antiquated rooms, some with private bathrooms, and good information on the local area. There is a small café serving decent breakfasts for US$2.

E Metropol, C 15, No 21-41, T721 2498. Decent hotel with small but clean rooms with cable TV and en suite bathrooms.

G María Belén, C 13, No 19-15, T723 0277. Basic but passable hotel with cable TV, en suite bathrooms with hot water and grumpy staff.

Ipiales *p328*

C Angasmayo, C 16, No 6-38, T773 2140, www.hotelangasmayo.com. The slick, minimalist lobby of this hotel is misleading as it appears to be the only part of the building that has seen a lick of paint in the last 10 years. However, the rooms will do and it also has internet access, parking, a restaurant with breakfast included, and a discotheque.

D Santa Isabel 2, Cra 7, No 14-27, T773 4172. Smart, centrally placed hotel with good services such as Wi-Fi in reception, an internet room, parking and a restaurant.

E Emperador, Cra 5, No 14-43, T725 2413. With good clean rooms with cable TV and private bathrooms with hot water, this hotel is the pick of the bunch of the budget options. Also has parking and is well placed 1 block from the Parque Principal.

E Metropol, Cra 2, No 6-10, T773 7976. Opposite the bus station, this basic hotel has passable rooms with cable TV and en suite bathrooms with hot water as well as a small café in reception. As with all hotels near bus stations, take care walking around at night.

E Señorial, C 14, No 4-36, T773 4610. Basic hotel with clean rooms, en suite bathrooms with hot water and cable TV.

F Belmonte, Cra 4, No 12-11, T773 2771. Basic but clean hotel offering rooms with cable TV and shared bathrooms.

🍴 Eating

Pasto *p323, map p324*

🍴 **El Gastronom'**, Av los Estudiantes, No 32A-68, T731 3477. Located in the northern part of town near the **Hotel Morasurco**, this French-run restaurant serves à la carte Gallic dishes as well as *almuerzo* for US$5. Home delivery is also available.

🍴 **Guadalquivir Café**, C 19, No 24-84, T723 9504. Another Pasto stalwart with more than 35 years' existence, this atmospheric café serves up home-made snacks such as *tamales*, *empanadas de añejo* and *envueltos de choclo*.

🍴 **Inca Cuy**, C 29, No 13-65, T723 8050. Tucked down a narrow corridor behind the Plaza de Bombona, a large statue of a guinea pig tells you what this restaurant specializes in. Be warned that fried *cuy*, as it is known, takes an hour to prepare, so it's best to phone ahead.

🍴 **Loto Verde**, Cra 24, No 13-79. Formerly known as Govinda's, this Hare Krishna-run café serves up vegetarian lunches for US$2.

🍴 **Parrilla Chipichape**, C 18, No 27-88, T729 1684. This is one of Pasto's most popular restaurants, renowned for its barbecued steaks and pork steamed in aluminium foil. On Sun it serves *ajiaco santafereño* and *sancocho de pollo*.

🍴 **Picantería Ipiales**, C 19, No 23-37, T723 0393. Despite its modern decor this restaurant specializes in typical food from Nariño, specifically pork-based dishes such as *lapigancho*. *Almuerzos* cost US$2.80.

Ipiales *p328*

🍴 **Mi Casita**, C 9, No 6-12, T773 2754. A local favourite, this canteen-style restaurant serves up typical Colombian specialities such as *mondongo* and several variations of *bandeja*.

🍴 **Rancho Grande**, Cra 7, No 14-51, T773 2665. With an interior built primarily in bamboo, **Rancho Grande** is an agreeable place to enjoy steaks, chicken, seafood and fast food.

🎭 Entertainment

Pasto *p323, map p324*

Teatro Agustín Aqualongo, C 16/Cra 16.

🎉 Festivals and events

Pasto *p323, map p324*

Christmas to 6 Jan New Year fiesta, with parades and general festivities.
4 Jan Parades commemorate the **Llegada de la Familia Castañeda**. Apparently this peasant family came from El Encano to Pasto in 1928. They are recreated in the parades.
5 Jan Día de los Negros. People dump their hands in black grease and smear each other's faces (nice!)
6 Jan Día de los Blancos. People throw talc or flour at each other. Local people wear their oldest clothes.
28 Dec and **5 Feb** Fiesta de las Aguas, when anything that moves gets drenched with water from balconies and even from fire engines' hoses. All towns in the region are involved in this legalized water war.
31 Dec Concurso de Años Viejos, in Pasto and also in Ipiales, when huge dolls are burnt. They represent the old year and sometimes lampoon local people.

🛍 Shopping

Pasto *p323, map p324*

Leather goods shops are on C 17 and 18. Try the municipal market for handicrafts.
Artesanía-Mercado Bombóná, C 14 y Cra 27.
Artesanías Mopa-Mopa, Cra 25, No 13-14, for *barniz*.
Artesanías Nariño, C 26, No 18-91.
Casa del Barniz de Pasto, C 13, No 24-9.
Instituto Geográfico Agustín Codazzi, in the Banco de la República building, C 18A,

No 21A-18. Maps of Colombia and cities, limited selection.
Ley on C 18, next to **Avianca** postal office. On the main plaza (C 19 y Cra 25) is a shopping centre with many shops and restaurants.
Los Dos Puentes, Cra 24 with C 21. Market selling fruit, vegetables and flowers.

▲ Activities and tours

Pasto p323, map p324
Every Sun a game of paddle ball is played across the border on the edge of the town (bus marked San Lorenzo) similar to that played across the border in Ibarra, Ecuador.
Emproturn, C 19, No 31B-44, T731 0975, emproturn@gmail.com. Tours in and around Pasto. Can arrange private transport from Cali.

◉ Transport

Pasto p323, map p324
Air
To **Bogotá**, 3 flights daily, 1 hr 55 mins, with Avianca and Satena. To **Cali**, 2 flights daily, 50 mins, Avianca.
   Airline offices Avianca, CC Galerías, local 214, T723 2320 or at the airport. Satena, Cosmocentro 2000, C 19, No 27-05, local 208, T729 0442.

Bus
To **Bogotá**, 18 hrs, US$49.50 (Bolivariano Pullman), 8 a day. To **Ipiales**, Cooperativa Supertaxis del Sur US$3, 2 hrs, frequent; by bus, US$2.70, sit on left hand side for the views. To **Popayán**, ordinary buses take 10-12 hrs, US$12.50; expresses take 5-8 hrs, cost US$14.50. To **Cali**, US$21, expresses, 8½-10 hrs. To **Bucaramanga**, 27 hrs, US$65, To **Medellín**, 18 hrs, US$47.50. To **Mocoa**, 8 hrs, US$7.25.

Ipiales p328
Air To **Bogotá**, **Medellín** and **Puerto Asis** with Satena. San Luis airport is 6.5 km out of town. Taxi to centre US$6.

Bus To **Popayán**, Expreso Bolivariano, Transipiales or Cootranar, US$15.50, 7½ hrs, hourly departures, 0730-2030, sit in the right-hand side for best views. Bus to **Cali**, US$22.50, 10-12 hrs. To **Pasto**, frequent, US$5, 1½ hrs. Buses to **Bogotá**9 a day with Bolivariano, 24 hrs, US$52 To **Medellín**, Expreso Bolivariano, 22 hrs, US$47.50, 3 a day.

❶ Directory

Pasto p323, map p324
Banks For changing TCs, BanColombia, C 19, No 24-52. Banco de Bogotá, C 19, No 24-68 will change TCs 0930-1130. If going to Tumaco, this is the last place where TCs can be cashed. **Davivienda**, CC el Liceo, C 17, No 25-12, gives largest advances on Visa. **Casas de cambio**, at Cra 25, No 18-97, and C 19, No 24-86, by the main plaza, changes US dollars into local currency. **Western Union**, CC El Liceo, Cra 26, No 17-12, Local 128. **Immigration** DAS: C 17, No 29-70, will give exit stamps if you are going on to Ecuador. **Internet** Pc-Rent, Pasaje Corazón de Jesús, C 18, No 25-36. **Medical services** Cruz Roja (Red Cross), Cra 25, no 13-26. **Post** Correos de Colombia, C 15 between Cra 23 and Cra 24. **Telecom** Long-distance calls, C 17 y Cra 23.

Ipiales p328
Banks It is not possible to cash Tcs, but cash is no problem; Bancolombia, cash against Visa. **Casa de Cambio** at Cra 6, No 14-09, other cambios on the plaza. There are money changers in the street, in the plaza and on the border, but they may take advantage of you if the banks are closed. Coming from Ecuador, peso rates compare well in Ipiales with elsewhere in Colombia. **Telephone** International calls from Cra 6 between C 6/7, opposite Banco de Occidente.

Contents

336 Los Llanos
  336 Villavicencio
  337 Around Villavicencio
  338 Listings

340 Amazonia
  340 Leticia and around
  341 Parque Nacional
        Natural Amacayacú
  343 Puerto Nariño
  343 Up the Río Yavarí
  345 Listings

Footprint features

334 Don't miss ...
337 Cowboy culture
341 Amazon forest

Border crossings

Colombia–Brazil and Peru
344 Leticia–Tabatinga and
        Santa Rosa

Los Llanos & Amazonia

At a glance

⊖ **Getting around** Walking or taxi in Leticia; river taxi to destinations on the Amazon. Buses or private car to explore Los Llanos.
◉ **Time required** 1-2 weeks.
☼ **Weather** Very hot all year round; driest between Jun and Aug in Amazonas.
✕ **When not to go** Good all year.

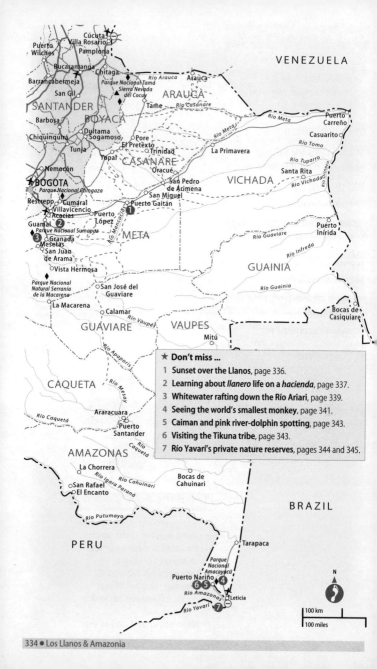

VENEZUELA

Villa Rosario
Cúcuta
Puerto
Wilches
Pamplona
Bucaramanga
Chitaga
Barrancabermeja
San Gil
Parque Nacional Tamá
Sierra Nevada del Cocuy
Río Arauca
Arauca
SANTANDER
Tame
Río Casanare
ARAUCA
BOYACA
Barbosa
Río Meta
Puerto
Carreño
Chiquinquirá
Duitama
Sogamoso
Pore
El Pretexto
Casuarito
Tunja
Topal
Trinidad
La Primavera
Río Tomo
Nemocón
CASANARE
Oracué
VICHADA
Santa Rita
★ BOGOTA
San Pedro
de Arimena
Río Tuparro
Parque Nacional Chingaza
San Miguel
Río Vichada
Río Orinoco
Restrepo
Cumaral
Villavicencio
Puerto Gaitán ❶
Acacias
Puerto
López
Guamal ❷
Parque Nacional Sumapaz
META
Puerto
Inírida
Granada ❸
Río Guaviare
Mesetas
San Juan
de Arama
Río Guaviare
GUAINIA
Vista Hermosa
Río Infreda
Parque Nacional Natural Serranía de la Macarena
San José del
Guaviare
Río Guainia
La Macarena
Calamar
Río Vaupés
Bocas de
Casiquiare
GUAVIARE
VAUPES
Mitú
Río Apaporis

★ **Don't miss ...**
1 Sunset over the Llanos, page 336.
2 Learning about *llanero* life on a *hacienda*, page 337.
3 Whitewater rafting down the Río Ariari, page 339.
4 Seeing the world's smallest monkey, page 341.
5 Caiman and pink river-dolphin spotting, page 343.
6 Visiting the Tikuna tribe, page 343.
7 Río Yavarí's private nature reserves, pages 344 and 345.

CAQUETA
Río Mesay
Araracuara
Río Caquetá
Puerto
Santander
Río Caquetá
AMAZONAS
La Chorrera
Río Igara Paraná
Río Cahuinari
San Rafael
El Encanto
Bocas de
Cahuinari
BRAZIL
Río Putumayo
PERU
Tarapaca
Parque Nacional Amacayacu
Puerto Nariño ❻❺ ❹
Río Amazonas
Leticia
❼
Río Yavarí

N

100 km
100 miles

A look at a map of Colombia reveals that an immense area east of Bogotá, with barely a town or road to be seen, makes up more than a quarter of the country's land mass. This is the Llanos, vast tracts of fertile cattle plains that stretch from the edge of the Department of Boyacá almost as far as the Amazon river and from the mountains of Bogotá as far as Venezuela (and beyond). Yet this region contains just a fraction of Colombia's population and much of the area is inaccessible by road. The Llanos' isolation has provided effective and convenient cover for guerrillas and cocaine-production factories and it is here that the war with armed groups such as the FARC continues. But impressive gains by the government in the last few years have made some of this cowboy country safe to visit again, particularly the main city, Villavicencio, and its immediate surroundings.

Further south, the grassy pastures make way for seemingly infinite hectares of pristine jungle, accessible only by boat or plane. The city of Leticia sits on the Amazon river and forms a three-pronged frontier with Brazil and Peru. This is the gateway to the Colombian Amazon and national parks such as Amacayacú and the impressively neat village of Puerto Nariño will give travellers the opportunity to observe some of this majestic river's wildlife at close range. Even better is a quick excursion to the Yavarí river in Brazil, whose private nature reserves provide excellent facilities for birdwatching, sports fishing and dolphin and caiman spotting.

Los Llanos

The vast plains that unfurl eastwards towards Venezuela like a green carpet from the mountainous folds of central Colombia make up almost a quarter of the country. These are the Llanos, comprising the departments of Arauca, Casanare, Vichada, Guainía, Meta, Vaupés and Guaviare – a land of cattle ranches, cowboys, música llanera, and spectacular sunsets. For many years this area has been at the heart of the guerrilla war and a centre of drug production. Much of it still is, but certain parts are beginning to open up thanks to increased security. In particular, Villavicencio and its immediate surroundings are safe and many Colombians take their holidays on the numerous cattle fincas that have been converted into very comfortable rental homes and hotels. With the construction of a new tunnel, the Buenavista, Colombia's longest, down the mountain from Bogotá, 'Villavo', as the locals call it, is a convenient 1½-hour drive from the capital.

The people are warm and hospitable, great horsemen with a touch of the Wild West. Once you hear the music of the llaneros, you will never forget it. ▸▸ For listings, see pages 338-339.

Ins and outs

If driving, plenty of reserve gasoline should be carried as there are few service stations. Also take food and plenty of water. Fishing tackle could be useful. Everybody lets you hang up your hammock or pitch your tent, but mosquito nets are a must. Roads are only tracks left by previous vehicles but are easy from late December till early April and the very devil during the rest of the year. More information on the *llanos* can be obtained from the office of the **Gobernación del Departamento de Meta** ⓘ *C 34/Cra 14, Bogotá*. We recommend you take good advice from reliable sources before driving around the Llanos independently.

Villavicencio → *For listings, see pages 338-339. Colour map 4, A1. Phone code: 8. Population: 384,000 Altitude: 467 m.*

Locally shortened to Villavo (Vee-a-bo), Villavicencio is the capital of Meta Department. This is where *llaneros* come to stock up on provisions and blow off a little steam in the city's bars and clubs. Founded in 1840 by Esteban Aguirre, it was originally a staging post and market for the ranching activities of the Llanos, conveniently on the way to Bogotá. Villavicencio is a good centre for visiting the *llanos* stretching 800 km east as far as Puerto Carreño and Puerto Inírida on the Orinoco. Cattle raising is the great industry on the plains, sparsely inhabited mostly by *mestizos*.

Ins and outs

A spectacular 110-km road runs south east from Bogotá to Villavicencio, at the foot of the eastern slopes of the Eastern Cordillera. A tunnel has reduced the journey by road from Bogotá to 1½ hours. The airport, **La Vanguardia**, is 4 km northwest of the town. The **bus station** is outside town on the ring road to the east, on Avenida del Llano. A taxi costs US$2.

Tourist information

Instituto de Turismo del Meta ⓘ *Cra 33, No 40-20, Edif Comité de Ganaderos, T661 4444, www.turismometa.gov.co.* Contact **William Restrepo** ⓘ *T310-766 3637*, who can organize guides and activities in the immediate vicinity of Villavicencio.

Cowboy culture

Llaneros have a distinct culture, worlds apart from the rest of Colombia. In fact, they share far more in common with their fellow ranchers across the border in the Venezuelan Llanos.

The first cowboys in the Americas – they preceded the gauchos of the Argentine *pampas* and the cattle herders of North America – they are predominantly a mixture of indigenous and Spanish heritage. They are known for their hardiness, appearing impervious to heat and cold and often riding their horses barefoot. They live an isolated life on these vast savannahs, tending their cows and returning to the few cities only for provisions and a spot of drinking.

They played an important part in the South American War of Independence, initially siding with the Spanish, who exploited their distrust of the aristocratic *criollos*, until Simón Bolívar, recognizing their value as skilled horsemen, went to live among them and won them over.

They nicknamed him *culo de hierro*, or 'iron buttocks' for his feats of endurance in the saddle.

Today *llanero* culture is known for its distinctive music whose main instruments are the harp, maracas and a small guitar called a *cuatro*. The *joropo*, a *llanero* dance, has become the national dance of Venezuela and of the Llanos of Colombia, and is celebrated during festivals such as the Torneo Internacional del Joropo in Villavicencio in late June/July.

Most important are the cattle. There are an estimated 12 million cows on the Llanos of Colombia and Venezuela, spread out over an area of 451,474 sq km. *Llaneros* are proud of their cattle-herding skills and there are annual tournaments that test their prowess at *coleo*, a kind of rodeo in which cowboys on horseback attempt to fell cattle by grabbing their tails and twisting them until they tumble. Villavicencio hosts the Encuentro Mundial de Coleo each October.

Sights

The attractive central **Parque de Los Libertadores** (also called Parque Santander) has busts of Francisco Santander and Simón Bolívar and many ancient *ceiba* trees. The mid-19th-century cathedral of **Nuestra Señora del Carmen** overlooks the plaza. Southwest of the city, the **Monumento a Cristo Rey**, off Calle 40, has good views. In the same direction, on the road to Acacias, is the **Monumento a Los Fundadores**, a sculpture by Rodrigo Arenas Betancur. There is a **botanical garden** 2 km from the centre.

Around Villavicencio

From Villavicencio, three roads run further into the Llanos. To the north is a popular route known as the **Ruta del Piedemonte Llanero** and on the road there are parks, indigenous communities and hot springs to visit.

Around 3 km northeast of Villavicencio on the road to Restrepo is the **Bioparque Los Ocarros** ⓘ *Km 3 via Restrepo, T670 9094, open Mon-Thu 0900-1600, Fri-Sun 0900-1700, US$4.50, children US$3.20, over 65s free with ID, guide US$5.30 (Spanish only)*, a 5.5-ha thematic park set around lakes and forests with nearly 200 species endemic to the Llanos. The park runs educational talks and workshops.

Two kilometres beyond the park is the **Centro Cultural Etno Turístico El Maguare** ⓘ *Km 5 Vía Restrepo, Vereda La Poyata, T664 8464, US$2.20*, a community project set up and managed by the Uitoto. The community puts on ancestral dances in a traditional *maloca* as well as talks about the state of Colombia's indigenous people and workshops in how to use some of their traditional tools and weapons. Some of the proceeds go towards supporting displaced and marginalized indigenous groups.

Further along the road is the pleasant town of **Restrepo**, famous for its salt mines and its pretty church. Beyond is **Cumaral** which has palm tree plantations and is known as the best place to eat meat in the Llanos. A few kilometres north of Cumaral, near Barranca de Upía, is the **Reserva Natural Aguas Calientes**, which has a natural pool set in exuberant forest.

Running south from Villavicencio, the Ruta del Embrujo Llanero passes through **Acacías**, **Guamal** and **San Martín**, a cattle town. To the west of Guamal is the **Río Ariari** and **Cubarral**, which are inside the Parque Nacional Natural Sumapaz and where adventure sports such as whitewater rafting, paragliding and abseiling can be practised, as well as *balsaje* (floating downriver on bamboo rafts). The road eventually leads to **San Juan de Arama**, gateway to the Parque Nacional Natural Serranía de la Macarena, an enormous rock similar to the *tepuis* of Venezuela. The Caño Cristales river runs through the park, which depending on the time of year and the amount of algae found in its waters, gives the river an incredible technicolour sheen. **Note** Currently the park should be considered strictly off limits as it is still under FARC control. Take careful advice before going there.

The road east from Villavicencio, known as the Amanecer Llanero, passes through the Apiay oil field before reaching **Puerto López** on the Río Meta. A few kilometres beyond Puerto López is the 21-m-high El Obelisco at Alto Menegua, built to mark the geographic centre of Colombia. This colourful monument, built in 1993, displays elements of local prehistory, cultural heritage and a relief map of Colombia. From here there are wonderful views of the Llanos. A further 150 km east is **Puerto Gaitán**, where there are good views and excellent sunsets to be seen from the bridge across the Río Manacacías. Nearby it joins the Río Meta where there are some beautiful white-sand beaches.

⊕ Los Llanos listings → *Phone code: 8.*

For Sleeping and Eating price codes and other relevant information, see pages 23-28.

🛏 Sleeping

Villavicencio *p336*
AL Don Lolo, Cra 39, No 20-32, T670 6020, www.donlolohotel.com. Like the **Gloria**, this hotel is no beauty. Rooms have cable TV, Wi-Fi, a/c, minibar and room service but are a little frayed round the edges. Restaurant and pool.
AL Hotel del Llano, Cra 30, No 49-77, T671 7000, www.hoteldelllano.com. Tucked under the forested hills of the Cordillera Oriental, this is Villavo's smartest option with good rooms and a host of extras such as a spa, sauna, pool, restaurant, tour agency and Wi-Fi throughout.

AL-A María Gloria, Cra 38, No 20-26, T672 0197, www.hotelmariagloria.com. In an ugly building, rooms feel a bit antiquated but have services such as a/c, flat-screen TV and Wi-Fi. Includes breakfast. Good pool area with sauna and Turkish bath.
B Savoy, C 41, No 31-02, T662 5007. Clean, simple rooms with a/c, cable TV and en suite bathrooms. Vegetarian restaurant downstairs.
C Hotel de Oriente, C 38A, No 29A-43, T662 6391. Good, large rooms, minibar, room service and en suite bathrooms, with fan instead of a/c is cheaper. Good security.
C San Jorge, C 38, No 31-21, T662 1682. Good, with clean rooms, a/c and cable TV.
D Delfín Rosado, C 35, No 23-15, T662 6896. The rooms may open up off dark corridors but they are comfortable with fan, cable TV and a restaurant serving decent breakfasts.

E El Caporal, C 39, No 33-35, T662 4011. Clean, simple rooms in a small hotel 1 block from the Parque Principal.
E Granja Los Girasoles, Barrio Chapinerito, T664 2712. Youth hostel, 160 beds, 3 km from bus station.
E Turista del Llano, C 38, No 30A-42, T662 6207. Rooms are a bit musty but it's in the centre of town, with cable TV, private bathrooms and towels and soap provided.

Fincas

One of the best ways to get to know the Llanos is to stay on one of the cattle ranches available for hire. **Fincas y Eventos**, C 47 Bis, No 28-09, T310-285 6641 (mob), www.fincas yeventos.com, has over 35 homesteads.

⊘ Eating

Villavicencio *p336*
Ⅱ Chop Suey, C 38, No 30A-44, T662 6852. Popular Chinese restaurant.
Ⅰ Asadero La Llanerita, C 35, No 27-16, T662 3001. Slow-roasted meats cooked on an open barbecue, including *falda de Costilla*.
Ⅰ Fonda Quindiana, Cra 32, No 40-40, T662 6857. One of Villavo's oldest restaurants, with a great atmosphere. Typical dishes such as *frijoles* and *lengua en salsa* as well as *parrillas*.
Ⅰ La Posada del Arriero, C 41, No 30-08, T664 1319. This restaurant serves typical dishes such as *mondongo* and *frijolada* as well as fish, chicken and steak, on a pleasant terrace painted orange and green.
Ⅰ Toy-Wan, C 40A, No 28-69, T664 1758. Smart oriental restaurant, does spring rolls and stir fries.

⊛ Festivals and events

Villavicencio *p336*
Jun-Jul Torneo Internacional del Joropo, www.torneointernacionaldeljoropo.com, involving parades, singers and over 3000 couples dancing the *joropo* in the street.

Mid-Oct Encuentro Mundial de Coleo. *Coleo* is a sport similar to rodeo in which cowboys tumble young calves by grabbing their tails and twisting them until they lose their balance.

⊘ Shopping

Villavicencio *p336*
Almacenes Ley, C 37, No 29-83 is a good place to stock up with provisions.

▲▲ Activities and tours

Villavicencio *p336*
Tour operators
Vergel Tours, Cra 30, No 49-77 (in **Hotel del Llano**), T682 5353, www.vergelaventura.com. Runs adventure-sport activities, including whitewater rafting, paragliding, horse riding and visits to hot springs. Recommended.

⊖ Transport

Villavicencio *p336*
Air To **Bogotá**, **Aires** 2 a day, **Satena** Sat only. To **Puerto Carreño**, **Satena** several a week. Satena also flies to a number of other destinations in Los Llanos.

Bus To Bogotá, *colectivos* and minivans leave 20 times a day from 0400-2000, US$10.50, 1½ hrs. Also regular services with Expreso Bolivariano, Arimena and Flota La Macarena.

⊙ Directory

Villavicencio *p336*
Banks Bancolombia and other banks near the Plaza. Most have ATMs. **Internet/ phone** CS&S Consultores, C 38, No 33-13. Internet and international calls. Ibérica, Cra 32, No 39-40. Skype, headphones and stationery. **Police** T112 or T662 5000. **Post** Adpostal, C 39/Cra 32.

Amazonia

The Colombian Amazon forms part of the largest ecosystem on the planet. More than one third of all the species in the world live in the Amazon rainforest, a giant tropical forest and river basin with an area that stretches more than 5,400,000 sq km. Its lifeline is the Amazon river, the largest river in the world that begins its journey in the Andes of Peru and Ecuador and flows for over 6000 km across almost the entire width of the continent before reaching the Atlantic in Brazil. By the time it passes Leticia, capital of Colombian Amazonas, it is already well into its stride, and this section of the Amazon provides plenty of opportunities for nature lovers to observe its flora and fauna up close. From Leticia, vast swathes of forest run northwards with little human activity to interrupt their quiet splendour. There are no roads and indigenous communities live off the fishing and transport provided by tributaries that feed into the Amazon. ▶▶ *For listings, see pages 345-348.*

Leticia and around → *For listings, see pages 345-348. Colour map 4, C2. Phone code: 8. Population: 35,000.*

Leticia is a port town on the Amazon that shares a border with both Brazil and Peru. The city is clean, modern and safe, though run-down near the river. It is rapidly merging into one town with neighbouring **Tabatinga** in Brazil (for day visits to Tabatinga there's no need to pass through immigration). The best time to visit the area is from June to August, the early months of the dry season. The river is at its highest level in May, lowest in September. At weekends, accommodation may be difficult to find. Leticia is a good place to buy typical indigenous Amazonian products, and tourist services are better than in Tabatinga or Benjamin Constant.

Ins and outs
The airport is 1.5 km from town, taxi US$2; small terminal, few facilities. Expect to be searched before leaving Leticia airport, and on arrival in Bogotá from Leticia.

There is an obligatory US$7 environment tax payable on arrival in Leticia. You may also be asked for a yellow fever certificate. If you do not have one, you may have an inoculation administered on the spot (not recommended). ▶▶ *For border crossings, see box, page 344.*

Leticia

To Airport & Tarapaca
Stadium
To Iquitos (Peru)
Rio Amazonas
MA
Brazilian Consulate
Parque Santander
Banco de la República Museum
DAS
Almacen Uirapuru
Productos Naturales del Trapecio Amazonico
Peruvian Consulate
To Manaus (Brazil)
BRAZIL
To Marco & Tabatinga

200 metres
200 yards

Sleeping
Amira 1
Decalodge Ticuna 2
Fernando Real 3
Hospedaje Los Delfines 5
La Frontera 4
Mahuta Guesthouse 6
Mochileros 7
Yurupary 8

Eating
Amazón Sazón 9
El Sabor 10
Tierras Amazónicas 11
Tierras Antioqueñas 12

Amazon forest

It may all look the same from above as you fly into Leticia but the Amazon has three types of tropical forest, each with distinct ecosystems: **Terra firme**, which is dry all year round and characterized by an abundance of tropical hardwoods, is where you are most likely to see large mammals. **Várzea**, which is flooded for half the year, contains fewer mammals but an abundance of birds. **Igapo**, which is always flooded and grows to a height of 3 m. This is where you are likely to see reptiles such as anacondas, caimans, boa constrictors and large fish.

The area immediately around Leticia is characterized by *várzea* and *igapo*, while for *terra firme* you will have to venture inland from the river or into Brazil or Peru.

For information, contact the **tourist office** ⓘ *C 10, No 10-47, T592 8065*. For a good account of local ecology and cultures of the northwest Amazon, see *The Forest Within: World-View of the Tukano Amazonian Indians* (Gerardo Reichel Dolmatoff, UK 1996).

Sights

There's precious little in the way of sights around town, but the **Banco de la República** ⓘ *Cra 10 No 10-15*, has a museum that covers local ethnography and archaeology, housed in a beautiful building with various workshops and talks as well as a library and a terrace overlooking the Amazon.

Around Leticia

On **Monkey Island (La Isla de los Micos)** visits can be made to indigenous Yagua and Ticuna. There are not many monkeys on the island now, those left are semi-tame. Agencies run overnight tours with full board. The price depends on the number of people in the group. If you choose to go on an organized tour, do not accept the first price and check that the equipment and supplies are sufficient for the length of the tour.

On night excursions to look for caiman, the boat should have powerful halogen lamps. You can swim in the Amazon and its tributaries, but do not dive; this disturbs the fish. Do not swim at sunrise or sunset when the fish are more active, nor when the water is shallow in dry season, nor if you have a wound that may open up and bleed. Take water-purification tablets with you since almost all the water here is taken from the river.

Parque Nacional Natural Amacayacú → *For listings, see pages 345-348. Colour map 4, C2.*

Some 60 km up the Amazon, at the mouth of the Matamatá Creek, is the entrance to the Amacayacú National Park, which is 100 km from north to south and a total of nearly 300,000 ha. It is bounded by several rivers flowing into the Putumayo and Amazon systems. At one point it touches the border with Peru. It is claimed that there are over 500 species of bird to be seen in the park, and 150 or so species of mammal, including pink dolphin, *danta* and *manatee*. The smallest monkey in the world, pygmy marmoset (*Cebuella pygmaea*), *titi leoncito* in Spanish, may also be seen.

Ins and outs

Boat from Leticia is US$10.50 one way, 1½-two hours; with **Tres Fronteras** (if you buy a return ticket, check that your operator runs the day you wish to return). Buy your ticket early to secure a seat. Boats leave at 1000 and 1400 and go on to Puerto Nariño.

The park entrance is 60 km upstream, at the mouth of the Matamata Creek, two hours from Leticia. It is open 0700-1700; day visits cost US$10.50 for foreigners, if staying overnight there is an additional charge of US$3.

Accommodation on two- to five-night packages is managed by **Aviatur** ① *C 7, No 10-78, T592 6814 in Leticia, or T01-900-331 2222/01-382 1616, reservasparques@ aviatur.com.co; for the park direct T592 5600.* The Leticia office is helful and will give information and arrange transport to the park.

Sights

There is a jungle walk to a lookout (guides will point out plants, including those to avoid) and a rope bridge over the forest canopy, with wonderful views over the surrounding jungle (US$25). There are various other guided day treks through the jungle. Boats go to a nearby island to see Victoria Regia water lilies. The park's main problem is that for much of the year it is flooded, thus restricting the mount of activities that can be done.

Around Leticia

The Colombian Amazon's second largest settlement after Leticia, this little riverside village has banned all motorized traffic. As a result, it's a tranquil place, its streets no more than pathways, immaculately swept and lined with flowers and herbaceous borders, while most of its houses are brightly painted with carefully tended gardens. There's also an emphasis on good environmental practice; Puerto Nariño has plans to become Colombia's first environmentally sustainable town.

Sights

In Puerto Nariño, be sure to visit **Fundación Natutama** ① *www.natutama.org, Mon and Wed-Fri 0800-1230, 1400-1700, free but contributions appreciated*. Natutama works to preserve the marine life of this part of the Amazon by organizing educational programs with local communities. At their visitor centre by the river there's an informative display of underwater life on the Amazon with life-size models of the various fish and reptiles, as well as videos. This is a good way to inform yourself about the Amazon's ecosystems before venturing out to see it in person.

Just beyond the village is **Lago de Tarapoto**, a popular place for seeing pink river-dolphins and caimans. Excursions in a *peque peque* (motorized canoe) cost about US$27-44 per person. Another, less well-known excursion is to **Lago San Juan del Socó**, a smaller lake but with a better chance of seeing wildlife due to Tarapoto's increasing popularity. Enquire at **Malocas Napü** (ask for Lorena, T313-483 1958).

There are also guided walks to various indigenous communities such as **San Martín de Amacayacú**, home to the Tikuna tribe who will talk about their customs. The Tikuna have also built a fine viewing tower in the village for wildlife spotting, US$2.70.

Up the Río Yavarí

West of Benjamin Constant, one of the Amazon's main tributaries, the Río Yavarí, forms the border between Peru and Brazil. This is one of the best places to observe wildlife on this section of the Amazon. There are several privately owned reserves here, with comfortable accommodation and excellent facilities for birdwatching, and dolphin and caiman spotting.

Ins and outs

There are no public river transport services up the Río Yavarí. **Palmarí** can organize private transport from Leticia, including transfer from the airport and stops at immigration to get your passport stamped. Boat trip takes 2½ hours in a fast boat and five hours in the slower, more scenic wooden boat, US$90. Alternatively, it is possible to make your own way there by catching a river taxi from Tabatinga to Benjamin Constant, 15 minutes, US$9.50, followed by a *colectivo* on the road to Atalaia do Norte, 40 minutes, US$9.50, where the reserve will arrange a pick-up for the final hour's journey by boat, US$16. This is quicker and cheaper than making the whole journey by boat, but less scenic.

Border essentials: Colombia–Brazil and Peru

Leticia–Tabatinga (Brazil) and Santa Rosa (Peru)

Colombian immigration DAS, Calle 9, No 8-32, T27189, Leticia, and at the airport. Exit stamps to leave Colombia by air or overland are given only at the airport. If flying into Leticia prior to leaving for Brazil or Peru, get an exit stamp while at the airport.

To enter Colombia you must have a tourist card to obtain an entry stamp, even if you are passing through Leticia en route between Brazil and Peru (the Colombian consul in **Manaus** may tell you otherwise; try to get a tourist card elsewhere). The Colombian consular office in Tabatinga issues tourist cards. Transit stamps can be obtained 24 hours at the DAS office. If visiting Leticia without intending to go anywhere else in Colombia, you may be allowed to enter without immigration or customs formalities (but TCs cannot be changed without an entry stamp). There are no customs formalities for everyday travel between Leticia and Tabatinga.

Brazilian immigration If visiting Brazil beyond Tabatinga you should pass through immigration. Exiting Colombia, get your passport stamped at the airport. Brazilian immigration is in Tabatinga on the main throroughfare from Leticia, open 0800-1200, 1400-1700.

Entry and exit stamps are given at the **Polícia Federal**, 10 minutes' walk from the Tabatinga docks, opposite **Café dos Navegantes** (walk through docks and follow road to its end, turn right at this T-junction for one block to the white building). If coming from Leticia, it is one block from the hospital on the road to Leticia. The office is open Monday-Friday 0800-1200, 1400-1800; also at airport, open Wednesday and Saturday only. Proof of US$500 or onward ticket may be asked for. There are no facilities in Benjamin Constant although it is possible to buy supplies for boat journeys. One-week transit in Tabatinga is permitted.

In this frontier area, carry your passport at all times. If coming from Peru, you must have a Peruvian exit stamp and a yellow fever certificate.

Peruvian immigration Entry/exit formalities take place at Santa Rosa. Every boat leaving Peru stops here. There is also an immigration office in **Iquitos** (Malecón Tarapacá 382) where procedures for leaving can be checked.

Reserva Natural Palmarí

ⓘ *T610 3514 (Bogotá), www.palmari.org (very informative website), US$70 per person, includes all food and alcohol, activities (except jungle walks greater than 24 hrs, sport fishing and canopy), and Wi-Fi and internet access. Transport from Leticia not included.*

On a raised bank looking out over the Javarí (in Portuguese) river, this jungle lodge has been designed to maximize the visitor's chances of seeing as many types of flora and fauna as possible, thanks to the reserve's access to all three types of Amazon forest within a 10-minute walk.

Accommodation is in simple cabins or a large communal *maloca*, connected by wooden gangways, while there's a viewing platform for observing river dolphins and the many birds and monkeys that inhabit the primary forest immediately behind. The reserve has over 20 guides, employed from local communities, and equipment for birdwatching fishing (over 20 species of gamefish, including peacock bass and *arowana*) and kayaking. Within its 40 ha there are canopy platforms and natural pools for swimming and fishing.

With jungle walks ranging from one to 72 hours, this is one of the best places in the area to observe the Amazon's wildlife up close.

Colombian/German owner Axel Antoine-Feill has set up an organization, the **Instituto de Desenvolvimiento Socioambiental do Vale do Javarí** ① *www.idsavj.org*, to work with local indigenous communities. All employees of the reserve come from five settlements close by and some of Palmarí's profits are invested back into these communities. The reserve takes a strong stance on responsible environmental practice, with non-eco-friendly shampoos and soaps banned during the visitor's stay (the reserve provides its own approved brands).

Reserva Natural Heliconia

① *T592 5773 (Leticia), www.amazonheliconia.com, US$420 per person (based on 2 people), including transport from Leticia and all food and activities (except canopy and massage treatments).*

Up a small tributary of the Javarí, about an hour by *peque peque* from Palmarí, this jungle lodge is about as isolated as you can get. It has several very comfortable *cabañas* (with bathrooms open to the forest behind) set around a jungle garden abounding in heliconia plants. The reserve organizes night-time caiman-spotting excursions as well as trips to visit local indigenous communities such as Santa Rita in nearby Peru. The forest behind provides opportunities for excellent walks, including a visit to an enormous *ceiba* tree, while there are also special birdwatching and fishing tours.

◉ Amazonia listings

For Sleeping and Eating price codes and other relevant information, see pages 23-28.

◓ Sleeping

Leticia *p340, map p340*

LL Decalodge Ticuna, Cra 11, No 6-11, T592 6600, www.decameron.com. Leticia's smartest hotel, run by the hotel chain **Decameron**, has comfortable rooms with a/c, cable TV and a large swimming pool but there have been reports of poor service. Can arrange stays in Amacayacu National Park and trips to Monkey Island, to which they hold concessions. Has all-inclusive packages, including all food and drink.

A Amira, Cra 9, No 9-71, T592 7767. This modern hotel has clean, comfortable rooms with a/c (almost half-price with fan), cable TV and private bathrooms with hot water.

A Yurupary, C 8, No 7-26, T592 4743, www.hotelyurupary.com. A good mid-range

option, the Yurupary has large rooms with private bathrooms and hot water as well as a lovely pool, fringed with tropical plants. Also arranges tours into the Amazon.

B Fernando Real, Cra 9, No 8-80, T592 7362. This hotel has an intimate atmosphere with rooms opening up onto a patio bursting with heliconias. The bathrooms are a little small.

B La Frontera, Av Internacional No 1-09, T592 5111, fronterahotelet@hotmail.com. As the name suggests, it's right on the border, so while it could be a bit noisy it's convenient if you are heading to Brazil. The rooms are clean with crisp, white sheets.

D Hospedaje Los Delfines, Cra 11, No 12-83, T592 7488, losdelfinesleticia@hotmail.com. This hotel has a lovely patio bursting with tropical plants and rooms with private bath, fan and Wi-Fi.

E Mahatu Guesthouse, Cra 7, No 1-40, T311-539 1265 (mob), www.mahatu.org. Another backpackers' hostel, this one is more

comfortable and better organized. It has 1 private room in a *maloca* in an overgrown garden out back and a couple of dorms with bunks, as well as a pool, kitchen and bike hire. Owner Gustavo René Alvarado speaks English, Flemish, French and Portuguese and organizes alternative tours of the Amazon.
E Mochileros, Cra 5, No 9-117, T592 5491. Basic hostel designed specifically for backpackers with bunks-only rooms and shared bathrooms. Organizes economical tours.

Tabatinga (Brazil)
Reais or pesos accepted. In Jun 2011 1 real = 1140 pesos.
B Takana, Rua Osvaldo Cruz, 970, T97-412 3557, takanahotel@hotmail.com. The lobby of this hotel is festooned with wooden figurines of Amazonian animals while the rooms are comfortable and clean with private bathrooms with hot water and a/c. Recommended.
C Vitoria Regia, Rua da Patria, 820, T973-412 2668. Basic rooms with cable TV and private bathrooms. Prices negotiable.
E Hotel Santiago, Rua Pedro Teixeira 49, T973-412 4680. Very basic but large rooms with private bathrooms.
F Hotel Pajé, Rua Pedro Teixeira 367, T973-412 2774. Next to the **Santiago**, this hostel is a little cheaper and a little cleaner.

Parque Nacional Amacayacú *p341*
Accommodation is managed by **Aviatur**, C 7, No 10-78, T592 6814 in Leticia (helpful), for the park direct T592 5600. There's a choice of private (**AL**) *malocas* or (**A**) dormitories. The Leticia office will also give information and arrange transport to the park.

Puerto Nariño *p343*
A Casa Selva, Cra 6, No 6-78, T311-201 2153, www.casaselvahotel.com. Very comfortable hotel with a fresh, airy feel about it. Rooms are spotless and it has a fine viewing platform on the roof. Can organize trips to nearby Lago de Tarapoto.

D Lomas del Paiyú, Cra 6 No 6-74, T313-237 0840. Small but clean rooms opening up off a long corridor. Ventilation could be a problem.
D Malocas Napú, C 4, No 5-72, T310-488 0998, olgabeco@yahoo.com, www.malocas napu.blogspot.com. This *maloca* has a couple of comfortable private rooms with fans as well as the cheaper option of hammocks. Staff are very helpful. Recommended.
E El Alto del Aguila, 20 mins' walk from the village or 5 mins by boat, Héctor, local school teacher/missionary has cabins, will arrange trips to indigenous communities and to see dolphins at Lago Tarapoto. He has pet monkeys, parrots, *gavilanes* and a pair of young caiman.
E Hospedaje Manguaré, Cra 5, No 5-52, T311-276 4873 (mob). This small hotel has comfortable cabin-style rooms with fans and shared bathrooms. It also doubles up as the town chemist.

🍴 Eating

Leticia *p340, map p340*
🍴 **Amazón Sazón**, Cra 9, No 7-56. Great little restaurant serving *comida corriente* as well as good-sized sandwiches, pizzas and hearty breakfasts.
🍴 **El Sabor**, C 8, No 9-25, T592 4774. *Menú del día* in several price brackets. *Bandeja paisa*, pork and chicken on offer.
🍴 **Tierras Amazónicas**, C 8, No 7-50, T592 4748. This restaurant has a good atmosphere, artisan decor and a varied menu of fish, chicken and steak dishes.
🍴 **Tierras Antioqueñas**, C 8, No 9-19. Good *almuerzos* of steak, chicken and *piracucu* fish (the largest freshwater fish in South America). *Bandeja paisa* is a speciality of the house.

Tabatinga (Brazil)
Reais or pesos accepted. In Jun 2011 1 real = 1140 pesos.
🍴 **Tres Fronteras Do Amzonas**, Rua Rui Barbosa, Barrio San Francixe, T97-412 2858.

Excellent restaurant with dining in a series of *malocas*. The menu is a mix of Brazilian, Peruvian and Colombian.
Ħ Te Contei?, Av da Amzide, 1813, Centro. Pay-by-the-kilo barbecued meats and salads from a buffet. By night they cook up excellent pizzas.

Puerto Nariño *p343*
There are 2 or 3 cheap restaurants near the waterfront, opposite the mini football pitch.

O Shopping

Leticia *p340, map p340*
Almacen Uirapuru, C 8, No 10-35, T592 7056. Enormous shop selling handicrafts from the Amazon region. It also has a small museum at the back with free entry if you buy *artesanía*.
Productos Naturales del Trapecio Amazónico, C 8, No 9-87, CC Shopping Center Centro, local 16-17, T592 4796. This natural chemists is packed with powders and herbs gathered from the forest. Ethno-botanist José Raúl Cuéllar has been making treatments from the Amazon's plants for more than 30 years and sells them all over the world.

▲ Activities and tours

Leticia *p340, map p340*
Tour operators
SelvAventura, Cra 9 No 6-85, T311-287 1307 (mob), www.selvaventuramazonas.com. This small operator does something a little different from the norm, with tailor-made trips to the Río Tacana to meet indigenous communities, sleeping in *posadas* and opportunities for kayaking, caiman spotting and observation of the forest from canopy platforms. Prices start from US$80 per person. English, Portuguese and Spanish spoken.
Steve McAlear, T313-313 1106, stevemcalear @hotmail.com. Englishman Steve McAlear

runs personalized tours to some of the area's more remote locations.

Puerto Nariño *p343*
Tour guides
Ever Sinarahua, Clarindo López and **Milciades Peña** are recommended for their local knowledge of flora and fauna and indigenous customs – enquire through **Casa Selva**. **Pedro Nel Cuello** – enquire through **Fundación Natutama**, www.natutama.org, is also recommended.

⊖ Transport

Leticia *p340, map p340*
Air Satena (C 11, No 5-73, T592 4845) and **Copa Airlines** (C 7, No 10-36, T592 7838) each fly to/from **Bogotá** (Tabatinga airport if Leticia's is closed) 1 a day. For good deals on Bogotá–Leticia flights we recommend the following agencies: **Doble Vía**, Cra 11, No 77-20, T211 2754; **Vivir Volando**, Cra 16, No 96-64, T601 4676, www.vivirvolando.com, best for **Satena**.

Tabatinga (Brazil)
Taxi Between Leticia and Tabatinga costs US$5.50 (more if you want to stop at immigration offices or exchange houses). Beware of drivers who want to rush you (expensively) over the border before it 'closes'.
Colectivo US$0.80 (more after 1800). If you ask for the port, you will be dropped where there is transport to **Benjamin Constant** (for Brazil and upstream boats to Peru).

Manaus (Brazil)
Boat From Manaus to **Benjamin Constant**, boats normally go on to **Tabatinga**, and start from there when going to Manaus. Boats usually wait 1-2 days in both Tabatinga and Benjamin Constant before returning to Manaus; you can stay on board. Tabatinga and Leticia

are 15 mins from Benjamin Constant by
river taxi, US$8.

From Tabatinga and Benjamin Constant
boats take around 3 days to Manaus, and
up to 8 days on the return trip up river.

Iquitos (Peru)

Boat Boats sail from Iquitos to a mud bank
called **Islandia**, on the Peruvian side of a
creek a short distance from **Benjamin
Constant**. The journey time is a minimum
of 2 days upstream, 8-36 hrs downstream,
depending on the speed of the boat.
Passengers leaving or entering Peru must
visit immigration at Santa Rosa when the
boat stops there. For entry into Brazil,
formalities are done in Tabatinga; for
Colombia, in Leticia. **Amazon Cruises and
Adventures**, www.amazoncruiselines.com,
operates a service between Iquitos and
Tabatinga/Leticia, US$795 per person,
based on 2 people sharing, 3 nights in a
110-year-old Scottish-built river cruiser.

Puerto Nariño p343
Boat from **Leticia**, daily at 1000 and 1400
(check times as they often change), 2 hrs,
US$12.50, with **Tres Fronteras**.

⊙ Directory

Leticia p340, map p340
Banks Banco de Bogotá, will cash TCs,
has ATM on Cirrus network, good rates
for Brazilian *reais*. There are street money
changers, plenty of *cambios*, and banks
for exchange. Shop around. **Internet**
Centel.net, C 9, No 9-09. Skype and
headphones as well as local and international calls. **AlohaNett**, C 11, No 7-22.
Skype and headphones. **Post** Adpostal,
C8, No 9-65, T592 7977. **Telephone**
Cra 11/C 9, near Parque Santander.

Puerto Nariño p343
Internet/telephone Internet and
international calls (expensive) next
to the school.

Contents

350 History

355 Modern Colombia
355 Recent history
357 The drugs trade
358 Government

359 Culture
359 Arts and crafts
361 Fine art and sculpture
365 Literature
368 Music and dance
370 Religion

370 People

371 Land and environment
371 Geology and landscape
375 Climate
376 Wildlife and vegetation
381 National parks

Footprint features

358 Colombian entrepreneurism
377 Flowers

Background

History

Pre-Columbian

Colombia was inhabited by various indigenous groups before the Spanish conquest. The most highly developed were the **Tayronas**, who had settlements along the Caribbean coast and on the slopes of the Sierra Nevada de Santa Marta. The Tayronas had a complex social organization, with an economy based on fishing, agriculture and commerce. They built paved roads, aqueducts, stone stairways and public plazas for ceremonies.

Another major group were the **Muisca**, a Chibcha-speaking people who dominated the central highlands of Colombia at the time of the conquest. Muisca and Chibcha can be considered the same language. Philologists identify the 'Chibchan' language as referring to a series of dialects extending from Nicaragua in Central America to Ecuador, almost all of which have now disappeared. Carbon dating places their earliest settlements at around BC 545. Their village confederation was ruled by the **Zipa** at Bogotá, and the **Zaque** at Hunza (now Tunja). The Zipas believed that they were descended from the Moon, and the Zaques from the Sun. Their livelihood came from trading at markets in corn, potatoes and beans. They were also accomplished goldsmiths, and traded emeralds, ceramics and textiles with other societies.

The **Sinú** had their chiefdoms in the present-day Department of Córdoba and parts of Antioquia and Sucre. They farmed yucca and maize on artificial mounds in the local marshlands with complex drainage systems to make the best use of high and low water levels. They also cultivated reeds used for textiles and basket-weaving, as well as working with gold. Much wealth was plundered from their tombs, known as 'guacas', by the Spaniards during the conquest.

The **Quimbayas** inhabited parts of the Valle del Cauca. They had a class system and society similar to that of the Muisca and Tayronas, except that some evidence suggests they practised ritual cannibalism.

'**Calima**' is a term used to classify the other indigenous groups living in the department of Valle del Cauca. They include the **Liles** (based near present-day Cali) and the **Gorrones** (based in the Cordillera Occidental). They were organized into small chiefdoms with economies based on fishing, hunting and cultivating beans, yucca and corn. They traded in gold, salt, textiles and slaves. Two other significant groups prospered in San Agustín and Tierradentro, in what is now the south of Colombia. Both left fascinating monuments but they had disappeared well before the conquest.

Spanish colonization

The first permanent Spanish settlement in Colombia was established in 1500-1507 by **Rodrigo de Bastidas** (1460-1527). He reached the country by sailing south along the Caribbean coast. After his return to Spain to face trial for insubordination, he was given permission to establish a colony. In 1525 he founded Santa Marta and named the river Magdalena. Cartagena was founded in 1533 by **Pedro de Heredia** and used as a central stockpile for the growing Spanish collection of treasure. Massive fortifications were built to protect it from pirate attacks. Santa Fe de Bogotá was founded by **Gonzalo Jiménez de Quesada** (c.1495-1579) in 1538. He arrived in Santa Marta in 1535 and continued up to the high plateau of Sabana de Bogotá with his men: 200 made the trip by boat, 670 by land. **Sebastián de Belalcázar** (c 1480-1551), the lieutenant of Francisco Pizarro, was given instructions to explore southern Colombia and the Cauca Valley in 1535. He founded Cali and Popayán in 1536 and 1537 respectively, and was made governor of Popayán in 1540. **Nicolás Federmann** (1506-1541), acting on behalf of the Welser financiers of Germany, led an expedition east to Coro and Cabo de la Vela, then back to Barquisimeto and Meta. He arrived in the Sabana de Bogotá in 1538, where he met Belalcázar and Jiménez de Quesada.

Jiménez de Quesada named the territory he had conquered Nuevo Reino de Granada, because it reminded him of Granada in Spain. Santa Fe de Bogotá was named after the city of Santa Fe in Granada. The first secular government to be established after the conquest was the Audiencia de Santa Fe de Bogotá, in 1550. After 1594, it shared ruling authority with the president of the New Kingdom of New Granada, the name given to the whole conquered area, which included Panama. The presidency was replaced in 1718 by a viceroyalty at Bogotá, which also controlled the provinces now known as Venezuela; it was independent of the viceroyalty of Peru, to which this vast area had previously belonged.

Independence from Spain

In 1793, a translation of *Rights of Man* was published in Colombia by **Antonio Nariño** (1765-1823), an administrator and journalist, known as 'el Precursor' for his important role in the Independence movement. He was imprisoned in Spain in 1794, but escaped and returned to Nueva Granada (as Colombia was then called) in 1797. He joined the patriot forces in 1810 and became president of Cundinamarca in 1812. In 1813 he led a military campaign in the south and was again imprisoned by the Spanish. Meanwhile **Simón Bolívar** (1783-1830) was leading a campaign for Venezuelan Independence. Following the collapse of the First Republic of Venezuela in 1812, he joined the Independence movement in Cartagena and had early successes in his 1812 Magdalena Campaign, which ended in Caracas, where the Second Republic was proclaimed. Again, the patriots lost control and Bolívar returned to Colombia, but was forced to flee to the West Indies when **General Pablo Morillo** launched the Spanish re-conquest.

Changes in Europe were also to affect the situation in Colombia. In 1808, Napoleon replaced Ferdinand VII of Spain with his own brother Joseph. The New World refused to recognize this, and several revolts erupted in Nueva Granada, culminating in a revolt at Bogotá and the establishment of a junta on 20 July 1810. Cartagena also bound itself to a junta set up at Tunja.

Simón Bolívar returned to the Llanos in 1816 and formed a new army. Their campaign for liberation involved a forced march over the Andes, in the face of incredible hardship. After joining forces with **Francisco de Paula Santander**'s Nueva Granada army, he defeated the royalists at the Battle of the Pantano de Vargas in July of 1819, winning the decisive victory at the Battle of Boyacá on 7 August. From 1819 to 1828 Bolívar was president of Gran Colombia, the new name for the union of Colombia, Venezuela, Panama and Ecuador, which lasted until the 1830s.

After the fall of Napoleon in 1815, the Spanish set about trying to reconquer the independent territories. The main Spanish general behind the task was Pablo Morillo (1775-1837), known as 'the Pacifier'. During his reign of terror (1816-1819), more than 300 patriot supporters were executed. Morillo set up the 'Consejo de Guerra Permanente' and the 'Consejo de Purificación'. The latter's aim was to punish crimes of treason. There was also a board of confiscations known as the 'Junta de Secuestros'. Morillo was linked to the re-establishment of the Inquisition, which saw many priests tried in military courts in South America.

The Spaniards created a considerable legacy in Colombia. Their main objective was to amass riches, notably gold, and ship everything back to Spain. Protecting what they had collected from their English, French and Dutch rivals led to the massive fortifications of their main port, Cartagena. Most of what they built is still intact and has to be experienced to be fully appreciated. However, they also brought with them culture and lifestyle, and some of their best colonial public and domestic architecture can be found in Colombia. Furthermore they brought their language, religion and many institutions, including universities, that continue to thrive today. The towns they planned and built are now being preserved. What they did not create, however, were political institutions, and the search for a durable formula continues, 200 years after Independence.

Gran Colombia

La República de Gran Colombia was established by the revolutionary congress at present-day Ciudad Bolívar (Venezuela) on 17 December 1819. A general congress was held at Cúcuta on 1 January 1821, and it was here that the two opposing views that later sowed such dissent in Colombia first became apparent. Bolívar and Nariño were in favour of centralization; Santander, a realist, wanted a federation of sovereign states. Bolívar succeeded in enforcing his view and the 1821 Constitution was drawn up, dividing Gran Colombia into 12 departments and 26 provinces. New laws were introduced to abolish the slave trade and allow free birth for the children of slaves born in Colombia, to redistribute indigenous lands and to abolish the Inquisition. This constitution lasted until 1830 when, following the breakaway of Venezuela and Ecuador, a new constitution was drawn up.

The next president after Bolívar was Francisco de Paula Santander, from 1832 to 1837. Formerly the vice-president, he had led a campaign of dissent against the alleged dictatorship of Bolívar, culminating in an assassination attempt on Bolívar on 25 September 1828. Suspected of having had a hand in the attempt, Santander was sentenced to death, but pardoned by Bolívar himself and instead sent into exile. later returning to hold the presidency. He played an important role in establishing the administrative structure of the new republic of Colombia, and went on to become leader of the congressional opposition from 1837 to 1840.

Colombia's civil wars

The new country, which still included present-day Panama, was the scene of much dissent between the centralizing pro-clerical Conservatives and the federalizing anti-clerical Liberals. The Liberals were dominant from 1849, and the next 30 years saw countless insurrections and civil wars. In 1885 the Conservatives imposed a highly centralized constitution that was not modified for over 100 years. Civil war had a disastrous effect on the economy, leading to the Paper Money Crisis of 1885, when Colombian currency suffered a dramatic fall in value and circulation had to be reduced to 12 million pesos in notes. Gold was not established as the standard for currency until 1903.

A Liberal revolt of 1899 against the rigidly partisan government of the Conservatives turned into the 'War of the Thousand Days', also known as 'La Rebelión'. It lasted from 17 October 1899 to 1 June 1903. The first Liberal victory was at Norte de Santander in December 1899, when government forces were defeated by rebel leader General Benjamín Herrera. The Battle of Palonegro, 11-26 May 1900, was won by the government forces, led by General Próspero Pinzón. This proved to be the decisive victory of the 'War of a Thousand Days'. 100,000 people had died before the Liberals were finally defeated.

During the Independence Wars, Panama remained loyal to Spain. Although it had been a state in Nueva Granada since 1855, it was practically self-governing until 1886, when the new Colombian constitution reduced it to a mere department. A bid for Independence in 1903 was supported by the USA. The revolution lasted only four days (3-6 November) and by 18 November the USA had signed a treaty allowing them to build the Panama Canal.

The authoritarian government of General **Rafael Reyes** (1850-1921), from 1904 to 1909, was known as the Quinquenio dictatorship. He created his own extra-legal national assembly in 1904. His territorial reorganization and his negotiations with the USA over Panama increased his unpopularity, leading to an assassination attempt in 1906. The new president from 1910 to 1914, **Carlos Eugenio Restrepo** (1867-1937), restored a legal form of government and began negotiations with the USA for the Urrutia-Thomson Treaty of 1914. This resulted in a US\$25 million indemnity payment to Colombia over US involvement in the Panamanian Revolution.

Colombia was also engaged in a dispute with its southern neighbour, Peru, over Leticia, capital of the Commissariat of Amazonas. Peru had repudiated the Salomón-Lozano Treaty of 1922 by occupying Leticia, a part of Colombia according to the treaty. The dispute was submitted to the League of Nations in 1933, who took over the Leticia area and handed it back to Colombia in 1934.

La Violencia

The late 1940s to mid-1960s were dominated by a period known as 'La Violencia', incited by the assassination of the socialist mayor of Bogotá, **Jorge Eliécer Gaitán**, on 9 April 1948. The riots that ensued were known as the 'Bogotazo'. La Violencia was characterized by terrorism, murder and destruction of property. Simultaneous, though uncoordinated, outbursts persisted throughout the 1950s. Among the many victims were Protestants, who were persecuted 1948-1959. Some 115 Protestants were murdered and 42 of their buildings destroyed. Other contributing factors to La Violencia were anti-communist sentiments, economic deprivation and the prevailing partisan political system. In 1957 a unique political truce was formed, putting an end to the violence. The Liberal and Conservative parties became the Frente Nacional, a coalition under which the two parties supported a single presidential candidate and divided all political offices equally between them. Political stability was maintained for 16 years. Ultimately the Conservatives gained more from this accord, and unforeseen opposition was provoked in parties not involved in the agreement.

Guerrilla Movements

One of the biggest guerrilla organizations active after La Violencia was the Movimiento 19 de Abril, known as M19. Their political wing was the Alianza Nacional Popular (ANAPO), founded by followers of the dictator **General Gustavo Rojas Pinilla** (1900-1975). His Peronist tactics during his 1953-1957 presidency had resulted in his trial by national tribunal and he was overthrown on 10 May 1957. ANAPO opposed both Liberals and Conservatives. They became a major protest force during the late 1960s and 1970s, believing that the 1970 presidential elections, in which Rojas Pinilla was a candidate, had been rigged, and that fraudulent results had placed **Misael Pastrana Borrero** in power. Ml9 took their name from the date of the election, 19 April 1970.

M19's agenda was to achieve a democratic socialist society. Seeking to identify themselves with the legacy of the hero of the Independence movement, their first public act was the theft of Bolívar's sword from Quinta de Bolívar in Bogotá. They also kidnapped José Rafael Mercado, president of the Confederation of Workers, in 1976, accusing him of fraud and misconduct in office, for which they tried and executed him. They then kidnapped Alvaro Gómez Hurtado, Communist Party leader and son of earlier president Gómez, to publicize demands for renewed talks with the government.

It was not until the late 1980s that negotiations got under way. A peace accord was reached in late 1989. The following year, M19 members surrendered their weapons and turned themselves into a bona fide political party, named Alianza Democrática, or M19-AD, with which they gained a significant percentage of the vote in the 1990 elections.

The other main terrorist organization after La Violencia was Fuerzas Armadas Revolucionarias de Colombia (FARC). Formed in 1964 under leader **Pedro Antonio Marín**, known as Manuel Marulanda or 'Tirofijo' ('Sureshot'), they were aligned with the Communist Party. After 20 years of guerrilla activity they signed a truce with the government on 24 May 1984. FARC joined forces with the legitimate Unión Patriótica and went on to win 10 seats in the 1986 election, while the Liberals took the majority.

In 1985 many of Colombia's guerrilla movements merged into the 'Coordinadora Guerrillera Simón Bolívar' (CGSB), together with all organizations that had refused to sign the government amnesty offered by **President Belisario Betancur** in 1985. Their aim was to co-ordinate their actions against the government and the armed forces. Most of their actions were based along the upper Río Cauca and the department of Antioquia. Peace talks with the government in the early 1990s collapsed, followed in 1992-1993 by several indecisive but destructive offences on the part of both the guerrillas and the armed forces.

The 1994 presidential elections were won by another Liberal, **Ernesto Samper**. The main thrust of his programme was that Colombia's current economic strength should provide resources to tackle the social deprivation that was causing drug use and insurgency. He placed emphasis on bringing the FARC and the other main guerrilla group, the **Ejército de Liberación Nacional** (**ELN**), to the negotiating table, while also increasing public spending on social welfare. Revelations during 1995-1997 that Samper's election campaign had been financed partly by a US\$6 million donation from the Cali Cartel saw the government's popularity decline. In 1996 further charges were brought against the president for links with the drugs mafia, although he was acquitted. The charges led to political instability and the attempted killing of Samper's lawyer. With the assassination of opposition leader Alvaro Gómez, Samper declared a state of emergency.

When it was revealed that other ministers had links with the drugs mafia, suspicion arose that Samper's acquittal had only been to protect their own positions. International confidence was lost. The USA decided, in March 1996, to remove (decertify) Colombia from its list of countries making progress against drug trafficking. This made Colombia ineligible for US aid.

Colombia was decertified for the second time in March 1997 partly because the Cali leaders were continuing their business from prison, having been given light sentences. Whatever progress was being made to eradicate drugs plantations and stocks, the denial of US aid permitted little scope for the establishment of alternative crops. Many rural communities were therefore left without any means of support.

In May 1997 the government admitted for the first time to the escalating problem of paramilitary groups and their links with members of the armed forces. The most infamous of these is 'Autodefensas Campesinas de Córdoba y Urabá' (ACCU), who receive financial support from drugs cartels. The state department admitted that 48% of violent episodes in 1997 were carried out by paramilitaries. This was confirmed by the annual report of the Inter-American Human Rights Commission in June 1997. In March 1998, congressional elections were relatively peaceful; and the US withdrawal of decertification restrictions the same month, were a welcome boost of confidence. Two rounds of presidential elections in May and June 1998 also passed without excessive guerrilla disruption. The new president, **Andrés Pastrana**, voted in on a promise to find a formula for peace, immediately devoted his efforts to bringing the guerrilla groups to the negotiating table. After a long, tortuous process with FARC, a large *zona de despeje* (demilitarized zone), was conceded, centred on San Vicente del Caguán in Caquetá. Not everyone was in favour of Pastrana's initiative, not least because FARC violence and extortion did not cease. In April 2000, the government proposed the ceding of a similar but smaller demilitarized zone to the ELN, situated on the west side of the Río Magdalena in the department of Bolívar and a small section of Antioquia, a *zona de encuentro*. Local communities of this agricultural area were dismayed and peacefully demonstrated by closing roads and causing disruption.

After a series of high-profile guerrilla terrorist actions, including the hijacking of a plane, attacks on several small towns and cities, and the kidnapping of several political figures, Pastrana ended the peace talks on 21 February 2002 and ordered the armed forces to start retaking the FARC-controlled zone.

Modern Colombia

Recent history

Alvaro Uribe succeeded Andrés Pastrana as president in May 2002, holding office for two terms, until 2010. A Harvard- and Oxford-educated lawyer, he came to power promising to eradicate the left-wing guerrillas' and right-wing paramilitaries' hold on the country.

To a large extent he succeeded. Using US funding from Plan Colombia (see below), he boosted spending on the military and armed peasants in vulnerable regions. He held formal peace talks with far-right paramilitaries and managed to bring security to most of the urban areas of the country within the mountainous centre. In so doing he effectively pushed the guerrillas, who at one point held territory within an hour of Bogotá, to the margins of the country – to the dense jungles around the borders with Venezuela, Ecuador and Panama.

In terms of the state's fight against the FARC, which has been going on for more than 40 years, 2008 was Colombia's *annus mirabilis*. Three major successes – each of which would have been considered a major, standalone coup in their own right – have shifted the balance of the conflict overwhelmingly in favour of the government.

In March, the Colombian army executed a raid just over the border into Ecuador in which Luis Edgar Devia Silva (normally known by his nom de guerre, Raúl Reyes), the FARC's spokesperson and a member of the Secretariat, was killed.

In May, it was revealed that the FARC's founder and leader, Pedro Antonio Marín Marín, aka Manuel Marulanda or Tirofijo ('Sureshot'), had died of a heart attack.

Then in July came the biggest blow of all – the dramatic rescue of Senator Ingrid Betancourt, who had been kidnapped six years previously while campaigning for the presidency. In many ways, Betancourt's imprisonment had come to symbolize the potency the FARC held over Colombia and her rescue severely dented the rebels' bargaining power.

These three strikes have led many analysts to sound the death knell of the FARC, but suggesting that the FARC have been neutralized may be premature. Alfonso Cano took over command after Marulanda's death and a number of bombings in late 2008 suggests they will continue to disrupt civilian life for years to come, while their bargaining power will remain intact while they still hold what was believed to be over 700 hostages in 2009.

Successes notwithstanding, Uribe was not without his critics when leaving office to successor Juan Manuel Santos in 2010.

A Human Rights Watch report released in October 2008 eg concluded that President Uribe's government has been putting obstacles in the way of the Supreme Court's efforts to investigate the paramilitaries' mafia-like networks and his cousin Mario Uribe was charged for alleged links to paramilitary groups.

In spite of these scandals, Uribe did during his eight years in office manage to improve security in most areas in Colombia. His successor Santos, a Harvard economist and former minister, took office in August of 2010 and appears to be following in Uribe's footsteps in terms of national security policies, while also recommencing a long-awaited land redistribution programme.

Relations with neighbours

In the last few years, diplomatic relations between Colombia and her neighbours have been at best frosty, at worst volatile. While much of Latin America has experienced a swing toward socialism and anti-American sentiment, Colombia has strengthened its ties with the USA and pursued a neo-liberal economical model. Uribe and the charismatic president of Venezuela, Hugo Chávez, the most outspoken critic of US 'imperialism', displayed a barely disguised disdain for each other and their diametrically opposed ideologies. New president Santos is, however, working to improve neighbourly relations with the country, having frequently met with Chávez since taking office. Border relations with Ecuador and Panama have at times also been fraught due to guerrilla and drug-trafficking activities in the border areas, particularly after the Colombian incursion into Ecuador in 2008.

Plan Colombia

Plan Colombia is a US-Colombian initiative designed to reduce the flow of cocaine into the USA. Conceived during the presidency of Andrés Pastrana, the original Plan Colombia asked for US aid to address the problem of social exclusion that has plagued Colombia since Independence from the Spanish and that has forced peasant farmers to cultivate coca, giving birth to guerrilla movements like the FARC in the first place.

A second draft, presided over by US President Bill Clinton's advisers, had an entirely more militaristic slant and aimed to reduce the drug supply by providing extra firepower to the Colombian army in its pursuit of drug-traffickers and supplying equipment and civilian agents for the destruction of coca plantations.

The plan has come under heavy criticism for its fumigation policy, which has seen farmers' legal crops destroyed alongside illegal ones, as well as causing adverse health effects on those exposed. NGOs also claim that the money provided by the US government, which tallies up to several billion dollars, has funded Colombian army units involved in extra judicial killings and other human rights abuses.

Despite the billions of dollars ploughed into the project, the plan has failed in its primary objective. A UN analysis has found that the eradication of coca plantations has been on a smaller scale than anticipated. What's more, the market price of cocaine has not increased significantly, something that would be expected if there were a shortage of the drug on the streets of the USA. Critics of the plan also argue that any eradication of coca production in Colombia would simply push cultivation back to countries such as Bolivia and Peru.

But the initiative has had a huge tangential success in that the money provided by the US government has helped the Colombian army in its victories over the FARC and for that has gained much approval in the eyes of many Colombians. The Plan Colombia budget for 2011 was being cut by 50 million dollars and it's uncertain how this will affect its future execution, but it remains in operation.

The drugs trade

In Medellín and Cali, two cartels transformed Colombia's drugs trade into a major force in worldwide business and crime. Their methods were very different; Medellín's was violent and ostentatious, while Cali's was much more low-key. The Medellín Cartel processed and distributed 60-70% of cocaine exported to the USA during the 1980s. It was headed by **Pablo Escobar Gaviria** (see box, page 218) and **Jorge Luis Ochoa Vásquez**. Many members of the Ochoa family were also working for the cartel. In the late 1980s both Jorge Luis Ochoa and Pablo Escobar were listed as billionaires by *Forbes Magazine*.

In 1981, **Marta Nieves Ochoa Vásquez**, Jorge's sister, was kidnapped. M19 were believed responsible. In response to the kidnapping, 'Muerte a Secuestradores' (Death to Kidnappers) was formed by leaders of the drugs trade. Their strong anti-Communist beliefs led to alleged support from factions of the military. In 1984 Muerte a Secuestradores assassinated Carlos Toledo Plata, an ANAPO congressman who had later joined M19.

President César Gaviria Trujillo, the Liberal candidate who had won the 1990 presidential election, put into motion a pacification plan to end the drugs cartels' offensive and establish a peace agreement with the guerrillas. In a further display of reformist government, he appointed **Antonio Navarro Wolff**, former guerrilla leader now of the M19-AD, to the post of health minister.

As a result of the reform of the constitution in 1991, a further general election was held in October 1991 (although not due until 1994) and the Liberals retained a majority in the Senate and the House of Representatives. By 1991 the government had secured the surrender, under secret terms, of senior members of the Medellín cartel, namely Pablo Escobar and Jorge Luis Ochoa. One of the publicized conditions for their surrender was immunity from extradition and reduced sentences. Some of the senior traffickers and murderers got only five to eight years. President Gaviria received international support, including from the USA, for his stance against the drugs problem, which contrasted with previous president Barco's tougher, and unsuccessful stand.

In the National Constituent Assembly elections of 1991 the M19-AD won 19 of the 70 contested seats; the Liberals won 24; combined Conservative factions won 20. These results were followed by attempts to legitimize and modernize the political system, in an effort to deny remaining guerrilla groups any cause for protest and therefore lead to peace. The judicial system was strengthened and extradition was banned. However, the early 1990s saw high abstention rates in elections: 60-70% of the electorate didn't vote. This was blamed on loss of confidence in the political system and disruption of voting by guerrillas in some rural areas.

During the Gaviria term, it was reported that Pablo Escobar was continuing to direct the Medellín Cartel from inside his purpose-built prison at Envigado. The Cali Cartel's trade was in turn growing in the wake of reduced activity by the Medellín Cartel. In July

Colombian entrepreneurism

Colombia is a nation of small businesses. Millions make their living by hawking their wares on the street. Street artists, photographers, people hiring out their mobile phones by the minute, and countless street stalls selling everything from fruit juices to iguana eggs – they're an enterprising bunch.

Step onto one of the colourful buses and you'll want for nothing. Fizzy drinks and snacks will keep you nourished, while travelling salesmen have perfected the art of the five-minute pitch. They usually wait outside bus stations to flag down a passing vehicle. You're handed the product to examine while they execute a carefully prepared speech. By the time the bus reaches the outskirts of town they've collected any unwanted merchandise and usually leave with a few thousand pesos in their back pocket. But don't switch off from the sales talk – sometimes what they have to offer is quite useful!

1992, Escobar escaped during a transfer to army barracks. Drug-related violence in Bogotá increased in 1993, thought to be Escobar's way of persuading the government to offer better surrender conditions for him. A paramilitary vigilante group was formed, called 'Perseguidos Por Pablo Escobar' (Los Pepes). This was allegedly made up of relatives of Escobar's murder victims and members of the Cali Cartel, and it targeted Escobar's family. Escobar was finally shot by the armed forces on 2 December 1993 in Medellín, giving a temporary boost to the government's popularity. The Cali cartel capitalized on the death of Escobar and the dismantling of his empire. By the mid-1990s they controlled 70% of the world market in cocaine. But in June and July 1995, six of the seven heads of the cartel were arrested. In 2006, the Rodríguez brothers, Gilberto and Miguel, were extradited to the USA and pleaded guilty in Miami, Florida, to charges of conspiracy to import cocaine. This put an end to cartel control over the Colombian drug trade and it has now splintered into many individual groups, including paramilitary and guerrilla forces, although this has not stopped production in any significant way.

Government

Senators and Representatives are elected by popular vote. The Senate has 102 members, and the Chamber of Representatives has 166. The president, who appoints his 13 ministers, is elected by direct vote for a term of four years, but cannot succeed himself in the next term. Every citizen over 18 can vote. Reform of the 1886 Constitution was undertaken by a Constituent Assembly in 1991 (see History, above). Administratively, the country is divided into 32 departments and the Special Capital District of Bogotá. Liberty of speech and the freedom of the press are in theory absolute but in practice more limited. The official language of Colombia is Spanish. Its religion is Roman Catholicism. There is complete freedom for all other creeds not contravening Christian morals or the law.

Culture

Arts and crafts

With the wide variety of climate, topography and geology, it is not surprising that Colombia has virtually all the materials, fibres, minerals and incentives to create useful and artistic products. Many of the techniques practised today have been inherited from the indigenous peoples who lived here before the conquest, some indeed have not changed much in the intervening centuries and are as appropriate now as they were then.

Gold

Gold is very much associated with Colombia. It was gold that brought the Europeans to the New World, and where they found it first. The indigenous peoples had been using it for many centuries though not as a simple 'store of value'. Only when it had been made into jewellery, body ornaments or items to be used for sacrificial rites for their gods did gold have value for them. It must have seemed incomprehensible to them, as well as a tragedy for posterity, when the Spaniards melted down the gold they obtained in order to ship it back to Europe.

Many of the *sierras* in the west of the country have traces of gold in the strata. Through erosion in the rainy climates of the region, panning for gold in the rivers was productive and has probably been practised here since around 800 BC. Even some deep shaft mines have been found in west Colombia.

The Quimbaya of the Cauca Valley produced 24 carat gold containers, helmets and pendants in their ascendancy from 1000-1500 AD and also worked with *tumbaga*, a gold-copper alloy. The Tolima of the Magdalena Valley made artefacts of pure gold, while the Wayúu of the Guajira made string beads, sometimes covered with gold, a tradition that continues today. When the Spaniards arrived, the Muisca of the Boyacá/Bogotá area were modelling figures in wax and covering them with clay. They then fired them, removed the melted wax and filled the mould with gold. By carefully prizing open the mould, they were able to make many replicas, thus inventing an early form of mass production.

Virtually all of today's techniques of the goldsmith were known to the early peoples of Colombia and there is a fine presentation on this subject at the museum in the Parque Arqueológico in Sogamoso, Boyacá, see page 100.

There are some good gold item bargains to be had in Colombia, notably in Bogotá and Cartagena. Perhaps the most interesting place, however, is Mompós, Bolívar, where there is a tradition of fine gold filigree work.

No one visiting Colombia should miss the Banco de la República's wonderful gold museums. The central collection of gold artefacts is in Bogotá but there are other smaller presentations in the main cities around the country, always worth a visit.

Textiles

Although Colombian textiles cannot rival those of Guatemala or Peru in terms of design and spectacular colour, certain areas of the country have very fine traditions. For the Wayúu, *'ser mujer es saber tejer'* (to be a woman is to know how to weave). Cotton was available in north Colombia and textiles were traded for wool from the Santa Marta *sierra* nearby, also used as a raw material. The Cuna of northwest Colombia still make the decorative panels for garments known as *molas*. A speciality is the *mola* made of many layers of coloured cloth sewn together, then cut out using the different colours to create a pattern or motif.

One striking costume is found in the south near Silvia, Cauca, where the indigenous Guambiano weave their own blue and fuchsia costumes as well as many other wool garments and blankets.

Basketry

By its nature, articles made of vegetable fibres do not survive for very long, but we know that the Spaniards found many examples of indigenous work in Colombia. The basket-weaving techniques of the Muisca have continued in Tenza, Boyacá, where people still use the giant reed *caña de castilla* (Arundo donax), which is easier to work with than bamboo. The whole local village works in this cottage industry.

Another similar community enterprise is in Sandoná, Nariño, where, in addition to basket weaving, Panama hats are a speciality. Panama hats are so named for where they were initially sold and shipped from, rather than where they were made. The workers on the canal in the early part of the 20th century were the first customers, followed by those passing through. They were made in Ecuador and in Sandoná where the local *iraca* palm fibre is used. Hats are also made in Sampués, Sucre, from 'arrowcane' which grows in the river lowlands nearby and good basket weaving using palma iraca can be found at Usiacurí, south of Barranquilla.

The finest quality basket weaving in the country is to be found along the northwest Pacific coast of Chocó where the women of the indigenous Waunana use *werregue* palm to weave a texture so fine that the finished product can look like clay and be used to carry water. They have a flourishing trade nowadays in coarser but more colourful palm weaving products.

Wood

The indigenous people of Chocó also make interesting 'healing sticks', said to have magical as well as healing powers. These are about 50 cm long with a pointed end and carved figures above. Held against the stomach of the patient, they can drive away evil spirits and cure illnesses. Carved wooden masks are a feature of indigenous crafts in the Sierra Nevada de Santa Marta in the north and the Sibundoy people of Putumayo in the extreme south of the country, used them for festivities and rituals. Interesting wood carvings are made by the Puinave people near Inírida. Wooden masks appear in the carnival in Barranquilla.

Perhaps the most important wood *artesanía* is found in Chiquinquirá (Boyacá). Carved musical instruments are a speciality and many other items including all sorts of items made of *tagua* nuts gathered in the forests of Chocó and Amazonas. Guitars are also found in Marinilla near Medellín.

Leather

Leather and woodwork often go together, and the arrival of cattle brought the necessary raw material. Now, finely engraved leather covering carved wooden chairs and other furniture is made in Pasto (Nariño), an important centre.

Barniz

An additional craft is that of the resin locally called *barniz*. This comes from seed pods of *Eleagia Utilis*, which grows at altitudes of over 2000 m in Putumayo. Nowadays, the resin is extracted by passing through a mill or by hammering. Previously this was done by chewing the seeds, commonly known as *mopa-mopa*, supposedly because of the strange sound made by the chewers attempting to speak as well as chew at the same time. After extraction, the resin is dyed and expertly stretched to paper thin sheets into which designs are cut to decorate wooden objects including masks, each colour produced individually, finally covered with a protective lacquer. Pasto is the most important centre for *barniz*.

Pottery

The best known pottery centre in Colombia is Ráquira, Boyacá. A large selection of products is made for household and ornamental use including many small items, all sold here and in surrounding towns. The large earthenware pots made here today are identical to those made by the Chibcha centuries ago. A similar pottery centre across the country, Carmen de Viboral, Antioquia, also produces ceramics that are known throughout Colombia.

Imaginative and amusing ceramics are made in Pitalito, Huila. This form of popular art, pottery adorned with scenes of everyday life, is typified by representations of the *chiva*, the omnipresent brightly coloured bus seen in many parts of Colombia.

A more unusual line of production is the 'blackware' made at La Chamba, Tolima. This small village, beside the Río Magdalena near Guamo, is not generally marked on maps. The process involves using closed kilns, thus cutting down the use of oxygen which thereby causes the iron in the clay to turn from red to black. La Chamba is now a household name in Colombia and is also becoming better known abroad.

Fine art and sculpture

The colonial art of Colombia is rich and diverse, perhaps reflecting its geographical position between the Caribbean and the Pacific, but also because of the early rivalry between the two first important colonial settlements of Bogotá and Tunja. Both cities boast numerous museums and religious foundations with good collections of painting, sculpture and decorative arts. Throughout the colonial period works of art were imported from Europe and elsewhere in the Spanish territories, particularly from Quito in the south. Artists came from far afield to work in the wealthy Colombian centres. In contrast to colonial practices in Mexico and Ecuador there seems to have been little attempt to train native craftsmen in the dominant European artistic modes of painting and sculpture, perhaps because indigenous expertise lay in pottery and metalwork rather than carving or painting.

Early art from Spain

The conquerors brought the Christian religion and, along with it, Christian art. The cathedral sacristy in Bogotá preserves what must be one of the first European imports: a fragile silk standard traditionally believed to have been carried by Jiménez de Quesada's troops at the foundation of Bogotá in 1538, and known as the **Cristo de la Conquista**. The emaciated, bloody figure of Christ is in a mixture of paint and appliqué, with a swirling length of loin cloth around his hips. This seems to billow in the breeze, an impression that would have been all the stronger in its original context. It is hard to imagine anything more alien to native beliefs or native forms of art. Other early Christian images, especially pictures of the Virgin, must have tapped into local beliefs because they soon became the focus of popular cults: the **Virgen de Monguí**, for example, is a 16th-century Spanish painting, which tradition holds was sent over by Philip II, while the **Virgen de Chiquinquirá**, the patron saint of Colombia, was painted by the Andalucían **Alonso de Narváez** who settled in Tunja in the 1550s. Neither is outstanding as a work of art but both have been attributed with miraculous powers and versions can be found all over Colombia.

Although religious commissions dominated artistic production throughout the colonial period some remarkable secular wall paintings survive in Tunja that show another side to colonial society. In the late 16th and 17th centuries the houses of the city's founder, Gonzalo Suárez Rendón, of poet Juan de Castellanos and of city notary Juan de Vargas were decorated with colourful murals based on a wide range of printed sources. Those in the **Casa Vargas** are the most sophisticated, the combination of mythological figures, exotic animals, grotesques, heraldic cartouches and occasional Christian monograms resulting in a complex humanistic programme, probably devised by Castellanos. The diversity of styles reflects the diversity of sources, which can be traced to French, Flemish, German and Spanish originals. The rhinoceros, for example, is derived from Dürer's famous woodcut of 1515 but reached Tunja via a Spanish architectural treatise by Juan de Arfe, published in Seville in 1587. The murals in the **Casa Suárez Rendón** derive in part from those in the Casa Vargas, but are less philosophical, more straightforwardly decorative. Nevertheless, these paintings imply that a highly cultured society imported the most-up-to-date books and prints from Europe.

Woodcarvings and sculpture

The new religious foundations in the Americas created a huge market for paintings and sculptures with which to adorn their altarpieces, and workshops in Andalucía flourished as a result. An outstanding example of imported polychrome sculpture is the dignified Crucifixion group of 1583 on the high altar of the chapel of the wealthy Mancipe family in the cathedral in Tunja, sent by **Juan Bautista Vázquez** (died 1589) from his workshop in Seville. Sculpture workshops were soon established in the Americas, however, and Colombian churches preserve a wealth of carved and polychrome wooden altarpieces, choir stalls, confessionals and pulpits, as well as decorative wooden ceilings, screens and wall panels. An early example is the ambitious high altar of the church of San Francisco in Bogotá. The central bays were redesigned in the late 18th century but the wings date from about 1620. The tightly ordered Renaissance structure frames panels of relief carving in two distinctive styles: in the upper storey each has a single, clearly defined saint, while in the lower storey the panels contain crowded narrative scenes, overflowing with energy (the torso of the figure of St Jerome leans right out towards the high altar) and lush vegetation. The unknown artist was probably trained in Andalucía.

Such altarpieces usually involved several different craftsmen. The carvings for that in the Jesuit church of San Ignacio in Bogotá (1635-1640), for example, were by an Italian, **Gian Battista Loessing**. Another important sculptor working in Colombia in the 17th century was **Pedro de Lugo Albarracín**, whose devotional images of the suffering Christ appealed to popular piety, and several, such as the powerful figure of the fallen Christ known as **El Señor de Monserrate** (1656) in the eponymous shrine on the hill above Bogotá, have become pilgrimage destinations. Records of other sculptors with the same surname working in Bogotá and Tunja in the 17th century suggest that Pedro de Lugo was the father of a dynasty of craftsmen. **Lorenzo de Lugo**, for example, executed the eight large reliefs for the high altar of the chapel of Rosary in Santo Domingo, Tunja (c 1686). The architectural frame of this outstanding altarpiece includes numerous anthropomorphic supporting figures, *atlantes*, a common feature of colonial church furnishings in Colombia, and a chance for craftsmen to indulge in fanciful invention constrained by Christian orthodoxy. A famous example is the androgynous figure on the pulpit stairs in San Francisco, Popayán, a basket of exotic fruit on its head, and a pineapple in its hand, but grotesque figures, sometimes semi-angelic, sometimes semi-demonic, can be spotted amongst the fronds of tropical foliage on almost any baroque altarpiece. In the 18th century, figure sculptor **Pedro Laboria** from Andalucía introduced a new lightness of touch with his sinuous, almost dancing saints and angels (examples in Tunja cathedral and Santo Domingo, Bogotá).

Early paintings

As with sculpture, the demand for painting was met from a variety of sources. Works were imported from Europe, particularly from Andalucía and from the Netherlands. In the 17th century, enterprising sea captains would find room in their holds for a roll or two of canvases from the workshops of Zurbarán or Rubens to sell in the colonial ports. Itinerant artists worked their way round the viceregal centres in pursuit of lucrative commissions such as **Angelino Medoro** (c 1567-1631) from Rome who also worked in Quito and Lima before returning to Europe (see the two large canvases in the Mancipe chapel in Tunja cathedral, 1598). Quito was an important source both of artists and of works of art. Born in Quito, the Dominican **Pedro Bedón** (c 1556-1621) worked in Tunja in the late 16th century and his influence can be seen in the *bogotano* miniaturist **Francisco de Páramo** (active in the early 17th century), while **Miguel de Santiago** (c 1625-1706) sent numerous works to Colombia, including his esoteric 'Articles of the Faith' paintings now in Bogotá's cathedral museum.

Santiago was an important influence on Colombia's best 17th-century artist, **Gregorio Vásquez de Arce y Ceballos** (1638-1711) who trained in the workshop of the extensive Figueroa family of painters but who was working independently by the time he was 20. A prolific and eclectic artist, Vásquez drew on a variety of sources: sometimes his stiff, hieratic figures reveal his debt to popular prints, sometimes his soft landscapes and sweet-faced Virgins demonstrate his familiarity with the work of Zurbarán and Murillo (good examples in the Museo de Arte Colonial, Bogotá). 18th century painting in Colombia follows the well-trodden paths of earlier generations of artists, with none of the confident exuberance found in sculpture. You will find his work in many of Bogotá's churches.

After Independence

Independence from Spain did not bring independence from the traditions of colonial art. A survey of the galleries of ponderous churchmen and other civic dignitaries in the various museums suggests a more or less seamless production from the 17th to the 19th centuries: some appear sophisticated, some brutish, and the artist is not necessarily to blame. But if artistic style changed little the struggle for independence did provide some new subject matter. Bolívar is endlessly celebrated in painting. An inventive example is that of 1819 in the Quinta de Bolívar in Bogotá, by **Pedro José Figueroa** (1770-1838), where he stands with a protective arm around the shoulders of a diminutive female figure personifying the new and newly tamed republic, dressed in a silk gown, but still with bow, arrows and feather headdress, and seated on a caiman. The events of the Wars of Independence are recorded by **José María Espinosa** (1796-1883) in a series of paintings of the 1813-1816 campaigns (examples in the Quinta de Bolívar and the Academia de Historia, Bogotá). The painting of the death of General Santander in 1840 by **Luis García Hevia** in the Museo Nacional is sincere in its naïveté, whereas **Alberto Urdaneta** (1845-1887) who studied in Paris with Meissonier and is a much more versatile artist, sometimes makes his subjects from recent history seem artificial and melodramatic (*Caldas marchando al patíbulo*, Museo Nacional). But Urdaneta is also remembered as an uncompromising caricaturist, so much so that on one occasion he was expelled from the country. The Museo Nacional in Bogotá has two contrasting portraits of the heroine Policarpa Salavarrieta, executed by the Spanish in 1817; one a popular anecdotal version shows her *en route* to the scaffold, the other attributed to **Epifanio Garay** (1849-1903) nicely contrasts the formal society portrait with the drama of the event: she sits poised and beautiful while the ominously shadowy figure of a soldier appears in a doorway behind.

Interest in Colombia's natural resources produced scientific missions that, although organized by foreigners (the first by the Spanish botanist **Celestino Mutis** in the 18th century and the next by the Italian geographer **Agustín Codazzi** in the 19th), nevertheless helped to awaken an appreciation of the landscape, peoples and cultures of Colombia, past and present. The Venezuelan **Carmelo Fernández** (1809-1887) worked for Codazzi in 1851, producing carefully observed watercolours of the peoples and traditions of different provinces (examples in the Biblioteca Nacional). **Manuel María Paz** (1820-1902) held the same position in 1853 and his drawings of the pre-Columbian culture of San Agustín are the first of their kind. **Ramón Torres Méndez** (1809-1895) was not a member of the mission, but like them he travelled extensively in the countryside and his scenes from everyday life helped to make *costumbrista* subjects respectable.

20th century

During the first decades of the 20th century Colombian artists preferred to ignore the upheavals of the European art scene and hold on to the established traditions of academic figure and landscape painting. Almost the only interesting figure, **Andrés de Santa María** (1860-1945), spent most of his life in Europe and developed a style that owed something to Cezanne and something to 17th-century Spanish art, but with an over-riding concern for a thickly textured painted surface that is entirely personal (*Self-portrait*, 1923, Museo Nacional, Bogotá). During the 1930s the more liberal political climate in Colombia encouraged the younger generation of Colombian artists to look for a more socially and politically relevant form of art which, conveniently, they found in the Mexican muralists. Instead of having to embrace the violent rupture with the past represented by modern European movements such as Cubism and Futurism, the muralists offered a way of continuing in a figurative tradition but now with a social conscience expressed in images of workers and peasants struggling against the forces of oppression. **Pedro Nel Gómez** (1899-1984) was the first to paint murals inside public buildings, particularly in his native Medellín, and he was followed by others such as **Alipio Jaramillo** (1913-1999) and **Carlos Correa** (1912-1985). The sculptor **Rómulo Rozo** (1899-1964) was also influenced by the rhetoric of the Mexican muralists, as well as by forms of Aztec and Mayan sculpture, and strove to achieve a comparable combination of simplicity and monumentality.

Only in the 1950s did Abstraction have any impact in Colombia. Born in Munich, **Guillermo Wiedemann** (1905-1969) arrived from Germany in 1939 and after a spell painting tropical landscapes began to experiment with an expressionist form of abstraction, full of light, space and colour. **Eduardo Ramírez Villamizar** (1922-2004) also began painting in a figurative mode but moved into abstraction in the 1950s and subsequently into sculpture, to create, alongside his contemporary **Édgar Negret** (born 1920), some of the most interesting Constructivist work in Latin America. Both work in metal and have produced large, often brightly painted pieces for public spaces. Another important artist of this generation was Barcelona-born **Alejandro Obregón** (1920-1992), who avoided pure abstraction, preferring instead to include colourful figurative references with nationalistic overtones: carnations, guitars, condors. The slightly younger and internationally famous **Fernando Botero** (born 1932) has also tended to favour national themes. Working both as a painter and a sculptor he takes figures from Colombian society – dictators, drug barons, smug priests, autocratic matrons, prostitutes, spoilt children – and inflates them to ludicrous proportions. His gigantic bronze figures and the angular, two-dimensional sheets of metal of Negret and Ramírez Villamizar represent the two poles of 20th-century artistic expression.

For the subsequent generation of artists Colombia's turbulent political history remains a recurrent preoccupation. **Luis Caballero** (1943-1995) was a masterful draughtsman who expressed his sympathy for the victims of officially sanctioned violence by the tender attention he devotes to their tortured, naked bodies. **Beatriz González** (born 1938) uses a pop idiom to present military and political leaders as big and bold but essentially empty. **Juan Camillo Uribe** (born 1945) manipulates the paraphernalia of popular religion – prayer cards, plastic angels, metallic trinkets – to construct wittily disturbing collages. Younger artists are exploring the tensions between the national and international demands of art, and are experimenting with a tremendous diversity of styles and media. There is certainly no shortage of talent. Many cities in Colombia now boast a lively art scene with regular public exhibitions of contemporary art and a good range of commercial galleries.

Rodrigo Arenas Betancur (1919-1995) followed in Rozo's footsteps (see above) to become Colombia's best known sculptor of nationalistic public monuments. His gigantic and often rather melodramatic bronzes can be found in towns and cities throughout the country, as, for example his heroically naked *Bolívar* in Pereira, *Monumento a la Vida* in the Centro Suramericano in Medellín and the complex *Lanceros del Pantano de Vargas* near Paipa which must have been quite a challenge to the foundrymen. His sculptures are eminently worth seeking out.

Literature

The indigenous Colombian written language was discovered to be at its earliest stages at the time of the Spanish conquest in the 16th century. Consequently there are practically no records of pre-conquest literature. The poetic tradition was oral; one of the few transcribed examples of spoken poetry is 'El Yurupay', an oral epic gathered from *indígena* in the Vaupés region in the 16th century, though not published until 1890.

The literature produced during the colonial period (1500-1816) was mainly by an ecclesiastical elite, written for the benefit of an upper-class minority. The predominant themes were the conquest itself, Catholicism and observations of the New World. The two major writers of this period had themselves been renowned conquistadores. **Gonzalo Jiménez de Quesada** (1495-1579), the founder of Bogotá in 1538, wrote *Antijovio* in 1567. The main purpose of this book was to defend Spain's reputation against accusations made by the Italian Paolo Giovio in his *Historiarum sui temporis libri XLV* (1552). Quesada sought to put the record straight on matters concerning the behaviour of his nation during the conquest of the New World.

Juan de Castellanos (c 1522-1607) wrote a lengthy chronicle of the conquest called *Elegías de varones ilustres de Indias* (*Elegy of Illustrious Men of the Indies*, 1589). It was written in the Italian verse style popular at the time, and has been called one of the longest poems ever written, 113,609 verses. The most important piece of narrative prose written during this period was *El carnero* (*The Butcher*, 1638) by **Juan Rodríguez Freyle** (1566-1640). This is a picaresque account of a year in the life of Santa Fe de Bogotá, using a blend of historical fact and scandalous invention to create a deliciously amoral book for its time. Mystic writing was also popular during the middle years of the conquest. **Sor Francisca Josefa de Castillo y Guevara** (1671-1742) was a nun who wrote baroque poetry, but was best known for her intimate spiritual diary *Afectos espirituales* (date unknown). Another Baroque poet of renown was **Hernando Domínguez Camargo** (1606-1659), who chronicled the life of Saint Ignatius in his epic *Poema heróica de San Ignacio de Loyola* (*Heroic Poem of St Ignatius of Loyola*, 1666).

The first major Colombian writer after the declaration of Independence in 1824 was **Juan José Nieto** (1805-1866). His *Ingermina, o la hija de Calamar* (*Ingermina, or the Child of Calamar*, 1844) is a historical novel about the conquest of the Calamar Indians in the 16th century. The mid-19th century saw the publication in Bogotá of *El Mosaico*, a review centred around a literary group of the same name, founded by **José María Vergara y Vergara** (1831-1872). The prevailing style in the capital was *costumbrismo*, the depiction of local life and customs in realistic detail. Major *costumbrista* novels were *Manuela* (1858) by **Eugenio Díaz** (1803-1865) and *María* (1867), by **Jorge Isaacs** (1837-1895). Romantic poetry also defined the early years of Independence, reflecting the strong influence Europe still had over Colombia. One of the exceptions was a poet from Mompós, **Candelario Obeso** (1849-1884), the first Colombian poet to use Afro-American colloquialisms in poetry. His *Cantos populares de mi tierrra* (*Popular Songs of my Land*, 1877) marked a progressive shift from the Romantic style, into a poetic language which reflected the true variety of Colombia's indigenous population.

An important region in the development of Colombian literature was Antioquia, the main city of which is Medellín. This region spawned the first crop of writers who were not of the upper-class elite which had dominated Colombian letters until the late 19th century. **Tomás Carrasquilla** (1858-1940) produced three major novels which reflected his humble middle-class background, and used a casual, spoken style to portray local customs and speech, and above all a love of the land. Another Antioquian of renown was **Samuel Velásquez** (1865-1941), whose novel *Madre* (*Mother*, 1897) gives a strong sense of the simple life of the countryside coupled with the religious passion of its inhabitants.

The beginning of the avant-garde in Colombia is marked by the publication of *Tergiversaciones* (*Distortions*) in 1925 by **León de Greiff** (1895-1976), in which he experimented with new techniques to create a completely original poetic idiom. Another important Modernist poet was **Porfirio Barba-Jacob** (the pseudonym of Miguel Angel Osorio, 1883-l942), who was influenced by the French Parnassian poets and published melancholic verse, typified by *Rosas negras* (*Black Roses*, 1935).

Other novelists of the same era were pursuing a much more social realist style than their avant-garde counterparts. *La voragine* (*The Vortex*, 1924) by **José Eustasio Rivera** (1888-1928) deals with the narrator's own struggle for literary expression against a backdrop of the Amazonian rubber workers' struggle for survival. **César Uribe Piedrahita** (1897-1951) also chronicled the plight of rubber workers, and in *Mancha de aceite* (*Oil Stain*, 1935) he looks at the effects of the oil industry on the land and people of his country. The problems facing indigenous people began to get more attention from socially aware writers and **Bernardo Arías Trujillo** (1903-1939) examined the lives of Afro-Americans in Colombia in *Risaralda*.

The late 1940s to the mid-1960s in Colombian society were dominated by La Violencia (see History, page 353). Literary output during this intensely violent period reflected the political concerns which had led to the violence; among the novels to stand out from the many personal tales of anger and disbelief was *El jardín de las Hartmann* (*The Garden of the Hartmanns*, 1978) by **Jorge Eliécer Prado** (born 1945), which charts the history of La Violencia in Tolima, one of the most severely affected regions. What makes this book readable is the lack of historical facts and figures, typical of books set during La Violencia, and a more generalized view of the troubles.

Two important poetry movements to come out of La Violencia were the 'Mito' group and the 'Nadaístas'. *Mito* was a poetry magazine founded in 1955 by **Jorge Gaitán Durán** (1924-1962). It included **Eduardo Cote Lemus** (1928-1964), **Carlos Obregón** (1929-1965) and **Dora Castellanos** (born 1924). Their influences were contemporary French writers such as Genet and Sartre, and the Argentinean José Luis Borges. *Mito* came out during the dictatorship of Rojas Pinilla, and was one of the few outlets for free literary expression in the country. The Nadaísta group was concerned with changing the elitist role of literature in the face of the violent conflict which affected everyone, and they felt should be addressed directly; they used avant-garde styles and techniques to achieve this.

By far the biggest influence on Colombian fiction was the publication, in 1967, of *Cien años de soledad* (*A Hundred Years of Solitude*) by **Gabriel García Márquez** (born 1927). He had published many short stories and novels in the 1950s and early 1960s. Among the most significant were *La hojarasca* (*Leaf Storm* in 1955) and *El coronel no tiene quien le escriba* (*No one Writes to the Colonel*, 1958), a portrayal of a colonel and his wife struggling to cope with the tropical heat, political oppression and economic deprivation in their final years. But it was with *Cien años de soledad* that he became recognized as the major exponent of a new style generic to Latin American writers. Events were chronicled in a deadpan style; historical facts were blended with pure fantasy, the latter written matter-of-factly as if it were the truth; characters were vividly portrayed through their actions and brief dialogues rather than internal monologues. The style came to be known as Magical Realism in English, a translation of the Spanish 'Lo real maravilloso'. In 1975 Márquez published *El otoño del patriarca* (*The Autumn of the Patriarch*), which was a return to a favourite theme of his, the loneliness that power can bring. *Crónica de una muerte anunciada* (*Chronicle of a Death Foretold*, 1981) was set in an unnamed coastal city, but no doubt not far from Márquez's birthplace of Aracataca. It captures the docility and traditional stubbornness of the people of Colombia's Caribbean seaboard, an area in which Márquez had worked as a journalist in the 1950s. *El amor en los tiempos de cólera* (*Love in the Time of Cholera*, 1985) is set at the turn of the century, and depicts the affair between a couple of septuagenarians against the backdrop of another fictional city; Márquez skillfully blends Cartagena, Barranquilla and Santa Marta into one coastal town. Márquez has published 21 works in total, as well as articles and essays.

Other important writers in the 1970s and 1980s include **Fanny Buitrago** (born 1945) and **Manuel Zapata Olivella** (1920-2004). In novels such as *Los Pañamanes* (1979) and *Los amores de Afrodita* (*The Loves of Aphrodite*, 1983), Buitrago contrasts the legends and culture of the Caribbean coast with the needs of young people to move on, at the risk of being swallowed up by modern North American culture. Zapata Olivella has published a monumental novel, *El fusilamiento del diablo* (*The Shooting of the Devil*, 1986) covering the six centuries of African and Afro-American history.

Colombian postmodern literature has followed European theoretical trends, with many of Colombia's more avant-garde writers living and working in Europe. While retaining the Magical Realist tradition of dispensing with a subjective, authoritative narrator, the post-modernists have greatly distanced themselves from the Colombian tradition of orally based colloquial storytelling. But it is García Márquez who has done the most to capture the public imagination. By borrowing from Colombian traditions with a modernist approach, he has created a style that has made him an internationally renowned literary figure.

Music and dance

No South American country has a greater variety of music than Colombia, strategically placed where the Andes meet the Caribbean. The four major musical areas are: the mountain heartland; the Pacific coast; the Caribbean coast; and the Llanos or eastern plains. See also page 29.

Mountain heartland

The heartland covers the Andean highlands and intervening valleys of the Cauca and Magdalena rivers and includes the country's three largest cities, Bogotá, Medellín and Cali. The music here is relatively gentle and sentimental, accompanied largely by string instruments, with an occasional flute and a *chucho* or *carángano* shaker to create the rhythm. The preferred instrument of the highlands and by extension Colombia's national instrument, is the *tiple*, a small 12-stringed guitar, most of which are manufactured at Chiquinquirá in Boyacá. The national dance is the **bambuco**, whose lilting sounds are said to have inspired Colombian troops at the Battle of Ayacucho in 1824. This dance can be found throughout the country's heartland and has long transcended its folk origins. The choreography is complex, including many movements, such as Los Ochos, La Invitación, Los Codos, Los Coqueteos, La Perseguida and La Arrodilla. Other related dances are the **torbellino**, where the woman whirls like a top, the more stately Guabina, the Pasillo, Bunde, Sanjuanero and the picaresque **rajaleña**. Particularly celebrated melodies are the *Guabina Chiquinquireña* and the *Bunde Tolimense*. The following fiestas, among others, provide a good opportunity to experience the music and dancing: **La Fiesta del Campesino**, ubiquitous on the first Sunday in June, the **Fiesta del Bambuco** in Neiva and **Festival Folclórico Colombiano** in Ibagué later in the month, the **Fiesta Nacional de la Guabina y el Tiple**, held in Vélez in early August, the **Desfile de Silleteros** in Medellín in the same month and **Las Fiestas de Pubenza** in Popayán just after the New Year, where the Conjuntos de Chirimía process through the streets.

Pacific coast

On Colombia's tropical Pacific coast (and extending down into Esmeraldas in Ecuador) is to be found some of the most African sounding black music in all South America. The **currulao** and its variants, the **berejú** and **patacoré**, are extremely energetic recreational dances and the vocals are typically African-style call-and-response. This is the home of the *marimba* and the music is very percussion driven, including the upright *cununo* drum plus *bombos* and *redoblantes*. Wakes are important in this region and at these the **bundes**, **arrullos** and **alabaos** are sung. Best known is the 'Bunde de San Antonio'. The **jota chocoana** is a fine example of a Spanish dance taken by black people and turned into a satirical weapon against their masters. The regional fiestas are the **Festival Folclórico del Litoral** at Buenaventura in July and **San Francisco de Asís** at Quibdó on 4 August. Quibdó also features a **Fiesta de los Indios** at Easter.

Caribbean coast

The music of Colombia's Caribbean lowlands became popular for dancing throughout Latin America more than 30 years ago under the name of **Música Tropical** and has much more recently become an integral part of the Salsa repertory. It can be very roughly divided into cumbia and vallenato. The **cumbia** is a heavily black influenced dance form for several couples, the men forming an outer circle and the women an inner. The men hold aloft a bottle of rum and the women a bundle of slim candles called *espermas*. The dance probably originated in what is now Panama, moved east into Cartagena, where it is now centred and quite recently further east to Barranquilla and Santa Marta. The most celebrated cumbias are those of Ciénaga, Mompós, Sampués, San Jacinto and Sincelejo. The instrumental accompaniment consists of *gaitas* or *flautas de caña de millo*, backed by drums. The *gaitas* ('male' and 'female') are vertical cactus flutes with beeswax heads, while the *cañas de millo* are smaller transverse flutes. The most famous conjuntos are the Gaiteros de San Jacinto, the Cumbia Soledeña and the Indios Selectos. Variants of the cumbia are the **porro**, **gaita**, **puya**, **bullerengue** and **mapalé**, these last two being much faster and more energetic. Lately cumbia has also become very much part of the vallenato repertoire and is therefore often played on the accordion. Cumbia has been superseded by vallenato in Colombia and today is probably heard more outside the country than in it, with Colombian migrants taking it with them to cities like Buenos Aires, Mexico City, Los Angeles – even London. While it has travelled, it has picked up influences to create new sub-genres such as **techno-cumbia** and **cumbia villera**, both popular in Peru and Argentina. **Vallenato** music comes from Valledupar in the department of César and is of relatively recent origin. It is built around one instrument, the accordion, albeit backed by *guacharaca* rasps and *caja* drums. The most popular rhythms are the paseo and the merengue, the latter having arrived from the Dominican Republic, where it is the national dance. Perhaps the first virtuoso accordionist was the legendary 'Francisco El Hombre', playing around the turn of the century. Today's best known vallenato names are those of Rafael Escalona (1927-2009), Alejandro Durán (1919-1989), Los Gigantes del Vallento and Calixto Ochoa. In April the **Festival de la Leyenda Vallenata** is held in Valledupar and attended by thousands.

Barranquilla is the scene of South America's second most celebrated **carnival**, after that of Rio de Janeiro, with innumerable traditional masked groups, such as the *congos*, *toros*, *diablos* and *caimanes*. The **garabato** is a dance in which death is defeated. Barranquilla's carnival is less commercialized and more traditional than that of Rio and should be a 'must' for anyone with the opportunity to attend. Other important festivals in the region are the **Corralejas de Sincelejo** with its bullfights in January, **La Candelaria** (Candlemas) in Cartagena on 2 February, the **Festival de la Cumbia** in El Banco in June, **Fiesta del Caimán Cienaguero** in Ciénaga in January and **Festival del Porro** in San Pelayo (Córdoba). To complete the music of the Caribbean region, the Colombian islands of San Andrés and Providencia, off the coast of Nicaragua, have a fascinating mix of mainland Colombian and Jamaican island music, with the calypso naturally a prominent feature. More recently two other genres have gained increasing popularity. **Champeta** originates in Cartagena and has roots in soukous, compas and reggae. It is characterized by very provocative dancing. **Reggaeton** has become a phenomenon throughout Latin America. Believed to have originated in Panama, it blends a merengue beat with rapping and influences from reggae and ragga.

Llanos

The fourth musical region is that of the great eastern plains, the so-called Llanos Orientales between the Ríos Arauca and Guaviare, a region where there is really no musical frontier between the two republics of Colombia and Venezuela. Here the **Joropo** reigns supreme as a dance, with its close relatives the **galerón**, the slower and more romantic **pasaje** and the breathlessly fast **corrido** and **zumba que zumba**. These are dances for couples, with a lot of heel tapping, the arms hanging down loosely to the sides. Arnulfo Briceño (1938-1989) and Pentagrama Llanera are the big names and the harp is the only instrument that matters, although normally backed by *cuatro*, guitar, *tiple* and *maracas*. Where to see and hear it all is at the **Torneo Internacional del Joropo** at Villavicencio in December.

Religion

The vast majority of Colombians (90%) are nominal Roman Catholics, and though observance is not particularly high, daily Masses in most town churches make it possible for visitors to see the interior of many churches. As elsewhere in Latin America, Protestant Evangelical Churches have made some progress in Colombia in recent years.

People

The regions vary greatly in their racial make-up. Antioquia and Caldas are largely of European descent; Nariño has more indigenous roots; while people from the Cauca Valley are more African, descending from the slaves brought to the area when sugar was introduced. Afro-Caribbeans are also prominent in the rural area near the Caribbean and the northwest Pacific coastline. No colour bar is legally recognized but is not entirely absent in certain centres. Population figures of cities and towns in the text are the best we can find but should not be relied upon. They will, however, give the traveller an idea of the size of the place and therefore the evel of facilities that may be expected.

The birth, death and infant mortality rates vary greatly from one area of the country to another, but in general they are similar to those of neighbouring countries. Hospitals and clinics are few in relation to the population. About 66% of the doctors are in the departmental capitals, which contain about half of the population, though all doctors have to spend a year in the country before they can get their final diploma. The best hospitals, notably in Bogotá and Medellín, are well equipped and have fine reputations attracting patients from other countries of Latin America.

Indigenous cultures

Guajira ..... Pre-Columbian
(Wayuú) ..... Present day

Not to scale

An estimated 800,000 tribal peoples, from 84 ethnic groups, live in Colombia. Groups include the Wayúu (in the Guajira), the Kogui and Arhauco (Sierra Nevada de Santa Marta), indigenous Amazonians such as the Huitoto, the nomadic Nukak and the Tikuna, indigenous Andean and groups of the Llanos and in the Pacific coast rainforest.

Although the national and official language of Colombia is overwhelmingly Spanish, many indigenous groups still use only their own languages. The largest ethno-linguistic group are the 150,000 Chibchas. On the Caribbean coast, especially the islands, English or Creole are widely spoken. The diversity and importance of indigenous peoples was recognized in the 1991 constitutional reforms when Indigenous Colombians were granted the right to two senate seats; the National Colombian Indian Organization (ONIC) won a third seat in the October 1991 ballot. State recognition and the right to bilingual education has not, however, solved major problems of land rights, training and education, and justice.

Land and environment

Geology and landscape

Colombia is the fourth largest in size of the 10 principal countries of South America,, slightly smaller than Peru and slightly larger than Bolivia at 1,142,000 sq km. In terms of Europe, that is the size of France and Spain combined. The latest estimate of population is 44.6 million, marginally more than Argentina and second only to Brazil in the continent. The people are concentrated in the western third of the country: nevertheless the population density of 39.3 per sq km is only greater in Ecuador within South America. To the east, it is bounded by Venezuela and Brazil, to the south, by Peru and Ecuador and in the northwest by Panama. It is the only South American country with a coastline on the Pacific (1306 km) and the Caribbean (1600 km), with two small offshore islands in the Pacific. In the Caribbean, there are various coastal islands including the Rosario and San Bernardo groups and the more substantial San Andrés/Providencia archipelago off the coast of Nicaragua, plus several cays towards Jamaica.

Its greatest width east-west is 1200 km and it stretches 1800 km north-south, from 12°N to 4°S of the equator, with virtually all of one of its departments, Amazonas, south of the equator. The borders of Colombia have been stable since 1903 when Panama seceded, though Nicaragua occasionally revives a claim for the San Andrés group of islands and there are three minute uninhabited reefs claimed by Colombia and by the USA: Quita Sueño Bank, Roncador Cay and Serrana Bank.

Structure

As with other countries on the west side of the continent, Colombia is on the line of collision between the west moving South American Plate, and the Nasca Plate, moving east and sinking beneath it thus creating the Andes. Almost 55% of the country to the east is alluvial plains on top of ancient rocks of the Guiana Shield dating from the Pre-Cambrian era over 500 million years ago. This was at one time part of the landmass called 'Pangea' which geologists believe broke up between 150 and 125 million years ago and the Americas floated away from what became Africa and Europe. It is presumed that prior to this, what is now the Caribbean Sea was an extension of the Mediterranean Sea and in the course of time this expanded to separate the two halves of the Americas.

During the Cretaceous period, around 100 million years ago, the Atlantic was undoubtedly connected to the Pacific Ocean, at least from time to time, but by the end of the Cretaceous, the Tertiary mountain building had begun and the emergence of Central America and eventually the Isthmus of Panama, sealed off the connection.

All the rest of Colombia to the west, apart from the islands, is the product of the Andean mountain building activity, which continues today. This began earlier in the Jurassic and Cretaceous eras with intense volcanic activity, but the maximum was in the late Tertiary (around 25 million years ago). Large areas of molten material were formed beneath the surface and were pushed up to form the large high plateaux with peaks formed from later volcanic activity. Some areas were folded and contorted and the original rocks metamorphosed to lose their former identity. In general, it is the mountain ranges to the west that were most affected in this way. Continuous weathering, especially during the ice ages of which the most recent was in the Pleistocene up to 10,000 years ago, has been responsible for deep deposits in the valleys and the plains of north Colombia and in the inland slopes of the Andes towards the Orinoco and Amazon.

Other than the coral islands just off the north coast, the Colombian islands of the Caribbean are all on a submarine ridge, which extends from Honduras and Nicaragua to Haiti, known as the Jamaica Ridge, which separates the Cayman Trench from the Colombia Basin, two of the deepest areas of the Caribbean Sea. Providencia is probably volcanic in origin but San Andrés has a less certain past, perhaps being an undersea mount which has been colonized by coral for millions of years, evidenced by the white sands and the limestone features. Little is known about the other reefs, banks and cays that belong to Colombia. The two Colombian island groups in the Pacific are quite different. Isla Gorgona is one of the few islands off the South American Pacific coast which is on the continental shelf and no more than 30 km from the mainland. There is evidence of past volcanic activity on the island and it may represent a point on an otherwise submerged ridge parallel to the coast. By contrast, the Isla de Malpelo is on one of the structural lines of the east Pacific which runs due south from west Panama along the line of longitude 81°W which peters out off the coast of Ecuador. There is a deep trench between this line and the coast with depths down to 5000 m and clear signs of tectonic activity along the ridge including Malpelo which is the top of a volcanic structure. Further to the west there is another ridge running south from Central America, the Cocos Ridge, which leads to the Galápagos Islands.

Andes

To the south of Colombia, the Andes of Ecuador are a single high range with volcanic peaks up to nearly 5000 m, but north of the border they quickly split into three distinct Cordilleras named Occidental, Central and Oriental. The first two are close together for 400 km but separated by a fault line occupied by the Río Patía in the south and the Cauca in the north. The Cordillera Oriental gradually pulls eastwards creating a valley basin for Colombia's most important river, the Magdalena. This range crosses the northeast border into Venezuela and continues as the Cordillera de Mérida. A subsidiary range, called the Sierra de Perijá, continues north within Colombia to reach the Caribbean at Punta Gallinas on the Península de Guajira, the northernmost point of the South American mainland. Near this point is the Santa Marta massif, one of the biggest volcanic structures in the world with the highest mountain peak in Colombia at 5775 m.

All three of the Cordilleras have peaks, mostly volcanic, over 4000 m, the Central and Oriental over 5000 m, with permanent snow on the highest. Many are active and have caused great destruction in the past, both with gas and ash explosions and by creating ice and mud slides. The whole of the western half of the country is subject to earthquakes, demonstrating the unstable nature of the underlying geology, and the significant situation of the country at the point where the Andes make a dramatic turn to the east. Also, in the northwest, another range to the west of the Cordillera Occidental appears, the Serranía de Baudó, which becomes the spine of the Darién isthmus of Panama, eventually continuing westwards. Thus north Colombia is at the tectonic crossroads of the Americas.

Valleys

A glance at the map of Colombia will show the physical dominance of the cordilleras and the human dependence on the valleys between them. The fact that they run more or less north-south was a great advantage to the earlier explorers interested in finding gold and silver and the later settlers looking for good arable land. Even the earliest inhabitants were interested in the protection that the rugged land offered them but also in ways to migrate further south. As a consequence, the eastern half of the country has, until very recently, been ignored and still remains largely unexplored.

The valleys are structural basins between the *cordilleras* and not simply products of river erosion. In some places they are many kilometres broad, as for example between Cali and Popayán, yet the Patía and Cauca rivers flow in opposite directions. Elsewhere, the rivers go through narrow passages, e.g. near Honda on the Magdalena where rapids interrupt river navigation. However, the basins have been filled many metres thick with volcanic ash and dust which has produced very fertile terrain. This, together with the height above sea level has made for an agreeable environment and one of the most productive zones of the tropics worldwide.

By contrast, the cordilleras create formidable obstacles to lateral movements. The main routes from Bogotá to Cali and Manizales must cross the Cordillera Central by passes at 3250 m and 3700 m respectively, and virtually all the passes over the Cordillera Oriental exceed 3000 m. Many of the volcanic peaks in these ranges are over 5000 m and are capped with snow, hence the name *nevados*. Such is the nature of the terrain that no railway was ever built to cross the cordilleras, except from Cali to Buenaventura.

The rivers themselves do not provide the most attractive human corridors as can be seen by the frequent diversions from the rivers by the main trunk roads. Fortunately, the surrounding countryside is frequently dominated by plateaux. These make good level sites for towns and cities (Bogotá itself is the best example). They also give long stretches of easy surface travel but are interrupted by spectacular descents and climbs where there are natural rifts or subsidiary river gorges. This makes for dramatic, but time-consuming scenic trips by road throughout this area of Colombia.

Caribbean lowlands

From the Sierra de Perijá and the Sierra Nevada de Santa Marta westwards are the great plains of the lower Magdalena, which collects most of the water flowing north in Colombia to the Caribbean. The Cordilleras Central and Occidental finish at about 4°N, 350 km from the mouth of the river at Barranquilla. About 200 km from the sea, both the Magdalena and the Cauca flow into an area of swamps and lagoons which becomes a vast lake when water levels are high. This lowland is the result of the huge quantities of alluvium that has been brought down over the years from the mountains in the south of Colombia. While not comparable in length with the major rivers of the world, the average discharge at the mouth of the Magdalena is 7500 cu m per second similar to that of the Danube or about one third of that of the Orinoco. To the north, the land slopes gently to the sandy beaches of the Caribbean and a string of inshore islands of considerable touristic appeal.

Beyond Barranquilla to the east, a sandbar encloses a salt lake that was formerly part of the Magdalena delta, now abandoned by the river which flows to the sea further west. On the far side of the lake, the Santa Marta massif comes down to the sea creating a interesting stretch of rocky bays and headlands. Further east again, the flatter land returns extending finally to the low hills of the Guajira peninsula at the northernmost tip of the continent. This is a sandy, arid region, and the modest northern end of the Cordillera Oriental.

At the west end of this section is the Gulf of Urabá and the border with Panama. The Río Atrato, which drains most of the area between the Cordillera Oriental and the Serranía de Baudó, reaches the sea here via another large swampy area where no land transport is possible. It is probable that this was formerly linked to the Gulf of Urabá which is itself now being filled up with material brought down by the Atrato and many other small streams. This was also probably an area where, in a much more distant past, the Atlantic was joined to the Pacific, a point not lost on the Colombians who periodically quote this as the site of a future rival to the Panama canal. There is little seismic activity in this region though there are occasional earthquakes and the mud lakes near Arboletes, Galerazamba and elsewhere near the coast are volcanic in origin.

Pacific coast

The Serranía de Baudó runs from Panama south to 4°N just north of Buenaventura. The basin between it and the Cordillera Occidental is drained by the Río Atrato to the north and the San Juan to the south with another river, the Baudó assisting the centre. This is an area of very high rainfall and access by any means is difficult. This coastline is very different from the north coast. Most of it is heavily forested but with very attractive small beaches interspersed with rocky stretches and affected with a wide tidal range, absent from the Caribbean. It has only recently been 'discovered' by the tourist industry and remains quiet owing to the difficulties and cost of getting there.

South of Buenaventura, there is another 300 km of coastline to Ecuador, but reasonable access is only possible at Buenaventura, and Tumaco in the extreme south. Rainfall here is still copious with many short rivers coming down from the Cordillera Occidental and creating alluvial plains along the coast typically with mangrove swamps, which continue into Ecuador. This part of the Colombian coast is also remote and unspoilt with a few fishing communities though tourism is beginning to take hold at the end of the two access roads. Further inland there are a few mineral deposits and gold mines which have attracted interest. There is no range of Tertiary hills here between the Andes and the coastline as in Ecuador.

Eastern plains

This section, representing more than half of Colombia, is divided into two parts. In the north are the grasslands known as *los llanos*, which stretch from the Cordillera Oriental across into Venezuela and on to the mouth of the Orinoco. Around 40% of the *llanos*, which means 'plains', are in Colombia. They are noted in both countries for the quality of the land for cattle raising which has been going on since the 16th century and are second only to the *Pampas* in Argentina for ranching in South America. Several important rivers, e.g. the Meta, flow from the mountains through this region to the Orinoco and act as transport routes. Slowly roads are being made into the interior but all-weather surfaces are virtually non-existent and land transport in the wet season is impossible. All important towns and villages and many *fincas* have their own airstrips. In the extreme north of the area, near the border with Venezuela, oil was found some years ago and new finds are still being made.

The southern part of the section is tropical forest associated with the Amazon Basin. As far as the vegetation is concerned, the transition is, of course, gradual. However, the Río Guaviare is the southernmost tributary of the Orinoco and, with headwaters (here called the Guayabero) rising near Neiva in the Cordillera Oriental, has its source some 350 km further from the sea than those of the official source of the Orinoco in the Sierra Parima on the Brazil/Venezuela border. Two important rivers join to form the Guaviare near the town of San José, the Guayabero and the Ariari. Between them is an extraordinary geological anomaly, the Serranía de Macarena. It is a huge dissected block of crystalline rocks partly covered with stratified later formations, 140 km long and 30 km wide, that stands isolated 2000 m above the surrounding undulating forest and has been identified as a chunk of the Guiana Shield, the rest of which is hundreds of kilometres to the east, forming the border area between The Guianas, Venezuela and Brazil. Although there are some other low formations in this area of the country which are founded on the ancient basalt rocks, as a remnant of 'Pangea', Macarena displays by far the oldest exposed rocks of Colombia.

South of the Guaviare Basin, all the waters of the region flow into the Amazon system. However, in the extreme east of the country, the Río Guainía drains the south part of the department of the same name which connects with another geographical curiosity, discovered by the great explorer Alexander von Humboldt. Some 250 km before joining the Guaviare, the Orinoco divides, with part of its flow going southwest as the 'Brazo Casiquiare', which eventually joins the Guainía to form the Negro and thence the Amazon. Other Colombian rivers feed the Negro, in particular the Vaupés, the longest tributary. Colombia therefore has the distinction of providing the true sources of the Orinoco and the Negro.

In the southern area, the climate becomes progressively wetter. Thick jungle covers much of it, though Colombia is no exception to the gradual destruction of the environment. The rivers Caquetá and Putumayo are important water routes to the Amazon proper but there is virtually no tourist traffic.

In the extreme south of Colombia is Leticia, on the Amazon itself, a reminder of the original drawing of the maps which allowed all the western countries of South America except Chile to have access to the river and an exit to the South Atlantic.

Climate

Temperatures in Colombia are mainly affected by altitude and distance from the north and west coasts. The highest average temperatures in South America are in the Maracaibo lowlands of which Colombia has the southwest corner and the northwest extension into the Guajira Peninsula. Average annual temperatures in the Caribbean Lowlands are typically in excess of 25°C, modified downwards on the coast, yet, within sight of the coast are the permanent snows of Sierra Nevada de Santa Marta due to its altitude of over 5500 m. The temperature becomes oppressive where there is also high humidity.

Rainfall depends on the migrating northwest and southeast trade wind systems, the effect of the Andes acting as a weather barrier and also on local situations along the coasts.

There is high rainfall in the southeast where the southeast trade winds bring moisture all year into the Amazon Basin that is continually recycled to produce heavy daily precipitation all along the east edge of the Andes. This however tails off northwards into the *llanos* especially November to March when the wind systems move south and the southeast Trades are replaced by the northeast system. This is less effective in bringing moisture into the area because of the protection of the Venezuelan Andes. The rainfall in the lower reaches of the Magdalena Basin is also high, aided by the large swampy area which keeps the air saturated. The highest rainfall in the country is in the northwest near the border with Panama, brought about by the convergence of the trade wind systems interacting with warm, saturated air coming in from the Pacific. Here it rains daily most of the year with some respite from January to March but with a total on average of 10,000 mm. This is one of the highest in the world. This heavy rain belt extends down the coast tailing off as Ecuador is approached. Unlike further south, the ocean here is warm and air over it readily condenses when it moves on to the land. However, this is a generalized pattern only.

Aberrations in the weather systems between November and March, when less rain normally falls, now labelled the El Niño phenomenon, also affect the western part of Colombia at least as far east as Bogotá. Large parts of the country, particularly the Caribbean coast and la Zona Cafetera, suffered from unusually heavy and prolonged rains in the autumn and winter of 2010, leading to extensive flooding, mud- and landslides.

Inland local features often determine the level of precipitation. To the east of Nevado de Huila (5750 m), for example, there is a small area of near desert caused by the effect of rain shadow. Near desert conditions also can be found on the tip of the continent, between Riohacha and Punta Gallinas which is probably caused by descending air collecting rather than expelling moisture. Although there are occasional storms here (Colombia was marginally affected by the heavy rains that brought disaster to the Venezuelan coast in 1999), the normal Caribbean hurricane track fortunately passes well to the north of the Colombian coast.

Wildlife and vegetation

This neotropical zone is a land of superlatives. It contains the most extensive tropical rainforest in the world; the Amazon has by far the largest volume of any of the world's rivers and the Andes are the longest uninterrupted mountain chain. The fauna and flora are to a large extent determined by the influence of those mountains and the great rivers, particularly the Amazon and the Orinoco. There are also huge expanses of open terrain, tree-covered savannahs and arid regions. It is this immense range of habitats which makes Colombia one of the world's regions of high biodiversity.

This diversity arises not only from the wide range of habitats available, but also from the history of the continent. South America has essentially been an island for much of its geological past, joined only by a narrow isthmus to Central and North America at various times between 50 million and 25 million years ago. The present connection has been stable only for a few million years. Land passage played a significant role in the gradual colonization of South America by both flora and fauna from the north. When the land-link was broken these colonists evolved into a wide variety of forms free from the competitive pressures that prevailed elsewhere. When the land-bridge was re-established a new invasion of species took place from North America, adding to the diversity but also leading to numerous extinctions. Comparative stability has now ensued and guaranteed the survival of many primitive groups like the opossums.

Flowers

An overabundance of floral species has helped make Colombia the world's second largest exporter of flowers, with over US$1 billion in sales annually. You name it, Colombia has it – everything from garden-variety roses and carnations to more exotic species like the bird of paradise and the heliconia. However, this country's undisputed crown jewel is the orchid. Over 3000 species of orchid are known to exist in Colombia, including the national flower, the majestic *Flor de Mayo*. A passion for these flowers led botanist Tom Hart Dyke into the treacherous Darién Gap in 2000, a harrowing journey, including kidnap by guerrillas, that he recounts in his bestselling book, *The Cloud Garden*. For those who do not wish to risk life and limb to experience the best of Colombia's flora, check out the **José Celestino Mutis Botanical Gardens** in Bogotá or the **Joaquín Antonio Uribe Botanical Gardens** in Medellín. The latter is particularly spectacular and contains a newly built 'orquideorama' that is not to be missed by orchid lovers. If you are lucky enough to be in Medellín during August, make sure to check out the flower festival that the city hosts every year.

There are three Cordilleras of the Andes dominating the western part of Colombia. The rivers draining the area are referred to as white water (although more frequently brown because they contain a lot of sediment). This is in contrast to the rivers that drain the Guiana shield in neighbouring Venezuela, which are referred to as black or clear waters. The forests of the latter are of considerably lower productivity than those of the Andean countries.

Llanos

Northeast of the Andes and extending almost to the Caribbean coast, the lowland habitat characterized by open grasslands and small islands of trees is called the *llanos*. Poor drainage leads to the alternation between standing water and extreme desiccation, leading to large areas being devoid of trees except for some species of palm. Fire has also been responsible for maintaining this habitat type. Above 100 m this gives way to predominantly dry forest with seasonal rainfall and a pronounced drought. Gallery forest persists only in the regions surrounding rivers and streams. In contrast, arid conditions are also found in the vicinity of the northern Caribbean coast.

Pacific West

The wet forests of the Pacific slopes of the western Andes provide an interesting contrast with the Amazon region by virtue of their high degree of endemism – species unique to an area. The region is often referred to as the Chocó and extends from the Darién Gap in Panama to northern Ecuador. The natural vegetation is tropical wet forest. Clouds that hang over the forest provide condensation, and this almost constant drenching by mist, fog and rain leads to a profusion of plants with intense competition for space, such that the trees and shrubs are all covered with a great variety of epiphytes – orchids, mosses, lichens and bromeliads. The area has been referred to by birders as the 'tanager coast', owing to the large mixed flocks of these colourful birds. There are many other species of endemic birds here apart from the tanagers. At La Planada, between Pasto and Tumaco, there is one of the highest concentrations of native birds in the continent and the forest reserve contains an immense diversity of orchids.

Overall, the fauna shows some interesting biogeographic patterns. Some species found here are those more common to Central and North America than to South America. The westernmost range defines a coastal strip with a fauna similar to Panama. Meanwhile, to the southeast, the fauna south of the river Guaviare is more typical of the upper Amazon Basin of Brazil and Peru.

High Andes

From about 3600 m to 4400 m, the high Andes are covered by *páramo* typified by the grass (*Stipa-ichu*) or *pajonal* which grows here. *Páramo* is a distinct type of high-altitude moorland vegetation comprised of tall grasses and *frailejones* (*Espeletia*) a member of the Compositae family, which are only found in the Colombian *cordilleras* and the Sierra Nevada de Mérida in Venezuela. These extraordinary plants that grow as high as 12 m, also frequently attract hummingbirds such as the black-tailed trainbearer and the great sapphirewing. Lakes and marshes are also a common feature since the ground is generally level. Interspersed among the grasses are clumps of club-moss and chuquiraguas. In the zone of the high *páramo* there are many lakes. Birds frequently seen in this area include the Andean teal, Andean coot and a variety of hummingbird species. **Andean condor** (*Vultur gryphus*) the largest land bird, weighing 12 kg and with a wingspan of 3 m, may be seen effortlessly gliding on the updraft from the warmer valleys below.

Some protection from the severe climate and the icy winds that can blast this harsh environment may be provided in the deeply incised gorges. Here there may be a lush growth of shrubs, orchids, reeds and dwarf trees providing a marked visual contrast to the superficially drier *páramo*. In the favourable sheltered micro-climatic conditions provided in the gaps between the tall clumps of grass, there nestle compact colonies of gentians, lupines and prostrate mosses. There is little evidence of mammal life here save for the occasional paw print of the Andean fox. **White-tailed deer**, once common has been over-hunted.

Under 3600 m, the condensation of the moisture-laden upwelling air from the warm humid jungles to the east creates cloudforest, with a similar wide variety of epiphytes as found near the west coast. Both giant and dwarf tree ferns are characteristic. These are highly resistant to fire, the traditional manner of maintaining grazing lands. Pollination is effected by a variety of agents. Fragrant odours and bright colours are used by some orchids to attract nectivorous birds, including some species of humming birds and insects. Others exude putrid smells to attract flies to carry out the same process. Tangled stands of bamboo intermingled with the *polylepis* forest are the dominant vegetation feature.

At high altitude *polylepis* forest clothes the deeply incised canyons and sides of the valleys. This is a tangled, lichen and fern be-decked world, dripping water from the moisture-laden air on to a mid-storey of tangled bamboo and lush tree ferns. A plentiful supply of bromeliads provide food for **spectacled bears**, now an endangered species. The steep slopes of the gullies are clothed in a dense blanket of giant cabbage-like paraguillas or umbrella plant. Tracks of mountain tapir are commonly found along river beaches, and the prints of the diminutive **pudu**, a small **Andean deer**, are also occasionally found. Mammals are rarely seen on the *páramo* during the day since most seek refuge in the fringing cloudforest, only venturing out on the open moors at night or under the protection of the swirling mists. But their presence is demonstrated by the tracks of **Andean fox** and marauding puma. Birds of the *páramo* include the mountain **caracara** and a variety of other raptors such as the **red-backed hawk**. Andean swifts, tapaculos, hummingbirds, finches and thrushes are common.

Masked **trogons** are also abundant in the *aliso* (birch) forests, evidence of recent colonization of areas devastated by the frequent landslides. Colourful tanagers and tiny hummingbirds are often encountered flitting between the myriad of flowers. At night the hills reverberate with the incessant croaks of frogs and toads.

Eastern slopes of the Andes

The cloudforests of South America are found in a narrow strip that runs along the spine of the Andes from Colombia, through Ecuador and into Peru. On the western side of the Central Cordillera between 2000 m and 3000 m are the remaining stands of the **wax palm** (*Ceroxylon alpinum*), the tallest variety of palm tree that grows dramatically above the surrounding forest and often appears above the cloud blanket. On the eastern side of the Cordillera Oriental the dense, often impenetrable, forests clothing the steep slopes protect the headwaters of the streams and rivers that cascade from the Andes to form the mighty Amazon as it begins its slow 8000 km journey to the sea. A verdant kingdom of dripping epiphytic mosses, lichens, ferns and orchids grow in profusion despite the plummeting overnight temperatures. The high humidity resulting from the 2 m of rain that can fall in a year is responsible for the maintenance of the forest and it accumulates and leaks from the ground in a constant trickle that combines to form myriad icy, crystal-clear tumbling streams that cascade over precipitous waterfalls. In secluded areas flame-red Andean **cock-of-the-rock** give their spectacular display to females in the early morning mists. **Woolly monkeys** are also occasionally sighted as they descend the wooded slopes. Mixed flocks of colourful tanagers are commonly encountered, and the golden-headed **quetzal** and Amazon umbrella bird are occasionally seen.

At about 1500 m there is a gradual transition to the vast lowland forests of the Amazon Basin; surprisingly less jungle-like but warmer and more equable than the cloudforests clothing the mountains above. The daily temperature varies little during the year with a high of 23-32°C falling slightly to 20-26°C overnight. This lowland region also receives some 2 m of rainfall per year, most of it falling from November to April. The rest of the year is sufficiently dry, at least in the lowland areas, to inhibit the growth of epiphytes and orchids which are so characteristic of the highland areas. For a week or two in the rainy season the rivers flood the forest. The zone immediately surrounding this seasonally flooded forest is referred to as *terra firme* forest.

Colombian Amazonas

The lowland Amazon region can be seen at its best as the river passes the Amacayacu National Park. Flood waters from the Peruvian catchment area inundate the forest for a short period starting in January in its upper reaches to create a unique habitat called *várzea*. *Várzea* is a highly productive seasonally inundated forest found along the banks of the whitewater rivers; it is very rich as a consequence of the huge amount of silt and nutrients washed out of the mountains and trapped by the massive buttress-rooted trees. One of the commonest trees of the *várzea*, the Pará rubber tree, is the source of latex. The Brazilian rubber industry foundered in the 19th century when seeds of this tree were illegally taken to Asia to form the basis of huge rubber plantations and flourished in the absence of pest species. In the still-flowing reaches of the *várzea*, permanently flooded areas are frequently found where vast carpets of floating water lilies, water lettuce and water hyacinth are home to the Amazonian manatee, a large herbivorous aquatic mammal which is the fresh-water relative of the dugong of the Caribbean. Vast numbers of spectacled caiman populate the lakes feeding on the highly productive fish community.

In the lowland forests, many of the trees are buttress rooted, with flanges extending 3-4 m up the trunk of the tree. Among the smaller trees stilt-like prop roots are also common. Frequently flowers are not well developed, and some emerge directly from the branches and even the trunk. This is possibly an adaptation for pollination by the profusion of bats, giving easier access than if they were obscured by leaves.

The vast river basin of the Amazon is home to an immense variety of species. The environment has largely dictated the lifestyle. Life in or around rivers, lakes, swamps and forest depend on the ability to swim and climb; amphibious and tree-dwelling animals

National parks & reserves

are common. Once the entire Amazon Basin was a great inland sea and the river still contains mammals more typical of the coast, e.g. manatees and dolphins.

National parks

Colombia established its first protected area in 1960 (Cueva de los Guácharos) and now has 56 reserves comprising 41 National Nature Parks (PNN), 10 Flora and Fauna Sanctuaries (SFF), two National Nature Reserves, one Vía Parque, one Fauna Sanctuary and one Unique Natural Area (ANU), spread throughout the country and in virtually every department. They vary in size from the tiny island of Corota in the Laguna de la Cocha near the border with Ecuador to large areas of forest in the eastern lowlands. All the significant mountain areas are National Parks including the Sierra Nevada de Santa Marta, El Cocuy, El Nevado de Huila, Los Nevados (Tolima and Ruiz) and Puracé. There are 15 on or near the Caribbean and Pacific coasts including the off-shore islands.

All except the smallest parks normally have one or more centres staffed with rangers (*guardaparques*) who offer information and guidance for visitors. Most, however, are remote with difficult access and few facilities. Unlike some Latin American countries, many national parks in Colombia are virtually free of 'tourism' and are thus of particular interest to those looking for unspoilt natural surroundings.

For various reasons, unlike many countries where the main problem for national parks is visitor overcrowding, many of the parks in Colombia are difficult to visit. Unfortunately, because of their remoteness, some have been sanctuary to guerrilla groups or drug traffickers, some are sensitive indigenous territories and many are of difficult access and have few or no facilities. Lovers of wilderness, however, will enjoy the richness of the natural attractions and the freedom from oppressive tourism.

Apart from the national parks, there are a considerable number of private nature reserves, some exclusively for research, others open to the general public. Many of these are worth visiting: details are given in the text.

200 km
200 miles

National parks & reserves ♦

Alto Fragua-Indiwasi PNN **46**
Amacayacu PNN **45**
Cahuinarí PNN **44**
Catatumbo Barí PNN **10**
Chingaza PNN **24**
Ciénaga Grande de Santa Marta SFF **7**
Corales del Rosario & San Bernardo PNN **8**
Cueva de los Guácharos PNN **39**
El Cocuy PNN **16**
El Corchal-El Mono Hernández SFF **47**
El Tuparro PNN **23**
Farallones de Cali PNN **28**
Galeras SFF **41**
Gorgona PNN **30**
Guanentá-Alto Río Fonce SFF **17**
Iguaque SFF **19**
Isla de La Corota SFF **42**
La Paya PNN **43**
Las Hermosas PNN **27**
Las Orquídeas PNN **15**
Los Colorados SFF **9**
Los Estoraques ANU **11**
Los Flamencos SFF **3**
Los Katíos PNN **12**
Los Nevados PNN **22**
Macuira PNN **2**
Malpelo SFF **25**
Munchique PNN **34**
Nevado de Huila PNN **29**
Nukak RNN **37**

Old Providence McBean Lagoon PNN **1**
Otún-Quimbaya SFF **48**
Paramillo PNN **13**
Picachos PNN **31**
Pisba PNN **18**
Plantas Medicinales Río Orito Ingi Andé SFF **54**
Puinawai RNN **38**
Puracé PNN **36**
Río Puré PNN **49**
Sanquianga PNN **35**
Selva de Florencia PNN **50**
Serranía de los Churumbelos Auka Wasi PNN **53**
Serranía de los Yariguíes PNN **51**
Sierra de Chiribiquete PNN **40**
Sierra de la Macarena PNN **32**
Sierra Nevada de Santa Marta PNN **4**
Sumapaz PNN **26**
Tamá PNN **14**
Tatamá PNN **21**
Tayrona PNN **5**
Tinigua PNN **33**
Uramba Bahía Málaga PNN **56**
Utría PNN **20**
Via Parque Isla de Salamanca **6**
Volcanes Doña Juana Cascabel PNN **52**
Yaigojé Apaporis PNN **55**

PNN Parque Nacional Natural
SFF Santuario Flora y Fauna
RNN Reserva Nacional Natural
ANU Area Natural Unica

Contents

384 Basic Spanish
for travellers

389 Index

395 Advertisers' index

396 Acknowledgements

397 About the author

400 Credits

Footnotes

Basic Spanish for travellers

Learning Spanish is a useful part of the preparation for a trip to Latin America and no volumes of dictionaries, phrase books or word lists will provide the same enjoyment as being able to communicate directly with the people of the country you are visiting. It is a good idea to make an effort to grasp the basics before you go. As you travel you will pick up more of the language and the more you know, the more you will benefit from your stay.

General pronunciation

Whether you have been taught the 'Castilian' pronounciation (z and c followed by i or e are pronounced as the *th* in think) or the 'American' pronunciation (they are pronounced as s), you will encounter little difficulty in understanding either. Regional accents and usages vary, but the basic language is essentially the same everywhere.

Vowels

a	as in English *cat*
e	as in English *best*
i	as the *ee* in English *feet*
o	as in English *shop*
u	as the *oo* in English *food*
ai	as the *i* in English *ride*
ei	as *ey* in English *they*
oi	as *oy* in English *toy*

Consonants

Most consonants can be pronounced more or less as they are in English. The exceptions are:

g	before e or i is the same as j
h	is always silent (except in ch as in *chair*)
j	as the ch in Scottish *loch*
ll	as the y in *yellow*
ñ	as the ni in English *onion*
rr	trilled much more than in English
x	depending on its location, pronounced x, s, sh or j

Spanish words and phrases

Greetings, courtesies

hello	*hola*	thank you (very much)	*(muchas) gracias*
good morning	*buenos días*	I speak Spanish	*hablo español*
good afternoon/		I don't speak Spanish	*no hablo español*
evening/night	*buenas tardes/noches*	do you speak English?	*¿habla inglés?*
		I don't understand	*no entiendo/ no comprendo*
goodbye	*adiós/chao*		
pleased to meet you	*mucho gusto*	please speak slowly	*hable despacio por favor*
see you later	*hasta luego*		
how are you?	*¿cómo está?* ¿cómo estás?*	I am very sorry	*lo siento mucho/ disculpe*
I'm fine, thanks	*estoy muy bien, gracias*	what do you want?	*¿qué quiere? ¿qué quieres?*
I'm called...	*me llamo...*		
what is your name?	*¿cómo se llama? ¿cómo te llamas?*	I want	*quiero*
		I don't want it	*no lo quiero*
yes/no	*sí/no*	leave me alone	*déjeme en paz/ no me moleste*
please	*por favor*		
		good/bad	*bueno/malo*

Questions and requests

Have you got a room for two people?
¿Tiene una habitación para dos personas?
How do I get to_?
¿Cómo llego a_?
How much does it cost?
¿Cuánto cuesta? ¿cuánto es?
I'd like to make a long-distance phone call
Quisiera hacer una llamada de larga distancia
Is service included?
¿Está incluido el servicio?

Is tax included?
¿Están incluidos los impuestos?
When does the bus leave (arrive)?
¿A qué hora sale (llega) el autobús?
When? *¿cuándo?*
Where is_? *¿dónde está_?*
Where can I buy tickets?
¿Dónde puedo comprar boletos?
Where is the nearest petrol station?
¿Dónde está la gasolinera más cercana?
Why? *¿por qué?*

Basics

bank	*el banco*	market	*el mercado*
bathroom/toilet	*el baño*	note/coin	*le billete/la moneda*
bill	*la factura/la cuenta*	police (policeman)	*la policía (el policía)*
cash	*el efectivo*	post office	*el correo*
cheap	*barato/a*	public telephone	*el teléfono público*
credit card	*la tarjeta de crédito*	supermarket	*el supermercado*
exchange house	*la casa de cambio*	ticket office	*la taquilla*
exchange rate	*el tipo de cambio*	traveller's cheques	*los cheques de viajero/*
expensive	*caro/a*		*los travelers*

Getting around

aeroplane	*el avión*	insured person	*el/la asegurado/a*
airport	*el aeropuerto*	to insure yourself against	*asegurarse contra*
arrival/departure	*la llegada/salida*	luggage	*el equipaje*
avenue	*la avenida*	motorway, freeway	*el autopista/la*
block	*la cuadra*		*carretera*
border	*la frontera*	north, south, west, east	*norte, sur, oeste*
bus station	*la terminal de*		*(occidente), este*
	autobuses/camiones		*(oriente)*
bus	*el bus/el autobús/*	oil	*el aceite*
	el camión	to park	*estacionarse*
collective/		passport	*el pasaporte*
fixed-route taxi	*el colectivo*	petrol/gasoline	*la gasolina*
corner	*la esquina*	puncture	*el pinchazo/*
customs	*la aduana*		*la ponchadura*
first/second class	*primera/segunda clase*	street	*la calle*
left/right	*izquierda/derecha*	that way	*por allí/por allá*
ticket	*el boleto*	this way	*por aquí/por acá*
empty/full	*vacío/lleno*	tourist card/visa	*la tarjeta de turista*
highway, main road	*la carretera*	tyre	*la llanta*
immigration	*la inmigración*	unleaded	*sin plomo*
insurance	*el seguro*	to walk	*caminar/andar*

Accommodation

air conditioning	el aire acondicionado	power cut	el apagón/corte
all-inclusive	todo incluido	restaurant	el restaurante
bathroom, private	el baño privado	room/bedroom	el cuarto/la habitación
bed, double/single	la cama matrimonial/	sheets	las sábanas
	sencilla	shower	la ducha/regadera
blankets	las cobijas/mantas	soap	el jabón
to clean	limpiar	toilet	el sanitario/excusado
dining room	el comedor	toilet paper	el papel higiénico
guesthouse	la casa de huéspedes	towels, clean/dirty	las toallas limpias/
hotel	el hotel		sucias
noisy	ruidoso	water, hot/cold	el agua caliente/fría
pillows	las almohadas		

Health

aspirin	la aspirina	diarrhoea	la diarrea
blood	la sangre	doctor	el médico
chemist	la farmacia	fever/sweat	la fiebre/el sudor
condoms	los preservativos,	pain	el dolor
	los condones	head	la cabeza
contact lenses	los lentes de contacto	period/sanitary towels	la regla/
contraceptives	los anticonceptivos		las toallas femeninas
contraceptive pill	la píldora anti-	stomach	el estómago
	conceptiva	altitude sickness	el soroche

Family

family	la familia	boyfriend/girlfriend	el novio/la novia
brother/sister	el hermano/la hermana	friend	el amigo/la amiga
daughter/son	la hija/el hijo	married	casado/a
father/mother	el padre/la madre	single/unmarried	soltero/a
husband/wife	el esposo (marido)/		
	la esposa		

Months, days and time

January	enero	Monday	lunes
February	febrero	Tuesday	martes
March	marzo	Wednesday	miércoles
April	abril	Thursday	jueves
May	mayo	Friday	viernes
June	junio	Saturday	sábado
July	julio	Sunday	domingo
August	agosto		
September	septiembre	at one o'clock	a la una
October	octubre	at half past two	a las dos y media
November	noviembre	at a quarter to three	a cuarto para las tres/
December	diciembre		a las tres menos quince
		it's one o'clock	es la una

it's seven o'clock	*son las siete*	in ten minutes	*en diez minutos*
it's six twenty	*son las seis y veinte*	five hours	*cinco horas*
it's five to nine	*son las nueve menos cinco*	does it take long?	*¿tarda mucho?*

Numbers

one	*uno/una*	sixteen	*dieciséis*
two	*dos*	seventeen	*diecisiete*
three	*tres*	eighteen	*dieciocho*
Four	*cuatro*	nineteen	*diecinueve*
five	*cinco*	twenty	*veinte*
six	*seis*	twenty-one	*veintiuno*
seven	*siete*	thirty	*treinta*
eight	*ocho*	forty	*cuarenta*
nine	*nueve*	fifty	*cincuenta*
ten	*diez*	sixty	*sesenta*
eleven	*once*	seventy	*setenta*
twelve	*doce*	eighty	*ochenta*
thirteen	*trece*	ninety	*noventa*
fourteen	*catorce*	hundred	*cien/ciento*
fifteen	*quince*	thousand	*mil*

Food

avocado	*el aguacate*	goat	*el chivo*
baked	*al horno*	grapefruit	*la toronja/el pomelo*
bakery	*la panadería*	grill	*la parrilla*
banana	*el plátano*	grilled/griddled	*a la plancha*
beans	*los frijoles/ las habichuelas*	guava	*la guayaba*
beef	*la carne de res*	ham	*el jamón*
beef steak or pork fillet	*el bistec*	hamburger	*la hamburguesa*
boiled rice	*el arroz blanco*	hot, spicy	*picante*
bread	*el pan*	ice cream	*el helado*
breakfast	*el desayuno*	jam	*la mermelada*
butter	*la mantequilla*	knife	*el cuchillo*
cake	*el pastel*	lime	*el limón*
chewing gum	*el chicle*	lobster	*la langosta*
chicken	*el pollo*	lunch	*el almuerzo/la comida*
chilli or green pepper	*el ají/pimiento*	meal	*la comida*
clear soup, stock	*el caldo*	meat	*la carne*
cooked	*cocido*	minced meat	*el picadillo*
dining room	*el comedor*	onion	*la cebolla*
egg	*el huevo*	orange	*la naranja*
Fish	*el pescado*	pepper	*el pimiento*
fork	*el tenedor*	pasty, turnover	*la empanada/ el pastelito*
fried	*frito*	pork	*el cerdo*
garlic	*el ajo*	potato	*la papa*

prawns	*los camarones*	spoon	*la cuchara*
raw	*crudo*	squash	*la calabaza*
restaurant	*el restaurante*	squid	*los calamares*
salad	*la ensalada*	supper	*la cena*
salt	*la sal*	sweet	*dulce*
sandwich	*el bocadillo*	to eat	*comer*
sauce	*la salsa*	toasted	*tostado*
sausage	*la longaniza/el chorizo*	turkey	*el pavo*
scrambled eggs	*los huevos revueltos*	vegetables	*los legumbres/vegetales*
seafood	*los mariscos*	without meat	*sin carne*
soup	*la sopa*	yam	*el camote*

Drink

beer	*la cerveza*	ice/without ice	*el hielo/sin hielo*
boiled	*hervido/a*	juice	*el jugo*
bottled	*en botella*	lemonade	*la limonada*
camomile tea	*la manzanilla*	milk	*la leche*
canned	*en lata*	mint	*la menta*
coffee	*el café*	rum	*el ron*
coffee, white	*el café con leche*	soft drink	*el refresco*
cold	*frío*	sugar	*el azúcar*
cup	*la taza*	tea	*el té*
drink	*la bebida*	to drink	*beber/tomar*
drunk	*borracho/a*	water	*el agua*
firewater	*el aguardiente*	water, carbonated	*el agua mineral con gas*
fruit milkshake	*el batido/licuado*	water, still mineral	*el agua mineral sin gas*
glass	*el vaso*	wine, red	*el vino tinto*
hot	*caliente*	wine, white	*el vino blanco*

Key verbs

to go	**ir**		there is/are	*hay*
I go	*voy*		there isn't/aren't	*no hay*
you go (familiar)	*vas*			
he, she, it goes,			**to be**	**ser**	**estar**
you (formal) go	*va*		I am	*soy*	*estoy*
we go	*vamos*		you are	*eres*	*estás*
they, you (plural) go	*van*		he, she, it is,		
			you (formal) are	*es*	*está*
to have (possess)	**tener**		we are	*somos*	*estamos*
I have	*tengo*		they, you (plural) are	*son*	*están*
you (familiar) have	*tienes*			
he, she, it,				
you (formal) have	*tiene*			
we have	*tenemos*			
they, you (plural) have	*tienen*			

This section has been assembled on the basis of glossaries
compiled by André de Mendonça and David Gilmour of
South American Experience, London, and the Latin American
Travel Advisor, No 9, March 1996

Index → *Entries in bold refer to maps*

A

Acacias 338
Acaime Natural Reserve 266
Acandí 162
accident and emergency 33
accommodation 23
Albarracín, Pedro de Lugo 362
Almacén de Pólvora (gunpowder store) 140
Alto de Idolos 319
Alto de las Piedras 319
Amacayacú National Park 341
Amazonia 340
Andean condor 378
Andes 241, 372
Andrés de Santamaría 364
Aquitania 101
Aracataca 180
Aratoca 116
Arboletes 161
  listings 165
Armenia 267, **267**
  ins and outs 268
  listings 277
  sights 268
arts and crafts 359
Bucaramanga   117

B

Bahía Agua Dulce 205
Bahía de Cartagena 140
Bahía del Suroeste 205
Bahia Malaga 295
Bahia Manzanillo 205
Bahía Solano 250
  listings 250
Baluarte San Francisco Javier 144, 147
Barichara 114, **114**
  listings 120
Barniz 360
Barrancas 193

Barranquilla 170, **170, 171**
  activities 174
  bars and clubs 173
  directory 174
  eating 173
  entertainment 173
  excursions 172
  festivals and events 173
  ins and outs 170
  shopping 174
  sights 171
  sleeping 172
  tours 174
  transport 174
basketry 360
Bedón, Pedro 363
Belalcázar, Sebastián de 304
Berlín 119
Betancur, Belisario 354
Betancur, Rodrigo Arenas 365
Biblioteca Bartolomé Calvo 146
Bioparque Los Ocarros 337
Boca Grande 327
Bocachica 147
Bocagrande 140, 141, 147
Bogotá 45-82, 50, 56, 64, 67
  bars and clubs 73
  Candelaria 54, **56**
  directory 80
  eating 71
  entertainment 73
  festivals 74
  getting around 49
  getting there 48
  Museo de Oro 62
  orientation 49
  safety 52
  shopping 74
  sights 54
  sleeping 68
  transport 78
Bolívar, Simón 127, 160, 351

border crossings
  Colombia–Ecuador
    Ipiales–Rumichaca 329
    Tumaco–San Lorenzo 329
  Colombia–Venezuela
    Cúcuta–Can Antonio 129
    Maicao 196
Borrero, Misael Pastrana 353
Botero, Fernando 222, 365
Boyacá Department 92
Boyacá, Battle of 94
Bucaramanga 116
  ins and outs 116
  listings 121
  sights 117
Buenaventura 294
  listings 298
Buga 292
Buitrago, Fanny 367
bus 20
business hours 38

C

Cabellero, Luis 365
Cabo de la Vela 194
caja vallenata 193
Cajamarca 269
Caldas, Francisco José de 304
Cali 286, **288**
  activities and tours 301
  background 287
  bars and clubs 299
  directory 303
  eating 299
  entertainment 300
  festivals and events 300
  ins and outs 286
  shopping 300
  sights 290
  sleeping 296
  transport 302

Camargo, Hernando Domínguez 366
Camarones 191
camping 24
Cañaveral 182
Cañón del Río Claro 238, 240
Capurganá 162
  listings 166
car 21
Carmen de Viboral 237
Carrasquilla, Tomás 366
Cartagena 138-169, **142**
  activities and tours 154
  around the old city 140
  background 139
  bars and nightclubs 152
  beaches 147
  Bocachica beach 147
  Bocagrande 147
  directory 156
  eating 151
  entertainment 153
  festivals 153
  fortifications 140
  getting around 138
  inner city 144
  ins and outs 138
  listings 148
  Marbella beach 147
  outer city 141
  ramparts 147
  security 139
  shopping 153
  sights 140
  transport 155
Cartagena and the north coast 135-169
Cartago 269
Casa Bolívariana 160
Casa de Gabriel García Márquez 146
Casa de la Aduana, Santa Marta 177
Casa de Núñez 146
Casa de Santander 130
Casa del Marqués de Valdehoyos 145

Casa del Virrey 270
Castellanos, Dora 367
Castellanos, Juan de 365
Cauca Valley 286
Centro Internacional de Convenciones 141
Cevallos, Gregorio Vázquex de Arce y 363
Chapinero 66
Chicó 67
children 33
Chinchiná 261
Chipre 255
Chiquinquirá 99
Chocó 248
Chucunez 326
Ciénaga 180
Ciénaga de Santa Marta 180
Circuito de Oriente 237
civil wars 352
climate 375
Cock-of-the-Rock 379
Coconuco 306
Codazzi, Agustín 364
Cojines del Zaque 94
consulates 34
Convento de Santo Domingo 178
Corcora 266
Correa, Carlos 364
Coveñas 161
cowboy culture 337
Cristo de la Conquista 361
Cubarral 338
Cúcuta 128, **128**
  listings 131
Cuestecita 193
Cueva de los Guácharos National Park 320
Cueva de Morgan 202
Ciudad Perdida 183
  trekking 184
culture 359
Cumaral 338
Curití 116
customs 33

D
dance 290, 223, 368
Darién Gap 161
de Bastidas, Rodrigo 350
de Belalcázar, Sebastian 350
de Heredia, Pedro 350
de Lugo, Lorenzo 362
de Paulo Santander, Francisco 351
de Quesada, Gonzalo Jiménez 350, 365
de Santiago, Miguel 363
Desierto de Tatacoa 309
  listings 313
Díaz, Eugenio 366
disabled travellers 33
diving 163, 180, 203
Doradal 240
  listings 244
Dosquebrados 261
drinking 25
drugs 34, 39
Duitama 100
Durán, Jorge Gaitán 367

E
eating 25
El Apostol de los Negros 144
El Bodegón de la Candelaria 144
El Cedral 264
El Cocuy 102
El Cove 201
El Cuzco 310
El Encanto 326
El Esclavo de los Esclavos 144
El Fósil 97
El Infiernito 97
El Peñol 238
El Poblado 226
  listings 227
El Retiro 237
  listings 244
El Tablón 319
El Valle 249
  listings 250

electricity 34
embassies 34
emergency services 33
Entrerríos 242
Espinosa, José María 363

F

Facatativá 83
Farallones National Park 293
Federmann, Nicolás 351
Fernández, Carmelo 364
festivals and events 29
Figueroa, Pedro José 363
Filandia 264
fine art 361
flights 17, 19
Floridablanca 118
flowers 377
Francisco de Páramo 363
Freile, Juan Rodríguez 366
Fuerte Castillo Grande 140
Fuerte San José 140

G

Galerazamba 157
Garay, Epifanio 364
García Márquez, Gabriel
    160, 180, 181, 367
Gaviria, Pablo Escobar 357
geology 371
Getsemaní 140
getting there 18
Girón 118, 119
    listings 122
gold 359
Gómez, Pedro Nel 364
González, Beatriz 365
Gorrones 350
government 358
gran Colombia 352
Greiff, León de 366
guacharaca 193
Guaduas 84
Guajira Peninsula 194
Guamal 338
Guane 115
    listings 121

Guatapé 238
    listings 244
Guatavita Nueva 85
Guerillas 40
Guevara, Sor Francisca
    Josefa de Castillo y 366
Güicán 102

H

Hacienda Nápoles 240
hammocks 195
health 34
Hevia, Luis García 363
history 350
homestays 24
hotels 23
Hoyo Soplador 201

I

Ibagué 269
Iglesia de la Tercera Orden
    141
Iguaque National Sanctuary
    98
immigration 42
Independence 351
Independence from Spain
    351
indigenous cultures 370
insurance 35
internet 35
Inzá 307
Ipiales 328
    listings 330
Iquitos 344
Isaacs, Jorge 366
Isla de la Aguja 178, 180
Isla de la Corota 325
Isla Fuerte 161
Isla Gorgona 296
Isla Grande 157
Isla Malpelo 296
Islas de San Bernardo 160
Islas del Rosario 157
    listings 164
Ituango 242
Iza 100

J

Jacob, Porfirio Barba 366
Jaramillo, Alipio 364
Jardín 241
Jericó 241
Juanchaco 295

L

La Boquilla 148
La Casa Museo de Simón
    Bolívar 146
La Ceja 237
La Chaquira 319
La Fe 238
La Gorda 145
La India Catalina 147
La Laguna 202
La Miel, Panama 163
La Pastora 264
La Pelota 319
La Popa hill 147
La Santísima Trinidad church
    141
La Violencia 353
La Zona Cafetera 252
Ladrilleros 295
Lago de Tota 100, 101
Laguna de Guatavita 85
Laguna de Navío Quebrado
    192
Laguna de Otún 264
Laguna La Cocha 325
landscape 371
language 36
Las Lajas 328
Lebrija 118
Legado de Piratas 202
Lemus, Eduardo Cote 367
Leticia 340, 340
    listings 345
Liles 350
literature 365
Loessing, Gian Battista 362
Los Angeles 182
Los Hoyos 310
Los Llanos 336
    ins and outs 336

Los Llanos and Amazonia
333-349
Los Nevados National Park
259, **259**

M

Macondo 180
Macuira National Park 195
Maicao 196
   listings 198
Makui 195
Manaure 194
   listings 197
Manaus 344
Manizales 252, **253**
   ins and outs 252
   listings 270
   sights 253
maps 22
Marbella 147
Marín, Pedro Antonio 354
Marmato 257
   listings 271
   sights 258
Marquez, Gabriel García
   See García Márquez
Marsella 264
Medellín 214, **216**, **225**, **235**
   around Medellín 237,
      239
   bars and nightclubs 230
   directory 236
   eating 229
   El Poblado 225
   entertainment 231
   festivals 231
   history 215
   ins and outs 214
   Metrocable 234, **235**
   safety 215
   shopping 232
   sights 218
   sleeping 227
   transport 233, **235**
media 37
Medoro, Angelino 363
Méndez, Ramón Torres 364
Minca 184

listings 187
Mirador Escalona 202
Modern Colombia 355
Mompós 159, **159**
   listings 164
Money 37
Monguí 101
Monserrate 63
Montenegro 269
Moore, Tyrell 219
Morgan, Henry 327
Morillo, General Pablo 351
Múcura island 160
mud volcano 158, 161
mudéjar 146
Muelle de los Pegasos 144
Muisca 350
Museo de Arte Moderno,
   Cartagena 144
Museo del Oro Zenú,
   Cartagena 145
Museo Naval del Caribe,
   Cartagena 144
music 193, 368
música tropical 193
Musichi 194
Mutis, Celestino 364

N

narcotics trade, the 357
Nariño, Antonio 96, 351
Narváez, Alonso de 362
national parks **380**, 381
Nazareth 195
Negret, Edgar 364
Neiva 308
   listings 313
Nevado del Tolima 267
New Frontiers Adventures,
   Colombia 189
Nieto, Juan José 366
Norte de Santander
   Department 126
North of Bogotá 89-134
Northwest Colombia
   211-282
Nuquí 248
   listings 250

O

Obeso, Candelario 366
Obregón, Alejandro 365
Obregón, Carlos 367
Old Providence 203
Olivella, Manuel Zapata 367
One Hundred Years of
   Solitude 180
Otún Quimbaya Flora and
   Fauna Sanctuary 264

P

Páez 307
Paipa 99
   listings 106
Palacio de La Inquisición 145
Palacio de la Proclamación
   145
Pamplona 126
   listings 130
   sights 126
Paraguaipoa 196
Parque Arqueológico 318
Parque del Centenario 144
Parque Ecológico Río Blanco
   256
Parque Nacional del Café
   269
Parque Nacional Ensenada
   de Utria 249
Parque Nacional Farallones
   293
Parque Nacional Los
   Nevados 259
   sleeping 271
Parque Nacional Natural Old
   Providence 204
Parque Nacional Puracé
   310
Parque Natural Nacional
   Macuira 195
Parque Ucumari 264
Paseo de los Mártires 144
Pasto 323
   background 323
   ins and outs 323
   listings 330
   sights 325

Pastrana, Andrés 355
Paz, Manuel María 364
Pedro Laboria 363
people 370
Pereira 261, **262**
  listings 272
  sights 263
Piedecuesta 118
Piedrahita, César Uribe 366
Pilimbalá 310
Pinilla, Rojas 353
Pitalito 320
Plaza de Bolívar 144
Plaza de la Aduana 144
Plaza de la Independencia 144
Plaza de las Bóvedas 146
Plaza de los Coches 144
Plaza de San Pedro Claver 144
Plaza de Santo Domingo, Cartagena 145
Plaza de Toros 146
Popayán 304
  background 304
  listings 312
  sights 305
post 39
pottery 361
Pozo de Donato 94
Prado, Jorge Elicier 367
Providencia 203, **204**
  beaches 205
  excursions 203
  ins and outs 203
  listings 207
public holidays 31
Puente de Occidente 244
Puente Heredia 141, 147
Puente Román 141, 147
Puerto Bogotá 84
Puerto Colombia 172
Puerto Gaitán 338
Puerto López 338
Puerto Nariño 343
Punta Gallinas 195
Punto Zero 223
Puracé 310

Q
Quibdó 248
  listings 250
Quimbaya 269
Quimbayas 350
Quinta de San Pedro Alejandrino 178

R
rail 20
Ráquira 99
religion 370
Reserva Natural Cañón del Río Claro 238, 240
  listings 244
Reserva Natural Heliconia 345
Reserva Natural la Planada 326
Reserva Natural Palmarí 344
restaurants 27
Restrepo 338
Restrepo, Carlos Eugenio 353
Reyes, Rafael 353
Ricaurte, Antonio 97
Río Ariari 338
Río Chicamocha 116
Río Yavari 343
Riohacha 191, **192**
  listings 197
Rionegro 118, 237
Riosucio 241
Rivera, José Eustacio 366
road 20
Rodadero 179
  listings 185
Rozo, Rómulo 364
Rumichaca 329

S
safety 39
Salento 265, **265**
salsa 290
Salto de Bordones 319
Salto de Honda 84
Salto de Versalles 84
Salto del Mortiño 319

Samper, Ernesto 354
San Agustín 317
  Bosque de las Estatuas 318
  eating 321
  Fuente de Lavapatas 318
  ins and outs 317
  Parque Arqueológico 318
  sleeping 320
  transport 322
San Agustín Monastery 146
San Andrés 201, **201**, **202**
  diving 203
  excursions 202
  ins and outs 201
  listings 206
  sights 201
San Andrés de Pisimbalá 307, 308
San Blas archipelago 163
San Cipriano 293
  listings 298
San Diego 141
San Fernando Fortress 140
San Francisco Monastery 141
San Gil 111, **112**
  activities 111
  listings 119
San José de Isnos 319
San José de la Montaña 242
San José de Manzanillo Fort 140
San Juan de Arama 338
San Lorenzo 185, 329
San Martín 338
San Pedro Claver 144
San Roque Chapel 141
Sandoná 325
Santa Bárbara 241
Santa Clara de Assisi 146
Santa Fe de Antioquia 242, **243**
Santa Marta 175, **177**
  activities and tours 189
  around Santa Marta 178, **179**
  background 176

bars and clubs 188
beaches 178
directory 190
eating 187
festivals 188
ins and outs 175
orientation 176
shopping 188
sights 177
sleeping 185
transport 190
Santa Rosa de Cabal 261
  listings 271
Santa Rosa de Osos 242
Santa Teresa Convent 144
Santander 293
Santander Department 111
Santo Domingo 145
Santo Toribio de Mongrovejo 146
Santuario Los Flamencos 191
Sapzurro 163
  listings 167
sculpture 361
Seaflower, The 200
Señor de Monserrate 362
Sierra Nevada de Santa Marta 184
Sierra Nevada del Cocuy 102, **103**
Silvia 306
Sinú 350
sleeping 23
snorkelling 163, 180
Sogamoso 100
Soledad 172
Southern Colombia 283-332
spa tourism 311
spectacled bears 378
student travellers 40
Supía 256
sustainable tourism 32

T
Taganga 180
  listings 186
Tamá National Park 127
tango 223
Tayrona National Park 180
  ins and outs 181
  listings 186
Tayronas 350
telephone 40
textiles 359
Tierradentro 307
  ins and outs 307
  listings 313
  sights 308
Tierradentro Archaeology Park 308
time 41
tipping 41
Titipán 160
Tolú 160
  listings 165
tour operators 41
tourist information 41
Trujillo, Bernardo Arias 366
Trujillo, César Gaviria 357
Tumaco 327
Tunja 92, **93**
  sleeping 104
Túquerres 326
Turbo 161
  listings 165

U
Urdaneta, Alberto 363
Uribe, Alvaro 355
Uribe, Juan Camilo 365
Uribia 194
Usaquén 68

V
vaccinations 34
Valdivia 242
Valle de Cocora 266
Valledupar 193
  listings 197
vallenato 193

Vásquez, Jorge Luis Ochoa 357
Vásquez, Marta Nieves Ochoa 357
Vázquez, Juan Bautista 362
vegetation 376
Velásquez, Samuel 366
Vergara, José María Vergara y 366
Villa Concha 178
Villa de Leiva 95, **96**
  listings 104
Villa del Rosario 130
Villamizar, Eduardo Ramírez 364
Villanueva 222
Villavicencio 336, 339
  listings 338
  sights 337
Villavieja 309
  listings 313
Villeta 83
Violencia, La 353
visas 42
Volcán de Lodo 161
Volcán del Totumo 157
Volcán Galeras 325
Volcán Puracé 311
volunteering 44

W
West View 202
Wiederman, Guillermo 364
wildlife 376
Wolff, Antonio Navarro 357
women travellers 40
woodcarvings 362

Y
Yarumal 242
youth hostels 24

Z
Zaque 350
Zipa 350
Zipaquirá 86
Zona Cafetera 252

Advertisers' index

Acknowledgements

Firstly grateful thanks must go to Peter Pollard for his work in compiling the original *Footprint Colombia* and to Charlie Devereux for his work on the previous edition. The author would also like to thank the following people for their invaluable support during the process of researching and writing this edition:

In Colombia: Thierry Forte and Marco de la Ossa Pizarro, Cartagena, Mathieu Perrot-Bohringer and everyone at Aventure Colombia, Cartagena/Bogotá, Francisco Huerfano Paez, Riohacha, Kelvin Leeming, Medellín, Simon Locke, Russell Coleman and Juan Pablo Echeverri, Manizales, Beatriz Botero, Pereira/Salento, Timothy Harbour and Jesús Bedoya, Salento, Roiber Vélez, Armenia, Nadia Diamond, Bogotá/Honda, Tony Lloyd, Germán Escobar and Gilma Madrid, Bogotá, Oscar Gilède, Villa de Leiva, Shaun Clohesy, San Gil (special thanks for San Gil map), Ignacio Megia and Dave Procter, Cali Tony and Kim, Popayán, René Suter, San Agustín, Stefan Schnur and Beatriz Rivera, Buga. Also thanks to the countless unknown Colombians, expats and fellow travellers who made the journey enjoyable throughout.

At Footprint: Alan Murphy and Felicity Laughton.

In the UK: Luisa Urueña and Emma Cashmore from Axis Travel Marketing, Juliana Torres from Proexport, Ben Box (editor of the *South American Handbook*), María del Pilar Fitzpatrick for inspiring my interest in Colombia in the first place, Laura Rendell-Dunn (Journey Latin America).

Elsewhere: Jenny and Christian (Stockholm, Sweden) for tips on San Andrés and Providencia.

Reader feedback: Raúl Rodríguez; Nik and Abby Nelberg; Angelique and Chris Williams (Hamburg, Germany) Peter Cleary; Ole Skjerven (Norway).

Special thanks to my good friends Bryony Addis-Jones and Elisa Sibille for constant encouragement, good cheer and patience during the whole book process.

About the author

Originally from Sweden, **Anna Maria Espsäter** first started discovering Latin America at 20, when she moved to Mexico to teach and work in an orphanage. Finally making it to Colombia, high on her travel wish-list for years, in 2009, she has already returned for her second spell, exploring the country thoroughly for the writing of this book. Based in London for many years, she works as a freelance travel and food writer. Having visited 85 countries to date, she remains undaunted despite surviving tropical disease, earthquakes, assault and armed robbery on the road. Latin America is still one of her favourite places to roam and write about and she hopes to return again before long.

Idlewild Books

12 W 19th Street
New York NY 10011
(212) 414 8888
www.idlewildbooks.com

Cust None

08 Apr 13 1 46p   Clerk ADMIN

Trans # 10043453   Reg 1

|||||||||||||||||||||||||||||||||||||||||

9781907263491   *Footprint Colombia Hbk 4e*

	1 @ $25.95	-20%	$20.76
Items 1		Sub total	$20.76
Units 1		Tax @ 8.90%	$1.84
		Discount	$5.19
		Total	$22.60

Non-Tax Items

Payment Via

VISA/MC/Discover $22.60

Titles available in the Footprint *Focus* range

Latin America	UK RRP	US RRP
Bahia & Salvador	£7.99	$11.95
Buenos Aires & Pampas	£7.99	$11.95
Costa Rica	£8.99	$12.95
Cuzco, La Paz & Lake Titicaca	£8.99	$12.95
El Salvador	£5.99	$8.95
Guadalajara & Pacific Coast	£6.99	$9.95
Guatemala	£8.99	$12.95
Guyana, Guyane & Suriname	£5.99	$8.95
Havana	£6.99	$9.95
Honduras	£7.99	$11.95
Nicaragua	£7.99	$11.95
Paraguay	£5.99	$8.95
Quito & Galápagos Islands	£7.99	$11.95
Recife & Northeast Brazil	£7.99	$11.95
Rio de Janeiro	£8.99	$12.95
São Paulo	£5.99	$8.95
Uruguay	£6.99	$9.95
Venezuela	£8.99	$12.95
Yucatán Peninsula	£6.99	$9.95

Asia	UK RRP	US RRP
Angkor Wat	£5.99	$8.95
Bali & Lombok	£8.99	$12.95
Chennai & Tamil Nadu	£8.99	$12.95
Chiang Mai & Northern Thailand	£7.99	$11.95
Goa	£6.99	$9.95
Hanoi & Northern Vietnam	£8.99	$12.95
Ho Chi Minh City & Mekong Delta	£7.99	$11.95
Java	£7.99	$11.95
Kerala	£7.99	$11.95
Kolkata & West Bengal	£5.99	$8.95
Mumbai & Gujarat	£8.99	$12.95

Africa	UK RRP	US RRP
Beirut	£6.99	$9.95
Damascus	£5.99	$8.95
Durban & KwaZulu Natal	£8.99	$12.95
Fès & Northern Morocco	£8.99	$12.95
Jerusalem	£8.99	$12.95
Johannesburg & Kruger National Park	£7.99	$11.95
Kenya's beaches	£8.99	$12.95
Kilimanjaro & Northern Tanzania	£8.99	$12.95
Zanzibar & Pemba	£7.99	$11.95

Europe	UK RRP	US RRP
Bilbao & Basque Region	£6.99	$9.95
Granada & Sierra Nevada	£6.99	$9.95
Málaga	£5.99	$8.95
Orkney & Shetland Islands	£5.99	$8.95
Skye & Outer Hebrides	£6.99	$9.95

North America	UK RRP	US RRP
Vancouver & Rockies	£8.99	$12.95

Australasia	UK RRP	US RRP
Brisbane & Queensland	£8.99	$12.95
Perth	£7.99	$11.95

For the latest books, e-books and smart phone app releases, and a wealth of travel information, visit us at: www.footprinttravelguides.com.

footprinttravelguides.com

Join us on facebook for the latest travel news, product releases, offers and amazing competitions: www.facebook. com/footprintbooks.com.

Credits

Footprint credits

Project Editor: Felicity Laughton
Layout and production: Emma Bryers
Cover and colour section: Pepi Bluck
Maps: Kevin Feeney

Managing Director: Andy Riddle
Commercial Director: Patrick Dawson
Publisher: Alan Murphy
Publishing Managers: Felicity Laughton
Nicola Gibbs
Digital Editors: Jo Williams, Tom Mellors
Marketing and PR: Liz Harper
Advertising: Renu Sibal
Finance and administration:
Elizabeth Taylor

Photograpy credits

Front cover: Jane Sweeney / AWL Images
(Magdalena, Parque Nacional Tayrona)
Back cover: Jon Spaull / Axiom (ice cream
seller, Cartagena)

Colour section: Page 1: Janos Csernoch /
Alamy (Cartagena); **Pages 2-3**: rm /
shutterstock.com (Caribbean beach);
Pages 6-7: Christian Kober / Robert Harding
(Sierra Nevada El Cocuy); **Page 8**: Sue
Carpenter / Axiom (Carnival in Cartagena)

Printed in India by Nutech Print Services

Footprint feedback

We try as hard as we can to make each
Footprint guide as up to date as possible
but, of course, things always change. If you
want to let us know about your experiences –
good, bad or ugly – then don't delay, go to
www.footprintbooks.com and send in
your comments.

Publishing information

Footprint Colombia
4th edition
© Footprint Handbooks Ltd
October 2011

ISBN: 978 1 907263 49 1
CIP DATA: A catalogue record for this book
is available from the British Library

® Footprint Handbooks and the Footprint
mark are a registered trademark of Footprint
Handbooks Ltd

Published by Footprint
6 Riverside Court
Lower Bristol Road
Bath BA2 3DZ, UK
T +44 (0)1225 469141
F +44 (0)1225 469461
www.footprinttravelguides.com

Distributed in the USA by Globe Pequot Press,
Guilford, Connecticut